MW00451849

A Naturalist's Guide to the Santa Barbara Region

A Naturalist's Guide to the

SANTA BARBARA
REGION JOAN EASTON LENTZ

Photography by Stuart Wilson
Maps and Illustrations by Peter Gaede

Joan Easton Lentz

Published in cooperation with the
Santa Barbara Museum of Natural History

Heyday, Berkeley, California

© 2013 by Joan Easton Lentz

All rights reserved. No portion of this work may be reproduced or transmitted in any form or by any means, electronic or mechanical, including photocopying and recording, or by any information storage or retrieval system, without permission in writing from Heyday.

Library of Congress Cataloging-in-Publication Data

Lentz, Joan Easton, 1943-
    A naturalist's guide to the Santa Barbara region / Joan Easton Lentz ; photography by Stuart Wilson.
        pages cm
    Includes bibliographical references and index.
    ISBN 978-1-59714-241-0 (alk. paper)
    1. Natural history--California--Santa Barbara Region. I. Title.
    QH105.C2L457 2013
    508.7283'85--dc23
                        2013006343

Cover photographs by Stuart Wilson
Book design by Lorraine Rath

Orders, inquiries, and correspondence should be addressed to:
        Heyday
        P.O. Box 9145, Berkeley, CA 94709
        510 549-3564, Fax 510 549-1889
        www.heydaybooks.com

Printed in China by Everbest Printing Co. through Four Colour Imports, Ltd., Louisville, Kentucky

10 9 8 7 6 5 4 3 2

This book is dedicated to my father, Robert Olney Easton,
who loved this land as much as I do.

Donor Acknowledgments

Contributions to *A Naturalist's Guide to the Santa Barbara Region* were a community effort spearheaded by the Santa Barbara Museum of Natural History. I wish to thank Caroline Grange, Director of Development at the museum, and her assistant Nicole Ketterer for their help in handling the gifts. Donations from hundreds of people made this book possible. I wish to recognize the donors listed below for their extraordinary generosity.

My special appreciation goes to Heloise and Sandy Power.

Joan Easton Lentz
March 2013

Joan and Lawrence Bailard
Catherine and Louis Bevier
Patty and Terry Bliss
Susan Bower
Candace Dauphinot and Richard Brumm
Julia and Lee Carr
Lisa and Stephen Couvillion
Nancy and Thomas Crawford, Jr.
Sally and Terry Eagle
Ellen Easton and Greg Giloth
Marsha and Jay Glazer
Jane and Thomas Kern
Bobbie and John Kinnear
Gilbert Lentz
Jennifer Lentz and Kevin Gerson
Judy and David Messick
Sharon and Stephen Metsch
Glen H. Mitchel, Jr.
Cynthia and Chapin Nolen
Leslie and Dennis Power
Heloise and Sandy Power
Joanne and Brian Rapp
Cathy Rose
Virginia Sloan
Melissa and Christian Stepien
John Storrer
Alice Van de Water

CONTENTS

Acknowledgments

This book is the product of many people who graciously shared their time and knowledge with me. I thank them for pausing in their busy schedules to talk, share publications, discuss issues, and answer questions: Genevieve Anderson, Susie Bartz, Michelle Berman, Ron Botorff, Andy Brooks, Andy Calderwood, Mark Capelli, John Carson, Mike Caterino, David Chapman, Dave and Sherryl Clendenen, Scott Cooper, Tom Dibblee, Tom Dudley, Jenifer Dugan, John Evarts, Krista Fahy, Kate Faulkner, Elaine Gibson, Bob and Carol Goodell, Bob Gray, Jan Hamber, Laurie Hannah, Laurie Harvey, Sandy Hedrick, Dave Hubbard, Larry Hunt, John Johnson, Kevin Lafferty, Paul Lehman, Andy Lentz, Kate McCurdy, Bob Norris, Tim Robinson, Sandy Russell, Cristina Sandoval, Santa Barbara Botanic Garden, Brad Schram, Dennis Sheridan, Michael Smith, Matt Stoecker, John Storrer, Sam Sweet, Paul Valentich-Scott, Adrian Wenner, Laura Wilson, and Jackie Worden.

Certain individuals were essential to the success of the book.

I thank Terri Sheridan of the Santa Barbara Museum of Natural History Library for her generous advice and support.

I want to express my extreme gratitude for the joint cooperation of Heyday in Berkeley, California, with the Santa Barbara Museum of Natural History, which resulted in publication of the *Naturalist's Guide*. Malcolm Margolin, the publisher at Heyday, and Karl Hutterer, the former executive director at the museum, believed in my project at a time when these sorts of endeavors are difficult to fund and to produce. Thank you for your faith in me. If it hadn't been for Gayle Wattawa at Heyday, who first saw my writing, this book would not have seen the light of day. In addition, Jeannine Gendar at Heyday was a terrific help during the editing process.

I wish to thank my sister, Ellen Easton, and my daughter, Jennifer Lentz, for their constant encouragement.

I wish to thank Stuart Wilson and Peter Gaede for their unfailing patience and hard work. I could not have had better partners going forward.

Last, there are certain people without whose support this book could never have been created: Paul Collins, curator at the Santa Barbara Museum of Natural History, Larry Ballard, research associate at the Santa Barbara Botanic Garden, and my husband, Gib. Their encouragement, knowledge, and wholehearted enthusiasm for the project helped make what started out as a dream become a reality—*A Naturalist's Guide to the Santa Barbara Region*.

Joan Easton Lentz
March 2013

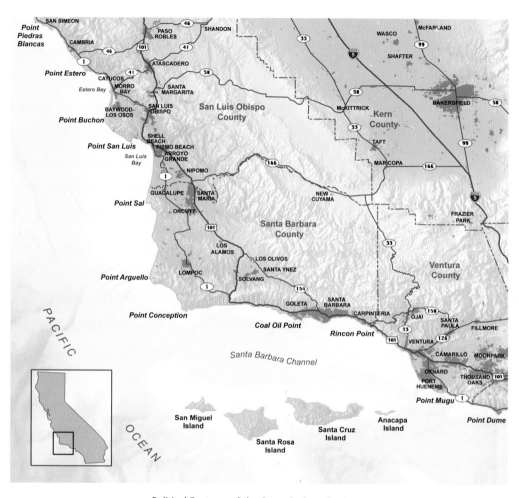

Political Features of the Santa Barbara Region

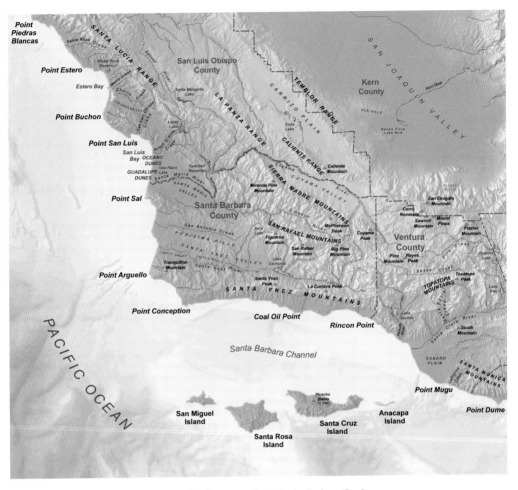

Topographic Features of the Santa Barbara Region

La Cumbre Peak sunset

Preface

The fog turns into a light rain on the windshield as I drive slowly up San Marcos Pass Road on an early May morning. A white mist wraps everything. Out of nowhere, the oncoming cars appear, passing with a muffled *whish*.

The backseat of the car is piled with binoculars, spotting scope, snacks, and a notebook. Field guides for local birds, flowers, and mammals litter the floor, sliding back and forth with the curves of the road.

Through the fog, I can see the tall, grayish-green shrubs of the chaparral on either side of the road. The bushes cling to the hillsides, flanked by tall slabs of sandstone rock.

This is part of Los Padres National Forest, but there's not a tree in sight. Instead, an impenetrable thicket of tall shrubs, their branches intertwined, make up the chaparral characteristic of a Mediterranean climate like ours.

As I drive higher to reach the summit, the mist begins to thin and finally dissipates. Soon, I am above the fog, at San Marcos Pass.

Turning onto East Camino Cielo, I follow the spine of the Santa Ynez Mountains. At every curve, the sweeping view shows a fog blanket nudging the mainland foothills, obscuring downtown Santa Barbara, the ocean, and most of the Channel Islands. Only the peaks of Santa Cruz Island poke above the marine layer.

The fingers of mist creeping up the canyons of the mainland resemble an ancient sea lapping a prehistoric shoreline. Half-drowned by a Pleistocene ocean, the Channel Islands and the Santa Ynez Mountains perhaps looked like this.

I pull over on the shoulder at a place where I can look north into the wild backcountry of the San Rafael Mountains, the Sierra Madre Mountains, and beyond. On a clear day, I would be able to see Mount Pinos way over in Kern County. I think of the pines that grow up there and the California Condor that once soared commonly over this country and will do so again, as reintroduction efforts succeed.

The next minute I'm out of the car. I have to get close to the smells of the sages and ceanothus growing in the chaparral. A branch of White Sage growing out of the roadcut unfurls its tiny white blossoms on a long stem. Grabbing a handful of leaves, I crunch them, then sniff the sagey odor. In the warm sun, the blue ceanothus gives off a honey fragrance. Salmon-colored Bush Monkeyflowers and lavender Woolly Blue Curls are in full flower; a Sara Orangetip butterfly, one of my favorites, flits by and is gone.

I sense the shadow of a large bird overhead, and I grab the binoculars to look at the hawk. It's a red-tail, in soaring flight, floating on the updraft. Beating the

The Sara Orangetip butterfly, one of the earliest to fly in spring

Hairy Ceanothus and Bush Poppy along East Camino Cielo

air with wings rowing and body held taut, the hawk maintains its position while turning its head from side to side, watching for the slightest movement below. At once, a slight stir in the roadside dust catches the hawk's attention.

In a second the red-tail dives, talons outstretched, wings tucked in full stoop. On the ground, the hawk battles with a rattlesnake. The snake, body writhing, puts up a fight. The hawk's claws and beak stab; she is big and strong. She must be a female intent upon gathering breakfast for a couple of fledglings in a nest nearby.

Finally, the red-tail overpowers the snake. The rattler, grasped in the hawk's talons, continues to squirm and buckle, but the powerful hawk lifts off, snake dangling. Stories are told that a hawk will pick up a rattlesnake, fly straight up, release the snake, and then, after the snake has dropped about a hundred feet, recapture it in midair. After a few minutes of this treatment, the rattlesnake will be more manageable for a meal back at the nest.

This time, however, the red-tail takes off slowly down the canyon, the snake's gyrating body making the bird wobble as it disappears out of sight.

I continue on the road towards La Cumbre Peak. Before 1900, there was no road along the top of the ridge here. It's hard to imagine our region without this road, because I have driven it in every kind of weather. I love the way it puts you on the edge of the continent and yet at the top of a mountain. On a clear day you can see from Point Conception to Point Mugu—the whole South Coast.

The Red-tailed Hawk, a common bird of prey in our region

Meanwhile, the mist has burned off, leaving a splendid panorama of the silvery Pacific and the islands of Anacapa, Santa Cruz, and Santa Rosa. San Miguel, furthest west, is still sunk in haze.

At length, I turn away from the view of the islands. But no matter in which direction I look, as far as my eyes can see I am surrounded by a landscape I know by heart. Or, to put it another way, a landscape of the heart.

In 1908 John Burroughs wrote, "One's own landscape comes in time to be a sort of outlying part of himself; he has sowed himself broadcast upon it, and it reflects his own moods and feelings."

xv

Santa Ynez Valley with the San Rafael Mountains in the distance

Northern Channel Islands from East Camino Cielo

Each of us has a place in the natural world that speaks to us. More than a collection of mountains and trees, wind and sky, birds and beasts, it is a personal landscape, imbued with memories and experiences. Beyond the science, outside the data, lies a sense of belonging that ties one forever to the natural world of a particular place.

Mine is the Santa Barbara region.

I love the rough peaks and dry canyons; the hot chaparral trails and cool rocky creeks with their sulfur smell; the Wrentit singing in the morning and the Coyote's cry at dusk; the sweaty hikes to Hurricane Deck and the overnight camping on Big Pine Mountain, listening for owls.

I love cruising the channel in a boat, watching for Humpback and Blue Whales; monitoring seabird migration past Goleta Point in spring; searching the tidepools below the bluffs at Cayucos on a sunny December day.

I have slogged through rain to find salamanders and toads in the Santa Maria Valley; gloried in the kaleidoscope of flowers that bursts from the dry arroyos of the Cuyama Valley after a wet winter.

I've walked on the west end of Santa Cruz Island to a windswept picnic site and trekked in snow on the back side of Mount Pinos among the quiet firs.

I've explored the chilly Carrizo Plain in winter to watch the Sandhill Cranes gather at Soda Lake; and waded into the Santa Clara River Estuary in summer, hoping for a glimpse of steelhead in the shallow waters.

I've exulted in the hundreds of shorebirds on Morro Bay's endless mudflats and climbed the "morro" known as Bishop's Peak to look down on Laguna Lake.

The Santa Barbara region is my personal landscape. I want to share it with you.

About This Book

The scope of this book is such that many aspects of the natural history of the Santa Barbara region had to be omitted or merely touched upon. For example, I have had to exclude material pertaining to the human history of the area. Santa Barbara's rich Chumash legacy has been discussed in many books, several of which have been written by Santa Barbara Museum of Natural History curators John Johnson and Jan Timbrook.

Also, this book is not a field guide. There are many of those available. Please go out and buy them all when you become interested in the myriad plants and animals that fill these pages.

This book *is* a guide to places to go in the field. Read, get excited, and get going. It's a journey unequaled anywhere on the planet.

Ocean sunrise

Introduction

> I shall never forget the impression which our first landing on the beach
> of California made upon me. The sun had just gone down; it was getting
> dusky; the damp night wind was beginning to blow, and the heavy swell
> of the Pacific was setting in, and breaking in loud and high "combers"
> upon the beach. We lay on our oars in the swell, just outside of the surf,
> waiting for a good chance to run in...We saw [the ship], sharp upon the
> wind, cutting through the head seas like a knife, with her raking masts,
> and her sharp bows running up like the head of a greyhound. It was a
> beautiful sight. She was like a bird which had been frightened and had
> spread her wings in flight.
>
> —Richard Henry Dana Jr., *Two Years Before the Mast*, 1840

Ever since 1840, when Richard Henry Dana described his ship's landing at the
beach at Santa Barbara on a voyage up the West Coast, this part of California
has captured the world's imagination. Renowned for its natural resources and
great physical beauty, the Santa Barbara region was subsequently visited by
early botanists, ornithologists, geologists, and anthropologists eager to record
details of this promised land and all its life-forms.

Over 150 years since Dana first chronicled his trip, the legendary scenery
and unique natural history of the California coast continue to lure visitors.
This book invites you to open your eyes and ears to the outdoor world, and
embark on an exploration of the Santa Barbara region's natural history.

* * *

Located between the southern end of Northern California and the northern
end of Southern California is a biogeographical area called the Santa Barbara
region. Some would say this is California's central coast, and others would clas-
sify it as the southern coast. Both are correct. It is a transitional zone situated
on the cusp of Northern and Southern California, where plants and animals of
the north mix with those of the south.

Point Conception, a rocky outpost jutting into the Pacific Ocean, is the
"elbow" symbolizing a general boundary between Northern and Southern
California. If you drew a horizontal line from Point Conception (34.5° north
latitude) along the ridge of the Santa Ynez Mountains, you would be tracing
a widely recognized floral and faunal boundary between plants and animals

The north-south trend of the coastline changes abruptly to east-west at Point Conception.
Photo by Bill Dewey

to the north that thrive in a cooler, moister climate and those to the south that have an affinity with a warmer, drier climate.

Due to its unique nature, the region is one of great biogeographical and ecological significance. Like only 2 percent of the world's surface, it has a Mediterranean climate and supports some of the most diverse communities on earth. It also produces endemic forms of life—those that cannot be found anywhere else.

Increasingly, the Santa Barbara region and portions of the California coast nearby are being identified as among the most valuable ecological hot spots in the world. At the same time, the population and urbanization pressures are enormous, threatening the very survival of many ecosystems.

Terrestrial habitats found in the region host a variety of species that live within its boundaries or pass through in migration. For example, nearly 490 different species of birds have found their way here over time. Pelicans, ducks, woodpeckers, hummingbirds, warblers, sparrows, and finches in colorful spring and drab winter plumages can be found on lakes and rivers, in weedy fields and willow clumps, contributing to a diverse avifauna.

Offshore, the marine life is equally rich. The northerly, cold California Current, which originates in Alaska, joins the warmer Davidson Countercurrent flowing up from Baja California. These currents attract species preferring colder temperatures, as well as those that live in warmer waters. There are creatures of all sizes and shapes: the largest mammals on

Oak woodland on the lower slopes of Figueroa Mountain

Rocky shoreline near Cambria

the planet, the whales, swim next to the tiny, one-inch krill on which they feed; the two-ton elephant seals lounge on the same rocks to which the minuscule barnacles cling.

The Santa Barbara region's location, positioned at the edge of a continent between land and sea, influences all aspects of its natural history: the ocean currents, the weather extremes, and the interplay of geologic forces.

Geologically, this border of the North American continent and the Pacific Ocean reflects the intersection of two plates of the earth's crust. Thousands of feet below the surface, the Pacific Plate is grinding against the adjacent North American Plate, with pressure relieved in the form of earthquakes. Movement along faults has thrust up the mountain ranges of the region in relatively recent geologic time.

Topographically, this is a land of contrasts: mountains cresting to over 8,800 feet, low alkaline sinks, sloping river valleys, terraced coastal headlands. You may awake in a tent beside a campfire on the slopes of Figueroa Mountain surrounded by coniferous forest and montane birds; then, hop in the car and in less than two hours you can be swimming side by side with dolphins at the beach.

The shape of the land creates a variety of habitats, each home to its own organisms. You will want to know what these organisms are and where to find them.

To help you, the book is organized in two parts. Part One consists of two chapters that describe the physical setting, weather, and geology of the Santa Barbara region. These big concepts are essential to

Soda Lake in the Carrizo Plain

Carpinteria Salt Marsh

Crest of the San Rafael Mountains as seen from East Camino Cielo

an understanding of what lives here and why.

Part Two of the book discusses the habitats where characteristic plants and animals can be found. The habitats are often, but not always, grouped together by their location. For example, the Shore chapter (Chapter 4) contains three different habitats: rocky shore, sandy beach, and dunes. These are clustered near each other at the shore. However, the Freshwater Wetlands chapter (Chapter 9) contains habitats such as rivers, lakes, and vernal pools that are scattered throughout the region.

Furthermore, the habitats are organized as much as possible in a gradient from the lowest, at sea level—the ocean—to the highest, the mountains.

Imagine you're on a journey through the region, starting at the ocean and traveling inland to the high mountains. As you pause on your journey at each location, the habitats you will encounter are described. Thus, you will begin at the ocean and proceed to the shore, the coastal wetlands, the coastal plain and foothills, the valleys (both coastal and interior), and finally, the mountains. But a complete view of the region must also include a visit to freshwater wetlands, the Northern Channel Islands, and urban parks and backyards. Obviously, these last three categories remain outside any elevation gradient.

Terrestrial habitats are characterized by their plant communities.

Please refer to the Plant Communities map on page 9. For example, the terms "coastal sage scrub" and "chaparral" describe two different habitats that you'll encounter in the Coastal Plain and Foothills chapter (Chapter 6).

Each habitat harbors plants that are indicators of climatic conditions and soils. In turn, the plants are part of ecosystems which include particular creatures. So, you start out by asking yourself, "What grows here?" The answer gives clues as to the insects, birds, and mammals that make a living there.

It's that simple. Go slowly and pay close attention to what's around you.

Know your location. Directions are important, so get situated. Which way are east, west, north, and south? Which mountain range are you looking at in the distance? Where is the closest creek or river?

Then ask yourself, "What's that tree? What shrubs grow under it? What's that big bug? Is that clicking noise an insect, a bird, or a mammal?"

When you begin to carefully observe what's around you, you begin to key into the world of nature.

PART ONE

THE LAND—INFLUENCES OF CLIMATE, WEATHER, AND GEOLOGY

Lake Cachuma and San Rafael Mountains. Photo by Peter Gaede

CHAPTER 1: LOCATION, LOCATION, LOCATION

Defining the Santa Barbara Region

Where is the Santa Barbara region? Setting boundaries in nature is complicated. Everything is tied to everything else. The lines of demarcation are blurred. Plants and animals have distributional limits depending upon watersheds and mountain ranges, not county lines.

A definition of the Santa Barbara region must spill over artificial human borders in order to reflect a mosaic of biotic communities. These natural boundaries may seem arbitrary to human eyes, but they outline the distribution of plants and animals, which are in turn influenced by climate, topography, and geology.

For this book, the Santa Barbara region is conceived of as spanning an area on the south-central coast of California.

The following are three different ways of looking at it.

A Bird's-Eye View

She was born in a zoo but grew up in the wild. She roosted and fed and learned to fly with others of her kind in steep Hopper Canyon in the Ventura backcountry. There, in the long, low light of winter, she practiced and honed her flying skills. Powerful dark wings spread wide, she soared for hours, circling above the barren cliffs and chaparral, exploring her new world.

Historic photo of a California Condor in flight. Condor Archives, Santa Barbara Museum of Natural History

3

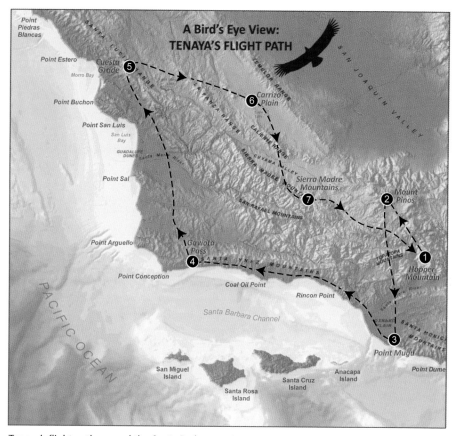

Tenaya's flight path around the Santa Barbara region

Her shoulder tag says she's No. 81, a young California Condor released to the wild months ago. We shall call her Tenaya. Like her ancestors for thousands of years, she is at home soaring above the mountains and valleys of this portion of California.

Now, on a clear day in April, she is ready to take her first long flight.

As the morning sun warms the updrafts, the bird takes off—running down a little slope in hops and skips to help herself become airborne. She's up! Wobbling from side to side at first, the condor hits her glide. Nine-foot wings held steady, now Tenaya is off, flying northwest to the highest point on the horizon, Mount Pinos.

After what seem like only a couple of flaps and a glide, she sees beneath her the open, rocky summit of the mountain, patches of snow nestling deep on its protected slopes. Circling high above Mount Pinos, she spots the dead trunk of an old Jeffrey Pine, long since shorn of needles, weather-beaten and isolated.

The condor slowly approaches for a landing, legs extended, wings braking. She almost overshoots, but at the last minute she grasps the snag and catches herself. Balancing and teeter-

4

ing, she clumsily turns around to face the west.

There, spread out before her, is the most beautiful view.

Her acute eyesight descries the far-off mountain ranges and fog-shrouded valleys of the Coast Ranges. The ridges seem to emanate from where she sits atop lofty Mount Pinos as from a central knot—with ribbons of mist in the low valleys running alongside the mountain ranges that border them.

To the north, she sees the pale white smudge of Soda Lake in the wide Carrizo Plain, flanked by the Caliente and Temblor mountains. If she looks over her shoulder, she glimpses a sliver of the flat San Joaquin Valley floor.

In the foreground, her gaze follows Lockwood Valley down to where it meets the Cuyama Valley, and thence all the way down the Cuyama River to Santa Maria and the sea. Way, way in the distance, she can just make out the Guadalupe Dunes. And from there, the glittering sea and curving coastline at Point Conception.

Between where the young condor sits atop Mount Pinos and the curving coastline so far away, there stretch the San Rafael and Santa Ynez mountains. In hazy silhouettes, their high peaks lie like stepping-stones along the ridge-lines, beckoning her to fly westward to the sea. Big Pine Mountain, Figueroa Mountain, La Cumbre Peak, Tranquillon Mountain: the farther away from Mount Pinos, the lower the peaks.

For now, however, Tenaya will fly along the southern border of this magnificent land which she accepts as her territory. She will head out towards Ventura, over the desolate Topatopa Mountains, over the Sespe Wilderness.

It is noon. The mists melting in the sunshine leave the valley floors. A breeze comes up.

She takes off, circles once to gain altitude, and glides to her cruising height of ten thousand feet. Beneath her, dry sandstone canyons fall steeply one upon another. A jumble of faults and scarps has given birth to a hodge-podge of ridges in the Topatopas.

In less than an hour, Tenaya sails high above the Santa Clara River Valley. Squares of fertile agricultural fields crowd the Oxnard Plain. Riding high above the freeways and busy shopping centers, the condor continues towards the blue Pacific. Perhaps she will fly along the ocean's edge to see what happens where the land meets the sea.

Down below, in a backyard in Port Hueneme, a little boy looks at the sky in disbelief. He squints. He sees a large dark bird with white wing patches. He thinks it may be an airplane at first, but then he notices that the bird has what looks like a large number on its wing. The little boy runs to call his father.

He has seen No. 81 on her maiden voyage.

Making a loop, she spirals higher and higher. Another slow flap and she'll be almost to the sea.

From here, she turns west and begins to follow the shore. The white sandy beaches, blue-green surf, and shale cliffs of the Ventura coast are like nothing she has ever known. Far below, fishing boats ply the glistening ocean. Occasionally, a whale spouts, then slides beneath the water.

On her left, the Channel Islands float above the horizon—the tips of a drowned mountain range. They rise parallel to the shore, just like the Santa Ynez Mountains looming on the other side of her flight path.

Following the coast, she approaches Carpinteria. She flies over a gray salt marsh threaded with channels of water. Another few minutes and the condor is over Santa Barbara: foothills sloping to a narrow coastal plain, red-tiled roofs and lush plantings.

Behind the town of Santa Barbara, the Santa Ynez Mountains form a craggy backdrop. The condor cruises along the ridge here, her wings buoyed by the afternoon updraft. On a clear day like this one, the country shines. The chaparral shows green highlights; yellow Bush Poppies grow along the ridge. The sea waits like a blue mirror.

Condor curiosity makes her turn north, following high, high above the path of US 101 as it cuts through Gaviota Pass.

The verdant hillsides of the Santa Ynez Valley, marked with oaks, spread below her. On the valley floor, the oaks are separated by grassy meadows.

Another three flaps and several glides propel the great bird towards the town of Santa Maria. Cool ocean breezes blow in from the Pacific now. Rich, dark earth nurtures broccoli and strawberries in field after field of plowed land. She sees the Santa Maria River winding its way to the ocean in a wide channel.

She circles slowly, trying to get her bearings.

The condor continues due north, flying towards San Luis Obispo. Now she's directly above the marshes and small lakes of the Los Osos Valley. A flock of fast-flying Cinnamon Teal passes many feet below Tenaya. They look like little specks compared to the huge condor.

Farms creep out from the town of San Luis Obispo up into the foothills. The tallest green hills are topped by rocky monoliths here. Fragrant sage scrub grows on the steep slopes right up to the base of these domes.

Suddenly, Tenaya finds she is battling the air. The wind swoops down the Cuesta Grade through this pass in the Santa Lucia Range, creating turbulence completely new to her. She must learn to cope with the rushing air currents and gain altitude to avoid them.

She banks and climbs higher into the sky.

If the young condor were to fly towards the coast, she would pass over the enormous mound of Morro Rock and perhaps be challenged by one of the Peregrine Falcons that live nearby.

But her instinct tells her to turn inland towards the wild, deserted mountains of the Santa Lucia Wilderness. Here in the rough country near a place called Castle Crags, Tenaya may find others of her kind.

All at once, a restlessness overtakes Tenaya.

The condor catches one of the thermals rising from the mountains beneath her and she's off again, this time heading over the backcountry around Santa Margarita Lake.

The Carrizo Plain, a vast grassland located to the east, lures the bird. It is a grazing patch for pronghorn, now reintroduced to their former range. Around the normally arid edges of shallow Soda Lake, patches of yellow daisies and blue heliotrope thrive.

A female Golden Eagle, perched on her nest high on a transformer tower, shows no interest as Tenaya passes overhead.

The condor, however, is always looking down, turning her head from side to side to scan the landscape. Her powerful vision spies a pair of ravens quarreling and hopping around a dead ground squirrel lying in the dirt beside Soda Lake Road. The carcass is small; her sense of smell picks up on its fragrance. It looks inviting.

But the sun is getting low in the west and she cannot continue to fly much longer. At last, hunger and thirst nudge Tenaya homewards. She loops back, flying south over the naked peaks of the Calientes towards the Cuyama River. The Cuyama Valley embraces the river. Dark juniper bushes dot the foothills; red rock canyons shelter big caves.

She crosses high over Bates Canyon as she follows the ridgetop of the Sierra Madre Mountains, and in doing so passes over a campground.

A man and a woman look up from their campsite. The late sun touches the silhouette of the condor in the evening sky above them. After the shadow of the bird passes over, they stare at each other, wondering if anyone will believe what they have just seen.

"It was a condor! It flew right over us in camp!"

Tenaya wheels into the next thermal and rides it high and fast. Her cruising speed kicks in. She's in flexglide. She's headed for Hopper Canyon and home, her huge wing tips reaching for the air waves.

A Hands-on View

Alas, we mortals cannot follow Tenaya's journey as she soars high above the perimeter of our region.

For a more hands-on method, here's a simple way to orient yourself to the major topographic features. The idea comes from Edward Selden Spaulding's wonderful book *Camping in Our Mountains*.

Put the palm of your right hand down flat on a table with your thumb parallel to your chest and your fingers spread out. The thumb represents the Santa Ynez Mountains; the index finger represents the San Rafael Mountains; the middle finger, the Sierra Madre Mountains; the ring finger, the Caliente Range; and the little finger, the Temblor Range. You will note how your thumb extends in a more horizontal direction and all of the fingers point slightly away from the thumb at an angle. The thumb (Santa Ynez Mountains) is part of the east-west-trending Transverse Ranges, whereas all the other fingers represent the northwest-southeast-trending ranges known as the Coast Ranges.

Returning to your outspread hand, look at the back of your hand near the wrist. Here's the big cluster of the highest mountains in our region, known as the Mount Pinos complex: Cerro Noroeste (formerly Mount Abel, 8,286 ft.), Mount Pinos (8,831 ft.), Sawmill Mountain (8,818 ft.), and Frazier Mountain (8,013 ft.).

The tabletop between your fingers represents valleys and watersheds. Between your thumb and forefinger lies the Santa Ynez Valley, threaded by the Santa Ynez River. Between the forefinger and middle finger, the Sisquoc River flows, eventually becoming the Santa Maria River. The space between the middle finger and ring finger can be the Cuyama Valley, through which the Cuyama River flows. And finally, the space between your last two fingers might stand for the Carrizo Plain.

Around your outspread hand, imagine the Pacific Ocean off your thumb—the Santa Barbara Channel—and then the coastline swinging around to skirt the left side of your hand. To the right of your little finger, imagine the vast expanse of the San Joaquin Valley.

This is an easy way to get your bearings. But such an oversimplified analogy is bound to leave things out. Parts of Ventura and San Luis Obispo counties are missing.

Still, this is the basic outline of the heart of our region.

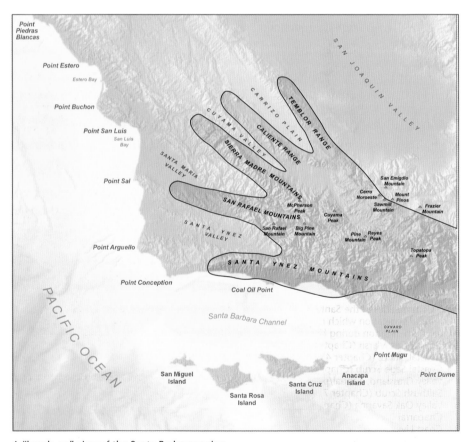

A "hands-on" view of the Santa Barbara region

If you've had enough of geography, skip to the climate section. For a more in-depth view, read on.

A Naturalist's View

The third view of our region is from the standpoint of a naturalist.

California as a whole is unique. Our state is considered one of the world's twenty-five most biologically rich and endangered ecoregions. It harbors more plant species than the central and northeastern United States and Canada combined (over

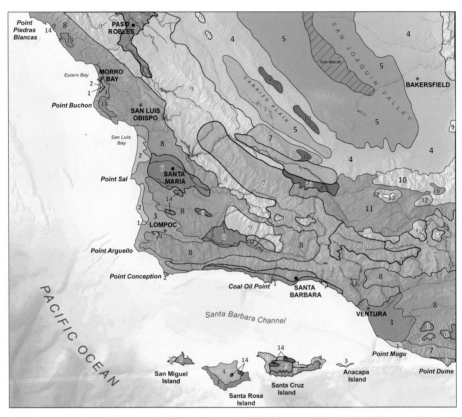

Plant Communities of the Santa Barbara Region (modified from Kuchler 1977): This map depicts the *natural* vegetation which is believed to have existed prior to modification by farming, grazing, and urbanization during historic times. Each habitat is designated by a number below.

1   Coastal Salt Marsh (Chapter 5)
2   Coastal Dunes (Chapter 4)
3   Coastal Sage Scrub (Chapter 6)
4   Valley Grassland, annual/perennial grasses (Chapter 7)
5   Saltbush Scrub (Chapter 7)
6   Valley Oak Savanna (Chapter 7)
7   Chaparral (Chapter 6)
8   Coast Live Oak Woodland (Chapter 7)
9   Blue Oak–Gray Pine Woodland (Chapter 7)
10 Juniper Savanna (Chapter 7)
11 Pinyon Pine–Juniper Woodland (Chapter 7)
12 Mixed Coniferous Forest (Chapter 8)
13 Subalpine Forest (Chapter 8)
14 Coastal Cypress and Pine Forest (Chapter 10)
15 Island Chaparral (Chapter 10)

forty-nine hundred native plants), and over 30 percent of the known insect species north of Mexico. Forty-four percent of the plant and animal species are endemic to California alone.

If you take a slice of the species diversity of California and place it in an area located approximately within San Luis Obispo, Santa Barbara, and Ventura counties, you are left with a rich and complex region for study.

Along the coast, the region stretches from Point Piedras Blancas in the northwest to Point Mugu on the southeast, and seaward to the edge of the continental shelf. The Santa Barbara Channel and the Northern Channel Islands are included.

Inland, the region is bordered on the north by the mountains of Southern San Luis Obispo County. Moving east from the coast, then across the Carrizo Plain and the Temblor Range, one comes to Interstate 5, which generally forms the region's eastern border. The high mountains of Ventura County are in the southern part of the region, with the Santa Clara River Valley forming the southern boundary.

One aspect stands out: the flora and fauna of the Santa Barbara region defy classification by a single method. Consider how the following scientific disciplines have variously categorized the area.

To botanists, the Santa Barbara region is a place where seven vegetation groups coalesce: those of the South Coast, North Coast, western Transverse Ranges, South Coast Ranges, San Joaquin Valley, tail end of the Sierra Nevada, and Northern Channel Islands. Even a small slice of the Mojave Desert laps over into the far eastern corner of the region.

To geologists, there are five geologic provinces found all or partly in the Santa Barbara region: southern Coast Ranges, Great Central Valley, southern Sierra Nevada, western Transverse Ranges, and Northern Channel Islands.

To climatologists, our region includes ten different horticultural climate zones, from the high-elevation cold interior to the South Coast mild marine belt.

To biogeographers, who define regions of California by patterns of animal distribution, the Santa Barbara region would be part of both the Central Coast bioregion and the South Coast bioregion.

To ecologists working with the US Department of Agriculture at the Forest Service, the Santa Barbara region would include eight separate ecological subregions.

Although the Santa Barbara region refuses to fit neatly into a single classification, there are historic and scientific precedents for describing an area with borders similar to those proposed in this book. Clifton Smith, in his indispensable *A Flora of the Santa Barbara Region, California* (1998) has used similar regional boundaries to describe the plants of our area. A conservation region outlined by the Conception Coast Project in 2005 included some of the same territory. It used watersheds and mountain ranges to define a rectangular portion of the Central Coast area. Furthermore, the Santa Barbara Museum of Natural History has concentrated its

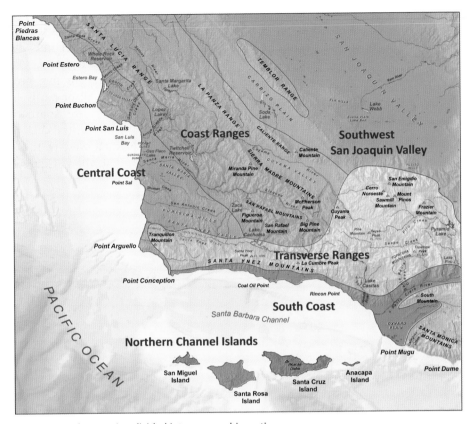

The Santa Barbara region divided into geographic sections

efforts over the years in a region with the general outline described above. Curatorial work, exhibits, and field study have centered upon the Santa Barbara Channel and its islands, and the watersheds of the Santa Maria, Santa Ynez, Ventura, and Santa Clara rivers, reaching inland to the Carrizo Plain and Mount Pinos.

Physical Geography: The Lay of the Land

For simplicity, let's divide the Santa Barbara region into six smaller sections in order to discuss their important physical features. Each subregion has characteristic plant communities and microclimates that set it slightly apart from the others. Please refer to the maps on pages 9 and 11.

However, it is essential to understand that the habitats outlined by their characteristic vegetation and described in depth in the following chapters may be found scattered throughout these sections. The following maps will also be a helpful reference for this discussion of physical geography: Political Features of the Santa Barbara Region (p. x) and Topographic Features of the Santa Barbara Region (p. xi).

Central Coast

Stretching from Point Piedras Blancas south to Point Conception, this section includes the coastal valleys, such as Los Osos Valley, Santa Maria Valley, westernmost Santa Ynez Valley, and the coastal terraces that end at Point Conception. From Piedras Blancas, rocky headlands occur south to San Luis Bay. From San Luis Bay to Point Sal, extensive sand dunes are found along the coast. From Point Sal south, the coastline resumes its rocky character to Point Conception.

The Santa Maria River flows through the Santa Maria Valley, a large coastal lowland basin, meeting the ocean near Guadalupe Dunes. South and southwest of the Santa Maria Valley, the Casmalia Hills extend to Point Sal. Here, Vandenberg Air Force Base covers approximately ninety-eight thousand acres and extends thirty-five miles along the coastline. It encompasses elevated mesas composed of ancient sand dunes on Burton Mesa and San Antonio Terrace.

The climate here is strongly influenced by the ocean and is cooler than that of the South Coast. The prevailing northwest winds regularly bring fog over the area.

Characteristic plant communities are dunes, annual grasslands, coastal sage scrub, chaparral, Coast Live Oak woodland, and Valley Oak savanna.

South Coast

This narrow coastal strip stretches from Point Conception south along the coast to Point Mugu.

Here, the western portion of the marine terrace is scarcely a mile wide, but to the east it broadens to five miles near the city of Santa Barbara. Small streams cut across the coastal plain as they drain the Santa Ynez Mountains. Occasionally, the coastline is broken by coastal wetlands, as at Goleta Slough and Carpinteria Salt Marsh.

Approaching the town of Ventura, the bluffs begin to recede, the coastal terrace widens, and the Ventura River swiftly debouches at the beach. Between Ventura and Oxnard, the Santa Clara River meets the ocean where it forms the Santa Clara River Estuary. The Santa Clara River watershed has created the fertile Oxnard Plain. To the south, Calleguas Creek flows into Mugu Lagoon, an important coastal wetland.

Once again, marine influence is great, but average temperatures are warmer than on the Central Coast. The south-facing location acts as protection from the strong northwest winds.

Characteristic plant communities are coastal sage scrub, chaparral, and Coast Live Oak woodland.

Coast Ranges

The southern portion of the Coast Ranges dominates the topography here.

In San Luis Obispo County, the northwest-southeast-trending Coast Ranges feature the southern Santa Lucia Range, the La Panza Range, the Caliente Range, and the Temblor Range.

If you travel east from Santa Maria on Highway 166, you will pass through the southern fringe of the Santa Lucias and La Panzas and arrive at the Cuyama Valley. The Caliente Range forms a ridge of rugged, sparsely vegetated mountains, with Caliente Mountain (5,105 ft.) as the high point. Beyond the Calientes, the Temblors are the last mountain range before the land dips down into the San Joaquin Valley.

The Caliente Range is the northern border of the Cuyama Valley. The Cuyama River, originating high in Lockwood Valley, forms this huge watershed. On the south side of the Cuyama Valley, the Sierra Madre Mountains and the San Rafael Mountains are the southernmost outliers of the Coast Ranges. The highest mountain is Big Pine Mountain (6,828 ft.) in the San Rafaels.

Where the Cuyama and Sisquoc rivers come together at the little town of Garey, they become the Santa Maria River. These rivers swell with runoff rainwater in winter, but in summer their flow is intermittent or sometimes completely dry.

The climate is a hot, interior one, modified only slightly by sea breezes. Snow falls on the mountains annually, but only lingers at highest elevations.

Characteristic plant communities are Juniper savanna and Pinyon Pine–Juniper woodland at lower elevations. Chaparral and Blue Oak–Gray Pine woodland are found on the slopes, interspersed with annual grassland. Small areas of mixed coniferous forest are found on the highest peaks.

Western Transverse Ranges

The mountains, hills, and valleys of the western Transverse Ranges are comprised of the Santa Ynez and Topatopa mountains, Pine Mountain, and Mount Pinos. These mountains trend in an east-west direction, "going against the grain" of most mountains in California, and in North America in general.

The Santa Ynez Mountains can be seen from Goleta, Santa Barbara, and Carpinteria as a bold, south-facing rampart above the coastal plain. Their westernmost peak, Tranquillon Mountain (2,170 ft.), is relatively low. East of Gaviota Pass, however, the crest gets higher to include Santa Ynez Peak (4,298 ft.) and La Cumbre Peak (3,985 ft.).

The Topatopa Mountains north of Ojai in Ventura County lie east of the Santa Ynez Mountains, their highest point being Topatopa Peak (6,210 ft.).

On the north side of the Santa Ynez Mountains, the Santa Ynez River winds westward through the Santa Ynez Valley to the sea. As it approaches Lompoc, it flows between the Santa Rosa Hills and the Santa Rita Hills, terminating at Ocean Beach Park near Surf.

The highest and most impressive mountains in the region are located in Ventura and southern Kern counties. Pine Mountain, a long ridge of sandstone, can be seen from Highway 33 as the road curves up through the backcountry near the Sespe Wilderness north of Ojai. Reyes Peak (7,510 ft.) is the highest point along the Pine Mountain ridge.

In the northeastern part of this section, the Mount Pinos area is made up of Frazier Mountain, Mount Pinos, Sawmill Mountain, and Cerro Noroeste. These four mountains are a result of geologic forces that reflect the histories of both the Transverse and Coast ranges, so they combine qualities of each. At 8,831 feet, Mount Pinos looms above the others. Much of the fauna and flora here has a strong affinity with the southern Sierra Nevada.

The climate is hot to temperate

with little marine influence. In winter, it's cold at higher elevations. Snow falls on the highest peaks in most years.

Characteristic plant communities are chaparral and Pinyon Pine–Juniper woodland on the lower ranges and mixed coniferous forest on the highest mountains.

Southwest San Joaquin Valley

This section is located on the southwestern fringes of the San Joaquin Valley, the southern portion of the Great Central Valley. Located in southeastern San Luis Obispo County and Kern County, the area includes the Carrizo Plain, an arid sink caused by a subsidence of the land between the Caliente and Temblor ranges. Soda Lake, an alkali playa, occasionally fills with rainwater. The Carrizo National Monument harbors a number of rare and endangered species of plants and animals.

Swinging around to form the southwestern portion of the "U" at the bottom of the San Joaquin Valley, a magnificent swath of grassland lies at the base of the Pleito Hills and now is set aside as the Wind Wolves Preserve.

There are no rivers here. Seasonal streams drain into basins and then dry up.

The climate is hot and semi-arid in summer and cold in winter.

California annual grasses and saltbush scrub are the characteristic vegetation here. At higher elevations are Blue Oak–Gray Pine woodland and Pinyon Pine–Juniper woodland.

Northern Channel Islands

The Northern Channel Islands—San Miguel, Santa Rosa, Santa Cruz, and Anacapa—are the tips of an undersea ridge that parallels the coast and the Santa Ynez Mountains. The highest point on the Northern Channel Islands is Picacho Diablo (2,450 ft.) on Santa Cruz Island.

These islands have a unique flora and fauna, much of it found nowhere else in the world.

Among the many plant communities found here are Bishop Pine forest, island chaparral, and dunes.

Climate

Climate is a collection of the prevailing weather conditions over time. Weather is the state of the atmosphere at a certain time or place: foggy, rainy, windy, or overcast.

Weather dictates the conditions under which plants and animals thrive or die.

Weather is strongly influenced by the ups and downs of local topography. On Big Pine Mountain, at over 6,800 feet, or at New Cuyama, at 2,160 feet, or on the pier at the Santa Barbara harbor, at sea level, you will encounter a variety of weather conditions. On a given day, it can be raining on Big Pine, dry and windy in New Cuyama, and foggy at the harbor.

To get the big picture, step back and take a moment to understand the patterns that create the Santa Barbara region's favorable climate.

Around the globe, regions with a location on the western border of a continent between 30 and 40 degrees latitude have a **Mediterranean climate**, named after those countries bordering the Mediterranean Sea. Found on only 2 percent of the earth's surface, areas with this climate are in California, near the Mediterranean Sea, in western and southern Australia, on the Chilean coast, and in the Cape region of South Africa. In a Mediterranean climate, mild rainy winters are followed by long dry summers. On balance, our region's climate is termed "semi-arid," due to the relatively low amount of average annual rainfall.

Most Mediterranean climates have less annual temperature variation than continental climates found inland. In our case, the presence of the Pacific Ocean nearby ameliorates temperature extremes, giving us cooler summers (see the "Summer Weather" section in this chapter) and milder winters than inland locations. Air traveling over the ocean acts as a modifier along the immediate coast, bringing with it cool temperatures in summer and mild temperatures in winter. This is because the ocean temperature varies only a few degrees from winter to summer (about 15°F at most); consequently, the ocean is cooler than the land in summer and sometimes warmer than the land in winter.

The marine influence on temperatures near the coast compared to sites farther inland illustrates how the shape of the land controls the airflow over its surface. The narrow coastal plains receive the most sea breeze, low valleys usher it farther inland, and mountain ranges often block the reach of the marine layer completely.

Thus, at locations farther inland and at higher elevations, the climate reflects more of a continental influence, with colder winters and hotter summers. In a couple of hours on a winter day, you can go from sun-bathing at the beach on the coast to cross-country skiing in several feet of snow on Mount Pinos.

Most winter days in the region average 55° to 65°F, although some inland spots have reached 10°F or lower. In July, on the other hand, the coastal valleys may have maximum readings of only 65° to 75°F while it could be 95° to 100°F in the inland valleys or 80° to 85°F in the mountains.

Seasons and Weather

People who move to the Santa Barbara region from other parts of the country lament what they perceive as the absence of seasons. With many temperate days of the year and an abundance of sunshine, those not attuned to nature's cycles assume that a day of comfortable temperatures in the winter is the same as a day in summer.

Santa Barbara's weather is less extreme than that of the rest of the continent, but there are certainly seasons: distinct times of the year when plants and animals grow, mate, reproduce, disperse, migrate, and hibernate. The rhythm of the seasons may vary from month to month depending upon many factors, but the seasonal clock is always ticking. Timing is everything in the natural world, and it's not always measured by the month of the year.

Seasons in our area are often triggered by a series of weather events. For example, on the rest of the continent, spring has been celebrated by writers and poets as beginning in March or April when the earth awakens after a harsh winter. But on Santa Barbara's coastal chaparral hillsides, the spring awakening starts

Lockwood Valley after a winter snowstorm

San Rafael Mountains looking north from Knapp Castle

Snow-covered conifers on Mount Pinos

after the first soaking rain, whether it be in November or February.

Winter

The winter season offers exciting opportunities to view nature at coastal locations and lowland valleys.

In the Santa Barbara Channel, **Gray Whales** (*Eschrichtius robustus*) swim close to shore on their return migration to Arctic waters, the calves nudging their mothers' sides. In February and March, watch for Gray Whales from Goleta Point or a boat in the channel. The whales exhale air in a plume of steam, then slowly dive, their long, slate-colored backs disappearing under the surface.

Onshore, **Harbor Seals** (*Phoca vitulina*) and **Northern Elephant Seals** (*Mirounga angustirostris*) begin the pupping season at rookeries in January and February. At a protected cove in Carpinteria, docents monitor female Harbor Seals; farther north at San Simeon, the elephant seal pupping event lures hundreds of visitors—intrigued at the chance to view these magnificent mammals on their breeding grounds.

Extreme low tides in December and January uncover otherwise hidden tidepool creatures. An exploration at Hazard's Cove at Montaña de Oro reveals orange **Ochre Sea Stars** (*Pisaster ochraceus*) clinging to the black rocks. In the green threads of **surfgrass** (*Phyllospadix* spp.), young kelp crabs scurry away. A reddish-brown, foot-long creature known as the **Gumboot Chiton** (*Cryptochiton stelleri*) glides slowly across the bottom of one of the deepest pools. A **California Two-spot Octopus** (*Octopus bimacu-*

East Beach in Santa Barbara after a storm on January 22, 2010

Kelp crab on surf-grass

loides) tenders a single tentacle from a hiding place. The minus tide days of winter make for great tidepooling.

Near the coast at Ellwood, in the eucalyptus groves, thousands of **Monarch** butterflies (*Danaus plexipus*) roost in heavy concentrations. The black-and-orange butterflies, tightly clustered together, cleave to the leafy branches of the tall trees. As sunlight warms them in the mornings, the butterflies depart their clusters, slowly flying about in the cool grove.

Harbor Seals at Carpinteria Bluffs

In the eastern Santa Maria Valley after a series of rainy nights, **Western Spadefoots** (*Spea hammondii*) and **California Tiger Salamanders** (*Ambystoma californiense*) crawl out of crevices and holes and travel overland, seeking mates in farm ponds and vernal pools.

At lowland freshwater lakes and reservoirs (such as at Lopez Lake, Lake Cachuma, and Lake Casitas), the calm waters host large flocks of wintering ducks and geese. Also, hundreds of swan-necked **grebes**, both **Western** and **Clark's** (*Aechmophorus* spp.), spend the winter here.

Western Spadefoots emerge on rainy winter nights to migrate overland to ponds. Their loud chorus attracts females.

Osprey soar over freshwater lakes in winter, adept at plunge-diving for fish.

When they dive, they leap forward and over, sending ripples across the glassy surface.

From a boat on Lake Cachuma, **Bald Eagles** (*Haliaeetus leucophelus*) can be spotted as they sit on prominent oak snags overlooking the water. Winter is the best time to watch the Bald Eagles and **Osprey** (*Pandion haliaetus*) as they hunt for fish in the lake and perch nearby to devour their catch. An Osprey will occasionally carry its fish to the top of a utility pole beside Highway 154, undeterred by the cars whizzing past.

For chaparral plants and birds, winter is the start of spring. Good rains in December and January stimulate the ceanothus, gooseberry, and manzanita to bloom. The songs of **California Thrashers** (*Toxostoma redivivum*) proclaim their territories among the sweet-smelling white blossoms of the ceanothus that cover the south-facing slopes of the Santa Ynez Mountains.

However, at higher elevations in the interior, winter brings much colder temperatures. Snow falls after the biggest storms. On the north slopes of Mount Pinos and Big Pine Mountain, three-foot drifts bury the thick conifer trunks.

In most years, only a few species of birds can withstand winter cold in the highest mountains. **Steller's Jays** (*Cyanocitta stelleri*) and **Clark's Nutcrackers** (*Nucifraga columbiana*) are year-round residents up there, subsisting on the nourishing seeds in pinecones. Other animals either hibernate or move to the lowlands.

Winter Weather

To understand our winter weather, imagine the global circulation of winds as they generally flow through the atmosphere from west to east across North America. (Winds are named according to the direction they come from, not the direction in which they are going.) Surface air flows from high pressure to low pressure; in the Northern Hemisphere, air is pulled clockwise around high-pressure cells and counterclockwise around low-pressure funnels—constantly forming and dissolving to affect our weather.

The all-important **westerlies** bring with them giant currents of air in the high atmosphere. The **jet stream**, the powerful inner core of the band of westerlies, steers these high-altitude winds.

In summer, when the days are long and the sun heats the earth more in the Northern Hemisphere, the westerlies retreat farther north, following the sun. But in winter, when cold air dominates, the storm-carrying westerlies move south. They travel across North America from west to east, controlling most of the weather in the United States and especially that of the West Coast.

After the long dry season, all eyes are on the sky to celebrate the first sign of winter rain in a Mediterranean climate. Most rain falls in December, January, February, and March, but beginning as early as October, a long-awaited rainstorm may invade the coast. The Pacific High (see "Spring Weather" section) has usually retreated far enough south so that the westerlies swing down the coast. Also during the winter, the jet stream is stronger and travels farther south, whipping up the westerlies and steering the storm tracks towards our region.

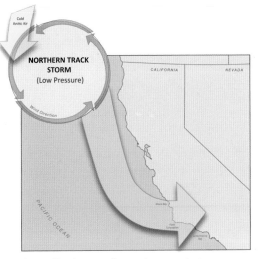

Generalized route of a northern track storm

As a winter storm moves onshore, the topography of the land affects rain totals. Rainfall amounts are enhanced by **orographic** effects: the clouds filled with moisture rise on the wind-ward side of the mountains and rain is squeezed out of them, because cooling air cannot hold as much moisture as warmer air. On the leeward side, the sinking air warms and has less relative moisture as it descends. Since a good deal of moisture has already been wrung out of the clouds, places in the lee of mountains are said to be in a **rain shadow.**

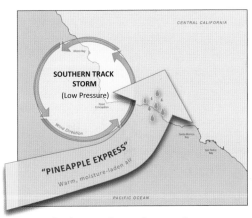

Generalized route of a southern track storm with "Pineapple Express"

The figures below show average annual rainfall for three locations on the coastal plain.

San Luis Obispo—24.36 inches
Santa Barbara—18.12 inches
Ventura—15.35 inches

Comparing these sites with some inland locations, you can see the effect of the Coast Range rain shadow on inland communities:

New Cuyama—8.39 inches
Taft—6.00 inches
Bakersfield—6.49 inches

At the crests of mountain ranges, locations such as San Marcos Pass or Refugio Pass, or Old Man Mountain, west of Ventura, benefit from oro-graphic uplift. On the other hand, locations in the lee of mountains, such as New Cuyama, experience the rain shadow of both the San Rafael and Sierra Madre ranges.

Because every drop of precipitation is so precious in a Mediterranean climate, winter storms merit further discussion.

Generally, there are two types of winter storms: those that originate in the Gulf of Alaska, the **northern track cold storms**, and those that originate off California, the **southern track warmer storms.** The northern storms are those that, depending upon their speed and size, come barreling down the coast, bringing with them moderate rain. Usually, San Luis Obispo and the northern portions of our region get more moisture from these northern storms, which tend to peter out, at least partly, by the time they get to the South Coast.

Since most of our storms come from the north, the extra rainfall provided to the region north of Point Conception is substantial, further reinforcing the landmark as not only a faunal boundary, but a climatological one as well.

In contrast, southern track storms are born not off Alaska but in the ocean off the California coast. When they move onshore, these warmer systems bring with them considerable amounts of moisture. If these storms are slow movers, they bump up against the south-facing slopes of the Santa Ynez Mountains and produce torrential rains due to the added orographic effects.

One of the signs of an approaching storm is a shift in the wind. Watch the palm trees along East Beach. When a storm approaches, the fronds bend with the wind from the southeast, and

sand blows across Cabrillo Boulevard. After the front passes through, the wind usually shifts around to the northwest.

Occasionally southern track storms tap into a plume of subtropical moisture, producing a third type of storm with an extra wallop. These **"Pineapple Express"** storms, so named because the plume they tap into often extends towards the Hawaiian Islands, deliver especially large amounts of rain to the South Coast; flooding and mudslides can occur because the earth is so saturated with water. These were the conditions in January of 2005, when the rain total at the top of San Marcos Pass was over twenty-four inches during a five-day period in which a series of Pineapple Express storms took place. The mudslide at La Conchita in which several people perished was a result of this same series of storms.

Spring

Spring spreads over the region gradually: from low elevations to high, and from west to east.

At the coast, strong northwest winds buffet the shore, especially north of Point Conception. The stiff winds invade the Santa Maria and Lompoc valleys in the afternoons. At the Santa Maria River mouth, the wind tears at the sand dunes; northbound shorebirds huddle in the lee of the dunes on the mudflats, their heads tucked under their copper-spangled wings.

Whitecaps fleck the ocean. Seabirds, flying north to their breeding grounds, pass by in thousands—a steady chain of **Pacific Loons** (*Gavia pacifica*), **Brant** (*Branta bernicla*), and **Surf Scoters** (*Melanitta perspicillata*).

Their urge to migrate is so strong they fly regardless of the wind, powerful wings pummeling the air. Often they land on the choppy seas off Shell Beach or Pismo Beach, bobbing and diving for fish in coastal waters. Due to the wind, ocean upwelling has forced cold, nutrient-rich water to the surface, where plankton blooms attract schools of small fish such as anchovies and sardines.

At rocky intertidal areas along the coast, creatures reproduce by broadcast spawning. Mussels, periwinkles, and anemones release clouds of sperm and eggs into the ocean when the tides are right.

On land, the spring bird migration is well underway by April at Nojoqui Falls County Park in the Santa Ynez Valley. Colorful warblers, tanagers, grosbeaks, and orioles perch in the oaks and sycamores as they make their way north from wintering grounds in Central America.

In the Cuyama Valley, along Cottonwood Canyon Road, a **Badger** (*Taxidea taxis*) trudges through the long grass towards its den, where it will soon give birth. **Western Rattlesnakes** (*Crotalus oreganos*) emerge from winter hibernation hungry, then coil in wait for careless **Deer Mice** (*Peromyscus maniculatus*). A pair of **California Ground Squirrels** (*Otospermophilus beecheyi*) refurbish their burrow, preparing for the arrival of a new litter.

In the Carrizo Plain, moonlit nights mean good hunting for the **San Joaquin Kit Fox** (*Vulpes macrotis* subsp. *mutica*) as it stalks kangaroo rats to take home to a litter back at the den. The cooing sound of **Burrowing Owls** (*Athene cunicularia*) wooing

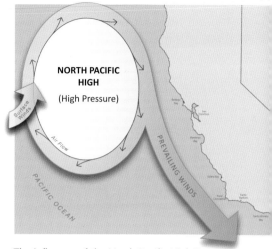

The influence of the North Pacific High Pressure system and its position, shielding the region from low-pressure disturbances from the north in spring and summer

The Badger is widespread but rarely seen.

The California Ground Squirrel: its abundance was noted by the earliest explorers.

21

California Poppies

Owl's Clover

Spring on the Carrizo Plain with goldfields in the foreground

Lupines on Figueroa Mountain

each other is the spring serenade of this wild, remote place.

The slopes of Figueroa Mountain shimmer with orange California Poppies and blue lupine. Farther north, at Shell Creek Road off Highway 58 near Santa Margarita, more wildflowers burst from the sandy soil. In a brilliant show, the blossoms of purple **Owl's Clover** (*Castilleja exserta*), orange-and-cream **Tidy Tips** (*Layia platyglossa*), bright yellow **goldfields** (*Lasthenia* spp.), pale blue-and-white **lupine** (*Lupinus* spp.), navy blue **phacelia** (*Phacelia* spp.), and white **popcorn flower** (*Plagiobothrys* spp.) blanket the grasslands between tall, wispy **Gray Pines** (*Pinus sabiniana*).

Spring Weather

Northwest wind and fog are the two harbingers of the spring season along the coast. Early spring days may be windy and clear, especially in the afternoons, but by May and June they give way to the fog cycle. Sometimes, for more than a week the sun is hidden by a deep marine layer. The mornings dawn cool and gray; often a light mist wets the streets and drips from the trees. In June many a graduation and Father's Day celebration suffer from sunless, damp afternoons.

What happened to the sunny Santa Barbara weather?

The answer is in the **North Pacific High**, a large dome of high pressure that lies about a thousand miles offshore. In spring and summer the North Pacific High moves slowly northward as daylight hours lengthen, taking up a position over the Pacific Ocean somewhere off Northern California. The surface winds, as they blow in a clockwise direction around this dome of high pressure, send alongshore winds towards the California coast. In addition, the Pacific High shields California from spring and summer storms.

Spring along Santa Rosa Road, Santa Ynez Valley

Onshore winds are at their strongest from April through July. The communities of Lompoc, Santa Maria, Pismo Beach, and Morro Bay, situated north of Point Conception, are more exposed to these spring northwest winds; Santa Barbara, on the South Coast, is somewhat protected. Ventura, located closer to the downwind end of the Santa Barbara Channel, may be windier in the afternoon than Santa Barbara.

Spring view of Sierra Madre Mountains from Cottonwood Canyon Road, Cuyama Valley

When the northwest wind contacts the streak of cold, upwelled water (see Chapter 3 for more on ocean upwelling) near the coast, its moisture condenses, forming **fog**. The fog, a collection of condensed water particles, soon becomes a marine layer which is sucked inland by the rising warm air from the land. Santa Barbara's air conditioner is now set up and ready to roll, cooling

Spring northwesterly winds blowing in the Santa Barbara Channel

Fog creeping in at Point Sal

Inland marine layer reaching to the base of Figueroa Mountain

all but the highest mountains and the farthest inland valleys.

The Santa Maria, Lompoc, and Santa Clara River valleys allow the cool air to seep inland, occasionally as far as sixty miles. These valleys are prime croplands for cool-season vegetables year-round. Some late spring days, the marine layer is so thick it will flow as far as the foothills and up the slopes of the San Rafael Mountains. On those mornings, you can stand on top of Zaca Peak or Figueroa Mountain and look out on a sea of fog which laps up against the 3,000 foot contour. All of Lake Cachuma and the upper Santa Ynez River watershed are socked in, hidden under thick fog.

Nothing is chillier than a Memorial Day picnic at Ocean Beach near Lompoc. A cold wind blows off the ocean, beachgoers shiver in sweatshirts, and the gray layer of fog prevents any sun from peeping through to warm the gathering. In contrast, a picnic at a park in Ojai in late May will feature a gentle breeze, warm temperatures, and plenty of sunshine. Or, go as far east as New Cuyama or Piru on Memorial Day and you'll be barbecuing in 90 degree temperatures. The farther inland you go, the less the sea air has a chance to mitigate the ups and downs of seasonal change.

Summer

In the Santa Barbara Channel, **Blue Whales** (*Balaenoptera musculus*) and **Humpback Whales** (*Megaptera novaeanglia*) gorge on the plentiful krill. Excited naturalists make trips towards Santa Rosa Island to observe these great beasts as they feed on the tiny, shrimplike krill that swarm in ocean waters.

Onshore at coastal salt marshes such as Morro Bay, a variety of clams squiggle deeper into their muddy homes. When the tide goes out, a female **Striped Shore Crab** (*Pachygrapsus crassipes*) stands watch at the entrance to her tunnel. She carries approximately fifty thousand eggs attached to the underside of her recurved carapace.

Humpback Whale fluke display with Santa Cruz Island in background

Meanwhile, most resident land birds have finished nesting by the end of June. Juvenile **Black Phoebes** (*Sayornis nigricans*), **Orange-crowned Warblers** (*Oreothlypis celata*), and **Bewick's Wrens** (*Thryomanes bewickii*) are on their own. Many immature birds wander upslope to cooler habitats. They forage for insects and nectar at higher elevations where plants are still flowering.

In the Cuyama and San Joaquin valleys, the grasslands have turned from green to gold to brown, seemingly overnight. Vernal pools dry up. Young salamanders and toads, matured from their larval stages, crawl into the nearest gopher hole or ground squirrel burrow to escape the heat and dryness.

Water striders are supported by surface tension in quiet pools.

Where perennial freshwater streams flow, **Southern Steelhead** (*Oncorhynchus mykiss*) swim along the bottom, gleaning mayfly and stonefly larvae from the streambed. **Common Water Striders** (*Aquarius remigis*) are quick to scoot to safety, avoiding the fish. At the bank of the stream, the **Common Green Darner** (*Anax junius*) dragonfly has just shed its plain larval exterior and is allowing its beautiful transparent wings to dry before a first flight.

Bewick's Wren. Photo by Robert Goodell

At the same time, spring is almost over for coastal sage scrub and chaparral on south-facing slopes of the Santa Ynez Mountains. The sages and buckwheats have begun to wither; their dead blossoms persist as tiny brown buttons on dried-out stalks.

In contrast, in the higher mountains springtime lingers into the summer months. In July on the slopes of Mount Pinos, crimson-flowered **Scarlet Penstemon** (*Penstemon rostriflorus*) lures hummingbirds; the delicate pink-and-white blossoms of **Parish's Snowberry** (*Symphoricarpos rotundifolius*) unfurl; bird song rings out from the pines. On the summit, dense mats of subalpine plants sport tiny pink, blue, and yellow flowers. Tall clumps of **Western Blue Flag** (*Iris missouriensis*) make a stunning show of purple at the meadow near Chula Vista Campground, further down the mountain.

Up here, mammals and birds still nurture dependent young. Juvenile chipmunks skitter around a dead fir trunk, chasing and fighting with each other. A female **Mule Deer** (*Odocoileus hermionus*) leads twin fawns to the spring at Sheep's Meadow on Sawmill Mountain. At the headwaters of the Sisquoc River on Big Pine Mountain, an **American Black Bear** (*Ursus americanus*) trailed by her cubs searches for grubs in the thick forest duff.

Summer Weather

The change from spring to summer weather along the coast is so gradual as to go unnoticed. The Pacific High still steers dry air across the ocean and the air still condenses as fog when it travels over the cool coastal waters. The daily fog cycle involves horizontal, or **advection** fogs, those that stay close to the ground in cumulus puffs and whiffs and smudges. They form overnight at sea and ooze inland over low spots in the coastal terrain. By late morning on a summer day they tend to burn off, as the heat of the sun warms the land and the mist dissipates.

Longer fog cycles involve advection fogs at the beginning, but soon the character of the fog changes. As cool air flowing in from the ocean piles up over the land, it pushes warm air that lies above it higher and higher. This warm layer of air, which acts as a ceiling above the marine air, is called an **inversion layer.** Colder air is usually found above warmer air, but not in this case; the usual layering of air masses is "inverted."

One of the most interesting aspects of summer fog is **fog drip.** When a stand of trees lies in the path of fog that carries a lot of moisture, tiny eddies of air above the trees dislodge the moisture in the fog. It collects on the leaves, from which it drops to the ground like a light rain. Fog drip provides much-needed moisture during the long, dry summer months. A study at Berkeley demonstrated that fog drip alone can produce up to ten inches of moisture beneath a single tree in one season. Several species of eucalyptus and conifer and the **Tanbark Oak** (*Notholithocarpus densiflorus*) are found at sites where fog drip increases moisture.

A fascinating experiment was done on Santa Cruz Island, where groves of **Bishop Pine** (*Pinus muricata*) reap the benefits of a heavy marine layer. Bishop Pines grow in rather poor,

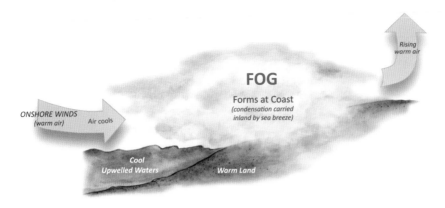

The movement of fog onshore on a typical summer day

sandy soil. On the mainland, they are found only near Lompoc and Orcutt, but the finest stands in our region thrive on Santa Cruz Island. Why?

Professor Douglas Fischer has studied the Bishop Pine forest on the island, where the maritime climate produces overcast conditions which shade plants, reduce water loss, and reflect solar radiation. When the cloud layer bumps up against the slopes, the moisture falls as fog drip.

Pine needles have the perfect structure to trap fog droplets. As the fog particles come swirling in, they slide down the pine needles and fall to the ground. Fog drip and the cool, moist influence of summer fog have allowed endemics or near-endemics of many plant species to persist on the Northern Channel Islands.

The same is true on the mainland, where fog drip in locations at the top of the Santa Ynez Mountains nourishes an association of plants with a more cool climate affinity (See Chapter 8).

But one day in early August, a subtle change creeps into the foggy mornings and hazy afternoons. About this time the North Pacific High begins to weaken, the force of its wind diminishes, and the temperature difference between the land and the sea decreases. The morning fogs are not as dense or as long-lived. Sometimes the days dawn clear and warm, perfect beach weather with highs of 75°F.

Occasionally in the afternoons, thunderheads bulge up over the Santa Ynez and San Rafael mountains. A humid, sultry feeling hangs in the air. This new type of disturbance swings up out of the Gulf of California, bringing with it a dose of subtropical moisture. These storms seldom bring substantial rainfall to the coast, but inland a few sprinkles may come down. In the mountains, thunder rumbles, and if lightning strikes it could start a forest fire.

Fall

In coastal lowlands, the first hot days dawn clear and calm. On some mornings, the Northern Channel Islands are stenciled against the horizon in sharp silhouettes. From time to time, warm winds from the northeast rake the

Brazilian Free-tailed Bats peek out from a maternal roost in crevices beneath a concrete bridge

Fall color: Fremont Cottonwoods

Fall color: Big-leaf Maple

landscape, which is parched and dry. Big, brown leaves begin to blow off sycamores. Hillsides studded with dusty oaks and pines wait for the first rain.

With no substantial precipitation since April, the lack of moisture has taken a toll on chaparral plants. The shriveled leaves of sumac and chamise persist; manzanitas have adapted to the Mediterranean climate by turning their leaves at an angle away from the punishing sun.

This passage by C. F. Macintyre, found in Lawrence Clark Powell's *Islands of Books*, describes it well: "Regard the withered buckthorn, dead deerweed, the rattling tambourines of lupine seed, the motherly yucca wilting with full pods, the moribund sagebrush mouthing earth's dry paps…then listen for the secret thoughtful rain."

Offshore, fish species following warmer waters tend to move northward into the Santa Barbara Channel in late summer and fall. **Pacific Bonito** (*Sarda chiliensis*) and **Dolphinfish** (*Coryphaena hippurus*)—otherwise known as Mahi Mahi—may sometimes venture into offshore waters. The strange-looking **Ocean Sunfish** (*Mola mola*), which resembles a large platter as it basks on its side at the surface, is another of the late summer and fall visitors.

At Tucker's Grove County Park in Goleta, **Acorn Woodpeckers** (*Melanerpes formicivorus*) cache acorns in tree trunks for retrieval later on; **Western Scrub-Jays** (*Aphelocoma californica*) grab acorns too and stuff them into the ground, where they will sprout after the rains. Nearby under a bridge, **Brazilian Free-tailed Bats** (*Tadarida brasiliensis*) roost in

Fall: dried flowers of California Buckwheat

Fall color: Willows, alders, sedges, cattails

the concrete crevices. Soon, their nightly insect-hunting trips will diminish, for they go into torpor as the nights grow longer and cooler.

For the woodrat and the **Coyote** (*Canis latrans*), inhabitants of the chaparral, September marks not the beginning of fall but of winter. The woodrat spends all of its time ensconced in its nest of sticks and rubble to avoid the heat. Dry conditions in the chaparral force the Coyote to descend into suburban gardens in search of water. It may seek prey in the form of domestic cats and dogs.

Golden-tipped rabbitbrush borders the roadways in the pinyon-juniper canyons of the Cuyama Valley and along Highway 33 in the upper Sespe Creek watershed. In higher canyons of the mountains, **Big-leaf Maples** (*Acer macrophyllum*) and **Fremont Cottonwoods** (*Populus fremontii*) turn shades of yellow. By November, pretty red berries cluster on **Toyon** (*Heteromeles arbutifolia*) shrubs, a sort of western color counterpart to the eastern hollies.

Some birds and mammals come down from higher elevations to seek water and avoid the winter cold.

Poison Oak in fall

Tule Elk at Wind Wolves Preserve

Red-breasted Sapsuckers (*Sphyrapicus ruber*) and **Yellow-rumped Warblers** (*Setophaga coronata*), which breed in local mountains, move to the coastal plain in fall.

Bears travel downslope to warmer canyons where berries and roots are not covered by snow.

The **Tule Elk** (*Cervus elaphus* subsp. *nannodes*) at Wind Wolves Preserve have finished the rutting season; the males go off together into the high, secret canyons, leaving behind the herd of females and yearlings.

Fall Weather

The transition from summer weather to fall is more noticeable here than the transition from spring to summer. By September, there's a definite change in the atmosphere.

According to the thermometer readings, especially along the coast, this is more like summer than fall. September, October, and November can have soaring temperatures in our region, depending upon the direction of the wind, the topography of

the land, and the location within the region.

The North Pacific High withdraws to the south, somewhat weakening the flow of cool northwesterly winds from the ocean. Although the sea breeze never completely dies, it is frequently replaced by drier air originating in the interior.

In fall the continental air, particularly of the Great Basin, plays a bigger role in the weather. This offshore flow from the interior deserts towards the Southern California coast is a prelude to what weather forecasters call a mild Santa Ana condition.

In this scenario, which typically results in bright, clear days in fall, the humidity of the air is low. The offshore breeze has traveled many miles across the interior and ended up at the coast, bringing with it the dryness of its Great Basin origins.

Meanwhile, in ocean waters, the influence of northwest winds blowing from the Pacific High decreases, accompanied by a subsidence in local upwelling. No longer quelled by

The two diagrams show the different locations of Santa Ana and Sundowner winds in our region

northwest winds, the more southerly, warmer Davidson Current flows north along the coast. Waters offshore are relatively warm, so fog forms less frequently in fall.

Extraordinary Weather Events

Long spells of sunny, calm days can lull you into forgetting that our region is subject to volatile weather from time to time. Meteorologists will be the first to admit that weather forecasts here can be challenging. That long stretch of the Pacific Ocean to the west and the high mountain ranges inland combine to add an element of the unpredictable.

Weather events that are outside the norm and occur irregularly are described by climatologists as **anomalous**. In this section we will discuss Santa Ana winds, Sundowner winds, El Niño—a condition properly called El Niño/Southern Oscillation—plus droughts and floods.

Santa Ana Winds

The dry winds known as Santa Anas

are the result of a massive high-pressure system over the Great Basin and/or the northern Mojave Desert. The air forms as a large dome of fair weather and takes on the qualities of the dry landscape beneath it. When conditions are right, this dry air rushes down through the mountain passes of Southern California. As the air descends, it follows the path of least resistance—squeezing through the passes and roaring down the canyons. This is a **katabatic wind** (from the Greek "to flow downhill"), and as it descends from the high deserts, the air further compresses and the wind becomes hotter and drier. It's like putting your thumb over a hose nozzle, forcing the water to come out faster. And for every thousand feet the air descends, it warms on average about 5.4°F.

Due to the topography and location of our region, the strongest of the Santa Ana winds are often felt in the Santa Clara River Valley and locations farther south. Although conditions may be dry and breezy below

Sundowner winds originate at the crest of the Santa Ynez Mountains and gather speed as they race downslope toward the coastal plain.

north-facing canyons along our South Coast, we do not bear the brunt of the true Santa Ana winds. Mild Santa Ana conditions, as described above under fall weather, may add a dryness and clarity to the air. At the same time it could be blowing a gale to the south in the Santa Clara River Valley and the Los Angeles Basin.

Sundowner Winds

Sundowner winds are similar to Santa Anas in this way: they are downslope winds. Otherwise, Sundowners are quite different. Unique to the Santa Barbara region, they originate in the late afternoon to evening. Unlike Santa Anas, they occur over a very small area.

Sundowners happen because of the east-west orientation of the Santa Ynez Mountains. When a complex and not fully understood set of conditions prevails, superheated surface air in the Santa Ynez Valley combines with a lessening of the marine conditions along the South Coast, setting the stage for potentially damaging winds.

The air, pent up behind the Santa Ynez Mountains, becomes a rushing river of wind once it descends through

the gaps in the ridgeline. Gaviota Pass, Refugio Pass, San Marcos Pass, and Romero Saddle (above Summerland) are a few of the low spots in the range where the Sundowners break through. Oddly, it can be dead calm at the very top of the ridge, but once the air heads downhill, it picks up tremendous speed. Each Sundowner event is slightly different, due in part to the effect of local topography. Some blow wildly from Gaviota to Montecito, while Carpinteria remains relatively calm. Rarely, a Sundowner wind consists of cooler air, rushing in gale force winds towards the coast.

Like Santa Ana winds, Sundowners occur most often in the fall but may blow at any time of year. In fact, a Sundowner on June 17, 1859, brought Santa Barbara's temperature to a record high of 133°F. And the Painted Cave Fire on June 27, 1990, was intensified by Sundowner winds and a temperature reading of 109°F at 6:00 p.m. at the Santa Barbara Airport. In the Santa Barbara area, both the Tea Fire of November 2008 and the Jesusita Fire of May 2009 were exacerbated by Sundowner winds.

But the Sundowner of December

31, 1995, was one of the most destructive of all.

Nature Journal
New Year's Eve, 1995

Sundowner

Last night I experienced one of the most frightening winds I have ever been through. Over the past thirty-five years—living as we do in the funnel of a coastal canyon—there have been times when I thought the wind would completely destroy the house. It blows so hard, rattling the windows, banging every door, the gusts so furious and so erratic that one minute they seem to come from one direction, the next minute another.

But those were more typical Sundowners. The one described here was an anomalous Sundowner—a redundancy if there ever was one!

During the day, I was completely absorbed in the compilation of our local Christmas Bird Count. Although it had been windy, it was not remarkably so. I was so relieved to have the census successfully completed that I scarcely paid attention to the weather.

But around nine p.m., the wind began to build. An hour later, the temperature was about 70°F, and I feared a Sundowner was in the making.

A raging Sundowner roared down our canyon. It felt as though the house would be lifted off its foundation. The wind whirled around the corners, snarling and fuming. I'm familiar with winds, but the force of this one was incredible.

Outside in the dark, windy night, the ominous thuds I heard above the howling gale were the echoes of tall trees hitting the ground, one after the other. The cracking of limbs breaking off, the hurtling of debris, the pinging noise of leaves and seedpods striking the windows: it was a maelstrom.

Later, the wind died down and I slept a bit.

This morning, by the light of day, the damage is shocking. It's as if nature has gone on a giant binge. The morning after is eerily quiet and dead calm.

I go outside to survey the surroundings.

Two eighty-foot-tall Deodar Cedars in neighboring backyards have been completely toppled. Eucalyptus and cypress trees, massive root balls ripped up out of the ground, lie across the main roads of Montecito and Santa Barbara. Downed power lines drape from utility poles. Electrical power has been cut off to thousands of households.

In my research for this book, I came across a paper by Dr. Warren Blier that featured three Sundowner winds in the Santa Barbara area, one of which was the one described here. He quoted an Associated Press report: "Strong winds—measured between 50 and 60 mph at Santa Barbara Harbor—caused several traffic accidents and wind also smashed windows of shops and restaurants at Santa Barbara's wharf."

Although the temperature gradient was lacking in this instance, and therefore the wind was not hot, the event goes down in the record books as being one of the most destructive Sundowners in history. A possible explanation was that in this instance, the air was a mass of high pressure aloft but not superheated. Then, it was funneled at high speed through local canyons towards low pressure at the coast.

El Niño/Southern Oscillation (ENSO)

Due to its location on the Pacific coast, the Santa Barbara region is in a position to have a front-row seat at El Niño events.

ENSO (El Niño/Southern Oscillation) is a condition in the atmosphere and ocean currents that begins in the tropical eastern Pacific Ocean (off Peru) and may spread its effects to other regions of the world. The terms for the warming phase, El Niño, and cooling phase, La Niña, refer to the temperature of the sea's surface in the eastern Pacific. Additionally, the atmospheric pressure of the tropical western Pacific (off Indonesia), compared with that of the tropical eastern Pacific (off Peru), can fluctuate. This is known as the **Southern Oscillation.**

Appearing at anywhere from two- to eight-year intervals, ENSO has been the cause of unseasonably high rainfall totals and flooding in the Santa Barbara area.

Scientists have identified the strongest recent ENSO events as those of 1982-83 and 1997-98.

What creates an El Niño event? The cold **Humboldt Current** is the counterpart of our cold California Current (See Chapter 3). Usually, the Humboldt Current flows north off the coast of Peru, where its cold, upwelled, plankton-rich waters support anchovies and other economically important fish harvested by Peruvian fishermen.

In El Niño years, the Humboldt Current weakens or stops flowing and the anchovy population moves to deeper waters or south off Chile, a disaster for the Peruvian fishermen.

Due to a complicated series of atmospheric events, the southeast trade winds cease to blow. The usual air-pressure pattern reverses itself in the phenomenon known as the Southern Oscillation; these changes affect global weather.

Here's how.

With the trade winds at bay, the top layer of the eastern Pacific off Peru begins to warm up due to the invasion of warmer water from the western Pacific. The warm water, normally kept far to the west off the coast of Indonesia by the trades, thus sloshes backwards in what's known as a **Kelvin wave** towards the coast of the Americas south of the equator. This invasion of warmer water actually swells, making a bulge about six inches higher on the surface of the Pacific Ocean.

When the warmer waters of the Kelvin wave approach the Peruvian coast, they block the upwelling of the Humboldt Current. The warm waters spread north, too, infiltrating California's offshore currents and elevating surface temperatures.

But that's not all. More clouds than usual form at the equator over the accumulated warm water brought by the Kelvin wave. Low pressure develops, drawing the subtropical jet stream farther north than normal. The jet stream carries the moisture-laden storms across the southern US. Santa Barbara and Southern California are right in its path.

What are the biological effects of an El Niño event? In addition to the climatological effects, the biological effects of ENSO can be devastating. Both north and south of Point Conception, water temperatures become four to six degrees higher than normal in an El Niño cycle. Warm water contains fewer nutrients, leading to less phytoplankton, the crucial base of the ocean's food chain. Seabirds and pinnipeds (seals and sea lions) are unable to find enough small schooling fish to feed on; the lack of nourishment for adults means they cannot successfully nurse their young.

After the 1997-98 El Niño, a strong La Niña in 1999 returned colder than normal temperatures to Santa Barbara's offshore waters. **California Sea Lion** (*Zalophus californianus*) and **California Brown Pelican** (*Pelicanus occidentalis* subsp. *californicus*) numbers rebounded, having been decimated by the lack of anchovy prey during the El Niño.

Commercial and recreational fishermen noticed a dramatic increase in the landings of subtropical fish species that prefer warm water during the 1982-83 El Niño.

Bottlenose Dolphins (*Tursiops truncatus*), usually a more southern species, were found regularly north of Monterey Bay in 1983. They arrived in the Santa Barbara Channel at that time and have stayed ever since.

Giant Kelp (*Macrocystis pyrifera*), brown algae that form forests underwater offshore, cannot survive long if water temperatures exceed 58°F, while during an El Niño episode water temperatures may reach 70°F. (See Chapter 3 for more on Giant Kelp.)

Giant Kelp also suffers from heavy storms that generate a higher wave surge. The heavy storms of the 1982-83 El Niño reduced surface canopies of Giant Kelp at study sites off the Northern Channel Islands.

Despite the above examples of El Niño's impacts, fluctuating environmental conditions such as El Niño and La Niña are still not well understood. La Niña dry years often follow El Niño wet years, but the severity of each remains unpredictable.

It's important to recognize that El Niño conditions and Pineapple Express events are distinct. They may or may not occur in tandem. For example, the storms of 2004-05 were warm-wet Pineapple Express events, but that was not an El Niño year.

Further complicating the weather picture is the **Pacific Decadal Oscillation**: warm and cool ocean temperature cycles that tend to last forty to sixty years. Some meteorologists believe that since the 1998 El Niño event, Santa Barbara offshore waters have been generally cooler, and they may stay that way for the most part for the next twenty-five years or so. Locally, cooler waters usually mean drier weather.

Droughts and Floods

Santa Barbara's highly variable rainfall regime produces weather cycles that include drought and flood. Droughts and floods aren't necessarily part of El Niño or La Niña conditions, but they can be.

As we saw earlier, the Pacific High plays a big part in controlling the mild weather and dry summers along the Pacific Coast. But, in winters when the Pacific High fails to weaken and move far enough south, storms from the Gulf of Alaska are blocked from delivering rain to Southern California. In these years, less than average precipitation falls in our region.

Mission Creek pouring over its banks during a winter storm

Sycamore Creek flooding after an El Niño storm, February 1998

A succession of these below-average rainfall years is considered a **drought.**

Historically, Santa Barbara's wet and dry cycles appear to have alternated. Missionaries at the Santa Barbara Mission kept climate records of events affecting local agriculture, such as the great floods of December 9, 1861, through January 10, 1862. Three storms during that time produced huge flood waters: erosion altered the canyons of the Santa Ynez Mountains, and silt deposited on the Goleta coastal plain filled in the harbor used by ships, resulting in the present salt marsh of Goleta Slough.

Following the floods of 1862, the worst drought in recorded history occurred, from 1862-64, devastating the cattle industry in Santa Barbara County. Over two seasons, the low rainfall resulted in the loss of two hundred thousand head of cattle— only five thousand head survived.

More recently, the term "drought" was applied to the years 1986 through 1990, when precipitation was well below average. In March 1991 the "March Miracle," an unexpected series of storms, rescued the region from a fifth year of drought. The decade of the 1990s can be characterized as a wet cycle, having had only two seasons with below-average rainfall. Since 2000, wet and dry winters have alternated, with 2004-05 being especially wet, although it was not an El Niño year. In contrast, the rainfall season of 2006-07 was one of the driest, with total precipitation of only 6.41 inches in downtown Santa Barbara.

During heavy rainfall, the steep slopes along the South Coast from Gaviota to Ventura may lead to **flooding.** For most of the year, the streams and rivers are dry; saplings and shrubs sprout in the watercourses. When the brief, stormy winter arrives, the creek waters swell with the force of the unaccustomed runoff from a heavy rain. Racing downslope, the creeks drag trees, shrubs, and boulders with them. When the debris becomes clogged under bridges and culverts or at bends in the stream, the waters pour out over the banks.

Along the South Coast, watersheds are small. The smaller the watershed, the less time it takes for the water to run from its peak rainfall at the top of the Santa Ynez Mountains to the ocean, where peak discharge occurs at the mouth of Mission, Sycamore, or Rincon Creek. In contrast, in the much larger watershed of the Santa Ynez River, the lag time between peak rainfall at Gibraltar Dam, for example, and peak discharge at the Santa Ynez River mouth is longer; but when the Santa Ynez River does flood, it will also take longer to subside.

In 1940-41, downtown Santa Barbara recorded the highest seasonal rainfall total ever, at 45.25 inches, until the 1997-98 El Niño storms topped that record with 46.52 inches.

Two of the most extreme flood years were those of January and February 1969, and January and March 1995, which caused millions of dollars' worth of property damage and forced evacuations.

Nature Journal

Flood of January 10, 1995

Today I measured more than nine inches of rain in the rain gauge in less than twenty-four hours. On top of a heavy rain of five inches a few days ago, this deluge was enough to send most South Coast streams over their banks.

Beginning at midnight the rain came down in sheets, pounding on the roof, pooling like a lake under the house, rushing away over saturated ground that could take no more. All night long, I listened to the rocks and boulders as they crashed and rumbled against each other in the creek down in the canyon. It was the sound of enormous rocks being picked

up by the power of the floodwaters as though they were pebbles.

By morning, freeway underpasses around town were deep in water. Schools and businesses closed, and still it poured. I eyed the front doorstep, as little by little the muddy water crept higher and higher. Any minute it could have come over the threshold. What then?

On the coastal slope, the water had to go somewhere as it roared down the mountainsides, into the gullies, and down the creeks as fast as it could to the sea. But the creeks and streams cannot carry a "hundred-year flood"! The water broke all the rules in its race to the sea. Suburban streets became rivers as the brown water surged down them, overflowing culverts, ripping out trees and debris, carrying boulders the size of small cars. Large street trees lay uprooted, pavements were lost to sinkholes. The fragile superstructure of urbanization was devastated by flood.

* * *

A study of the natural history of the Santa Barbara region depends upon a knowledge of our location in the south-central portion of the state. The region is unique due to its position on the border of northern and southern weather regimes, which affect the habitats where animals and plants live. In addition, the region's varied topography results in wide contrasts between temperatures at the coast and those inland.

In the big picture, the Santa Barbara region is particularly sensitive to climate change. Our location near the coast is vulnerable to El Niño/Southern Oscillation events. Global changes can be measured just offshore by monitoring the fluctuations of sea surface temperatures.

The concept of the relationship between weather conditions and the topography of the land is vital to an understanding of the natural world. The northwesterly winds of spring and summer blow over the ocean, bringing cooling fog and enhancing the marine influence. In fall the Santa Barbara region may be affected by conditions in the Great Basin and interior deserts, where our strongest offshore winds originate. In winter, storms dump the most precipitation on the windward slopes of the east-west Santa Ynez Mountains and north-south Coast Ranges, depending upon the origin of these low-pressure systems.

Learn the lay of the land—the topography. It's the first step in this wonderful journey through our region.

The Santa Ynez Mountains form a wall behind the city of Santa Barbara

CHAPTER 2: GEOLOGY—LAYING THE FOUNDATION

Picture a scene from millions of years ago. You are standing in the middle of a lush grassland with scattered subtropical trees. Plant-browsing mammals such as camels and titanotheres move slowly as they graze. (A titanothere looks like a horse crossed with a tapir.) Nearby, a marsh threaded with stream channels empties to a warm sea. On the banks of the stream, soft-shelled turtles sun themselves. A group of oreodonts—small, piglike beasts with flexible snouts—crop the grasses. They squeal as a giant vulture swoops over and perches nearby. In the distance, a hyena-like dog crouches, ready to pounce on a tortoise.

This isn't the Serengeti. It's an environment that existed 34 million years ago as depicted in the Sespe Formation fossils found in our region's backcountry.

More recently, forty thousand years ago, you are strolling along the Carpinteria bluffs near the location of the present town of Carpinteria. A pine forest thrives here and dense shrubbery hides a natural spring. The spring, as it turns out, is in the middle of a thick pool of black tar, or asphaltum. The eerie moaning sound of an animal in distress carries over the air. Kneeling, you part the bushes and watch as an awkward, furry mammal lunges and fights, trapped in the asphalt ooze. It is a very large bison. As the bison thrashes helplessly, other carcasses float to the surface. Among them are a mastodon, a camel, and a saber-toothed cat. These Pleistocene animals, approaching for a drink, met the fate of the bison. Several vultures and an eagle watch from the treetops, attracted by the stench and noise.

By far the best way to journey back in geologic time, however, would be to rent yourself a boat—but there would be nothing to see. There was no land where the Santa Barbara region is today. It was submerged beneath the Pacific Ocean. In fact, coastal California as we know it is a comparatively recent creation. For millions of years before that, the sea covered everything. It was sometimes a shallow sea, sometimes a deep one, and land lay eastward. And,

39

Pillow basalts near Figueroa Mountain are an example of igneous rocks. The pillow shape is characteristic of underwater eruptions.

because dinosaurs were extinct before local sediments were deposited, their remains have never been found here.

Geologists and paleontologists seek to recreate what the natural world looked like in the past. To do this, they look at the rocks.

Rocks are the history books of nature. By knowing the language in which these books are written—geology and paleontology—earth scientists unravel the origins of the rocks and fossils we see on the ground today.

Geology is the foundation of our knowledge of the shape of the land, and the flora and fauna that existed a hundred thousand years ago or a hundred million years ago. The spectacular landforms of the Santa Barbara region are a result of geological forces. Our steep mountains, river valleys, and offshore islands have a fascinating geologic history. (See Chapter 10 for more on island geology.)

Two words—**plate tectonics**—explain the origins of the Santa Barbara region. According to this con-cept, giant plates move about on the earth's surface. These plates, carrying ocean floors and continents, bump into each other, expand, or disappear, and are at the root of mountain building. Where two plates collide, huge mountains can be thrust up, or volcanoes erupt. Where two plates slide past each other, earthquake faults can develop and the crust can be torn and deformed.

Plate tectonics explains why earthquake faults crisscross our region and how they got there. The south-central coast of California is one of the most active mountain-building, crustal-folding areas of the earth. At this moment, the forces of the Pacific and North American tectonic plates are grinding slowly against each other, dragging Santa Barbara off in a northwest direction towards San Francisco.

Geology is not static. It is happening now, and it is of vital importance.

Rock Types

An understanding of geology hinges on a few basic ideas.

The earth is made up of minerals. A rock is a collection of these minerals, sometimes in grains, sometimes in crystals. Rocks come in three basic types: igneous, sedimentary, and metamorphic.

To start with, the earth's crust was **igneous**. Igneous rocks are created from molten magma under the crust. When these rocks cool, they crystallize. Granite is one of the most familiar igneous rocks. It forms slowly and crystallizes into a coarse-grained rock beneath the earth's surface. Rhyolite and basalt are finer-grained igneous rocks that come to the surface and quickly cool. They are ejected by active volcanoes.

Igneous rocks are rare in the region, but on the drive up Mount Pinos you can see granitic rocks that were molded deep in the earth's crust 145 mya (million years ago) and pushed up to its surface relatively recently. Other igneous rocks, such as rhyolite and andesite, spewed out by volcanoes less than 23 mya can be found on Vandenberg Air Force Base (Tranquillon Mountain) near Lompoc and at other locations.

The "morros"—the chain of volcanic plugs that form peaks between Morro Rock and Islay Peak near San Luis Obispo—are composed of igneous rocks. These peaks were formed when congealed lava oozed up through ancient volcanoes. Weathering has eroded the softer rocks around them. The morros dominate the landscape and provide a scenic backdrop for the beautiful Los Osos Valley.

Sedimentary rocks are consolidations of particles transported when other rocks weather and erode. They're described by the size of the particles. If the rock's particles are minuscule, as with mud, it is called shale. Silt, with somewhat larger grains, comprises siltstone. Sand, larger still, makes up sandstone.

About 95 percent of the rocks in our region are sedimentary. They are found in layers or beds, each bed differing slightly from the other. Each layer (**stratum**) of sedimentary rock represents a depositional event, such as a flood or an underwater landslide.

Through careful study of sedimentary rocks, geologists are able to reconstruct ancient geography, or **paleoge-**

The morros, a chain of volcanic plugs extending from San Luis Obispo to Morro Bay, are another example of igneous rocks.

Serpentine outcrop along Figueroa Mountain Road

ography. They do this by examining the particles in the rock layers and figuring out their source and place of deposition. Geologists can tell if the sedimentary layer originated as a nearby highland or a rushing river, thereby reconstructing the topography of millions of years ago.

For example, the Santa Ynez Mountains represent a series of more than forty thousand feet of sedimentary rocks. The layers accumulated at the bottom of the Pacific Ocean as the

The reddish-brown rocks in the middle foreground are the Franciscan Formation, part of the oceanic crust now exposed on Figueroa Mountain.

rock particles washed off nearby land and settled on the ocean floor.

Metamorphic rocks have been changed from their original form by either high heat or intense pressure, usually in connection with the movement of tectonic plates on the earth's surface. Metamorphic rocks are not molten, so they retain some of the characteristics of their original form.

The best example of metamorphic rocks is found in the **Franciscan Formation** exposed along the flank of Figueroa Mountain. Metamorphics of the Franciscan Formation—serpentine, blueschist, and chert—were once at the bottom of a deep ocean trench. Tremendous tectonic pressure altered them from their original substances. Along Figueroa Mountain Road, the outcrops of greenish serpentine, California's state rock, are easy to see. Serpentine is soft and smooth when polished or carved and is prized by local sculptors.

Mapping the Rocks

In order to read the past through rocks, geologists can examine an exposed roadcut or a core sample from a well and tell which rocks are youngest and which are oldest. Two principles they use which give them a relative age dating are that the oldest rocks were deposited first, the principle of **superposition**; and that those first rocks were laid down in nearly horizontal layers, the principle of **original horizontality**.

Sound simple? In theory, yes. But the earth's crust is a dynamic, pliable material over the long stretches of geologic time. The pressures of crustal movements create upfolds (**anticlines**) and downfolds (**synclines**), faults, and volcanoes. Mountain building (**orogeny**) continues to hurl up peaks and weathering erodes them, washing the sediments over alluvial plains, down through the river drainages to the sea.

The rocks we see on the ground today have not always been at that location. Geologists must look beyond topography to recreate the rock layers that lie buried or are only partially visible.

For example, the big outcrops near the top of La Cumbre Peak are part of that forty-thousand-foot pile of sedimentary rocks that were once at the bottom of the sea. They belong to the **Matilija Formation**, sandstone deposited on the ocean floor 50 mya and finally upended by faulting and compression only 5 mya. Many of the lovely sandstone walls found throughout the region are carved from the Matilija rocks.

Geologists use the term "formation" to identify a distinctive type of rock

Arlington Peak, also known as Cathedral Peak, is resistant sandstone of the Matilija Formation, which has provided sandstone for many of the rock walls in the region.

formed by the same geologic processes at about the same time. By looking at the composition of the mineral grains, the color, texture, and thickness of rocks, and the fossils in the rocks, geologists recognize and map the groups of similar rocks called formations. Formations are named after the location at which they were first described; sometimes they stretch for miles throughout a region, and sometimes they are quite restricted.

In order to map the landscape, a three-dimensional geologic picture of the underlying rocks must be drawn from what is visible on the surface. Thomas W. Dibblee Jr., one of the best-known geologists of the region, hiked every inch of the mountainous backcountry, mapping the geologic formations. He had an uncanny ability to recognize formations in the field, much as you and I would know the face of an old friend.

Geology in the Santa Barbara area is especially interesting because it is composed of both **continental** and **oceanic basement** rocks overlain by an enormously thick series of mostly marine sedimentary layers.

Continental basement rocks are a part of the ancient North American continental crust. They are the igneous (granite) and metamorphic (gneiss and schist) rocks exposed on Mount Pinos and Cerro Noroeste. The rocks on Cerro Noroeste, formed 1.2 billion years ago, are by far the oldest in our region.

Oceanic basement rocks underlie most of the remaining area. They are part of the oceanic crust that was scraped off during the collision of the Pacific and North American plates and embedded under the Santa Ynez and San Rafael mountains 200 mya. Oceanic basement rocks are visible on Figueroa Mountain as part of the

Franciscan Formation. In most other places, they are buried under deep layers of younger sedimentary rocks.

Nature Journal
April 29, 2001

Geology Field Trip to Figueroa Mountain

On a fresh morning I meet the group in Los Olivos, in the Santa Ynez Valley. There are forty-five of us—geology students of all ages and skills—led by the enthusiastic Helmut Ehrenspeck. In a caravan, we set off up Figueroa Mountain Road, passing foothills of oaks and grasses. As we near each roadcut, I watch for the white streamlaid gravels and sediments of the Paso Robles Formation, which blankets most of the Santa Ynez Valley. It is rocky, poor soil, but vintners love the Paso Robles; it's marvelous for wine growing.

At the first stop, the bridge over Alamo Pintado Creek, we leave our cars and begin the hike up Birabent Canyon. A steep hillside lies above us on the other side of the creek. On the left side of it is a band of whitish soil (Careaga sandstone) sporting a profusion of Purple Sage, Black Sage, California Sagebrush, and other shrubs. On the right side, the rock is brown and bare with only a thin clump or two of vegetation.

Helmut explains this is the work of the Little Pine Fault. The dull, brownish rock with scarcely anything growing on it is thrust up against the much more recent rock of the Careaga Formation. The Franciscan Formation—the barren, brown stuff—is ancient. Once a piece of the ocean floor, it got plastered onto North America from the Pacific Plate when the two collided 200 million years ago. The

Franciscan is basalt and chert and serpentine from the depths of a 10,000-foot-deep sea which existed where we're standing now.

This is the southernmost expanse of easily accessible Franciscan rocks in California. Pretty impressive.

As we walk on, the chocolate Franciscan cliffs rise against a blue sky. A rolling meadow with tall grass appears. We have arrived at a former Chumash village site, Sohtonok'mu.

The meadow is part of an ancient landslide, typical of our Franciscan Formation: hummocky, bumpy, and lumpy. Helmut explains that the Chumash often settled near landslides. Water seeped out around the edges of the landslide and formed little pools where waterfowl congregated and tules grew.

If we'd been Chumash we would've jogged up Birabent Canyon and come out on the shoulder of Figueroa Mountain. But being twenty-first-century geology students, we hop in our cars and continue up Figueroa Mountain Road to the pull-out where you look directly across to Grass Mountain—still blazing with orange poppies in late April.

The chilly north wind blows our jackets and whips at our hair as we stand looking across at Grass Mountain. But Helmut isn't talking about the poppies. In fact, what Helmut has to say sounds positively threatening. The concepts overwhelm me as I stand, notebook out, pencil scratching away.

You see, he explains, the Santa Ynez Valley is being squeezed up against the San Rafael Mountains. The Santa Ynez Fault and the Little Pine Fault are converging towards each other, wrinkling up everything in between. Also, he says, the whole Transverse Range block, which used to be near San Diego, has been rotated up here by 90

Some highly metamorphosed and contorted rocks of the Franciscan Formation on Figueroa Mountain

degrees and as this continues it is jamming itself into the San Rafael Mountains.

How fast? At about the rate your fingernails grow.

He shows us dramatic evidence: a big dip and fold in the strata of Zaca Peak called the Zaca syncline. If the rocks don't fault under pressure, they bend the way this Monterey shale has done, making a big roller-coaster pattern. With the morning sun behind us, it's easy to see.

Our next destination, Soapstone Hill, is a great mound of serpentine rising up between Figueroa Mountain and Ranger Peak. More Franciscan Formation.

We cling to Soapstone Hill, scrambling up on hands and knees so as not to get blown away. Only a few bunchgrasses grow on the serpentine. Helmut says serpentine and other Franciscan rocks contain minerals toxic to many plants. Plants that do survive on serpentine are often rare or endemic.

As I totter around in the windy blasts on Soapstone Hill, listening to Helmut's animated explanations, I look out on the view with new eyes. I begin to understand how the geology underneath controls the vegetation. Looking back at Figueroa Mountain, I notice that Coulter Pines, Big-cone Spruce, and Coast Live Oaks grow lush and fine on the Monterey shale, but on the Franciscan Formation, only scattered Gray Pines and skinny Blue Oaks survive. The line of demarcation comes right across on the fault where the Davy Brown Trail drops down into Fir Canyon.

Imagine. I've hiked that trail for years and I never knew what lay beneath.

Not long after this field trip, Helmut Ehrenspeck passed away unexpectedly. His invaluable contributions to local geology are greatly appreciated and he is greatly missed.

How Old Are the Rocks?

Not only are rocks the history books of nature, they serve as calendars, too. The question of how long ago events of prehistoric time occurred is central to our discussion.

The **geologic time scale** is a way of measuring the history of the earth since its beginning some 4.6 billion years ago. One of the most difficult concepts in all geology is the vastness of geologic time.

Geologic time is overwhelming. A trickle of water etches a steep canyon. A glacier scoops out a valley. Inch–by–inch movement along a fault scarp shoves mountains sideways or up and down.

By examining fossils, we know life changes over time. Charles Darwin

Fossil sand dollars found in the Cuyama Valley, the site of an ancient sea

got his first glimmerings of the idea of evolution from studying geology. As Steve Jones says in *Darwin's Ghost*:

> Geology persuaded Darwin that there was no need to call on ancient cataclysms, be they biblical floods or gigantic earthquakes, to shape the earth. A tiny stream, given long enough, could carve

a giant valley and a shallow sea make, as it dried, a plain a thousand miles across….If landscapes could be transfigured by slow change, so, surely, could flesh.

The geologic time scale gives us reference points in millions-of-years-ago segments. See the Geologic Chart on page 50 for a summary of some of the rock formations in our area and where to see them. Keep it handy to track developments in the past as we skip around in our discussion of what happened when.

A helpful quote from Robert P. Sharp and Allan F. Glazner in *Geology Underfoot*:

> Suppose we let a yardstick represent all of geological time. Precambrian time would measure 30.5 inches, Paleozoic time 3.6 inches, Mesozoic time 1.4 inches, and Cenozoic time about .5 inch. The human race originated about 2.5 million years ago, only .02 inches down the yardstick.

Rocks can be dated in two ways. The most reliable—radioactive age determination—involves a chemical analysis as the radioactive elements decay into other elements. It provides us with a reasonably good means of discovering the absolute age of a rock. Another method of dating rocks involves examining the rock sequence—**stratigraphy**—to figure out a rock's age in relation to its surroundings.

Fossils, animal or plant evidence naturally preserved in the rocks, play a big part in age determination. Since older rocks contain more primitive fossils, and younger rocks more advanced ones, relative age can be determined depending upon what fossil-bearing formations lie above and below the layer in question. **Index fossils** represent life-forms that only survived for a restricted period of time and are thus reliable measures.

Steve Jones, in *Darwin's Ghost,* talks about the inadequacy of paleontological collections, and how much of the earth's fossil record has been lost:

> The turmoil of the rocks means that fossils are not laid down in neat sequence in an ordered world....The Passenger Pigeon flourished in North America as late as the Civil War. At the time of the *Mayflower,* nine billion were alive. Nobody has ever seen the fossilized bones of a Passenger Pigeon. Without a written record we would never know of its existence. Untold numbers of other beings have accompanied it into oblivion. Like the products of past labor, too much has been made for it all to be preserved.

Because most of the Santa Barbara region spent so much time underwater, the majority of fossils here are marine. Fossils of mollusk shells, such as a three-and-a-half-inch clam uncovered in the **Jalama Formation** near Point Conception, are typical of the region. The clam lived at the bottom of the sea 75 million years ago.

Clams, like many invertebrates, have been in the fossil record for millions of years; they have not changed significantly over geologic time. Thus, they are not as good an index fossil as some other marine creatures.

The most useful are **foraminifera.**

Layers of radiolarian chert, representing millions of years of deposition of the remains of microscopic organisms living in open oceans, have been found in the Franciscan Formation. Note the bending and warping that testify to tremendous tectonic pressure.

These microscopic animals secrete exoskeletons of calcium carbonate arranged in a variety of shapes, each species tied to a specific time period. If traces of a particular foram can be detected in a layer of marine rock, such as a mudstone or a clay, that will be a clue to that formation's age.

Radiolaria, other microorganisms found in deep oceans, build their skeletons of silica. When their remains settle out of the water column, they are compacted on the ocean floor, forming a sedimentary rock known as chert. Although greatly altered in the Franciscan Formation, some radiolarian fossils in the chert may still be identified as to species. The presence of radiolarians helped geologists confirm that the Franciscan Formation was once at the bottom of the sea.

Further evidence of the Franciscan Formation's deep sea origins comes in the form of ancient fossils discovered near what was once a

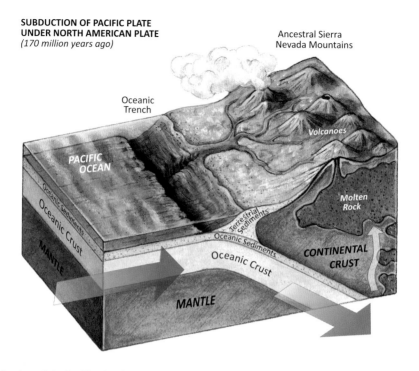

**SUBDUCTION OF PACIFIC PLATE
UNDER NORTH AMERICAN PLATE**
(170 million years ago)

Ancestral Sierra
Nevada Mountains

Oceanic
Trench

Volcanoes

PACIFIC
OCEAN

Oceanic Sediments

Oceanic Crust

Molten
Rock

MANTLE

Terrestrial
Sediments

Oceanic Sediments

Oceanic Crust

CONTINENTAL
CRUST

MANTLE

Subduction of the Pacific Plate beneath the North American Plate about 170 million years ago

hydrothermal vent at the bottom of the Pacific Ocean, in Jurassic times. What remains of the vent is visible in the Figueroa Mountain area. It's called the "black smoker" and around it lived worms and gastropods (snails). These are the oldest fossils in the region.

Plate Tectonics: When Portions of the Earth's Crust Collide

The concept of plate tectonics is now regarded as essential to an understanding of Santa Barbara's geology. However, as recently as the 1970s it was considered revolutionary. Renowned local geologist Tanya Atwater, whose work was instrumental in the final acceptance of plate tectonics, continues to fine-tune its applications. Mean-

while, other earth scientists explore the full ramifications of these ideas.

The earth resembles a round fruit with a relatively thin outer crust and a core at the center. The crust averages about fifteen miles thick, and beneath it lies the **mantle**, eighteen hundred miles thick. The crust and the rigid upper part of the mantle—the outer sixty miles of the earth—make up the **lithosphere**. At the center of the earth is a core with a radius of roughly twenty-two hundred miles.

Suppose you took a paring knife and carved the fruit. By delicately carving the outer surface into a dozen patterns, you could replicate what the earth looks like when the lithosphere is broken up into tectonic plates. These tectonic plates, which are quite rigid, move about over the remainder of the more plastic mantle rocks—the **asthenosphere**—beneath them. The plates have no pattern in their movements, but instead drift about, either by pulling apart, colliding against each other, or sliding past each other.

Some plates are huge, some smaller; some carry continents and parts of the ocean, some carry only ocean. If the plate has ocean on top of it, it will be six miles thick, but if the plate carries a continent, it can be twenty to thirty miles thick.

The plates can move up to two inches per year. Where they pull apart, they form a ridge known as a **rise**, or **spreading center**. When fissures crack the ridge, molten lava seeps out of the mantle to make new crust.

Where plates collide, a long, deep trench can form at the bottom of the ocean with a chain of volcanoes inland from it. This is called a **convergent** plate boundary. One of the plates slides under the other, a process called **subduction**. In Santa Barbara's case, it was the oceanic plate which slid under the continental plate and returned to the mantle millions of years ago. This recycling of crustal material is the earth's way of balancing the new crust at spreading ridges with the disappearance of old crust at subduction zones.

As subduction draws the oceanic plate deeper under the continental plate, some of the oceanic plate gets scraped off and stuck onto the edges of the continental margin. This smaller unit of rocks is called an **accreted terrane**.

In this way, much of California and the western margin of North America grew. Each subduction episode ended in an accreted terrane, which expanded the coastline to the west.

When tectonic plates bump against each other obliquely, then slowly grind past, the pressure is transformed into numerous faults and folds, called a **transform** plate boundary. This is happening in Santa Barbara and all of Southern California, the most studied transform plate boundary in the world. The Pacific Plate, on which Santa Barbara, part of Southern California, and most of the Pacific Ocean rides, is pushing hard against the North American Plate. The movement of the Pacific Plate is northwestward in relation to the North American Plate. The **San Andreas Fault** and its associated faults make up this transform plate boundary, which covers a wide zone.

Geologic History

North America

Prior to 542 million years ago, in **Precambrian** times, an ancient continent existed whose west coast shoreline ran from western Idaho across eastern California through the Mojave Desert and into parts of the San Gabriel and San Bernardino mountains. Extremely old rocks can be traced which were part of the **crystalline basement** of this ancient continent, but not much else is known about it. Possibly, the continental basement rocks of Cerro Noroeste were part of this continent, since they are old enough.

In the late **Paleozoic**, a continental shelf had developed along the

Age of Local Formations and Where to See Them

Era	Period	Epoch	Time*	Event	Representative Location
Cenozoic	Quaternary	Holocene	11,700	Dune Sands (younger)	Morro Bay, Oso Flaco Lake, Guadalupe Dunes
				Dune Sands (older)	Nipomo Mesa; La Purísima State Historic Park
		Pleistocene	2.6m	*Paso Robles Formation:* Terrestrial alluvial detritus of Monterey Formation	Rolling hills and raised flats above Santa Ynez and Los Alamos valleys
	Neogene	Pliocene	5m	*Sisquoc Formation:* Whitish marine diatomaceous sediments	Casmalia and Purisima Hills; quarry at Miguelito Canyon near Lompoc
		Miocene	23m	*Monterey Formation:* Light-colored marine sedimentary shale	Bluffs along South Coast; Arroyo Burro, Gaviota
				Morros: Igneous plugs of congealed lava	San Luis Obispo County from Morro Rock east to Islay Peak
	Paleogene	Oligocene	34m	*Sespe Formation:* Often reddish-colored terrestrial sedimentary shales, conglomerates	Highway 154 three miles north of US 101
				Coldwater and Cozy Dell Formations: Sandstone and shale	Front-country canyons of Santa Ynez Mountains
		Eocene	56m	*Matilija Formation:* Erosion-resistant light-colored marine sandstone	La Cumbre Peak, Montecito Peak, Santa Ynez Peak
		Paleocene	66m	*Pozo Formation:* Shallow marine sandstone	Small outcrops on Santa Cruz Island
Mesozoic	Cretaceous		145m	Igneous plutonic rocks, granitic	Mount Pinos: roadcuts on the way to the summit
				Jalama Formation: Marine sedimentary	Nojoqui Falls
				Shales, sandstones	
	Jurassic		200m	*Franciscan Formation:* Mixture of serpentine, basalts, sandstones, chert, peridotite	Hills around San Luis Obispo, Cuesta Ridge, Figueroa Mountain Road
	Triassic		252m		
Paleozoic			542m		
Precambrian			older than 542m	*Gneiss:* Metamorphic rock appearing banded due to recrystallization under high pressure and/or partial melting	Cerro Noroeste; roadcuts along middle and upper portions of road to summit

*Starting dates refer to years before present

western edge of a slowly coalescing continent known as **Pangaea**. After that, not much happened to the outlines of Pangaea. Its western margin, where California now lies, was underwater and free of tectonic activity. A low shoreline lay along the present foothills of the Sierra Nevada.

Then, during the **Jurassic**, Pangaea began to break up. Its borders assumed the shape of present North America. The whole west coast, including the Santa Barbara region, entered a time of turbulence.

An oceanic trench formed west of our region, and the Pacific Plate accelerated its rate of sliding beneath the North American Plate. The melting rock beneath the North American plate formed a reservoir of magma which forced up the volcanoes of the ancestral Sierra Nevada range miles away.

In our area, the terranes which were scraped off the oceanic crust by the continental crust ended up as the basement rock for the San Rafael Mountains. Geologists recognize that the melange of rock fragments making up the Franciscan Formation on Figueroa Mountain was once part of the oceanic crust beneath the sea. Much more recently, Figueroa Mountain was thrust upwards by compression and faulting, exposing the Franciscan.

Santa Barbara Region

As the subduction episode began to subside, mud, sand, and other sediments were deposited on the continental shelf. In the **Eocene**, a layer cake of sandstones and shales built up underwater: the **Juncal**, **Matilija**,

Note the difference in vegetation as the Rincon Formation (foreground), composed of shale and covered by grassland, abuts the Vaqueros Formation (background), composed of sandstone and covered with chaparral at Arroyo Hondo Preserve.

Cozy Dell, and **Coldwater formations**. Although they were deposited in that order, today if you were to hike up Rattlesnake Canyon behind Santa Barbara, you would be approaching them in reverse order. In more recent time, these rocks have been squeezed up and overturned by tectonic forces.

Excellent fossils from the Ventura backcountry show that the shallow Eocene ocean bottom had early forms of sea stars, brittle stars, cone shells, sea urchins, oysters, even lobsters. Throughout our region, the Pacific Ocean invaded the land in shallow embayments and deeper straits, ebbing and flowing around a few uplifted highlands. Then, the highlands eroded, the sea transgressed, and little dry land remained.

Finally, in the **Oligocene**, sea levels lowered and the land rose for the first time. The **Sespe Formation** was part of a big delta with steep flowing streams, broad floodplains,

The reddish Sespe Formation as seen from Highway 154. Many terrestrial fossils have been recovered from this formation, especially in Ventura County.

and slow-moving rivers. (If you skip ahead you will see that the rocks that ended up as the Sespe Formation in our backcountry originally formed 250 miles south of here.) One of the rivers was the paleo-Colorado River (an ancestral Colorado River), which then dumped into the Pacific, not the Gulf of California as it does today. Geologists can see this by examining the gravel and cobbles in the Sespe Formation.

The Sespe Formation is named for Sespe Creek in Ventura County. It's a thick sequence of rock outcrops from Gaviota to north of Fillmore. Its distinguishing red color is due to oxidation of the rocks. It is especially interesting because it reflects a terrestrial landscape. Fossils of titanotheres and oreodonts are contained in the Sespe rocks, which is how we know these strange life-forms existed at that time.

In the Sespe Formation's red beds, paleontologists have unearthed many interesting fossils. At a location in the

Upper Sespe Gorge/Sespe Creek area, a partial list included the aforementioned titanotheres as well as:

- Plant-browsing mammal—*Duchesneodus californicus*
- Rhinoceros-like mammal—*Amynodontopsis* spp.
- Gar—*Lepisosteus* spp.
- Soft-shelled turtle—Family Trionychidae.
- Tortoise—*Testudo* (*Hadrianus*) spp.
- Bird—Class Aves

Also, fossilized remains of rodents, pocket gophers, and jumping mice were well represented. However, these creatures' time above water was short-lived, geologically speaking. After only three hundred thousand years, the sea inundated the region once more.

Beginning in the **Miocene**, big changes were in store. The Pacific Plate was still shouldering its way past the North American. But the zone where the most pressure was being exerted—coastal California—started to show the stress of this pressure in a different way: by faulting. The San Andreas Fault system was gradually born.

Extreme turbulence accompanied the birth of the San Andreas Fault system. Volcanoes on land and underwater erupted as the crust was torn apart in some areas. Tremendous force pressed against our whole region. The stage was set for one of the most dramatic events in local geologic history—an amazing 90 degree crustal rotation of the Western Transverse Ranges.

Recall that the Western Transverse Ranges—the Santa Ynez, Topatopa, and Santa Monica mountains and the Northern Channel Islands—have an anomalous east-west trend at present, different from the usual north-south direction of North American mountain ranges.

When the Pacific Plate rubbed against the North American Plate in the mid-Miocene, a portion of the North American Plate—our Transverse Range block—got broken off and carried away. As Tanya Atwater says in her *Plain English Field Guide to the Geology of the Western Santa Monica Mountains,* "As the rim of the continent broke apart, one sliver of the continent...got caught up in the shear between the plates. It rotated, much like a floating plank that has one end snagged on the river bank while the other end is dragged along by the current." (For more on plate tectonics, see Atwater's downloads at http://emvc.geol.ucsb.edu.)

In sum, 10 million years ago, the Western Transverse Ranges were farther south, perhaps near the San Diego region, and lay in a northwest-southeast configuration parallel to the coastline. After being rotated approximately 90 degrees over millions of years, the Santa Ynez Mountains and the south coastal portion of our region arrived at the present east-west configuration. Picture a large block of land with a hinge point over near Santa Clarita whose outer end has swung clockwise, from lying due south along the coast to its present east-west orientation.

As the Transverse Range block approached the Santa Maria Basin, it squeezed the Franciscan Formation from the subsurface up onto

The Santa Ynez Mountains, part of the Western Transverse Ranges, underwent an astonishing 90 degree crustal rotation to end up at their current east-west position during the Miocene.

the western flank of the San Rafael Mountains and the Cuesta Ridge, and it crumpled the basin sediments into the washboard structure we see today. The Santa Rita Hills, the Purisima Hills, the Solomon Hills, and behind Avila Beach, the Irish Hills are the upwarps, and the Santa Ynez, San Antonio, Santa Maria, and Los Berros valleys are the downwarps.

Our crustal block is still being squeezed by compression. The North American and Pacific plates alternately concentrate pressure through faulting and folding of the rocks.

Subsequently, sea level rose again and the shoreline retreated eastward. Present-day Ballinger Canyon, Quatal Canyon, and Apache Canyon, located in the badlands of the Cuyama Valley, mark an ancient shore and coastal lagoon. The coarse gray sands and red clays, known as the **Caliente Formation**, have preserved evidence of another group of extinct land mammals, including mastodons and grazing-browsing primitive horses, that roamed

Eroded sandstone cobbles of the Gaviota Formation at the base of uplifted bluffs of the Monterey Formation

the land. Three kinds of camels fed on the grasses and shrubs: a long-necked giraffe camel, a camel similar in size to today's one-humped dromedary, and a gazelle-camel, which was more like a deer in size. The piglike oreodonts were there, and so was a type of pronghorn. Early forms of the pocket mouse, cottontail, ground squirrel, and fox have been found, as well as a strange doglike creature.

The climate throughout was milder than it is now, with summer rains and frostless winters. Much of the flora was similar to that of northern Mexico, a live oak woodland and subtropical scrub interspersed with grasses.

The rest of the region lay once again underwater. The Santa Clara River Valley was inundated by the sea. The Santa Maria Valley was underwater, too. Over time, these marine embayments filled with deposits of organic-rich mud called the **Monterey Formation**, now well known for yielding oil. Oil drilling operations near Ventura, in the Santa Barbara Channel, and near Santa Maria plumb the depths of the Monterey. The tar you step on as you walk on our beaches comes from natural seeps from this same layer of rock.

Near Lompoc, the **Sisquoc Formation**'s silica-rich layers of sediment contain diatoms. The remains of diatoms, single-celled marine plankton, accumulate in deep ocean basins as marine snow (see Chapter 3). Today, **diatomites** are used in a variety of products from ceramics to insulation to filters. The quarry at Lompoc is one of the biggest suppliers of diatomaceous earth in the world.

In the **Pliocene** a tremendous

episode of mountain building began. Mount Pinos, Pine Mountain, the San Rafaels, the Sierra Madres, the Santa Ynez range, the Topatopas, and the Northern Channel Islands were further elevated. The steep new mountains, blocking rainfall, created rain shadows; drier habitats formed inland. A Mediterranean climate took hold. The cold California current brought coastal fogs.

Santa Barbara's modern topography began to take shape.

Despite erosion, the compressive forces of the North American and Pacific plates pushed most of the mountaintops even higher than they are today. The Pacific Plate began to move in a more northerly direction, intensifying the squeeze. The Caliente Range was heaved up out of a

Beginning in the Pliocene our region's steep mountains, such as the San Rafaels and the Sierra Madres, were uplifted.

lowland. Present drainage patterns and watersheds emerged. Alluvium, washed down by creeks and rivers, blanketed the land from Gaviota to Oxnard. Santa Barbara's coastal plain rose to its present position.

The onset of the **Pleistocene** brought numerous glacial-interglacial cycles. The last major period

of glaciation, the Wisconsin, began 120,000 years ago. In our region there were no glaciers, although the climate cooled considerably. Moisture-loving plants that preferred cooler conditions partially replaced chaparral scrub and oak, which had spread here from the Southwest. Torrential rains and floods brought quantities of material down from our mountains, forming big alluvial fans.

Since much of the earth's water accumulates in glaciers during these cold cycles, sea levels dropped. During the **Tioga glaciation**, which was at its maximum twenty thousand years ago, sea levels were approximately three hundred feet lower than today, according to recent calibrations by geologists.

The current epoch, the **Holocene** (beginning about eleven thousand years ago), is a warm period. Chaparral and oaks dominate our flora, while some of the pines and other moisture-loving plants have receded to cooler canyons and mountaintops.

Geologic trends in Santa Barbara's past continue into the present. Warm-cool climate cycles, mountain building, erosion, and northward movement of the Pacific Plate—these will persist long into the future.

Famous Fossils of Our Region

To learn more about fossils, come behind the scenes at the Santa Barbara Museum of Natural History and explore the paleontology collection. Drawer by drawer and cabinet by cabinet, exquisite fossils—many of them millions of years old—lie waiting to usher you back in geologic time. Some are so tiny they must be enclosed in vials cushioned on cotton. Others, like the six-foot-long Columbian Mammoth tusk, cannot fit in the cabinets.

These bones are beautiful: a blue-gray jaw of a Pleistocene mastodon dug up at the former Corona del Mar Ranch in Goleta; a delicately reconstructed skeleton of a young Pygmy Mammoth from Santa Rosa Island; an imprint of a fish species preserved in a white square of diatomaceous rock from Lompoc.

On a shelf by itself, a cast of the skull of a large marine mammal (*Paleoparadoxia*) rests. This peculiar creature, an ancestral form of the manatee with a head that resembles a hippopotamus, swam off our shores 20 million years ago.

The fossil of a giant toothed bird that had a wingspan of fourteen to sixteen feet was found in the Monterey Formation in Tepusquet Canyon east of Santa Maria by Santa Barbara Museum of Natural History curator Phil Orr in the 1950s.

From the museum's collection, three fabulous fossil finds stand out: a gigantic toothed marine bird from Tepusquet Canyon, a group of birds, mammals, and plants from the Carpinteria Tar Pits, and the Pygmy Mammoth remains from the Northern Channel Islands (See Chapter 10).

The giant toothed marine bird was flying above present Tepusquet Canyon, northeast of Santa Maria, when it plunged to its death in a saltwater bay 10 million years ago. In the mid-1950s, this rare fossil was discovered from a flagstone quarry; the bird's complete skeleton lay between two slabs of Monterey Formation shale.

The bird, with a wingspan of fourteen to sixteen feet, had short legs and a long, thin bill with a hook at the tip. The bill, complete with a series of bony projections resembling teeth on the upper and lower jaws, suggests the bird caught live fish. Entombed in the same quarry, fossils of a porpoise, whale, fish, and two other bird specimens—a shearwater and a thrushlike passerine—were discovered.

The fossil of the giant toothed bird, so crisp you can see the feather imprints on the shale, is not only a **"type specimen"** but a **"type genus."** Throughout the history of the natural sciences, species of all sorts have been described as from a **"type locality"** (the location where they were first found) and designated as type specimens, the first example of its kind to be described and identified. The new genus was called *Osteodontornis orri*, or Orr's Bony-toothed Bird. (*Osteo*, bony; *odonto*, toothed; *ornis*, bird. The species name, *orri*, honors Phil Orr, then Curator of Paleontology at the Santa Barbara Museum of Natural History). Only two other fossils of bony-toothed birds have been found, one from London and one from Brazil.

Exciting stuff—to come upon an undescribed insect, animal, or plant embedded in rock and to tell the world about it for the first time. Paleontologists thrive on these discoveries. When a new fossil is brought to light, the gap between prehistoric and modern flora and fauna shrinks. Modern evolutionary biologists depend upon these links to explain how lifeforms have changed over time.

Carpinteria Tar Pits: The largest assemblage of Pleistocene fossils in our region comes from the Carpinteria asphalt deposits on the Higgins Ranch property. Asphalt had been mined on the coast at this spot east of Carpinteria Creek since 1887. It helped pave the streets of Carpinteria, Montecito, Santa Barbara, Goleta, and San Francisco. It was mined hydraulically, then shipped out either by sea from the Smith Brothers' pier at Carpinteria or by the newly completed Southern Pacific Railroad to Los Angeles.

It was here, in 1927, that workers searching for oil made an exciting discovery: a collection of fossils preserved in the aphaltum, lying buried beneath many feet of sand and gravel. Faulting through centuries had allowed seeps of asphalt to reach the surface, mix with the sand, and form pools which trapped unsuspecting animals. (Unfortunately, after paleontologists removed what fossils they could, the area was dug out and used as a refuse dump.)

Two other tar pit locations for fossil remains in Southern California, one at McKittrick, near Taft, and the other at the well-known Rancho La Brea location in Los Angeles, are of similar age. The fossils at McKittrick reflect a drier, inland fauna, and those at La Brea—extraordinary in their number—reflect an open coastal plain. At all three sites, the tar had effectively mummified the specimens, preserving in liquid asphalt the most minute structures of the skeletons.

The Carpinteria site included plant, bird, and mammal remains, although a lot of it was severely fragmented. The asphalt traps were unique. As Miller and DeMay explained in 1941, in "The Fossil Birds of California":

> The asphalt accumulations approach as nearly the work of an active collector as can well be attained by a geological agency. The locality acts as a trap that can be sprung by an elephant or a song sparrow and could retain either victim. It is automatic in that the victim is removed, prepared, and the trap reset by the upwelling of new crude oil from below, and by slow submergence of the animal's body. The bait used was of greatest diversity—water for the thirsty or the dabbler, green herbage for the ungulate or the hiding small folk, live bait [with] uplifted complaining voice to attract the predator, and finally the quieted victim to send positive odors trailing long down the wind to arrest the passing carrion feeder who might chance to cross that wind. This almost personified trap worked day and night at all seasons, and through a long succession of years.

At Carpinteria, the fossils represented largely immatures of carnivores (meat eaters) and ungulates (grazers). Perhaps inexperience led them to seek water from the spring, oblivious of the deadly asphaltum immediately adjacent.

A partial list includes:

- Ground-Sloth—*Glossotherium* (spp.) (possibly not in the pit but nearby)
- Dire Wolf—*Canus dirus*
- Saber-toothed Cat—*Smilodon californicus*
- American Mastodon—*Mammut americanum*
- American Horse—*Equus occidentalus*
- Camel—*Camelops* (spp.)
- Antique Bison—*Bison antiquus*
- Elk-like Deer—*Cervus* (spp.)

Other mammals were modern-day species of the coyote, fox, striped and spotted skunk, weasel, and various mice, gophers, squirrels, and rabbits.

The highest percentage of land birds were birds of prey. Six species of eagle, seven species of hawk, and four species of vulture, including the **California Condor** (*Gymnogyps californianus*), were represented in the tar pits. Such a large proportion of predators indi-

Bones of the extinct California Turkey were found at the Carpinteria Tar Pits and are now housed at the Santa Barbara Museum of Natural History.

cates they must have been trapped in the asphaltum pools while hunting. They met their own fate while waiting patiently for their prey's demise.

The most common bird from the pits was the extinct California Turkey (37 individuals). In addition, there were 108 small, perching birds identified. As for marine birds, only one bone, that of a Brown Pelican, was

This tar-coated Monterey Pine cone was once embedded in the Carpinteria Tar Pits, indicating a different climate in the recent past.

discovered.

The asphaltum deposits at the Carpinteria Tar Pits give clues about the climate and vegetation there. In the tar-coated seeds, needles, cones, and wood, fragments of **Monterey Pine** (*Pinus radiata*), Bishop Pine, and **Gowen Cypress** (*Callitropsis goveniana*) were well represented. They appeared to have been washed down from higher elevations during floods. The few **Douglas-Fir** (*Pseudotsuga menziesii*) and **Redwood** (*Sequoia sempervirens*) specimens were water-worn and may have been transported by storm runoff from another location. However, Douglas-Fir is known to have grown on Santa Cruz Island. Many species of chaparral plants, such as poison oak, manzanita, elderberry, and yerba santa—which grow onsite or within several miles today—showed up, too.

From this evidence, researchers think the climate and vegetation of Carpinteria forty thousand years ago were more like those of today's Monterey peninsula, two hundred miles to the north; during the Pleistocene, perhaps a cooler, moister climate reached further south. The landscape was apparently a pine forest with shrubby undergrowth.

Then, as now, a delightful place to live.

Asphaltum, or tar, oozes from the bluffs near Carpinteria Tar Pits Park.

Nature Journal
July 6, 2001

Carpinteria Tar Pits

Early on a warm, gray morning I set out to visit Carpinteria's Tar Pits Park. Crossing the railroad tracks, I head for the beach along a well-worn path across the bluffs. I pass one great pit where most of the asphalt mining occurred in the late nineteenth and early twentieth centuries.

I am near the site of what was once a thriving Chumash village, Mishopshnow, about which Crespí wrote in his diary on the Portolá expedition in 1769. He observed the Chumash caulking plank canoes with asphaltum from the springs and, so the story goes, he named the place Carpinteria (carpenter shop).

At Tar Pits Park, the trail leads me to a low, shady spot. It is lush and green here with sycamores and willows. This was the ancient spring where freshwater lured the Pleistocene mammals and birds to their demise.

The strong, petroliferous smell of tar assails my nostrils. Tar lies all over the ground around me. Over there, a cut in the cliffs leads down to the beach. On either side of the trail, blackish mounds of asphalt blanket the rocks. Some of it is in smooth flats that look as though a paving company had just finished. Others are solid, pillar-like mounds with sagging gray fronts. If the sun were out, the pillars of asphalt would slowly start to slump.

Next to the pillars, an active tar leak oozes from a gully. The gooey tar forms a runnel of black down the cliff face, making a puddle in the white beach sand at the bottom.

Liquid asphalt is like thick maple syrup, but inky-black and smelly. And, like syrup, it sticks to everything.

Having studied the tar and its current cache of sticks, stones, a beer bottle, and a paper cup, I return to the small seep. Basket Rush grows around the low points of the seep in dark, green spikes. The white, cone-shaped blossoms of the Yerba Mansa nestle nearby. No wonder the mammals and birds of long ago were fooled into approaching good drinking water, when, in fact, death lurked nearby.

I turn to walk back along the bluffs, looking out on an overcast sky, the sea so calm the waves are like ripples. In Pleistocene times, the shoreline would have been further out.

I try to picture a forest here with scattered stands of Bishop Pine and Monterey Pine. The climate would have been cooler, moister.

Otherwise, the tar pits might have been much like this on a July day forty thousand years ago.

Except for the extinct mammals.

I will miss seeing the American Mastodon, the Antique Bison, and the last of the American horses as they stepped unwarily into the soft asphaltum. I will miss the pack of Dire Wolves that gathered on the sidelines, hoping to bring down a large camel as it struggled in the tar. I will miss the Asphalt Stork, the Errant Eagle, and the Fragile Eagle, all waiting for the struggling animals to perish so they can begin their next meal. And the Merriam's Teratorn; I would have liked to see this enormous vulture with a fifteen-foot wingspan.

Walking back, I think about the geology here, and how it intersects with other branches of science. Geology, paleontology, anthropology, and archaeology come together at the Carpinteria Tar Pits.

Over my shoulder, I see the modern oil operations continuing today, with boats ferrying supplies to and from offshore oil platforms.

Since Miocene times, geology has influenced life along this Carpinteria shore.

Earthquakes

To experience an earthquake is to feel the pace of geologic time quicken, if only for a minute. Who can forget the unsettling emotions as you watch the walls of your house shake, the books in the shelves fall out, and the windowpanes buckle during a major quake? Everybody in Santa Barbara has an earthquake story. Longtime local residents accept the uncertainty of living in earthquake country.

On the other hand, outsiders regard the constant threat of earthquakes as one more crazy aspect of Southern California living.

To the uninitiated, all quakes are catastrophic. Unfounded fears run wild.

Indeed, because of our location on the edge of the Pacific Plate, earthquakes will always be a fact of life in the Santa Barbara region, where movements on the San Andreas and related faults are caused by crustal pressures where the two continental plates intersect.

When rocks are stressed by tectonic forces beyond their ability to bend or fold, they break at weak points called fault planes. At these planes, pressure bears on the rocks and then is released in the form of **seismic waves**. The original rupture point, the focus of the earthquake, is usually shallow, less than sixty miles beneath the surface of the earth.

There are several ways to measure earthquakes, but the oldest is a **seismograph**, which documents earthquakes by recording incoming earthquake waves as lines on a paper drum. The **Richter scale** measures the magnitude of an earthquake in terms of the amplitude of the waves recorded on the seismograph.

A major earthquake, defined as over 7.0 on the Richter scale, can be destructive. The ground may rupture at the surface, involving several feet of vertical or horizontal displacement. If the shaking of the ground is violent, it may cause buildings to collapse. Liquefaction occurs when seismic waves move through areas underlain by fine sand. Sometimes land on steep hills slides. And, a rupture in the ocean floor may cause a **tsunami** to flood low-lying coastal areas.

Besides the San Andreas Fault, major faults in our area are the Santa Ynez Fault, Big Pine and Garlock faults, the Santa Cruz Island and Santa Rosa Island faults, and the San Cayetano and Oak Ridge faults.

San Andreas Fault

In 1895 Andrew Lawson described what he thought was a local fault in the San Francisco area, which he named the San Andreas Fault. It turned out, however, to slice through

seven hundred miles of western California. The San Andreas Fault is called a right-lateral strike-slip fault. This means that if you stand on any side of the fault, apparent movement of the opposite side will be to your right. Cumulative right-slip movement on the San Andreas Fault system is 196 miles. It may sound like a lot, but it works out to an average of a half-inch per year.

Since its role in the 1906 San Francisco earthquake, the San Andreas Fault has attracted worldwide attention from geologists and seismologists. The fault traces a path onshore from Mendocino south through the Coast Ranges, where it follows a northwest-southeast direction. Beginning at the Carrizo Plain, the fault makes the "Big Bend," following an anomalous east-west direction as it intersects the Garlock Fault near

Aerial view of the San Andreas Fault, looking southeast towards Mount Pinos. Photo by Bill Dewey

Wallace Creek, in the Temblor Range, shows the offset of the creek channel due to movement along the San Andreas Fault.

Frazier Mountain and then skirts the edge of the Mojave Desert. The Big Bend is centered where the Garlock, Big Pine, San Gabriel, and San Andreas faults come together. This spot is a focus of intense tectonic pressure, reflecting the underlying movements of the Pacific and North American plates.

The destructive Fort Tejon earthquake that struck on the San Andreas Fault in 1857 was estimated to be 7.9 on the Richter scale; it ruptured the ground for two hundred miles. A cowboy on the Carrizo Plain described a formerly circular corral across the fault zone which ended up in the shape of an "S" as the two halves were separated by right-lateral slippage. In Santa Barbara and Lompoc, the 1857 quake shook violently, damaging both the Santa Barbara and La Purísima missions.

One of the best ways to see the San Andreas Fault on the ground is to visit the Carrizo Plain National Monument. Here, in these wide grasslands with no trees, the bare bones of the earth stand out. At the base of the Elkhorn Hills, a long scarp face traces the San Andreas Fault for many miles. Alkali puddles called "sag ponds" border the scarp face.

Stream channels in the Carrizo Plain issuing from the foothills of the Temblor Range have been abruptly offset by the fault. The channels resume their courses after being shifted to the right at a 90 degree angle.

At Wallace Creek, which moved

thirty feet during the 1857 earthquake, you can walk a trail up to a good vantage point, reading the excellent informational signs along the way. From this hilltop you see how the dry, rock-strewn lower channel of Wallace Creek has slid a total of 420 feet towards San Francisco along the fault plane over the last ten thousand years.

In addition to the Fort Tejon quake of 1857, several major earthquakes and scores of minor ones have shaken the Santa Barbara area since the early 1800s. In 1812, 1902, 1925, 1927, 1952, and 1978, earthquakes damaged the missions, destroyed buildings in downtown Lompoc and Santa Barbara, and rattled residents' nerves.

The 1925 Earthquake in Santa Barbara

A great deal has been recorded about the 6.3 magnitude earthquake which struck downtown Santa Barbara at 6:44 a.m. on June 29, 1925.

For example, "an unidentified early-morning golfer at the La Cumbre Golf and Country Club in Hope Ranch" is quoted in Christine Palmer's article "The 1925 Earthquake":

I was held spellbound by a roar, the like of which I have never heard, cannot intelligently explain, or ever expect to hear again, and was then picked up and shaken violently as if some monster had me by the shoulders with the sole intent of shaking my head from my shoulders. It was all that I could do to stay on my feet. The hills seemed to rise and fall...the rolling of the landscape being plainly visible on all sides of me. It was not the little jerks once in a while felt in many parts of the state, but a long drawn out roll that I believe would put many of our beach roller coasters into a class below it. The roar which seemed to precede the actual shock by two or three seconds seemed to be coming from a long distance away and came with the rapidity of a bullet.

On the same morning, Julia Morgan, the famous architect of William Randolph Hearst's castle, had just arrived in Santa Barbara on the train to meet with Pearl Chase, community activist. Standing on the sidewalk, waiting for the streetcar, Morgan was thrown to the ground by the shock of the earthquake. Afterwards she described walking for blocks through the rubble of smashed cars and tumbled buildings as she made her way up lower State Street.

As it turned out, the 1925 earthquake in Santa Barbara had a silver lining. Civic-minded residents succeeded in changing the face of the community by rebuilding in tile-roofed Mediterranean architecture. The Spanish-Moorish atmosphere they created proved a boon to tourism and economic development, attracting people from all over the world.

Downtown Santa Barbara lies between the Mesa Fault and the Mission Ridge Fault. Between the two are floodplain deposits of silt, sand, and gravel. The epicenter of the quake was somewhere offshore of Carpinteria, causing slippage on these two faults. Recall that liquefaction of areas underlain with unconsolidated material is a chief cause of earthquake damage to structures. The low areas where the majority of the commercial buildings in Santa Barbara stood were full of loose soils. Buildings constructed there shook violently, due to the movement of seismic waves through the shifting sediments.

Liquefaction was also blamed for the collapse of Sheffield Dam. Constructed northeast of the city at the base of the foothills, the dam was built on sandy soil. When it collapsed it sent forty million gallons of water down Sycamore Canyon. Lower Milpas Street became a lake two feet deep.

The quake of 1925 killed thirteen people, injured sixty-five, and caused $15 million in property damage in 1925 dollars. Casualties would have been a lot worse had the quake hit during regular working hours.

Tsunamis

Tales of tsunamis hover around Santa Barbara's historical earthquake accounts. Firsthand evidence, though, is hard to come by. After the 1812 earthquake, a fifty-foot-high tsunami supposedly invaded Refugio Canyon. The account published in a newspaper long after the event is likely an exaggeration.

After the 1925 Santa Barbara quake, Pearl Chase (quoted in Palmer's article) and several other observers remembered that a tsunami rose above the West Beach seawall (there was no breakwater then) and came up State and Chapala streets "nearly as far as the railroad tracks." Others, however, recalled nothing unusual. If the 1925 wave took the form of a rapidly rising tide, perhaps nobody noticed the surge amid the general commotion and the bursting of Sheffield Dam.

Another tsunami, after the 7.3 magnitude quake of 1927 near Lompoc, sent a wave approximately six feet high ashore between Point Arguello and Surf. The quake shook Lompoc, Santa Maria, and Los Alamos. Captain Williamson of the SS *Floridian* described great quantities of dead or stunned fish floating on the surface of the sea a few miles from Point Arguello.

On August 13, 1978, a 5.9 earthquake occurred southwest of Santa Barbara beneath the Santa Barbara Channel. Most of its energy was directed toward Goleta, particularly at the University of California Santa Barbara campus. Hundreds of thousands of books were thrown from the shelves of the UCSB library. In downtown Goleta, stores suffered broken windows and fallen merchandise. On San Marcos Pass, a landslide blocked the roadway.

Predicting Earthquakes

The best way to predict earthquakes on active faults is to know the pattern of their history. Since energy accumulates between earthquakes, seismically quiet sections of active faults pose the greatest threat.

In the past two millennia, movement has occurred at intervals of 145 years along the south-central portion of the San Andreas Fault, the area nearest Santa Barbara. That puts us overdue for a major quake, "the Big One."

As John McPhee says in his outstanding book on California geology, *Assembling California*:

In 1906, the great earthquake was an unforeseeable Act of God. Now the question was no longer *whether* a great earthquake would happen but *when*. No longer could anyone imagine that when the strain is released it is gone forever. Yet people began referring to a chimeric temblor they called "the big one," as if some disaster of unique magnitude were waiting to happen. California has not assembled on creep. Great earthquakes are all over the geology. A big one will always be in the offing. The big one is plate tectonics.

Phylogeography

Earthquakes aren't the only reminder of how the concept of plate tectonics has revolutionized our understanding of the natural world.

In the 1960s and 1970s, when the theory of plate tectonics began to be accepted, scientists sought to explore the implications of geologic history for the current distribution patterns of organisms. This expanding field, **phylogeography**, attempts to correlate aspects of paleogeography— what California looked like thousands to millions of years ago—with the origins of the distribution of plants and animals today. This is a new frontier in molecular biology and much work lies ahead, but the fascinating part is the linkage between what our region looked like in the past and how that is reflected in where species live now.

Phylogeography is really an extension of the field of **biogeography**, which has been around for a long time: the study of how species are dispersed across continents and how they got there. Alfred Russel Wallace, a contemporary of Charles Darwin, is considered the father of biogeography.

With the discovery of DNA, today's biologists can trace the genetic lineage of an organism. But could they also measure the age at which the organism diverged in the geologic past from other closely related organisms—find a molecular clock, so to speak? It turned out that they can.

Up to this point, biologists have classified species by physical structure (**morphology**) and geographical distribution, but now they have a unique opportunity to go deeper. What if two species appear to be similar in every way, but their genetic markers are completely different? This is the miracle of experiments with DNA. After numerous studies, some of the animals that we thought were related or even the same are turning out to be distinctly separate species. This is due, in part, to their past geographic distribution.

One more point: many of these studies refer to **clades**. A clade is an evolutionarily distinct genetic lineage, a group of organisms that all descended from the same genetic ancestor.

Phylogeography and Slender Salamanders

Recall that the geologic history of our region has been one of major events: over millions of years, blocks of continental crust have been moved about, the ocean has invaded the land and retreated, and mountain ranges have been thrust up and eroded. These events have affected how species differentiated from other species over time.

Hold on while we go for a wild

The Channel Islands Slender Salamander (genus *Batrachoseps*) may have become geographically isolated and distinct from mainland counterparts due to its geologic history

ride through the labyrinth of scientific experiments that may have changed forever how we look at species formation.

So far, these studies have been most successful with sedentary organisms, such as certain reptiles and amphibians. One of the first works suggesting phylogeographic principles was done on the genetic origins of lungless salamanders of the family Plethodontidae. These tiny, wormlike slender salamanders (*Batrachoseps* spp.) have a small home range and are endemic to the Pacific Coast.

In 1966 there were only two species of slender salamander recognized in California. Recent studies using DNA research that was linked to paleogeography hypothesize that there are likely twenty species in California. The slender salamanders are secretive and structurally similar. So where did all the new species come from? They were here all the time, it's just that molecular measurements discovered they were genetically different, did not interbreed, and stayed isolated because of their geologic history. Thus, the genetic markers for

each species are different; though they look very similar, they are separate species.

There is evidence that the distribution of several of the slender salamanders reflects the movements of blocks of land—terranes—millions of years ago on which these ancient forms of life "rode" to their present locations. When the terrane became attached to the mainland after movement north, the salamanders did not interbreed with neighboring populations. Thus their genetic lineages are intact and can be traced from millions of years ago.

Our Region 8 to 2.5 Million Years Ago

Phylogenetic experiments employing more recent geologic reconstructions have concentrated on where, in the current landscape, we can see breaks in population groups that might reflect the geologic history of our region.

At 2.5 million years ago, our region can be described as having had two large ocean embayments: one covered the present Santa Maria River and Santa Ynez River valleys and extended inland to what is now the Gibraltar Dam area; one flooded the current Santa Clara River Valley and reached inland almost to the town of Northridge. These two arms of the sea were divided by the future Western Transverse Ranges (Santa Ynez, Topatopa, Pine Mountain, etc.), which had already assumed their current east-west position, although they were not as high in elevation.

In "Toward a Better Understanding of the Transverse Range Break," coauthor Michael Caterino, Curator of Entomology at the Santa Barbara Museum of Natural History, states:

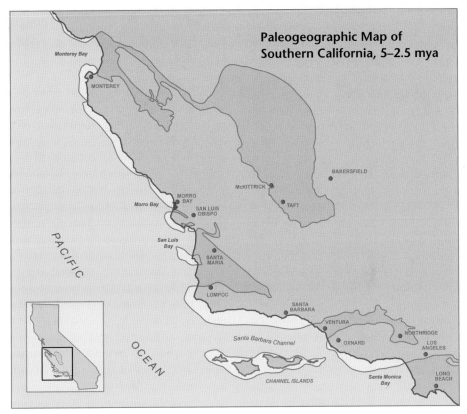

A hypothetical reconstruction of what our region may have looked like 5–2.5 mya. Note the submergence of the Santa Maria, Santa Ynez, and Santa Clara River valleys (as well as the San Joaquin Valley and the Los Angeles Basin) by marine embayments, which may have isolated populations of animals. (after Hall 2002)

The Transverse Ranges have been a major focus of phylogeographic studies in California. The mountains extend from the Pacific coast inland to the Mojave and Colorado deserts, perpendicular to the common north-south orientation of the mountain ranges in western North America. They effectively divide the California Floristic Province, and many species show distinct north-south or east-west breaks across the Transverse Ranges.

The faunal north-south break in marine life at Point Conception—the westernmost tip of the Transverse Ranges—is easily observed due to differences in climate, weather, sea surface temperatures, and currents. But now we have this terrestrial faunal break that appears to echo on land what we knew from the ocean. It turns out that the region where the present Western Transverse Ranges are located has been a barrier to north-south animal distribution for several million years, not so much due to the mountains, which were not elevated until more recently, but to the presence of the two marine embayments.

Pacific Pond Turtle

Recent scientific papers have compared the DNA of a variety of organisms to see if this contact zone between northern and southern clades of a population holds up. A sharp population break at the Transverse Ranges was documented for the **Southern Alligator Lizard** (*Elgaria multicarinata*) and the **California Mountain Kingsnake** (*Lampropeltis zonata*). Further recent studies show north-south breaks at the present Western Transverse Ranges for other species, such as the **California Legless Lizard** (*Anniella pulchra*), **California Red-legged Frog** (*Rana draytonii*), and **California Newt** (*Taricha torosa*).

Interesting work has been done with the phylogeography of the **Pacific Pond Turtle** (*Actinemys marmorata*). An analysis of the DNA showed a large northern clade extending from Washington south to San Luis Obispo County; a San Joaquin Valley clade extending from the southern Great Central Valley; a geographically restricted Santa Barbara clade from a limited region in Santa Barbara and Ventura counties; and a southern clade that occurs south to Baja California along the coast. This new knowledge may indicate that the Pacific Pond Turtle is in the process of speciation, whereby at least some of

these distinct populations would be split into totally new species, reflecting their original geologic isolation. Evidently, the deep marine embayments were physical barriers that the Pacific Pond Turtle could not cross.

Results of phylogeographic studies of mammals are not as strong as those found for reptiles and amphibians, but there are a few examples. The **California Vole** (*Microtus californicus*) shows a pronounced north-south break, indicating a northern clade and a southern clade with an intermediate zone of contact in Santa Barbara and Ventura counties. Knowing that the land where the Santa Ynez Mountains now stand was bordered by two ocean embayments, it's not surprising the voles did not move back and forth over this barrier.

California Tiger Salamanders

One of the reasons biologists have increased their analysis of phylogeographic variation is to help in understanding the biodiversity of our region. Also, if we can fine-tune our knowledge of how species are formed and where they exist, we can protect species that may have been overlooked. In most cases we need DNA studies to assist in solving these puzzles.

The California Tiger Salamander, a Santa Barbara County endemic, is a perfect example. (See Chapter 9 for more on tiger salamanders.) In 2004, H. Bradley Shaffer and his colleagues examined the genetics of California Tiger Salamanders and showed that the salamanders found in the Santa Maria Valley were genetically distinct from those found elsewhere in the state.

Shaffer postulated that when the Santa Maria Valley's ocean embayment began to recede, it became a lowland filled with alluvial sediments surrounded by recently emerged upland mountainous regions that lacked appropriate salamander habitat. This suggests that the current range of the Santa Barbara population of tiger salamanders has likely existed in an isolated lowland habitat for a few million years.

The questions: How did the Santa Barbara tiger salamander population become so isolated from other populations, and why are its closest relatives found in the more distant populations?

Enter reconstruction of the geologic past. About eight million years ago, a large marine embayment covered most of what is now the San Joaquin Valley. As the southern Coast Ranges began to emerge, the embayment was gradually cut off from the ocean, but seaways persisted near Monterey in the north and the Cuyama Valley in the south. Tiger salamanders in the Coastal Ranges were unable to cross the seaway. Meanwhile, the San Joaquin Valley population likely pioneered a land route westward along the southern margin of the seaway, through the area presently occupied by the Cuyama Valley, eventually reaching the newly exposed lowlands of the Santa Maria Valley area.

Jump forward about four million years, when the suitable tiger salamander habitat that once extended from the southeastern side of the San Joaquin Valley to the coast was fragmented as the Tehachapi, San Emigdio, and Sierra Madre mountains began to rise up. The Cuyama pathway no longer existed, and the Santa Maria Valley tiger salamanders were now cut off geographically and genetically from those in the San Joaquin Valley, left to evolve in isolation for a few million years.

In support of this, biologists have detected a phylogeographic break for several species of reptiles and amphibians that coincides with the present east-west Cuyama Valley.

Certainly, the location of the Santa Barbara region has put it at the center of many phylogeographic discoveries. The more we learn about what our region looked like in the past, the more we can understand species distribution today. The study of phylogeography is young, but that's what makes it fascinating. The research described above needs to be expanded before these genetic findings result in the establishment of new species. Regardless, it is evidence of how relevant the geologic past is to the future of our understanding of biodiversity. With the great assistance of recent genetic studies, species that have yet to be recognized may still be discovered.

* * *

Take a deep breath. You survived the geology chapter.

The geology of coastal Southern California is perhaps more complex than any other region of comparable size on earth. It is the foundation for much of what we know about how our region looked millions of years ago.

Geology is responsible for the topography of our region. The topography influences the weather. The weather has a hand in the vegetation that grows here. The vegetation is the basis for the habitats. The habitats are where the spectrum of insects, reptiles, amphibians, birds, and mammals live. All of these comprise the natural world of the Santa Barbara region.

PART TWO

THE HABITATS—WHERE THE PLANTS AND ANIMALS LIVE

CHAPTER 3: THE OCEAN—WONDERS OF OFFSHORE WATERS

 Beneath the wind-chopped waves and blue-green waters of the Pacific Ocean off our shores lies one of the world's most significant ecosystems. Few visitors realize the global importance of the sea at this location along the west coast of the continent. The power of the winds and currents to influence marine life results in unusually high species diversity. For example, more species of whales, dolphins, seals, and sea lions can be found in our own Santa Barbara Channel than almost anywhere else in the world.

Ninety percent of the astoundingly rich underwater life, however, is invisible. It consists of millions and millions of microscopic, free-floating organisms—the plankton. Just like a rich, nutritious soup, the patches of ocean where plankton flourishes will serve as a food base for all sea creatures, from the smallest invertebrates to the largest whales.

Straddling Point Conception at the crossroads of the cold, murky, nutrient-rich waters from the north and the warmer, sheltered waters to the south, our region hosts a mix of northern and southern marine species. In addition, the underwater topography of the Santa Barbara Channel, particularly the presence of the Channel Islands, offers a variety of depths and underwater surfaces that attract a plethora of life-forms.

But there's more: consider the productivity of Giant Kelp, the brown algae we know as "seaweed" that grows only in certain areas of the world's oceans, forming canopies across the surface that stretch for miles. You may have noticed the kelp as it lies spent on the sandy beach in brown piles. When alive, it forms an underwater forest famous for the species of invertebrates, fish, and mammals it attracts.

Looking south across the Santa Barbara Channel with islands in the distance

If we were all experienced divers, our examination of the ocean would be more straightforward. But most of us must be content to study the waters of the Santa Barbara Channel from the surface, usually from the deck of a boat.

Oceanography

Bathymetry: What Does the Ocean Floor Look Like?

Landlubbers gazing at the sea have a misconception that underneath the surface, the land slopes gradually from shallow to deeper waters, just as it does at the beach at low tide. But a submarine topographic map, a **bathymetric map**, reveals the ocean floor off our region is not a gentle slope at all. It is a maze of basins, shelves, trenches, and ridges, formed by geo-logic forces millions of years ago when the Pacific and North American plates collided. Just as the surface of the land has valleys and mountains, so too does the ocean floor.

The underwater topography of our region is divided into two distinct parts. North of Point Conception, the ocean floor is a narrow shelf—the **continental shelf**—after which it drops off to the deep ocean. The con-tinental shelf north of Point Concep-tion is narrow, probably no more than eighteen or twenty miles wide, and deep submarine canyons cut into the shelf in certain places. These canyons carry sediment and debris (both min-eral and organic) from the beaches out into the deep ocean, where they come to rest in large fans spread out on the ocean floor. For example, off Point Arguello a submarine canyon cuts through the continental shelf and culminates in the Arguello Deep-Sea Fan.

In contrast, south of Point Conception, the ocean floor consists of a series of elevated mesas and basins which eventually give way to a steep escarpment and the deep ocean. Geologists call this area between Point Conception and Mexico the **Continental Borderland**. It is a checkerboard pattern unique to this portion of the west coast, with deep, closed basins interspersed with elevated ridges. Some of these ridges emerge as islands, like the Northern Channel Islands. Others remain underwater, mountain chains that never breach the surface.

Off Santa Barbara and Ventura shores, a five-mile-wide shelf gives way to a series of basins, such as the Santa Barbara Basin, and ridges, such as the Santa Rosa–Cortes Ridge. The basins are fed by submarine canyons that carry sand and organic matter to the bottom. Basins closest to the shore are shallower, those further out are deeper. The Santa Barbara Basin is fairly shallow, at 2,056 feet, with a floor area of 420 square miles. At the seaward edge of the Continental Borderland, the basin and ridge formations end at an abrupt trench, the Patton Escarpment, which leads to the true deep ocean.

Marine biologists use another term when talking about the area from Point Conception to the Mexican border, **Southern California Bight**. The bight is that portion of the Pacific Ocean that forms the big open bay off Southern California. Looking at the way the California coastline curves

The Humpback Whale is a summer visitor in the Santa Barbara Channel.

southeast from Point Conception, one can imagine a giant fish grabbing a big bite out of the land.

The Santa Barbara region, then, encompasses offshore waters north of Point Conception as well as those in the northwest corner of the Southern California Bight.

Ocean Currents Driven by Winds

Ocean currents, driven largely by winds, are essential to life in the sea. Currents vary in temperature and degree of salinity, which is reflected in the kinds of marine plants and animals they nourish.

Most people don't realize that much of the world's ocean is barren; life in the oceans isn't distributed uniformly. On the contrary, the **Eastern Boundary Current Regions**, of which the waters off California are one (others include the west coast of South Africa, the Canary Island region, and the Peru-Chile coast), occupy less than .1 percent of the world's ocean and account for 17 percent of the world's fish catch. These regions have

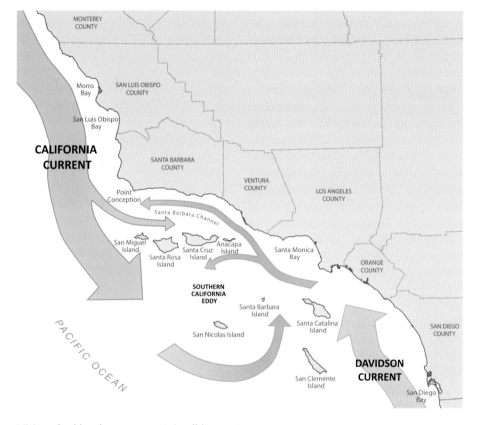

Mixing of cold and warm currents in offshore waters

one thing in common: ocean currents that create a spectacular upwelling phenomenon. In order to understand upwelling, let's begin with the all-important currents.

The **California Current** is a broad, slow surface current coming from Alaska that flows south along the California coast. Its cold, green waters are high in nutrients and oxygen, conditions conducive to marine life in more northerly climates. At Point Conception, where the coast bends sharply east, the California Current keeps on flowing south, but it now runs along the outer edge of the Channel Islands. For instance, north of Point Concep-

tion the California Current comes within 25 to 95 miles of the coast, but to the south it is some 125 miles offshore.

South of Los Angeles, the California Current splits, one arm continuing south, the other flowing back north. The northern arm, known as the **Southern California Countercurrent** or **Coastal Eddy**, is a giant counterclockwise gyre that circulates the waters of the Southern California Bight. Part of the Southern California Countercurrent flows back north through the Santa Barbara Channel and up to Point Conception. The other part of the Southern California

Countercurrent ends up circulating in a surface area centered over the Santa Rosa–Cortes Ridge near San Nicolas Island.

Meanwhile, yet another current, the **Davidson Current** (named after a naval officer who mapped much of the west coast for sailors) flows northward from Baja. It is deep and hugs the California coast, carrying relatively warm, salty, low-oxygen water with it, characteristics favoring more southerly marine life.

Depending upon the strength of surface winds and other weather conditions, the three major currents wax and wane seasonally. The deep Davidson Current is always present, but throughout spring and summer the colder California Current and Southern California Countercurrent dominate it. From late fall through winter, however, when the California Current weakens, the Davidson Current strengthens.

In summary, the waters off our region are a mixture of cold and warm, truly a transition zone. Depending upon the prevailing winds and the season, these northern and southern currents merge and separate, flow fast or slow. In the northwest section of the Southern California Bight, at the western entrance to the Santa Barbara Channel, the influence of the California Current is strong. Having just passed Point Conception, it bathes the marine life off San Miguel and parts of Santa Rosa Island in cold water. In contrast, at the southeastern entrance to the channel, the warmer, more sheltered waters off Anacapa Island and the mainland near Ventura attract more southerly marine species.

Important biological research in the last thirty years shows that the general area around Point Conception is the most pronounced break for marine fauna and flora on the West Coast. For example, several studies have proved that marine fishes, benthic mollusks (shelled animals), and other marine invertebrates that were common south of Point Conception became less abundant and eventually quite scarce in waters to the north. Conversely, species that preferred the colder waters of the Central and Northern California coast stayed mostly north of Point Conception. Interestingly, the Point Conception area is more of a barrier for southern species than those to the north. This is due to the cold California Current swinging southwest, which encourages a few of those cold-water forms of life to move south of Point Conception and inhabit the waters of the Northern Channel Islands and the western portion of the Santa Barbara Channel.

The Upwelling Phenomenon

From April through July, the northwest winds blow parallel to the California coastline, especially north of Point Conception. And as they blow down the coast, they drive the surface ocean waters before them.

But the surface waters are subject to the **Coriolis effect** as Earth spins, so instead of staying parallel to the coast, the waters veer offshore at a 45 to 90 degree angle, to the right of the blowing wind. (In the Southern Hemisphere, waters veer to the left.) When warmer nearshore surface waters are pushed out to sea, a vacuum is created

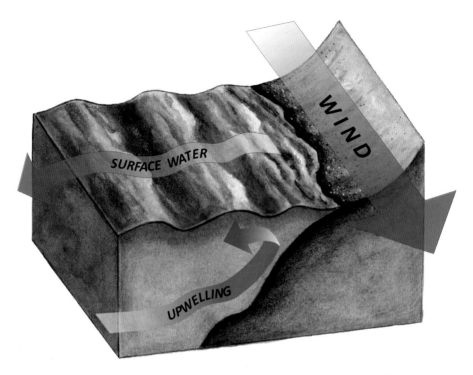

Upwelling: In spring and early summer, strong northwesterly winds and the Coriolis effect steer surface waters away from the coastline, bringing plumes of colder, nutrient-rich water up from the ocean depths.

close to shore, and plumes of colder water well up from below. This important process, called **upwelling**, brings water rich in nutrients up from the bottom of the ocean. The upwelling is most vigorous north of Point Conception, but it also occurs at certain places in the Santa Barbara Channel and near the Northern Channel Islands.

For example, a very strong northwesterly wind event occurred on April 14, 2009, along the coastline near Avila Beach (as measured by the Center for Coastal Marine Sciences at Cal Poly San Luis Obispo). Peak winds were measured at 50 mph and sustained gusts were to 63 mph. Immediately after the wind event, water temperatures close to shore dropped from 57°F to 50°F. By April 19, however, calm winds and warm temperatures had increased the sea surface temperatures back up to 60°F along the coast.

Newly upwelled cold water, carrying nutrients, will foster a bloom of the tiniest organisms of the ocean— the phytoplankton—when the water has warmed again. Usually, nutrients are continuously depleted by marine life in the water column. The upwelling phenomenon brings the nutrients back up to the surface, as fertilizer if you will, which promotes an increase in phytoplankton growth and thus fuels the food chain from the tiniest larval octopus all the way up to the whale.

The Basis of Life in the Ocean

Plankton: Soup of the Sea

Like the majority of life in the ocean, the enormous baleen whales found in our region, such as the Blue, the Humpback, and the Gray, depend directly or indirectly on **plankton**, the stuff that makes up "whale food."

The term "plankton" refers to organisms that float in water currents throughout the ocean. (This is in contrast to **nekton**, the larger animals that are capable of swimming against the dense property of seawater, like fish, sharks, and whales.)

There's an extremely important difference between organisms that live in the sea and those on land. In the ocean, the whole ecosystem is based on the microscopic plankton that are at the base of the food chain (everything eats them). So the medium—the ocean—in which every creature exists is also the source of nourishment. By contrast, on land the food source is not just suspended in the air; trees, flowers, and grasses form the base of the food chain and they must be harvested in all sorts of ways.

Plankton can be subdivided into two groups: the **phytoplankton**, free-floating photosynthesizers; and **zooplankton**, various floating animals. (Current molecular biology has classified some of the phytoplankton as neither animals nor plants, but unicellular creatures in the kingdom Protoctista. For example, some phytoplankton, such as algae, can both photosynthesize and take in organic material, so they cannot be classified as either plants or animals, but are rather a little of both. Thus, when we say "phytoplankton," we are not strictly talking about plants, but about one-celled forms of life.)

Phytoplankton are the do-it-yourselfers: these microscopic unicellular organisms need only light, carbon dioxide, and nutrients to grow. Recent studies show they take in bacteria as well, consuming up to 90 percent of all the bacteria eaten in the top layer of the ocean!

Of the phytoplankton, major components are **diatoms** and **dinoflagellates**. Diatoms differ from dinoflagellates in their "housing" structures. Diatoms are encased in little odd-shaped boxes constructed of silicon dioxide, the same material found in glass. Their unique shapes are beautiful under a microscope.

It turns out, however, that a few species of diatoms can be poisonous.

Two of the diatoms that we know of in the genus *Pseudo-nitzschia* are responsible for carrying the neurotoxin **domoic acid** at certain stages of their life cycle. Domoic acid accumulates in shellfish and fish and can cause ill health or death in marine mammals, especially seals and sea lions, as well as fish, birds, and humans.

Recent scientific studies in the Santa Barbara Channel tie the blooms of the diatom *Pseudo-nitzschia* to the wind-driven spring upwelling events that occur around Point Conception and in the channel itself. For example, in the spring of 2002 and 2003, two blooms of *Pseudo-nitzschia* in the Santa Barbara Channel resulted in fifteen hundred pinniped (seal and sea lion) deaths. Some years are worse than others, but it appears that the wealth of nutrients released by upwelling can increase populations of these diatoms to the detriment of sea mammals.

When marine mammals come ashore and appear disoriented or die, it is termed a **stranding.** Furthermore, according to curator Michelle Berman-Kowalewski at the Santa Barbara Museum of Natural History, stranding is officially defined as any animal out of habitat, so that a pinniped in a rookery with symptoms of domoic acid is not officially stranded because the rookery is its normal habitat. Berman-Kowalewski has tallied strandings in the Santa Barbara region over time and found that most took place in the spring.

The other component of phytoplankton, the dinoflagellates, propel themselves through the water with two flagella (swimming appendages). They, too, are capable of producing toxins. The concentrations, harmful to fish and invertebrates, known as **"red tides"** are outbreaks of red-pigmented dinoflagellates. A filter feeder, such as a mussel, might feed on toxic dinoflagellates which, though not harmful to the mussel, could cause paralytic shellfish poisoning in humans. The blooms occur near shore, usually from May through October, and are not tied to upwelling phenomena. You may have seen the signs posted: mussel quarantine. They should be taken seriously.

Both diatoms and dinoflagellates emit light, a phenomenon called **bioluminescence.** Some species of dinoflagellates, as well as larger animals like squids and fishes, produce a greenish-blue light when they are disturbed. You can see this at night, when breaking waves appear to give off phosphorescent light. This mysterious glowing is caused by a chemical reaction in each minuscule dinoflagellate, probably an adaptation to ward off predators in some way.

Turning now to the zooplankton, picture innumerable microscopic forms of all sorts of marine animals floating about like miniature snowflakes. Vital to the life of the ocean, zooplankton are the chief "grazers" that feed on the phytoplankton. A majority of the zooplankton are larval forms (immatures) of many types of marine dwellers. One day these tiny creatures will mature into adult anemones, worms, snails, crabs, or lobsters, but in their larval forms they look quite different.

One of the most common zooplankters is the tiny **copepod** (*Calanus pacificus* is the one off our coast), a crustacean about one-half to three-quarters of an inch long. Copepods have oval-shaped bodies with long antennae. Some scientists think they form the largest animal biomass on earth, a title which has also been mentioned in connection with their larger (two and one-half inches long) cousins, the **krill** (*Euphausia pacifica* in our region).

Krill

Krill (the name comes from the Norwegian word meaning "young fry of fish") are at the large end of the zooplankton size scale. This shrimplike crustacean is familiar to many of us as a mainstay of the diets of baleen whales, seals, and seabirds. Most krill are filter feeders, taking in dia-

Krill is the most important food source for Blue Whales.

toms through fine combs on their front appendages. They are also bioluminescent.

Krill are unique because the size difference between them, the food they eat, and the predators that eat them is huge. Krill graze on tiny phytoplankton cells, smaller than the width of a hair, therefore much, much smaller than they are. In turn, they are devoured by the largest animals to have ever lived, the Blue Whales. In the natural world, it is customary to have more intermediates between such a large consumer and a much smaller one.

Zooplankton's daily migrations have puzzled biologists for more than a century. **Diel migrations**—daily, vertical migrations—involve the movement of masses of zooplankton up to the surface of the water at night and then down to the lower regions of the ocean during daylight hours.

The major stimulus controlling the diel migrations appears to be light. With sonar equipment, it's possible to trace the sound reflected off the animals. As they move up and down in the water column, their bodies form a distinct layer. One of the explanations put forward for the diel migration of zooplankton is that the movement into more dimly lit, deeper waters during daytime avoids predation by surface-feeding birds, fish, and squid.

A related migration is that of the **deep scattering layer.** Back in the days when sonar was first tested, echoes came from sources in the water which were thousands of feet above the bottom. These mid-water sound layers were called DSLs, or deep scattering layers. At night the layers moved to the surface, where they became a single broad band. Scientists discovered the layers were mid-water fishes that spend their days in the middle of the water column but move at night to the surface of the water. At dawn, these animals return to deeper water. Thus, members of the deep scattering layer somewhat reflect the diel migration of the zooplankton (krill, copepods) on which they feed.

Nature Journal
August 15, 2000

Whale Watching for Blue Whales in the Santa Barbara Channel

I've taken my seasickness pills, but my stomach is still queasy at the thought of my first boat trip in the channel in years.

The day is perfect: summer-calm, enough haze to keep the wind down. We chug out of the harbor on the "old" Condor, the old-fashioned, slower boat— not the Condor Express now in use.

We're headed directly southwest to a place just off the passage between Santa

Rosa and Santa Cruz islands. Here the upwelling of the currents produces a bloom of plankton and thus krill and thus Blue Whales! How exciting is this? I've never seen a Blue Whale before—a life mammal.

"Bottlenose Dolphins at ten o'clock," the skipper shouts.

Although I'm on board with a group of birders, the rest of the passengers are there to sample other forms of sea life. The birders perk up at the presence of our first Sooty Shearwaters cruising above the dolphins. The friendly dolphins come right up to the boat and swim alongside us as we plow forward, rising gently up and down with the southern swell.

Before we get too much farther into the channel, we come upon a strange creature with a single fin visible, swimming in an odd way. This is the Ocean Sunfish, or Mola Mola, a flattened fish with a single fin above and below it. When it swims, the upper fin goes forward and backward like a pathetic little oar. When it lies down and suns itself, it looks like a big, pale, elliptical pancake floating out in the ocean, but it can weigh up to five hundred pounds! Sometimes birds come and perch on the Mola Mola, investigate it for parasites, and pick them off. The Mola Mola is a warmwater fish.

At last, we're beginning to see some birds: Black Storm-Petrels, an Ashy Storm-Petrel. Binoculars bouncing around, some salt spray on our glasses, all part of the pelagic experience.

"Look, Pink-foots!" someone yells. The Pink-footed Shearwaters, white underneath and pink feet tucked behind them, flush low over the heaving sea. Their slow and lumbering flight sends them stiff-winged, skimming the waves as they go.

The chop is rougher now and we've fled the bow to go up above. The skipper announces that the first person to spot the blow of a Blue Whale will receive a free cocktail at the galley. The idea of a cocktail in this swell is not appealing, but we redouble our efforts with the binoculars. After all, we birders should be the ones to see the first whale. We're told the blow of a Blue Whale is thirty feet high. Hmmm.

I can't wait to see these enormous mammals. All my life I've heard about the immense Blue Whale, but how can one really imagine it? The idea of these ninety-foot-long beasts floating around in our channel is absurd. How many tons of water do they displace? How can they subsist on the same food that the tiny phalarope (a migrating shorebird) eats, the krill? Amazing.

A woman sitting next to me—with no binoculars and certainly a first-time whale watcher, screams out, "There it is—a blow—a whale—over there!"

She's right. The skipper cuts the engine.

We loll about, the waves rocking the boat. We're a couple of miles north of the west end of Santa Cruz Island. This is the place, the favored Blue Whale feeding spot. Year after year the Blues visit offshore here to gulp the tiny krill in copious mouthfuls.

The captain tells us to watch closely as the cow and calf swim nearby. How can we miss them?

A long, low, submarine-like object with a smooth, bluish-gray body eases up out of the water. It's the mother, the cow, and she's lazing around before she makes her next dive. The mom is ninety feet long and the calf by her side is fifty feet.

The captain informs us that the calf, feeding on its mother's milk, gains nine pounds an hour. The mom herself could weigh close to two hundred tons! Unbelievable!

These leviathans roll over and then back.

"Ph-whooooosh!" When they're close to the boat you can hear and see the blow as the Blue exhales a plume of salty breath. What a sound! What a smell!

Although the bulk of the adult is hidden beneath the water, you get the impression of length in the shallow, lolling dives. That's when you see the whale's body close to the surface, and you learn the look of the ocean patch underneath which the Blue Whale swims—for when the whale is just beneath the ocean's swell, the water above it becomes a light, aquamarine blue—a calm slick that remains long after the animal has moved on. This is the footprint of the Blue Whale.

The Blue Whale—the largest species that has ever lived on the planet—in Santa Barbara Channel. Photo by Robert Goodell

As the adult and youngster lounge about in shallow arcs, exclamations go up from the whale watchers and birders on board.

"Whoooosh!" Another high spume from the cow's blowholes, this time even closer to the boat.

At last, the mother tires of her rolling. The frontal portion of her huge body begins a deeper dive. We can see this from the boat, and the knowledgeable among the passengers predict a "good fluke show."

As the Blue Whale dives deeper and deeper, her midsection comes almost completely out of the water. And now, the grand finale: the tail of the great Blue. Those twin flukes we've read so much about rise gracefully and flip backward as the whale finishes the deep dive and disappears.

"Ooooooh—ahhhh!" goes up from the whole boatload.

We have seen what we came for. The day is a whopping success. Looking around us, we spy through binoculars the spoutings of at least six or seven other Blue Whales. We're in the midst of the krill—the feeding ground of the Blues!

It's magical.

Ecology Lesson—How Natural Communities Operate

This book takes an ecological approach to studying the natural world. Using marine organisms as examples, here are some basic concepts.

Ecology is a way of describing the interrelationships between organisms. All organisms interact among each other and with the environment they live in.

A **species** is a group of individuals that breed only among themselves. The number of individuals in a species in any given area is a **population.** Several populations of different species might constitute a **community.**

An **ecosystem** is usually comprised of several communities. An ecosystem can be big and complex or small and simple. Since we are discussing the oceans, let's take an example from offshore. An ecosystem could consist of all of the organisms in the Santa Barbara Channel, or all of the organisms that live in a kelp forest, or all of the organisms that live in a tidepool. In fact, all of life on earth could be considered one giant ecosystem.

What fuels the ecosystem? How is energy transferred from one organism to another within the ecosystem? That is, how does each member of the ecosystem survive? Who eats whom?

On land and at sea, energy from the sun is captured by **autotrophs,** which are green plants, bacteria, or algae that can make their own food from the sun by photosynthesis. All other life-forms are called **heterotrophs,** those that must obtain food from other sources. Heterotrophs eat the autotrophs, or they consume other heterotrophs, or they absorb dissolved organic matter from the environment. Such an organization of an ecosystem is known as a **trophic structure** in which each successive feeding level is a **trophic level.**

The first trophic level is the **producer.** These are the algae and unicellular phytoplankton, autotrophs, which use the sun's energy to make their own food. In the marine environment, the autotrophs are microscopic organisms that float throughout the ocean (except for the kelps, which are big, but they only grow in nearshore waters). This is hugely different from on land, where autotrophs are large and visible: grasses, shrubs, trees. In the marine environment you cannot see the producers, but on land you certainly can.

The second level includes animals known as **herbivores.** Herbivores devour plant material. In turn, herbivores are eaten by **carnivores,** which are eaten by other, larger carnivores or by **omnivores** (animals that eat both plants and animals). Finally, the **decomposers** (the bacteria) break down the dead organisms, making them re-usable by the autotrophs or heterotrophs that can absorb organic molecules. Each pathway that transfers energy from a given source through a series of consumers is called a **food chain.** Putting together all the food chains in an ecosystem results in a **food web.**

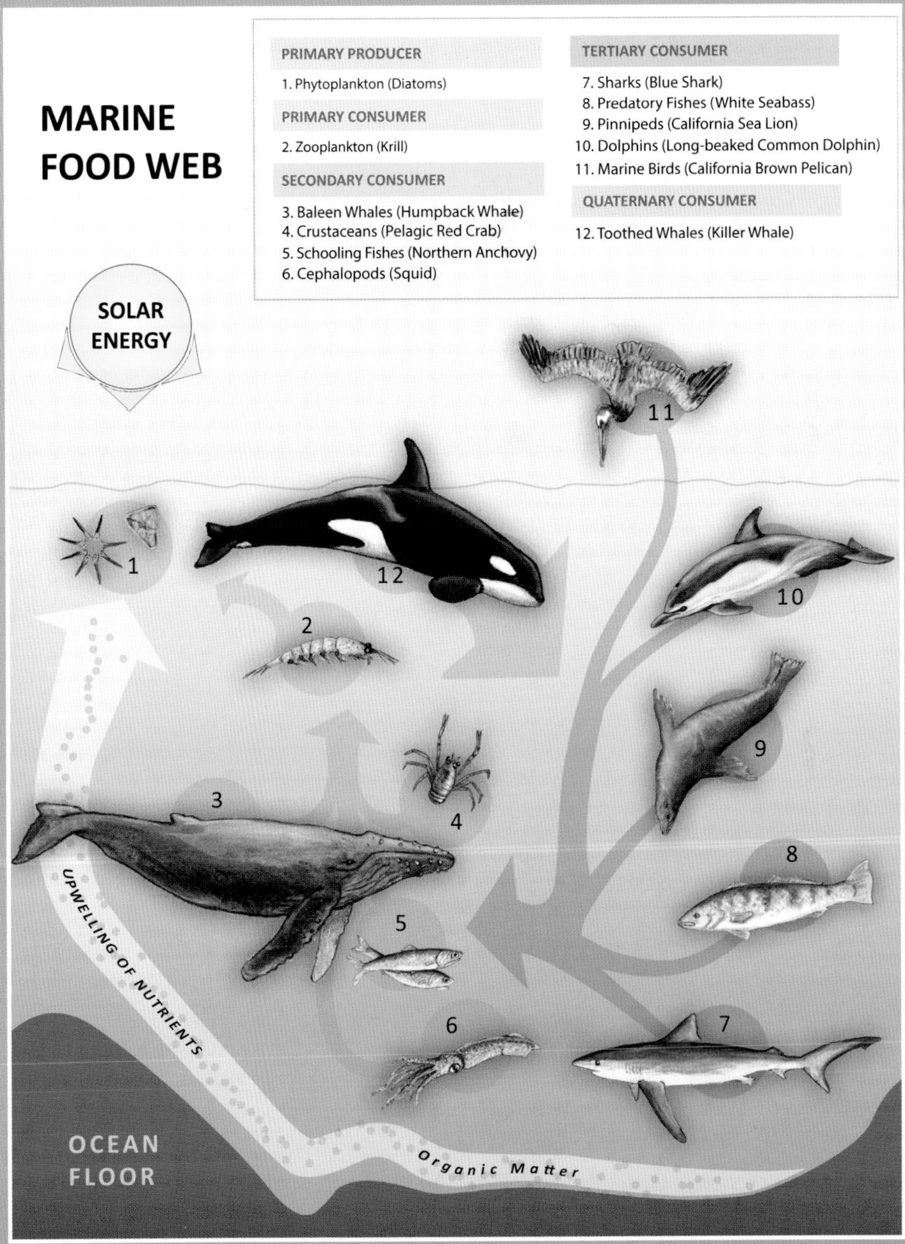

MARINE FOOD WEB

PRIMARY PRODUCER
1. Phytoplankton (Diatoms)

PRIMARY CONSUMER
2. Zooplankton (Krill)

SECONDARY CONSUMER
3. Baleen Whales (Humpback Whale)
4. Crustaceans (Pelagic Red Crab)
5. Schooling Fishes (Northern Anchovy)
6. Cephalopods (Squid)

TERTIARY CONSUMER
7. Sharks (Blue Shark)
8. Predatory Fishes (White Seabass)
9. Pinnipeds (California Sea Lion)
10. Dolphins (Long-beaked Common Dolphin)
11. Marine Birds (California Brown Pelican)

QUATERNARY CONSUMER
12. Toothed Whales (Killer Whale)

SOLAR ENERGY

UPWELLING OF NUTRIENTS

OCEAN FLOOR

Organic Matter

A marine food web

A food web maps out how each organism in the system makes a living—in other words, its **niche** in the food chain. For example, phytoplankton (autotrophs) are fed on by microscopic marine crustaceans like the copepods (heterotrophs). The copepods are herbivores: that's the niche they occupy. However, the place where they live, the ocean, is their **habitat**. A habitat, then, is the place where an organism is found.

If this all sounds a little too pat, it probably is.

The patterns of nature involved in ecology and biodiversity may be more complex than we originally thought. Recently, scientists have grappled with what they call "ecological surprises"—the hint that randomness and even chaos may underlie certain ecosystems. More often than not, of course, major human manipulations of natural communities produce surprising results. (See Chapter 10 for examples of these.)

One of the most astonishing ecological surprises was the discovery of deep sea hydrothermal vent communities. Nearly every aspect of their existence has been unexpected. In a 2008 article, "Understanding and Predicting Ecological Dynamics," Daniel F. Doak and his coauthors explain that the "population densities, species composition, and chemical energy source of these communities all contradicted universally accepted generalities about the ecology of the deep ocean regions as low-density, low-productivity ecosystems reliant only on sparse fallout from the distant photic zone [above]."

In other words, scientists were unable to predict from what they knew of ocean ecosystems that these high-temperature vent communities living in complete darkness on the ocean floor would be filled with all sorts of creatures.

As we move forward in our exploration of the Santa Barbara region, keep in mind that the ecological principles outlined above are subject to the randomness of weather (El Niño/Southern Oscillation), trophic cascades (when a keystone predator is removed or, perhaps accidentally, replaced by another), and climate shift, among other phenomena. As much as we'd like to impose patterns on nature, a lot of our observations only touch the surface. This becomes extremely important as biologists seek to predict the outcome of experiments that impact the management of natural populations.

In some instances, scientists may know more, but understand less, than Charles Darwin did a century and a half ago.

Giant Kelp: Big Brown Seaweed

Speaking of Darwin, on first sighting Giant Kelp he wrote, "I know of few things more surprising than to see this plant growing and flourishing amidst those breakers of the western ocean, which no mass of rock, let it be ever so hard, can long resist."

Darwin was fascinated by the forests of Giant Kelp he saw in the Southern Hemisphere, their canopies floating in brown bundles on the surface of the sea. Early mariners considered them a signal that land was not far off.

Forests of Giant Kelp are subtidal beds of a perennial brown alga which, in the Northern Hemisphere, grows near shore only from Santa Cruz, California, to Baja California. (In the Southern Hemisphere, it can be found along the Pacific coast of South America.)

Giant Kelp is the largest marine plant on earth, and a single plant can survive up to ten years, reach 120 feet in length, and weigh 700 pounds.

A thin band of rich underwater kelp forest thrives in our region at locations seventeen to sixty-five feet deep and water temperatures generally below 68°F. The "roots" of Giant Kelp, called **holdfasts**, grab onto the ocean floor (substrate), preferably in rocky areas but sometimes in sandy ones. From the holdfast, a "trunk," or **stipe**, grows upward, ending in one or more flat blades. At the base of the blades are **pneumatocysts** (floats) filled with gases, which allow the blades to keep upright in the water. These blades may form a canopy as much as four feet thick, preventing light from penetrating to the ocean floor in certain places. The blades stream out on the surface of the ocean in the direction of the current flow.

Just like phytoplankton, Giant Kelp absorbs energy from the sun in order to thrive, processing the carbon which fuels the food web. Just like phytoplankton, kelp is stimulated to grow extraordinarily fast—as much as a foot a day—when essential nutrients, particularly nitrogen, upwell from the ocean floor. The next time you take a walk on the beach, pick up a piece of "seaweed" and notice the surface of the blades: they are bumpy with

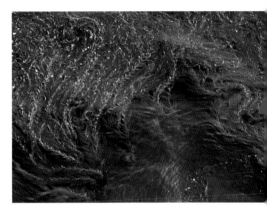

Giant Kelp near Anacapa Island

A holdfast anchors kelp to a rock.

Inhabitants of the Giant Kelp forest

little ridges. These striations help the blades move with the surge, and they facilitate photosynthesis by increasing the surface area of the blade.

A study in 1983 that measured thirty-two kelp forests along the mainland and Channel Islands found that Santa Barbara Giant Kelp forests were larger and had a greater canopy than other forests in the Southern California Bight. Our region accounted for 65 percent of kelp coverage, although it represented only 18 percent of the study area.

There used to be a thriving industry in Southern California which extracted **alginic acid** from the cell walls of Giant Kelp. Algin, a substance used in a number of products such as icings, ice creams, and pharmaceuticals, has gel-producing, emulsifying properties. Special kelp-cutting barges pruned the tops of the Giant Kelp forest, trimming the plants. In recent years, however, overharvesting has been a concern and now the kelp industry is much reduced.

One of the reasons for the decline of the kelp industry is the increase in threats to the survival of Giant Kelp forests. The force of catastrophic winter storms tears the plants loose from the ocean floor. Warm sea surface temperatures associated with El Niño events can cause die-offs. Human encroachment, pollution of the ocean, and overfishing all have had an effect.

A different kind of kelp, **Bull Kelp** (*Nereocystis luetkeana*), thrives from Point Conception (where it coexists with Giant Kelp in the northern part of our region) to Alaska. Well-suited for the rougher swells, Bull Kelp is extremely resistant to breakage. Unlike Giant Kelp, which can propagate from its holdfast year after year, Bull Kelp is an annual; when the upper portion of the plant is destroyed, the plant dies. (See Chapter 4 for more on marine algae)

Life in a Giant Kelp Forest

The structure of a Giant Kelp forest community is much like that of forests on land. There is an understory of a variety of smaller kelps, some of which hug the ocean floor or are only two or three feet above it.

This subtidal forest attracts many forms of life. Over 800 species of animals—some 50 species of fishes, as well as invertebrates, birds, and mammals—and 130 species of marine algae depend upon Giant Kelp to some degree.

Looking at the kelp forest as an ecosystem, note that primary production is available in three forms: living tissue on whole plants; drift in the form of whole plants or detached pieces; and dissolved organic matter (**DOM**, tiny pieces of detritus) and particulate organic matter (**POM**, made up of minuscule pieces of detritus).

Each morsel of kelp is a bite of energy for a juvenile fish, a slurp of carbon for a filter-feeding scallop, or a munched meal for a sea urchin. At the same time, detritus falls to the bottom of the kelp forest and decomposes. This decomposition releases nutrients back into the water column once again—assisted by upwelling, which circulates them up from the ocean floor.

Despite the enormous productivity of the kelps, it has been estimated that only 10 percent of the net production enters the food webs of the kelp bed through grazing. The remaining 90 percent enters the food chain in the form of detritus.

Two of the grazers, those that feed directly on the kelp, are the **Purple Sea Urchin** (*Strongylocentrotus purpuratus*) and **Red Sea Urchin** (*Stronglyocentrotus franciscanus*). In areas where sea otters are absent, unchecked sea urchins can be destructive to kelp forests, creating "urchin barrens."

The **Southern Sea Otter** (*Enhydra lutris* subsp. *nereis*) has been called a

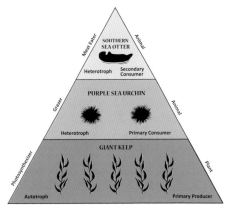

Marine food web with the Southern Sea Otter as a keystone species

The Sunflower Star, a large and active sea star found on the Northern Channel Islands

Purple Sea Urchins

keystone species in the Giant Kelp forest: its presence or absence results in important consequences for the whole kelp community because it preys on sea urchins.

However, the picture is not quite so simple. Scientists have been studying kelp forest ecosystems, particularly in the rich beds off the Northern Channel Islands, to find out the significance of predators other than sea otters on sea urchins. Researchers discovered that there was a big difference between kelp forests that were fished and kelp forests that were in reserves where fishing had been banned. They took long-term monitoring data from Channel Islands National Park, which has a thirty-year-old Anacapa marine reserve and many five-year-old marine reserves throughout the islands, and compared them with adjacent areas where fishing was permitted.

They found that in the fished sites, where sea urchin predators had been removed, urchins were much more destructive. Typically, there are three main species that prey on sea urchins (other than the sea otter): **Spiny**

Lobster (*Panulirus interruptus*), **California Sheephead** (*Semicossyphus pulcher*, a fish), and **Sunflower Star** (*Pycnopodia helianthoides*, a sea star). Of course, the Sunflower Star would not have been fished, but the point is that these natural urchin predators, if left undisturbed, are able to control urchin grazing rates, leading to an overall increase in kelp.

This is a "trophic cascade," a top-down effect, in which the act of fishing cascades down the food chain to produce a community shift: fishing removes the lobster and the sheephead, which leaves the urchin free to destroy the kelp unchecked. In a marine reserve where predators are not fished, they eat the sea urchins and the kelp is not destroyed. Furthermore, sea urchin disease is more prevalent in fished areas because the carrying capacity for their population has been stretched to the breaking point, making them more susceptible to disease.

Southern Sea Otter

Hunted for their fur until a mere fifty to one hundred individuals were all that remained in the early 1900s, sea otters are now fully protected and are staging a slow comeback, although they remain on "threatened" status under the Endangered Species Act. The Southern Sea Otter is the genetically distinct subspecies found on the south-central California coast, from Half Moon Bay to Point Conception. Otters seen south of Point Conception are usually young, solitary males that wander at the northern and southern limits of their range in late winter and early spring.

The sea otter is one of our smallest

A Southern Sea Otter gives a ride to its youngster.

marine mammals. It has exceptionally thick fur to keep warm—nearly one million strands of hair per square inch!—because it has no blubber to protect it from cold ocean waters. Long, waterproof guard hairs trap air, keeping the shorter layer of fur dry, which repels the cold. The guard hairs must be kept scrupulously clean, which is why otters spend a good portion of their time grooming.

Seen from shore, a sea otter looks like a small brown bear floating on its back amid the kelp. The sea otter often uses a large rock, which it carries on its chest, to crack the hard shells of the creatures it eats. These include animals that humans also find tasty, such as sea urchins, abalone, and a variety of clams. This has led to conflicts between those who wish to protect the sea otter and commercial fisheries that see the otters as a threat.

In the late 1980s the US Fish and Wildlife Service relocated a small population of sea otters to San Nicolas Island (approximately thirty animals survive there now), in order to establish an experimental group of otters that lived away from the mainland coast. The reason? Sea otters are especially vulnerable to oil spills. Oil mats their long hair and poisons their prey. The translocation was finally declared a failure, however, because the sea otters often perished during the process and others migrated back to their original home near the mainland.

In 2007 Southern Sea Otters were at a peak of three thousand individuals, but since then, biologists have noted an increase in the deaths of young pups and females. Multiple factors affect otter survival, and at first the stalled recovery of this species was blamed on parasites, bacteria, and toxins found in stream runoff and dumped into the ocean by storms. But some ecologists disagree. Emerging evidence suggests that the rates of disease are a symptom of a bigger problem—insufficient prey resources and malnutrition. The otter population around Monterey, in particular, appears to be stressed and spending more time searching for prey. Nobody knows why the animals don't spread out to unoccupied territories within their range where food is more abundant.

Biologists are wrestling with the question of whether infectious disease in the sea otter is an emergent phenomenon destined to get worse, or a long-term feature of Central California's ecosystem.

No single answer to the mysterious sea otter deaths applies, but keeping human-caused pollution out of the ocean would be a good first step.

Ocean Fishes

Over 85 percent of all California marine fishes are found in the Southern California Bight. Like marine algae, marine fishes—especially the southern species—show a significant break at the area around Point Conception. The same complex topography, convergence of ocean currents, and changeable weather patterns that make the Santa Barbara offshore region so dynamic apply to its rich ichthyofauna.

Life histories of fishes reflect extensive migrations as warm and cool water events come and go in the Santa Barbara Channel. Invasions of tropical fishes during warm-water years associated with El Niño and invasions of northern fishes during cool-water years take place from time to time.

Recall that the entire area of the open ocean is divided into the **pelagic** realm, which contains organisms that live in the open sea, and the **benthic** realm, comprising organisms that live at the bottom of the sea. **Epipelagic** fishes are those that live in the **photic zone** (lighted part) of the ocean, usually between five hundred and six hundred feet.

Populations of epipelagic schooling fishes such as **Northern Anchovy** (*Engraulis mordax*), **Pacific Sardine** (*Sardinops sagax*), **Pacific Chub Mackerel** (*Scomber japonicus*) and **Jack Mackerel** (*Trachurus symmetricus*) are unique to Eastern Boundary regions such as ours. Short-lived and with populations that are highly unpredictable from one year to the next, these small schooling fish—sometimes called "forage fish"—reproduce prolifically and are extremely important as food for natural predators such as tuna, salmon, marine mammals, and seabirds.

The famous collapse of the booming sardine fishery in the mid-twentieth century taught us how overfishing and shifting environmental conditions can affect the seemingly endless supply of forage fishes.

These slivers of silver tend to move in dense schools, called "bait balls," which makes them easy prey for larger fish below the surface and seabirds above. A swimming, whirling bait ball attracts a feeding frenzy of tuna, dolphins, pelicans, and gulls— all preying on the little oily sardines and anchovies.

We know a lot about the Northern Anchovy because one of its most

Northern Anchovies are an important food source for marine birds and animals.

Pacific Sardine

abundant population centers is offshore in the Southern California Bight. Indeed, anchovy larvae are the most common fish larvae in the California Current. Anchovies live for about five years and grow quickly to be six to eight inches long. They spawn in the water column and have no parental care; 80 percent of the spawning occurs from winter to spring. Females may spawn twenty times per year; during the peak season adults spawn every six to eight days between sunset and midnight.

El Niño/Southern Oscillation (ENSO) events alter the ocean ecosystem; Northern Anchovies are just one example. With the influx of warmer ocean waters, anchovies redistribute themselves. In the 1982-83 El Niño, Northern Anchovies moved their spawning grounds offshore and farther north to deeper, cooler waters. In this and subsequent ENSO years, the reduction and loss of the anchovy population reverberated throughout the marine food chain. California Brown Pelicans, which breed on Anacapa Island, suffered a marked downturn in 1997-98 due to the lack of available prey to feed their young. (See Chapter 10 for more on pelicans.)

California Sea Lions and Northern Fur Seals, both of which had been hit hard by the 1982-83 warm water temperatures, underwent another blow in the 1997-98 El Niño that resulted in a three-fourths reduction in the survival rate of juveniles of both species at their rookeries on San Miguel Island. The scarcity of prey caused thousands of the year's pups to die because their mothers were so weak and undernourished they could not

Marine Mammal Calendar for Santa Barbara Channel

Year-round
Most dolphins and porpoises
Minke Whale
Fin Whale
Harbor Seal
Northern Elephant Seal
California Sea Lion
Northern Fur Seal

Winter
Gray Whale (December to mid-February: southbound migration)
Harbor Seal (at rookeries breeding)
Northern Elephant Seal (at rookeries breeding)

Spring
Southern Sea Otter (February to early May)
Gray Whale (February to early May: northbound migration)
Harbor Seal (at rookeries molting)
Northern Elephant Seal (at rookeries molting)
Humpback Whale (start to arrive in May)
Blue Whale (start to arrive in May)

Summer
Humpback Whale feeding
Blue Whale feeding

Fall
A few Blue Whales linger
Southbound Gray Whales begin

produce milk. Northern Elephant Seals suffered losses for a different reason: their young were washed away from pupping grounds by the heavy surf of El Niño storms. (For more on El Niño, see Chapter 1.)

Marine Mammals

In the ocean environment, the closest relatives to humans are the marine mammals: seals, sea lions, whales, dolphins, porpoises, and sea otters. As such, they hold a special fascination. Their long migrations, their haul-outs at deserted beaches, their unique adaptations to deep sea life, and their eerie vocalizations underwater all lure naturalists from around the world to study marine mammals here.

The Santa Barbara region is renowned for its marine mammal viewing opportunities because it's at the intersection of northern and southern waters, the Northern Channel Islands provide good rookeries, food sources are rich, and major migration routes pass nearby. At least twenty-seven species of marine mammals have been regularly sighted in our channel, and over forty have been recorded in the larger Southern California Bight. These are world-class totals.

An important fact to remember is that North Pacific populations of most of our marine mammals were under siege by hunters and whalers until quite recently, with some species only receiving complete protection since 1966. Tracking population cycles and learning more about the life histories of marine mammals is crucial to completing the recovery of marine mammals from their pathetically low numbers early in the twentieth century.

Pinnipeds

Seals, fur seals, sea lions, and walruses are considered pinnipeds.

California Sea Lions are the most abundant pinniped in the Santa Barbara Channel. Their northernmost rookery on San Miguel Island shelters thousands of sea lions.

True seals differ from sea lions in that they have small front flippers and they lack the external ear flaps (**pinnae**) that sea lions have. Seals, marvelously streamlined in the water, roll helplessly about on

Bull Northern Elephant Seal at the colony near San Simeon

land. Sea lions, having larger front flippers, propel themselves on land more easily.

Putting aside sea lions for another discussion (see Chapter 10), let's talk about Northern Elephant Seals and Harbor Seals, which have rookeries you can see on nearby mainland beaches.

The life cycle of the Northern Elephant Seal is astonishing. Where do they go when they leave the rocky bay at Piedras Blancas? Male elephant seals travel up to thirteen thousand miles a year, from California and Baja to the North Pacific to feed, and back—the first time to breed, and the second time to molt.

When male elephant seals (they get their name from that long nose that hangs down over the lip) depart after coming ashore, they spend many months at sea. But they are not just swimming along casually. A male dives two or three times per hour, and each dive lasts twenty minutes. They plumb the depths, foraging at 1,000 to 2,500 feet, a zone packed with fish and squid.

Elephant seals' adaptations for deep diving astound researchers. To decrease oxygen consumption, the seals constrict the flow of blood to muscle, tissue, and internal organs, keeping it only in the brain and central nervous system (and to some extent the liver). Their lungs collapse as they dive; with no air, there is no exchange of gas (nitrogen) between lungs and blood, which prevents the bends that human divers so fear. Furthermore, most diving mammals suffer high-pressure nervous syndrome, a state that occurs between 350 and

Harbor Seal colony at Carpinteria Bluffs

700 feet deep and feels like being squeezed to death. But elephant seals show no ill effects.

One of the reasons male elephant seals dive to such depths is that they must replenish the protein and fat stores they lose by fasting during breeding and molting. Consuming one hundred to two hundred pounds of food a day, these bulls are tapping into a deep feeding zone that whales and fishermen can't reach. But deep dives may take a toll in the long run. Elephant seals, at thirteen to twenty years, have shorter lives than their shallower-diving Harbor Seal cousins, which live to twenty-five or thirty years.

Regardless, Northern Elephant Seals have made a swift comeback to a current population of about 150,000. In our region, they have rookeries at San Miguel Island and Santa Barbara Island, as well as at Point Piedras Blancas north of San Simeon.

From the Carpinteria Bluffs, you can watch the Harbor Seals as they come ashore to a historic haul-out location for breeding and pupping. And since 1991, watchful docents

have been monitoring this colony, successfully keeping people and dogs away from the seals during the crucial months from December through May, when the seals give birth and care for the young. The pups are born on land but can immediately swim if they have to. Harbor Seals are long-lived—if they survive human interference and ocean predators. For example, on March 9, 2008, two Harbor Seals were killed by a fifteen-foot **White Shark** (*Carcharodon carcharias*) approximately thirty yards offshore of the Carpinteria rookery. In recent years, shark attacks on Harbor Seals appear to be increasing. Probably a greater threat, however, is unleashed dogs on the beach, because when the colony is disturbed the seal pups get trampled to death.

The Carpinteria Harbor Seal colony appears to be holding its own, with a total of approximately one hundred pups born annually in recent years. How fortunate we are to have the only publicly accessible Harbor Seal colony between here and La Jolla.

Nature Journal
November 21, 2002

Northern Elephant Seal Rookery, Piedras Blancas Lighthouse north of San Simeon

At a vista point along Highway 1 north of San Simeon, a "wildlife viewing" binocular symbol directs us to a now-famous Northern Elephant Seal colony. Since 1992, these huge seals have come ashore here to breed and give birth. Lying on the sand beneath the bluffs and very close to human onlookers, the elephant seal females and young are pale yellow or gray—enormous, streamlined lumps. The adult males, weighing about four thousand pounds, are much larger and darker, with protuberant snouts. They grunt, belch, and snort in displays of masculine authority. Two young bulls skirmish in the water among the breaking waves, lunging and biting at each other. Finally, an enormous old bull comes lumbering down from the sand, humping along like a log with ripples in it. Scarred and bloodied from earlier battles, the old bull nudges and shoves at the two sparring males, signaling his superiority. The youngsters aren't disputing it; they leave.

A view of the Northern Elephant Seal colony near San Simeon

An alpha male such as this large bull can expect to impregnate many females in one season.

As the tide ebbs and the gulls scream, the groaning and grunting noises of the elephant seals become louder; the bulls raise their snouts and roar. It is so vital, so exciting. And yet the seals appear oblivious to tourists and traffic.

Come here for a ringside seat at the pinniped lovefest.

Sparring immature male Northern Elephant Seals vie for dominance in the colony.

Same Location, May 5, 2009

The spring wind whips at our hats and jackets and puffs of fog hover just off the dark rocks. Onlookers are everywhere, from all over the world. A new boardwalk has been added since our visit in 2002, and the scene at the rookery is quite different in May from what it was in November.

There are no young males roaring and splashing and making a commotion in the water. This time it's just the mothers and their weaned youngsters (termed "weaners") that dominate the sandy beach like a collection of large, sleek sausages lying in the sun. The adult females

Young Northern Elephant Seals during the spring molting season

are of all colors, because the "cata-strophic molt," as opposed to a gradual molt throughout the year, is taking place now, over the next three or four weeks. The older fur—brownish or pale yellow—will become sleek, silvery gray when the molt is finished.

With binoculars from the viewing board-walk, I notice that each seal is literally peel-ing. Patches of exposed skin and ridges of older skin curling away make room for the new, rich fur that enables these animals to withstand cold, deep water.

As I get to the far end of the boardwalk, I spy one seal so close I can look into her large, dark eyes. It's a big female lying half-buried in the sand. She arches her back to look at me, then yawns, exposing a gap-ing, pink maw. She and many of the other seals scoop up the sand with their flippers and throw it onto their backs, which cools them down and discourages flies.

A well-informed docent tells me that by summer, these females and their young will be gone, off foraging in deep water to the far west. (During their molt here on the beach, the adults are fasting.) Mean-while, the male elephant seals are in the Gulf of Alaska, feeding, and will return in summer to claim the beaches for their own molting session.

Looking down the curve of coastline in this rocky, shallow bay, I marvel at the rookery tightly packed on the narrow beach. The colony now numbers sixteen thousand individuals.

Dolphins and Porpoises

Whales, dolphins, and porpoises comprise the order Cetacea, which is divided into two groups: the Mys-ticetes, or **baleen whales** (see next sec-tion), and the Odontocetes, or **toothed whales**, dolphins, and porpoises. Due

to the shape of their faces, dolphins and porpoises may look as though they have noses. They don't. Like all aquatic mammals, they use lungs and a blow-hole in the top of their head to breathe.

Intelligent, active, and highly vis-ible, dolphins are a first Cetacean sighting for most of us. Strolling along the beach, scanning offshore from a promontory, or watching from a boat, we thrill at the beauty and grace of dolphins gliding through the water or plunging beside the bow of the boat. Their subtle patterns of gray and white and black against the sea serve as reminders that dolphins are readily identifiable by their shape and coloring, and the Santa Barbara Chan-nel attracts many species. Dolphins, like whales, use underwater sounds to communicate.

What is the difference between a dolphin and a porpoise? Some people are embarrassed to ask this question or use the terms interchangeably, but the two species are in completely sep-arate families. Porpoises are smaller, chunkier, and lack a rostrum, or beak.

Long-beaked Common Dolphin, the most numerous marine mammal in the Santa Barbara Channel. Photo by Robert Goodell

In contrast, the larger dolphins are more streamlined and have a prominent beak. However, as Michelle Berman-Kowalewski states, "not all dolphins are larger than porpoises and not all dolphins have a beak. The biggest difference is their teeth shape, conical versus spatulate."

Dolphins are seen more often than porpoises in the Santa Barbara Channel: there are more dolphin species here, and porpoises shy away from boats and human interactions, unlike dolphins.

Our most numerous Cetacean offshore is the common dolphin, now divided into the **Short-beaked Common Dolphin** (*Delphinus delphis*) and the **Long-beaked Common Dolphin** (*Delphinus capensis*) species, but the difference is difficult to discern unless you're an expert.

Common dolphins gather in herds of hundreds, if not thousands. From far away, large groups will swim over to hitch a ride on the bow wave of a whale-watching or fishing boat. Looking out from the deck, you see the entire surface of the ocean churning, alive with the energy of hundreds of jumping and diving dolphins. Leaping into the air, twisting and turning and playfully slapping at the water, common dolphins delight in accompanying boats. This might have been the species of which Herman Melville wrote that they "upon the sea keep tossing themselves to heaven like caps in a Fourth of July crowd."

It has been thought that the Short-beaked Common Dolphin feeds mostly at night, following the vertical migrations of the deep scatter-

Long-beaked Common Dolphins riding the bow wave of a boat.

ing layer of fishes and other organisms. The long-beaked, however, is diurnal—feeding on small, schooling fish. They can be harbingers of a feeding frenzy, when the anchovies and sardines start schooling near the surface. With seabirds such as pelicans and cormorants diving, and dolphins rippling up a ruckus underwater, the frenzy soon attracts other species to the food source. It's exciting to watch this from shore. Use binoculars or a spotting scope to track the distant birds as they follow the moving fish, plunge-diving from the air and scooping mouthfuls from the water.

In addition, the following species are often seen from whale-watching boats in the Santa Barbara Channel: Bottlenose Dolphin, **Pacific White-sided Dolphin** (*Lagenorhynchus obliquidens*), **Risso's Dolphin** (*Grampus griseus*), **Northern Right-Whale Dolphin** (*Lissodelphis borealis*), and **Dall's Porpoise** (*Phocoenoides dalli*).

Gray Whale showing blowholes and barnacles.
Photo by Robert Goodell

Whales: Grays, Humpbacks, and Blues

Of all the marine mammals, it is the enormous whales that instill the deepest passion in many of us. "Whales, we now know, teach and learn. They scheme. They cooperate, and they grieve. They recognize themselves and their friends. They...fight back against their enemies," wrote Charles Siebert in a 2009 article titled "Watching Whales Watching Us."

The more scientists learn about whales, the more they are able to draw parallels between whale and human behavior. Whale brain structures are surprisingly similar to those of humans. In 2006 a study of the brains of two baleen species—Humpback and Finback whales—revealed large numbers of cells that have a link to higher cognitive functions like self-awareness, compassion, and language communication. The same study noted that Sperm, Killer, and Humpback whales show complex social patterns, cooperation, and cultural transmission, a finding which may be related to the similar brain structures of whales and humans.

A baleen whale feeds by scooping up a large quantity of water that contains its prey, then sieving it through a "curtain" of baleen that hangs from the roof of its mouth in place of teeth. The flexible plates of baleen trap the prey, letting water pass through. Baleen plates are a form of keratin, somewhat like human fingernails.

Three species of baleen whale, the Gray Whale, the Humpback Whale, and the Blue Whale, frequent our region, providing a rare opportunity to observe these giants as they feed and migrate offshore.

California Gray Whale: California Gray Whales, familiar to many of us because we can spot their blows from shore, were the first species to get the public interested in watching whales. In late fall, they travel south through the Santa Barbara Channel, often navigating around the south side of the Channel Islands. After giving birth and mating in the shallow lagoons off Baja California, the Grays return north in spring, bound for foraging areas in the Bering and Chukchi Seas. En route, they hug the California coast to protect their calves from dangerous predators such as Killer Whales and sharks. Another reason to stick close to shore is their preference for benthic (sea-bottom) crustaceans. Making shallow dives and usually feeding on its right side, a Gray Whale sucks up muddy sediments, then filters out tiny prey items which stick to the baleen fringe in its mouth.

Gray Whales Count, a group of volunteers in the Santa Barbara region, has been conducting Gray Whale counts since 2005. The valuable information gathered from their sea watch on the bluffs at Coal Oil Point at UC Santa Barbara reflects Gray Whale population trends. They are part of a network of whale-count stations located up and down the California coast. The closest stations to our region are at Palos Verdes to the south and Point Piedras Blancas to the north. At Piedras Blancas, counters can expect to see close to the total Pacific population of Gray Whales as they go by along the coast—about twenty thousand individuals.

Endangered Humpback Whale breaching—forty tons of acrobatics! Photo by Robert Goodell

On the other hand, at Santa Barbara whale counters saw approximately 960 adult whales and 237 calves in the 2012 northbound migration. Although most whales migrate north using the Santa Barbara Channel, some choose to go around the Northern Channel Islands on the south side, and thus they are not tallied at this station.

Whale counters are especially interested in calf totals, i.e., how many juvenile whales travel north each season. When calf totals are down, it may indicate a bad year for birthing in the Baja lagoons.

Lately, however, experts have learned that conditions in the Bering Sea due to climate change have an impact on Gray Whale migrations and births. If the whales go north of Alaska into the Beaufort Sea—the ice pack is melting and foraging is good there—their return migration to birthing areas in Baja is much longer. In fact, scientists have discovered that some female Grays have begun giving birth en route before they reach the lagoons in Mexico. This can be measured at monitoring stations which total both

northbound *and* southbound migrations, where they find that there are more calves on the southbound (fall and winter) route than formerly.

Yes, giving birth in migration in the open ocean carries risks. Hypothermia, having to learn to swim in rough seas, difficulty in nursing, and predation by Killer Whales are just some of them. But it might be evidence of what is called "behavioral flexibility" as the Gray Whale adapts to climate change. At the American Cetacean Society biennial conference in 2008, biologists proposed that the Gray Whale be designated an "indicator species," one whose health and survival in response to climate shifts make this species a unique reflection of the changing environment in which it lives.

From 2007 to 2010, Gray Whale cow/calf pair numbers past Coal Oil Point were low to very low. In 2011 and 2012, apparently, the totals were way up. It's difficult to pick out trends, but the more we gather the raw data, the more we learn.

A lot of scientific assumptions about Gray Whale behavior even ten years

Aerial photo of endangered Blue Whale mother and calf. Mothers and their calves are often seen feeding in the channel in summer. Photo by Robert Goodell

ago have been turned upside down by marine biologists with revolutionary new tracking and identification methods. Some of these changes in behavior may be due to the whales' adaptations to new environments, and others are surely a response to climate change.

Humpback Whale: Because they are so active, Humpback Whales are a favorite of whale watchers. Breaching—throwing more than a third of its body out of the water and splashing down on its back—and slapping the water with extra-long pectoral fins are part of the Humpback's repertoire. Their flukes (tail fins), which they fling skyward as they dive, have individual patterns of black and white with wavy margins.

These fluke patterns allow biologists studying Humpbacks to distinguish one individual from another, because each fluke pattern is unique.

After thousands of hours of photographing Humpback Whales during three seasons (2004, 2005, and 2006), researchers with a program called SPLASH (Structure of Populations, Levels of Abundance and Status of Humpback Whales) in the North Pacific were able to identify 7,971 individuals by comparing tail fluke photos. The number of Humpback Whales was estimated to be 18,300 for the Northeast Pacific (over 50 percent of this population winters in Hawaii). The number of Humpbacks frequenting California and Oregon is estimated at 1,400 to 1,700. Fortunately, the population of Humpbacks is considered to be steadily increasing at about 6 percent per year.

When you look at the size of these baleen whales, you ask how they can possibly sustain themselves. What kinds of feeding strategies do they use?

Humpback Whales consume krill, but they eat other prey as well. When small schooling fish like Northern Anchovies are running in the Santa Barbara Channel, the whales' diets will shift to take advantage of the feast. Humpbacks use several feeding techniques, but the one they're most famous for is the "bubble net." The Humpback, either alone or together with others, dives down and then swims upward in a spiral while blowing bubbles through its blowholes. The bubbles rise up, surrounding the trapped group of fish in a circular "net." Once the net surrounds the fish, the whales swim quickly upward, their gaping mouths swallowing thousands of fish in one gulp. As many as a dozen whales may cooperate to create rings or nets as wide as one hundred feet in diameter.

Blue Whale: Gray and Humpback Whales, big as they are, look puny beside a Blue Whale. Visit the exhibit of the Blue Whale skeleton at the Santa Barbara Museum of Natural History and walk around under the huge bones to get an idea of how immense these beasts are.

Ponder the following: the Blue Whale's heart is six feet wide; its lungs weigh one ton; its brain weighs fifteen pounds; its tongue weighs as much as an elephant; it is longer than three school buses; its blow is almost three stories (thirty feet) high. We know all these facts about Blue Whales, but when it comes to their lifestyles, much continues to be discovered with every research trip biologists undertake.

For example, exactly where does the eastern North Pacific population (to which the Blue Whales of our region belong) spend the winter? Where do they give birth? What methods of feeding do they use? And what do their sounds mean?

By using satellite and acoustic tags and photography, scientists on an expedition in 2008 were able to track several Blue Whales from their summer feeding grounds in the Santa Barbara Channel to a wintering area off the coast of Central America known as the Costa Rica Dome. Here, an upwelling of nutritious cold water fertilizes the growth of phytoplankton which in turn is eaten by zooplankton (krill), the preferred diet of the Blue Whale. Other Blues, from Antarctica and elsewhere, join the feeding concentration at the dome.

This scientific venture successfully documented the Costa Rica Dome as a winter feeding area, but only one cow/calf pair appeared. (Nobody has ever witnessed the birth of a baby Blue Whale.) So, although courtship behavior was observed, we still don't know exactly where most Blue Whales mate and give birth in winter months.

There are now considered to be approximately two thousand Blue Whales in the California/Oregon/Washington stock. New research has found that some of these Blues along the coast have begun to wander further north, replicating historical patterns of foraging off British Columbia. By photo identification, biologists can recognize individual whales that were first seen off Central California and then traveled to the Pacific Northwest in a relatively recent range extension. It had been more than fifty years since Blue Whales were documented in these northern waters where, before 1966, the species used to be regularly found (and hunted).

Beginning in about 1990, large numbers of Blue Whales began to frequent the Santa Barbara Channel in spring and summer. A study of their feeding habits in the channel recorded over three hundred Blue Whales feeding there in August 1996. The Blues were discovered to be feeding on dense patches of krill associated with the north and west sides of San Miguel Island and the north side of Santa Rosa Island, where it is thought that circulation in the Santa Barbara Channel may support an abundance of krill. Here, where the phytoplankton and associated krill have drifted south from a center of upwelling off Point Conception, cool water overlays the shelf bottom that forms around the islands. The species of krill taken (*Euphausia pacifica, Nematoscelis difficilis,* and *Thysanoessa spinifera*) are all cold-water species found as far north as the Gulf of Alaska.

Both at the Costa Rica Dome and in the Santa Barbara Channel, Blue Whales feed by diving deep, usually between three hundred to seven hundred feet, sinking headfirst beneath a patch of krill. Abruptly, the whale switches direction and lunges upward while opening its mouth and forcing water and krill into its pleated throat pouch. A feeding whale will repeatedly lunge from beneath towards the krill, then surface to breathe after ten minutes or so before attempting the next dive. As twilight approaches and the krill move to the surface, Blue Whales feed more shallowly, rolling over on their sides with their mouths open to scoop up these crustaceans.

And how much can an adult Blue Whale eat in a day? Forty million krill. Contemplating that amount makes one realize the importance of the health of our oceans and the fragility of this whole ecosystem. It is not something we can take for granted, for our oceans are vulnerable, as are these enormous Blue Whales.

One of the facts about the Blue

WHALE FACTS

SPECIES	LENGTH	WEIGHT	POPULATION IN NO. PACIFIC	CONSERVATION STATUS
Gray Whale	49 ft.	36 tons	20,000	Protected
Humpback Whale	50 ft.	40 tons	18,300	Endangered
Blue Whale	100 ft.	190 tons	2,000	Endangered

Whale the general public may not know: its vocalizations are louder and carry farther than those of any other living animal. However, most sounds are given at too low a pitch for the human ear to hear. For example, Blue Whale bulls give a thumping, deep pulse "A" call, followed by a continuously toned "B" call, both of which can be heard for thousands of miles underwater. These A and B calls have been classified as song (Humpback and Fin whales also sing). Furthermore, a new study shows that Blues' songs reflect their particular geographic region like dialects. Thus each song group may be characteristic of a certain Blue Whale subset of the total population.

By affixing acoustic recording tags to Blue Whales in the Santa Barbara Channel and at Monterey Bay in 2007, scientists found out there was a correlation between a whale's song and its behavior. They discovered that besides the A/B song, Blues utter a downswept "D" call, as well as a highly variable group of frequency-modulated calls. Lone, traveling males produced A/B songs, and single A and B calls were typically given by pairs. This suggests that these calls have something to do with reproduction. D calls were heard from both sexes during foraging, usually when the whales were in groups. All calls were produced at shallow depth, and calling whales spent more time in shallower water than non-calling whales. Since traveling whales do not typically dive deep, they would experience little extra energetic cost by uttering long song bouts as they swim from one place to another.

There is an urgency to the search for the secrets of the lifestyles of all the giant baleen whales, because new threats crop up as human pressures affect what goes on in the ocean. Ship strikes—ships striking whales—in the Santa Barbara Channel are a major concern, as is pollution of the ocean by fuel emissions and ship noise.

In order to preserve and protect these magnificent cetaceans, biologists continue to carefully monitor their movements and lifestyles. Not that long ago, their populations were so decimated that current numbers would have been unthinkable.

* * *

On an overcast spring day off Point Conception, the sea is smooth, but the underlying swell heaves and sighs, up and down, up and down—pushed by the rhythm of the northwest wind. It is a dull, metallic sea. For miles and miles, the distant horizon blends with the gray ocean. For miles and miles, there is no sign of life.

All at once, a flock of dark specks bobbing on the water becomes a group of **Sooty Shearwaters** (*Puffinus griseus*). The birds are pecking and diving and slurping at the krill just beneath the surface. Common dolphins materialize out of nowhere, splashing their way in silver arcs. Murrelets and auklets—tiny seabirds of black and white that nest on the Channel Islands—join the fray. One murrelet has a downy chick in tow that can't be more than a few days old. The murrelets disappear underwater, then pop up.

Red-necked Phalaropes (*Phalaropus lobatus*), tiny shorebirds on their way to nest in the Arctic, stab at the water with needlelike bills as they float in flocks. They are gorging themselves on the same prey that lures the Humpback Whale: krill.

Close by, the blow of a Humpback Whale sprays.

A "current break," where warm and cold masses of water meet, draws a feeding frenzy. Krill, copepods, and juvenile fishes swim in layers, stacked like a cake, trapped by the sheer velocity of opposing currents. In eddies and gyres, fast and slow, where currents collide they bring life to the ocean.

We landlocked souls cannot read the signs, but the seabirds with their sense of smell are the first to arrive at the feeding frenzy. Seals, dolphins, and whales join in as if on cue.

What's going on here is the very stuff a naturalist seeks to understand: the wondrous way the wind pushes the surface of the ocean; the friction of warm against cold currents; the bountiful aspect of a healthy ocean that feeds a multitude of creatures.

The incomparable diversity of life in the Pacific Ocean off our shores is a realm of its own, and it is a key frontier of natural history in the region: although much work has been done, scientists are still searching for a better understanding of how the ocean functions and how to protect it.

In the last chapter, we explored the underwater realm of the ocean. Most forms of life in the ocean are difficult to see, much less touch. To many of us, the ocean is inaccessible, a strange and vast world, difficult to experience if you aren't accustomed to oceangoing adventures.

The shore, on the other hand, is inviting to all. Here lies a sweep of pale sand, with rocks jumbled together or slanted in low reefs, seaweeds lush in tidepool gardens or heaped as wrack at the bases of cliffs. At last, you can examine up close some of the creatures and algae that are normally hidden at the bottom of the sea.

This major transition zone between marine and terrestrial ecosystems takes place in a narrow strip in our region—sometimes only several yards wide, sometimes more than a mile wide, yet it stretches the whole length of the coast from Point Mugu on the south to Point Piedras Blancas on the north, hundreds of miles long. So narrow, so long, and so exceptionally rich in species, the seashore is the dynamic interface between the two great ecosystems on the planet: marine and terrestrial.

At the shore, waves hurl themselves at rocky cliffs, sands drift and pile in small grains or bigger cobbles, dunes are destroyed and created, and the tides surge and recede. Life here is ruled by the force of the waves, the temperature of the water, the substrate (rocky, muddy, or sandy), and the tidal level. Whether we're discussing rocky coasts, sandy beaches, or dunes, organisms living with these harsh conditions will only survive if they can adapt.

The Santa Barbara region has excellent examples of every kind of seashore habitat. Generally speaking, rocky shores are more common north of Point Conception, in northern Santa Barbara County and San Luis Obispo County.

Tides

Before setting out on a field trip at the shore, study a tide table. In our region, the minus tides of late fall and winter, which occur in the afternoon, are the best times to go tidepooling.

The position of the moon and the sun in relation to Earth influences the tides. The moon, lying closer to Earth than the sun, has the most influence. When there is a new moon or a full moon, the sun, moon, and Earth are in alignment, and the gravitational pull on the water increases, meaning a greater extreme between low and high tides. These are called **spring tides**, a reference to the upwelling of the water during a high tide. The less extreme tides that occur when the moon is in its quarters—the sun, moon, and Earth are not in line—are referred to as **neap tides**, from an old English word meaning "scarce."

Along our coast, there are two high tides and two low tides each day, of different heights: the "higher high water," "lower high water," and so on. These will cycle through in a twenty-five-hour period, each tide being about an hour later the following day.

At certain times of the month, the shore undergoes extreme tides. In the Santa Barbara area, the highest high tide averages over five feet above sea level, and the lowest low tide is at sea level. **Minus tides**, those below sea level, expose the creatures in the lowest tide zone. These animals and plants are usually inaccessible except during minus tides.

On a field trip, you can safely count on tidepooling an hour before and an hour after the listed time for the minus tide.

The coast here is more exposed to strong westerly winds, the waves are higher, and the water is colder.

On the other hand, in southern Santa Barbara and Ventura counties, sandy beaches are more common. The rocks are sedimentary (usually sandstone and shale) and crumble easily, becoming sand. The shore here is in the lee of the west winds because the coast has taken that turn at Point Conception and it now faces south instead of west. It is protected by the Channel Islands, and storm surf is not as strong as to the north.

But the South Coast lacks the great expanse of sand dunes seen in northern Santa Barbara and southern San Luis Obispo counties. Why? The answer lies in the wind and the shape of the coastline to the north. The intense northwest wind that blows in spring and summer north of Point Conception feeds sand to the dune systems. If you look at the shape of the coast behind which these dune sheets form, you can see that the sand gathers behind the bays formed by

Coal Oil Point Reserve tidepools

headlands and, blown by the wind, creeps inland to form the dunes that cover the low landscape behind those headlands.

Each of these terms: the rocky intertidal, the sandy beach, and the wind-formed dunes, describes a portion of the seashore.

We begin with the rocky coast.

Rocky Shore

Life in a Wave-Swept Environment

For just a minute, imagine you are a mussel or barnacle permanently cemented to a rock. You cannot move, so how are you going to get food? How can you reproduce, stuck for a lifetime on a lonely ledge? How can a creature the size of a dime or less withstand the constant battering of the waves at high tide and the hot, dry sun when the tide is low? And if you're a crab, won't you get washed away because you aren't stuck down?

The successes of animals and plants in the rocky intertidal zone include an array of body plans with design criteria that have fascinated naturalists for centuries.

In the previous chapter, we talked about ecological niches—the role an organism plays in order to live within the set of ecological conditions that surround it.

The tidepools and the creatures that exist there are an excellent example of **adaptive radiation** (see also Chapter 10). Adaptive radiation means that from a common ancestor, a wide variety of species has diversified over eons to fill a variety of ecological niches. From a single descendant, say a snail or a crab of one species or another, come multiple species of snails or crabs that have diverged over time to coexist in the same small area. When closely related species inhabit the same geographic area, it is known as **sympatry**. Thus, these species have evolved over millennia to coexist, reducing competition by using similar ecological resources in different ways (their niches).

So when we say an animal has an "adaptation" for a certain environment,

Rocky shore at Goleta Point, a wave-swept environment

we are talking about millions of years of gradual change.

The most challenging physical factor that organisms have to live with on the rocky coast is **wave shock**. Most of the plants and animals in the rocky intertidal zone are subject to wave force pulling and pushing them, inundating them with life-giving seawater and at the same time tearing at them with deadly power.

Marine algae (seaweeds) and animals somehow manage to live in these conditions. For animals, size and shape are adaptations. Limpets, barnacles, and chitons have streamlined, low-profile shapes that minimize the force of the smashing waves.

To move or not to move—each has advantages. Crabs, shrimps, lobsters, and other crustaceans that walk using jointed legs can seek shelter from the waves in crevices or under rocks. These organisms must hide from the strongest surf, however, because they can easily be dislodged and washed away.

Many animals are **sessile**, fixed in place—once situated, they cannot move. Barnacles, oysters, and certain worms are permanently attached to the rocks. Limpets and chitons have an extra large "foot" that helps them hold on despite being clobbered by waves. Most marine algae have holdfasts, instead of roots, which fasten them to the surface of a rock.

During a low tide, intertidal organisms are exposed to air. If they lose too much water during evaporation, they will not survive. Thus, water loss (**dessication**) is important to their design. Once again, mobile animals like crabs can move into moist cracks or go where water has gathered in deeper tidepools. But most organisms that live at higher tide levels conserve moisture by clustering in dense groups. Evidently, living side by side decreases water loss in barnacles, mussels, and sea anemones.

Limpets and periwinkles protect against water loss by clinging tightly to the rock's surface.

During a prolonged low tide, seaweeds may suffer from severe water loss. But many have tissues in their blades and stipes that will wither and shrink during dry periods, but then recover quickly once they are hydrated again. Experiments have shown marine algae can lose 60 to 90 percent of the water in their tissues and still recover.

Respiration, or the ability to obtain oxygen, proves challenging because these marine organisms need to extract oxygen from water. In many kinds of snails and bivalves, the gills that enable them to breathe in water are enclosed in a cavity to prevent them from drying out. The cavity is protected by a shell.

In the case of a small tidepool fish, such as the **Tidepool Sculpin** (*Oligocottus maculosus*), its breathing can take place through the skin. Almost 50 percent of the sculpin's oxygen intake is through its skin, so that the gills are fairly small.

Some tidepool organisms can only feed when the tide is in. Grazers, filter feeders, detritus feeders, or other predators must be covered by water in order to feed.

The turbulent waves make repro-duction a challenge, too. How do animals of the opposite sex get together? Often, they don't; but with **broadcast spawning**, they can release eggs and sperm into the ocean and, in the circulating water, fertilization occurs. For example, limpets, mussels, and sea stars release millions and millions of eggs and sperm at various times of the year. This is one of the major differences between life on land and in the sea: can you imagine animals on land throwing sperm and eggs out into the air?

One of the ways that intertidal

Rocky shore habitat at Mussel Shoals, Ventura County

organisms increase the chances their eggs will be fertilized is by clumping together in aggregations and then releasing their sperm and eggs all at once. Also, they spawn using the rhythm of the tides. For example, mussels use synchronized spawning, only releasing sperm and eggs during neap tides.

Internal fertilization is another way of reproducing (see the buckshot barnacle account in this chapter). Finally, some creatures use a combination of broadcast spawning and

asexual cloning. The Clonal Anemone (see account in this chapter) releases eggs or sperm into the water twice a year. The juveniles (planktonic larvae) then settle on a rocky surface and from there reproduction is by cloning.

Life in the Tidepools

If you investigate rocky areas of the coast at low tide, notice that the animals that cling to the sunny, dry tops of the boulders are different from those found in the middle of the rocks or those at the base of the rocks in tidepools.

Just as, when climbing, you see particular trees and shrubs at lower elevations that you do not find as you progress up the mountain, so it is in

Tidal zonation on a single rock, with upper portion rarely submerged and lower portion regularly submerged

intertidal zonation. You can examine one big rocky outcrop at the shore and see bands of organisms of different kinds as you go from the bottom dwellers in the shallow water to those high on the tops of the rocks.

This is intertidal zonation: the arrangement of plants and animals

at the seashore in horizontal bands according to each organism's ability to withstand tidal exposure, heat, light, and desiccation. The term "tidal exposure" means the amount of time a certain snail or anemone or crab is exposed to air between tides. Remember, these animals are marine organisms, not terrestrial ones, and they need to be bathed in salt water at intervals or they will die.

The upward range of an animal or plant is related to physical conditions. The lower limit of an organism's distribution is more a result of competition with other animals, especially those that will eat them. For example, shelled organisms such as mussels and snails dare not venture down to lower tidal zones, due to predation by sea stars. The sea stars, on the other hand, will not venture upwards, because their ability to withstand water loss is not great. They will dry out and perish if they climb up to feed on the mussels.

In the tidepools, the number and variety of living things is almost unbelievable.

"Ferocious." "Survival of the fittest." "Competition." "Cauldron of life." These terms describe what goes on in the rocky intertidal: teeming forms of life in a fixed amount of space. Indeed, nearly every known animal phylum is represented in this habitat. Only by running for cover (crabs, shrimps, small fishes), fighting (anemones, with their stinging-cell wars), crowding (mussels and gooseneck barnacles piled high onto each other), and hanging on relentlessly (barnacles, limpets, snails) do the organisms survive.

Nobody can describe the tidepools at low tide as well as John Steinbeck did. The great friend of renowned marine biologist Ed Ricketts wrote, in *Cannery Row:*

> On the exposed rocks out of water, the barnacles bubble behind their closed doors and the limpets dry out. And down to the rocks come the black flies to eat anything they can find. The sharp smell of iodine from the algae, and the lime smell of calcareous bodies and the smell of powerful protean, smell of sperm and ova fill the air. On the exposed rocks the starfish emit semen and eggs from between their rays. The smells of life and richness, of death and digestion, of decay and birth, burden the air. And salt spray blows in from the barrier where the ocean waits for its rising-tide strength to permit it back into the Great Tide Pool again.

Indicator Species

Local marine biologist Genevieve Anderson has taught students for years about tidal zonation by choosing two or three indicator species in each zone or horizontal band of rocky shore that can always be found. If it's your first time tidepooling, it's a good way to remember which organisms can be found where. Much of the information below is based upon Professor Anderson's lessons.

The Splash Zone gets very little wetting, even by the highest tides, and is dry most of the day. Animals up here at the top of the rocks and away from the surf must be able to withstand dry conditions.

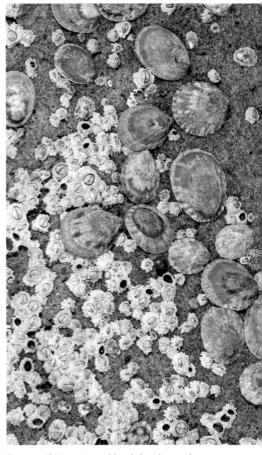

Fingernail Limpets and buckshot barnacles thrive in areas that remain dry most of the day.

You will always see the **Eroded Periwinkle** (*Littorina planaxis*) in the splash zone. This little snail spends most of its life closed up behind its **operculum**, a special trap-door structure that protects its shell from drying out. The snail then secretes mucus which cements its body to the rock. On rare occasions, when the tide is very high, periwinkles will come out to feed on patches of algae.

Like many others in the snail family, the periwinkle has the equivalent of a mouthful of razor-sharp teeth,

The Eroded Periwinkle lives high on the rocks in the splash zone.

Dense clusters of Leaf Barnacle are found with clumps of California Mussels in the high tide zone, away from predatory sea stars.

for life. Thousands exist side by side, high up on the dry rocks. They aren't bothered by predators, which is one advantage. And when the tide is high, they stick out their specialized feet to rake in food from the seawater. This adaptation prompted Thomas Henry Huxley to describe the barnacle as "a crustacean fixed by its head and kicking food into its mouth."

Like many marine creatures, buckshot barnacles are hermaphroditic—having both male and female organs. However, most individuals cannot get their sperm to their own eggs. Like most barnacles, the buckshot barnacle has an inflatable penis that may extend as much as two inches (twenty times the size of its body) from the animal in order to fertilize a neighbor. These barnacles produce up to sixteen broods a year, released as thousands and thousands of tiny larvae shed into the water.

The *High Tide Zone*, washed by the high tide half the day, is home to the limpets. An indicator species here is the **Rough Limpet** (*Lottia scabra*). If you get lucky you might find the **Owl Limpet** (*Lottia gigantea*), our largest limpet, with a length of up to four inches. Owl Limpets aggressively bulldoze intruders off their own patch of green algae, which can extend as much as one square foot over a rock's surface.

Here's what Martin Wells, H. G. Wells's grandson, has to say about the limpet in his *Civilization and the Limpet:*

Limpets sit about, doing nothing much, most of the time. When

with which it scours the rocks for algae. This is really a specialized organ called a **radula**, so sharp it makes marks on the surface of the rock as it scrapes off the algae. The serrated teeth of the radula are continually being replaced—no need to worry about them wearing out.

The **buckshot barnacle** (*Chthamalus* spp.) is the other indicator species of the splash zone. This tiny, gray barnacle—looking like a flat-topped volcano—is affixed to its rock

the tide is up, or the seashore still wet enough to do so without risk of desiccation, they potter off to browse the thin coating of algae growing on the rocks around them. And then, after a while, they return to the spot they left, settle down, and concentrate on digestion. Day after day. Not an exciting lifestyle, but interesting because limpets turn out to be remarkably adept at returning to exactly the place they quit several hours before. They have to be. It is the only place in the vicinity where the individual's shell exactly fits the contours of the rock. It has grown to do so precisely because the animal keeps returning to the same home. A snug fit is essential if it is to avoid drying up between tides.

How does the limpet find its way back to its original rock scar? The mystery has never been conclusively solved, but the implication is that the limpet has highly sophisticated senses of smell and taste that enable it to trace a return route.

Another indicator species of the high tide zone, the **Leaf Barnacle** (*Pollicipes polymerus*)—formerly known as the Gooseneck Barnacle— is attached to a fat stalk and lives in mounded colonies crowded together on the rocks. The gooseneck name originated from the medieval belief, propounded by the monk Giraldus Cambrensis, that these were the eggs of geese. Leaf Barnacles are long-lived (twenty years) and secrete new gleaming white calcium plates annually.

The **California Mussel** (*Mytilus*

Clonal Anemones: where two colonies meet, each competes for space, creating a no-man's-land between the two clonal groups.

californianus) is the most numerous indicator species in the high tide zone. The mussel attaches itself to a rock by **byssal threads**, which it deposits onto the rock from its soft foot. Once the glue-like substance hardens, the threads, which are composed of a strong protein similar to human hairs, hold the mussel in place. Mussels like to grow close together and on top of each other, creating their own mussel habitat, which attracts lots of creatures. Crabs, barnacles, and limpets affix themselves between and on top of the shells of the mussels, forming communities of their own on the mussel clumps.

The Mid Tide Zone, dry only a portion of the day, is dominated by the **Clonal Anemone** (*Anthopleura elegantissima*)—formerly known as the Aggregate Anemone. Water here gets to about 2.5 feet above sea level (zero tide), and the rocks are devoid of shelled animals because they would be eaten by sea stars if they ventured down this low. This leaves the territory free for the Clonal Anemones, which look like low mounds of mud

The Ochre Sea Star (seen here in two color phases) is an indicator species of the low tide zone.

The Surf-grass Limpet subsists on microscopic algae found on the long, narrow blades of surf-grass.

The Starburst Anemone lives in the low tide zone.

with broken shells stuck to them to protect them from the sun and keep them from drying out. The center of the animal is its mouth, which is surrounded by stinging tentacles that trap small crustaceans and fish.

When the high tide is in, these animals can split down the middle and clone themselves. Each anemone in a single colony is related to the other. When one group of clones meets another group, war breaks out. Special fighting tentacles are inflated and used to sting the opposing clone colony until they move or die. These anemone battles create free zones down the middle, like paths on the rocks, and they can be easily seen in the mid tide zone: wherever two clone groups meet, an anemone-free zone of bare rock shows that war has been waged and each side has retreated to its own colony, at least for now.

The Low Tide Zone is revealed only at minus tides; most of the organisms here are usually covered with seawater. An indicator species is the Ochre Sea Star. Uniquely adapted for pulling bivalve shells apart, the sea star uses its hundreds of tubed feet with suckers on the ends to grab onto a shell and pull for hours until the mussel gives up. Once the shell is even the tiniest crack apart, the sea star slides its stomach into the mussel and consumes it. Typically, a sea star takes six hours to devour a mussel. Interestingly, we now know that snails and limpets may exhibit a "running response" when they sense the presence of a sea star. A sea star's chemical trace in the water is enough to set these creatures moving (albeit slowly!) away from this powerful predator.

The Giant Green Anemone lacks the radiating lines found on the oral disk of the Starburst Anemone.

The Ochre Sea Star is very important as a top predator, or keystone species, in the rocky intertidal. If not for the Ochre Sea Star, our rocks might be dominated by mussels. Experiments have shown that if the sea stars are removed from an area, mussels will spread down into the low tide zone and beyond.

Now that we have reached the low tide zone, look for one of the few flowering plants in the intertidal: surf-grass. Surf-grass grows in long strands over the rocks like a bright green, extra-long meadow of grass exposed at the lowest tides of the year. Surf-grass meadows nurture juvenile fishes, as well as crabs and snails. The **Surf-grass Limpet** (*Notoacmea paleacea*) lives only on the long, thin leaves of the surf-grass, where it feeds on microscopic algae.

Also in the low tide zone, the **Starburst Anemone** (*Anthopleura sola*) appears to be a round, green flower when it's covered with seawater. The "petals" are actually tentacles that sting prey. If two Starburst Anemones touch tentacles, they will fight until one of them withdraws.

Looking similar to the Starburst Anemone, but usually found in the cooler waters north of Point Conception, the **Giant Green Anemone** (*Anthopleura xanthogrammica*) is another solitary anemone to watch for. It has no radiating lines on the oral disk like those of the Starburst Anemone.

The low tide zone at a minus tide contains a collection of splendid treasures—animals and algae that you won't find every time you visit the tidepools. Unlike the indicator species mentioned above, which you can count on seeing at certain tide levels, these specialties dwell in the deepest pools and are only found at extreme low tides. One of the most difficult to locate is the octopus. Visit the Ty Warner Sea Center on Stearns Wharf to study an octopus up close.

The Two-spot Octopus

The **California Two-spot Octopus** (*Octopus bimaculoides*) is a small octopus that shelters in crevices beneath rocks at low tide. It has two false eye spots located below its real eyes.

Here's what Santa Barbara Museum of Natural History curator emeritus Eric Hochberg has to say about the cephalopods (octopuses and squids) in the *Light and Smith Manual:*

California Two-Spot Octopus at the Ty Warner Sea Center on Stearns Wharf in Santa Barbara.

The octopuses, squids, cuttlefishes, and relatives that make up the Class Cephalopoda are unique among mollusks in a number of ways. Their highly developed nervous systems and correspondingly complex behaviors have fascinated observers for centuries. Who cannot be intrigued by stories of octopuses escaping the most cunningly sealed aquaria to steal crabs from neighboring tanks? However, the escape artistry of octopuses is due as much to their lack of a shell as to their cranial capacity.... Shell loss allowed cephalopods to become swift, agile predators in a variety of marine environments, but it also revealed their soft, tasty mantle to a host of potential predators.

Octopuses swim by a jet propulsion system, shooting water from beneath their mantle cavity from a siphon tube. They can also move rapidly over sand or rocks using their eight arms covered with suckers. As a substitute for the protection of a shell, the animal can emit a blackish ink that effectively screens and confuses predators.

When hunting, an octopus waits quietly beneath a rock in a dark pool. Camouflaged in hue and texture to match exactly the pebbly background, the animal is difficult to pick out. When a crab sidles by, the octopus grabs it, subdues it with paralyzing venom, then devours the crab with the two hidden, beaklike jaws concealed in its mouth.

The octopus's method of reproduction is unusual: one of the male's arms enlarges and is modified to carry sperm. During copulation, the sperm is deposited under the mantle of the female. The female then faces a long period—two to four months—of caring for the eggs. Looking like tiny bunches of grapes, the eggs are suspended from the roof of a sheltered cave or dark cavity among the rocks. Here, the female octopus guards them. Once they hatch, her duty is done, and she dies.

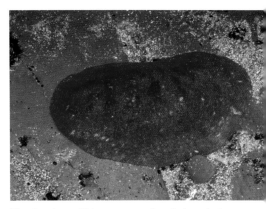

The Gumboot Chiton, up to a foot in length, is the largest chiton in the world.

Recent experiments show that individual octopuses have different temperaments, responding to stimuli in lab aquariums in different ways. One researcher examined three-week-old Two-Spot Octopuses to measure their temperamental traits. Temperament dimensions were scored on four behaviors: Active Engagement, Arousal/Readiness, Aggression, and Avoidance/Disinterest. Results showed that related octopuses, those in the same brood, were more similar in temperament than those that were unrelated. Evidently, "it runs in the family" applies to octopuses too.

Brown Rock Crab at Hazard Canyon, Montaña de Oro State Park

Stories of an octopus's ability to figure out new situations abound. In 2006 a female **Giant Pacific Octopus** (*Enteroctopus dofleini*) at the Seattle Aquarium was given a childproof pill bottle containing herring and took fifty-five minutes to figure out how to push down and turn the bottle cap to open it. In subsequent trials, she was able to decrease the average opening time to five minutes.

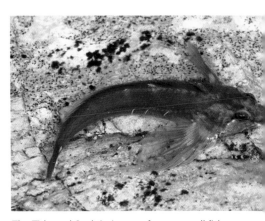

The Tidepool Sculpin is one of many small fish that inhabit tidepools.

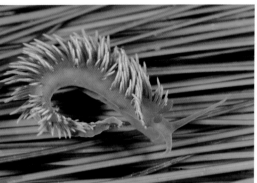

Two species of colorful nudibranchs. Left, Spanish Shawl; right, two Hermissendas meet.

Nature Journal
October 18, 2009

Near Hazard Canyon, Montaña de Oro State Park

I walk down the steep, sandy path from the bluffs, and suddenly I am there.

Stretching far, far out to the receding waves is a massive rocky reef, terraced and slanted seaward to form the most abundant tidepools I have ever seen. The variety of life is a sensory overload spread before me in the soft light of this October afternoon.

It is like wandering in a pristine kingdom. Channels of water interlace the rocky ledges. Seaweeds in all shapes and colors cover the ground, shining in the sun. The brownish-green rockweed, the bright green sea lettuce, the fat-strapped, brown laminarians, the delicate pink coralline algae. Some have a dark purple iridescense, others show ruffled edges; some grow high on the ledges as green fuzz; others stain the rocks like gobs of oil, but they aren't oil, they're black, living algae!

Gingerly, I negotiate the first slippery rocks. Progress is slow. Every channel of water has a new treasure for me to examine, every rock face is draped with algae. At a minus tide, this secret world is revealed for a short while. Where to pause in the maze of life beneath my feet?

Here at Montaña de Oro, north of Point Conception, you can see the same tidal zonation you'd find down on the South Coast. On an enormous rock close to shore, buckshot barnacles coat the surface like a nubby carpet of gray. On the north side of the rock, more sheltered from the sun, tiny limpets and periwinkles pock the ledges and cluster in the cracks. Nothing can tear them from the rock, but heat and sun could be their demise.

The Giant Green Anemones, however, are different from the ones we see to the south. They are a deep green, and many are four to six inches wide. I spotted two beginning to fight: their special stinging cells (acrorhagi) look like white dots nestled in between the rays of their oral disks. When you see these white dots unveiled, you know that a stinging war has broken out between two of these big anemones.

Interestingly, there are only small patches of mussels and Leaf Barnacles here and there. Why? Because the algae have covered the rocks so completely there's not much space for the mussels and barnacles to settle. Also, high surf is a factor.

We are lucky enough to discover two fantastic specimens, the likes of which you will not find south of Point Conception.

The first one I almost step on. I am tramping along in my waders, farther out now towards the retreating surf line, when I stop and look down. An animal the size of my boot, a foot long, lies before me. It is a reddish-brown rock, but it moves!

A Gumboot Chiton. Never in my life have I dreamed I would come across one of these fascinating animals, the largest chiton in the world. I pick it up gently, and it begins to curl up into a ball like a pillbug. Placing it back in the water, I watch as the chiton slowly slides away on its big foot. It is related to the snails, but with a shell inside—a series of bony plates that you can't see. Tonight, when the tide is in, it will use its sharp radula to graze on the abundant algae.

At this point, my companion comes running up. Another extraordinary find, a Sunflower Star, has been located farther seaward.

Slipping and sliding, I scramble over to the pool where the super-sized sea star lies. This gorgeous, purplish-red creature is a keystone predator on sea urchins and almost any other shelled creature it gets its arms (legs?) around. This one has twenty-one rays and measures over two feet across—a grand specimen. I notice that most of the Black Turban Snails in the pool where it lies have moved well away, sensing its presence.

The sun is getting low.

My mind is struggling with the whole concept of this intertidal landscape. "Fecund," "ferocious," and "cauldron of life" seem feeble compared to the overwhelming numbers of animals and algae

I've observed today. And I haven't even mentioned the tidepool fishes: the blennies and the sculpins. And the octopus that got away before we could identify it. And the bat stars and the leather stars... and on and on...

Marine Algae—Colorful Gardens in the Tidepools

In the midst of searching for tidepool creatures, take a moment to notice the lush gardens of seaweeds—marine algae—that grow about the rocks. Studying the rocky intertidal environment without discussing the variety and beauty of the various marine algae would be like going for a walk in the woods without mentioning the trees, or hiking through the chaparral without commenting on the shrubs.

Algae growing on the rocky intertidal shore are at the base of the food chain for the animals that reside there—one of the main sources of sustenance for the grazers and the filterers upon which so many other animals prey. Also, by releasing oxygen into the seawater, algae enrich the whole ecosystem.

Like the animals of the rocky shore, algae have distributional zones: some are found at higher levels, able to withstand desiccation and exposure to wind and rain. Others grow only in deeper waters, concealed unless a minus tide provides an opportunity to study them.

Whether the substrate is sand or rock, whether the coast is open or sheltered, and what type of herbivores graze on the algae: these are all variables that determine the kinds of algae you might see at any given

Sea lettuce is one of the more common species of green algae in the high tide zone.

Seaweed Limpet with grazing scars on the central stipe of Feather Boa Kelp

place. Marine biologists can make a few generalizations, however. Just like the invertebrates we've been studying, certain species that prefer colder water will be found in greater abundance north of Point Conception and on the Channel Islands of Santa Rosa or San Miguel, due to the presence of the cold California Current system that bathes those shores. South and east of Point Conception, on the other hand, a more southerly flora thrives. Furthermore, the mix of warm and cold currents in the Santa

Barbara Channel encourages an enormous variety of algae, and different sites along the rocky shore create microhabitats which foster myriad species.

Marine algae can be classified based on three dominant pigments: the **green algae** (Phylum Chlorophyta), the **brown algae** (Phylum Phaeophyta), and the **red algae** (Phylum Rhodophyta). Unfortunately, these colors aren't always obvious in nature. The greens are the easiest to recognize, but the browns and reds can get bleached or combined with other pigments so that color alone is not sufficient for identification. Still, it's a place to start.

The green algae have the smallest representation on our shores because they require sunlight and can't grow at depths. They are much more common in freshwater and in the tropics. The few species we do have are abundant: **sea lettuce** (*Ulva* spp.), bright green with ruffled edges, sprawls over tidepool ledges; **enteromorpha** (*Enteromorpha* spp.) is light green and drapes itself in stringy sheets over boat docks, boat hulls, and buoys, as well as high intertidal rocks.

The brown algae are the largest of the marine algae. They include the kelps (Order Laminariales—see also "Giant Kelp Forest" in Chapter 3). Able to withstand the stronger wave action and colder waters to the north, many varieties of brown algae grow all the way from Point Conception to Alaska. The biomass of algae, especially the kelps, in colder waters is greater, but the diversity of species there is somewhat less than in waters to the south.

The **Feather Boa Kelp** (*Egregia menziesii*), commonly found in shallow tidepools in our region, is one of the most easily recognized. A special limpet, the **Seaweed Limpet** (*Notoacmea insessa*), feeds on the central stipe of the Feather Boa. The limpet makes a series of shallow pits as it grazes along, and you can see these if you examine a piece of the Feather Boa.

Red algae, abundant in warmer waters, are the most numerous of the three algal types. Smaller than the brown algae, the red algae come in various shapes and sizes—jointed and intricately branched, splashed like pink paint on the rocks, or paper-thin and elegant. Most look pink, purple, or reddish, but some look black or even greenish-brown.

Certain species of red algae are commercially important for **agar**, a thickening substance used in culturing bacteria. Others possess **carrageenan**, a stabilizing and gelling agent used in milk products like ice cream.

One of the most beautiful red algae, **Nori** (*Porphyra perforata*), is grown commercially for wrapping sushi—the large production of Nori in Japan shows how big the edible seaweed industry has become. Nori grows on mid-intertidal rocks in our region and can be seen at certain seasons.

Pink coralline algae

Another fascinating red alga is *Plocamium cartilagineum*, or **Sea Comb**. This is the red alga that the **California Seahare** (*Aplysia californica*) feeds upon, and which is responsible for the color of the seahare's dark purple ink (see Chapter 5). The Sea Comb contains certain bromine hydrocarbons that predators avoid; bromine compounds are passed on in the sea-

hare's ink, a deterrent to attackers. (The seahare itself is immune to the compounds.) The bromine also interferes with any bacteria that might form a slime on the surface of the Sea Comb.

One afternoon in January 2010, Professor Emeritus of Biology at UC Santa Barbara David Chapman, who hails from New Zealand, spoke of his enthusiasm for his specialty, marine algae. The study of marine algae is known as **phycology** (derived from the Greek word *phykos,* meaning

Tar Spot is a dark brown alga that looks like a glob of tar

"seaweed"). In the herbarium at UCSB's Cheadle Center for Biodiversity and Ecological Restoration, Chapman assists with the maintenance of over ten thousand specimens of marine algae, all carefully pressed on special herbarium sheets. The sheets are shelved in cabinets, labeled, and filed for easy access. Chapman is one of the great old-timers and a gifted teacher. He helped discover, back in the 1960s, the fact that the pneumatocysts of certain brown kelps contain carbon monoxide.

If you have a chance to go over the exquisitely preserved specimens, you will be surprised at how true the colors remain and how lifelike they appear. A specimen of **chondria**, its thin branches punctuated by the parasite **janczewskia** (named after the French-Polish botanist Edward Janczewski) is amazing: the parasite

clings to the alga, and it is so evenly spaced, it seems part of the regular structure of the plant.

And the lovely coralline algae—those pink **corallina** and **bossiella** which tinge the tidepools at Coal Oil Point, shone as vividly as ever. *Corallina vancouveriensis* has an interesting history. It was named after Captain George Vancouver, whose expedition to the Pacific Coast of North America from 1791 to 1795 collected important algae specimens.

As David Chapman summarizes our algae, "Cold temperate waters are very, very rich in algal flora, but what makes Santa Barbara unique is that the cold current swings out at Point Conception and then you have the warm currents coming up from the south and they all mix together offshore."

A classic book, *Marine Algae of Cal-*

The diversity of life in a tidepool

ifornia by Isabella Abbott and George Hollenberg, is still the best reference book written on the subject, according to Chapman. Several smaller, current guidebooks are available too. It's time we learned more about our region's lovely marine algae.

To sum up, here's John Steinbeck again, this time from *Sea of Cortez: A Leisurely Journal of Travel and Research:*

> And it is a strange thing that most of the feeling we call religious, most of the mystical outcrying which is one of the most prized and used and desired reactions of our species, is really the under-standing and the attempt to say that man is related to the whole thing, related inextricably to all reality, known and unknowable.... It is advisable to look from the tidepool to the stars and then back to the tidepool again.

Birds of the Rocky Shore

Those shorebirds that are specialists in prying, turning, and snatching make a good living on the rocky shore. Except for the Black Oystercatcher, most are wintering birds or migrants.

Black Oystercatchers (*Haematopus bachmani*) locate mussels that

A sandy beach, looking south towards Morro Rock

High tide at a sandy beach between Coal Oil Point and Isla Vista

Hours later at the same beach

have their shells slightly apart. With a quick jab of its long red bill, the oystercatcher severs the abductor muscles, thus popping the mussel open. **Black** and **Ruddy Turnstones** (*Arenaria melanocephala* and *A. interpres*), true to their name, glean the rocky shore by turning over stones and bits of seaweed to find the tiniest amphipods in the wake of retreating waves. Like the **Surfbird** (*Aphriza virgata*) and **Wandering Tattler** (*Tringa incana*), these bird species seek the slippery, wave-washed rocks. They fly up just in time to avoid the drenching surf, then settle back to search the wettest, most exposed parts of the wave-swept shore. Any animal not firmly attached is fair game, including little limpets, crabs, and worms.

A completely different set of birds stays to breed on our rocky shores, the majority choosing the Channel Islands over the mainland for nesting. The isolation and inaccessibility of island nesting colonies prove attractive to the three species of cormorants—Brandt's, Double-crested, and Pelagic—as well as the California Brown Pelican (see Chapter 10).

However, north of Point Conception there are a few areas where you can spot nesting cormorants on offshore islets and stacks, particularly along the San Simeon coast. On the cliffs at Shell Beach, **Pelagic Cormorants** (*Phalacrocorax pelagicus*) nest in a loose colony. Each cormorant picks an individual niche in the rock, lining it with seaweed. From the nest, they make forays to nearshore waters to fish. The **Pigeon Guillemot** (*Cepphus columba*), another rocky cliff nester, chooses sea caves and dark caverns.

They have nested under the San Luis pier and in burrows at Shell Beach.

At extreme low tides other birds, such as sandpipers, herons, egrets, and gulls, explore the rocks before the tide comes back in. They take advantage of the exposed tidepools, where prey is uncovered and available for the watchful birds.

Sandy Beach

After tidepooling in the rough–and-tumble atmosphere of the rocky shore, a walk on the sandy beach is a peaceful respite. Aside from the shorebirds, the beach looks pretty empty of life; but beneath the surface of the sand, a lot is going on.

Beach wrack teems with invertebrates. Here Michael Caterino, Curator of Entomology at the Santa Barbara Museum of Natural History, examines kelp.

While humans tramp over the beach down to the tide line—set up their umbrellas, throw Frisbies for dogs, make sandcastles with their children, swat at kelp flies, or dig for sand crabs—are they aware that they are guests in a community that belongs to millions of beach organisms?

Among the rounded, light-colored sand grains of the beach live many, many more individuals than those that inhabit the rocky shore. Thousands of animals live in the sand. Density on a sandy beach is usually far greater than on the rocky shore, but there is much less diversity.

Living on the sandy beach is even more rigorous than living in the rocky intertidal zone. **Interstitial** organisms (those able to live between the grains of sand) exist in a constant state of flux. Sand is always moving, shifting, piling up, or drifting away. There's no stability. Every time a wave breaks, the sandy beach changes. Conditions alter from one minute to the next,

depending upon the waves and the weather. It takes a very special organism to survive the constant fluctuation of sand on a beach. But those organisms who manage to survive have little competition and their populations can be huge.

Zones of a Sandy Beach

The movement of sand along the coast is called **longshore transport**. Driven by storms originating in the Gulf of Alaska, sand is gradually transported from north to south by the angle of the waves striking the coast.

In winter, large waves from storms usually remove much of the sand from a beach, sometimes leaving only cobblestones or bedrock. If large waves are combined with high tides, sandy beaches can be washed completely away. In summer, smaller waves gradually return sand to the beach, where it gets built up over the rocks that lie underneath.

Just as the rocky shore has zones, so does the sandy beach.

The **foreshore** is the part of the beach between the drift line and the

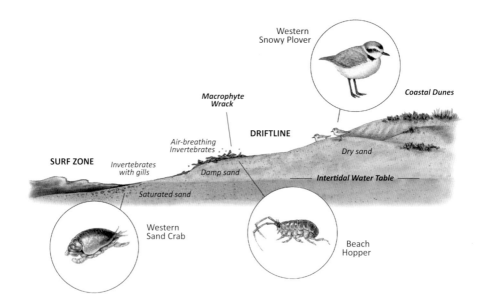

Cross section of a sandy beach

surf, sometimes called the **swash** zone. The **drift line** is where the highest high tide waves reach, a general borderline between the dry sand, where invertebrate animals live that draw oxygen from the air, and the wet sand, where animals live that have gills and draw oxygen from seawater. Behind the drift line, which is often marked by clumps of stranded seaweed **(macrophyte wrack)** deposited by the high waves, lies the dry sand, or **backshore**.

Life on the Sandy Beach

Our sandy beaches in Southern California, when compared to similar ones in Australia, South Africa, Chile, and Oregon, are much richer in species. One of the reasons for this is the macrophyte wrack. The piles of drifted, dead seaweed are a source of food for many sandy beach creatures

and the predators that feed on them.

An area about ten square feet along the shore on one of our local beaches boasts the following peak densities: up to 7,700 beach hoppers, 7,900 Western Sand Crabs, and 10,600 Bloodworms. Granted, these are maximums and don't all occur at once, but just the fact that our beaches can support this number of creatures is staggering.

In the highest zone of the sandy beach, insects and crustaceans swarm around rotting piles of kelp. **Kelp flies** (*Coelopa* spp.), which may annoy beachgoers, are delectable for shorebirds such as the Western Snowy Plover.

Beach hoppers and Beach Pillbugs are crustaceans related to shrimps. **Beach hoppers** (*Megalorchestia* spp.), known as **amphipods**, look like little shrimps as they hop around on the dry sand with their pink antennae, then burrow in headfirst to hide.

Beach hoppers' bodies are squeezed laterally—they are long and narrow. They feed voraciously on the decaying mounds of Giant Kelp, especially at night. **Beach Pillbugs** (*Tylos punctatus*), flattened from top to bottom, are a type of **isopod**.

Move down the beach now, closer to the surf. If you start digging in the wet sand, you'll find **Bloodworms** (*Euzonus mucronata*). Bloodworms crawl through the sand in enormous numbers, to a depth of about eight inches. Somewhat like earthworms on land, Bloodworms subsist by passing sand through their digestive tracts. These harmless worms—they don't bite—get their name from their red color. If you pick one up it will coil into a spiral; they are so adapted to burrowing that they do not crawl or swim when removed from their sandy homes.

Perhaps the most well known of the sandy beach animals is the hippid crab known as the **Western Sand Crab** (*Emerita analoga*). These little crabs continually bury themselves as they move along with the sand in the swash zone. Using specialized hair bristles along their antennae, they sift the phytoplankton brought up by each surge of the surf.

The Pismo Clam

Further down still, buried beneath the roughest waves, lives the **Pismo Clam** (*Tivela stultorum*). "Pismo" is from the Chumash word *pismu,* meaning tar. Pismo Clams thrive in the surf zone.

Positioning itself with its hinged side toward the ocean, the Pismo Clam burrows down less than two inches below the surface of the sand.

Kelp flies are found near piles of beach wrack. The flies are a crucial food source for migrating and wintering shorebirds.

Close-up of a beach hopper

A Western Sand Crab buries its hind end in the wet sand, which allows it to use its antennae for collecting minute organisms brought in by the waves.

Its incoming siphon has an interesting net of tiny flaps (papillae) that screen out grains of sand and permit seawater filled with plankton, bacteria, and detritus to enter. Despite this, half of the clam's stomach content is usually sand.

Pismo Clams can grow to be more than seven inches long. Growth is continuous throughout the clam's life and can be measured by counting the growth rings on its shell. At Pismo Beach, clams reach four and a half inches between ages seven and eight.

From 1916 to 1947, commercial diggers harvested nearly fifty thou-

Pismo Clam specimen photographed at the Santa Barbara Museum of Natural History

sand clams per year at Pismo Beach. Now, recreational clamming is tightly regulated there and elsewhere, due to the steep decline of the Pismo Clam population. Often the heaviest concentrations of Pismo Clams, which range from Monterey to Baja California, are in the vicinity of Pismo Beach, although this varies annually.

Biologists still do not know the ideal conditions for Pismo Clam spawn-

ing; some years are good and some are not. From 1986 to 1988, spawning was successful and record numbers were reproduced. In 1990, young Pismo Clams appeared to be abundant from San Diego to Pismo Beach. But surveys in the Pismo Beach and Morro Bay areas from 1992 to 2000 indicated low levels of reproduction.

Pismo Clams have many predators besides humans, including Southern Sea Otters, sharks, rays, and some surf fishes.

Paul Valentich-Scott, Curator of Invertebrate Zoology at the Santa Barbara Museum of Natural History, points out that you can go and have a look at the **neotype** of the Pismo Clam at the museum. When a scientist names a species, a classic or "type specimen" of the organism is designated, usually located at a museum. But in the case of the Pismo Clam, which was named by J. Mawe in 1823, no type specimen had been found. Thus in 1996, Eugene Coan, a noted biologist specializing in mollusks, designated one of the Pismo Clams in the museum's invertebrate collection as the neotype of the Pismo Clam— an example to show all the world that this particular organism is what the Pismo Clam looks like.

Birds on the Beach

Sandy beach ecologists Jenifer Dugan and David Hubbard have been sampling bird life on the South Coast at Isla Vista Beach, east of Coal Oil Point, for many years. They've discovered that numbers of shorebirds observed here are extremely high for a sandy beach in the temperate zone anywhere in the world. Ninety-seven percent of this abundance consisted of eight species: **Sanderling** (*Calidris alba*), **Semipalmated Plover** (*Charadrius semipalmatus*), **Marbled Godwit** (*Limosa fedoa*), **Black-bellied Plover** (*Pluvialis squatarola*), **Western Sandpiper** (*Calidris mauri*), **Willet** (*Tringa semipalmata*), Surfbird, and **Whimbrel** (*Numenius phaeopus*).

Peak use of the sandy beach comes in fall and winter. In fall, shorebird migration south to Central America brings many bird species to our beaches, some of which remain here for the winter. Between August and October, twelve to seventeen species of shorebirds can

Marbled Godwits forage at depth with their longer bills.

Sanderlings move up and down the sandy beach at the edge of the waves.

Sanderlings, like many shorebirds, have sensory organs at the tips of their bills that help them locate prey in the wet sand.

be found on one kilometer (.62 miles) of open beach shoreline, with a maximum of about 280 individuals.

By contrast, the beach is nearly empty of shorebirds in May and June, when most of the birds have departed for nesting grounds to the north. Maximum counts in May and June reflect only two species of shorebirds representing eleven individuals per kilometer of shoreline.

During El Niño events when much of the sand is washed away, leaving only cobblestones and rocks (such as in 1997-98) the Surfbird, a species that prefers rocky shores, is unusually abundant.

Nature Journal
October 13, 2007

El Capitan State Beach

I am on a field trip with sandy beach experts Jenny Dugan and Dave Hubbard. Sandy beach ecology used to be the poor stepchild of the study of the shore. But

Beach Grooming—an Ecological Disruption

If you pay an early morning visit to a Southern California beach, you might witness a process called grooming.

From May to September, mechanical grooming devices leave an unnaturally wide swath of barren sandy beach. Based on evidence from important experiments by Jenifer Dugan and David Hubbard, some Southern California communities have suspended this practice.

When you groom a sandy beach, you lose the washed-up piles of kelp, which provide sustenance for numerous creatures, such as kelp flies and beach hoppers. And when there are fewer invertebrates for the birds to eat, there will be fewer birds.

Raking a sandy beach takes away the bits and pieces of driftwood, the cobbles, any object which might help form small dunes or hummocks in the sand. Wind transports the sand constantly, and where sand stabilizes behind an object, native plants can colonize. Grooming destroys any seeds or seedlings of native plants. By measuring plots of groomed and ungroomed portions of beaches in Santa Barbara, Ventura, and other Southern California counties, Dugan and Hubbard were able to prove that frequent beach grooming turned a normal coastal strand ecosystem into a barren, unvegetated desert.

Conservation of our precious sandy beaches will maintain their biodiversity and wildlife.

Go see for yourself the difference in wildlife on groomed versus ungroomed beaches.

---

now, squeezed by rising sea levels on the one hand and development on the other, the sandy beach is being taken seriously by researchers.

Today, on the narrow strand at El Capitan State Beach, we walk west, making our first stop just beyond a group of rambunctious youngsters playing in the surf.

I watch as Dave digs a series of holes in a transect. The holes closest to the sea are filled with much more seawater than those up near the dry sand. Eventually, if you moved all the way up to the cliff, you'd have freshwater underneath.

Between the holes closest to the waves and those up by the dry sand lies the swash zone, where the waves wash up and back. The swash zone is jam-packed with Western Sand Crabs. These egg-shaped little crabs are often found together in dense groups, burrowed into the sand side by side. The crabs move up and down along the beach with the tide, always staying in the breaking wave zone. Wherever they go, whether it's swimming, crawling, or burrowing, they move backwards.

Dave releases one of the big female sand crabs he's been holding to show us.

She quickly digs in backwards, facing the surf. On the backwash of the wave, which is gentler than the surge, the crab extends her two antennae, making a "V" against the water. The antennae gather microscopic plankton, the nourishment delivered from the sea.

After one of the millions of eggs of the female sand crab is fertilized, it develops and hatches and then swims away as a larva. After journeying as far as perhaps Oregon, it settles down and becomes an adult crab. Young sand crabs tend to burrow in up higher on the beaches, as do the small males. The females, which can get to be over two inches long, brave the heavier surf down closer to the waves.

I am familiar with sand crabs—as any child growing up in a beach town would be—but I have completely forgotten the beach hoppers! These interesting terrestrial creatures are like little shrimps, but they live in the drier sand.

Jenny Dugan is ready to teach us about beach hopper behavior. As we stand around waiting, she tells each of us to gather two small sticks of driftwood. Holding our sticks in one hand and a tiny beach hopper in the other, we get our assignment: mark the spot where you place your hopper on the sand with one stick, then see which direction it hops before burrowing in, and mark that with the other.

I put the one-inch-long beach hopper, its pink antennae tickling my hand, down on the sand. It begins to hop vigorously towards the upper part of the beach in the direction of the looming cliff. When I look around, I see the rest of the people in the group exclaiming as their beach hoppers all head for the hills too!

Jenny explains that orienting themselves like this is a beach hopper specialty:

Beach hoppers on a summer night. Bring a light and watch the amazing show as thousands and thousands of these creatures feed on the kelp washed up during the day.

in each tiny body is a sun compass. Since they are air breathers, they avoid the surf, hiding under masses of stranded kelp on the beach during the day.

At night beach hoppers are attracted to light, and I quote this marvelous passage from Ricketts in Between Pacific Tides:

Observers with a trace of sympathy for bohemian life should walk with a flashlight along a familiar surfy beach at half-tide on a quiet evening. The huge hoppers will be holding high carnival—leaping about with vast enthusiasm and pausing to wiggle their antennae over likely-looking bits of flotsam seaweed. They will rise up before the intruder in great windrows, for all the world like grasshoppers in a summer meadow.

Beach hoppers feast on stranded kelp, and their favorite variety is the brown Giant Kelp. These rotting, smelly mounds washed up on the beach are a magnet for all sorts of beach species. As we walk back, we see the margins of the kelp fronds lying on the sand, completely surrounded by

View of the freshwater Oso Flaco Lake outlet as it makes its way through the dunes of the Guadalupe-Nipomo Complex to the sea.

the pin-prick burrow holes of beach hoppers. Sometimes, only this outline of the kelp frond remains on the sand: the kelp itself has been completely devoured.

A hundred pounds of wrack can be deposited on the beach at night and by morning it will be completely gone, eaten by all the creatures that live on it.

For our last stop of the field trip, we are headed a half-mile east, where a seawall was built in 1932. Patches of seawalls have been built at locations all along our region's coast.

Jenny and Dave have researched beaches with and without seawalls. Looking at the beach in front of the wall, I see that there is no high tide refuge for birds or animals; only the wet sand lies in front of the wall. There is no drift line, no backshore with dry sand. Indeed, no kelp litters the beach.

What does that mean for beach hoppers? They're fewer. What does that mean for Western Sand Crabs? They're fewer. And where are the birds? The shorebirds you expect on the sandy beach just aren't there. Even the gulls don't like it.

Up to now, I've never been aware of the complexity of life on a sandy beach. This field trip has opened my eyes.

* * *

On the evening of August 23, 2011, I was able to observe the phenomenon Ed Ricketts described. If you walk along a beach laden with wrack on a summer night, the masses of beach hoppers feeding and jumping on the piles of moist kelp are astounding. The dense multitudes swarm amid the wrack, and when you put a light down on the sand, the hoppers fly up like popcorn popping—an extraordinary sight.

Dunes

If you stand on the sandy beach looking back towards the shore, you see either steep bluffs backing the beach or low, rounded dunes. Or, especially along the South Coast, human encroachment with buildings and parking lots.

Where the sandy beach is not backed by cliffs or bluffs, **dunes** may accumulate.

Suppose you're standing at the dunes at the Santa Maria River mouth. Now, reach down and pick up a handful of dry sand. Watch the grains of sand as they drain through your fingers. How does the sand get to the beach, and how did it end up as part of a dune?

A Grain of Sand: the Journey

Your imagination can run wild with

134

this one: let's trace the journey of a grain of sand from its origins.

Individual grains of sand come from rocks, most likely from our local mountains. We know that these mountains were upthrust in the recent geologic past, but the rocks found there can be much older.

Perhaps our grain of sand began as a fleck on the surface of a piece of billion-year-old granite lying at the summit of Cerro Noroeste. As bedrock is eroded and transported by streams, it becomes finer and finer. Jostled and pounded along the way, rocks and pebbles end up as grains of sand. Washed down off Cerro Noroeste into a creek in Lockwood Valley, then into the Cuyama River, then into the Santa Maria River, our grain of sand is finally deposited into the ocean at the river's mouth.

Over thousands of years, the action of the waves pushed the grain of sand back towards the land from which it had come. It lay as a particle of sand on the ocean beach. Succumbing to the prevailing northwest winds off the ocean, that grain of sand from Cerro Noroeste began the next phase of its journey.

Lying on the beach, the grain of sand was in a perfect position to be taken up and blown by the constant sea breeze. Typically, a grain of sand moves forward by bouncing. The wind carries it, lifts it, and then it falls back down to the ground again. As it moves along in this bouncing movement, called **saltation**, the grain of sand covers distances inch by inch.

Any obstruction to the wind, such as a bush, rock, piece of driftwood, or a mass of sand, may be enough to make the sand grains pile up on top of each other. A gentle mound or hillock forms.

A dune is created.

Wind moves our grain of sand up to the top of the dune until the dune becomes so steep it collapses and the grain rolls down the other side. A dune is only as steep as its angle of repose, usually about 30 to 34 degrees.

This process of windblown sand piling up and rolling down the lee side creates a dune that migrates inland. Rates of advance are close to two feet per year, but it takes thousands of years to form a whole sheet of dunes.

And it may have begun with that grain of granite washed down from the summit of Cerro Noroeste.

Aeolian Dune Sheets

The expansive sand dunes of our region are the largest Aeolian (meaning wind-driven, after the Greek god of the winds, Aeolus) dune sheets found anywhere on the California coast.

Three huge dune sheets—one near Morro Bay, one in the Santa Maria Valley, and one in the Santa Ynez Valley—make up a thousand square miles of dunes. All of the dune complexes form behind beaches that are backed by a flat landscape of river basins and low hills. The northwest wind blows the sand from the beach into the shallow-bottomed valleys, which are oriented in a northwest-southeast direction. Over eons, the sand builds a dune system; these northwest winds have been forming dunes for thousands of years.

For now, we are interested in two

Aerial view of the Aeolian dune sheets between Guadalupe and Oso Flaco Lake. Note the shape of the parabolic dunes, which are created by winds blowing from the northwest. Photo by Bill Dewey

categories of dunes: recent, active dunes being created just behind the open coast; and those that formed during Holocene times—twelve thousand years ago to present. At the mouth of the Santa Maria River Estuary and at Oso Flaco Lake—both considered portions of the Guadalupe-Nipomo Dunes Complex—you can explore the dunes we discuss. (See Chapter 6, "Burton Mesa Ecological Reserve," for more on older dunes.)

What Grows on a Dune?

Dune plants, brave pioneers of the inhospitable dune environment, breach the borders of the coastal strand. Outliers, they represent the first phalanx of seed-bearing plants. Behind them come all the vegetative habitats that are described in this book: the grasslands, the chaparral, the oak woodland, and the forests,

as we proceed farther and farther inland.

Constantly battered by salt-laden, sand-bearing breezes, deprived of freshwater, and growing in a humus-poor medium, dune plants must be hardy.

Let's divide the dunes into **coastal strand**, **foredune**, and **backdune**.

On the coastal strand, little ephemeral (temporary) beach mounds or shadow dunes form. For the most part, they will be washed away by rough winter waves, but they may harbor a few plants temporarily.

A foredune needs special conditions in order to develop. A foredune is a vegetated ridge of sand parallel to the beach, rising above the ordinary high tides. It supports more species than the coastal strand, but fewer than a backdune. Backdunes are the stabilized, older ridges of sand often formed in a parabolic shape, like an

136

Clockwise from top left: Dune Lupine; Seacliff Buckwheat; Beach Evening-Primrose; Beach Sand-Verbena

open horseshoe with the mouth facing the direction of the wind. Among some stabilized dunes in our region, freshwater wetlands can be found—such as at Oso Flaco Lake and other lakes in the dunes north of it.

Pioneer dune plant communities creep across the sand, held together by a network of dense branches. Tolerant of repeated burial due to shifting sands, they have deep taproots to get water. Their leaves are small, grayish-colored, sometimes succulent, often hairy to protect against the sun. Many of these foliage characteristics are shared with desert plants.

A Walk in the Guadalupe-Nipomo Dunes at Oso Flaco Lake

You can view the succession of dune vegetation if you visit Oso Flaco Lake in the Guadalupe-Nipomo Dunes Complex in southern San Luis Obispo County. The beauty of the dune plants, many of them rare and endangered or at the northern or southern limit of their ranges, is stunning from the boardwalk at Oso Flaco.

Start out by traversing classic dune scrub.

These are the backdunes of Holocene age, having been laid down in the past twelve thousand years. They comprise a portion of the Guadalupe-Nipomo Dunes and feature the largest expanse of Holocene dune scrub in California.

On these backdunes, soils are slightly richer, retain more water, and are more fertile than on the foredunes. Plants are bigger and more shrub-like, and the leaf litter attracts a variety of animals. Some of these shrubs are the same as those found in coastal sage scrub (see Chapter 6), but most are unique to the dunes. **California Sagebrush** (*Artemisia californica*), **Coyote Brush** (*Baccharis pilularis*), **Mock Heather** (*Ericameria ericoides*), **Seacliff Buckwheat** (*Eriogonum parvifolium*), **Deerweed** (*Acmispon glaber*), **Bush Lupine** (*Lupinus arboreus*), **Dune Lupine** (*Lupinus chamissonis*), and **Black Sage** (*Salvia mellifera*) are found in the dune scrub.

Dune scrub blooms from April through October: the beauty of the Dune Lupine, with its blue candelabra blossoms, the bright yellow **Western Wallflower** (*Erysimum capitatum*), pink **Paintbrush** (*Castilleja affinis*), and a host of other shrubs makes for a resplendent display. Where moisture collects in swales, specialized tiny dune sedges and rushes thrive, sheltered by taller willows and dark green wax myrtle.

On this walk at Oso Flaco, you will see three kinds of sand-verbena. The first one you come to is **Pur-**ple **Sand-Verbena** (*Abronia umbellata*), with a light purple flower, low-growing and the most inland of the three. Out closer to the beach—often right on the strand—you will come to **Yellow Sand-Verbena** (*Abronia latifolia*), which reaches the southern limit of its range at nearby Surf (west of Lompoc). Also on the strand, find **Beach Sand-Verbena** (*Abronia maritima*), a sticky plant with succulent leaves and deeply colored reddish-purple flowers. It is the rarest of the three.

As you near the open beach, and views of blue sea appear and disappear beyond the dunes, a low-growing, gray-foliaged shrub called **Beach Bur-Sage** (*Ambrosia chamissonis*) covers the sand. It may be accompanied by **Beach Evening-Primrose** (*Camissoniopsis cheiranthifolia*), with its gray, creeping stems, the cheeriest yellow primrose that you'd ever expect to see, and yet it can take the punishment of salt spray and blowing sand.

Pale purple–flowered **Sea Rocket** (*Cakile maritima*) wins the prize for the hardiest of the hardy, however.

The hardy Sea Rocket grows closer to the sea than any other beach plant.

Often growing closer to the sea than any other beach plant, Sea Rocket has succulent stems and leaves that store water, and the plant grows low enough to avoid abrasive wind. Its fruit resembles a two-stage rocket: when the upper stage falls off, it may float for days in salt water like a cork, and if washed up on the upper beach, it will sprout a new plant. The lower stage of the rocket dies with the existing plant, but it can germinate in place. Therefore, Sea Rocket can spread itself everywhere, as well as continue to expand in its own space.

Because dunes are shifting mounds of sand often existing close to human dwellings, it is understandable that introduced plant species have been employed as a means of controlling the wayward sand. Several kinds of **ice plant** (mostly *Carpobrotus* spp.) have been introduced from South Africa and other regions. Their fleshy green leaves and bright flowers have become naturalized in many locations along the coast. Restoration efforts have been remarkably successful in eradicating ice plant invasions in some, but not all, areas.

A more damaging and widespread European invader known as **European Beachgrass** (*Ammophila arenaria*) can be found in nearly all dune systems. European Beachgrass was introduced to North and South America and New Zealand to stabilize sand dunes. It spreads by a powerful network of underground stems (**rhizomes**), ideal for controlling the shifting sands of foredunes. However, the dunes' dynamic ecosystem suffers when a wall of European beachgrass blocks the addition of new sand. And growing in dense stands, European Beachgrass crowds out native species, including **American Dune Grass** (*Elymus mollis*), which is found north of Morro Bay if at all.

Western Snowy Plover and California Least Tern

The dune ecosystem is a harsh one for animals. Human influences have not helped the situation, but they have also been the cause of recovery, especially when it comes to birds.

Species that once nested and roosted along the coastal strand and adjacent foredunes—the **Western Snowy Plover** (*Charadrius alexandrinus* subsp. *nivosus*) and the **California Least Tern** (*Sternula antillarum* subsp. *browni*)—were the first to feel the threat of disturbance by man. Along the smooth, warm sands of the coastal strand, often backed by a lagoon or a river estuary, California Least Terns used to nest in undisturbed colonies. Plunge-diving for fingerling-sized fish, the adults brought back food to fledglings on the sand.

Western Snowy Plovers chose the same sandy areas for nesting and for winter roosts, often spreading into the swales and hummocks of the foredunes. They fed on kelp flies attracted to the nearby clumps of seaweed on the beach. The pale gray backs of the plovers matched perfectly the pale gray stones they huddled against.

And then came the surfers, sunbathers, recreational vehicle drivers, picnickers, and swimmers. With one footstep, a plover's clutch of eggs could be instantly destroyed. And the terns, sensitive to the slightest disturbance, were constantly disrupted by

Threatened Western Snowy Plover, which nests at beach areas, is now monitored for its protection.

Endangered California Least Tern often nests on the same beaches as the Western Snowy Plover. Photo by Marlin Harms

Both the tern (endangered on federal and state lists) and the plover (threatened on the federal list), protected by law, have made remarkable comebacks from steep population declines in the 1970s. "Critical habitat" on beaches where nesting and roosting occurred has been set aside for them, inspiring biologists and volunteers to new monitoring efforts. As an example, portions of beaches up and down the coast in our region from southern San Luis Obispo County to the Ventura–Los Angeles County line are closed to the public during the breeding season, from March through September.

On the South Coast, at Coal Oil Point Reserve, a colony of Western Snowy Plovers has succeeded in reestablishing itself at Sands Beach, at the mouth of Devereux Slough, after forty years. In 2001, one nest was found. Mustering a group of volunteer docents and setting up symbolic fencing consisting of a rope fastened to stakes in the sand around the colony, Reserve Manager Cristina Sandoval was able to protect the plovers and their nests from destruction and grow the colony to a stable level of approximately thirty-five chicks fledged per year since 2002. Despite urban predators such as skunks and crows, Sandoval and her volunteers demonstrated that coastal strand and dunes—even on the heavily used South Coast—can still shelter the snowy plovers that belong there.

unleashed pets and urban predators such as the **Northern Raccoon** (*Procyon lotor*) and **Virginia Opossum** (*Didelphis virginiana*).

Ironically, it is human intervention that has helped the two species recover. What appeared to be an unavoidable disaster is now generally considered a success story, after years of work on the part of government agencies, biologists, and volunteers.

Associate Curator of Vertebrate Zoology at the Santa Barbara Museum of Natural History Krista Fahy wrote her doctoral dissertation on the Western Snowy Plover. At the Santa Maria

River Estuary, she studied the relationship between plover nest success and the habitats that the nests are built in. Plovers chose to nest in areas near vegetation, driftwood, and scattered rocks. Those nests with vegetation nearby were less preyed upon than those on open rocky ground.

California Least Terns breed only from San Francisco to Baja California and are concentrated mostly in Los Angeles, Orange, and San Diego counties. With protective efforts in place since 1973, the tern population soared from a total of six hundred pairs to roughly seven thousand pairs in 2005.

In our region, California Least Tern nesting colonies are protected at Pismo Beach, Oso Flaco Lake, the Santa Clara, Santa Maria, and Santa Ynez river estuaries, Vandenberg Air Force Base, Ormond Beach, and Mugu Lagoon. Interestingly, most of these sites are used by Western Snowy Plovers as well. Many of them are dune-backed beaches.

Other Wildlife of the Dunes

An undisturbed dune ecosystem consists of patches of sand dotted with shrubs of various sizes. The habitat is strange, seemingly bleak. Many of the life-forms here are considered endangered or threatened because dune areas are so limited in California.

One of the most interesting species to inhabit coastal dunes is the California Legless Lizard, designated a species of special concern by the state. It looks like a six-inch silvery snake, but unlike a snake, this lizard has eyelids. Although the legless lizard has remnant hip and shoulder bones, it has totally done away with legs and arms. Instead, it slides through the sand by "swimming" in undulations rather than digging or burrowing. Tiny, silvery scales make a smooth outer skin, so that the lizard negotiates subterranean sandy soil easily.

Legless lizards prefer the older, stabilized dunes covered with dune scrub, where they seek shelter under Dune Lupine or Mock Heather. The density of these lizards can approach two thousand per acre in suitable dune habitats. Legless lizards are not always confined to the dunes, however, and may be found in oak woodland and chaparral habitats, hiding in damp soil under rocks or rotting logs.

Recent research carried out as a genetic survey of the legless lizard

California Legless Lizard, one of the most common denizens of the dunes, is difficult to see because it lives beneath the surface.

reveals more diversity within the animal's populations than previously reported. Evidently, there are five major lineages of this wormlike reptile. Two of the lineages correspond to the typical north-south split found in our region for many reptiles. However, other populations were discovered in

The Globose Dune Beetle feeds on plant roots.

central California, including two that are endemic to the San Joaquin Valley and Carrizo Plain. (See Chapter 2 for more on phylogeography and animals in our region.)

The **Globose Dune Beetle** (*Coelus globosus*), a threatened species in California, is about one-quarter inch long. Found on the foredunes immediately back from the open beach, this beetle spends its time underneath the sandy surface, burrowing down to feed on native plant roots and detritus. It avoids areas invaded by ice plant and European Beachgrass.

Globose Dune Beetles aren't the most mobile of insects—they are usually restricted to moving in the sandy substrate from one plant to the next. The larvae go through several stages as they grow, then pupate; the adults lack functional wings. A related species of dune beetle has also been found on the Channel Islands.

Another endangered species, the **Morro Shoulderband** (*Helminthoglypta walkeriana*)—a snail—eats decaying vegetation found under bushes and in the leaf litter. Two centers of popula-

tion of the Morro Shoulderband are at Montaña de Oro State Park and Morro Strand State Beach. Although it is restricted to areas of dunes, it appears not to avoid ice plant and European Beachgrass.

The **Morro Bay Kangaroo Rat** (*Dipodomys heermanni* subsp. *morroensis*) survives only as a single population in a small dune complex near Morro Bay and is considered endangered. The more common **Lompoc Kangaroo Rat** (*D. heermanni* subsp. *arenae*) is the subspecies found in the remainder of the dunes in our region. (See Chapter 6 for more on kangaroo rats.)

* * *

The waves and the rhythms of the tide seem as far away from the tall sand dunes as the Clonal Anemone is from the Globose Dune Beetle. The transparent fronds of Nori that swish back and forth holding tightly to the tidal rocks can have nothing in common with the hardy Sea Rocket growing in a hummock of sand on the open beach. How can we talk about a Western Sand Crab—its lifestyle in the surf, its antennae snatching food from the seawater—in the same chapter as a California Legless Lizard that glides beneath a blue-flowering lupine bush, nibbling at dead leaves?

The paradox of life at the seashore originates at the waves' edge and carries inland to the highest dunes. Proximity to the sea, with its warm and cold currents; the influence of a fierce wind blowing from the northwest or a gentle breeze from the south; the rocky shores, with their shelled, sessile limpets hanging on for dear life, and the sandy beach, with its beach hoppers jumping and jawing in the mounds of wrack: these are the pieces of a food chain that begins at the surf's margin and eventually peters out on a distant backdune.

In the end, it is the spell of the shore that weaves the magic. Now you've learned the descriptions and details, the facts and the figures, but they are like spent mounds of kelp on the strand. What really matters is a walk on the beach on a clear winter day, your toes feeling the wet sand and the wiggle of the sand crab. Spend an hour in the tidepools at a minus tide, where every discovery is a breakthrough to another world that you never knew existed. Hike along a dune face in spring surrounded by a

Morro Shoulderband: a land snail endemic to two very small areas of dunes around Morro Bay. Photo by Dennis Sheridan

burst of purple and yellow and blue flowers growing from small greenish-gray shrubs.

Go towards the shore. Bring your friends and family. It's one of the best introductions to the natural world.

 On a chilly November day, when fog hangs heavy on the salt marsh at Carpinteria, the landscape is a dull one. The gray-green of the low-growing Pickleweed is broken only by dodder, the parasite that drapes itself over patches of the marsh like an orange spiderweb. Pickleweed, a succulent perennial found in most of California's coastal wetlands, is dominant here. It holds the marsh together against winter's fierce storms and high tides, shelters migrant birds, elevates the burrows of hundreds of crabs and shrimps, and protects tiny fish among its roots.

A few taller shrubs may punctuate the scene, and reeds grow in the more upland freshwater areas, but the salt marsh is largely a grayish-brown monochrome of Pickleweed and mud. From a distance, the vegetation appears to blend with the mudflats and the mudflats to merge with the channels filled with salt water.

It is a drab sight—perhaps a desert, even—to the uninitiated.

On the contrary, the salt marsh and its accompanying mudflats are one of the most productive and rare ecosystems in the Santa Barbara region.

The salt marsh is a major layover for migrating and wintering waterbirds. It harbors a unique collection of invertebrates—worms, crabs, clams, and shrimps. It shelters numerous fish species, particularly the gobies and the California Killifish, which are especially well adapted to survive in brackish water. And, because there are only a handful of viable coastal wetlands with salt marshes in our region, many of the species that inhabit these wetlands are endangered or threatened.

What Is a Coastal Wetland?

California's coastline, with its rugged topography of steep bluffs, is geologically young. Bays and estuaries of the kind found in the extensive wetlands along the east and gulf coasts of North America have not yet had a chance to form. However, where the larger estuaries create wetlands with constant tidal influence, such as at Morro Bay, Goleta Slough, Carpinteria Salt Marsh, and Mugu Lagoon, a rich assortment of plants and animals thrives. Indeed, temperate zone estuarine wetlands have a greater variety of plants than arctic, boreal, or even tropical marshes, especially in areas where winter rainfall adds to freshwater input as it does in Southern California.

The largest estuary is at Morro Bay, with 2,300 acres; Mugu Lagoon (surrounded by the Naval Air Weapons Station, which restricts public access) is the second largest, with an approximate total of 1,474 acres. Situated between the two is Carpinteria Salt Marsh, with a wetland of about 230 acres.

Coastal wetlands are biologically important: they dissipate rushing floodwaters after heavy rains; reduce erosion by slowing runoff; recharge groundwater and surface water; and absorb nutrients while removing toxic substances.

Over the last century, however, nearly 90 percent of California's coastal wetlands have disappeared. They have been filled in by sedimentation due to upstream development, degraded by chemical runoff, "reclaimed," and urbanized, so that many of the plants and animals that depended upon these surroundings have lost their habitat.

Carpinteria Salt Marsh at high tide

The same view of Carpinteria Salt Marsh, at low tide. Note the difference in water levels in the main channel.

The ecosystem at a coastal wetland, where the freshwater of a stream or river meets the salt water of the sea, is formed of several elements: freshwater marsh, salt marsh, mudflat, and lagoon. (See Chapter 9 for more on freshwater wetlands.) Shifting with the tides twice daily, the balance of freshwater and salt water changes constantly at this intersection of river and ocean. Some of the wetland will always be underwater, and some of it will always be above the high-water mark. In between are the mudflats, which are usually exposed at

145

Coastal wetlands may look uninteresting, but beneath the mud they're filled with life. Carpinteria Salt Marsh is one of the few remaining coastal wetlands on the South Coast.

In winter, Devereux Slough fills with brackish water, a mixture of rain runoff and tidal seawater.

Aerial view of Devereux Slough showing the sandbar that blocks the mouth of the slough in spring through fall. Photo by Peter Gaede

low tide, and the lagoons, which fill as the tide comes in.

The salt marsh—located on the landward side of the estuary—encompasses the mudflats and the surrounding vegetation. Drained by a network of little creeks and channels, freshwater from the stream or river flows through the salt marsh and out to the sea. At the same time, the salt marsh accommodates the tide laden with saltwater rushing inland. At this meeting place, ocean water sinks to the bottom because it is heavier, and freshwater floats above, creating an area of turbulence, which stirs up nutrients. Nutrients take the form of microscopic cellular plants and animals that live in the water column or grow in the mud, furnishing food for a variety of invertebrates.

In our region, however, a majority of the estuaries are blocked by sand berms; where a stream meets the ocean, a seasonal sand barrier forms at the stream's mouth. This is the case at the Santa Maria River, the Santa Ynez River, Shuman Creek, San Antonio Creek, Devereux Slough, Carpinteria Creek, and the Santa Clara River. Lack of rain runoff during Southern California's long dry season leaves the creek or stream with intermittent access to the sea, unable to break through the sand berm at its mouth. If winter rains increase the flow to breach the blockage, then tidal activity may be restored for a few months. But typically these estuaries are low in diversity of plant and animal life; they lack the daily tidal flushing required for a richer wetland.

The Salt Marsh

Plants of the Salt Marsh

Life in a coastal wetland is tough. It is a story of organisms that can survive challenging conditions and constant change; the plants and animals that live here are equipped to handle the unique physical and biological rigors of life in the salt marsh. They have evolved these adaptations over time, and they are a testament to the success of living things that seek to occupy every habitable corner of our planet.

Salt marsh plants have a suite of abiotic (physical) factors affecting them. Tidal fluctuation is the major one. Inundation by tides affects oxygen and salinity. Therefore, plants are distributed in bands of elevation within the marsh, depending upon their ability to withstand tidal flooding. Salt marshes in our region have basically two zones: the high marsh and the low. The low part of the marsh at Mugu Lagoon and Morro Bay contains submerged **Eel-Grass** (*Zostera marina*), which is not present at Carpinteria Salt Marsh. The next layer up consists of **Pickleweed** (*Salicornia pacifica*), which dominates the low marsh. Due to its tolerance for salt water, it is more widespread now than it used to be.

At the higher parts of the marsh, various other plants grow that cannot handle being submerged by tidal flood as well as Pickleweed does. They are **Jaumea** (*Jaumea carnosa*), **Alkali Heath** (*Frankenia salina*), **Salt Grass** (*Distichlis spicata*), **Sea-Lavender** (*Limonium californicum*), **Seaside Arrow-Grass** (*Triglochin concinna*), and **Parish's Glass-wort** (*Arthrocnemum subterminale*, also sometimes called pickleweed). **Salt-marsh Bulrush** (*Bolboschoenus maritimus*) occupies a portion of the high marsh where freshwater influence somewhat dilutes saline soil.

Freshwater input affects plants because it dilutes the salinity of the wetland. During the rainy season, precipitation dilutes the salinity of the water, enabling certain kinds of plants to grow well in winter and spring, before the hypersaline (extremely salty) conditions of summer and fall set in, with no natural freshwater input. Salt marsh plants have difficulty getting seeds to germinate in marsh soil without the help of winter rains to reduce the salinity.

In the upper marsh, where freshwater streams flow into the salt marsh and conditions are less salty, such as at the borders of Santa Monica and Franklin creeks at Carpinteria, or along Los Osos and Chorro creeks at Morro Bay, watch for tall, skinny stands of bulrushes, cattails, and sedges.

Soils are another key physical factor influencing the survival of marsh plants. Finely textured soils have poor drainage rates and create unique chemical conditions: very little oxygen is available and toxic compounds, such as sulfides, build up. Interestingly, the actual salinity of the pores in the soil, which is driven by evaporation rates, is likely to be higher in the high marsh areas than where soils are regularly covered by tidal flushing. For example, Pickleweed, which is frequently submerged by saltwater, is less tolerant of high salinities *in the soil* than Parish's Glasswort, which

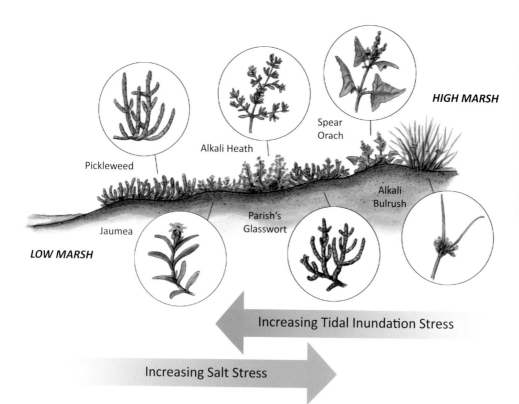

HIGH MARSH

Spear Orach

Alkali Heath

Pickleweed

Alkali Bulrush

Parish's Glasswort

Jaumea

LOW MARSH

Increasing Tidal Inundation Stress

Increasing Salt Stress

Adaptation of salt marsh plants to differences in soil salinity

grows at a higher elevation in the marsh and is submerged infrequently.

Adaptations of Salt Marsh Plants

How do salt marsh plants withstand these conditions? Their biotic (biological) responses take many forms: over millennia, they have evolved a variety of structural adaptations to allow them to live in an environment where oxygen is limited due to an abundance of salt and mud.

Certain species of bulrushes and cattails send oxygen to their roots via pressurized ventilation and convective gas flow. Other plants may be able to shift between aerobic (oxygen) and anaerobic (absence of oxy-

gen) methods of respiration, depending upon whether oxygen is available or not.

Plants that tolerate salt in their tissues are called **halophytes**. Look closely at the segmented stems of Pickleweed. (Although the stems resemble little green pickles, the plant is actually named for its use as a pickling agent in kitchens throughout the world.) Pickleweed, like many halophytes, has a special adaptation to reverse the flow of water into its roots, excluding salt. Also, many marsh plants, including Pickleweed, are succulent. They store water in their tissues in order to help dilute the concentration of salt.

Salt Dodder, a parasite, drapes itself over Pickleweed.

Other halophytes—Salt Grass, Arrow-Grass, and Sea-Lavender—rely on glands which excrete salt, leaving a white film covering the leaves. Another plant, **Spear Orach** (*Atriplex patula*), a species of saltbush, has tiny glands on its leaves that store salt until the glands burst open and the salt is blown or washed away.

Salt marsh plants have another biotic strategy: passive shading, in which one species of plant reduces soil salinity by shading areas where a winter annual such as **Coulter's Goldfields** (*Lasthenia glabrata* subsp. *coulteri*) can later germinate.

Competition is a fact of life, as neighbor elbows neighbor for optimum space in this ecosystem. **Salt Dodder** (*Cuscuta salina*), a creeping parasite with threadlike bright orange stems, climbs over stands of Pickleweed, sucking out the moisture and eventually killing it in certain patches. This allows new species of salt marsh plants a chance to gain footholds in what otherwise might become a monoculture of Pickleweed. And diversity—the presence

of an array of plant species, not just one or two dominants—makes for a more dynamic, healthy salt marsh community.

A recent experiment, in which researchers varied the growing conditions of certain plant species at Carpinteria Salt Marsh by watering them, concluded that variation in total annual precipitation promotes variation in plant species. Some plants will thrive in dry years, and yet even more will benefit from a year with heavier precipitation. These results agree with other scientific papers that have concluded that species richness for plants increases in estuarine wetlands from south to north in our region, largely due to more winter rainfall north of Point Conception. In addition to species richness, coastal wetlands in the Santa Barbara region reflect an important gradient in northern versus southern salt marsh plant species. Several species of plants reach their northern limits here, and others are at their southern limits.

Beneath the Mud: Invertebrate Animals of the Salt Marsh

Many of the most interesting organisms in the salt marsh live out of sight. These are the invertebrates: the crabs, snails, clams, and worms that hide in layers of mud, creep along under cover of the incoming tide, and dig deep burrows in the sides and bottoms of the channels. Some of the creatures are also found in the rocky intertidal habitat on open shores, but most have established themselves in the shelter of the estuary, taking refuge from the surf in these calmer waters.

Invertebrate animals face some of

Salt Marsh Bird's-beak is one of the most beautiful plants of the salt marsh.

Salt Marsh Bird's-beak

One of the most famous and beautiful plants found in our region's salt marshes is the **Salt Marsh Bird's-beak** (*Chloropyron maritimum* subsp. *maritimus*). It grows as an annual, eight to sixteen inches tall, and the flower resembles a kind of paintbrush, with purple sepals and white petals ending in a closed, beak-like little hook at the top. Salt Marsh Bird's-beak is in the Broomrape family and is a root parasite. It inserts its own tiny haustoria, or roots, to penetrate the tissue of the host plant and obtain nutrients. At Morro Bay, Carpinteria, and Mugu, the Salt Marsh Bird's-beak blooms from May to October in the higher portions of the salt marsh. It is listed as endangered by both the state and federal governments.

the same challenges that plants do in the salt marsh: seasonal changes in the salinity of water and soil, lack of oxygen in the mud, and competition from neighbors. Many invertebrates are **euryhaline**, that is, they are able to live with changes in the salinity of the water. Interestingly, most organisms from the sea can adjust to reduced salinity better than freshwater organisms can adjust to higher salt concentrations.

Life for a crab or worm in the salt marsh has advantages. Protection from violent wave action, lots of sunlight, shallow water, tidal exchange for bringing in nutrients and carrying off wastes, and a relatively mild climate: all these foster a favorable place to live. Burrowing into the mud helps conceal these animals from enemies, keeps them from drying out, and surrounds them with potential food.

Let's return to Carpinteria Salt Marsh and get our hands dirty.

A majority of invertebrate animals in the marsh feed in one of two ways. They are either **suspension feeders** or **deposit feeders**. Suspension feeders, including the mussels, clams, and cockles, strain microalgae and other microorganisms from the water column by opening their shells and directing food particles across their gills. They position themselves below mean high tide so that they have access to seawater much of the time. Deposit feeders, on the other hand, ingest decaying detritus and other organic morsels found on the surface of the mud itself. Deposit feeders form two groups: those that feed at the surface, such as the **California Horn Snail** (*Cerithidea califor-*

150

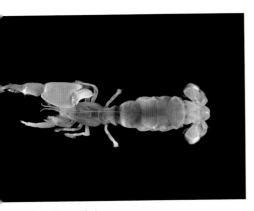

Bay Ghost Shrimp

California Horn Snail is an abundant resident of the salt marsh mudflats.

in order for Pickleweed to be accessible to invertebrate animals, it must first be decomposed by bacteria or other **detritivores** (organisms that eat fragments). And along the same lines, researchers have just discovered that Western Sandpipers feed on biofilm, the minuscule film of bacteria, detritus, and sediment that grows on the surface of the mud. It was previously assumed that the birds ate only small crustaceans.

Omnivores are secondary consumers; they feed on the primary consumers. These predators devour just about anything, including carrion. In this group are found the crabs, a few of the snails, like the **California Aglaja** (*Navanax inermis*), and the rather fierce polychaete worms. Surprisingly, the worms are armed with terminal jaws made for biting whatever prey they come upon.

The segmented polychaete worms, represented by eighteen species, form the largest group of invertebrates found in Carpinteria Salt Marsh. They are followed by the clams and mussels, with fourteen species; the

nica), and those that feed below the surface, such as the burrowing **Bay Ghost Shrimp** (*Neotrypaea californiensis*). Some animals, of course, feed both at the surface and beneath it. Deposit feeders can live almost anywhere, since all they require is the nourishing mud.

Both suspension feeders and deposit feeders are primary consumers in the salt marsh food chain. They eat green algae and the floating unicellular organisms called diatoms. Decomposed plant material is another source of food. For example,

California Aglaja, often referred to by its genus name, *Navanax*: a marsh predator that tracks its prey by following mucus trails

151

The Striped Shore Crab is easily observed along one of the channels at low tide.

shrimps and crabs with eleven species; and the snails with ten species. Following is a discussion of these invertebrates grouped by the intertidal zones in which they make their muddy homes.

On a field trip to Carpinteria Salt Marsh, you will see some of the creatures discussed below. Others will be hidden from view. Begin at the higher elevations and work your way down onto the mudflats.

High Intertidal Zone: The first invertebrate that catches your eye is a reddish crab with two large claws, the **Striped Shore Crab** (*Pachygrapsus crassipes*). Standing in front of their mud-burrow entrances along the banks on either side of a watery channel, these crabs are formidable scavengers and omnivores. They even eat their smaller neighbor, the **Yellow Shore Crab** (*Hemigrapsus oregonensis*), which is found lower on the banks in the marsh and thus closer to tidal influence. Striped Shore Crabs

have an aggressive manner of rearing up when disturbed but are actually rather timid when forced into a "fight or flight" situation. They can be found on the rocky open shore as well as in the marsh, but here they position themselves higher up in the intertidal zone than they would on the open coast. This is true of many salt marsh creatures.

A crab that you will never see but is of interest to know is the **Fiddler Crab** (*Uca crenulata*). Among the rarest crabs in our region because they are at the northern limit of their Southern California distribution at Carpinteria, the fiddlers live in a small colony in the highest portion of the marsh. They make a deep, permanent burrow with a chamber at the end. They could hardly be farther from the sea, but here they dine on small plants and animals contained in the surrounding moist soil. The males sport one claw much larger than the other, helpful in digging but used chiefly in signaling to females during breeding season: the male, when a female appears, stretches out his largest claw to its maximum length and then whips it suddenly back to his body in a show of bravado (the "fiddling" motion).

Middle Intertidal Zone: Now, dig down into the mud just beneath the surface of the marsh, known as the middle intertidal zone. Here you begin to see several examples of **commensalism**, an interaction wherein burrow-constructing animals take in "roommates." The commensal animal is one that lives with and takes advantage of the host animal but does not appear to harm the host.

Two deposit feeders, the Bay Ghost Shrimp and **Blue Mud Shrimp** (*Upogebia pugettensis*), are common. The Bay Ghost Shrimps look like miniature lobsters and grow up to four inches long. Their burrows are complex, with many tunnels, and the shrimps are constantly digging and improving upon them. According to marine biologist George MacGinitie, quoted in *Between Pacific Tides:*

> The animal digs its burrows with the claws of the first and second legs, which draw the sandy mud backward, collecting it in another receptacle formed by another pair of legs. When enough material has been collected to make a load, the shrimp backs out of its burrow and deposits the load outside. All of the legs are specialized, some being used for walking, others for bracing the animal against the sides of the burrow, and still others for personal cleansing operations.

Their constant digging overturns the sediments of the mudflats, in a manner similar to the way earthworms work the soil.

Bay Ghost Shrimps take in boarders—living in their burrows with a species of **polychaete worm** (*Hesperonoe camplanata*), **pea crab** (*Scleroplax granulata*), and **red copepod** (*Clausidium vancouverense*). They feed by gleaning detritus from the flow of mud that passes through their digestive tracts, also gaining nutrients in the form of plankton moving through the water in their burrows. Bay Ghost Shrimps are long-lived, at up to sixteen years.

The **Lewis's Moon Snail** (*Euspira*

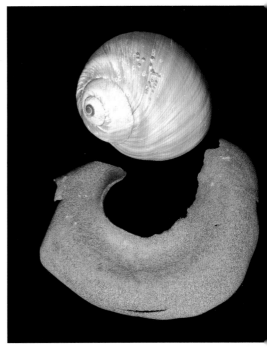

Lewis's Moon Snail shell with sand-covered egg mold in the shape of a collar. Specimens from the Santa Barbara Museum of Natural History

lewisii), one of the predators at the top of the food chain in the marsh, looks like a large lump buried under the sand. Uncovering it reveals a four-inch shell with a big foot that looks too large to withdraw into the comparatively small shell. It may do so, however, and close the door (operculum) behind it when disturbed. One of the ways to recognize the presence of moon snails is by their egg cases, which resemble circular pieces of cast-off rubber. The eggs, extruded from the mantle cavity in a gelatinous sheet, form a sand-covered mold around the foot of the moon snail. When the young hatch, the egg cases are no longer needed and can be seen lying about on the mudflat in odd, sandy collar shapes.

Arrow Goby, one of the commensals that live in the burrows of Fat Innkeepers

When a moon snail goes hunting, it clamps its large foot around a clam or mussel and then drills a perfect hole through the shell with its sharp radula, sucking out the internal organs and leaving only the penetrated shell as evidence of its skillful attack.

Also numerous in the middle intertidal area of the marsh are the segmented worms of the class Polychaeta. *Capitella capitata*, a favorite prey of many shorebirds, is a common polychaete found at Carpinteria Salt Marsh. The Greek word "polychaeta" means "many bristles," an apt description of these worms, as each segment possesses a tuft of bristles that protrude from the worm's footlike organs, which paddle them forward through the water.

The **Fat Innkeeper** (*Urechis caupo*) is well known for its lifestyle, which tolerates several commensals occupying its unique burrow. Found at Morro Bay and Mugu Lagoon but not at Carpinteria, this cigar-shaped worm is usually eight to ten inches long. It constructs a U-shaped bur-

row beneath the low tide line with entrances sixteen to thirty-eight inches apart. These entrances are narrowed, so that they are smaller than the width of the burrow.

The amazing aspect of the whole setup is the spinning of a slime net which is used for food capture. At the entrance to the vertical part of the burrow, the innkeeper attaches an extremely fine mucous net that traps microscopic particles. When the animal wants to feed, it moves up the burrow, swallowing the net as it goes. It digests the net, along with the detritus caught there, but it discards any large or unwanted particles. They do not go to waste, however. Like the Bay Ghost Shrimp, the Fat Innkeeper takes in at least three commensals that share the burrow: in this case a reddish segmented worm (*Hesperonoe adventor*), a miniature pea crab, and a small fish, the **Arrow Goby** (*Clevelandia ios*). The crab and the worm are in competition for the innkeeper's leftovers, with the worm usually getting the worst of it. The goby and the crab, however, seem to have a more friendly relationship: gobies have been seen to carry large pieces of food to a crab and then eat the smaller crumbs as the crab tears up the morsel.

Low Intertidal Zone: At last, shovel in hand, you may want to explore the deepest levels of the mud at the marsh.

In this habitat beneath the lowest tides, clams hide themselves from predators by living deep in the muck. Clams feed and breathe through two siphons on one end of the animal. Water passes through one siphon and out the other, giving this filter feeder a chance to grab small bits of food from the water. Two gills on each side of the clam's foot have a surface area to absorb oxygen and are equipped with small cilia that push the food towards the clam's mouth. In this way, a clam has solved two of the problems of life deep in the mud: receiving oxygen and getting food.

The third problem for clams is predators, which they escape by digging deep. As a rule, the deeper the clam digs, the thinner its shell needs to be, because it is safer from predators at lower elevations. Higher up, clams arm themselves with thicker shells to shield them from hungry gulls, shorebirds, and other enemies.

Two extra-large clams, the **Geoduck** (*Panopea generosa*) and the **Pacific Gaper** (*Tresus nuttallii*), are found at Carpinteria. The Geoduck lives in a deep, deep burrow from which it sends two extremely long siphons upwards, through which it feeds and breathes. This clam's shell can be up to eight inches long and its maximum weight is twelve pounds! More frequently found at Carpinteria is the gaper, easily recognized by its siphon, from which it can shoot a jet of water two or three feet into the air when perturbed.

Other common clams at Carpinteria Salt Marsh are the **Pacific Littleneck** (*Leukoma staminea*), the **Bent-nosed Clam** (*Macoma nasuta*), and the **Pacific Razor Clam** (*Tagelus californianus*). The Bent-nosed Clam uses its siphon like a little vacuum cleaner. The incurrent siphon bends over very slightly so that its tip just touches the surface of the sand and can glean

An assortment of bivalves found in the marsh. Left to right: Pacific Littleneck, Bent-nosed Clam, and Pacific Razor Clam

detritus from the surface. When the clam has vacuumed all of the nearby surface, it moves on to another spot.

With the exception of Goleta Slough, Morro Bay, and Mugu Lagoon, all other coastal wetlands in our region are too small and lack the tidal influence to harbor any of the marine invertebrates mentioned above. At Goleta Slough, however, the California Horn Snail and a high density of Pacific Razor Clams have been found.

At least five of the invertebrate species found at Carpinteria Salt Marsh are warm temperate (southern), reaching the northern limits of their range here: the Fiddler Crab, **Olive Ear Snail** (*Melampus olivaceus*), and three kinds of clams—**Frilled Venus** (*Chione undulata*), **California Fat Tellin** (*Psammotreta obesa*), and **Pacific Egg Cockle** (*Laevicardium substriatum*). As noted in Chapter 4, our region is a transition zone for marine invertebrates; those inhabiting coastal wetlands reflect this geographic north-south division.

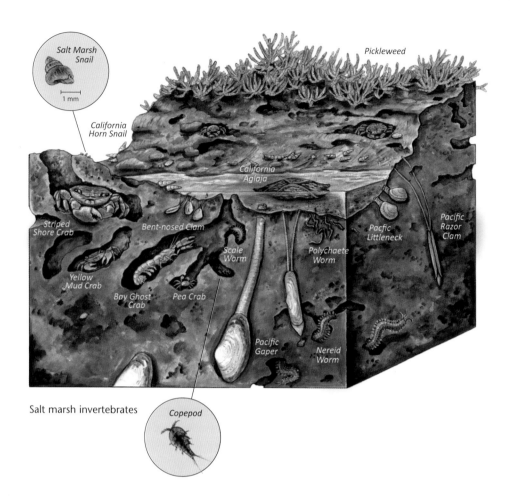

Salt marsh invertebrates

Labels in image: Salt Marsh Snail, 1 mm, Pickleweed, California Horn Snail, California Aglaja, Striped Shore Crab, Bent-nosed Clam, Pacfic Littleneck, Pacific Razor Clam, Yellow Mud Crab, Scale Worm, Polychaete Worm, Bay Ghost Crab, Pea Crab, Pacific Gaper, Nereid Worm, Copepod

Insects of the Salt Marsh

Mosquitoes, as one might suspect, are a big presence, with ten kinds of mosquito larvae having been observed in the pools and drainage ditches of Carpinteria Salt Marsh. The **California Salt Marsh Mosquito** (*Aedes taeniorhynchus*) is found in the winter, and in summer the **Summer Salt Marsh Mosquito** (*Aedes squamiger*) is common.

Another insect frequenting the salt marsh is the **Western Pygmy-Blue** butterfly (*Brephidium exilis*), which you might see hovering near one of the nonnative **Australian Saltbush** (*Atriplex semibaccata*) plants. This minuscule butterfly (not quite a half-inch long from one wing tip to another) is an indicator of saline soils because it lays its eggs on salt-loving plants, which are food for the young caterpillars. The **Wandering Skipper** (*Panoquina errans*), is also considered a salt marsh specialist. The larval stages are dependent upon Salt Grass; the caterpillars are evidently able to withstand a good deal of salt in their diet.

Western Pygmy-Blue, one of the world's smallest butterflies

The Wandering Skipper, found only in salt marshes, reaches its northern limit in our area.

Nature Journal
November 4, 2007

A Visit to Carpinteria Salt Marsh

I am walking along the berm road at the UC Santa Barbara Reserve portion of Carpinteria Salt Marsh this afternoon.

As the ebbing tide exposes muddy channels, I watch the marsh change. The shorebirds, once huddled together in a far corner of the Pickleweed to loaf and preen, rouse themselves in anticipation of the coming feast. As the seawater recedes, Willets and Long-billed Curlews, Greater Yellowlegs and Dunlins fly to their feeding spots along the banks of the main channel.

The banks are honeycombed with crab burrows. Striped Shore Crabs stand at their burrow entrances, waving their two large claws. One of the shore crabs quickly sidles off in search of detritus uncovered by the ebbing tide; another scuttles back into its burrow to avoid the marauding birds.

Through binoculars, I see a Willet grasp a juvenile crab by the carapace, dismember it, and quickly gulp down the remains. Then a Long-billed Curlew, wielding its lengthy, decurved bill, walks into view. It need not bother with surface prey, because a bill this long can plumb the deeper burrows where the Bay Ghost Shrimps hide. The tall curlew plunges its bill full-length into the slime, swiveling it around in search of prey.

On the higher mudflats, green algae is stranded in large chartreuse mats. Hundreds and hundreds of dark, cone-shaped shells of the California Horn Snail—the most numerous snail in the marsh—litter the surface of the green algae. Able to withstand the harshest conditions of

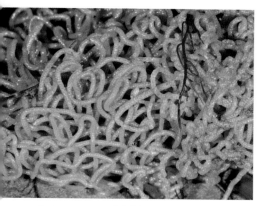

Stringy masses of California Seahare eggs

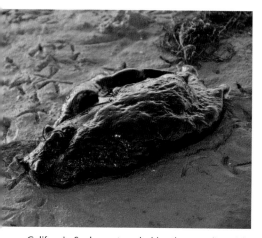

California Seahare stranded by the receding tide

of the estuary, where the water is quickly draining to the ocean. Gulls scream on the rocky shore. Cormorants stand with wings akimbo.

All at once a Peregrine Falcon makes a daring attack. Flying faster than fast, the falcon approaches out of nowhere. The flock of Western Sandpipers is up in an instant, flinging themselves in unison from one corner of the sky to another. The falcon will only succeed at catching a sandpiper if one can be separated from the tight flock. No luck today. The flock escapes by fleeing towards the open beach, banking and quickly gaining altitude. The peregrine, having strafed and missed, flies off as if this was only a morning warm-up drill.

Once I'm out at the deepest channel, I peer down into the turbid water. Shadows are moving beneath the surface. It's a group of California Seahares. Nearly a dozen of these interesting, foot-long creatures have come to spawn in the shelter of the salt marsh.

Seahares are hermaphroditic, producing both eggs and sperm, thus playing the role of male and female at the same time. The submerged seahares often form a long, circular chain of mating individuals. An animal can serve as the male for a mate in front of it and a female to an animal behind it. I am witness to an underwater reproductive orgy!

These orgies last from several hours to several days and result in masses of eggs. Long after I leave the salt marsh tonight, millions and millions of microscopic eggs will be laid. When the eggs hatch, little larval seahares will circulate in the water—most to be devoured by other animals. When the juvenile hares do settle, it will be on a special red alga (Plocamium). After feeding on the red-

the salt marsh, horn snails proliferate on exposed banks and flats.

Out towards the estuary inlet, the channels still hold water. I notice little holes along the bottom of these waterways. These are the tips of Bent-nosed Clam siphons. The fleshy tubes poke up above the ooze, proving irresistible to juvenile Diamond Turbots, a salt marsh fish. Since the siphons regrow, this is a nice little farm from which the turbots continue to reap a tasty harvest.

At last, I find myself out at the mouth

dish pigments in the algae, an adult sea-hare is able to emit a noxious purple ink when touched or disturbed. Presumably, the presence of a bunch of red algae in the channel has touched off this mating spree.

I can't stop thinking about the seahare and its marvelous inner construction. It has no outer shell, but an internal one. The digestive system is complicated: the seahare uses its sharp radula (tongue) to eat the algae, which then proceeds to one of three stomachs; the second and third stomach are lined with teeth to continue the grinding process begun by the radula.

My marsh walk must come to an end. I want to stay and study more of the marsh inhabitants, like the Bay Seahare (now called California Aglaja). Related to the California Seahare, the aglaja is another one of the opisthobranchs, but it is not an herbivore. Instead it is a vicious predator of various snails and even small fish, following underwater scent trails to locate prey.

Who would have thought these strange hares, which are basically snails without shells, would dwell in the channels of Carpinteria Salt Marsh?

Fish Stories

Tidewater Goby

Seasonal coastal estuaries that are blocked by a sand berm and backed by a lagoon serve as refuges for a special Southern California fish—the **Tidewater Goby** (*Eucyclogobius newberryi*). These two-inch-long, gray-brown fish are especially adapted to survive in shallow lagoons with a healthy amount of freshwater input. They thrive where salinity is under 10 percent. For example, the Tidewater

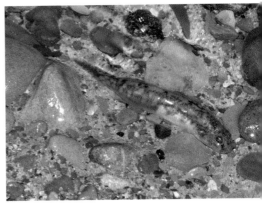

Tidewater Goby, found only in the shallow lagoons formed at the mouths of coastal streams. Photo by Peter Gaede

Goby is not found at Carpinteria Salt Marsh because it is too saline there.

Goby populations in lagoons blocked by sandbars are endemic to low-salinity water. With coastal wetlands under pressure, the Tidewater Goby has received endangered status in San Luis Obispo, Santa Barbara, and Ventura counties, and acreage has been set aside to preserve the impounded coastal creek mouths which they prefer.

Gobies employ a number of tactics for success in these land-locked lagoons, including their small size and their ability to spawn year-round.

The life history of the Tidewater Goby is highly unusual. Females are aggressive and dominant during the breeding season, when they assume a striking blue-black color. The reproductive process begins with the males digging vertical burrows in the coarse sand in water less than three feet deep. They do this by entering the burrows, then emerging with tail and body undulating in a backward swimming motion as they carry mouthfuls of wet sand, which they arrange around the entrance to the burrow. Once the burrow has been excavated, the male waits inside. He may block the entrance with a plug made of mucus and sand, playing hard to get. But the ripe females are on the prowl and they will enter a male's burrow if at all possible. A female will erect her dorsal fins, hop around the entrance, and make short dashes, and still she is lucky if she is able to enter the male's burrow. When she is finally allowed in, the two mate and the female suspends her eggs, one by one, from the roof and sides of the burrow. The male goby guards the eggs until they hatch, in about ten days.

In their cut-off lagoon habitats of low-salinity water, Tidewater Gobies have an advantage because there are no commensal organisms to bother them, predators are few, and they do not have to cope with tidal fluctuations. However, each Tidewater Goby population that flourishes at the mouth of one of these creeks is genetically unique and isolated, so that care must be taken to protect not only the larger populations, for example at the Santa Ynez River mouth, but the smaller ones that exist at Jalama Creek, Gaviota Creek, Arroyo Burro Creek, Mission Creek, Carpinteria Creek, and Ormond Beach, to name a few.

Other Fishes of Coastal Wetlands

In the larger estuaries, the common resident fishes are Arrow Goby, **Shadow Goby** (*Quietula y-cauda*), **Longjaw Mudsucker** (*Gillichthys mirabilis*), **California Killifish** (*Fundulus parvipinnis*), **Pacific Staghorn Sculpin** (*Leptocottus armatus*), and **Topsmelt**

(*Atherinops affinis*). Like the plants and invertebrates of the salt marsh, these resident small fishes are highly adapted to living in salty, shallow water and mud.

Longjaw Mudsuckers have large upper jaws and are a bit bigger than the gobies. After devouring a Yellow Shore Crab—their preferred food—they will take over the crab's burrow, where they will nest and defend themselves against other males. In confrontations, male mudsuckers open their jaws wide and push each other around mouth to mouth.

Mudsuckers are successful in the marsh because they know how to deal with the lack of oxygen in muddy pools. When the oxygen level is too low, mudsuckers are able to breathe air. They swim to the surface, gulp air, then hold it in their throats, which contain blood vessels that transfer the oxygen to their bloodstreams.

Most of the fish living in coastal estuaries consume plants, detritus, or small invertebrates. Topsmelt and California Killifish are in turn preyed upon by larger fish, as are Arrow Gobies and Shadow Gobies. Fish-eating birds, such as mergansers, diving ducks, cormorants, herons, gulls, and terns, harvest these surface-dwelling, schooling fish. At low tide, willets, godwits, and curlews probe the burrows and eat the Arrow Gobies hiding there.

Perhaps the Arrow Goby is the best example of a resident estuarine fish. It lives in a burrow individually or with commensal hosts. It attaches its eggs to the walls of the burrow and, at low tide, can go from one burrow to another as long as there is even a thin film of water overhead. The

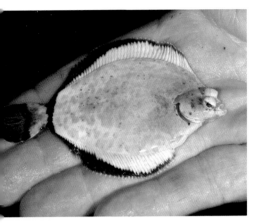

This juvenile right-eyed flatfish, the C-O Sole, may reach fourteen inches as an adult. The "C" and "O" refer to faint markings, a spot and crescent, on the tail, barely visible here.

Arrow Goby eats polychaete worms and copepods and is itself an important source of food for larger fishes.

The Flatfishes

At Morro Bay, Carpinteria Salt Marsh, and Mugu Lagoon, **California Halibut** (*Paralichthys californicus*), **Diamond Turbot** (*Hypsopsetta guttulata*), and **Starry Flounder** (*Platichthys stellatus*) swim in from the sea. The adults spawn in or near these calm waters, after which they return to the ocean, leaving behind the juveniles. The sheltered waters of the salt marsh protect the young fish, acting as their nursery until they reach a size where they can compete in the open ocean.

Halibut, turbot, and flounder are called flatfish because their bodies are flattened from top to bottom (dorso-ventrally) rather than from side to side (laterally). Flatfish are born with eyes on either side of the head. As they mature, one eye "migrates" so that they have both eyes on the upper

side of the head. This side, the exposed side, is also the one with coloration, the downside being pale white, which aids in camouflage from predators.

The most abundant flatfish and the one most esteemed for its commercial and recreational value is the California Halibut. When the young halibut are small, they feed on crustaceans such as amphipods and mysids—tiny, shrimplike creatures—in the marsh. But once they reach approximately two inches, their diet shifts to gobies. By the time they are two years old, they have left the estuary's protection for the open seas, where adults can grow to five feet and weigh about seventy pounds.

The Starry Flounder is a member of the "righteye flounder" family, which also includes the Diamond Turbot. Supposedly, all righteye flounders lie on the sandy bottom on their left side with both of their eyes on the right side. However, this appears to vary throughout populations, and some have both eyes on their left side. The Starry Flounder has been found occasionally at Carpinteria Salt Marsh, a southern limit, but it is much more common north of Point Conception.

Fish that use the salt marsh seasonally, such as the flatfishes described above, have good reason to do so. Studies at Mugu Lagoon show that fish abundance in the salt marsh compared to the open ocean is highest in the summer months, peaking in June, due to three factors: food is abundant, predators are relatively scarce, and water temperatures are high. In winter, on the other hand, Mugu Lagoon is much less hospitable for fish: major winter storms make

Shorebirds feed at low tide at Morro Bay

the water less salty, there is sediment in the water column, and fish-eating birds abound.

A Smorgasbord for the Birds

Birds are the most conspicuous members of a coastal wetland community. Secondary and even tertiary consumers in the salt marsh ecosystem, they feed on animals that have already partaken of food at another trophic level. Birds are more mobile than the plants and invertebrate animals that inhabit the salt marsh year-round: they frequent coastal wetlands at certain times of the year and are absent at others.

Migrant Shorebirds, Wintering Waterfowl

The Pacific Flyway, bordered on the east by the Rockies and on the west by the Pacific Ocean, is a broad area used by birds passing through en route to their Canadian and Alaskan breeding grounds in spring, and to wintering grounds in Central and South America in fall. The location of the Santa Barbara region on the Pacific Coast places it on one of the best-traveled routes of the Pacific Flyway. More than 80 percent of the species in the Sandpiper family (Scolopacidae) migrate, including curlews, godwits, dowitchers, and phalaropes.

Shorebirds use the rich estuaries as stopovers to rest and refuel during their long-distance journeys. With advances in radiotelemetry tracking devices, ornithologists have been able to learn more about the migration habits of sandpipers. One study focused on four species, all of which move through our region in spring and fall: Western Sandpiper, **Dunlin** (*Calidris alpina*), and **Long-billed** and

Short-billed Dowitchers (*Limnodro-mus scolopaceus* and *L. griseus*). The Western Sandpiper and Short-billed Dowitcher nest in Alaska and winter as far south as South America. The Dunlin and Long-billed Dowitcher also nest in Alaska, but they winter in Mexico.

Most of the banding and telemetry work has focused on the migratory behavior of the little Western Sandpiper, which weighs less than an ounce. It is the most abundant shorebird on the Pacific Flyway. In one study, Western Sandpipers were banded on their wintering grounds in the estuaries of Mexico before they began to migrate. The males left first, anxious to capture the best breeding territories in the far north. The females followed several days later.

Large flocks of Western Sandpipers arrive in late March and early April at Mugu Lagoon, Carpinteria Salt Marsh, Devereux Slough, and Morro Bay. They make short flights (about 135 miles per day), stopping to rest for two to four days—sometimes up to a week—at coastal estuaries. The protein and fat they have stored up to make the long journey must be supplemented along the way by the worms, snails, and other fare offered at the salt marsh smorgasbord.

Although in spring shorebirds hurry to make their way north, the pace of migration south to wintering grounds is more leisurely. Indeed, at all of the coastal wetlands in our region, fall is the season when birds are most abundant and species richness is highest. Augmented by the juveniles of the year, the shorebird flocks comprise the majority of species

Eel-Grass beds exposed at low tide inside Morro Bay

Brant, which overwinter at Morro Bay in good numbers, rely on Eel-Grass for food.

American White Pelicans, another wintering bird species at Morro Bay, require the still waters of the bay for fishing.

found at coastal wetlands, although other waterbirds can be found, too. For example, Mugu Lagoon is the southern destination for a number of diving ducks, grebes, and coots, as well as shorebirds.

At Morro Bay in winter, groups of Brant—elegant black-and-white geese—feed chiefly on Eel-Grass. Eel-Grass is a submerged flowering plant with green, strap-like leaves. It grows in lush beds at Morro Bay. An assortment of snails and other creatures cling to the Eel-Grass, providing extra nourishment for the Brant. Come spring, these birds will depart for nesting grounds in the high Arctic.

Another winterer at Morro Bay is the **American White Pelican** (*Pelecanus erythrorhynchos*). In stately groups, these enormous white birds dip their bills into the water as they fish from a

sitting position. They do not plunge-dive like their relative the Brown Pelican.

Birds are subject to the rhythm of the tides. When the tide is in, shore-birds roost in vegetation at the high end of the marsh, while out near the mouth of the estuary at the deeper lagoons the swimming and diving birds gather to feed. At Goleta Beach near the mouth of Goleta Slough, **Red-breasted Mergansers** (*Mergus serrator*) and **Double-crested Cormorants** (*Phalacrocorax auritus*) dive for fish when the lagoon is full and the water deep.

As the tide recedes, a different scene unfolds: long-legged waders such as the **Great Blue Heron** (*Ardea herodias*) and the **Great Egret** (*Ardea alba*) pose along the muddy banks. Patiently, they await their chances to fish as the water level lowers. The sharp, thick bills of the heron and egret are attached to their long, flexible necks, helping them to assume a posture called "peering over" when fishing. Often, they will raise their wings halfway to block the glare of the sunlight on the water.

At low tide, the watchful gulls descend, fearless scavengers. They're game for an opportunity at the left-overs table. The scraps inadvertently dropped by the plunge-diving or wading birds do not escape the keen-eyed gulls.

A Great Blue Heron stalks prey at Carpinteria Salt Marsh.

Nor are the clams safe. Clams living in the shallows, though their shells are thick, are at risk from gulls. A **California Gull** (*Larus californicus*) will snatch a clam from the surface of the mud and carry it in its bill to an area of hard substrate (stones, rocks) near the mouth of the estuary. Here, the gull will repeatedly hover above the rocks, dropping and then retrieving the clam until its shell has finally cracked open to reveal the juicy prize inside.

How Shorebirds Forage in Coastal Wetlands

This Snowy Egret has succeeded in catching a good-sized fish.

How do shorebirds sort themselves out at a coastal wetland, where the habitat is rather uniform and the competition for prey is high?

Among the sandpipers, variable bill length and leg length provide the species with different feeding strategies. Tall sandpipers—**Long-billed Curlews** (*Numenius americanus*), Marbled Godwits, Whimbrels, and Willets—plumb the mudflats with longer bills. Their longer legs enable them to explore in deeper water. Curlews and whimbrels, with long, decurved bills, are able to wrestle with ghost shrimps buried in

The Black-crowned Night-Heron forages in the salt marsh from dusk to dawn.

The salt marsh at Morro Bay at high tide, with Morro Rock in the background

their burrows beneath the surface. Smaller sandpipers use their shorter bills and shorter legs to feed in shallower waters. Dunlin, Western Sandpipers, and **Least Sandpipers** (*Calidris minutilla*) resort to probing and picking at the edges of tidal pools. Here, prey is much smaller and includes tiny fish larvae and floating crustaceans.

Interesting studies done in the 1990s showed that probing birds like the sandpipers use sensory organs in their bill tips to detect vibrations or pressure in the mud or sand. The upper and lower parts of shorebird bills are lined with small sensory pits.

As Tim Birkhead says in his fascinating book *Bird Sense:*

When the bird pushes its beak into wet sand it generates a pressure wave in the minute amounts of water lying between the sand grains. This pressure wave is disrupted by solid objects, such as bivalves, which block the flow of water, thereby creating a "pressure disturbance" detectable by the bird. Rapid and repeated probing, so typical of these wading birds, is thought to allow them to build up a composite three-dimensional image of food items hidden in the sand.

Nature Journal
November 21, 2002

A Visit to the Salt Marsh at Morro Bay

We have just arrived at the little beach town of Baywood Park late on a clear, warm November day. Offshore breezes ruffle the cypresses, and the sun is beginning to set. The great rock of Morro Bay looms in the distance.

The mudflats of the salt marsh lie entirely exposed, the tide so far out that every channel and every lump on the muddy bottom is stripped bare, uncovered.

We walk to the north end of 4th Street, where a wooden platform allows good views of the masses of shorebirds feeding. Bathed in the golden light of the setting sun, the subtle shorebird plumages of gray and brown take on brilliant highlights. Against that muddy background, the whirling flocks wheel and turn, flashing white underparts, uttering wild cries, then settling once more to probe what lies beneath the mud.

I try to imagine all the buried creatures the birds can sense with their highly tactile bills. All I can see is the surface of the mudflat: pocked with mysterious air holes, punctured by little volcanoes, lumpy with underground burrows partially exposed. Occasionally a clam squirts off.

Underlying the surface of the marsh, this nether world exists. I can't see it, but I know it's there. Beneath the mud, the hungry Fat Innkeeper waits for the tide to come in again; the Geoducks and gapers retract their siphons to withstand the temporary lack of seawater; the gobies swim to the few remaining shallow puddles and wait.

At the shore, colorful wooden boats lean on their sides, stranded on the mud.

It is dead low tide.

By the next morning, all has changed. Gone are the golden sunset, the groups of shorebirds, the exposed mudflats. The weather has turned and so has the tide. The quiet overcast of a marine layer settles over the landscape. During the night, the mudflat has become a lagoon filled with water, packed with ducks and geese. The muttering and murmuring of the Brant geese in their flocks is a special sound I haven't heard since my last visit to the Northwest.

Several of the geese come onshore at a nearby sandspit, where they appear to be eating bits of gravel to aid their digestion. Others are out in the middle of the bay, slurping up the Eel-Grass. The Brant lean over and grasp the bright green straps of Eel-Grass in their bills with a twisting motion. Often, it dangles from their bills as they nibble away at the nourishing blades. And all the while they are talking to each other in low tones.

Ducks float by. Some dive in the deeper water, others only dabble at the edge of the marsh.

The menu of the estuary has changed. The shorebirds must roost elsewhere at high tide, leaving the marsh to the waterfowl. This juxtaposition of the mudflat and the flooded lagoon, the freshwater of creeks joining the saltwater of the ocean, the land meeting the sea—this is what's so exhilarating about spending time at an estuary.

The Invisibles—the Power of Parasites in the Salt Marsh

At Carpinteria Salt Marsh on any given day, you can watch as the California Horn Snail lies scattered about on the muddy shores, the silvery killifish darts up a murky channel, and a Snowy Egret waits for a killifish and stabs it with its bill at exactly the right moment to make the catch. Simple ecology of the salt marsh: a primary producer, the microalgae (cyanobacteria and diatoms on the surface of the mud), being eaten by a primary consumer, the horn snail; and a secondary consumer, the killifish, being eaten by a top predator, the Snowy Egret.

But underlying the day-to-day activities of life in the salt marsh, there is a phenomenon that was unknown even twenty years ago. UC Santa Barbara researchers Kevin Lafferty, Armand Kuris, and their colleagues have evidence that the ecology of the marsh may be governed by its invisible and most powerful inhabitants—its parasites.

The parasitic mode is widespread among animals, and their relationships to the host species are incredibly intricate and varied. Parasites outnumber all other species on our planet. They are smart and specialized; each variety picks the host that will best serve its needs. Some castrate their hosts, some live in their hosts' brains, and some fiddle with their hosts' immune systems.

The Light-Footed Clapper Rail and Belding's Savannah Sparrow

After the migrant shorebirds and wintering ducks have departed, coastal salt marshes are the domain of the only two species of birds that live there year-round: the **Light-footed Clapper Rail** (*Rallus longirostris* subsp. *levipes*) and the **Belding's Savannah Sparrow** (*Passerculus sandwichensis* subsp. *beldingi*). These particular subspecies of the rail and the sparrow are found only in coastal wetlands south of Point Conception. Threatened by urbanization and the destruction of their ancestral breeding areas, both are listed as endangered.

At Devereux Slough (Coal Oil Point Reserve), the brown, streaky Belding's subspecies of the Savannah Sparrow reaches its northernmost breeding grounds in California. Living out its entire life in the midst of the Pickleweed, this unobtrusive sparrow is most easily seen in late winter and early spring, when it perches up to sing.

In May 2006, a survey of Belding's Savannah Sparrows at Carpinteria Salt Marsh turned up fifty-three territories.

Although the sparrow appears to be holding its own at salt marshes from Devereux Slough to Mugu Lagoon in our region, the fortunes of this little bird follow closely those of the salt marshes in which it dwells.

The light-footed subspecies of the clapper rail, a former resident and breeder at Carpinteria Salt Marsh, has not been regularly observed there since 2004. Because this was the northernmost location where the Light-footed Clapper Rail nested, the salt marsh at Carpinteria is a candidate for future reintroduction of the species. Successful captive breeding programs are in place in other Southern California marshes, and it's hoped the species will one day be able to relocate here.

The problem? Non-native **Red Foxes** (*Vulpes vulpes*), along with Northern Raccoons, Virginia Opossums, and stray pets, all prey on rail eggs and young. At Carpinteria Salt Marsh, these aspects of urbanization must first be mitigated before reintroduction can take place. It is a huge task.

Not all the news is bad, however. In a 2004 survey of Light-footed Clapper Rail numbers throughout Southern California, a census at Mugu Lagoon showed 19 pairs were exhibiting breeding behavior. This is the third-largest breeding population of the species in the state, and it is evidence of the dedication to management and wetlands restoration for the study area at the naval base there. Indeed, throughout Southern California, a total of 163 pairs range-wide in 1989 had grown to a record of 443 pairs by 2007.

Clapper Rails are chestnut-colored,

The endangered Light-footed Clapper Rail has been extirpated from Carpinteria Salt Marsh and is now found only at Mugu Lagoon in our region. Photo by Monte Stinnett

chicken-like birds with long bills. They are secretive, foraging in the marsh in Pickleweed and in nearby brackish water where bulrushes (*Schoenoplectus* spp. and *Bolboschoenus* spp.) and cattails (*Typha* spp.) grow. Rails seek crabs, insects, ghost shrimps, snails, killifish, and even tadpoles for food.

The "clappering" sound that Clapper Rails make, like two wooden sticks beaten together, echoes over the salt marsh, signaling their presence as they sneak through the vegetation. But do not expect to see a Clapper Rail—even if you are surrounded by suitable habitat—unless a particularly high tide flushes one out.

Good nesting habitat is critical to the survival of a rail population. In recent years, Clapper Rails at Mugu Lagoon have nested in scattered stands of **Southwestern Spiny Rush** (*Juncus acutus* subsp. *leopoldii*). In other Southern California marshes, Clapper Rails utilize **California Cord Grass** (*Spartina foliosa*). Nests are subject to flooding in heavy tides and must be situated above high water in order to be successful.

Sunset at Carpinteria Salt Marsh

In a study published in 2008, Lafferty and Kuris estimated the numbers of parasites in salt marshes along the coasts of California and Baja California as follows: approximately 40 percent of the species in any location are parasitic on the 60 percent of species that are free-living.

At Carpinteria Salt Marsh, one particular parasite, a **bird liver fluke** (*Euhaplorchis californiensis*)—a flatworm-like invertebrate—plays a critical role.

First, a fish-eating bird, such as a Snowy Egret, releases the fluke's eggs in its droppings on a mudflat. A California Horn Snail, an intermediate host, eats the feces. The eggs hatch, and the young flukes castrate the horn snail and produce their own offspring. The offspring (cercariae) break out of the snail and swim around, searching for a California Killifish, which is the next host. Entering the fish's body through its gills, the cercaria makes its way through blood vessels to a nerve, which then leads to the brain, where it forms a thin film. This does not harm the killifish—except that it makes the fish perform in a way that is likely to get it caught by a bird: the fish flips and shimmies, swims close to the surface, and maybe even jumps out of the water. These behaviors are not seen in normal killifish in experiments comparing them with parasitized killifish. Thus, the fluke is controlling its host's behavior to facilitate its transmission to the next host—the Snowy Egret. Once the egret devours the killifish, the fluke is transferred from the fish's brain to the bird's gut, where it lives and sends its eggs out to the world in the bird's droppings, and the cycle is complete.

The benefits to the Snowy Egret—the ease of catching more fish and the increased nourishment—offset the disadvantages of having a parasite living in its stomach. The California Horn Snail population benefits similarly: a percentage of their numbers are unable to reproduce due to castration, but this reduced population is kept healthy by having more than enough microalgae on which to feed. If flukes were absent from the marsh, the snail population would nearly double, thinning out the supply of microalgae and making it easier for the snails' predators, such as crabs, to thrive unchecked.

This extraordinary discovery implies that parasites are indeed at the top of some food chains and can function like keystone species. They can control the dominance of some competitors and allow others to coexist. This explains why parasites have been linked to the health of the marsh: if the fluke's life cycle is operating as it should, then it is being transmitted from one host to another. Would there be fewer birds in the marsh if not for the readily available supply of California Killifish, and could the birds catch the fish as easily were the fish not parasitized?

The bird liver fluke is only one of many parasites living in the salt marsh that affect the lives of waterbirds and other animals. *Sacculina carcini*, a type of barnacle, starts out as a free-swimming larva and then, when it finds a crab host, crawls in and takes up residence. As it settles into the crab's body, it grows rootlike tendrils that feed on nutrients dissolved in the crab's blood. Eventually, the barnacle forms a bulge on the underside of the crab's shell. The crab goes about life seemingly unchanged, but it cannot reproduce, nor can it molt or grow. It simply eats to feed itself and the parasite that controls it. As a parasite, *Sacculina carcini* changes the crab's life completely. One difference between it and the bird liver fluke is that *Sacculina* only lives within one host, while *Euhaplorchis* must transmit itself via several hosts in the salt marsh.

* * *

At the end of the day, as the sun sets on the salt marsh, most of the birds have departed. The remaining shorebirds cease their clamoring and fly to the higher stands of Pickleweed to roost together. Egrets and herons have gone, leaving only the occasional Black-crowned Night-Heron to stand silently on the edge of the bank, hoping for a last unwary killifish to swim its way.

Meanwhile, the rising tide floods the mudflats. All the shallow channels are full of seawater now, and the deeper ones in the high marsh are inundated as well.

Striped Shore Crabs retire to their burrows and close off their entrances. The tiny, conical horn snails look motionless, but they are entwining themselves in the green algae for shelter from the advancing water. Other snail species retreat into their shells completely.

A stillness settles over the marsh. The sea breeze has calmed. Pickleweed and Jaumea, their pores under stress of hot sun during daylight hours, welcome the cool night.

But beneath the mud, it might as well be midday. The clams, sensing the approach of a fresh supply of nutrients, prepare to receive the meal of microscopic diatoms and algae delivered to them twice a day on the rising tide. Their siphons are open and ready.

Likewise, the worms prepare to reap the benefits of the influx of seawater. They wriggle to the tops of their burrows or let the surge carry them, swimming freely.

Welcoming the oxygen-fresh tide, the commensals—crabs, worms, and fish living in the burrows of other organisms—become alert at the prospect of leftovers from the host's next meal.

Soon, dusk envelops the salt marsh entirely. The watery channels and dark vegetation become one featureless landscape. The only sound to disturb the silence is the gentle lapping of the rising tide against the muddy banks.

Although it is night, a coastal wetland never sleeps.

CHAPTER 6: COASTAL PLAIN AND FOOTHILLS—OUR SPECIAL SHRUBS

 Most of us in the Santa Barbara region live on the coastal plain. From here, we have a view of the foothills, then upwards to the steeper mountain slopes. Whether you live in Ventura, Santa Barbara, or San Luis Obispo, you see on those foothills a patchwork of shrubs. Some are gray, some green, some waist-high, some taller, but trees are mostly absent. Here, the sun is too hot, the soil too poor, and the rainfall too sparse to support many trees.

These hardy bushes, however, are known for their resilience. They can withstand drought and fire; they thrive in long, hot summers and short, wet winters. When it does rain, these shrubs help control flooding on steep slopes; their roots stabilize the soil and rocks, preventing erosion.

Composed of two major types—**coastal sage scrub** and **chaparral**, these plant communities are similar to shrublands found in the few other spots in the world where a Mediterranean climate predominates. They are the signature vegetation types found in much of Central and Southern California.

Furthermore, these two habitats—coastal sage scrub and chaparral—often border suburban residences. These native shrubs may grow right outside your door, across the street, or in a neighboring open space. And, they harbor unique insects and animals.

Birds of coastal sage scrub and chaparral may scratch in the leaf litter under bushes outside your window, while butterflies and beetles feast on flowers in your backyard. Snakes and lizards may bask in the sun on your patio or hide in your woodpile. These birds, insects, and animals are the companions of daily life in much of the Santa Barbara region.

Furthermore, coastal sage scrub and chaparral will be the first native vegetation you come to as you explore our wilderness trails.

Coastal sage scrub on the south-facing slopes of the Santa Rita Hills east of Lompoc

Park at trailheads at Montaña de Oro, or on the coastal slope of the Santa Ynez Mountains behind Santa Barbara, or at Arroyo Verde Park in Ventura. Look around you. Gaze upslope at what's growing there. Follow the trail as it threads upward through a maze of gray, pungent sagebrush, and then winds higher still into the tall bushes of chaparral. Listen for the songs of chaparral birds. Absorb the warmth and the smells of these wild brushlands in late winter and spring.

Understand that this scrub vegetation is a part of California's special heritage, a form of wilderness found nowhere else in North America.

Coastal Sage Scrub

If you follow a path inland from the beach or start hiking at a trailhead at the base of our coastal foothills, you'll be surrounded by coastal sage scrub.

Once you are familiar with the soft stems and fragrant leaves of coastal sage scrub crumpled in your hand or brushing against your jeans, they become an essential and beautiful part of the hiking experience. Many

of the leaves look gray because they have minute hairs that protect from the sun. The smell and feel of the shrubs, combined with the understated beauty of their flowers, transform "boring, gray bushes" into a habitat worth exploring.

Coastal sage scrub is made up of soft-leaved subshrubs that grow waist-high on shallow soils, usually from sea level to 3,000 foot elevation. These plants are adapted to soil that retains little water. Their roots are not deep. They rely on moisture from summer fog to reduce the stress of evaporation.

In order to withstand the long, dry summer, some of the shrubs are drought-deciduous; their leaves may shrivel up and fall off during the summer, but the plant will not die.

In typical coastal sage scrub, the three dominant plants are California Sagebrush, Black Sage, and **Purple Sage** (*Salvia leucophylla*). California Sagebrush smells like spicy licorice. Black Sage and Purple Sage exude a more delicate odor, similar to lavender. A fourth species, **White Sage** (*Salvia apiana*), has long stalks of tiny flowers; the leaves are delicious to flavor food.

Colorful blossoms lure hikers to coastal sage scrub, especially from March through June. The delicate orange flowers of **Bush Monkeyflower** (*Mimulus aurantiacus*) mix with the pale pink puffballs of **California Buckwheat** (*Eriogonum fasciculatum*). Yellow-and-orange-petaled Deerweed forms thickets. More noticeable in fall is Coyote Brush, with its bright green leaves and white tufts at the tips of the branches—not flowers but the

Purple Sage is a fragrant component of coastal sage scrub.

Coastal sage scrub contrasting with mustard along Suey Creek Road near Santa Maria

seed crowns, or pappi, of the female plants.

One plant of coastal sage scrub that should be avoided by humans is **Poison Oak** (*Toxicodendron diversilobum*). The oils contained in this shrub with shiny, green leaves in clusters of three cause severe skin irritation. It often grows in moister areas, at the base of little swales and in sheltered arroyos, and sometimes like a vine, reaching high into the canopy. In fall the leaves of Poison Oak turn vibrant red, dropping off by winter.

Birds, however, are immune to Poison Oak. Many species eat the berries of Poison Oak because of their nutritious, waxy coating. Some swallow the berries, digest the coating, and later defecate the seeds. Also, Poison Oak provides a tangled understory that ground-nesting birds, such as Wrentits, towhees, and juncos, use for cover and protection.

Coastal sage scrub includes a number of plants that are not sages; in fact, we could simply call it coastal scrub in some parts of the Santa Barbara region, where the sages are not as dominant.

For example, if you're driving south along US 101 between Santa Barbara and Ventura, notice the plants that grow on the ocean bluffs there: **Lemonade Berry** (*Rhus integrifolia*), **Giant Wild-Rye** (*Elymus condensatus*), **Coast Sunflower** (*Encelia californica*), and **Coastal Prickly-Pear** (*Opuntia littoralis*). This is coastal sage scrub, minus the sages.

Coastal sage scrub may grow near the coast or farther inland. Whether bordering the salt marsh at Morro Bay or growing along the hillsides of the wide Santa Maria, Santa Ynez, and Santa Clara valleys, coastal sage scrub forms patterns on the lower hills, often interfingering with chaparral or grassland.

Inland, in the upper drainages of the larger rivers, such as the Cuyama or the Santa Clara, coastal sage scrub survives on dry ridges or rocky outcrops—places where the soil is poor and the sun is hot. But always it is within reach of cooling fogs which sneak in from the ocean on summer mornings, often as far as sixty miles from the coast in some of the larger valleys.

Coastal sage scrub at Cerro Cabrillo trailhead in Morro Bay State Park, with Bush Monkeyflower and Purple Sage

Lemonade Berry is one of the more common shrubs in coastal sage scrub.

One of the best examples of pure coastal sage scrub habitat can be found at Cerro Cabrillo trailhead in Morro Bay State Park. Here, along the Park Ridge Trail off South Bay Boulevard, you can enjoy the view of Morro Bay while walking through a classic, fragrant collection of coastal sage shrubs.

Chaparral

In South Africa, they call it "fynbos," in Chile it is "mattoral," in the Mediterranean "maquis" or "garrigue," in Australia "kwongan," and in California it is "chaparral." Our chaparral is unique, but it is similar to other shrub vegetation types that flourish in Mediterranean climates.

California chaparral is a taller, stronger, more resilient neighbor of coastal sage scrub. It reaches higher on mountain slopes and it can take a lot of abuse. It has been misunderstood as our "enemy" because it is prone to wildfires. But chaparral forms the backbone of an ecosystem so special and fragile that scientists everywhere are concerned for its preservation.

Chaparral has been called an "elfin forest" by several authors, including Francis M. Fultz, who in 1927 wrote one of the first books describing it, *The Elfin-Forest of California:*

A typical chaparral-covered hillside along Upper Sespe Creek, with a Bigcone Spruce in the middle distance

> The chaparral is very dear to me now, but when I first "hit the trail" that led me into it, it did not strike me at all favorably. And everything about it was so new and strange that I almost felt as if I were in another world. Of the "brush" of which it was composed, there was scarcely a familiar form, and it was all so harsh and unyielding that it aroused a certain feeling of hostility within me. I knew, however, that the feeling was unjust, for I was fully aware the chaparral was a forest-cover designed by Nature as the best possible means for the conservation of the land. I knew, too, the proper thing for me to do was to down the unfriendly feeling and make an honest effort to get acquainted.

View from the top of Refugio Road with Woolly Paintbrush and Chaparral Clematis in foreground

We look at the chaparral every day if we live in almost any portion of the Santa Barbara region, but how many of us take the time to understand what it is, how it works, and what animals live there?

Chaparral is not the name of a particular plant. Over one hundred species of plants comprise chaparral. The term "chaparral" comes from *chaparro*, a word Spaniards in California used to describe places where scrub oaks grew.

Chaparral shrubs are rugged and woody. They grow in patches on south-facing slopes of the coastal foothills and interior mountains of San Luis Obispo, Santa Barbara, and Ventura counties. Examples of chaparral are found on the Santa Lucia, San Rafael, Santa Ynez, and Topatopa mountains, and the Upper Sespe Creek drainage. Our region's backcountry includes miles and miles of watershed, much of it wild and unpopulated, which is covered by chaparral.

Because many of our mountain ranges run in an east-west direction, there can be a distinct difference between vegetation on the south side versus the north side. Direct sunlight on south-facing slopes contributes to warmer air, warmer soil, less available moisture, and shorter plant stature. In contrast, the north slopes of mountains, with cooler air and cooler soil, retain more moisture and produce taller, denser vegetation. Therefore, many of our foothill slopes are covered with coastal sage scrub or chaparral on the south side, but on the north side they support oaks or even conifers (especially at higher elevations). One study site in a fifty-meter transect at Sedgwick Reserve in the Santa Ynez Valley found fifty-five species of plants on a north-facing slope, but only twelve on the adjacent south-facing slope.

Red Toyon berries brighten winter chaparral and serve as an important food source for birds and mammals.

Chaparral Shrubs

Chaparral is made up of thick, impenetrable stands of evergreen shrubs six to fifteen feet high, with stout trunks and tightly braided branches. As the bushes age, the dead branches may drop off and die—a sort of self-pruning adaptation to conserve energy. Chaparral does most of its growing in the winter rainy season. Deep taproots allow the plants to use subterranean water, while horizontal surface roots are able to lap up a passing thundershower.

From June until the first winter rains, the merciless sun beats down on chaparral shrubs. Their defense is in their evergreen, **sclerophyllous**

Chamise is one of the most widespread chaparral shrubs and forms extensive stands throughout the region.

178

leaves (reinforced with sclerenchyma, a special supportive, protective tissue). Although these shrubs are not summer-deciduous, like some of those in coastal sage scrub, their leaves may grow at a vertical angle to the sun. This diminishes the direct effect of the sun's rays. When the shrubs reach maturity, many of the leaves are naturally protected by the shade the tall crowns form when interlaced with neighboring shrubs.

For this discussion, let's pick five of the dominant chaparral shrubs.

Chamise (*Adenostoma fasciculatum*) is one of the most abundant. Its small, needle-shaped leaves of green are arranged in clusters along the erect stems. Creamy white miniature flowers form a mass of blossoms at the ends of the stems. Compared to many other chaparral shrubs, Chamise is a relatively late bloomer, flowering in June, after which the plants take on a reddish-brown hue from the dried-up flowers and fruits. Chamise is the top chaparral shrub in its ability to survive drought, heat, and fire, and as such it can be found in extensive stands throughout the region.

Toyon is known for beautiful red berries and dark green leaves that grace chaparral hillsides from November through March. In winter, American Robins, Hermit Thrushes, Cedar Waxwings, and other birds strip the berries from the bushes for food, thereby spreading them here and there throughout the chaparral.

Ceanothus (*Ceanothus* spp.) rivals Chamise as the most widespread shrub of the chaparral. When in full bloom, the ceanothus display is superb. To quote Francis Fultz, "The slopes of the Santa Ynez Range, back of Santa Barbara, are famous for their widespread Ceanothus. In late February and early March the mountains just back of the town are usually white for miles with its bloom."

In this passage, he is describing **Big-pod Ceanothus** (*Ceanothus megacarpus*) shrubs, which boast pure white, fluffy cloaks of blossom. Each little flower is tiny, but when clustered on the ends of the branches, they cover the plants

Greenbark Ceanothus is often found on north-facing slopes of local mountains.

Big-pod Ceanothus cloaks the south-facing chaparral slopes of the Santa Ynez Mountains with masses of white, fluffy blossoms every spring.

Hoaryleaf Ceanothus (blue) and Hairy Ceanothus (white) along East Camino Cielo

Older specimens of Bigberry Manzanita can attain a height of twenty feet or more.

cream, blue, or purple depending upon the species. Up on East Camino Cielo, look for the creamy **Hoaryleaf Ceanothus** (*Ceanothus crassifolius*) and the deep blue **Hairy Ceanothus** (*Ceanothus oliganthus*).

If you walk through a ceanothus patch in bloom, the sweet smell of the flowers is overpowering. Clouds of a variety of native bees hover at the blooms; listen to the loud humming of insects going about the important business of pollination.

Another noise, that of the ceanothus fruits popping, takes over later in the season when ripe, dried-out seeds burst from their pods, flying through the air to land beneath the shrubs. Chaparral dwellers such as mice, woodrats, and a variety of birds feed on the ceanothus seeds.

Of all the chaparral shrubs, **manzanita** (*Arctostaphylos* spp.) is the easiest to recognize. Its lovely reddish-brown bark peels away from a thick, tall trunk. Like ceanothus, many varieties of manzanita grow in our area. **Bigberry Manzanita** (*Arctostaphylos glauca*) may attain a height of twenty feet or more. Manzanita flowers, usually pinkish-white and shaped like little lanterns, hang down from the branches. They attract a variety of insects and hummingbirds.

The fruits of manzanita—"little apple" in Spanish—nourish several chaparral animals. The common name Bearberry reflects the fondness of the American Black Bear for these berries. The scat of many chaparral animals, including the black bear, Coyote, and **Common Gray Fox** (*Urocyon cinereoargenteus*), shows the

in a white mist. Gradually, over a period of days, the white mist works its way up the hills to the very top of the ridge, a steadily rising tide of what is sometimes referred to as "Santa Barbara snow."

Ceanothus blossoms may be white,

remains of the manzanita fruits they have eaten.

Both ceanothus and manzanita are represented by many species in California. Botanists tell us that they have evolved very recently, and a number of species of each are found in small areas on particular soils in our region, and nowhere else in the world. Another characteristic ceanothus and manzanita have in common is that the many, many different species are split fifty-fifty in the way they reproduce after a fire. Half **resprout** from a burl (a woody, underground part at the base of the plant) and half of them are **nonsprouters**, or "seeders," reproducing from seeds buried in the soil. This anomaly within a certain type of plant is highly unusual and may indicate they are still developing in their response to fire. (See "Fire in Shrublands" in this chapter.)

There are seven species of **scrub oak** in the region. This may be the prickliest, toughest plant of all. A miniature oak, from the same genus as the majestic oak trees of oak woodlands, it looks nothing like them. It is squat and head-high, with green leaves often edged in miniature spines. Like those of all oaks, its fruits are acorns that fall out of the cups that hold them to the branchlets. Chaparral animals relish the fallen acorns.

On serpentine soils (see Chapter 2), the **Leather Oak** (*Quercus durata* var. *durata*) can occasionally be found. Look for it on the hike to Goat Rock from Ranger Peak east of Figueroa Mountain, here at the southern limit of its range.

Many other shrubs of the chapar-

ral plant community are beautiful, important, and cannot be mentioned here due to space limitations. A good reference book on the subject is *Introduction to California Chaparral* by Ronald Quinn and Sterling Keeley, in the California Natural History Guides series from the University of California Press.

Nature Journal
June 15, 1954

Hike to Manzana Narrows out of Nira Campground, San Rafael Wilderness

(This account is written from memory, with help from a little notebook I wrote in and saved all these years.)

My father taught me to love the chaparral. Since childhood, he was fascinated by the wild, isolated backcountry of the upper Sisquoc River—what is now the San Rafael Wilderness.

Dad was at home in chaparral. The spiny shrubs and the silence spoke to him. Like the Western Fence Lizard, he could withstand hot temperatures easily and he survived on a swallow or two of water, even during the longest hikes.

Dad knew the secrets of chaparral country: the best swimming holes on Manzana Creek, the hidden caves with Chumash paintings that only a few had visited. He had bushwhacked his way through all this country. No trail was too steep or too brushy.

The land of the chaparral filled his imagination. His enthusiasm for what others considered a hot, dry wasteland was boundless.

I will never forget my first backpacking trip into chaparral country with Dad and my sister, Ellen.

Knowing the backcountry as well as he did, he was sure we would be thrilled to be hiking along the hot, dusty trail up the Manzana to the Narrows, where we were to camp overnight, then go up onto the lower portion of what's called Hurricane Deck.

To get ready for the backpacking trip, Dad had gone downtown to the old Army surplus store on State Street and purchased "backpacks" for us two girls. They were actually made of two small wooden dowels with straps between them, designed to hold a sleeping bag. This was long before recreational camping gear of the type we have today had been invented, and, having served overseas for four years in World War II, Dad had plenty of his own gear, including his original sleeping bag, that he wanted to keep using.

So we set off one hot, hot June morning, and I'll never forget the smell of the chaparral and how it came right down to the creek. Sycamores and alders gave shade by the creek, but the trail wandered up and down, as I recall, often leaving the creek for long distances.

This is when I got to know the chaparral. This is when I got a good case of poison oak. This is when I learned what it was like to be tired and thirsty.

But with Dad, you forgot how tired and thirsty you were, because nothing was boring or taken for granted. His enthusiasm for the natural world, the endless exclamations of joy when he was hiking in the chaparral country, were contagious. He told us stories of California Condors soaring over these rugged cliffs. He told us about riding with vaqueros (wearing "chaps") through the toughest scrub-oak brush imaginable to round up wild cattle that had escaped from the ranch.

And then he conjured up the Chumash and all that he knew, which was considerable, about their lifeways and the ceremonies held, perhaps, in nearby rock formations.

The hot, deserted chaparral backcountry was transformed into a faraway kingdom for us girls. Its mythology, its wonders, revealed only to those who spent time there, were infused with our father's reverence for it.

At last, when we reached the Manzana Narrows, we set up camp. Dad produced dinner from his backpack. No open fires were allowed and we didn't have a camp stove, so dinner consisted of dried fruit, crackers, and a snack bar.

I lay awake most of the night, listening to Manzana Creek as it tumbled through the boulders nearby. The smell of the big bay trees growing there filled the cool night air.

Next morning, we walked up the White Ledge trail towards the Deck. It was another warm day. Ellen and I were dragging.

But Dad would have none of it. He promised to show us a secret cave. He hadn't been to this spot in thirty years, but he remembered exactly where it was. Barging right through the thickest patches of chaparral, Dad unerringly led us to the cave.

We were enchanted. We peeked past the shadowed opening of the sandstone rock to where a pastel, reddish drawing was barely discernible in the gloom.

A god, proclaimed my father. A sacred spot where the Chumash worshipped. We stepped back in awe.

The hissing sound of a juvenile rattlesnake broke the silence. Engrossed in the magic, I had nearly stepped on the little snake, which lay coiled at my feet. Some say that the bite of a young *rattlesnake is even more venomous than an adult's.*

Suddenly, we had plenty of energy to discuss our experience as we walked all the long miles home.

Dad said the snake was guarding the sacred place.

We didn't argue.

A Special Kind of Chaparral at Burton Mesa

Where the sandy soils have been blown by the wind far inland and the cooling fogs provide relief from summer sun, a unique type of chaparral has evolved. Called **maritime chaparral** and locally known as Burton Mesa chaparral, it is found on coastal lowlands and exposed ridges from Monterey to Point Arguello.

Burton Mesa—an area stretching from San Antonio Creek to the Santa Ynez River and inland to La Purísima Mission—is an ecological island of sorts, containing chaparral plants and animals found nowhere else. Among them, thirty-nine animals and twenty-two plants are rare, threatened, or endangered.

Although the reserve is located on private property (much of it on Vandenberg Air Force Base), it includes La Purísima State Historic Park. If you follow trails throughout the park, you will find an accessible portion of the Burton Mesa Ecological Reserve and some of the species described below.

Recall when we were talking about the Aeolian dune sheet in Chapter 4. Here at the state park you are walking

Specialty shrubs found in Burton Mesa Chaparral, clockwise from left: Lompoc Ceanothus, Santa Barbara Ceanothus, and Shagbark Manzanita

Blending perfectly into a background of dry, sandy soil, the Blainville's Horned Lizard can be found in open areas of coastal sage scrub and chaparral.

on the oldest dunes (paleodunes); parts of the sandy soil underfoot were deposited twenty-five thousand to eighty thousand years ago.

The Burton Mesa chaparral is dominated by local endemic species of ceanothus and manzanita. For example, **Lompoc Ceanothus** (*Ceanothus cuneatus* var. *fascicularis*), fluffy bluish-white in bloom, and **Santa Barbara Ceanothus** (*Ceanothus impressus* var. *impressus*), with deep purple blossoms and minuscule leaves with impressed veins, are found nowhere else; and **La Purisima Manzanita** (*Arctostaphylos purissima*) is considered seriously endangered and very rare. You can recognize it by the way

the leaves clasp around the stems of the plant.

One of the most interesting aspects of the reserve is the link to plants that are usually found in the desert. Here, at least a hundred miles away from desert habitat, grows the **Sand Almond** (*Prunus fasciculata* var. *punctata*); its nearest relative is found in the Mojave and Colorado deserts. Similarly, the **Blainville's Horned Lizard** (*Phrynosoma blainvillii*, formerly called Coast Horned Lizard) is related to the **Desert Horned Lizard** (*Phrynosoma platyrhinos*). It is believed that desert forms of life spread this far west and this close to the coast during a warming period that occurred in

California's climate twenty-five hundred to five thousand years ago.

Research at Burton Mesa has recently uncovered two forms of life found only here: the **Lompoc Small Blue** (*Philotiella speciosa* subsp. *purisima*) and the **Vandenberg Monkeyflower** (*Mimulus fremontii* var. *vandenbergensis*). The Lompoc Small Blue, one of the tiniest butterflies in California, has pale turquoise underwings bordered by tiny black dots. When it opens its wings, from above they show dark navy blue bordered by white. The monkeyflower, a small annual plant with yellow flowers, was not formally recognized as a separate taxon (a subspecies, in this case) until 2005 and is considered highly endangered.

Fire in Shrublands

In 1836 Richard Henry Dana described Santa Barbara after a fire in *Two Years Before the Mast:*

> The town is certainly finely situated, with a bay in front, and an amphitheatre of hills behind. The only thing which diminishes its beauty is, that the hills have no large trees upon them, they having been all burnt by a great fire which swept them off about a dozen years before, and they had not yet grown up again. The fire was described to me by an inhabitant, as having been a very terrible and magnificent sight. The air of the valley was so heated that the people were obliged to leave the town and take up their quarters for several days upon the beach.

Brushlands do not need to burn, but they frequently do. Lightning strikes or human activities, aided by dry, hot winds and low moisture content in chaparral shrubs, cause wildfires to ignite.

When a wildfire roars through our coastal foothills or erupts over acres of backcountry, destroying almost everything in its path, one's first reaction is of sympathy and sorrow for the lost landscape. These days, unfortunately, the damage may include human structures and even lives. We mourn these disasters.

However, when any ecosystem is disturbed, such as in a massive fire, the terrible destruction is followed by an astonishing renewal of life.

"Rising from the ashes" is a phrase used to denote a new beginning, a fresh start, after adversity or tragedy of some kind. Chaparral plants have a suite of adaptations that assure this: deep root systems, underground structures that assist resprouting, and seeds that can lie dormant for long periods of time.

For example, Toyon is a resprouter. It has an underground structure—a

The Tea Fire near Santa Barbara in November 2008 destroyed many homes.

root crown or burl—which stores water and carbohydrates. After a fire, Toyon resprouts from its base, an advantage because the plant is already well situated, roots are well developed, and the first-year growth is greater than that of a seedling. Most chaparral plants are resprouters.

In contrast, some species of ceanothus and manzanita do not resprout, but instead rely on a dormant seed bank that accumulates during long, fire-free intervals. **Buckbrush** (*Ceanothus cuneatus*) is an example of a seeder.

A few shrubs, such as Chamise, reproduce by both resprouting and seeding. This may be why Chamise is such a widespread shrub in California chaparral.

The Fire Regime

The term "fire regime" refers to the overall pattern of fire in a particular location. The pattern depends upon the **frequency**, **intensity**, **seasonality**, and **spatial pattern** of each fire. The discussion below deals with chaparral, but it also applies to coastal sage scrub.

In earlier times, Native Americans used fire in various habitats to flush deer, clear the ground of shrubs under oaks, and encourage new growth of herbaceous plants, rather than woody plants. They set surface fires in a patchwork, as needed, to clear out shrubbery and promote the new shoots of grasses that would attract game animals, which they hunted for food.

Recently, scientists have taken core samples from sediment deposited in the Santa Barbara Channel and found that over the past six hundred years, large fires—not the small ones set by Native Americans—burned approximately every sixty-five years. Alarmingly, the frequency of chaparral fires increased during the twentieth century and has shot up even more in recent decades.

With human activities making further inroads into chaparral habitats, there appears to be a correlation between human presence and the alarming rise in the frequency of wildfires; humans or their activities start the majority of fires in shrublands, and because residential development breaks up the chaparral into smaller patches, it has become more difficult for the ecosystem to recover after a fire.

There is a myth that chaparral needs frequent fire. Granted, chaparral is resilient to occasional fires, but it must have long intervals in which to recover. Resprouters need time to replenish their underground resources, and seedlings need time to grow tall enough to reproduce on their own.

Human-caused fires are burning the chaparral too often. Modern fires are larger and occur more often than at any other time in our region's history. The first fire that comes through may burn the tops of the plants, but a second fire following, say, in five years—much too soon—may burn all of the seedlings and resprouts.

Another myth is that old stands of chaparral are decadent and pose a significant fire hazard. In other words, they need to burn. Biologists are beginning to examine old-growth chaparral and have found it may be more productive than younger stands. For example, more seeds were produced on a ninety-year-old manzanita than on a twenty-five-year-old. And some manzanitas with burls may be centuries old.

Fire suppression in chaparral ecosystems, unlike in forest ecosystems, does not lead to large fuel accumulations or bigger fires. Big fires will continue to occur, not because of unburned, old-growth chaparral, but because of the millions of people who live in or near this habitat, increasing the likelihood of fires.

Type conversion, a situation where chaparral that has burned too frequently may gradually be replaced by another vegetation type, is a threat. If fire sweeps through the same area more than once in five to ten years, weedy, non-native grasses will begin to infiltrate and take over. Non-native grasses dry out sooner in the spring than the natives and provide a fuel base that promotes additional fires. And soon, the coastal sage scrub and chaparral ecosystems just disappear, leaving a wasteland of annual grasses and weeds.

In addition to frequency, the intensity of fire affects the size and destruction of the burn. South-facing slopes burn more fiercely than north-facing ones, because north-facing slopes are more mesic (moist). Windy, dry Santa Ana conditions produce a fast, hot fire that leaves little unscorched, as do Sundowner winds, which blow over the Santa Ynez Mountains down onto the coastal plain of southern Santa Barbara County—a unique meteorological condition local to our region.

The time of year is important. A majority of fires start in September through December, when Santa Ana winds exacerbate fire conditions. In some ways, however, fall fires are not the most destructive for chaparral. Fires in spring, such as the Jesusita Fire in Santa Barbara in May 2009, are much more damaging. Spring is a time of chaparral growth, and it is the time of year when mammals, birds, and insects first produce their young; what's more, the wait for the rejuvenating moisture of winter rains is longer in spring than in fall.

A mosaic pattern of fire damage, such as burned areas interspersed with non-burned terrain, usually helps in post-fire recovery.

A section of chaparral burned by the Jesusita Fire of May 2009, with only charred stalks remaining

The Fire Cycle

After a fire, the nature of chaparral changes. Gone are the tall, woody, shade-producing shrubs; a moonscape remains. The bare ground is littered with charred pieces of wood from the fire. Ash lies everywhere and gets on your shoes and in your eyes when the wind blows. The dead skeletons

Chamise resprouting from its root crown in February 2010, less than a year after the Jesusita Fire

of burned shrubs stand as depressing reminders that a major disturbance has changed this once-thriving ecosystem into a barren desert.

But wait! This is a chance for renewal. After winter rains, fresh growth brings a mix of different species. An outrageous jumble of colorful blooms turns the wasteland into a flower garden. A temporary spike in biodiversity follows fires, giving rise to **fire followers.** The seeds of these beautiful **annuals**—plants that grow, set seed, and die in one season—may have lain dormant for years, decades, or even centuries, just waiting to be released by certain cues.

Fire followers only bloom after a fire. Their seeds don't respond to typically favorable conditions to germi-

nate, but must wait for the exact cue that breaks their dormancy. For many it is heat shock, but for some it is **scarification** (damage to the seed coat). Also, recent studies show that smoke chemicals, called **karrikins**, stimulate light sensitivity in plants, which encourages germination.

For example, heat shock stimulates **Coastal Lotus** (*Acmispon maritimus*), **Succulent Lupine** (*Lupinus succulentus*), **Caterpillar Phacelia** (*Phacelia cicutaria*), and **Large-flowered Phacelia** (*Phacelia grandiflora*). Charred wood and smoke affect **Whispering Bells** (*Emmenanthe penduliflora*) and **Common Eucrypta** (*Eucrypta chrysanthemifolia*).

Post-fire succession in chaparral regrowth involves different species. First come the fire followers, brightening the hillsides with their multicolored blossoms in the first year or two after a fire. Look for a show of phacelias, lupines, lotus, mariposa lilies, fire poppies, and morning glories.

By the second or third year after a fire, half-shrubs begin to take over. Two to five feet high, they are fast-growing **perennials** (plants that bloom year after year). Five to ten years after a fire, these lower shrubs are shaded out by the true, tall chaparral shrubs.

However, chaparral may respond differently depending upon the severity of a fire and its location. For example, driving up San Marcos Pass (Highway 154) on the south slopes of the Santa Ynez Mountains, you will notice **Coast Morning Glory** (*Calystegia macrostegia*), which has dominated the landscape for many years. It smothers fifteen miles of an area

The Fire Poppy is one of the beautiful fire followers that sprout after a chaparral burn.

Large-flowered Phacelia is another of the plants with seeds that germinate following the heat shock of a wildfire.

Numbers of Lawrence's Goldfinches increase dramatically in post-fire shrublands because they feed on the seeds of fire-following plants. Photo by Peter Gaede

burned by the Gap, Tea, and Jesusita fires in a mass of vines.

Bird response to chaparral wildfire has been studied very little. However, ornithologist Phil Unitt of the San Diego Natural History Museum, surveying chaparral areas burned in 2002 and 2003 in large wildfires in San Diego County, has found that certain birds—like plants—are "fire followers." The most conspicuous is the migratory, sky-blue and rust **Lazuli Bunting** (*Passerina amoena*). The bunting favors the charred branches of previously burned shrubs as excellent lookout perches from which to sing. **Lawrence's Goldfinch** (*Spinus lawrencei*) is another species that increases in numbers in post-fire shrublands, feeding heavily on seeds of fire-following plants. In the case of the **Black-chinned Sparrow** (*Spizella atrogularis*), another migrant, numbers jumped sharply during the second year after the fires.

In an ongoing bird study in Santa Barbara County on the slopes of Big Pine Mountain, which burned in the 2007 Zaca Fire (California's second largest fire in recorded history), a similar phenomenon was noted. In the three years post-fire, large increases in Lazuli Buntings and Lawrence's Goldfinches were recorded. Also, these species were breeding at higher elevations than usual, in patches where the coniferous forest had burned and shrubs were colonizing.

Birds that were most deeply affected by wildfire in the San Diego surveys were the resident birds of the chaparral: **Bushtit** (*Psaltriparus minimus*), **Wrentit** (*Chamaea fasciata*), California Thrasher, and Bewick's

Recent Fires in the Santa Barbara Region

Ventura County

Name	Date	Acreage
Simi Fire	October 2004	108,204
School Fire	November 2005	3,891
Day Fire	September 2006	167,702
Shekell Fire	December 2006	13,600
Sequoia Fire	December 2006	367
Nightsky Fire	October 2007	35
South Fire	October 2008	30
Guiberson Fire	September 2009	17,500

Santa Barbara County

Gaviota Fire	June 2004	7,440
Perkins Fire	June 2006	15,043
Rancho Fire	June 2007	482
Zaca Fire	July 2007	240,207
Mariposa Fire	September 2007	176
Sedgwick Fire	October 2007	710
Tea Fire	November 2008	1,940
Jesusita Fire	May 2009	8,733
La Brea Fire	August 2009	89,489

San Luis Obispo County

El Cerrito Fire	November 2008	60
Lake Fire	July 2009	123

Wren. (See "Birds in the Bushes" in this chapter.) All are weak flyers and could not escape the path of the fire. Being completely suited to mature chaparral, they were slow to reinhabit the more open, post-fire landscape.

Insects of Shrub Communities

Many insects that live in these brushy plant communities have evolved particular adaptations for chaparral life, including their response to periodic wildfires. One of the most interesting has been dubbed the **Fire Beetle** (*Melanophila occidentalis*) because of its attraction to byproducts of combustion. Fire beetles are attracted to fires over long distances by a pair of specialized infrared sensory organs. Detecting the infrared radiation produced by chaparral fires, they immediately fly to the scene, eager to partake of the charred wood and damaged trees, often landing on firefighters.

Fire beetles mate and lay their eggs on the still-warm branches of burned shrubs. The females have glands that exude a special wax on the undersides of their bodies to protect them from getting burned while they deposit eggs deep into the damaged wood. When the eggs hatch, the larvae eat the wood, which helps to decompose it.

A well-known research paper published in 1957 documented the presence of Fire Beetles at cement plants in Southern California, where they congregated in the vicinity of kilns and were known as "stack bugs." They have also been observed swarming around barbecues and football games, the latter in the 1940s and 1950s, when cigarette smoking was in vogue.

Male rain beetles fly low over chaparral, searching for females, soon after the first rain of the season begins to fall.

Another insect unique to chaparral foothills is the **rain beetle** (*Pleocoma* spp.). As soon as the first heavy rain of the season begins to fall, the male rain beetle is stimulated to leave its earthen burrow and fly low over the ground, searching for a female. Some species fly only at dusk and dawn, others fly any time of day as long as it's raining.

The female seldom leaves her burrow, which may be up to six feet underground. However, when the rain begins, the female comes to the burrow's entrance. She emits a strong scent, a **pheromone**, which attracts the male. Down he flies to mate with the female, after which the female plugs the burrow's entrance and retreats deep into the ground to lay her eggs; then she dies. During the following spring, the eggs will hatch and the larvae will feed and grow underground for ten or twelve years. They subsist on the roots of a variety of plants, especially oaks. During the final stage, the larva pupates for

Common Butterflies of Coastal Sage Scrub and Chaparral

1. Pale Swallowtail, *Papilio eurymedon*
2. Sara Orangetip, *Anthocharis sara*
3. California Ringlet, *Coenonympha tullia*
4. Mormon Metalmark, *Apodemia mormo*
5. Gabb's Checkerspot, *Chlosyne gabbii*
6. Mylitta Crescent, *Phyciodes mylitta*
7. Gray Hairstreak, *Strymon melinus*
8. Echo Blue, *Celastrina ladon*
9. Checkered Skipper, *Pyrgus communis*
10. Northern White Skipper, *Heliopetes ericetorum*
11. Callippe Fritillary, *Speyeria callippe*
12. California Dogface, *Colias eurydice*
13. Painted Lady, *Vanessa cardui*
14. Variable Checkerspot, *Euphydryas chalcedona*
15. Common White, *Pieris protodice*
16. Buckeye, *Junonia coenia*

An Insect Primer

The story goes that a prominent theologian once asked a well-known biologist, J. B. S. Haldane, what one could infer about the nature of the Creator from his creation, and the reply was "an inordinate fondness for *beetles!*" He could have responded by saying "insects." Insects are so successful that individuals within a species may number in the millions. Species exist in such numbers that many remain undescribed or unnamed, especially in tropical forests.

One of the secrets to insect success is metamorphosis.

We all learned about metamorphosis in grammar school. The teacher brought the silkworm eggs to class and we watched the eggs hatch into caterpillars (larvae), which then devoured mulberry leaves. Eventually, the larvae spun their silk cocoons (pupae). And then, voila!—a beautiful moth emerged. Metamorphosis is easy to study in the order Lepidoptera, the moths and butterflies. The striking difference in appearance between the homely larva and the gorgeous adult butterfly is a visual delight.

Many insects undergo four stages of life: adults lay eggs, which hatch into caterpillars, maggots, or other larval forms. The **larva** grows by molting several times. Larvae feed on leaves, grasses, even carrion. At the last molt, the **pupa** forms, a stationary, case-like structure—a little purse.

Usually hanging from a branch or other object, the pupa breaks open when the adult insect issues.

Other insects, such as grasshoppers and true bugs, undergo a partial metamorphosis: the immature, called a **nymph**—a subadult resembling the adult—grows in stages, or molts, the last stage being an adult.

Evolutionarily, insects' adaptation to metamorphosis is a key development. By separating the various stages of growth in this way, insects utilize a range of living situations; the larvae exist in a different niche from the adults. In between, the resting stage (known as the **diapause**, which can occur at any of the four stages) provides an opportunity for the insect to wait out unfavorable conditions, such as drought or cold weather. Certain species of insects may wait several years before they complete their life cycle if conditions are not good. What an advantage this is in harsh terrain or an unfavorable climate.

Angiosperms, or flowering plants, have coevolved with animals—particularly insects, but also birds and bats—in pollination partnerships. By visiting flowers to collect nectar and pollen, insects carry pollen from one blossom to another. Thus, at the same time the insects search for food, they contribute to the genetic diversity of the plants by depositing pollen and fertilizing the flowers.

Ceanothus branch with native bumblebee

a short time, then transforms into an adult. Once the larva becomes an adult, it will never eat again: its mouthparts are atrophied and its sole purpose is to reproduce.

By tying its mating cycle to that of the rain, this beetle can remain underground for long periods of time in case of drought.

Pollination in Chaparral

Flower-visiting insects are more abundant and more species-rich in chaparral than in any other type of California vegetation. In a research project in 1977 in Southern California, the numbers of flower-visiting insect species were 309 in mature chaparral, 254 in post-fire chaparral, and 119 in coastal sage scrub. Of those insects, the chief pollinators are the native bees.

Native bees, as differentiated from the well-known non-native **Honey Bees** (*Apis mellifera*), are unfamiliar to the general public. Except for **bumblebees** (*Bombus* spp.), most of our native bees are solitary and do not form hives or have the social organization of the Honey Bee. Native bees build their individual nests in the ground, in cavities in dead wood, or in pithy stems of shrubs. The female bee builds her nest and provides nectar and pollen, which will be used by the larvae once they hatch from eggs. Having done this, she seals up the nest and leaves.

Native bees represent nine major families, including the bumblebees, large carpenter bees, digger or mining bees, small carpenter bees, leafcutter bees, mason bees, and sweat bees.

In a study conducted from 1997 to 1999 at Pinnacles National Monument, located north of our region in one of the inner South Coast Ranges, Olivia Messinger and Terry Griswold found an amazing array of nearly four hundred bee species of fifty-two genera. The rugged landscape, dominated by chaparral, proved incredibly productive for research into the habits and importance of native bees as pollinators.

While bees visit flowers for both nectar and pollen, it is pollen for nest provisions that drives the females in

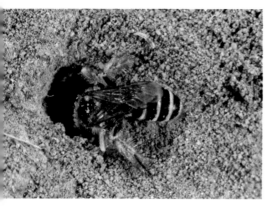

A digger bee entering a burrow in the soft substrate of a trail in the chaparral

particular. Some bees, including the bumblebee, are generalists, collecting from a wide array of plants. Others are specialists, consistently gathering pollen from a single genus or a closely related group of plants.

The bees have tongues of different lengths that determine from which flowers they can best obtain nectar while harvesting pollen. Some bees have structural adaptations for certain plants. Most have an area of stiff hairs, called a pollen brush, into which pollen grains are pushed. One kind of specialist bee, *Diadasia*, accommodates the large pollen grains of **Elegant Clarkia** (*Clarkia unguiculata*) and Coast Morning Glory with

widely spaced hairs in its pollen brush.

Native bees frequent flowers that are bright white, yellow, or blue or have ultraviolet properties. They have keen vision in the UV spectrum. Nectar guides, colorful markings on the petals of a flower, tempt the bees to enter.

Butterflies, moths, birds, and flies are other pollinators of the chaparral. All have their preferences, but most visit a variety of flowering plants. Hummingbirds can see red but bees cannot, so hummers thrust their long bills into red, tubular flowers like the perennials **Scarlet Bugler** (*Penstemon centranthifolius*) and **California Fuchsia** (*Epilobium canum*). Butterflies fly to deep purple or red flowers, usually with petals that have a wide landing pad. Moths prefer white or pink flowers with a strong, sweet odor emitted at night, such as California Buckwheat or **Jimson Weed** (*Datura wrightii*). Flies are attracted to pale, purple, or dark brown flowers. They may pollinate Chamise and various species of ceanothus.

Interestingly, ceanothus and California Buckwheat attract the greatest diversity and number of insect pollinators.

More about Insects of Shrub Communities

Of the thousands of insects found in chaparral, most are inconspicuous. The insects described below are either easy to see or have particularly unique lifestyles suited for shrublands.

The first insect you notice on a hike in the chaparral is the **stink beetle** (*Eleodes* spp.). These large (one inch or more) black beetles belong to the

Darkling Beetle family. When a stink beetle walks slowly across the trail, it often elevates the tip of its abdomen, especially when touched gently with a stick. By displaying its hindquarters in this fashion, the beetle is warning you and any nearby predators that it will emit a stinky, noxious substance as a defense mechanism. And this will happen if, indeed, you have found a true stink beetle. However, other darkling beetles—there are one hundred species in California!—will imitate this stance even if they aren't able to produce the smelly stuff, because it has proved so effective at deterring enemies. So whether you have found a true stink beetle or one of its imitators is up to you to discover.

Stink beetles are a familiar sight on front-country trails through the chaparral.

Keeping your eyes on the trail in more open areas, away from the dense chaparral, you will find one of the native ants of our region, the **harvester ant** (*Messor* spp., named after the Roman god of crops and harvest).

Harvester ants eat the seeds of chaparral plants. They have elaborate underground nests. You might spot the entrance to a nest in the middle of a clearing, marked with a ring of discarded chaff from harvested seeds. The ants work in an area within about thirty feet of their burrow, leaving the husks of the seeds above ground. The presence of this litter enriches the soil, encouraging the growth of microorganisms beneath the surface such as mites, roundworms (nematodes), bacteria, and fungi.

Whenever harvester ants cross your path, you can expect to find Blainville's Horned Lizards. Harvester ants remain the chief food for these lizards and when they are scarce—either

These harvester ants are attempting to move a carabid beetle carcass into their underground home.

because of urban development or an invasion of non-native ants—the lizard population declines and eventually disappears.

In sandy, open areas, perhaps more likely in coastal sage scrub than in thick chaparral, watch for the cone-shaped depressions made by **antlions** (*Myrmeleon* spp.). Like the Blainville's Horned Lizard, the antlion relishes harvester ants.

The antlion itself is a larval form (sometimes called a "doodlebug") of

Funnel-shaped pit created by an antlion larva to trap wayward insects. Inset is a closeup of the antlion larva.

the beautiful, lacy-winged adult. The adult antlion resembles a damselfly or dragonfly, and it does not eat, but only reproduces after a short life of night-flying. The strange-looking larva, however, is a totally different creature. A pale gray, oval-shaped beast with grasping jaws, the antlion larva does all the eating for this species.

By digging a little pit in the soft, sandy soil, the antlion lures the ants to their doom. It hides at the bottom of the pit, concealing itself and its sickle-shaped jaws beneath the sand. When an ant walks into the pit, the sand grains begin to slip inward, trapping the prey. Immediately, the antlion grasps the harvester ant with its jaws and begins to throw more sand onto its victim. The ant is now done for and usually gives up, destined to become food for the ferocious doodlebug. After the antlion has grown

to a certain stage, it makes a cocoon underground, out of which the adult will eventually emerge.

Another interesting bug of coastal sage scrub, often found on Coyote Brush and California Sagebrush, is the **spittle bug** (*Aphrophora* spp.). You can't help but notice the frothy "spit" that the juvenile bug, or nymph, emits as a protective nest as it develops. In certain years, these spittle bug nymphs are everywhere, using their webs of foam to conceal themselves before they eat the leaves of the shrub they were hatched upon. When mature, the very ordinary-looking grayish-brown bugs are capable of flight.

One creature you definitely do not want to touch, if you see it scurrying across the ground, is the **velvet ant** (*Dasymutilla* spp.). This is not an ant, but a female wasp that lacks wings (the males do have them). Velvet ants look

198

The foamy blobs of juvenile spittle bugs are a familiar sight on Coyote Brush. If you push aside the "spit," you can observe the nymph, pictured in the close-up.

so soft, with their bright red, plush bodies. They are seen singly in sandy openings in the chaparral. Don't pick them up because they have a very painful sting.

Another family of wasps, the **gall wasps** (family Cynipidae), is not found on the ground. They leave evidence of their presence on the stems and leaves of chaparral and a variety of other plants, in the form of galls. Galls are swollen plant tissue and come in an array of mind-boggling shapes, from pin-sized pimples to lumps to misshapen bumps on the leaves or stems of a plant.

A female gall wasp pierces the surface of the plant tissue with her **ovipositor** (egg-laying body part, also the stinger in bees, ants, and stinging wasps), then lays her eggs. A gall forms to envelop each wasp egg after it is deposited. Each species of gall wasp can be recognized by the shape and color of the gall that encases it, which is fortunate because the tiny adult wasps are rarely noticed.

The gall really starts to become larger once the hungry larva hatches and begins feeding. It's the chewing

The velvet ant is not an ant but a wasp.

The tiny gall of the Urchin Gall Wasp

"Oak apples" are conspicuous galls on oaks.

of the larva that releases chemical compounds which redirect the plant tissues to form the protective outer parts of the gall. After several months of development in these perfect larval nurseries, the adult wasps emerge to live for about a week without feeding.

In the chaparral, round, red "oak apples" are common on scrub oaks. On the inside the galls are corky, full of nutrients for the larvae to feed on. Interestingly, gall wasps may produce one generation with both male and female offspring in the spring, and then in the fall they may asexually (without fertilization from a male) produce another generation, of wingless females only. Also, several species of gall wasp may share the same gall without harming the wasp that first formed it. Others may lay eggs that parasitize the first wasp. Another may parasitize the parasite (a hyperparasite), and a moth larva may even eat the whole gall. It is reported that California has more recognized Cynipid wasps than North Africa, Northern Europe, and Asia combined.

Evidently the galls do not harm oaks unless the trees are diseased or stressed.

Two Moths: The Yucca and the Ceanothus

These two moths have fascinating lifestyles completely adapted to the chaparral. One, the Yucca Moth, is so tiny it's difficult to see. The other, the Ceanothus Silk Moth, is so large it's difficult to miss, but it flies only at night.

The **Yucca Moth** (*Tegeticula maculata*) has a partnership with the **Chaparral Yucca** (*Hesperoyucca whipplei*) that benefits both of them, a perfect example of **symbiosis**. "Obligate mutualism" is another term that means each of the two species needs the other to survive.

The tall Chaparral Yuccas that march up and down our hillsides with their creamy spires of blossoms are pollinated by the Yucca Moth. Until recently, scientists thought that each yucca species was pollinated by its own moth species, but they are now finding, with the help of DNA, that there may be more than one species involved.

In order to pollinate a flower, an insect must climb into it to reach the pollen. But yucca pollen is particularly difficult to deal with: it's sticky and comes in long strands. Most insects avoid it. The female Yucca Moth has a specially curled mouthpart that she uses to roll the pollen into a neat ball after scraping it from the anther of the male flower. She then flies off to the next yucca flower.

Here, she places the pollen on the female part of the flower, the stigma.

Chaparral Yucca: an "insect hotel"

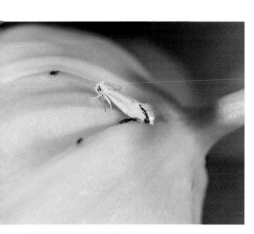

Female Yucca Moth

Then the Yucca Moth moves to the base of the ovary, where the seeds will develop following fertilization, and here she lays her eggs by piercing the ovary wall with her ovipositor. In this way, she has deposited her eggs as near as possible to the place where the seeds will develop. The larvae eat yucca seeds in order to survive.

Inside the ovary, the seeds and the Yucca Moth larvae grow. When the larvae emerge from the ovary, they drop to the ground and burrow into the soil. After a year, when the yucca plant blossoms again, they come out as short-lived adults.

The special point to remember: there are many more seeds produced by the yucca plant than are eaten by the Yucca Moth larvae. The plant gives up a few seeds, comparatively speaking, in exchange for efficient pollination by the moth.

All of the yuccas in a given spot may bloom simultaneously, but we don't know why, or what month they can be counted upon to bloom in. Perhaps by flowering all at once, the yucca sends a signal to the Yucca Moth that now is a good time for pollination. Or maybe the moths themselves are the impetus for mass bloom, visiting the flowers and keying them to bloom in unison.

The **Ceanothus Silk Moth** (*Hyalophora euryalus*) has a completely different lifestyle. It is large, with a five-inch wingspan, and splendidly marked. Ceanothus is the host plant for its frightening-looking caterpillar. Thus, it is a true chaparral native. The stunning adults are difficult to spot unless you see them flying at dusk or dawn.

The Ceanothus Silk Moth has a five-inch wingspan.

During spring nights, the female Ceanothus Silk Moth emits a chemical scent from glands protruding from her abdomen. These pheromones spreads far and wide over the chaparral, beckoning the males. Once a male has found her, and mates, the female withdraws the glands. Then other males will not be attracted to her.

The adults have thus completed their sole purpose—to mate and reproduce. Once the eggs are laid, the adults will die. They have no mouthparts and cannot feed. But watch for the green, four-inch caterpillars as they devour ceanothus leaves in late spring and summer, before they spin their cocoons on the plant in fall.

The Famous Local Timema

Most people have never heard of a timema. This green, brown, or pinkish creature is an atypical member of the Walkingstick clan (Order Phasmatodea) and it has local significance.

In 1993, when UC Santa Barbara biologist Cristina Sandoval was a graduate student, she discovered a new species of the timema, subsequently named *Timema cristinae* in her honor. But that alone wasn't enough to satisfy Sandoval, who wanted to do further research on timemas.

Some timemas are green with stripes on them, some are plain. Some are brown, some are gray. Sandoval was intrigued by whether these characteristics were passed on to the insects' offspring. Much to her and her colleagues' surprise, they found a possible example of how a species is formed.

Part of the answer may be in the mating habits. When a male timema is looking to mate, he crouches on top of the female and tickles her antennae with his own, while stroking her abdomen with his feet. If this feels good, she'll mate with him, but if not, she'll run from him. Somehow, the genes that influence mating preferences are passed along with the genes that determine what the timema looks like. Thus, if striped timemas only mate with other striped ones, and plain timemas mate with plain, two separate species of timemas will be created over time.

The species formation is reinforced by predators, because either you're a plain-backed timema that blends perfectly with your green ceanothus leaf, or you're a timema with a yellow stripe down the back, perfect for straddling the needle-like Chamise leaf. Any timema with an "in between" appearance (i.e., a product of the striped and the plain timema) will be gobbled up by a bird or a lizard, while any timema that is perfectly camouflaged will survive to reproduce more of its kind. If interbreeding between striped and plain varieties ceased, then two species would exist, not one.

Cristina Sandoval proved this in experiments with timemas. Over and over, the striped timemas, when placed on the wrong bush, were eaten. The striped *Timema cristinae* dominated on Chamise because it matched its background completely, and birds and lizards didn't notice it. On the other hand, the plain *T. cristinae* dominated on ceanothus.

Cristina's Timema, named after biologist Cristina Sandoval, who first described the species

Nature Journal
June 1, 2010

Trip up Highway 33, Ventura County

On a day of deep, wet marine layer at the coast, we leave the June gloom and set out to explore up Highway 33 in Ventura County. This is one of the emptiest and most beautiful highways in our region; it weaves its way through undisturbed, pure stands of chaparral. And, as the road leaves the citrus orchards of Ojai behind, the sun peeks out.

Following Highway 33, we snake through the tunnels at Wheeler Gorge, where water glistens as it runs down the steep rock face right by the highway.

For the next eight miles or so, the road climbs steeply in hairpin turns. If you go, be sure to notice the thick, solid covering of chaparral on these south-facing slopes. The green mantle of shrubs is uniform until you look at it through binoculars and realize that the different colors of green and the different growth habits translate into a collection of many species. The dominant shrubs are Chamise and scrub oak.

Along the roadway, white Matilija Poppies with orange centers burst from the rocky cliffs or grow in clumps at the turnouts.

An interloper in the form of Spanish Broom—an introduced non-native shrub—shows bright yellow blossoms. Too many of our hillsides host this invader from the Mediterranean.

But back to the chaparral. What other vegetation could take the punishment of the sun on hot summer days here, or keep these precipitous hillsides from eroding away after heavy rains? This is chaparral at its finest, burgeoning with new growth after a wet winter.

At the top of the grade climbing out of the Matilija North Fork drainage, the view of the immense sandstone rock formations of Pine Mountain Ridge makes you realize you're in another watershed, that of the wild Sespe Creek. Fed by tributaries issuing from the mass of Pine Mountain Ridge, the Sespe will make its way far to the east of us before it enters the Santa Clara River at Fillmore.

At this pass from the Matilija into the Sespe you are on Dry Lakes Ridge, where a steep firebreak trail leads west up the hill. Botanists hike up there to study the rare flowers around the dry lakes.

Today, we are bound for one of the shallow creeks that flow into the Sespe: Derrydale Creek. This creek is particularly inviting, although it lacks a maintained trail. The Wolf Fire swept through here in 2002, but you can still squeeze through gaps in the resprouted chaparral shrubs and some of the fire-following annuals persist in more open places.

Climbing up into the canyon, we tally three species of milkweed. The common one is narrow-leaved and green, the other two have gray, hairy leaves and purple-centered flowers. The Palmer Mariposa Lily, a pale white cup with a little yellow cross inside, found chiefly in Ventura County, is on the endangered list.

Two male blue-and-orange Lazuli Buntings sing their buzzy trills perched on the tops of the burned stalks of scrub oaks, which are now almost engulfed by growth at their bases.

Penstemons and gilias add purple and pink to the color scheme; I have never seen the chaparral this beautiful. The creek is flowing well, the day is cool and sunny, and the place is deserted. Perfect.

Looking back from where we've come, we can see the north side of the chaparral ridge where we left the car down on Highway 33. From this distance, it's easy to understand the difference in moisture between north and south slopes in the chaparral. Bigcone Spruce trees cling to the shady, moist canyons, and healthy, big ceanothus bushes covered in blue blossoms proliferate on the north slope.

But the outstanding feature of this hike turns out to be the insect life.

The California Dogface Butterfly (the California state butterfly) would be a new one for me. At last we spot several of them: medium-sized butterflies, constantly on the move, but I get my binoculars on one and see the dog-face pattern on a bright orange background. A life butterfly! The host plant for the California Dogface is False Indigo, a common shrub of montane chaparral, and we notice several.

On the return down the trail, we discover a tall yucca that cries out for inspection. This is the highlight of the day! So many insects in the white-petaled flowers of the yucca, and so many insects crawling up and down the stem! It's an apartment house of insect activity from top to bottom.

At the top of the yucca, much higher than my head, are red dots of Convergent Lady Beetles feeding on the aphids that coat the blossoms up there. Examining the open white flowers farther down the stalk, we see soldier beetles, a few California Carpenter Bees (which often nest in dry, dead yucca stalks), some tiny black thrips, and the most sought-after of all: the female Yucca Moth. This delicate moth, three-eighths of an inch long, is pure white with black wing tips. Watching the moth, it hardly seems a candidate for the important task of pollinating the yucca. Of course, there are many, many of its kind hard at work on that same yucca, but it seems a Herculean task.

Along with the true Yucca Moth, we probably saw bogus yucca moths. Difficult to identify because they can be variously colored, they don't have a role in yucca pollination. They simply live on the yucca and their larvae burrow into the stalk.

Further "downstairs" in the yucca, at the base of the stem where it rises from the rosette of spiky leaves, big black Yucca Weevils feed off the sticky sap. Carpenter ants scurry up and down the thick stalk.

Another new insect for me, the Timema cristinae, scuttles away into the base of the plant. It's the brown form, not the typical green one, but I don't care. Just the fact that I know the biologist after whom this timema is named is a thrill.

By the time we leave, we have decided that the Chaparral Yucca in bloom wins the prize for the busiest, most compelling "house of insects" in the chaparral ecosystem.

Insect Species We Saw

- California Dogface
- Convergent Lady Beetle (Hippodamia convergens)
- Soldier beetle (Cantharus spp.)
- California Carpenter Bee (Xylocopa californica)
- Thrips (Order Thysanoptera)
- Yucca Moth (Tegeticula maculata)
- Bogus yucca moth (Prodoxus spp.)
- Yucca Weevil (Scyphophorus yuccae)
- Carpenter ant (Camponotus spp.)
- Cristina's Timema

Itchy Insects of the Chaparral

Exploring the chaparral in springtime has some challenges, among them the **canyon flies** (*Fannia* spp.), also known as **eye flies**.

Canyon flies drive hikers crazy because they hover annoyingly around your head. These are tiny flies (one-eighth inch or less), and they look for moisture by trying to get into your eyes, ears, nose, or mouth. Never seeming to land, and not biting, they are still a nuisance. However, they are a fixture in dry chaparral, especially in spring.

Ticks, on the other hand, should be taken seriously. Related to spiders, ticks live in brushy areas where they cling to the tips of plants, searching for a host animal. They are sensitive to vibration and carbon dioxide levels, and if a deer, dog, or human passes by, they wave their legs in the air, hoping to clasp on. After attaching itself to the skin of the host, the tick feeds on the host's blood. As the tick feeds, its sack-like body becomes engorged with blood, often tripling in size. When full, the adult tick falls off and goes through a number of stages and successive molts as it matures.

The **Pacific Coast Tick** (*Dermacentor occidentalis*) is the common one found here, but several other

Southern Alligator Lizard with ticks attached to the side of its head. Ticks that feed on alligator lizards or Western Fence Lizards are less likely to spread Lyme disease than others.

species live in the chaparral as well. One of these, the **Pajaroello** (pa-har-way-o) **Tick** (*Ornithodorus coriaceus*) has a fearsome reputation which it doesn't deserve. It is large (up to half an inch long) but difficult to see. In a paper written in 1972, local medical doctor Robert M. Failing and his colleagues described the true nature of the Pajaroello Tick bite. Dr. Failing, having experienced the bite of the dreaded Pajaroello on a camping trip into the San Rafael Mountains, was anxious to dispel the myth that surrounds the animal. "A bite more feared than that of a rattlesnake..." is part of the frightening folklore. However, Dr. Failing found that in his case, conservative treatment was in order, and no ill effects occurred. Severe systemic reactions are rare and the idea that this tick bite is fatal is completely untrue.

Check your clothing if you've been out in the chaparral. Fortunately, ticks don't attach themselves immediately, so you have plenty of time to brush them off before they get settled in. In all my years of hiking, I have seen many ticks and have only been bitten by one, which was later easily removed. If a tick does bite you, you should attempt to remove the animal.

Ticks may carry serious diseases, such as **Lyme disease**, which is transmitted in only 3 to 5 percent of tick bites in Southern California. One of the fascinating aspects of the Lyme disease tick, the **Western Black-legged Tick** (*Ixodes pacificus*), is that in the subadult stage it can be detoxified if it bites a **Western Fence Lizard** (*Sceloporus occidentalis*) or a **Northern** or **Southern Alligator Lizard** (*Elgaria coerulea* and *E. multicarinata*, respectively) and then drops off. These lizards contain proteins in their blood that destroy the spirochaetes of the bacterium *Borrelia burgdorferi,* which causes Lyme disease. In other words, if you are bitten by a subadult or adult tick, either of which has been cleansed by biting one of these lizards, you will not contract Lyme disease. (See below for more on lizards.)

Scientists believe this may be one of the reasons the rate of Lyme disease infection in California has been much lower than that of other states, particularly on the East Coast, where these lizards are not found.

The Bobcat is one of the common predators in shrublands.

Other Animals of Shrub Communities

One of the best ways to look at an ecosystem is to look at a cross section of the habitat. In chaparral and coastal sage scrub, a collection of reptiles, rodents, and other animals thrives. The problem: many live underground, many are camouflaged and move quickly away when disturbed, and many have evolved to hunt nocturnally. You would be lucky to observe even a fraction of the common species. But they are all there. The lizards and snakes, mice and rats, and the **Bobcat** (*Lynx rufus*), **Mountain Lion** (*Puma concolor*), and Coyote.

If you walk into the chaparral at first light, or at dusk, you will observe the most animal life. Midday is the quiet time. To avoid the intense heat, lizards, snakes, and birds hide under bushes or in rock crevices. Late winter and early spring yield the most sightings. By early summer, many animals estivate (hibernate to avoid heat), spend more time in their burrows, move upslope to follow the spring bloom on the hillsides, or wander widely into neighboring habitats, such as oak woodland.

But back to that slice, that snapshot we might take if we could see beneath the surface, peer into the thickest bushes, follow the wildest animals to their secret spots.

The Woodrat

The one rat that is exclusive to shrublands in our region lives aboveground.

How many times have you looked at a scrub oak with a messy bunch of sticks protruding from the upper branches and thought it was an abandoned bird's nest? It's a nest all right, but a true rat's nest.

This is the abode of the **Big-eared Woodrat** (*Neotoma macrotis*), formerly called the Dusky-footed Woodrat (*Neotoma fuscipes*), now found only from northeastern San Luis Obispo County north into Oregon. Both the Big-eared Woodrat and **Bryant's Woodrat** (*Neotoma bryanti*) live in our region, the latter frequenting drier habitats in the inland portion, the Big-eared living in moister habitats.

Woodrats use whatever sticks and

The Big-eared Woodrat is found in our region, along with Bryant's Woodrat.

Woodrats build elaborate nests in trees, on the ground, or in caves.

der to store available berries and seeds, and a central area lined with soft grasses where the occupant sleeps during daylight hours. It has been reported that the bigger houses in the scrub oaks are those of the male, while the female has her own smaller nest on the ground.

Some woodrats in dry regions stuff their nests into shallow caves in cliff faces, protected from weather. These nests, occupied for many years, are full of sticks and branches preserved by the woodrat's urine. Scientists have dated some of the sticks and branches to be thousands of years old.

Woodrats reach peak numbers in mature chaparral, where the shrubs are large enough to support their nests and their voracious appetites. The density is up to sixteen individuals per acre; each woodrat only forages in a small territory adjacent to its nest.

Lizards

Choose a big rock near a trail in the chaparral and sit there quietly on a sunny morning. Listen patiently until the leaf litter under a nearby bush rustles. At first, you won't see a thing, but in fits and starts, the lizard will move out from under the thick shrubbery into the clearing in front of you. Haltingly, it will cross the ground, then makes a dash for the closest stump.

If it's a Western Fence Lizard, commonly called a blue-belly, the lizard will sit motionless on the stump for a long time. Blue-bellies are great baskers in the sun. They pick an exposed perch, such as a fence post, tree trunk, or log, from which to observe their surroundings. The males often

branches are around to build their nests, which are up to five feet tall. Also known as pack rats, woodrats are legendary for their love of bright, shiny objects, which they will collect and take back to their nests. Often, they leave something in exchange for the item they've taken, such as a couple of acorns or a sprig of sage.

The nest of a woodrat, an elaborate structure, contains several entrances, little balconies for defecation, a lar-

The Western Fence Lizard is a frequent visitor to suburban backyards bordering shrublands.

perature, this process is governed by an amazing third eye, called the **parietal eye**. A dot in the middle of the large scale behind the eyes, it interacts with the part of the brain that controls color. This automatic control button tells the lizard when to adjust its skin color and when to move in or out of the sun.

Western Fence Lizards reach peak abundance in recently burned, relatively open chaparral according to one study, probably because of the increased numbers of insect prey there.

The Western Fence Lizard and the Southern Alligator Lizard, both mentioned previously in their role in controlling Lyme disease, are common visitors to suburban backyards bordering shrublands.

The alligator lizard, its tail almost as long as its body, takes people aback with its snakelike, writhing movements. It has a big, triangular head and small legs; when it moves, its whole body wriggles from side to side like an alligator's. This can be frightening if one happens to get into your house and scamper across the kitchen floor, which they occasionally do.

do push-ups to show off their blue throats and declare dominance. With patient observation, you'll see the metallic blue belly and throat and the yellow-orange undersides of their hind legs.

In the breeding season (March through June), male and female fence lizards will share a basking site. After mating, the female digs a nest where the soil is moist and lays six to twelve eggs. She buries the eggs and then takes off, never seeing them again. The little hatchlings look like inch-long miniatures of the adults. You'll see them running around in midsummer.

The Western Fence Lizard changes color depending upon the time of day. It must regulate the amount of heat it absorbs by adjusting pigments in its skin. When the lizard turns black, it soaks up more solar radiation. As the day progresses, the lizard may appear pale brown. Allowing the lizard to maintain a steady body tem-

Along with many other lizard species, Southern Alligator Lizards have the ability to detach their tails to escape enemies. The broken-off tail will writhe around for several minutes, presumably a distraction to whatever predator is pursuing the lizard. A new tail will grow back, although it is never quite as good as the first one.

Southern Alligator Lizards feed on insects found in chaparral. They also consume other lizards and even small

With the expansion of the suburban-wildland interface, the Coyote has become a common sight in many neighborhoods.

mice. Alligator lizards are special because they can be more active at cooler temperatures than most other lizards and will hunt earlier and later in the day. They have a powerful bite, so be careful if you catch one, but otherwise they are harmless.

Coyotes in Our Backyards

Every animal mentioned above is potential prey for the "top dog" in shrublands: the Coyote. Coyotes are especially abundant in young chaparral, rarer in chaparral that hasn't burned in over twenty years.

Coyotes originally evolved in a grassland environment, where **ungulates** (hooved mammals) such as deer and pronghorn antelope browsed. In this setting, the Coyote formed packs, often comprised of a dominant male and female accompanied by nonbreeding members of last year's brood—"aunts and uncles" of the current year's batch of pups. Hunting was a cooperative endeavor, with two or three Coyotes working together to hunt prey. Back at the den, one of the pack members would be left to guard the six or seven young waiting for their food to be delivered. Food was carrion, or a fresh kill of anything from rabbits to gophers to deer.

But in recent decades, life has changed for some populations of the Coyote. One of the most adaptable of all mammals, it has discovered the easy living to be had near human developments, where shrublands close to suburbia provide shelter, and prey is readily available nearby.

The suburban-wildland interface

is expanding, especially in Southern California. The Coyote, once seldom glimpsed, has become a familiar sight at dawn or dusk. Using steep chaparral-covered canyons as daytime retreats, Coyotes patrol adjacent suburban settlements. And why not? The Coyote is an opportunist. This clever animal is drawn to human-landscaped environments that abound with rodents, rabbits, water sources, pet food, and household refuse.

Where prey size is small, such as in chaparral, Coyotes hunt alone or in pairs, not in packs. Their sight, hearing, and sense of smell are highly developed. Their haunting, high-pitched bark, ending in a quavering, wailing howl, echoes far into the night. The bark may sound like it comes from a pack of animals when there is, in fact, only one individual making all the noise.

Researchers in one experiment in Southern California observed what happened when housing developments left "islands" of chaparral surrounded by suburban lots. The first thing they noticed was that bird life diminished in the chaparral patches. No surprise there. But in the patches frequented by Coyotes, there were more birds than in those without. The reason? The Coyotes were eating the house cats, raccoons, and foxes that were preying on the birds. Thus, in the patches of chaparral where no top predator like the Coyote was there to control them, the medium-sized predators had run amok killing birds.

The Coyote is a victim of its own success. It figured out that it was easier to prey upon domestic livestock in open rangelands than on the more cautious wild animals, and in suburban habitats the Coyote has become equally audacious. In open rangelands, Coyotes are poisoned and trapped—but this has not controlled them. In suburbia, fencing and vigilance have not been entirely successful. This situation is not the Coyote's fault.

Birds in the Bushes

Birds of shrublands are drab in color. Their subdued tones of brown and gray, buff and cinnamon reflect the muted colors of their surroundings and help camouflage them. Bird species here must blend in with their background, for many dwell on or near the ground within easy reach of predators. Birds living in the dense brush are also good ground foragers. Protected by the chaparral canopy, they can locate food in the leaf litter or on low branches. Rather than fly from one spot to another, they run or hop.

A Wrentit in Poison Oak

John Davis and Alan Baldridge, in *The Bird Year: A Book for Birders*, cite interesting studies showing that an unusually large proportion of the resident chaparral birds have short, rounded wings and long tails. Birds inhabiting this type of vegetation make only short flights and don't require strong wings; many never migrate.

The Wrentit and its echoing song have come to symbolize chaparral in our region. As Ralph Hoffman wrote in 1927 in his inspiring field guide, *Birds of the Pacific States*, "Even those who ordinarily have no ear for bird songs often comment on a loud, ringing voice from the chaparral-covered hillsides in the foothills that repeats the same staccato note, finally running the series rapidly together. This is the Wrentit, heard a hundred times before it is once seen."

The hot, close, impenetrable thickets of mature chaparral, buttressed by Poison Oak and choked with ceanothus, are the home of the Wrentit. Here, it goes about its sedentary ways. Wrentits have very short wings and a weak flight; they are reluctant to cross even a fuel break or a wide spot in the trail. The Wrentit's only companion is a mate that is chosen for life. The males and females are constantly together, flitting quickly and quietly from one twig to another in the densest bushes, never perching up to sing like other birds. Together they travel the unknown passages of a secret landscape, one that looks thoroughly uninviting to humans, but one for which the Wrentits are perfectly fitted.

Male and female Wrentits look alike: small, round-bodied birds with long tails held cocked at an angle.

The Wrentit's upperparts are grayish-brown and its breast, faintly streaked, is washed with cinnamon. At close range you can see the pale iris of each eye.

The California Thrasher, another iconic bird of chaparral hillsides, is not shy about singing its rich, loud song while perched up for anyone to see on top of a shrub. As he throws his head back and enunciates "*kick*-it-now, *kick*-it now, *shut*-up, *shut*-up, *dor*-o-thy, *dor*-o-thy," the thrasher's long, sickle-like bill opens and shuts vigorously. Rather than fly, the thrasher runs underneath the entangled twigs of chaparral, counterbalanced by its long tail. It uses this tail like a rudder, steering upwards or sideways as it climbs through the brush. Along with thrashers, Bushtits, Bewick's Wrens, **Spotted Towhees** (*Pipilo maculatus*), and **California Towhees** (*Melozone crissalis*) all have proportionately short wings and long tails, enabling them to negotiate the dense scrub.

Although the variety of species is not great, bird numbers are high here. Particularly in winter and early spring, the shrubs are loaded with food. Buds, berries, nectar, bulbs, corms, and seeds, plus a healthy insect population, provide the birds with nourishment. Should this food supply become sparse due to lack of rainfall in a particular year, some species will not nest. The **California Quail** (*Callipepla californica*), for example, will reproduce only in years when available food is sufficient for their needs, or those of their dozen or more chicks.

Resident chaparral birds begin to display courting behavior by January after the first rains. Bushtits leave

The California Towhee is a ground feeder.

After the first rains in January, the male California Thrasher climbs to the tops of chaparral shrubs and begins to sing.

their flocks and separate into pairs, searching for spots to hang their pendant nests. Bewick's Wrens utter their full repertoire of spring songs, perhaps confusing to beginning birders, but female wrens are attracted to a lusty singer. California and Spotted Towhees, ever-present in suburban gardens bordering shrublands, become more visible now as they scratch in the leaf litter with their special two-step: feet together forward and feet together backward.

The male California Quail assumes a position of prominence atop a post or bush, performing the duty of sentinel for his hidden mate. His sleek black head plume shakes every time he gives his single-note warning call.

In March through May, food supplies are plentiful, resident birds are nesting, and summer visitors such as the **Costa's Hummingbird** (*Calypte costae*), **Ash-throated Flycatcher** (*Myiarchus cinerascens*), Lazuli Bunting, and Black-chinned Sparrow arrive from wintering grounds in Central America.

During the breeding season, the male California Quail acts as a sentinel for his hidden mate.

The months of July and August are like autumn in the chaparral. Many birds drift upslope to search for food and moisture in the cooler climates of higher vegetation, even to the forests. Thus certain chaparral birds, such as the Ash-throated Flycatcher, Lazuli Bunting, and Costa's Hummingbird, might be considered to migrate three times in one year: in spring they fly north from Central America; in summer they move upslope from their chaparral environs to higher elevations in the mountains; and in early fall they migrate south once again to Central America.

* * *

Find the trailhead nearest where you live and explore the country of coastal sage scrub and chaparral. This may be at Montaña de Oro State Park, at Sage Hill Campground in the Upper Santa Ynez River drainage, at Santa Paula Canyon in back of Ojai, or anywhere along Sespe Creek in Ventura County. This is the way to immerse yourself in the shrublands discussed in this chapter.

Learning the names of the various shrubs and animals is only the first step. Chaparral habitat is not easy to love, but once you have experienced the upward climbs and the sandstone boulders, the spiny branches pulling at your jeans and the dust sticking in your throat, you go beyond identification and move into the realm of the animals and plants that give this unique place life.

To stand quietly on a spring morning and see the light creep down the ridgetops into the canyons; to hear the *"pit-pit-pit-pit-tr-r-r-rrrr"* song of the male Wrentit reverberating from the hillsides; to lie in a sleeping bag and listen to the mice as they pitter-patter underneath the shrubs all night; to scale the ridge and look back down at the distant Pacific Ocean; to contemplate the beauty of this harsh land: these are the rewards of those who venture into the elfin forest.

Chaparral and coastal sage scrub must be held precious, as the finest examples in North America of vegetation in a Mediterranean climate. Threatened by fire, drought, and human alteration, this "unlovable" collection of plants and animals should be defended. It is the hallmark of the Santa Barbara region and if it is imperiled, so are we.

CHAPTER 7: VALLEYS—A JOURNEY FROM THE COAST TO THE INTERIOR

The view from the top of the Santa Ynez Mountains is one of hills and valleys that stretch from the coast towards the interior, north and east. The rivers that flow to the sea sculpt valleys. The valleys contain bottomlands with deeper soils, while shallower soils cleave to the surrounding hillsides. What grows here? What animals will we find here? Following the river valleys from west to east, our journey inland will trace an idealized transect from a coastal western valley like the Santa Ynez towards an interior eastern valley like the Cuyama.

This chapter is divided into two parts: the first deals with valleys located closer to the coast, such as the Los Osos, Los Alamos, Santa Maria, Santa Ynez, and Santa Clara. Coastal valleys, with their majestic Valley Oak bottomlands and Blue Oak–Gray Pine woodlands, are classic California landscapes. Nowadays these valleys are well known for their agriculture, ranch-style developments, and vineyards.

The second part of this chapter describes the inland valleys, which contain different habitats from those closer to the coast. In the Cuyama and Lockwood valleys, a mix of pinyon pines and junipers cloaks the higher hillsides, with an understory of **Great Basin Sagebrush** (*Artemisia tridentata*). Being in the rain shadow of the San Rafael and Sierra Madre mountains, these valleys get less rainfall than the coastal valleys; the climate is hotter and dryer. Few people live here.

By extending this hypothetical journey into the Carrizo Plain and the southwest edge of the San Joaquin Valley, we will encounter two more types of interior valley: one with desertlike scrub habitat and one supporting prairie grasslands.

But first, the coastal valleys.

Coastal Valleys: Coast Live Oak Woodland, Valley Oak Savanna, and Blue Oak–Gray Pine Woodland

Atop "Hadrian's Wall": A Relict Association of Plants

If you stand on the crest of the Santa Ynez Mountains, botanically speaking you are on the cusp of Northern and Southern California. Elna Bakker, in her wonderful book *An Island*

Tanbark Oak leaf litter. Note the unique fuzzy acorn cups, different from those of true oaks.

Kinevan Road, with the Tanbark Oak–Madrone relict association typically found in wetter climates

Called California, explains that "The mountains of Santa Barbara County have been repeatedly mentioned as having the southernmost extensions of a number of important species. The Santa Ynez Mountains, in particular, are the Hadrian's Wall of California flora."

Some of the plants we will study are not found south of the Santa Ynez Mountains; some will not attempt to go north and cross over the mountains. This wall is an imaginary line and, while not exact, is a way to understand the significance of this east-west-trending mountain range for plant distribution.

As an example of plants not found south of the Santa Ynez Mountains, take the special pockets, or **relict associations,** that grow at the top of the Santa Ynez Mountains. They contain several species with cool weather requirements more suited to the redwood forests of Northern California. When the climate became drier and warmer, most plants retreated farther north, but a few of them have survived here due to the extra rainfall as well as fog drip found on the ridgeline of the Santa Ynez Mountains.

The plant community along Kinevan Road at the summit of San Marcos Pass is a good example. Here, you get a sense of being in a shady evergreen woodland. Get out of your car and walk over to the red-barked **Madrone** (*Arbutus menziesii*) trees— not manzanitas, although their bark is similar. Madrones are tall trees with shiny leaves and delicate white flowers. The lovely **Tanbark Oak** (*Notholithocarpus densiflorus*), not a true oak, is another of the northern species.

Dense Coast Live Oak woodland is visible on the north slopes of the Santa Ynez Mountains at the right side of the photo in this view from Highway 1.

These trees, with few exceptions, are not found south of "the Wall."

North of Point Conception along the road to Jalama Beach, a similar relict plant community grows at Jualachichi Summit on the slopes of Tranquillon Mountain. The fog-laden breezes provide suitable micro-habitat in the understory for **Sword Fern** (*Polystichum munitum*), **Huckleberry** (*Vaccinium ovatum*), and **Salal** (*Gaultheria shallon*)—none of which grow south of the Santa Ynez Mountains.

Coast Live Oak Woodland

From the summit of the Santa Ynez Mountains, you have a good vantage point. The north slopes boast a woodland of deep green, round-canopied oaks. These are the famous **Coast Live Oaks** (*Quercus agrifolia*). They are common in our region within a fifty-mile belt of the coast. Of all the oaks, this is the most well known and beloved for its ubiquitous presence in the California landscape.

Coast Live Oaks are easily identified by their dark green, shiny leaves—curled under and spine-tipped. If you look at the undersides of the leaves, you will see fuzz at the base of the veins.

Coast Live Oaks have extensive root systems that reach thirty feet down for moisture, adapting them to a long dry season. Their thick bark protects from fire, although the trees readily stump-sprout and branch-sprout after a fire. Some trees have been known to live for 150 to 250 years.

The leafy canopy of the oaks shelters a community of plants and animals that live in dappled light and

Hummingbird Sage, an understory plant in the Coast Live Oak woodland

Coast Live Oak is common near the coast.

shade. The leaves of such understory plants as Poison Oak, **Hummingbird Sage** (*Salvia spathacea*), **currants** (*Ribes* spp.), and **Fuchsia-flowered Gooseberry** (*Ribes speciosum*) can absorb sunlight in shady surroundings.

In the understory, birds and animals find protection from predators. Ground-nesting birds conceal their nests here. Spotted Towhees choose Poison Oak thickets and **Dark-eyed Juncos** (*Junco hyemalis*) nest in tufts of **bedstraw** (*Galium* spp.) or **Miner's Lettuce** (*Claytonia perfoliata*). **Anna's Hummingbirds** (*Calypte anna*) time their first brood to coincide with the early crimson blooms of the Fuchsia-flowered Gooseberry in late December and January.

Fallen leaves, twigs, and branches contribute nutrients to the forest floor. Termites, beetles, fly larvae, millipedes, and slugs crawl through the decaying matter.

In contrast to the silent creatures working the soil, **woodland cicadas** (*Platypedia* spp.) are noisy. In March and April, the males of this slender, winged genus (Order Homoptera) vibrate the membranes of their abdomens at a high frequency, setting up sound waves which attract females. Most woodland cicada species in California have reduced sound-producing organs, so they only emit an incessant clicking, not the high-pitched buzz heard in many other parts of the world. Although the constant clicking emanates from woodland shrubs and trees close by, the cicadas themselves are surprisingly difficult to locate.

Cicadas lay their eggs in plant stems or trees. After emerging from the egg, the immature stage, or nymph, drops to the ground and buries itself. Here, it feeds on tree roots and sheds its exoskeleton (outer covering) as it grows. After two to five years, the long-lived nymph emerges and transforms into an adult with clear, delicate wings. After mating and egg deposition, the adults soon die.

The other noticeable insect of Coast Live Oak woodland is the **California Oak Moth** (*Phryganidia californica*). Oak moth larvae, which look like little green worms with reddish heads, devour the leaves of the oaks. Since there are three generations each year, by the end of summer some oak trees near the coast may be completely denuded.

The first evidence of an oak moth infestation is the fluttering of pale tan moths around groves of Coast Live Oaks in spring and summer. But these are the adults, and it's the larvae that do the damage. Particularly in years of little rainfall, Coast Live Oaks may look almost lifeless after the ravages of the oak moth. Although the trees are stressed, they are not dead, and they should recover after the following winter. Inland, Coast Live Oaks are not as affected because the moths cannot survive cold winters.

California Oak Moth caterpillars can quickly denude a Coast Live Oak of its leaves. Inset: an adult

Miner's Lettuce is easy to recognize. Its leaves have a mild peppery taste.

The woodland cicada emits a constant clicking noise in spring in Coast Live Oak woodland.

Valley Oak: countless animals use these magnificent oaks for shelter and sustenance.

Our Precious California Oaks

Oaks, in the family Fagaceae, have been on earth for 45 million years. They grow throughout the Northern Hemisphere. Some attain an age of four hundred years. The majestic tree oaks—as opposed to the scrub oaks (see Chapter 6)—reign over California's landscape in such a way that a newcomer is immediately struck by their beauty and variety.

Dark green Coast Live Oaks cluster in canyons and dot golden grasslands. Enormous **Valley Oaks** (*Quercus lobata*), deciduous in winter, spread their bare branches wide over open valleys, conjuring a more rural California. On hillsides, **Blue Oaks** (*Quercus douglasii*) blend with Gray Pines to lead us upward on a tour towards the higher mountains.

One of the best resources for learning about these and other magnificent oaks is *Oaks of California*, published in 1991 by the fine, local Cachuma Press. Much of the information here is gleaned from this book.

Most of our dominant oaks are endemic (found nowhere else) to the state of California. If chaparral is the signature vegetation type of Central and Southern California, perhaps oak woodland could be said to be the signature vegetation type of the whole state.

Oaks are unique: their fruit is an acorn.

On each oak tree, the male, pollen-bearing flowers grow in early spring as hanging catkins. The female flowers are smaller, inconspicuous, and scattered about in the new twigs. Oaks are wind-pollinated: they disperse clouds of pollen on the wind. Eventually, the pollen finds its way to female flowers, preferably on another tree of the same species. Once fertilized, the acorn begins to develop from the ovary of the female flower.

The acorn is extraordinary. Its tough outer shield not only protects the seed inside but makes it possible for a bird or rodent to carry the acorn away from the parent plant. To sprout, the acorn needs sunlight, which is not often found underneath the parent oak.

Once that acorn is buried in the ground by, for example, a Western Scrub-Jay and watered by winter rains, it has the potential to become a seedling oak. From there it grows into a sapling.

In some years ("mast years"), oaks produce thousands and thousands of acorns, essential nutrition for an array of insects, birds, and mammals. In a relationship similar to the pollination bargain some plants have struck with bees and butterflies (see Chapter 6), oaks feed a multitude of other organisms. Their acorn dispersal mechanism is dependent on hungry animals, and many thousands of acorns are eaten before they can germinate. Still, the oak must gamble with its acorn crop, because dispersal is the key to successful regeneration.

Unfortunately, successful regeneration—the survival of saplings to evolve as adult oaks—and loss of habitat have been a challenge for California's oaks. The Valley Oak and the Blue Oak are considered species of special concern because their populations are threatened.

Valley Oak savanna: trees interspersed with grassland

Valley Oak Savanna

Continuing our journey down the north slope of the Santa Ynez Mountains, we soon reach the Santa Ynez Valley.

The enormous Valley Oaks have a different aspect from the round-crowned, dark-green Coast Live Oaks. A Valley Oak grows taller, has a thicker trunk, and spreads its branches wider—somewhat like an oversized umbrella, but one that you can see through; between the bunches of leaves, spaces of sky appear. The leaves themselves are a duller green and larger, with deep lobes. Valley Oak leaves lack the characteristic spines found on Coast Live Oak leaves.

The term "savanna" refers to regions where scattered trees let in enough sunlight to support grasses beneath them. A savanna differs from a woodland, where the canopies of the trees touch, or nearly so. Valley Oak savanna, characterized by grasslands with widely spaced oak trees, is one of the most beloved and, perhaps, one of the most endangered of all our oak landscapes.

In San Luis Obispo County, you can find Valley Oak savanna in the upper Salinas Valley east of Paso Robles, and in the Los Osos and Edna valleys. In Santa Barbara County, Valley Oak savanna occurs in the Santa Ynez Valley and portions of the upper Santa Maria Valley near Sisquoc and Garey. In Ventura County, the Valley Oak is at the southernmost tip of its range in Thousand Oaks.

The Valley Oak: a Keystone Species

The Valley Oak's massive structure, majestic canopy, and renowned longevity make it the keystone species of the Valley Oak savanna ecosystem. From the tips of its roots deep in the ground to the ends of its branchlets waving in the breeze, a Valley Oak supports a community of fungi, insects, birds, and mammals.

Fungi, the most familiar form of which are mushrooms, thrive in the leaf litter underneath the Valley Oak. Mushrooms come in a fascinating assortment of shapes, colors, and sizes. They can be bright

Chanterelles, although uncommon, thrive in the leaf litter under Valley Oaks.

The Monterey Ensatina (left) and the Arboreal Salamander (right) live in damp places near oaks.

Yellow-billed Magpies, which build their stick nests in the tops of Valley Oaks, are one of California's endemic birds.

223

This juvenile Western Skink inhabits the moist ground at the base of a Valley Oak.

Mule Deer feed on the leaves and acorns of Valley Oaks.

The delicate shapes of Lace Lichen can be seen hanging from the limbs of Valley Oaks.

orange, butter yellow, caramel, charcoal, or pure white. Some have the familiar umbrella shape on a stalk, while others resemble little black pellets, scrunchy pieces of wool, or miniature lollipops. Some mushrooms are a gourmet's delight, others are extremely toxic. The mushroom panoply is full of look-alikes, so it's essential to know your fungi before you go out collecting! For example, the delectable **chanterelle** (*Cantharellus* spp.) mushroom has a look-alike called the **Jack-O-Lantern** (*Omphalotus olearius*) which is poisonous.

Fungi cannot take in food as animals do, nor can they make their own food as plants do (photosynthesis); they absorb their food from their surroundings. By growing in damp soil, the threadlike feeder roots, or **hyphae**, give off enzymes which break down the substrate and thereby absorb the nutrients from the soil itself. Most fungi are **saprophytes**, important decomposer organisms feeding on dead material in the leaf litter and soil.

When you pick a mushroom from the floor of an oak woodland, you aren't destroying the fungus, whose hyphae are underground, but you are picking the fruiting body, like picking an apple from a tree.

Fungi play a special role in the success of oaks. Deep in the soil, the roots of the oak gather water with the help of special fungi—a white covering known as **mycorrhizae**. These fungi help the tree roots take in water and nutrients from the soil, while at the same time gaining sugars from the tree for their use—a mutually beneficial situation. Truffles are an example of mycorrhizal fungi, as are chanterelles.

Where the leaf litter is thick and the soil damp after recent rains, decaying logs or old slabs of bark on the ground hide creatures. Dig around in the wet soil and you may see literally hundreds of **springtails** (Order Collembola), a primitive wingless insect. These minute (quarter-inch-long) insects have extended tails that allow them to hop into the air like fleas when they sense danger. One of the chief components of healthy soil, springtails feed on detritus (decaying matter) in the oak litter, thereby recycling nutrients helpful to the tree.

But the springtails are themselves a tasty morsel for lungless salamanders. In the nooks and crannies of the trunk of a Valley Oak these chief predators of springtails hide. Lungless salamanders obtain oxygen through their skin and the lining of their mouths. If they dry out, they are unable to breathe, so lungless salamanders venture about only in wet weather and at night. During the day, they rest in dark crevices of the bark of an oak, or in the soil.

Lungless salamanders have a unique **chemoreceptor** in the form of two grooves, one on either side of the snout between the nostril and the upper lip. These grooves allow the salamander to take in sensory information about other salamanders and the chemistry of the environment (moisture levels, etc.). In males, the grooves are especially well developed and are used to recognize females during the mating season.

Two lungless salamanders found in our region, the **Monterey Ensatina** (*Ensatina eschscholtzii*) and the **Arboreal Salamander** (*Aneides lugubris*), lay their eggs in damp places near oaks. When the little salamanders hatch, they look like tiny versions of the adults. Unlike newts and other salamanders, lungless salamanders do not have an aquatic phase, so they need not lay their eggs in water.

Climbing now higher up into a Valley Oak, you wonder at those soft-gray pieces of **Lace Lichen** (*Ramalina menziesii*) that hang from the tree's limbs. Lace Lichen is not a parasite; these delicate swags, composed of both a fungus and an alga, do not harm the tree. Lace Lichen helps the Valley Oak by enhancing the capture of wind or fog-borne nutrients such as nitrogen. After the first rains, nitrogen washes off the lichen, falling to the base of the tree. Here bacteria can convert it into a useful form for the host tree. Lace Lichen is very sensitive to air pollution and no longer grows in some sections of Southern California.

In contrast, **mistletoe** (*Phoradendron* spp.), which also grows in clumps high in the Valley Oak's upper branches, is a true parasite. Its modified roots

Years of prolific acorn production are known as "mast years."

(haustoria) invade the oak's bark, penetrating it to receive nourishment. Luckily for the mistletoe, its berries and seeds attract numerous birds. (See Chapter 5 for another plant parasite, dodder.)

Birds, especially **Western Bluebirds** (*Sialia mexicana*), consume mistletoe berries whole. Inside the berries are seeds surrounded by a sticky pulp. When the bird defecates, the sticky pulp acts as a cement and the whole mess sticks firmly to a tree branch. Thus cemented, a few of the seeds will eventually germinate and penetrate the host tree.

Mistletoe cannot kill an oak, but if the tree is old or dying, this parasite might hasten the oak's—as well as its own—demise.

At the top of a Valley Oak, many species of birds make nests in the branches. The **Yellow-billed Magpie** (*Pica nuttalli*)—one of California's two endemic birds (the other being the **Island Scrub-Jay** (*Aphelocoma insularis*)—is closely tied to the Valley Oak. The magpies build their globular nests in oak boughs, often camouflaging the nests in or near clumps of mistletoe. They are colonial nesters, so you may see up to ten or twelve of their unruly bundles of sticks in several adjacent oak trees.

To further understand the distribution of the Yellow-billed Magpie, volunteers for California Audubon have conducted statewide surveys since 2009. The southernmost populations occur near Solvang in Santa Barbara County. San Luis Obispo County traditionally is in the top three California counties in terms of the numbers of these birds sighted. In 2011 San

Luis Obispo County totaled 293 birds, while Santa Barbara had 179. For more recent information go to www. ca.audubon.org.

Among the other birds that nest in Valley Oaks are Red-tailed Hawks, which make platform nests of sticks that they may reuse from year to year. Nesting Nuttall's Woodpeckers excavate cavities in the oak that are appropriated in other years by Western Bluebirds, **Oak Titmice** (*Baeolophus inornatus*), **Violet-green Swallows** (*Tachycineta thalassina*), and even the occasional **Purple Martin** (*Progne subis*).

The most important function of the Valley Oak, as is true of many a keystone species, is to provide food for herbivores. Herbivores, which eat the leaves, roots, and acorns, are in turn consumed by carnivores. For example, the California Ground Squirrel, which collects acorns, is preyed upon by Badgers, Bobcats, and Common Gray Foxes. Mule Deer, which browse on leaves and twigs, are preyed upon by Mountain Lions.

Of all the California oaks, the Valley Oak provides more food and shelter to a greater variety of insects, birds, and mammals than any other.

Acorn Adventures

For birds and other animals, acorns— each a marvelous package of carbohydrates and fats—remain the most sought-after product of the Valley Oak.

A smooth, brown acorn resting in its cup high in a Valley Oak in late September is destined for an adventurous life. First, an Acorn Woodpecker, its red head shining in the sun, flies into the tree and, clasping one of the thick limbs tightly, plucks that acorn from its cup. In undulating flight, the Acorn Woodpecker heads out towards the granary tree where the woodpecker colony stores its acorns.

But en route to the granary tree, the Acorn Woodpecker accidentally drops its prize, the acorn, on the ground. Undaunted, the bird will return to gather more, but this particular acorn now has a new owner, a California Ground Squirrel. The squirrel has been scouring the grassland in the vicinity of its burrow. Seizing the acorn between its teeth, it bobs up and down as it gallops across the ground towards the burrow's entrance. Caching acorns underground is a great survival mechanism for a ground squirrel; if stored away now, the nuts provide nourishment throughout winter and early spring.

So engrossed was the ground squirrel in delivering its newly acquired acorn, it failed to notice the shadow crouched against the ground. A Bobcat has been stalking the ground squirrel, and, as soon as the rodent heads for its burrow, the Bobcat pounces. Alas for the squirrel, the Bobcat's hunting skills, honed by hunger, are excellent. As the cat grabs the squirrel, the acorn drops to the ground. The Bobcat fades quietly into the tall grasses, carrying its furry prey.

But this acorn will not lie unclaimed for long. A Western Scrub-Jay, perhaps a juvenile and not experienced in gathering food, has been watching from afar. Looking for an easy find, the jay flies over from the Valley Oak branch on which it was perched and, alighting on the ground, picks up the acorn. Gingerly, it rotates the acorn round and round in its bill, assessing the freshness and size of the nut. Satisfied that this acorn is worth collecting, the scrub-jay positions the nut lengthwise in its bill and carries it off.

At some distance from the original Valley Oak, and slightly up the hillside, a **Blue Elderberry** (*Sambucus nigra*) creates a patch of shade, and it is here that the Western Scrub-Jay chooses to bury its acorn. Beside the bush, the scrub-jay places the nut in the soil, then covers it. Generations of jays have buried acorns in this manner so as to retrieve them later on. If the scrub-jay doesn't return, an oak sapling may sprout here.

Perhaps due to inexperience, the young jay failed to notice an important reason not to bury an acorn there: the telltale mound of fresh soil where a pocket gopher had just expanded one of its underground tunnels. The earth here is pockmarked with gopher burrows.

And gophers love acorns.

Coming upon the newly buried acorn in the course of its digging, the gopher grabs it, scurries back to the underground chamber where it stores food, and adds this acorn to its stash.

Our acorn has traveled an adventurous path. It will end up as a packet of nourishment for the pocket gopher. Like the overwhelming majority of acorns from the Valley Oak, this one will not sprout and grow to maturity.

Blue Oak–Gray Pine Woodland

On this journey through coastal valleys, if you travel eastward or decide to climb to higher elevations, expect to encounter Blue Oak–Gray Pine woodland. Ascending the slopes of Figueroa Mountain from the Santa Ynez Valley, or climbing up the Cuesta Grade out of San Luis Obispo, notice that the oaks start to look different; they are Blue Oaks. What's more, the oaks will be interspersed with wispy, long-needled pines.

This particular combination of Blue Oak and Gray Pine is unique to California. Neither tree is found south of the Santa Ynez Mountains (Hadrian's Wall again). Sometimes called "foothill woodland," this vegetation community adapts well to the shallower soils of the foothills adjacent to coastal valleys.

Blue Oaks tolerate hot temperatures and dry conditions better than Coast Live Oaks or Valley Oaks, so they occur farther inland. They have roots that grow rapidly, but not as deep as those of other oaks. After October or November rains, Blue Oak acorns immediately begin to sprout, not waiting until the drenching storms of winter.

Although the Blue Oak is deciduous in winter, it can also be drought-deciduous; that is, the tree becomes partially dormant, dropping many of its leaves, in especially hot, dry summers. The blue-gray color of the leaves is caused by a waxy coating that helps the tree to withstand dehydration. The leaves, much smaller than those of Valley Oaks, have shallower indentations at the edges.

If you eye a Blue Oak from a distance, notice its color and shape. The whole tree has a bluish cast. The canopy of the Blue Oak is smaller than that of the huge Valley Oak, and not as dense and rounded as that of the Coast Live Oak. Often, a Blue Oak

Foothill woodland

The Blue Oak, a California endemic

looks less imposing than other oaks. Its success at combating a slew of difficult environmental conditions has made the Blue Oak one of the most numerous species of oak in California.

The Gray Pine is equally well adapted to hot, dry foothills. It can live on ten inches of rain a year, the deep roots making do with whatever moisture comes their way.

Gray Pine doesn't look like a typical pine. It has multiple trunks, which divide not far above the ground, and the branches are supple, almost floppy. Along the branches, wispy, long needles sprout in bunches of three. The cones of Gray Pines are unforgettable: big, heavy, and pineapple-shaped, they have spines on the tips of the scales and are sticky with pitch. The nuts, however, are a favorite of **Western Gray Squirrels** (*Sciurus griseus*). With their lovely, full tails helping

them balance, gray squirrels jump from one branch to another high in these feathery pines.

Similar to that of Valley Oak savanna, the understory of Blue Oak–Gray Pine woodland consists mostly of introduced annual grasses (See "Grasslands" later in this chapter).

Gray Pines reach their southern limit of distribution in the Santa Ynez Mountains.

Nature Journal
March 17, 2001

University of California Sedgwick Reserve

On one of the most lovely of all the early spring days I've ever known, a group of us from the Museum of Natural History take a bus to Sedgwick Reserve for a special field trip.

It has just rained, and the greens and the grays in the landscape make us gasp. The greens: bright green wild oats; bronzy-green tips of new Coast Live Oak leaves; pale yellow-green tips of new Valley Oak leaves against dark, wet-barked trees; dark green of mature Coast Live Oaks. The grays: pale gray clouds in the sky deepening the intensity of the colors below; gray-blue of feathery Gray Pines scattered among the oaks; dusky gray of chaparral sage scrub, some blending to lavender, some to white.

Our leader, Paul Collins, Curator of Vertebrate Zoology at the museum, asks us to notice the difference between the Coast Live Oak woodlands we have seen on the north slopes of the Santa Ynez Mountains and the Blue Oak–Gray Pine woodlands on the higher north slopes at Sedgwick.

Once at the entrance to the main canyon, we gaze up to the lower reaches of Figueroa Mountain, with its serpentine ledges and grassy swales. A smudge of orange at the base of Grass Mountain shows California Poppies are starting to bloom.

Spring wildflowers push up through moist soil. Early patches of lavender-and-yellow Shooting Stars, deep blue Brodiaea, tiny scarlet Red Maids, white Popcorn Flowers, and yellow Fiddlenecks grow on the mesa

above the barn. They have a head start on the grasses and they are going to blossom as soon as they can.

A Red-tailed Hawk swoops and dives overhead, making shadows on the green slopes. The hawk displays with legs dangling while it circles and cries. Later, I discover a Red-tailed Hawk nest in a Gray Pine, the female sitting patiently—half-buried into the nest platform as she looks out over this beautiful, wild valley.

A male Phainopepla silhouetted in a mistletoe-laden Valley Oak sits up straight to show its black crest and ruby red eye.

We begin walking up the main canyon on a dirt track. The tall, brown stalks of last year's annual grasses shelter the young green grass in the ungrazed portion of the pasture. On the grazed side of the fence, all the grasses are clipped and short.

Suddenly Paul stops, putting his forefinger to his lips to quiet us. He gestures towards the hillside.

There it is: a Badger. It has chosen a nice, east-facing slope for its den and is putting the final touches on the entrance, its powerful claws raking the dirt away. Stunned, we watch, wide-eyed, as this seldom-seen mammal works away. His black-and-tan snout hides sharp teeth.

Ground squirrels beware! One of the badger's chief prey is the California Ground Squirrel. The squirrels run about like fat, brown sausages, popping up out of burrows, then down again.

Unexpectedly, an adult Bald Eagle, its wide brown wings bracketed by white head and tail, flies right over our heads! Everyone exclaims. Here we are, miles from any large body of water. Where is the bird headed? Subsequently, we realize that Lake Cachuma isn't that far away. And who knows? Perhaps the eagle *was contemplating nesting in one of the Gray Pines. I've seen photos of an eagle nest, seven feet deep and three feet wide, weighing hundreds of pounds, supported in the crotch of a Gray Pine.*

As we return to the ranch house for lunch, I gaze around me at this exquisite piece of oak woodland, this reserve where the public can visit and university researchers can work. These magnificent oaks, the Gray Pines, the lush wildflowers, Figueroa Creek running fast and fresh: how lucky we are to have such a haven for study of the fauna and flora of our oak woodlands.

* * *

(Note: Sedgwick Reserve is open to the public on a limited basis for scheduled hikes.)

The Latest on Acorn Woodpeckers, Western Scrub-Jays, and Oaks at Sedgwick

Recent research concerning oak woodlands, much of it conducted at Sedg-

An Acorn Woodpecker on a Valley Oak, a favored granary tree

wick Reserve in the Santa Ynez Valley, has widened our understanding of oaks. At Sedgwick, all three oak habitats discussed in this chapter can be studied: Coast Live Oak woodland, Valley Oak savanna, and Blue Oak–Gray Pine woodland.

One important area of investigation is the habits of Acorn Woodpeckers and Western Scrub-Jays in relation to oaks.

Acorn Woodpeckers have a fascinating lifestyle: not only do they share mates and raise their young in groups, but they harvest acorns and store them in a central granary tree that can be used by any member of the group.

The granary tree, usually a massive Valley Oak or Coast Live Oak, can have several hundred to several thousand holes, furnishing protection from weather and predators. The furrowed bark of the granary tree is studded with hundreds and hundreds of acorns, each of which is fitted into a custom-made hole drilled by the woodpeckers of that colony. This does not appear to harm the trees; sometimes the birds use dead snags, but more frequently the granary is a live tree.

Research has shown that woodpeckers gather acorns from trees within about five hundred feet of the granary tree, although one individual woodpecker was known to have carried an acorn a mile and a half away from its source!

At first, it was thought that Acorn Woodpeckers were storing acorns to eat insects that might invade the nuts—not the nuts themselves. But closer examination showed that woodpeckers take great care to move the acorns from hole to hole to keep them from becoming riddled with insects. The birds reject acorns that are infested. In addition to acorns, Acorn Woodpeckers also consume flying ants, sap, oak catkins, fruit, flower nectar, and occasional grass seeds.

The number of acorns stored is reflected in the size and reproductive abilities of the woodpecker colony. Acorn Woodpeckers occupy a permanent territory near the granary tree. They are cooperative breeders: the colony has only one nest, which is shared by the sexually mature males and females, and the nonbreeding birds are helpers, sharing in the duties of raising the young.

Along with cooperation comes competition. The woodpeckers don't form pairs, but co-breeding males (the dominant males of the colony) mate with any and all dominant breeding females. Furthermore, co-breeding females routinely remove each other's eggs from the cavity, tossing them out in favor of their own. At some point, however, the demolition derby ends, and a female leaves her co-breeder's egg in the nest while laying her own beside it.

Western Scrub-Jays are another species intimately involved with oaks. One of the first to write about jays and oaks was Joseph Grinnell, California's famous zoologist. In a well-known 1936 *Condor* article, "Up-Hill Planters," Grinnell describes walking among oaks growing on a slope in a woodland in the Southern Sierra Nevada. As he notes the way the acorns roll downhill, he wonders why oak saplings are growing upslope,

The Western Scrub-Jay propagates oak woodlands by caching acorns in the ground.

above where most of the source trees are located:

> The birds were gathering the acorns and carrying them up the slopes, to be ensconced in various hidey-holes, some of them to be buried…in the ground of open spaces on the hillsides…Every bird going up-slope bore an acorn lengthwise in its bill; every bird in return course was empty-billed.

Moreover, researchers watching scrub-jay behavior with peanuts find that the birds will sample several nuts to ascertain which one is the plumpest and, presumably, most nutritious. (This behavior has also been noted in Pinyon Jays with pine nuts.) Results illustrate that jays do not randomly select just any acorn from the crop, but employ certain standards of quality. Furthermore, if the jay has found a particularly healthy source tree, it will use that fact, that "updated information," revisiting that particular oak regularly rather than waste time with acorns of a lesser quality from another tree.

In sum, biologists are revealing the complex relationships between oaks and Western Scrub-Jays, and the role of the jays in propagating the trees by burying the healthiest acorns.

Oak Regeneration

Experiments at Sedgwick and elsewhere have revealed a slow decline in the regeneration of Valley Oaks and Blue Oaks due to a combination of factors. The Coast Live Oak appears to be holding its own, at least for now.

At Sedgwick, scientists have done amazing studies of how oaks reproduce and what affects their success or failure to sprout. A group of oaks has been genetically mapped so that the DNA of all the oak trees in a certain area is known. In this way, the acorns of the parent trees can be tracked and their fate observed. For example, using this information, scientists can tell exactly where each acorn in a granary tree originated, thus measuring the distance a woodpecker traveled to carry it there.

One of the key elements of acorn survival is adequate rainfall in late winter, which enhances the sprouting of acorns and seedlings. In dry years, fewer acorns sprout and fewer seedlings thrive.

Another difficulty for oaks revolves around gophers and ground squirrels eating and storing large numbers of acorns. Of the enormous volume of acorns produced by oaks in a normal year, a huge percentage are consumed by these rodents and do not sprout.

Last and perhaps most surprisingly, the experimental plots at Sedgwick that were protected from grazing cattle and deer had sprouting results similar to those that were not protected from grazing. There may be more damage done where the grass and herbaceous cover is left alone than where they are mowed or grazed. Gopher activity is greater in ungrazed areas, because there is more vegetation to munch on. It is possible that grazing has an indirect, positive effect on oak seedling survival by encouraging fewer gophers.

Interior Valleys: Pinyon Pine–Juniper Woodland, Grasslands, and Desert Scrub

To see the progression from coastal western valleys to inland eastern valleys, travel Highway 166 from north of Santa Maria east towards Taft and Bakersfield. Following the winding Cuyama River as it meanders back and forth through Santa Barbara and San Luis Obispo counties, this journey leads us away from the oak woodlands towards more inland landscapes.

At first, the Coast Live Oaks cover the north-facing slopes; coastal sage scrub blends into chaparral. But past Twitchell Reservoir, and over the crest of the southern tip of the La Panza Range, the Cuyama Valley begins to

Grasslands at the eastern end of the Cuyama Valley with ruins of an old adobe

widen. Here, where rangelands and vast ranches still exist, look south and see the Sierra Madre; the slopes are dark with a variety of oaks and some chaparral. In contrast, look north at the Caliente Range—a barren, eroded series of canyons and rugged ridges.

The Cuyama is an inland valley. In its natural state, the flat terrain of the Cuyama Valley floor was a patchwork of annual grasses mixed with arid salt-bush scrub in the lowest parts. When Joseph Grinnell described it in his journal of an expedition there in 1912, up to two hundred Pronghorn roamed the valley; deer were plentiful.

In the late nineteenth century, this was a hardscrabble land, suitable for cattle grazing or dry farming. For a long time, nothing much grew except oil wells—nothing much until water was added. Now, a patchwork of cultivated crops enhanced by massive irrigation systems has almost entirely replaced the native vegetation. In order to see the type of vegetation that once covered the valley floor, it will be necessary to move on to the Carrizo Plain, which we will do later in this chapter. But before that, let's get off the main highway and explore a wonderful side canyon of the Cuyama Valley.

The Caliente Range as seen from the south side of the Cuyama Valley looking north

Pinyon Pine–Juniper woodland

Pinyon Pine–Juniper Woodland

To see classic Pinyon Pine–Juniper woodland, take a trip up Santa Barbara Canyon. This type of woodland is found on the inland side of interior mountains from 4,000 to 6,000 feet. It represents the extreme western extension of a Great Basin type of vegetation found more typically in Utah, Arizona, and Colorado. In our region, Pinyon Pine–Juniper woodland is found in the Upper Sespe watershed, the side canyons of the Upper Cuyama Valley, and Lockwood Valley near Mount Pinos.

California Juniper (*Juniperus californica*), a chunky, dark green tree that looks more like a large shrub, grows slowly and lives a long time. Junipers can survive with little rainfall and withstand extreme heat and cold. The berries of this tree provide food for several montane bird species in winter. **Townsend's Solitaires** (*Myadestes townsendi*) and **Mountain Bluebirds** (*Sialia currucoides*) descend to the valleys, where winter temperatures are warmer, to feed on them. Juniper berries are actually the fleshy

cones of the tree with a seed inside. They're blue and spicy-tasting; some varieties of juniper are crushed to flavor gin.

Junipers pioneer new woodland by providing shade in which the seeds of their companions, the pinyon pines, can germinate. However, at lower elevations where there isn't enough moisture for the pines, junipers may form a savanna, where junipers are scattered among grasslands, such as on the higher slopes of the Cuyama Valley and on the Temblor Range.

The **Singleleaf Pinyon Pine** (*Pinus monophylla*) is the pinyon pine found in our area. It is the only pine in the world that has a single needle in each bundle; all other pines have two or more needles in a bundle.

Pinyon pines aren't huge, and they may look like tall, blue-gray shrubs when nestled among the large sandstone boulders of this country.

Pine nuts, those tasty nuts called for in so many recipes, also provide essential food for other animals. Chipmunks, ground squirrels, woodrats, and **Pinyon Mice** (*Peromyscus truei*) forage at pinyon pinecones in fall.

Singleleaf Pinyon Pines have only one needle in each bundle.

Clark's Nutcrackers, **White-breasted Nuthatches** (*Sitta carolinensis*), and **Mountain Chickadees** (*Poecile gambeli*) relish pinyon pine nuts. When the cone crop fails at higher elevations, the **Pinyon Jay** (*Gymnorhinus cyanocephalus*)—not often found in our region—may be spotted locally. Like other members of the Corvid family (crows, jays, ravens), Pinyon Jays cache pine nuts in autumn by burying them, then return to retrieve them in early spring.

The Pinyon Mouse forages on the nuts of pinyon trees.

Nature Journal
October 20, 2000

Trip up Santa Barbara Canyon to Cuyama Peak

The urgency of a bird chase is a gnawing in the pit of your stomach: anticipation mixed with fear of disappointment. Can you find the right area? Will the bird fly over? Can you recognize its call?

I'm searching for a Pinyon Jay, which would be a new addition to my Santa Barbara County bird list. The chances are slim...

Traveling up the bumpy road in Santa Barbara Canyon, we pass yellow cotton-wood trees highlighted by the morning sun. Red cliffs on the canyon walls show whitewash where a Prairie Falcon nested one year. At the intersection of Dry Creek Road, we hit dirt, and the way gets more treacherous. Fat juniper bushes display their blue-green berries. Two kinds of rabbitbrush, one with tall whitish stems and one with shorter green stems, show bright yellow blooming heads.

All the Desert Mountain Mahogany shrubs have pale halos around them, standing out from the background of junipers and pinyons. The halos come from the white, feathery curlicues attached to the seeds, perfect for wind dispersal.

The quietness of fall is upon the land. The pinyon pine branches hang heavy with cones. Surely, sometime soon, a Pinyon Jay will fly over? Stopping frequently, we scan for flocks of jays. We head up the rough track in the direction of Cuyama Peak (5,875 ft.), where the Pinyon Jays were seen only two days ago.

Clark's Nutcrackers, normally absent at this low elevation, seem to be everywhere.

The yellow blooms of Common Rabbitbrush brighten Pinyon Pine–Juniper woodland in fall.

Pinyon Pine–Juniper woodland with Great Basin Sagebrush in the foreground

Their insistent "caw" resounds from the hillsides. Fooling us temporarily, the call is similar to that of the Pinyon Jay, but not as nasal. Still, the excitement builds as we realize that, indeed, it is an "invasion year" for nutcrackers, meaning the cone crop has failed in the higher mountains, so the birds have wandered far out of range. This offers hope for seeing Pinyon Jays as well; they've been seen accompanying the nutcrackers.

At the summit of Cuyama Peak, we get out and stretch. We walk over and climb the rickety stairs of the old-fashioned fire lookout

Desert Mountain Mahogany as seen on the drive up to Cuyama Peak. Feathery plumes attached to the seeds aid in wind dispersal.

building. From the top there's a great view. In every direction, you can pinpoint a familiar mountain or valley of the backcountry.

Opposite us, across the Cuyama Valley, the dry slopes of the Caliente Range lie bare and exposed. The ridges of these desert lands, like boney fingers, clasp the valleys. In October, when no green grass softens the hills, the essence of the earth's formation is revealed. Golden grasses grazed to stubble; shrubs shriveled from summer heat. Bare rock, bare land...

From this vantage point, the green checkerboard of agricultural fields in the Cuyama Valley below contrasts with the Upper Cuyama and Lockwood valleys, where native sagebrush still dominates.

Here on Cuyama Peak, the north-facing slope phenomenon is easy to see. It's as though the mountaintop has a split personality. The south side is a mélange of chaparral shrubs, but on the shady, cooler north side a thick forest of Bigcone Spruce and tall, healthy pinyon pines grows.

From our spot on the lookout balcony, we can see that the forested slope below is jumping with birds! We watch as they fly from one conifer to another. Steller's Jays, Western Scrub-Jays, Common Ravens (Corvus corax), and Clark's Nutcrackers. A feast of corvids, all feasting on the pinyon pine and Bigcone Spruce cones. Fantastic!

And, to my bitter disappointment, not a single Pinyon Jay did we spot that day. Nor have I seen any in our county since.

Grasslands

Some grasslands are in the interior, directly in our path as we travel Highway 166 eastwards. Other grasslands are found as coastal prairie in San Luis Obispo County, in high meadows on

Interior grasslands at Painted Rock on the Carrizo Plain

Purple Needlegrass is the most common native bunchgrass in the Santa Barbara region.

the mountains (potreros), and in the various savanna landscapes.

The most extensive grasslands grow on the alluvial plains that slope to the interior valley floors. What little water flows out of the nearby mountains collects in dry lakes, or sinks—such as at Soda Lake on the Carrizo Plain and Buena Vista Lake at the southern end of the San Joaquin Valley. The lakes may hold water in the spring, but by fall and winter, they are bone dry.

To the casual observer, all grasslands look alike: golden, nodding heads blowing in the wind. Abounding in wildflowers in a wet year, short and brown too soon in a dry year, the grasslands seem to serve more as a backdrop for grazing livestock than a habitat in their own right. But once you know the history of grasslands and their importance to a variety of animals, they assume tremendous significance.

Grasslands in California are famous for their native perennial bunch-grasses, species found only in western North America. Bunchgrasses, adapted to winter rain and summer heat, grow with tufts of stems arising from a perennial root crown. One of the most common is **Purple Needlegrass** (*Stipa pulchra*), the state grass of California.

At present, most California grasslands are a mixture: a small percentage of these rare bunchgrasses and a much larger percentage of annual grasses that were introduced from the Mediterranean area in the 1800s with the advent of extensive cattle grazing. Representative introduced annual grasses are oats (*Avena* spp.), bromes (*Bromus* spp.), barley (*Hordeum* spp.), and rye grass (*Festuca* spp.).

Negative impacts of these livestock herds included overgrazing, trampling, and erosion, which decimated the native flora while providing a perfect environment for the non-native grasses to thrive in. Non-native grasses were adapted to a Mediterranean climate, and they could withstand heavy grazing; they grew faster and seeded out faster than native bunchgrasses.

We don't know what the native flora looked like in these vast areas prior to the 1800s, as there is no historical record of its demise. In the early twentieth century, some botanists speculated that these sites were dominated by native perennial bunchgrasses—a theory that is no longer in favor. The perennial "grasslands" of old California also con-

tained a dazzling variety of perennial and annual wildflowers (forbs).

This is supported by a number of brief historical accounts. Fray Juan Crespí, who accompanied Gaspar de Portolá on the first Spanish land expedition to Alta California, recorded many details in his journal, including fine descriptions of the vegetation. Alan K. Brown's translation in *A Description of Distant Roads* includes an entry from May 7, 1770, describing an area near the Santa Ynez River in what is now Santa Barbara County:

> A great plenty of white, yellow, red, purple and blue blossoms: a great many yellow violets...such as are planted in gardens, a great deal of larkspur, a great deal of prickly poppy in bloom, a great deal of sage in bloom; but seeing all the different sorts of colors together was what beautified the fields the most.

In a marvelous, old-fashioned book written in 1927, *The Wild Gardens of Old California*, Charles Francis Saunders gives his version of what Crespí described on that first trip:

> On mesa and valley floor and treeless loma, the mantle of vivid green is overlaid riotously with color—the orange of California poppies; the blue and lavender of sturdy lupines and lolling wild heliotrope; the mauve of owl's clover; the pale gold of sun-cups—trickles and rivulets and broad rivers of color. Down from the foothills of the purple Coast Range, it leaps and streams, gathered now into pools

Clockwise from top: Mariposa Lily; Sky Lupine;
Baby Blue-eyes; Cream Cups; Tidy-tips

and lakes, now breaking in cascades and ribbons over the brink of the arroyos and barrancas, to reappear on the hither side and spread illimitably in kaleidoscopic flood, until it is halted at last by the barrier of the sea....

Dainty nemophilas of a heavenly blue; fringed gilias yellow throated and pink; pallid creamcups and collinsias lifting pagoda-like spires in purple and lilac and white. More aloof are the mariposa tulips, which, like the aristocrats that they are, shrink from the touch of other elbows. They lift cups of varied color here and there among the taller grasses, upon which as upon an emerald sea, billowed and tossed by the breeze, the lovely flowers ride and dance like cockle shell boats tugging at their anchors.

Can there be any doubt that the glory of California's grasslands was its native wildflowers, even when viewed centuries ago by the earliest explorers?

Animals of Grasslands

Grazers and Browsers: The grasslands featured here are those at Wind Wolves Preserve, Bitter Creek National Wildlife Refuge, and the Carrizo Plain National Monument. They form a wildlife corridor of grasslands from the southern end of the San Joaquin Valley—the far eastern corner of our region—west to the Carrizo Plain. All are accessible from Highway 166. At this writing, Bitter Creek is not open to the public.

California Mule Deer, Tule Elk, and **Pronghorn** (*Antilocapra americana*) are

ungulates (hooved mammals) that forage in grasslands. As we preserve our region's grasslands and restore them to a more natural state, Tule Elk and Pronghorn are being reintroduced to some areas. Mule Deer appear to be more adaptable to human disturbance and habitat loss than the others. For the most part, they have maintained their populations, and they are closely monitored by the California Department of Fish

Grasslands at Wind Wolves Preserve with Tule Elk herd

and Wildlife with regulated hunting seasons.

Although Mule Deer eat mostly grasses, they also browse on shrubs and small trees, particularly in fall and winter; Tule Elk and Pronghorn graze on grasses and forbs year-round. All of these ungulates have two white "mittens" on their rumps which, when erected, fan out beyond the body's contours and act as a warning signal to other members of the herd.

Close cousins of Mule Deer and members of the same family, Cervidae, Tule Elk once roamed the southern San Joaquin Valley in great numbers.

243

Tule Elk at Wind Wolves Preserve. Note bull in middle distance.

With the onslaught of the gold rush in the late 1840s, these beautiful creatures were killed for meat and hides in greater numbers than ever before to supply the growing population of settlers. By 1873, when elk hunting was finally banned, only a few elk remained in the marshes of Buena Vista and Tulare lakes.

The Tule Elk, one of three subspecies of elk found in California, is the only one endemic to the state; it has made a great comeback. Thanks to intensive conservation efforts, there are now about thirty-nine hundred Tule Elk statewide in twenty-two herds. Tule Elk have probably done so well in reintroduction because their historic predators, the **Gray Wolf** (*Canis lupus*) and the **Grizzly Bear**

(*Ursus arctos*), are extinct in California.

The best places to see Tule Elk in our region are at the Carrizo Plain National Monument and at Wind Wolves Preserve. This preserve, located in Kern County at the southern end of the San Joaquin Valley, is relatively new. Comprised of ninety-seven thousand acres of the historic San Emigdio Ranch, Wind Wolves was purchased in 1996 by The Wildlands Conservancy and is now open to the public on weekends. The name "wind wolves" refers to the waving of windblown grasses, as though an unseen wolf were walking through them. Wind Wolves Preserve is a perfect example of foothill and valley grasslands. There are several colonies of native perennial bunchgrasses.

Nature Journal
October 31, 2010

Wind Wolves Preserve

The van heads out along the dirt road as we climb higher and higher into the rolling foothills above the San Joaquin Valley. The bumps in the road jostle my binoculars; I want to stop every five minutes to examine the wildlife. A Prairie Falcon perches on the edge of a water tank. A Northern Harrier glides and dips along the top of the hill. The view out to the north, of agricultural cropland, contrasts with these undulating hills of nothing but grass, grass, and more grass.

Today, Wind Wolves ecologists Dave and Sherryl Clendenen have agreed to take us on a special guided tour of this enormous piece of preserved grassland. In 1806, when the first Spanish expedition to the San Joaquin Valley camped at the mouth of what is now called San Emigdio Canyon, they were traveling the original inland road between Los Angeles and San Francisco. San Emigdio is the patron saint of earthquakes, which is fortunate because the San Andreas Fault runs right along the southern edge of the tall ridges of the San Emigdio Mountains to the south. As we look up, we can see a dusting of new snow among the shadows of the conifers growing on top.

Our goal is to see the Tule Elk herd. Slowly, the van inches up over the lip of a grassy hill. The photographers among us are ready.

A herd of nearly a hundred calves and cows with half a dozen big bulls appears in a bowl of the hillside. As we come to a stop, they slowly move off.

Dave decides that a better approach will be to park the van and hike up another rise, just out of eyesight of the animals. We get out and begin climbing up through the springy wet grass. (This month's record-setting rainfall has made the grass grow, and the trails are muddy.)

On hands and knees, we crawl onto a high bench above the elk.

They don't see us. And, to our joy, a lone Coyote, which does see us, is setting up a racket over in the opposite direction. The Coyote is yapping and howling a warning the elk are not heeding. Great. This focuses the elk herd on the Coyote. The cows fear Coyotes, because they know the danger to their calves. Slowly all of the animals begin to stalk the Coyote.

We are transfixed by this chance to observe the elk.

The bulls sport massive racks of antlers. The biggest elk weigh over six hundred pounds. Rutting season, which began in August, is now nearly finished. With the breeding season over, the bulls will leave their harems and form a "boys' club" high up in the hills somewhere. The cows will stay together until April, when each will produce a single calf.

Meanwhile, the Coyote, intimidated by the herd's approach, has disappeared.

We listen to the sounds of the elk. High, whistling bugles issue from the bulls—not at all what I'd expected from these huge animals. The calves bleat plaintively, staying close to their mothers.

At last, we walk back down the hill and continue the tour by van. Around every corner, there's a vista of wispy clouds, huge blue sky; the sprawling San Joaquin Valley lies behind us.

Next stop is Reflection Pond. Here, where a low sump holds water in wet years, giant rock formations push up from the grasslands. The outlook is superb in every direction.

We are reminded that, in the days before The Wildlands Conservancy purchased this land and saved it from development, this area was slated to become a toxic dump!

The day warms up; we sit eating lunch. I am thinking one thought: now is the time for a condor to fly over. I try to keep it to myself, but Sherryl, she of the sharp eyes, knows how much it would mean to me to see one of the reintroduced California Condors.

Sherryl spots it first—the black speck that will become an adult condor if you see it magnified through the spotting scope! Sherryl and Dave, both experienced condor observers, can recognize the birds as condors soaring far, far away. Two more show up, slowly banking and occasionally flapping, using the thermals to help them. Finally, I'm able to focus in on the big white patches of the underwings as the dark birds glide in the blue sky above the distant ridgetop.

It's been many, many years since I've seen a condor in the wild. Places like Wind Wolves, with its elk herds, condors, and undisturbed grasslands, fill me with hope for the future.

Pronghorn, we know from early accounts, existed in the Cuyama Valley and the San Joaquin Valley up into the 1890s. Someday they may be reintroduced at Wind Wolves. Currently, Carrizo Plain National Monument is the only grassland area in our region where you can see Pronghorn.

Pronghorn are different from elk and deer, being in a uniquely North American subfamily, the Antilocaprinae. The fastest mammals in North America,

Pronghorn again roam the Carrizo Plain. Photo by Marlin Harms

Pronghorn are built for speed, with long, slim legs. Their pointed hooves are cloven and have special cartilage to cushion the shock of running over rough ground. Their speed may have evolved because they were chased by a Pleistocene predator, the **American Cheetah** (*Acinonyx trumani*), which has since become extinct.

Pronghorn have tan-and-white bodies and dark markings on their heads and necks. They carry their heads upright, displaying blackish horns with small, protruding prongs and hooks. Like elk, Pronghorn are polygamous, mating with more than one female. A breeding male Pronghorn will stake out and defend a territory where there are plenty of plants on which to forage, such as a succulent patch of grasses. They favor a mixture of sagebrush, grasses, and forbs.

Pronghorn gather in groups to escape predators. When running, they form elliptically shaped herds and may achieve speeds of over fifty miles per hour.

Pronghorn have been reintroduced into the Carrizo Plain National Mon-

Mountain Lion

ument. Their populations fluctuate from year to year and are closely monitored by biologists. Fences and other such artificial barriers are detrimental to Pronghorn because they are hesitant to jump over them and this facilitates predation by Bobcats and Coyotes, especially of their young.

The Grazer's Predator, the Mountain Lion: The chief predator of ungulates is the Mountain Lion.

Being the most powerful predator in our region, it's at the apex of the food pyramid in grasslands and many other ecosystems. According to old accounts, even a grizzly could be vanquished by a lion, which could jump on the bear's shoulders and cut its throat in a fight to the death.

Species like the Mountain Lion are capable of taking down prey several times their own size. Members of the dog family (Canidae), the cat family (Felidae), and the hyena family (Hyaenidae) possess this ability. There appears to be a body threshold of around forty pounds beyond which a predator must begin to tackle larger prey in order to get enough calories. At that weight, the metabolic costs of hunting rise more steeply than the energy gained. Smaller predators, because of their lower energy requirements, can subsist on insects or rodents. By examining the fossil record, researchers have discovered that larger and larger species repeatedly evolved in many lineages. These top predators are called **hypercarnivorous**, that is, purely meat-eating. They cannot get enough nourishment from any other diet. For this reason, some scientists believe that large carnivores run a bigger risk of extinction than smaller carnivores or herbivores.

The Mountain Lion is free of natural enemies. Specializing in stealth, it stays out of sight because that's its hunting mode. Built to stalk prey and surprise it, the Mountain Lion is tremendously agile and strong. Its heavy, well-developed forelegs enable it to strike and hold prey. Its claws are long and retractable, good for ripping into and holding onto another animal. Males average 140 pounds and are 6 feet, 10 inches from head to tail tip. Females are slightly smaller and weigh less. Reports of a 76-pound Mountain Lion tackling an elk that weighed nearly nine times as much are undoubtedly true.

Lions are especially adapted to killing deer, which form 75 percent of their diet. Deer are often found along canyon ridges, where, in order to catch the scent of approaching danger wafting upwards on air currents, they customarily bed down. Mountain Lions hunt along these ridges, often resting on "lion ledges," rocky formations from which they may launch an attack.

Lions eat only that which they have killed—almost no carrion. After killing, the lion covers the carcass with dirt and leaf litter; it will return to feed over the next few days, moving and concealing the dead prey each time.

Mountain Lions have been targeted for predator control ever since the 1600s, when early Spanish settlers paid bounties for lion pelts in order to protect their livestock.

In 1990 a coalition of conservation organizations, including the Mountain Lion Foundation (www.mountainlion.org), placed Proposition 117 on the statewide ballot. The initiative was passed and the Mountain Lion was reclassified as a "specially pro-

tected mammal," and sport hunting of lions was permanently banned in the state. However, depredation permits may be issued against any offending lion, if a resident requests one and if there's proof that domestic animals or humans have been attacked. (The latter is rare.)

Somewhere between four thousand and six thousand Mountain Lions roam California. Their home ranges vary in size from twenty-five to two hundred square miles. In San Diego County, researchers have captured and radio-collared some fifty-three lions in order to track individuals and learn more about their lifestyles. One lion roamed sixty miles and another traveled a hundred miles, both undetected by humans and yet close to human habitation.

Mountain Lions need wild landscapes. Urban planners are already implementing bridges designed to work as wildlife corridors. The structures allow the lions to pass under busy freeways (usually at night) from one wild area to another. Remote cameras record these passages, so we know that the structures are definitely working. In our region, Ventura County has been a leader in this regard.

Mountain Lions are not tame; they will avoid humans, if given the chance. We need these top predators, critical for keeping deer herds healthy. Without them, the deer population may skyrocket, then plunge due to lack of food or prevalence of disease. Mountain Lions, seldom seen, are everywhere.

Grassland Engineers: Gophers and ground squirrels are essential to the health of grasslands, as was the Grizzly Bear until late in the nineteenth century.

If you've ever observed activities of a gopher in your garden, you will understand the impact of burrowing rodents on the landscape. One of the most widespread rodent species, **Botta's Pocket Gopher** (*Thomomys bottae*), has a profound effect. The burrowing of the gopher loosens hard soils, increases soil aeration, and helps rainwater to penetrate into the ground.

Botta's Pocket Gopher, an ecosystem engineer

The abundance of burrowing rodents such as pocket gophers and ground squirrels in grasslands was remarked upon by early explorers, settlers, and naturalists. In 1923, Joseph Grinnell wrote, in "The Burrowing Rodents of California as Agents in Soil Formation," an important article about the pocket gopher:

A gopher is loath to leave its shelter and ordinarily does not venture as far even as the length of its body from the open mouth of its burrow....The haunches of the animal, when it forages, remain in contact with the orifice of the burrow, as a sort of anchor by means of which the gopher can pull itself back into safety at an instant's warning....

In digging, the earth loosened by the strong incisor teeth and stout front claws is swept back underneath the body until a considerable amount has accumulated. The animal then turns around (being able to do so apparently almost within the diameter of its own body, which is the diameter also of its burrow), and pushes the earth along the tunnel to the surface opening where it is shoved out on top of the ground....Only the fore feet, in conjunction with the broad furry face below the level of the nose, are used in moving the earth. The...fur-lined cheek pouches, with which the animal is provided, and which are situated at each side of the mouth, are not used to carry earth, but solely to carry clean food materials.

Individual gophers have tunnel systems one to two feet deep, averaging sixteen feet in length. Moreover, gophers dig year-round. Acting somewhat like rototillers, they have been estimated to completely turn over the topsoil in their habitat areas every three to fifteen years.

By comparing areas disturbed by burrowing mammals and those undisturbed nearby, researchers have concluded that, beginning soon after California's first contact with European explorers, rodents played a role in spreading the non-native annual grasses that now dominate grasslands. In the disturbed areas, soil temperatures are warmer and there are often higher levels of nitrogen. And because non-native annuals produce seeds soon after the first rains, more quickly than native bunchgrasses, burrowers eat and store them in great quantities. The conclusion appears to be that areas disturbed by rodents favor annual grasses over perennial bunchgrasses.

Unlike the pocket gopher, which does its work out of sight, another ecosystem engineer, the California Ground Squirrel, sits up in plain view beside the entrance to its burrow. Ground squirrels inhabit a veritable maze of underground tunnels extending down into the ground more than two yards in some places, and stretching for an average of thirty-five feet. They prefer to establish their network of tunnels on a sloping piece of ground to avoid flooding.

Ground squirrels are enormously important in grasslands for three reasons: they are diligent soil movers and aerators; they form a prey base for many other animals, such as rattlesnakes, Coyotes, foxes, Bobcats, Badgers, hawks, and eagles; their abandoned burrows provide shelter for toads, Burrowing Owls, skunks, snakes, and salamanders.

Ground squirrels gather seeds, nuts, fruits, and the stems and leaves of grasses, then carry them to their burrows in inner cheek pouches, storing their provisions for times when food is scarce, especially during hibernation in cold weather. Chipmunks

also have inner cheek pouches, but tree squirrels do not.

An interesting study on ground squirrel communication has revealed that the chattering vocalizations among members of a colony vary depending upon the kind of predator that has been sighted. For example, the chatter notes in response to snakes were different from those warning of carnivores. Furthermore, Bobcats, Coyotes, and dogs were greeted with one kind of response call, and another was reserved for Badgers—the squirrel's archenemy. By vocally warning each other of the approach of danger, ground squirrels receive a social benefit. And, since males and females usually remain in the area where they were mated, and where young are born, these vocalizations are passed down to the next generation, somewhat like a local dialect.

Although it may strike the reader as incongruous, another soil disturber, the Grizzly Bear, will be discussed here. Few people are aware of the ecological role the grizzlies played in open areas, such as grasslands and oak savanna, prior to 1900. Extirpation of the California grizzly was complete by 1924. (The last capture of a live Grizzly Bear—"Monarch"—occurred in 1889. Monarch ended up at the zoo in Golden Gate Park in San Francisco and died in 1911. The bear was something of a legend, weighing 1,127 pounds and measuring over seven feet from nose to tip of tail. The mounted pelt is still on exhibit at the California Academy of Sciences in San Francisco.)

Grizzlies were a common sight in open grasslands before hunting pressure from early settlers forced them up into the chaparral to take refuge. For example, when Grinnell passed through the Cuyama Valley on his 1912 expedition, grizzlies had already disappeared from the lowlands. He recounts hearing that "a grizzly and two cubs are ranging in the [Sierra Madre Mountains] between here [Cuyama Valley] and the Sisquoc; the foot tracks are 11 inches long. The country the bears live in is impenetrable."

In earlier times the bears, with their extra-long claws, dug up large areas of grassland soil to search for rodents, roots, bulbs, and insect grubs. They also ate grasses, wild clover, berries, nuts, acorns, and carrion, including elk and whales. Gophers in particular were important prey for grizzlies.

Tracy Storer and Lloyd Tevis, in *California Grizzly,* quote John Xantus de Vesey, the Hungarian zoologist who was stationed in 1860 at Fort Tejon, not far from today's Wind Wolves Preserve: "This bear sometimes amuses himself with digging, like the pigs, and sometimes during a moon-light night, he will dig up many acres of lands, so that not one blade of grass is to be found on it." Xantus also noted that "The land was well-stocked with rodents" and "only the badger could vie with the bear in digging rodents from the soil."

Grizzly Bears also played a role in the Valley Oak savanna ecosystem. Captain John C. Frémont and his party in 1846 recorded the astounding sight of young Grizzly Bears feeding in the tops of Valley Oaks:

Suddenly we saw among the upper boughs a number of young grizzly bears, busily occupied in breaking off the smaller branches which carried acorns, and throwing them to the ground. Dismounting quickly and running into the open we found the ground about the trees occupied by full-grown bears, which had not seen us, and were driving the young ones back [up into the trees] until the jingle of our spurs attracted their attention.

The acorn was always a mainstay of the grizzlies' diet, and early writers mentioned this food more than any other in describing the bears' preferences.

Although the grizzly survives elsewhere in North America, it is too late to compare its ecology in other regions with that of its former place in the ecosystem of California. A keystone species of such magnitude—being a carnivore, herbivore, and digger of the soil—must have had a sizeable effect.

Carrizo Plain: Our Region's Special Desert

We now turn off Highway 166 and back to the northwest into southern San Luis Obispo County. The hot, dry, unforgiving yet fascinating landscape of the Carrizo Plain is the closest thing to the desert in our region. Comprising the western portion of the San Joaquin Valley, the Caliente and Temblor ranges, and the Carrizo and Elkhorn plains, the landscape is alien to any we have met so far.

A case could be made that this region is so distinct it could be characterized as a "West San Joaquin Desert." After

The Temblor Range, from Carrizo Plain looking east

the grasses and wildflowers of spring have shriveled and died, the relentless sun and lack of summer rainfall create a land of barren ground dotted with shrubs—many of which are typical of desert habitats.

Fifty years ago Ernest Twisselmann, member of a longtime ranching family in the Temblor Range, wrote *A Flora of Kern County, California*. He began by quoting Mary Austin describing this country:

> You will do well to avoid that range uncomforted by singing floods. You will find it forsaken of most things but beauty and madness and death and God. Many such ranges quicken the imagination with a sense of purpose not revealed, but the ordinary traveller brings nothing away from them but an intolerable thirst.

And yes, you will be thirsty. But, like all naturalists, you are not an ordinary traveler. And you must visit the Carrizo Plain.

The Carrizo Plain is a rift valley bordered on the northeast by the San Andreas Fault. On the alluvial slopes of the surrounding Temblor and Caliente mountains and on the valley floor, elements of foothill and valley grassland mix with scrubby desert plants.

Wet winters are a rarity here; dry winters and summer drought are the norm. In wet years, surface runoff from the hills collects in Soda Lake or forms ephemeral ponds known as vernal pools (see Chapter 9).

At the margins of Soda Lake, the soil has a high salt content. The whole basin is part of a broad alkali sink. Shrubs found here—**Iodine Bush** (*Allenrolfea occidentalis*), saltbush, and **Mormon tea** (*Ephedra* spp.)—are all able to withstand hot, dry, desertlike conditions.

Occasionally, in spring after a wet winter, the Carrizo Plain's typical aspect of gray shrubs and short grasses is transformed into a palette of fantastic wildflowers. Deep blue **Great Valley Phacelia** (*Phacelia ciliata*), yellow **Hillside Daisy** (*Monolopia lanceolata*), and tall, crimson **Desert Candle** (*Caulanthus inflatus*) are but a few of the outstanding ones. In these years, even the poorest, driest soils give rise

Clockwise from top: Hillside Daisy; Great Valley Phacelia; Desert Candle

to carpets of goldfields splashing brilliant yellow over the seemingly barren ridges.

Nature Journal
May 4, 2001

Carrizo Plain Natural Area

We are camped on the Carrizo Plain tonight. The sounds carry so far in the immense quiet.

All night beneath the moon, I hear the Burrowing Owls calling to each other. I'd never heard their song before, a soft "cooing" coming from the silent distance: "coo-COOOO, coo-COOOO."

The full moon over the plain is a sight—dark hills and stars and the rustle of kangaroo rats out searching for food. On a full moon, the goings-on in the grasslands are no longer secret.

The force of the land pushes everything else aside. The niceties of overcivilized society are in abeyance here. What houses there are—trailers or shacks—lie broken and abandoned.

In the early morning when the sun peeps over the Temblors and the sky is as wide as can be, the shadows still lie in the creases of the rounded hills. A pair of Loggerhead Shrikes, intent on crafting a nest in a dead tree—the only one for miles—swoop by, making their harsh call. The air is fresh, laden with that smell of dew on the grasses.

I watch as a family of ground squirrels plays at their burrow. Mama is keeping a lookout on her dirt platform, while around her tumble and play three little ones. They scuffle with each other, typical youngsters, while she watches—with a wide view of the sky and the mountains.

I have memories of visiting the Carrizo in 1993, when the phacelia—a deep, dark blue variety—was knee-high. And now, as I look off to the north of Soda Lake Road, in a few low spots—several lakes of flowers emerge. At first I think it's a mirage, like the "water" I've seen in some of the low basins that turned out not to be water at all, but an expectation of water. But this breathtaking blue patch was the marvelous phacelia of '93! It lingers in low places even this late in the spring.

We pack up and head out to drive up the McKittrick Grade into the Temblors. As we approach a dirt pull-out by the roadside, we see two rattlesnakes briefly entangled, perhaps as a prelude to mating? We stop the car, and one slithers into the grass. The other snake remains, coiling and even rattling. It is a good-sized adult—four feet long and four inches wide at its middle, with at least ten rattles. This is rattlesnake country, lest we forget.

Animals of the Carrizo Plain

Carrizo Plain National Monument consists of 250,000 acres in the heart of this arid scrubland. More endangered and threatened native species live here than perhaps any other spot in California. The **Blunt-nosed Leopard Lizard** (*Gambelia sila*), **Giant Kangaroo Rat** (*Dipodomys ingens*), **San Joaquin Antelope Squirrel** (*Ammospermophilus nelsoni*), and **San Joaquin Kit Fox** (*Vulpes macrotis* subsp. *mutica*) are the familiar ones. They are joined by various species of rare plants. The monument contains many of the habitats we've discussed: alkali sink, desert scrub, foothill and valley grassland, and juniper savanna.

As in all desert areas, animal activity takes place at night or underground.

Four of the threatened and endangered inhabitants of the Carrizo Plain (clockwise from top): San Joaquin Kit Fox, Giant Kangaroo Rat, Blunt-nosed Leopard Lizard, and San Joaquin Antelope Squirrel

When the sun sets, Giant Kangaroo Rats (measuring six inches, not counting the tail) scramble out of their burrows and hop about, searching for seeds. Like their smaller relatives, the **Agile Kangaroo Rat** (*Dipodomys agilis*) and the **Heermann's Kangaroo Rat** (*Dipodomys heermanni*), both of which are found in our region, Giant Kangaroo Rats have elaborate burrow systems known as warrens.

Equipped with super-long tails that have a tuft of fur on the end, kangaroo rats get their name from their style of locomotion: they jump, using long hind legs, holding their tails curved up over their backs. When they run, their tails wave back and forth—a distraction for predators, who may end up snapping at the rat and getting a mouthful of tail.

The most important feature of a kangaroo rat's life is its burrow. The burrows protect against predators and the weather; soil is a great buffer. Recent experiments show that the temperature of these burrows is warmer than originally thought, although cooler than the outside air. The air may reach 113°F just above the surface of the ground, but the temperature in the burrow is a comfortable 86 to 90°F.

During the day the entrance to a kangaroo rat burrow is usually blocked. By trapping the moisture from the rats' own breath, the interior of the burrow remains relatively humid compared to outside air. Furthermore, the rats' metabolic rate is lower than that of other mammals. Because less oxygen is required to maintain this lower rate, the kangaroo rat inhales less dry air and thus experiences less evaporative water loss.

Kangaroo rats gather seeds in fur-lined cheek pouches and carry them back to their burrows. Their metabolism, especially suited to a diet of seeds, breaks down the oils and fats which provide energy as well as water. Because they absorb and retain the water derived from their food, and because they secrete concentrated urine and dry feces, the rats never need to drink a drop of liquid.

Giant Kangaroo Rats are different from others of their kind. They make granaries, which are piles of seedheads harvested from herbaceous plants. They set the seedheads out to cure in the sun for four to six weeks before moving them underground to larders in the burrow. These granary mounds can be four or five feet wide and four inches high.

After many years of occupancy by Giant Kangaroo Rats, the topography becomes lumpy, with the burrows of the rats sticking up in mounds above intervening low places. The mound is the rat's "precinct." It supports lusher, greener vegetation that, due to fertilization by rat droppings, is richer in nitrogen and produces bigger seeds than the surrounding growth. After the Giant Kangaroo Rat has harvested the seeds from its granary, it clears all the dead plant litter from the precinct, leaving a bare space in the immediate area.

A rapid drumming on the ground with the large hind feet designates Giant Kangaroo Rat territoriality. They will defend their precincts and granaries. Sometimes, though, San Joaquin Antelope Squirrels and

The Gopher Snake, one of the species that shelter in rodent burrows

Blunt-nosed Leopard Lizards get away with sheltering in the burrows of Giant Kangaroo Rats to escape the heat.

In the ecosystem of the Carrizo Plain, Giant Kangaroo Rats play a crucial role. They are food for the vertebrate hunters, such as the endangered San Joaquin Kit Fox. This petite fox, with its oversized ears, is ecologically adapted to an open habitat where desert shrubs grow. Kit foxes excavate more than one den per family, sometimes as many as twenty. Dens are used to escape predators, such as the Coyote and the non-native Red Fox. The natal den, where the typical litter of four or five pups is born, is smaller than the brood den, in which the family spends the winter months. The foxes' construction of more than one den results in vacant dens, which are often occupied by Burrowing Owls.

Kit foxes are nocturnal, emerging

Juvenile Burrowing Owls imitate the sound of Western Rattlesnakes, making a buzzing sound called the "rattlesnake rasp" to frighten predators away from the nest burrow.

Borrowers of burrows on the Carrizo Plain

at sunset to hunt. Sometimes different family groups will use the same hunting area, but not at the same time. However, during the drought conditions on the Carrizo Plain between 1989 and 1991, biologists observed that home ranges did not overlap. In addition, they noted the reduced reproductive rate of kit foxes, a reaction to the effects of drought. Lack of vegetation during drought means fewer rodents and rabbits for the foxes to eat, forcing them to forgo breeding.

During this same drought period, kit foxes were studied in relation to their chief predators. Eighteen out of twenty-three kit fox deaths were attributed to Coyotes and Red Foxes. On the other hand, in some circumstances Coyotes and kit foxes showed that they could coexist. Overall, kit foxes may not need to avoid Coyotes: the foxes' hunting skills and multiple dens allow them to do better in this desert habitat than the Coyotes can.

Nevertheless, some San Joaquin Kit Fox populations have discovered a way to avoid Coyotes altogether. A recent news story describes their adaptation to human environments on the outskirts of Bakersfield. Here, in the open country surrounding suburban homes and schools, the foxes are not in competition with Coyotes, which prefer brushier habitat. Kit foxes have learned that burrows and shelters can be found in culverts, irrigation channels, and in crawl spaces under portable classrooms. Too, hunting is a lot easier in suburbia than in the dry grasses; human leftovers and pet food put out by fox lovers take the place of kangaroo rats in the foxes' diets. Interestingly, biologists have tested these urbanized kit foxes and found that besides being fatter than their wilder relations, they also have higher cholesterol readings.

But let's return to the Carrizo, where the kit foxes truly belong.

Foxes and other animals make burrows that are used by non-digging animals, such as Burrowing Owls, various rabbits, rattlesnakes, gopher snakes, and tarantulas.

The little Burrowing Owl occupies abandoned kangaroo rat and ground squirrel burrows. Often seen perched on fence posts, the Burrowing Owl spreads its wings and flies when a car approaches, eventually landing at its burrow entrance. It stands guard on spindly-looking legs, watching for enemies. The eggs and young are hidden underground in a nest chamber off the main tunnel.

The young Burrowing Owls, if alarmed, will utter a cry called the "rattlesnake rasp" which sounds exactly like a Western Rattlesnake. Experiments by researchers suggest that this acoustic mimic of a rattlesnake rattle deters predators—for example ground squirrels, which are afraid of rattlesnakes—from entering nest burrows.

This is a natural phenomenon called **Batesian mimicry**, whereby a harmless species, in order to deter a predator, imitates a species that is harmful to that predator. Named after Henry Walter Bates (1825–1892), an English naturalist who spent many years in the Amazon rainforest, Batesian mimicry was first studied in butterflies, where visual rather than acoustic mimicry was observed to deter predation.

Burrowing Owls, unlike most other owls, hunt during the day. In the spring breeding season, they feed chiefly on insects. In fall and winter they switch to small mammals or even birds for sustenance.

Western Rattlesnakes are classified as "pit vipers" because they have a deep pit, or opening, on each side of the head that aids in sensing warm-blooded prey.

The Carrizo Plain is one of the few places in our region where you can still see Burrowing Owls. They are designated a species of special concern in California, due to declining numbers in developed areas, especially along the coast.

Folklore has it that Burrowing Owls, rattlesnakes, and ground squirrels all live together in the same burrow. This is not true.

The snakes do not live in the burrows, but they may shelter there to escape the heat, to hibernate, or to bear young.

Being the chief venomous snake found in our region, the rattlesnake is often clouded in myth and misinformation. An excellent book, *Rattlesnakes, Their Habits, Life Histories, and Influence on Mankind* by Lawrence M. Klauber, is a good reference for this species. Try the abridged version, since the original work is in two volumes and fills fifteen hundred pages.

Another myth about rattlesnakes is that each rattle at the tip of the tail represents a year of the snake's life. In order to grow, the snake must shed its skin several times a year, and each time, a rattle segment is added. Therefore, especially in its younger years, a rattlesnake may shed two to four times and add two to four segments per year. Regardless, after about twelve rattles have formed, the older rattles begin to erode due to wear and tear. (In captivity, fifteen to sixteen rattles are not uncommon.) Rattlesnakes have been known to live up to twenty years in the wild, but if you see one this old, you aren't likely to see twenty segments at the end of its tail.

Rattlers must eat live prey, and they must devour it whole. In order to locate prey, since they are virtually deaf and see well only at close range, they must rely on their sense of smell. And that sense is especially keen. The forked tongue of the snake, which flickers in and out of the mouth, is used as an organ to detect odors.

Rattlesnakes are called **pit vipers** because they have a deep pit, or facial opening, on each side of the head. These pits have been called ears or extra nostrils, but their purpose is to aid in locating and striking prey. Each pit is a temperature differential receptor—that is, it is sensitive to objects having a higher temperature than the snake's surroundings: in other words, warm-blooded creatures. The pit aids the snake in locating the prey and following its movements closely enough to strike it.

Rattlers are ambush hunters; they have no need to go chasing long distances for prey, but simply lie coiled and ready to strike should the opportunity arise. When they strike, venom is delivered via retractable fangs located at the front of the upper jaw. In biting, the rattlesnake stabs and injects poison into its victim in a quick thrust. When the venom is injected, the victim is paralyzed, so the rattler does not need to struggle to subdue it.

Rattlers are most active in spring, when they are hungry after hibernation. In our region, hibernation lasts from late fall through early March. After mating, a female rattlesnake does not lay eggs, but bears live young, each of which has been encased in a flexible covering retained in the body of the mother until it is ready to be born. Although the mother snake may go into a burrow or crevice to bear the young, she does not care for them after birth. The highly venomous little six-inch wrigglers must mature on their own.

Rattlesnakes are dangerous to humans because of their poisonous bite, but they do not seek confrontation. It is up to you to watch where you walk in the backcountry. If you hear the sound of a rattlesnake, stand still and try to locate the snake. Don't move or run away; you might inadvertently step on the animal. Watching for rattlesnakes is a part of experiencing nature.

Any discussion of rodent burrows in arid grasslands (and in chaparral, too) would be incomplete without mentioning the **tarantula** (*Aphonopelma* spp.).

Newcomers to the area are shocked when they meet with this giant, hairy spider. Its appearance is enough to alarm even the most seasoned outdoor enthusiast. Once you under-

Tarantulas inhabit rodent burrows in open country. Males are more easily seen in fall, when they come out of their burrows to search for females.

The tarantula has a trick for self-defense: it rubs its hind legs against its hairy abdomen, which releases the hairs, making them fly all over the place. The hairs may inflame the skin or eyes of a predator. A tarantula may have a bald spot on its back where the hairs have been rubbed off.

Male tarantulas are more active than females, have longer legs, and do not live as long. Females have been known to live over twenty years in captivity, and they molt many times; after maturity, the males molt only once.

In late summer and fall, male tarantulas "go walkabout" in search of females. An experiment in 1999 using radio telemetry to track the males' journeys found that they traveled just under a mile in a circuitous route, searching for burrows of female tarantulas. When they found a female burrow, they entered it and mated with its occupant, often then moving on to burrows of other females. There was little evidence of a synchronized, directional movement—in other words, a migration—of all the males together. Each male appeared to wander randomly, until certain cues provided by the females enticed him into a female's burrow. The wandering was observed over a significant period of time, up to eighteen days.

Tarantulas are benign creatures, worthy of our respect and study. Please don't harm them, for they are a vital part of the arid grassland ecosystem.

* * *

stand the tarantula's lifestyle, however, perhaps it will not seem so fearsome. Its bite is certainly nothing to worry about.

Tarantulas live in loose colonies, inhabiting rodent burrows or other holes in the ground. They partially line their burrows with silk and close them at the top with a thin webbing of silk. The tarantula does not spin a web to catch prey, but waits at the entrance to its burrow. When a victim appears, the spider strikes and injects poison with powerful fangs. It eats beetles, sowbugs, and crickets.

We have come a long way on our journey through the heartland of the region. So varied and rich is the plant and animal life of our coastal and interior valleys, much has had to be omitted.

Above all, understand that the gradient of vegetation is not only from north to south in our region, but west to east. Plants requiring cooler conditions tend to drop out south of the Santa Ynez Mountains (Hadrian's Wall), and when you travel west to east, you will see plants that require moister conditions giving way to those able to stand a hotter, drier environment. In describing the lush coastal valleys replete with oaks and fertile soils, we began our journey. By the finish, we were in the saltbush scrub of the arid Carrizo Plain.

Some species are so specially adapted they remain tied to a particular habitat only. The Acorn Woodpecker cannot live in saltbush scrub. The Giant Kangaroo Rat cannot live in Pinyon Pine–Juniper woodland. In contrast, the Mountain Lion, the Mule Deer, and the Western Rattlesnake will occur throughout these valleys, from the coast to the interior.

It is this extraordinary richness of flora and fauna that sets our region apart. Cool groves of Coast Live Oak with Acorn Woodpeckers and Western Scrub-Jays hustling for acorns; pinyon pines and junipers clinging to steep hillsides in canyons of the Cuyama Valley, where wintering birds feed on juniper berries; grasslands in the foothills at the southern tip of the San Joaquin Valley, where Tule Elk roam; and a slice of desert scrubland on the Carrizo Plain, where endangered species thrive.

These are the landscapes of the heartland of the Santa Barbara region. If you have never visited them, you have a lot to look forward to...

CHAPTER 8: THE MOUNTAINS—PINES ON SKY ISLANDS

Leaving behind the foothill woodlands of the valley slopes, we now travel up toward the summits of our high mountains. It is a land of sweet-smelling conifers and unclouded skies. The air is fresh. The scent of the pines and the gentle breeze trigger childhood memories of mountain vacations in other forests.

The view of the streams and valleys below gives meaning to the names found on maps and transforms them into real landmarks. That ridge, that mountaintop, that riverbed, that canyon—they spread before you now in an unforgettable scene. More than simply arriving at the summit, you have gained an overview of the region's landscape. For a sense of the topography of the land, you must venture atop our highest mountains.

To those of us who live in the flatlands, the mountains hold special mysteries. Over these summits, California Condors have begun to soar once more. Through the forest understory, black bears shuffle along, stopping to sample juicy currants. Chipmunks scamper up and down the Jeffrey Pine trunks.

And the birdlife: so different from that of the lowlands. A more northerly avifauna is found here. Relicts of a time when the climate was wetter and cooler, these forests in isolated pockets on the highest peaks create a microhabitat for bird species more commonly found in the Sierra Nevada. Many of the trees, shrubs, wildflowers, and mammals found here are also denizens of the Sierra.

One of the paradoxes of Southern California and its Mediterranean climate is the surprising presence of coniferous forests. In contrast to the coast, with its mild, maritime influence, inland mountain ranges are governed by the extremes of a more interior climate regime. Snow and cold temperatures—unheard of on

Jeffrey Pines grow in open, parklike stands on Mount Pinos.

the coast even in winter—are a fact of life in the high mountains.

The term "sky islands" has been used to describe the mountaintops in our area. Many of the mountains are completely surrounded by chaparral, just as islands are surrounded by water. But on their summits, above the sea of chaparral, small patches of verdant forest survive. Imagine a landscape like that of the Sierra Nevada within two hours of the coast.

This is the magic of our high mountains. With no warning, you round the next corner of a boulder-clad, chaparral-covered slope and find yourself in another world.

The stark contrast between the sea of chaparral and the shady coniferous forest is unique to Southern California mountains. Often, chaparral marches right up to the 6,000 foot level on the south-facing slope of a mountain, while on the north side grows a lush coniferous forest.

Mountains, with their endless views and towering conifers, are rare in our region. Just as John Muir was drawn

to the Sierra Nevada, so we seek the beauty and solace of our montane forests closer to home.

Montane Mixed Conifer Forests

Where are these high mountain forests and how can you get to them? In Chapter 2 we discussed the mountain ranges of our region, including the San Rafael range, where patches of coniferous forest can be found on the highest peaks: Figueroa Mountain, which is reached by car from the Santa Ynez Valley, and Big Pine Mountain, a remote peak with restricted access in the San Rafael Wilderness. Another area of coniferous forest is at Pine Mountain Ridge, a succession of summits, the highest of which is Reyes Peak. Pine Mountain Ridge is accessible by car from Highway 33. The Mount Pinos complex includes Mount Pinos, Sawmill Mountain, Grouse Mountain, and Cerro Noroeste. This area is accessible by car from the west via Lockwood Valley and from the east via Interstate 5, exiting at Frazier Park.

Bigcone Spruce (foreground) grows on the north-facing slope at Ranger Peak near Figueroa Mountain.

Mixed coniferous forest on the north slope of Big Pine Mountain; chaparral-covered slopes of the Sierra Madre Mountains in the distance

Singleleaf Pinyon Pines in snow near Pine Mountain summit

In Chapter 7 we discussed Gray Pine, Pinyon Pine, and California Juniper, all of which are cone-bearing trees that grow at lower elevations. Now let's focus on those that grow higher up—from about 4,000 to 8,000 feet. This is known as the mixed conifer forest. In our region, it is the finest forest with the greatest variety of trees.

The pines, firs, and cedars that make up the mixed conifer forest bear their seeds in cones and have needles or scalelike leaves. Conifers bear two sets of cones: tiny pollen cones (male), which are seldom noticed; and the more familiar, much larger seed cones (female). The male pollen cones tend to grow near the bottom of the tree, while the female seed cones are attached higher up.

The process of pollination occurs when the wind blows the pale yellow grains of the pollen cones and one tiny speck lands on a female cone.

Pollen cones quickly fall off the tree when pollination is finished, but the seed cones persist for a long time. In the pine genus, seed cones can vary from one inch to more than twenty inches in length. After the seeds have been fertilized, the cones of most conifers open and the seeds are then borne away on the wind and eaten or dispersed by animals. When growing conditions are favorable, the seeds sprout in the forest duff and young trees form an understory.

Depending upon topography, soils, and elevation, the species composition of a mixed coniferous forest differs from one mountain to another, and from one site to another on that mountain. Often, the trees cling to steep, rocky slopes with poor soils. As with the oaks, mycorrhizal fungi are essential to the health of conifers. The decaying litter of conifers tends to be acidic, so bacteria are absent. The fungi assist in decomposing organic litter on the forest floor, permeating the soil to absorb nutrients and water for the trees.

The Coulter Pine bears the largest cone in our region.

Like deciduous trees, these evergreens lose their needles—just not all at once. They must withstand the adversity of drought and freezing temperatures, and because they continuously shed and replace their needles, they can carry out photosynthesis all year—although at a slower rate in winter. The length of time the needles remain on the branches varies from one species to another.

Conifers are among the most long-lived organisms on earth. Some Bristlecone Pines, for example, have weathered more than forty-seven hundred growing seasons, surviving one of the most inhospitable habitats in North America.

Trees of the Mixed Conifer Forest

Traveling up the mountainside, let's take the conifers in the order in which they might appear, from those occurring at lower elevations to those at higher ones.

The **Coulter Pine** (*Pinus coulteri*), with long needles in bundles of three, is found chiefly in California. Within the state, its range is from San Francisco to Baja; it is absent from the Sierra Nevada. Coulter Pine cones are massive, among the heaviest in the world. Don't place your sleeping bag beneath a Coulter Pine, because the huge cones can weigh up to eight pounds—a rude awakening indeed.

Coulter Pines are sometimes **serotinous**, meaning they need the heat of fire to open up and release their seeds. This is an advantage in Coulter Pine groves, which are often adjacent to chaparral and subject to wildfires. The nourishing bed of ashes left behind after a fire enables the seedlings to grow deep roots the first year and mature quickly. Coulter Pines will bear cones within ten to fifteen years after they've taken root. On Big Pine Mountain, where the Zaca Fire of 2007 burned heavily in patches of Coulter Pine forest, seedlings have sprouted on much of the forest floor. They are surrounded by the burned trunks of a ghost forest of parent trees.

Coulter Pines frequently form a transition from foothill woodland or chaparral to the true montane forests higher up. A good place to see Coulter Pines is at the intersection of Figueroa Mountain Road and the road up to the Pino Alto Picnic Area on the summit of Figueroa Mountain, or on the top of La Cumbre Peak behind Santa Barbara.

Bigcone Spruce (*Pseudotsuga macrocarpa*), often found at the same lower elevations as Coulter Pine, is a true Southern California specialty. From the Santa Ynez Mountains south (Hadrian's Wall again!), Bigcone Spruce replaces Douglas-Fir, a more northerly species. These two trees are the only *Pseudotsugas* in North America. *Pseudotsuga* means "false hemlock" and refers to the Bigcone's drooping foliage and papery-scaled cones—similar to those of a hemlock tree.

Bigcone Spruce likes the shady slopes, whereas Coulter Pine goes for the sunny ones. In steep, north-facing canyons where moisture lingers, tall, raggedy Bigcone Spruce, with their outstretched dark limbs, can be identified from a great distance. Occasionally they are interspersed with oaks and even chaparral, so they have a kinship with Coulter Pines in that regard.

Bigcone Spruce on north-facing slopes along Upper Sespe Creek

Cones of Bigcone Spruce (above) and Ponderosa Pine

On Figueroa Mountain, drive along the north side of Ranger Peak or hike down the Davy Brown Trail into Fir Canyon and you'll encounter Bigcone Spruce. Its name notwithstanding, its cones are only big in comparison to those of its cousin the Douglas-Fir, so don't be disappointed when you see they're only five inches long. The cones are really pretty, with tiny

267

Canyon Live Oak, with bicolored leaves and large acorns

three-pronged bracts growing out of the scales.

While you're up on Figueroa Mountain, look for the **Canyon Live Oak** (*Quercus chrysolepis*), which frequently consorts with these lower elevation conifers. This oak can have large spreading limbs, or it can grow like an oversized shrub, but it is the brownish-gold fuzz on the underside of the younger leaves that makes it unique. The old-fashioned name "Golden-cup Oak" aptly describes the outer scales of the wide acorn cups, which are covered with the same brownish-gold fuzz. The acorns are big and sturdy. Canyon Live Oaks are similar to the various scrub oaks in their response to fire, resprouting from the root crown.

Moving now up to the summit of Figueroa Mountain at Pino Alto Picnic Area, you notice the tall spires

of **Ponderosa Pine** (*Pinus ponderosa*). Ponderosa Pine grows throughout the West, but in our region it is not abundant. In contrast, **Jeffrey Pine** (*Pinus jeffreyi*), which is largely restricted to California, is the staple of mixed coniferous forests on our highest mountains. Above 6,000 feet, Jeffrey Pines, with their thick, reddish-brown trunks and spreading, scraggly crowns, reign supreme. Jeffrey Pines are common on the four peaks we will study in this chapter, with the exception of Figueroa Mountain, which has only Ponderosas.

Some naturalists find it difficult to tell Jeffrey Pines from Ponderosa Pines in the field, because they are very similar in appearance. Both have long needles in bunches of three. The phrase "gentle Jeffrey and prickly Ponderosa" is a reminder: when you

Jeffrey Pine seedlings

(*Abies concolor*) mix with Jeffreys in the shadiest areas. White Firs have stiff, short, bluish-gray needles. They look like typical Christmas trees, with straight branches graduated from top to bottom. The barrel-shaped cones, sitting erect on the topmost branches, make the White Fir easy to recognize. In our region, the White Fir is found only on the highest mountains. You can picture its boughs laden with snow all winter, a California Christmas tree in its natural surroundings—unlike the ones for sale at Christmastime in parking lots downtown.

A case can be made for the **Sugar Pine** (*Pinus lambertiana*) as the most beloved of our high-mountain conifers. Everybody knows the Sugar Pine, with its super-long, narrow cones (up to twenty-four inches, the longest of any pine) hanging at the tips of graceful, sweeping branches. The straight, gray trunk reaches very tall, over one hundred feet in our region and taller in the Sierra Nevada. This majestic tree grows sparingly on the shady slopes of Big Pine Mountain, Reyes Peak, and Mount Pinos.

handle Jeffrey cones, the spines point down and do not prick you. When you grasp Ponderosa cones, the spines stick out and are uncomfortable to the touch. Another difference is that the undersides of the scales on the cones of Ponderosa Pine are much darker than they are above, whereas the cone scales of Jeffrey Pine are the same color above and below.

And then there's always the smell test. If you get up close to the bark of a Jeffrey Pine you will find it has the delicate, sweet scent of vanilla, which the Ponderosa Pine doesn't have.

Jeffrey Pines are the dominant conifer in our high-elevation forests, but at moister sites on the north slopes, especially where deep snow lies well into spring, the beautiful **White Firs**

White Fir in winter on Mount Pinos

269

Sugar Pine, with long cones hanging from the ends of the branches

Sugar Pine cones

Incense Cedar (*Calocedrus decurrens*) is not a pine, but a tall, cinnamon-barked member of the Cypress family. The leaves are pressed flat and lightly scaled, and the cones so small you hardly notice them. Incense Cedar has become more common in forests over the last hundred years than in the past because its wood was not considered good for lumber; while pines were logged, Incense Cedars were left. They were a weed tree, taking over disturbed soils after logging or bulldozing. Just like White Firs, young Incense Cedars don't mind growing in shady conditions; they like a moist forest.

In its natural state, our mixed conifer forest is open and sunny, allowing for a variety of trees and shrubs to grow. When fire has not burned in many decades, however, White Fir and Incense Cedar crowd out other species of trees, preventing the sun-loving shrubs, seedling oaks, and other pines from sprouting.

Incense Cedar is somewhat immune to patchy wildfire, but where fire burns hot and heavy, as the Zaca Fire did on Big Pine Mountain in 2007, the hardest hit trees are completely destroyed. Now, the formerly dense Incense Cedar–White Fir forest in certain areas on the north slope of Big Pine has been completely opened up. Among the stark, black trunks, a three-foot-high growth of burgeoning ceanothus and other shrubs creates a vital understory. Conifer seedlings push up through the ashes next to charred logs. Much as we mourn the loss of the tall conifers here, it's an excellent example of forest rejuvenation and the importance of the fire cycle.

Incense Cedar on Big Pine Mountain

The Understory in a Mixed Coniferous Forest

Look around as you walk through the forest. Between the trunks of towering trees, the forest floor is largely bare. Shrubs are sparse. The shallow soils and steep slopes do not encourage a wealth of vegetation. More importantly, the lack of rainfall all summer means only the most drought-tolerant shrubs will flourish. Unlike in the Sierra Nevada, where summer thunderstorms bring occasional moisture, our montane shrubs and herbs must endure the summer without any refreshing rainfall.

Most understory plants are components of montane chaparral. In several cases, they are high-elevation forms of chaparral species we already met in Chapter 6. **Parry Manzanita** (*Arctostaphylos parryana*) is joined by various ceanothus species, such as **Mountain Whitethorn** (*Ceanothus cordulatus*) and **Deer Brush** (*Ceanothus integerrimus*). Parish's Snowberry is a

Bush Lupines and California Poppies on open slopes of Figueroa Mountain

Rabbitbrush grows in open areas between the Limber Pines that dominate the subalpine forest at the summit of Mount Pinos.

Clockwise from top left: Parish's Snowberry, Wax Currant, and Snow Plant

bushy ground cover of the Honeysuckle family, common in sunny portions of the forest. Several species of currant and gooseberry provide succulent, reddish berries when ripe. On Pine Mountain Ridge and on Mount Pinos, the aromatic Great Basin Sagebrush and in fall, **Yellow Rabbitbrush** (*Chrysothamnus viscidiflorus*) comprise elements of the understory. Though not in huge variety, these shrubs provide crucial shelter and fruits for many birds and mammals.

One of the greatest joys of exploring our coniferous forests is discovering familiar wildflowers blooming here that you might have first identified on walks in the Sierra Nevada. The Scarlet Penstemon, pale white **Plain Mariposa Lily** (*Calochortus invenustus*), **Red Columbine** (*Aquilegia formosa*), orange Western Wallflower, and blue-and-white **Collinsia** (*Collinsia childii*), to mention a few, are present; you're likely to see them if you visit several mountaintops in June.

Under the shadiest patches of the forest, red **Snow Plants** (*Sarcodes sanguinea*) pop up out of the pine needles covering the forest floor. Snow Plants

Wind-pruned Limber Pines on Mount Pinos

are saprophytes, which get their food from the roots of the pine trees by way of a fungus. The fungus is similar to the mycorrhizal fungi that aid conifers in absorbing organic matter.

Montane Meadow

Iris Meadow on Mount Pinos is the only accessible montane meadow in our region. Located on the north slope of the mountain, the meadow is ringed by Jeffrey Pine forest. Here, where an ephemeral snow-melt seep trickles out of a wide swale, tall white **Corn Lilies** (*Veratrum californicum*) and **Ranger's Buttons** (*Sphenosciadium capitellatum*) stand with masses of Western Blue Flag iris. In late spring and early summer, the meadow echoes with bird song; chipmunks and squirrels scuttle up and down the Jeffrey Pine trunks. This is our region's version of a Sierra Neva-dan alpine meadow, and you can drive right up to it.

Subalpine Forest

A short walk from the parking lot at Iris Meadow up to the summit of Mount Pinos brings you to the only example of subalpine forest in our region. At over 8,800 feet elevation—almost to timberline here—the trees are shorter and the forest is open and windswept. Winter temperatures are frigid, and precipitation in the form of snowfall is close to forty inches per year; strong winds in fall and winter shear the trees, pruning their tops and stunting their growth. The resulting **krummholz** (meaning "twisted wood") aspect of the trees near timberline can be seen in Jeffrey Pines and White Firs that grow sideways with gnarled branches touching the ground.

Limber Pines inhabit the rounded, exposed summit of Mount Pinos.

But it is a different species, **Limber Pine** (*Pinus flexilis*), that dominates this exposed forest. On dry, windy mountaintops, where growing conditions are extremely difficult, Limber Pines do well. With their crooked, short branches and flexible boughs, Limber Pines recall the **Whitebark Pine** (*Pinus albicaulis*), which grows at timberline in the Sierra Nevada.

Clark's Nutcrackers and Limber Pines

Limber Pines have a mutually beneficial relationship with the Clark's Nutcracker, a gray bird with striking black and white wings. All nutcracker-dependent pines, like the Limber Pine and Whitebark Pine, have large, wingless seeds that aren't dispersed by wind. When the seeds within the cones are ripe, the nutcrackers will harvest them. Standing on a cone or on an adjacent branch, the nutcracker uses its long, sharp bill to jab between the cone scales to remove the seeds. Upon removing a seed, the bird tests to see if it is healthy by moving it up and down in its bill, a process known as "bill clicking." If the seed is sound, the nutcracker places it in a pouch located beneath its tongue. The bird may carry up to a hundred seeds at once in the pouch, swelling its throat.

As its relative the Western Scrub-Jay does in oak woodland, the nutcracker stores Limber Pine seeds for future use by burying them. Distances vary, but sometimes the birds will fly several miles to find the perfect spot to cache the seeds. Often it is on a south-facing slope, where spring snow will melt earlier than in other places. Here, the nutcracker disgorges the seeds from its pouch and, after digging a little trench in the forest litter, deposits its treasure. Caches typically contain one to fifteen seeds, sometimes as many as thirty.

Beginning in early February, Clark's Nutcrackers retrieve the seeds from the caches. Snow or ice often cover the ground, but the birds will locate many of the seeds they buried, even if it was as long as six months before. Research has proven that nutcrackers possess a sophisticated spatial memory. Using visual cues such as rocks, logs, and trees, the bird that buried those seeds returns and digs them up.

Clark's Nutcrackers, found on Mount Pinos, are important dispersers of Limber Pine seeds.

The Fell-field Community of Cushion Plants on Mount Pinos

Once you've admired the Limber Pines and the spectacular view from this mountaintop, turn your attention to the little flower garden beneath your feet. Watch where you step. Everywhere, the cushion plants grow in rounded masses over the rocky soil between the granite slabs.

Because of its location at the junction of the Southern Coast Ranges to the northwest, the Transverse Ranges to the east, and the San Joaquin Valley to the northeast, Mount Pinos is at a unique crossroads, and its high elevation and isolation made it atypical of Southern California mountains. All these conditions make for interesting plant life on the mountain.

Fell-field is a European term meaning "stony field." Fell-fields occur on high, barren slopes where soils are thin and sandy, and where strong winds carry away the finer particles, leaving only gravel. The special aspect of the Mount Pinos fell-field is its relatively low elevation, below 9,000 feet; fell-fields are found in areas above 11,500 feet in the Sierra Nevada.

Frequently, however, more seeds are cached than can be recovered, and those are the ones that will sprout.

Limber Pines' growth habits reflect the forgotten caches of the Clark's Nutcracker. The trees sprout in clusters and mature as a small group of pines. And, since caches are often seeds gathered from the same tree, chances are that the pines in that cluster are related. In this way, the genetic traits of successfully dispersed Limber Pines are passed on, which is why Limber Pines have ascending branches with prominently displayed cones at their tips—making it as easy as possible for the Clark's Nutcrackers to find the cones and disperse their seeds.

In our region, Limber Pines comprise a subalpine forest on Mount Pinos; they can be found sparingly on Reyes Peak and Sawmill Mountain, too. Interestingly, Limber Pine is the only species of pine that grows side by side with the ancient Bristlecone Pines in the White Mountains east of Bishop.

In 2008, botanists from UCLA published an important paper on the ecology of the subalpine fell-field atop Mount Pinos. They examined the leaves and growth habits of four key alpine cushion plants: **Kennedy's Buckwheat** (*Eriogonum kennedyi*), **Western Mountain Phlox** (*Phlox austromontana*), **Brewer's Lupine** (*Lupinus breweri*), and **Pursh's Locoweed** (*Astragalus purshii*). Each of these is a tiny, low-growing plant with minuscule leaves and lots of flowers.

Kennedy's Buckwheat (top) and Brewer's Lupine (bottom) are part of the rare fell-field plant community at the summit of Mount Pinos.

The buckwheat is a mass of pink puff-ball flowers; white star-shaped blossoms cover the phlox; the blue lupine is miniaturized; and the white loco-weed has marvelous, large seedpods covered with whitish hairs.

The scientists found that each of these cushion plants had **amphistomatic** leaves—there were pores, or **stomata**, on both sides of the leaves—to facilitate photosynthesis: the leaves can absorb more carbon dioxide and release more oxygen this way. Most plants have stomata on only the bottom surface of the leaves. But these cushion plants atop Mount Pinos, like many desert plants, survive by photosynthesizing quickly, maximizing the short growing season at this altitude.

Studying the Montane Birds of Our Region

Before the 1980s, little attention had been paid to the bird life on the highest mountains of our region, with the exception of Mount Pinos. Because the mountains are situated between the lofty Southern Sierra Nevada to the northeast and the high San Gabriel, San Bernardino, and San Jacinto mountains to the southeast, they may have been overlooked by earlier ornithologists. Indeed, the forested areas on these summits are relatively small, and in the case of Big Pine Mountain, they are rugged and difficult to access.

In 1981 I set out with several other birders to census the montane breeding birds of four isolated mountain-tops in our region: Figueroa Mountain (4,528 feet), Big Pine Mountain (6,828 feet), Pine Mountain (7,510 feet), and Mount Pinos (8,831 feet).

The Steller's Jay is a common, year-round resident of the coniferous forests.

These mountains are of great ornithological interest. They are surrounded at lower elevations by chaparral. When a montane bird attempts to colonize one of these mountaintops, it must fly over inhospitable habitat for many miles to reach the coniferous forest on the summit.

Some questions we wanted to answer were: Is there a difference in the number of montane species inhabiting the four mountains? What similarities could we find between the

White-headed Woodpeckers are rare away from the higher mountains.

In the 1970s, scientists were excited about the theory of island biogeography. Although it originated as a study of true islands, it soon became popular as a way of studying islands of montane habitat surrounded by barren desert, such as occurs in the Great Basin. Island biogeography yielded some interesting hypotheses. First, larger islands were predicted to have a greater variety of species, and larger populations of those species, than smaller islands; and second, islands closer to a source of potential colonizers were predicted to have more species than distant islands.

In examining our sky islands of montane habitat, we found that the single most important factor influencing the distribution of montane birds was the extent of suitable habitat for a species. Three variables contributed to this: extent of coniferous forest, rainfall, and elevation. Another factor, proximity to neighboring mountains, was more difficult to measure.

Not surprisingly, we found the greatest number of montane species on Mount Pinos: it has the largest acreage of montane coniferous forest, and it is closer to a source for montane birds (the Southern Sierra Nevada) than the other mountains in the study.

Generally, the number of montane species declined from east to west and from the highest mountain to the lowest, but the drop-off was not uniform.

Species such as **Golden-crowned Kinglet** (*Regulus satrapa*) and **Red-breasted Nuthatch** (*Sitta canadensis*) were more dependent upon a moist forest habitat than upon elevation or location. For example, on Big Pine Mountain, Golden-crowned Kinglets

avifauna of these peaks, the nearby Sierra Nevada, and the other Southern California mountains mentioned above? Would the number of montane species drop off as we moved from east to west and from highest to lowest—Mount Pinos to Figueroa Mountain? What factors affected the bird populations on each mountain: Altitude? Size of forested area?

Although we recorded all the bird species we found to be present, we were especially interested in those defined as "montane": generally, those found above 5,000 feet and associated with the coniferous forest.

Birds of Four Isolated Mountains

	Mt. Pinos	Pine Mtn.	Big Pine Mtn.	Figueroa Mtn.
Northern Goshawk	B+	—	—	—
Blue Grouse	E?	—	—	—
Mountain Quail	B	B	B	B
Flammulated Owl	B	—	B'	B
Northern Pygmy-Owl	B	B	B	B
Spotted Owl	B	B	B	B
Northern Saw-whet Owl	B	B"	B	B
Calliope Hummingbird	B	SV	SV	—
Red-breasted Sapsucker	B	B	B	—
Williamson's Sapsucker	B"	B+	—	—
White-headed Woodpecker	B	B	B	SV
Olive-sided Flycatcher	B	B	B	B
Dusky Flycatcher	B	B	B	—
Steller's Jay	B	B	B	B
Clark's Nutcracker	B	SV	—	—
Mountain Chickadee	B	B	B	B
Red-breasted Nuthatch	B	B"	B	B"
Pygmy Nuthatch	B	B	B	B
Brown Creeper	B	B	B	B
Golden-crowned Kinglet	B	B'	B	—
Ruby-crowned Kinglet	E	—	—	—
Mountain Bluebird	SV	—	—	—
Townsend's Solitaire	B	B	—	—
Hermit Thrush	B	—	SV	—
Solitary Vireo	B	B"	B	B
Nashville Warbler	B"	—	B+	—
Yellow-rumped Warbler	B	B	B	—
Hermit Warbler	SV	—	—	—
MacGillivray's Warbler	B"	—	B"	—
Wilson's Warbler	B+	SV	—	—
Western Tanager	B	B	B	B
Green-tailed Towhee	B	B	B"	—
Fox Sparrow	B	B	B	—
Lincoln's Sparrow	B+	—	—	—
Dark-eyed Junco	B	B	B	B
Purple Finch	B	B	B	B
Cassin's Finch	B	B	B+	SV
Red Crossbill	B	SV	SV	SV
Pine Siskin	B	—	—	SV
Evening Grosbeak	SV	—	SV	SV

Breeding status of montane species in four areas of Santa Barbara, Ventura, and Kern Counties: B confirmed breeding; B+ confirmed but irregular, not annual; B' probably breeding; B" possibly breeding; SV summer visitor, no breeding evidence; E extirpated, formerly bred.

The Flammulated Owl is one of the birds the author surveyed on local mountaintops. Photo by Peter Gaede

We were especially interested in one species of tiny owl, the **Flammulated Owl** (*Otus flammeolus*). These six-inch gnomes carry a mystique: they're long-distance migrants, but little is known about their wintering range and habitat in Mexico. Every spring the owls make a journey north to montane areas of the West, returning to established territories year after year.

Flammulateds are equipped with a special vocal chord anatomy that makes them even more difficult to locate by sound than most other owls. They produce hoarse, low-frequency notes which are ventriloquial; one of these birds can be calling repeatedly from a tree right over your head all night long and you may never locate or see it. What's more, when you hear these deep hoots in the forest, they sound as though the bird were far away, but it could be quite close.

Flammulated Owls, being strictly nocturnal, are always a challenge to find, and because they're so difficult to see, censusing is done by calls alone. The deep hoots are territorial calls, a warning to intruders and a lure to female owls.

Biologists who study Flammulateds have discovered that they prefer open forests with little understory—similar to some of the habitat in the mountainous areas of our region. The owls locate prey visually, and they feed on a variety of insects. In early spring, they go after owlet moths (Family Noctuidae), but later in summer they subsist on beetles, crickets, and grasshoppers. They use their talons to snatch prey, then transfer it to their bills.

were more common than on arid Pine Mountain and Mount Pinos, despite the fact that the latter mountains are higher and support more forest.

When cataclysmic changes occur in the montane coniferous habitat, as happened on Big Pine Mountain with the Zaca Fire of 2007, bird populations are greatly affected. Golden-crowned Kinglets have yet to return to Big Pine Mountain. But newcomers from other montane species, including Townsend's Solitaire, have been sighted there. (See Chapter 6 for more on post-fire changes on Big Pine Mountain.)

Nature Journal
June 1–3, 1990

Bird Survey on Mount Pinos and Cerro Noroeste

Tonight we are camped at the Mount Pinos Campground. The smell of the warm earth, the clear air, the wonderful open stands of Jeffrey Pines—this is where my heart lives.

We arrived about 6:30 p.m., driving from Santa Barbara. The rest of my (tolerant) birding friends are already here, ready to begin the two-day census on this, the highest mountain in our study area. The smell of the pines and the still night remind me of many June nights camping out on other mountains. The coastal girl, I am drawn to the mountains. I can't get enough of the cold and the freshness, the sense of adventure in a new place.

On this absolutely calm, clear night, the half moon rises and the stars fill the clear sky from one horizon to the other.

It is time to begin the nocturnal portion of the survey. We must census the owl species. First, we drive over to McGill Campground, pile out of the car, and listen. The dark shapes of the trees mock us in stately silence. They seem almost human, standing in judgment of our crude efforts to attract the owls. Nothing. No response.

We shiver; it's getting colder, later, and the owls are absent.

Next stop: Fir Ridge Road, a deserted track through the middle of the forest. Every quarter-mile, we listen for the call of the Flammulated Owl and the Northern Saw-whet Owl. Neither of these species has been found on Mount Pinos since the 1930s. We need to know if

they still frequent this monster of a mountain.

I am getting tired and discouraged. It's near midnight and the silence, like the cold night, presses in on us from every direction.

As a final effort, at the far end of the track we stand patiently, ears straining.

What was that noise? A faint, muffled hoot from far, far upslope. The Flammulated Owl! I can hardly contain my excitement.

"Hoot...hoot....hoot"—very deep and distant from the dark, fir-clad hill. This tiny, tiny owl has a powerful voice. After about five minutes, the hooting begins to come closer.

And yes, there's another. One seems to be answering with a single, low hoot while the other responds in double hoots, so it really sounds like "whoo-WHOOT, whoo-WHOOT, whoo-WHOOT." If you listen long enough, you hear a measured rhythm, like a minuet.

Eventually, one of the owls comes near. It is probably in one of the closest pines, looking down at us. We feel the brush of air as it flies overhead. We don't attempt to see it or disturb it. We have our evidence and I am thrilled beyond words.

As we are about to leave, another type of call, from downslope, breaches the silence. It is the constant staccato call of a Northern Saw-whet Owl, "Toot-toot-toot-toot." Wow! More good data here.

Suddenly, right beside us, a wrenching, terrifying scream breaks the night. Sounding like a Halloween witch's screech, or the death throes of a small mammal, this is just another of the calls of the Northern Saw-whet Owl. I am unnerved by the eerie sound, but elated at the response. Now we have good evidence of these two species of owls on Mount Pinos—for the first time in sixty years!

The dark trees stand quiet and tall and the moon is so bright you can walk back without a flashlight. I might as well be walking on the moon itself, I am so happy, and awed at the bravery and ferocity of these little owls. We simply wait and look on in wonder as, invisible but so close by, the birds approach us and call out in defense of their breeding territories.

Morning comes quickly after a night of owling. I lie in my sleeping bag, listening to the melodies of Green-tailed Towhee and Fox Sparrow in the campground. Steller's Jays chatter and bicker at each other around the campsite. An Olive-sided Flycatcher on top of a nearby pine sounds off, "quick-THREE-beers!" I treasure the dawn chorus of the mountain birds coming to life after the cold night.

At the picnic table, coffee and oatmeal have never tasted so good.

After driving up to Iris Meadow, we decide to explore this special place. We watch as a male Calliope Hummingbird displays in fine fashion: a great ascending flight upwards, and then a downward-rushing arc. At the base of the loop, the Calliope makes a small sound like a rubber band vibrating. This, our smallest hummingbird, breeds sparingly—only on Mount Pinos, of all the mountaintops in the study. And there he sits on a Wax Currant bush, king of the mountain—his purple throat feathers flared out to catch the morning sun.

The day is utterly calm again, perfect for censusing birds. And our luck never quits. Hiking towards the summit from Iris Meadow, we decide to take a side trip where the road forks. The north-facing slope of the mountain drops off steeply here; Limber Pines cling to the rocky soil.

The continuous, rollicking, melodious song of a Townsend's Solitaire, an uncommon bird anywhere in Southern California, makes us stop in our tracks. It sings on and on from the top of a scraggly Limber Pine.

And so began two days of intense, productive bird surveying. We drove over to nearby Cerro Noroeste and camped there the second night. It was like being in the Sierra, but different. The forest is drier here, where loads and loads of flat-topped old Jeffrey Pines grow.

There's a secret spring on Cerro Noroeste where all the birds come to drink. Here we sat on a boulder and watched as crimson-headed Cassin's Finches bathed, Pine Siskins drank, and a pair of White-headed Woodpeckers brought their two juveniles to the running water.

The deep, quiet night on Cerro Noroeste yielded no owls whatsoever. But I didn't care. I was in the mountains and it was glorious.

Other Animals of the Coniferous Forest

Endemic Subspecies of Mount Pinos

One of the birds I searched for in vain during the montane bird surveys was the **Mount Pinos Sooty Grouse** (*Dendragapus fuliginosus* subsp. *howardi*), a subspecies endemic to the Mount Pinos area. The last confirmed sightings were in the 1970s.

Although tantalizing reports of sightings of this bird persisted throughout the time we were conducting our studies, neither I nor any of our other observers could confirm them. Biologist James Bland, who conducted surveys from 2002 through 2009, is at work on a paper soon to be published:

"Surveys and Habitat Assessments Indicate Extirpation of Mount Pinos Sooty Grouse from the Sky Islands of South-Central California." Sadly, as his title indicates, this unique subspecies of the Sooty Grouse (formerly known as the Blue Grouse) can no longer be found in the Mount Pinos forests. The closest population to us is in the Greenhorn Mountains in northern Kern County.

Another endemic subspecies, however, has fared better. The **Mount Pinos Chipmunk** (*Tamias speciosus* subsp. *callipeplus*), a subspecies of the Lodgepole Chipmunk, is a beautiful, deep chestnut-colored chipmunk living at the highest elevations on Mount Pinos only. Above 7,000 feet, this little chipmunk scurries in the open forest underneath the tall Jeffrey Pines. Mount Pinos Chipmunks can be found around old logs, rotting stumps, and rocky outcroppings on the forest floor. They avoid a thick understory, which is preferred by their cousin the **Merriam's Chipmunk** (*Tamias merriami*), farther down the mountain.

The Mount Pinos Chipmunk is an endemic subspecies.

All chipmunks have five dark stripes alternating with four lighter stripes that run from the nose to the rump. The Mount Pinos Chipmunk has wide, bright white outer stripes and a rich, chestnut-brown coloration. This differs from the Merriam's Chipmunk, which has a duller coat and less contrast in its stripes. An illustration of what's called **Gloger's Rule**—that mammal species in humid areas are more heavily pigmented than those in drier areas—can be seen by comparing the fur pattern of Merriam's Chipmunk with that of the Mount Pinos Chipmunk. In the moist, coniferous forest, the light-and-dark pattern of the Mount Pinos Chipmunk reflects the patterns of light and shade on the forest floor. In the drier areas at lower elevations, the duller coats of Merriam's Chipmunks blend into the monochrome of chaparral shrubs.

It appears the playful Mount Pinos Chipmunk has nothing to do but chase around a pine stump all day. But if a predator approaches, the chipmunk is off in a flash. It races up the trunk of the nearest tree, flicking its tail from side to side, and scurries to safety in the higher branches.

The chipmunk is easiest to see in fall, when it busily gathers and stores pine seeds, grasses, and berries for winter. Stuffing its cheek pouches with food, the chipmunk carries supplies to its den, located underground beneath a rock or log. Chipmunks don't truly hibernate; they assume a state of torpor, slowing down their metabolism to endure the winter cold. Occasionally, they come out of torpor to consume bits of stored food.

More about Chipmunks and Squirrels

The Mount Pinos Chipmunk's lower-elevation relative, Merriam's Chipmunk, is found just about anywhere, particularly in brushy chaparral habitats and on up through oak woodlands, all the way to the coniferous forest. On all the other high mountains in our region, except the summit area of Mount Pinos, the expected chipmunk is Merriam's.

Merriam's Chipmunk squeaks, chatters, and scolds to communicate alarm or aggression. One sound in particular, a sharp, staccato "hoot" or "chuk" is very similar to that of the **Northern Pygmy-Owl** (*Glaucidium gnoma*), a small montane owl that eats other birds. Many an inexperienced naturalist, when censusing for pygmy-owls, has heard Merriam's Chipmunk and been fooled. These owls may call during the day, so confusion between the two sounds is understandable.

High above the chipmunk's haunts, the arboreal Western Gray Squirrel jumps from one tree to another as it moves through the upper boughs of the conifers. Its long, furry tail acts as a rudder and helps the squirrel negotiate its favorite overhead routes. The gray squirrel is shy, tending to avoid people. It goes about its business of harvesting pine seeds by chewing the cones off the tree, letting them fall to the ground, then chiseling out the nutritious seeds. Lacking cheek pouches, the squirrel must eat most of the pine seeds on the spot. It will, however, carry a few to a nearby location and bury them, to be excavated later when food supplies dwindle. These mammals have very strong teeth that grow continuously: the incisors may grow six inches per year, but constant wear and tear keep them from growing too long.

In the tops of conifers, female gray squirrels build globular nests of sticks, each with a central cavity. Here they usually have one litter in the spring and one in the fall, with three to five young in each. Once the young have left, squirrels are not territorial about their nests; a neighboring squirrel may stop by to use another's nest for shelter from time to time.

Black Bears

The American Black Bear is seldom seen on an outing to our local mountains, and this is as it should be. Our black bears, mostly nocturnal and always shy, disappear like shadows down the steepest of ravines.

But bear sign abounds if you know where to look. Their footprints make deep, round depressions in the pine needles of the forest floor. Their territorial scratch marks reach seven feet high on Incense Cedars, where the bark has been shredded and left hanging. Piles of lumpy, dark scat containing berries occasionally mark forest trails. And a large basin of cleared

These American Black Bears were photographed by a trail camera at Sedgwick Reserve. Photo by Grant Canova-Parker

pine needles tells us where a bear has taken a nap or spent the night.

Because Grizzly Bears formerly dominated our region, black bears were unknown in the Coast and Transverse ranges of California prior to 1950. In 1935 there was a report of bears being transplanted from Yosemite to areas in Los Angeles County. Other records document shipping of "bad" bears— bears with behavioral issues toward humans—out of Yosemite to the Los Padres National Forest about this time.

Only 10 percent of the statewide black bear population inhabits the Central Western–Southwestern California bioregion, which includes our region. Currently, the California Department of Fish and Wildlife estimates there are over thirty-five thousand black bears in the state, which translates to around three thousand bruins in Southern California.

Black bears' vital statistics are as follows: adult males weigh from one hundred and fifty to four hundred pounds and stand three feet high at the shoulder. Records exist of heavier individuals, some weighing over six hundred pounds. Male bears lose weight in the spring, when they travel for miles, looking for female bears with which to mate. From July until they den up for hibernation in the fall, they steadily gain weight. Females, on the other hand, are at their lowest weight just after hibernation but gain pounds steadily throughout the year. Sows with young are lighter than those without cubs.

Black bears are not always black. They are customarily some shade of cinnamon or brown; only about 5 percent are black. The average lifespan of a bear is eighteen years.

Bear scratch marks on Incense Cedar at Big Pine Mountain

Let's follow in the footsteps of a female black bear as a way of understanding the lifestyle of these interesting animals. Most of the information below was gleaned from *Black Bear: Spirit of the Wilderness* by Barbara Ford.

Biography of a Black Bear

Our female black bear began life as a blind, helpless cub in her mother's den sometime in December, January, or February. She and her sister nuzzled their mother for milk. They snuggled together to keep warm in a den located in a hollow Jeffrey Pine high on Reyes Peak. While hibernating, the mother bear had given birth in the den to the twin cubs. She had not had anything to eat since fall, and yet she was able to nurse her cubs with highly nourishing milk.

By mid-March or early April, the mother and cubs had left the den. The cubs, now three months old, quickly learned how to climb trees and how to turn over rocks and logs to look for insects.

Like all bear cubs, they engaged in play fighting. They communicated with their ears, flattening them completely during aggressive encounters, but only partly in other play. They tried to knock each other off balance using their paws. When one cub was downed, the other would give it a quick swipe with its paw, but they were careful not to hurt each other.

Our female cub spent the first year and a half of her life with her mother and sister. This was the only time she would be with other bears, for black bears are basically solitary creatures. However, the family unit made up of the mother and her two cubs is a strong one. During this time, the mother was never more than a few feet away from the cubs. She led them everywhere: she even ripped apart logs and turned over boulders, teaching the cubs how to find food.

By the time her second winter arrived, our female cub weighed somewhere between thirty and one hundred pounds. Once again she and her sibling nestled in with their mother in the den. This winter the den was different, a bigger space under a pile of boulders, hidden by shrubs. After this second hibernation, when she emerged as a yearling, she was almost as big as her mother.

Regardless of their size, yearling cubs still receive the constant care of the mother bear. But in late spring or early summer of our cub's second year, the formerly inseparable family will suddenly split up.

The mother's physiology will change; she will enter her fertile period, or estrus. When an adult male black bear, perhaps one that has wandered a great distance to find a fertile female, comes into the mother bear's territory, our cub will be forced to leave, driven off by her mother or because she fears the adult male. The adult bears, too, will go their separate ways after mating.

As for the cubs, yearling females will often stay in a territory fairly near the mother bear, but yearling males will travel far and wide, looking for a new place to establish themselves.

Black Bears and People

In November 2010, I talked with wildlife biologist and Sedgwick Reserve manager Kate McCurdy. McCurdy has worked with bears in Yosemite for years. She has a keen sense of what is currently going on vis-à-vis black bears and their interactions with people.

When I asked McCurdy about bears and people, she said, "Bears can get along with people, but can people get along with bears?"

In Yosemite, she was instrumental in making it mandatory for backpackers to store their food in bear-proof canisters, which has proven successful for avoiding bear incidents in the Sierra Nevada and many other locations in California mountains.

Problems arise, however, when a bear, usually a young male looking for easily available food, is found up a tree in someone's backyard or raiding the garbage cans in a suburban community.

Bears are opportunistic; most can habituate to people. This sometimes gets them into trouble, as they take readily to human food and trash and to being around people in general. "Rogue" or bad bears are extremely rare, but those are the ones people tend to remember.

Most of the bears that turn up in urban or suburban areas are males less than three years old. They are looking for a new home range. The best course of action is to leave them completely alone and prevent them from getting into trashcans or sources of food left outside, such as pet or bird feeders, so that they won't learn to be a nuisance.

Maybe, with education, people will change their old attitudes, attitudes that have been retained long past their usefulness. For example, some people look on all bears as monsters that eat people. Many see bears as the enemy, to be shot on sight. Others treat them like pets to be photographed and fed.

Kate McCurdy says that there are more black bears in the state and fewer truly wild bears than ever before. She emphasizes that the best way for people to avoid conflict with bears is to keep them away from unnatural food sources. After all, if black bears had not been able to coexist with people, they'd be gone by now, like the grizzlies. Apparently they are willing to put up with all the harassment they receive in the more urban areas; they have even become nocturnal to avoid humans.

Dormancy: Hibernation in Black Bears as an Example

Dormancy is usually triggered by environmental conditions, such as extreme heat or cold. Just as plants go dormant to prepare for freezing temperatures when growth would be risky, so hibernating animals go dormant by slowing down their metabolism and lowering their body temperature to withstand cold. By responding to inhospitable conditions in this way, animals are able to remain in places where they can make a good living the rest of the year, once conditions become tolerable again.

Hibernation is the term used for dormancy in animals, by which they survive winter cold and lack of food. A black bear goes into hibernation from December through March, lowering its body temperature by several degrees.

Black bears can do this successfully because they load up on fat calories in the late summer and fall. Such foods as manzanita berries, pine nuts, and acorns provide huge amounts of calories. A pound of acorns contains over two thousand calories and a bear can eat ten pounds of acorns in a day.

Because black bears do not reduce their body temperature as much as other true hibernators, such as bats and rodents, and because they can react to disturbances and become aroused during hibernation, some biologists consider their hibernation to be atypical. The smaller mammals are able to lower their body temperatures more dramatically than bears, but they do arouse themselves to urinate or defecate every ten days or so.

A black bear does not eat, urinate, or defecate during hibernation. Researchers have discovered that the bear has a **fecal plug**, a wad of material held within the colon that consists of vegetation the bear ate just before hibernating and hair it swallowed while licking itself in the den.

Astonishingly, a mother bear is able to give birth to her cubs and produce milk for their nursing while her body is in this state of hibernation. In addition, black bears are able to recycle calcium back into their bones during hibernation, which prevents osteoporosis during this period of inactivity.

Some other forms of dormancy are estivation, diapause, brumation, and torpor. **Estivation** refers to dormancy in the summer months, when outside temperatures become too hot and too dry. California Red-legged Frogs and California Tiger Salamanders bury themselves in underground crevices or burrows in order to keep their skins moist.

We have mentioned **diapause** (Chapter 6), which occurs in the life cycle of insects. This form of dormancy is characterized by the suspension of development of immature insects so they can live through temperature extremes or drought. Cocoons are an example of the diapause phase of an insect's development.

Brumation is the hibernation that cold-blooded animals go through during winter. For example, snakes crawl into rock crevices or caves to shelter from the cold. They become lethargic, seldom moving, for long periods of time.

Last, **torpor** is a state of suspended animation whereby the body temperature is reduced for a short period of time. It is really an abbreviated hibernation and lasts for several hours. Hummingbirds that are active during the day are able to drop their body temperature during cold nights to conserve energy. Chipmunks are another example, going into torpor in winter but awaking to nibble on food they have stored in their burrows.

Not all of the black bears in our region are thought to go into hibernation in the strictest sense of the term, but since no studies have been done on local populations, it is hard to know for certain. Bears inhabiting chaparral at lower elevations are not as affected by cold temperatures and lack of food as those that live in the coniferous forests. However, it appears that a majority do undergo a period of prolonged inactivity, and those that give birth will usually den up during winter months.

McCurdy hopes her prediction is wrong, but she says, "In our lifetime, it's going to be a rare thing to see a truly wild black bear."

California Condor: Flying over Our Mountains Once Again

Mount Pinos, that highest of our mountaintops, used to be frequented by California Condors. Back in the 1970s, stories were told about numbers of these giants coming to the open area at the summit to loaf and perch on late summer afternoons. Biologists and birders knew this was *the* place to see condors, many of

Two California Condors in flight. Historic photo courtesy of Santa Barbara Museum of Natural History Condor Archives

which were soaring overhead on their way from nesting spots in the Sespe area to likely foraging acreage on the Tejon and San Emigdio ranches.

But that was over thirty years ago.

So much has happened in the colossal effort to save the California Condor that we have forgotten how

natural it was to just go up to Mount Pinos on an August day and scan the horizon and actually see these amazing birds.

Today, the California Condor has become a symbol of the natural history of the whole Santa Barbara region. This immense bird, which inhabited California and much of western North America for thousands of years, made its last stand for survival in the wild in our rugged backcountry. Just like the Grizzly Bear, the California Condor retreated to the mountains of Central California. Unlike the grizzly, the condor was plucked from the brink of extinction in one of the most hard-fought conservation stories of all time. The struggle continues, as we seek to help the species recover.

The condor saga is a long and complicated one, but it is fascinating: required reading for those of us who wonder how reintroduction and restoration can succeed. An excellent book on the subject is *The California Condor: A Saga of Natural History and Conservation* by Noel and Helen Snyder. Up-to-date information can be found on the Internet (see "useful Websites" in Bibliography).

California Condor: Biology and Lifestyle

The California Condor is an immense bird. It has the longest wingspan of any North American bird, at nine to ten feet. It weighs sixteen to twenty-five pounds. It is only slightly smaller than the **Andean Condor** (*Vultur gryphus*), its closest living relative in the family of New Word Vultures (Cathartidae). The **Turkey**

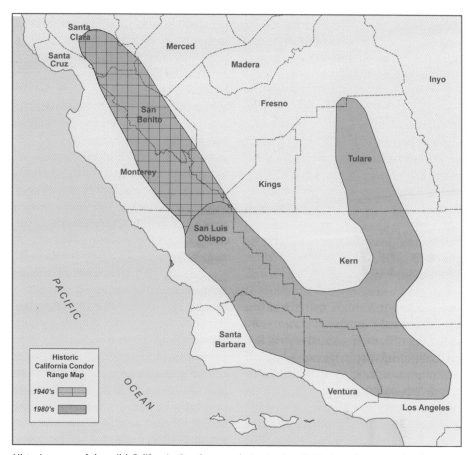

Historic range of the wild California Condor population in the 1940s, based on records of Koford (1953) and Robinson (1940), and the range of the species in the 1980s as determined from records in the modern program (after Snyder 2000).

Vulture (*Cathartes aura*) is another cousin.

Beginning back in Eocene times (50 million years ago), large vulture-type birds became established in North America because the carcasses of herds of grazing ungulates provided easy pickings for these scavengers. Then, during the Pleistocene, California Condors and their ancestors soared across much of the southern United States. Even by the end of the Pleistocene, some ten thousand years ago, they were present in Southern California, as the fossil remains at the La Brea Tar Pits in Los Angeles indicate: *Teratornis merriami* and *Breagyps clarki*—both similar to the California Condor—have been found in numbers there.

Vultures are carrion feeders; their feet are not adapted for carrying prey. They have naked, featherless heads to help keep themselves clean when feeding on the inner recesses of messy carcasses. Also, the exposure of the naked head to sunlight kills any lingering bacteria a bird might acquire.

Like Turkey Vultures, California Condors do not make nests. Eggs are

291

simply laid on the bare ground of a cave or a hollow stump. Big differences between Turkey Vultures and condors occur in their breeding habits, however. Condors lay one egg per clutch; they undergo a long incubation period (fifty-four to fifty-eight days), and the juveniles are dependent upon their parents for up to eighteen months. Because the breeding cycle takes so long, condors often manage to lay only one egg every two years. (Occasionally a female condor, having laid an egg early enough in the previous year, will be able to produce another one during the next breeding season, though probably not until late spring.) If something happens to the first egg of the season, a replacement egg will be laid, a process called "double clutching." A condor cannot breed until it is at least six or seven years old. In captivity it may live for over forty years.

With such a low reproductive rate and a slow path to maturity, condors cannot withstand a high mortality rate if they are to survive as a species. When condor deaths reach more than 10 percent of their population annually, the whole population is in danger of extinction. This is why poisoning, shooting, and collisions with power lines pose such a threat to the birds. Their existence is extremely fragile.

Condors soar great distances—up to 150 miles in a day—looking for food. They may travel as fast as forty to sixty miles per hour when soaring, but more slowly in flapping flight. During takeoff, the birds often run downhill to give themselves a boost into the air, then flap their wings to get going. Once in flight, wingbeats are few.

Typically, Turkey Vultures and Common Ravens find carcasses first. Since condors do not possess the keen sense of smell that Turkey Vultures do, they use their superb eyesight to observe where and when Turkey Vultures and ravens descend to feed, following the other birds to the carcass.

Scavengers, unlike birds of prey, must compete on the spot with others for their food. At the carcass, the condor has to adapt to the situation or starve. There's literally a pecking order, or "dominance hierarchy." Experienced, older birds have an advantage. Interestingly, scientists have found that scavenging birds have a remarkable ability to learn new tasks. For juvenile condors, however, it is often difficult to get their fair share of the proffered feast.

Food consumption varies from one condor to the next. For example, on a short winter day in bad weather, it's difficult for a condor to find food, because it cannot soar. Fortunately, it doesn't need to eat every day; it fills its crop (the food pouch below its throat) with three or four pounds of food, enough to sustain it for several days.

One unique aspect of condor behavior is their inquisitiveness and playfulness. Young birds, especially, will show curiosity about shiny objects. They will pick up pebbles and toss them, or play tug-of-war with twigs. They are social, occasionally approaching groups of people—a trait that has made it very difficult for recovery efforts at times. Never let a condor approach you; any habituation to humans is disastrous for the bird's future survival.

Condor Research and Early Recovery Efforts

This quotation from the Snyders' *The California Condor* encapsulates our enormous interest in this charismatic bird: "Perhaps more than any other North American bird, the condor has attracted conservation attention from a great variety of individuals and organizations. The seemingly endless debates and controversies over its plight are in part a product of this diversity."

Think of it: you have field biologists, a host of government wildlife agencies on both the state and federal level, private conservation organizations, captive-breeding specialists in various zoos, plus active citizens— all passionately involved in the same goal: to save the California Condor.

The questions are: how, when, and under whose authority?

We are still looking for all the answers and it has taken years and years to chart a successful course. What follows is only a summary of these efforts.

Early explorers, settlers, ornithologists, and egg collectors wrote briefly of their encounters with this mysterious, giant bird. But misinformation was rife. One article in the *Los Angeles Times* in 1934 had a drawing with the following caption: "This drawing by *Times* Staff Artist Bernard Garbutt shows how a California Condor is capable of carrying a fawn in its talons." Obviously, the artist had a vivid imagination.

Up until the 1930s, nobody seemed to know for certain how many condors remained in Southern California. Some experts pronounced the species doomed, with only ten remaining. Others, such as Cyril Robinson, deputy supervisor of the Los Padres National Forest (known as the Santa Barbara National Forest until 1938), estimated perhaps sixty were still to be found in the mountains northwest of Los Angeles.

Robert E. Easton, my grandfather, a Santa Maria businessman and manager of the Sisquoc Ranch, took an interest in the condor and decided to act on the bird's behalf. A 1986 *Noticias* article by Ray Ford details efforts to assess the condors' situation:

On Friday, June 29, 1934, a light breeze stirred along the slopes of the Sierra Madre Mountains in northern Santa Barbara County, providing the characteristic currents which made them the primary flyway of the California Condor. The cavalcade of friends, which included Robert E. Easton and his son Bob, proceeded slowly up the steep, angular trail by horseback.

Anticipation rose with the gain in elevation. The miles seemed to drag on, but then suddenly, a high grassy ridge could be seen out of which rose rounded masses of weather-sculpted sandstone. Circling above were the large dark birds.

Three days before the trip, Lamar Johnston, another local rancher, along with my grandfather and father, had prepared a blind, in front of which

Falls at Sisquoc Condor Sanctuary in the San Rafael Wilderness after the Zaca Fire of 2007. Photo by Greg Giloth

the San Rafael Wilderness known as Hurricane Deck. The road would have passed dangerously close to Condor Falls, a known bathing and roosting area for California Condors. In May 1936, as many as twenty-one birds were observed at one time at the falls.

Robert E. Easton persuaded the Forest Service, thanks to the cooperation of Cyril Robinson, to relocate the fire road up on Montgomery Potrero, then owned by the Sisquoc Ranch, thus averting disturbance to the condors down at the falls.

After that, it seemed essential to create a sanctuary around the falls. In 1937 the Secretary of Agriculture set aside the Sisquoc Condor Sanctuary, a twelve-hundred-acre portion of chaparral and remote cliff faces—a first important step in condor conservation.

In 1939 an Audubon Fellowship was established at the University of California to support research on the California Condor. Several years later, the fellowship research of wildlife biologist Carl Koford helped lead to the creation of a second reserve, the Sespe Condor Sanctuary in Ventura County.

Ian and Eben McMillan, rancher friends of Koford's, were sympathetic to his belief that condors were extremely wary of human disturbance and that disturbance was one of the greatest threats to their survival; if enough habitat could be preserved, the California Condor would survive without intervention on the part of humans.

Koford was the first modern-day wildlife biologist to devote a lifetime to the field study of the habits of the condor; his notes were meticulous and voluminous, and his research

they placed the carcass of an old ranch horse as bait for the condors.

In the words of one of the observers, Ernest Dyer, an ornithologist and retired chemical engineer: "Across, and around, and in and out of the circling mass of lesser birds: crows, ravens, and turkey vultures, we descried greater forms gliding steadily and majestically in wider and unwavering orbits." Dyer was later to write an article for the Cooper Ornithological Union about this sighting.

The immediate threat to the local condors was the US Forest Service's plan to put a fire control road right through what is now the portion of

John Borneman and Fred Sibley on a condor survey, April 1967, on the cliffs of West Big Pine. Photo from the author's collection

was groundbreaking. By 1953, he estimated there were forty to sixty condors left in the wild. In the 1960s and 1970s, outstanding condor researchers such as Fred Sibley and Sandy Wilbur spent months in the field and discovered incredibly remote condor nest sites. Koford's population figures were revised upward, to about 150 birds in the wild. Wilbur began a program of feeding the condors by putting out carcasses at the Sespe sanctuary. Still, it was difficult to come up with a consensus on the numbers of wild condors and thus to judge how fast the Southern California population was dwindling.

At that point researchers, government agencies, and the National Audubon Society, as well as citizen activists, had only an inkling of the enormous role that lead poisoning was already playing in the demise of the free-flying California Condor. Most authorities blamed the slow reproductive habits of the species for its problems.

Efforts to protect condor habitat continued. A group of National Wildlife Refuges (NWRs) was established. The largest is a group of four, the Hopper Mountain National Wildlife Refuge Complex, which includes Hopper Mountain NWR, Bitter Creek NWR, Blue Ridge NWR, and Guadalupe–Nipomo Dunes NWR (which is not condor habitat and is the only one accessible to the public).

Hopper Mountain NWR, located about six miles north of Fillmore, was established in 1974. Its steep rock formations and complete isolation were perfectly suited for condor nesting, and it would later become one of the first locations where captive-hatched condors were taken to become acclimatized to the wild. The site of the old Hopper Ranch, where Carl Koford once studied condors, it is adjacent to

California Condor taking flight. Photo by Dennis Sheridan

the original Sespe Condor Sanctuary and now includes more than twenty-four hundred acres of chaparral and cliff-scarred canyons.

Bitter Creek NWR, established in 1985 and comprising much of the former Hudson Ranch, is a much larger swath of a totally different type of habitat. It is open grassland, valuable for condor soaring and foraging. Situated just north of the high ridges of Mount Pinos and Cerro Noroeste and adjacent to Wind Wolves Preserve, Bitter Creek includes the grasslands of the Southern San Joaquin Valley.

Both these areas of rolling foothills attract other soaring birds, such as Golden Eagles, Common Ravens, and Turkey Vultures.

The California Condor Recovery Program

In *The Condor Question, Captive or Forever Free?* edited by David Phillips, David Ross Brower, and Hugh Nash, Ian McMillan is quoted as saying:

> The real importance of saving such things as condors is not so much that we need condors as that we need to save them. We need to exercise and develop the human attributes required in saving condors; for these are the attributes so necessary in working out our own survival.

By 1979, an estimated twenty-five to thirty-five condors remained in the wild. California Condors require remote areas of rugged country for nesting and foraging. And yet the remaining birds were concentrated in an area seventy-five miles north of ultra-urban Los Angeles.

One wild-hatched, abandoned condor had been found, given the name Topatopa, and taken to the Los Angeles Zoo. The Condor Research Center was formed, a cooperative effort of the US Fish and Wildlife Service and the National Audubon Society.

On a spring day in 1982, a female condor in the Sespe Condor Sanctuary gave birth. Known as Adult Condor No. 8 (AC8), she was the last free-flying, wild-born female condor. Her male chick, Xolxol (pronounced "hol-hol"), would become the first addition to the captive breeding pro-

California Condor with radio tag protruding on left side of bird. Photo by Dennis Sheridan

gram, joining Topatopa at the Los Angeles Zoo later in 1982. And so began the California Condor Recovery Program.

Despite all efforts, including captive incubation of wild-collected eggs, from 1980 to 1987 the population of the California Condor took a seemingly irreversible downturn. Debate ensued as to whether to take all the remaining nine birds into captivity or leave some out to keep the wild population going. As one disaster followed another, the wild population shrank. Lead poisoning from carrion was the suspected culprit, but no condor bodies were ever found to autopsy.

In late 1986, the call came to take in the remaining three wild condors. Adult Condor No. 9 (AC9) was the last wild condor to be captured. Born in the wild in 1980, he has since become something of an icon for condor followers. He has sired numerous offspring, both in zoos and, when he was at last released, in the wild.

But back then, nobody knew that AC9 or any other condor would ever grace the skies of our region again.

For eons these birds had soared over our mountains. Regardless of past mistakes, our only hope for saving the species and its genetic diversity was to enter a period of captive breeding in various zoos.

The first successes were sweet. A condor chick hatched in captivity in 1988. Female Andean Condors—captive-bred birds from zoos in the US—were released into areas that had been the habitat of California Condors. Because their population is more stable than that of California Condors and their behavior is similar, Andean Condors proved helpful to scientists preparing for the anticipated release of California Condors.

By the early 1990s, all Andean Condors had been taken in, and then came the great moment, in 1992, when two captive-bred California Condors were released in Ventura County. Successful releases took place over the next few years in Santa Barbara County, San Luis Obispo County, Monterey County, and Northern Arizona.

The road to recovery has not been straightforward for the condor. In the early years, one of the chief problems was collision with power lines. Now, a pole-aversion training program for all releasable condors features a mock power pole placed inside the flight pen where the young birds are held prior to a release. The power pole gives off a small electrical charge whenever a condor starts to land on it. The birds quickly learn to avoid the power pole, and condor deaths in the wild from collisions with wires have been reduced.

Before a condor is released, a numbered tag is affixed to its wings, along with a small transmitter, and often a GPS unit which gathers information on the bird's location.

The goal of the Condor Recovery Plan is to establish three separate populations, one in California and one in Arizona (each with 150 birds and at least fifteen successfully breeding pairs), and a captive group of condors in zoos. You can find a Condor Program Monthly Status Report on the Hopper Mountain NWR website. As of October 2012, the total population of the California Condor was 232 wild birds and 177 captive birds, which adds up to an impressive 409. One of the most significant figures is the number of wild-fledged chicks: 33.

The biggest problem still facing the condor is not a low reproductive rate, reluctance to breed in captivity, or human disturbance, but the ingestion of lead: condors feeding on carrion contaminated with lead will sicken and die. Scientific studies document that the primary source of this lead is spent ammunition in the carcasses of animals that have been shot. When a lead bullet hits an animal, it expands into hundreds of tiny specks. Lead bullets are also hazardous to Bald Eagles, Golden Eagles, Turkey Vultures, and Common Ravens.

Assemblyman Pedro Nava introduced Assembly Bill No. 821, now known as the Ridley-Tree Condor

California Condor in flight, with patagial tags for identification. Photo by Dennis Sheridan

Preservation Act, which became effective July 1, 2008, and requires the use of non-lead centerfire rifle and pistol ammunition when taking big game and Coyotes on public lands within the range of the California Condor.

Hunters and ranchers, long interested in wildlife conservation, are the key to helping get the lead out of the condors and out of the environment. An alternative to lead bullets is pure copper bullets. Copper bullets do not fragment the way lead bullets do.

On a more cheerful note, our local Santa Barbara Zoo has become active in the Condor Recovery Program. Currently, five young condors not suitable for release into the wild are part of an educational exhibit there. It is exciting to think that our zoo has embraced the California Condor and is assisting these great birds in their comeback.

Another local institution, the Santa Barbara Museum of Natural History, has become the repository for the California Condor Archives: videos, slides, photographs, films, and a computerized document retrieval system which is continually updated. The collection is managed by ornithologist Janet Hamber.

Where to View Condors

Where's the best place to view condors in Southern California? It's the same spot frequented by the last free-flying condors in the 1980s, a place called "The Sign" along Cerro Noroeste Road. Approximately 9.7 miles from the intersection of this road with Highway 166, you come to a large "Los Padres National Forest" sign. Here, you're atop a grassy ridge with views in every direction. To the east are the rolling hills of Bitter Creek National Wildlife Refuge, which has become one of the chief release sites for condors. The updrafts from the floor of the San Joaquin Valley make it an ideal place for condors to forage as they drift up against the slopes of the Mount Pinos–Cerro Noroeste complex.

The Southern California condor flock resident at Hopper Mountain often travels along this route over to Bitter Creek, where clean carcasses are provided for the birds. Your chances are good for spotting condors, since the birds follow the ridgelines as they travel between Hopper and Bitter Creek.

Nature Journal
September 6, 2002

Trip to Hopper Mountain NWR

I have never seen so many California Condors in one day!

We are invited to visit Hopper Mountain National Wildlife Refuge, located in the dry, rugged foothills of Ventura County. As the jeep traverses the rocky, reddish-hued landscape, I recall what I've read about the Sespe Formation and the rhinoceros-like titanotheres that might have grazed here eons ago, although in a completely different habitat.

As we climb higher and higher I relish the view from the shoulder of Hopper Mountain. The whole Santa Clara River Valley spreads before us: South Mountain and the Oxnard Plain, and the knobby Santa Monica Mountains in the distance to the south. Beyond that, the Channel Islands.

Just looking at the Santa Clara River Valley conjures another, more recent geologic time, when the whole valley formed the bottom of an inland embayment of the Pacific Ocean.

The road we follow winds up through a large oil field, another testament to undersea origins. The Monterey Formation here yields rich oil deposits; the giant praying mantis shapes of the pumps on either side of the road seem incongruous, but they have been here since the 1920s and coexist with the condors in a surprisingly peaceful way.

This is the heart of condor country. The barren hillsides are peppered with chap-

arral; prickly, scrubby bushes space themselves over rocky ridges. Rocks are everywhere. The pale cliffs, studded with potential condor "caves," or nesting sites, form honeycombs of dark holes and ledges. They rise steeply from the floor of Hopper Canyon.

Our first stop turns out to be a magnificent experience. The OP (observation point) here is occupied by a young intern holding a telemetry unit. She's monitoring eight condors perched on a rock formation known as "the pinnacles" far below us. Through the spotting scope, we discern the enormous black forms sitting on the rocks.

But overhead, the action is even more exciting. Three condors fly low above us. We follow them with binoculars as they soar out over the Fillmore foothills and Oat Mountain below. Each bird has a tiny antenna and a two-color tag attached to its wings.

We learn that individual condors do, indeed, have personalities: some are aggressive, some adapt well in the wild, others "just don't get it," and so on.

The birds are fed a carcass at one of three feeding sites on the refuge. They are also provided with water in a small tub.

The "pinnacles" rock formation was the site of the first Andean Condor release, in 1989-90. Now, ten adults and twelve young condors are seen frequently at Hopper, and there are eighteen condors up at Ventana near Big Sur. The two populations go back and forth between the locations. [Years later this is still true, although condor numbers have increased greatly since this journal entry.]

The most exciting aspect of all is three *condor nests and* three *chicks waiting to fledge somewhere on the refuge. [Sadly, lead poisoning took all but one of these.]*

We get back into the truck and drive down to the Hopper Ranch house, a hard-scrabble, tough-luck, bare-bones sort of place. They have put some ugly vinyl siding up—simulated wood—to protect the old wooden ranch house, but otherwise, it is much the way it has been since the early days. A huge stone fireplace, quite a few bedrooms, a bathroom with a rickety shower, an old-fashioned kitchen with a gas stove standing up on its legs like the one my grandmother used to have. A large, blue, triangle-shaped coffeepot sits on top of the stove.

In the living room, littered with notes and books and various indications that outdoorsy individuals live there, are all the charts of the condor comings and goings. Each bird's movements are tracked on a huge schedule sheet. Beneath that are bunches of old, crinkled topo maps pinned up side by side.

We walk around and explore the place.

I am in awe of all the dedicated young biologists living in this isolated spot without an ounce of luxury, getting paid a pittance. They're on six-month shifts.

We eat lunch on the concrete porch under a walnut tree. Old sycamore trees with naked branches stand in back of the house. We notice one immature bird perched there—sitting and looking rather befuddled. One of the interns says it is a bird that "just couldn't get it together."

After lunch we drive down the hill to an area where the recovery team has built a large, two-story structure as a holding pen for the condors. The structure has one wall of solid metal and there is open screening over the top and sides of the rest of the enclosure. The recovery team brings the condors here from the zoo to observe them before releasing them.

We finally leave, driving up to a higher OP. Here we look out over the edge of middle Hopper Canyon, and on the west side we see a clump of bare Bigcone Spruce trees covered with whitewash, another favorite roosting site of the condors.

Scanning over the canyon, we spy two condors on the east side, gliding just above the canyon wall. With the barren cliffs and scruffy shrubs as a background, through the binoculars we get good views of the enormous vultures soaring steadily. For minutes, I never see them flap. The slightest movement of the tips of its flight feathers is enough to steer the condor in one direction or another. You can see the bright white patches on the underwings easily.

We drive on to the trailhead for "Koford's OP," where we park and walk out the jeep road for about forty-five minutes. At last we arrive at a couple of sweeping viewpoints where you are able to look right down into Hopper Canyon.

A giant cave, known as "Hole in the Wall" by the condor cognoscenti, lies across the canyon on the opposite wall of rock. This spot is in Koford's (and others') field notes from way, way back. There's something special about it. Through the spotting scope we notice that the full-grown Bigcone Spruce trees are dwarfed by the gaping hole in the rock.

Surely California Condors have used this cave for thousands of years.

* * *

From fell-fields to Clark's Nutcrackers, Limber Pines to Mount Pinos Chipmunks, American Black Bears to California Condors: this journey along the summits of our highest mountains has been a whirlwind of discovery.

When you live in chaparral country, you don't dream these islands of coniferous forest exist. Coming upon them holds that special magic reserved for those whose thirst for knowledge of our region's natural history is not easily slaked. At the top of these mountains, you walk among many of the flowers, trees, and birds of the Sierra Nevada.

Recall that our mountains are sky islands. Surrounded by chaparral, these oases of refreshing, green forest leave the first-time visitor astonished.

Beneath the trees, black bears den up in winter. From one branch to another, chipmunks and squirrels run their highways. Among the pine needles, yellow-and-red Western Tanagers flit about making nests in spring. And overhead, the mighty condors have begun to fly once more.

For those who venture to the summits, these are the rich rewards.

CHAPTER 9: FRESHWATER WETLANDS—PRECIOUS WATER IN A DRY LAND

 Raindrops send life-giving moisture through all of nature. The trickle of a tiny seep down a parched arroyo becomes a waterfall in a rushing creek, which in turn feeds into the sweeping flow of a big river in flood. Water oozing through the tules on the margins of lakes and reservoirs; water collecting in ponds that have been dry for months; water puddling in the low places—in drainage ditches, in the side channels of our big rivers, in wet agricultural fields: everywhere water brings with it new life. In this land of short-lived winters and dry summers, water stimulates plants to new growth, insects to move forward in complex cycles, other animals to forage and thrive, and humans to prosper.

Freshwater wetlands are found throughout all the habitats described in this book, but in this chapter we examine them apart from their surrounding habitats.

The richest zones for insects, birds, reptiles, amphibians, and mammals are located in and around freshwater wetlands. An **ecotone,** or edge situation, is created where streams wind their way through chaparral, oak woodland, grassland, or forest. And in another example, at the edges of lakes and reservoirs, freshwater marshes harbor abundant species of all kinds. Furthermore, the insects and fishes living in the water are a valuable source of nourishment for a myriad of other organisms. Insects wriggle and float on the surface of the water. Fish come up to snatch these tempting morsels. Ducks, grebes, and cormorants dive headfirst after the fish while herons and egrets stalk them from the bank. Toads, frogs, and salamanders make annual migrations to ponds and vernal pools, where they mate and lay eggs.

Our streams, lakes, and ponds are indispensable to wildlife and to the well-being of those of us who live here.

Let's learn why.

303

Nojoqui Falls

Creeks and Rivers

Along the southern coast of Santa Barbara County, from Point Conception to Rincon, approximately sixty creeks drain small watersheds. They come tumbling out of narrow-sided canyons and have short, steep gradients. In less than seven miles creeks may drop four thousand feet from their headwaters in the Santa Ynez Mountains down to the Pacific Ocean.

Hike the trails beside some of these creeks to observe the narrow canyons and the seasonal flow of water. After torrential rains, the creeks swell their

banks. By the end of a long, hot summer, however, the water slows to a trickle and many creeks may dry up completely.

North of Point Conception the watersheds are larger and wider. Two of our major rivers, the Santa Maria River and the Santa Ynez River, drain large watersheds with headwaters in the rugged backcountry of Los Padres National Forest. The Santa Maria River and its tributaries, the Cuyama and the Sisquoc, flow for a distance of over ninety miles. Twitchell Reservoir is the only impoundment.

San Jose Creek, one of the numerous creeks that run south from the Santa Ynez Mountains and across the coastal plain

Santa Ynez River below Bradbury Dam

Like the Santa Maria, the Santa Ynez River runs in an east-west direction for approximately ninety miles. There are three dams on the Santa Ynez: Juncal (Jameson Lake), Gibraltar (Gibraltar Reservoir), and Bradbury Dam, which forms the largest reservoir, Lake Cachuma.

The other two major rivers lie in Ventura County. The Ventura River, flowing north-south, descends fairly steeply from its headwaters at Matilija Creek down to the ocean. Matilija Dam's reservoir has filled with silt. Advocates for restoration of the Ventura River are seeking to remove the dam because it blocks access to upstream spawning for steelhead trout.

The longest river in our region is the Santa Clara River, stretching over one hundred miles from east to west. The watershed of the Santa Clara River comprises some sixteen hundred square miles—a vast network of creeks, the largest of which is Sespe Creek. Other major tributaries are Santa Paula, Hopper, and Piru creeks. Santa Felicia Dam is on Piru Creek, and the Vern Freeman Diversion Dam is on the main channel of the Santa Clara.

Intriguingly, the headwaters of three of these big rivers are located within a few miles of each other, high in the eastern portion of the Santa Ynez Mountains near the Santa Barbara–Ventura County line. If you were to stand on a ridge near Monte Arido (6,003 ft.), you could look west into the Santa Ynez River watershed, south to the Ventura River watershed, and east to the Santa Clara River watershed. The Cuyama River headwaters aren't far away, over on the slopes of Cerro Noroeste.

Cuyama River drying with summer's approach

Santa Clara River, February 2011, with deciduous cottonwoods and willows at its edge

San Luis Obispo Creek reaches the ocean at Avila Bay.

Creeks in southern San Luis Obispo County drain the foothills of the southern Santa Lucia Mountains. Chorro Creek flows westward to Morro Bay; San Luis Obispo Creek flows southward, reaching the ocean at Avila Bay. Arroyo Grande Creek enters the ocean at Oceano.

North of the town of San Luis Obispo, the Salinas River flows from its headwaters in the La Panza Range out of our region into Monterey County to the north.

Structure of Creeks and Rivers: The Riparian Habitat

The **riparian habitat** (from the Latin *ripa*, meaning bank or shore of a stream or river) is an ecosystem which includes stream channels and areas on either side that may flood periodically.

On the bottom of the **streambed**, sand, gravel, and rocks move, depending upon the force of the water running through the channel. Pools are deep areas produced by scouring during storms. Riffles are shallow areas where gravel accumulates. Pools and riffles divide stream gravels so that finer materials are found in pools and coarser ones in riffles. The shallow, bubbling water of riffles contrasts with the slower water of pools. Riffles may be more sunlit, while pools tend to be well shaded by the trees on the banks, especially in narrower watersheds. The different riverine habitats attract different fish and insects.

The **stream channel** contains the flowing water. On either side of the streambed is a **stream bank**, the sloping area between the water's edge and level ground. The **riparian corridor**

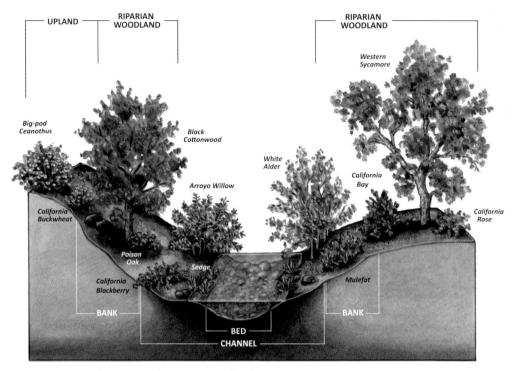

Cross section of a stream with riparian woodland

consists of the streamside vegetation that's located along the bank and on the level ground immediately adjacent to the creek. In the case of a river, both the channel and the riparian corridor will be wider than those of a creek, sometimes extending many hundreds of feet from the center of the streambed.

Away from the stream and the riparian corridor is an **upland** area, which may or may not be part of the **floodplain**. Only in certain years, when the stream flows over its banks, will the floodplain receive water.

Humans interfere with creeks and rivers by altering the flow of water and sediment to prevent flooding. But channelization and damming rob the streambeds of the natural variability that often helps absorb floodwaters.

In addition, dams and reservoirs disrupt the ecosystem of a river. Reservoirs trap sediment and eventually fill up. When a stream is transformed into a concrete conduit with no riffles or pools, no sandbars or tree roots, the biological communities that inhabit the stream can't thrive. Dams and reservoirs reduce the stream's flow, lessening the necessary scouring. The water never rushes through the channel, and therefore the important highs and lows of the streambed get evened out to the detriment of many organisms living there.

Riparian Corridor

The plants of a riparian corridor are different from those of the neighboring ecosystems. If you were to fly over our region on a summer day, you'd see that the land below is largely brown, gold, or gray, except where corridors of green trace the patterns of streams over the countryside. A riparian corridor consists of the tall trees and understory of associated shrubs found in the fertile, well-watered soils on the banks of streams. It is a transition zone between an aquatic community—the stream—and an upland community, which might be chaparral, coastal sage scrub, or even suburban houses.

The vegetation in a riparian corridor stands out in our typical summer-dry landscape. The mature trees, reminiscent of places in the Midwest or East rather than California, are deciduous. In spring the trees produce shade, creating a cool oasis. In summer a luxuriant green tangle of scrambling plants and blackberry thickets grows as an understory. By fall, as the leaves on the trees begin to turn, the corridors of green along the stream bank become ribbons of yellow. In winter, the sycamores, alders, and cottonwoods lose their leaves, and their bare branches allow the sunlight to penetrate through to the water's surface.

Riparian vegetation provides the shade that cools stream water. Cooler waters have more oxygen and are more attractive to fish. The trees shed leaves and branches into the stream, creating habitat for insects, which means more food for fish. When riparian trees die, they fall into the stream channel and create saturated logs and mounds of woody debris. These obstacles help to form the deeper pools in the streambed as the

river scours around them, so they are crucial to fish.

Native Plants of Riparian Corridors

Willows (*Salix* spp.) grow in the middle of streambeds or on the damp banks. They spread rapidly from root sprouts. Four common willow species are found along the Santa Clara River: **Narrow-leaved Willow** (*Salix exigua*), **Red Willow** (*Salix laevigata*), **Arroyo Willow** (*Salix lasiolepis*), and **Yellow Willow** (*Salix lasiandra*). Red Willows grow to be immense trees with dark bark. Arroyo Willows make a tight forest of willow woodland adjacent to the river channel. All willows have wind-dispersed seeds that blow through the air in little tufts every spring.

A narrow-leaved shrub resembling a willow, **Mule Fat** (*Baccharis salicifolia*), is another plant that grows right in or near the streambeds of most watercourses. The pungent odor of Mule Fat evokes riparian areas throughout our region.

Of the tall trees, the **White Alder** (*Alnus rhombifolia*) takes root right at the water's edge, requiring cool, well-oxygenated water. White Alders are reliable indicators of a permanent stream.

Next up the bank are the beautiful cottonwoods. **Black Cottonwood** (*Populus trichocarpa*) is found along the coast, while Fremont Cottonwood grows further inland. Both have heart-shaped leaves, but the Black Cottonwood's leaf margins are smooth and the Fremont Cottonwood's are scalloped. Fremont Cottonwoods mature to tall, furrow-barked trees. Their shimmering, pale green leaves and

Arroyo Willow catkins

Streamside vegetation of the Santa Clara River: willows and other riparian shrubs bend with the flow of the river, then recover quickly after flooding.

branched canopies characterize many a western scene.

Like willows (they're in the Willow family), cottonwoods must be able to survive the siltation, bank erosion, and sandbar shifts of a river. Even if a destructive flood has wiped away mature trees, many streamside species can sprout from roots or trunks. Quick regrowth is part of their survival strategy.

Western Sycamore (*Platanus racemosa*), with its broad leaves and angular growth, is another common tree of the West that marks a subsurface water source. Sycamores can sustain themselves at some distance from a streambed, as long as there is sufficient groundwater. With their pale, gray-and-white bark, trunks gnarled with age, and distinctive leaves that turn brown in fall, sycamores take their place beside cottonwoods as one of the signature trees of riparian corridors.

Non-native Plants of Riparian Corridors

Unfortunately, the presence of water has made it easy for several non-native plants to colonize the riparian plant community. Three in particular are worth a mention: **salt cedar**, or **tamarisk** (*Tamarix* spp.), **German-Ivy** (*Delairea odorata*), and **Giant Reed** (*Arundo donax*). All three were introduced from Europe or Africa in the seventeenth and eighteenth centuries, and in many riparian areas they threaten to engulf native species.

The most destructive of these invaders is Giant Reed, sometimes just referred to as Arundo. It resembles

Giant Reed, one of the invasive, non-native plants of riparian corridors, grows tall near the Santa Clara River.

bamboo or sugar cane. Introduced into Mediterranean lands from the Indian subcontinent, it was abundant by 1820 in the Los Angeles Basin. Evidently, Arundo was used for roofing material and to "control" erosion (in fact, it does just the opposite). While its tall, hollow stalks may be useful as reeds for woodwind instruments, for which it has been cultivated, the plant has escaped and formed thick stands that dominate most of Southern California's riparian woodlands.

Biologists at UC Santa Barbara have done a good deal of research along local streams and rivers, studying Arundo's effects on wildlife and how we might get rid of this scourge. The researchers have confirmed that Arundo does not spread by seed propagation, but by exceptionally robust rhizomes (underground stems) that take hold quickly. They also note that Arundo displaces native vegetation and is generally avoided by wildlife. Litter from the leaves and twigs of Arundo does not support the insect fauna that is so important to native fish.

On the Santa Clara River, Arundo removal efforts begin with machines, which mow down the mature plants. Volunteers apply chemicals to the bare stalks and then bundle and stack them so they will dry out. Immediately, new green shoots pop up in the infested area, but these can usually be controlled. This laborious process is the only way known to eradicate Arundo. It is an ongoing battle, and vigilance is essential; the plant resprouts again and again unless properly treated.

One encouraging note comes from studies by Professor Tom Dudley at UCSB. He found that three non-native insects cause moderate damage to Arundo along the Santa Clara River: a stem-boring wasp, *Tetramesa romana*; a shoot-fly, *Cryptonevera* spp.; and an aphid, *Melanaphis donacis*. After further experiments have been carried out, these herbivores may form part of a biological control program targeted at the worst tracts of Arundo along the Santa Clara River.

Examples of Riparian Corridors

Arroyo Hondo Creek is one of many coastal streams that drain the southern slope of the Santa Ynez Mountains.

Pristine section of Arroyo Hondo Creek at Arroyo Hondo Preserve, where riparian habitat thrives

Located west of Santa Barbara between Refugio State Beach and Gaviota, the creek is the centerpiece of Arroyo Hondo Preserve, an undisturbed example of riparian habitat. The tree canopy meets above the water, completely shading the creek in spring and summer. White Alder, Western Sycamore, Black Cottonwood, several kinds of willows, and **California Bay** (*Umbellularia californica*) line the stream bank. The shrubby understory includes **Western Virgin's Bower** (*Clematis ligusticifolia*), **California Coffeeberry** (*Frangula californica*), **California Blackberry** (*Rubus ursinus*), Poison Oak, and Mule Fat.

At Arroyo Hondo Preserve, the public is welcome on some Saturdays. This historic rancho, owned by the Hollister family until 2001 and thus exceptionally pristine, is one of the best places on the South Coast to study creekside habitat.

The Santa Clara River: The lower reaches of the Santa Clara River are so wide that the tree canopy cannot reach across and instead forms forests on either side.

The riparian corridor along a river is a rich and important place: the vegetation acts as a biofilter to prevent agricultural toxins from seeping into the water; it reduces sedimentation, which is necessary to protect spawning beds for fish; and it strengthens the river's bank, lessening erosion.

Efforts are progressing to restore riparian vegetation along the Santa Clara River, which has suffered from human encroachment. Friends of the Santa Clara River have teamed with The Nature Conservancy to initiate the Santa Clara River Parkway project.

Santa Clara River, with braided channels. Friends of the Santa Clara River seeks to restore riparian vegetation along the river by setting aside key parcels for protection.

The goal is to purchase several thousand acres of private land along the river in order to revegetate and enrich the riparian woodland, while eradicating invasive exotics such as Arundo.

At the Hedrick Ranch Nature Area, the public can visit by prior arrangement in order to see the impressive results of the wildlife restoration project begun there in 2001 and now fully completed. The former owner, Sanger (Sandy) Hedrick, was raised on the property and sold his 223 acres to the California Coastal Conservancy, which then deeded it to Friends of the Santa Clara River.

Another parcel owned by The Nature Conservancy is located at the terminus of Briggs Road, further west on the river. Here, a twelve-hundred-acre slice of riparian habitat is slated for restoration; volunteers regularly help with Arundo eradication and other activities, but the area is not yet open to the public.

Birds of the Riparian Habitat

More species of birds nest in riparian habitats than in any other ecosystem. The trees and shrubs provide excellent cover for nests, and dead snags supply nest holes for cavity nesters. Several layers of vegetation, from tall canopy trees to medium-sized shrubs to low, tangled undergrowth, offer a selection of nesting heights. The bird life is rich and varied, consisting of bark gleaners, aerial foragers, nectar feeders, fruit and berry feeders, and ground foragers. A plethora of insects, both in the water and on land, offer nourishing protein destined for the mouths of hungry nestlings. For example, on the grounds of the Santa Barbara Botanic Garden—

along a small riparian section of Mission Creek—a recently published checklist shows nearly fifty species of birds breeding there over the years.

On the Santa Clara River at Hedrick Ranch Nature Area, the restored riparian habitat is a magnet for birds. On a spring day, in a single robust Red Willow, a pair of Ash-throated Flycatchers fly back and forth from a hole in a horizontal branch, carrying insects to a brood inside. From high in the leafy dome of the willow, a male **Blue Grosbeak** (*Passerina caerulea*) sings in melodic phrases. And around the base of the thick willow trunk, a **House Wren** (*Troglodytes aedon*) explores the bark for bugs.

Two indicator species for riparian zones—the **Yellow Warbler** (*Setophaga petechia*) and the **Yellow-breasted Chat** (*Icteria virens*)—breed at Hedrick Ranch. The Yellow Warbler is common and easily seen as a patch of bright yellow contrasting with the green foliage. Males and females flit from willow to cottonwood, searching for the perfect place to position their delicate, fibrous nests. The Yellow-breasted Chat, that largest of all wood warblers, with its striking black mask and yellow underparts, remains hidden in the blackberry thickets. You know it's there, because it taunts you with a repertoire of whistles and chatter as it skulks out of view.

Riparian woodlands attract resident and seasonal nesting birds, but they also function as crucial highways for migrating birds. In spring, land birds that migrate north from Central and South America through California find food, water, and cover by stopping over at our rivers. In fall, many of the same migrants seek the watercourses on their return trip southward, hop-scotching their way from one riparian area to another.

Beginning in the 1940s in Southern California, the quality of riparian woodlands started to decline due to damming, channelization, invasion by non-native plants, and urban development. Eventually, over 90 percent of Southern California's riparian woodland disappeared. Several species of birds that depended solely upon lowland streamside habitat could no longer find suitable places for breeding.

One bird in particular, the **Least Bell's Vireo** (*Vireo bellii* subsp. *pusillus*)—a unique subspecies of Bell's Vireo that nests only from Santa Barbara County south into Baja California—was considered a barometer of riparian systems. While almost nobody was paying attention, the population of this tiny songbird dived. In 1986 state and federal authorities declared it to be endangered.

Observers saw the decline of the Least Bell's Vireo as a symbol of a bigger problem—loss of riparian habitat. In addition, livestock grazing and increased agriculture had ushered in a damaging nest predator, the **Brown-headed Cowbird** (*Molothrus ater*).

Brown-headed Cowbirds are brood parasites; they lay their eggs in the nests of other bird species. Cowbirds in California have increased phenomenally in the past hundred years, flourishing in fragmented, open woodlands where urban development has carved up wildlands into smaller parcels. Although Brown-headed Cowbirds parasitize the nests of many

Female Least Bell's Vireo feeds a large Brown-headed Cowbird nestling. Photo by Jim Greaves, June 6, 2006

The same female Least Bell's Vireo later in the season, with her own nestlings. Photo by Jim Greaves, July 19, 2006

birds in various habitats, the Least Bell's Vireo is much sought-after as a foster parent in riparian corridors.

When a cowbird egg hatches in the vireo nest, its larger size and aggressive behavior mean the cowbird will be fed first, at the expense of the vireo nestlings. The hatched cowbird survives, but the host nestlings usually perish.

Fortunately, biologists who advocate cowbird control have successfully trapped and removed cowbirds along much of the Santa Clara River. Without that effort, the vireo would likely have been wiped out. Once the bird was declared endangered, riparian habitat restoration efforts began. Giant Reed has responded to eradication efforts, and a dense understory of Mule Fat and other shrubs now attracts Least Bell's Vireos to nest.

While searching for Least Bell's Vireos in a riparian area, listen for their buzzy song first. Often described as a two-phrased sound, with the first part asking a question and the second part answering it, the song goes something like this: *"Cheedle cheedle chee? Cheedle cheedle chew!"*

Least Bell's Vireos aren't especially shy, and thus are not difficult to spot if they are present. Although they are a nondescript, grayish color, their cocked tails and busy habits endear them to those of us who appreciate seeing birds at home in their natural surroundings.

At Hedrick Ranch Nature Area you can sometimes locate vireo nests. Habitat restoration and cowbird trapping have made a huge difference in the vireo population. In a survey conducted in 2002, three pairs of Least

Bell's Vireos plus three other individuals were tallied in this area. Compare this with a 2010 census at the same location which counted seventy-one pairs plus three single males.

The Southern Steelhead, a Special Kind of Salmon

The **Southern Steelhead** is our region's special species of salmon—adapted to seasonally dry streams in the arid climate at the southern end of the steelhead range.

Southern Steelhead and **Coastal Rainbow Trout** are the same species. The steelhead is the **anadromous** form of the trout; it is able to spend part of its life in the ocean but returns to freshwater streams for breeding.

Historically, the Southern Steelhead was the only salmon species living in every major watershed in our region. The Santa Ynez River had the largest population of steelhead in Southern California, with estimates of thirteen thousand to twenty-five thousand in the early 1940s. On the Santa Clara River, up to nine thousand adults were recorded in some years. But now, their population has dwindled to less than one percent of its former size.

Southern Steelhead, however, are tough and highly adaptable to the vagaries of riverine life. Given a chance, they'll survive because they have evolved several strategies.

Steelhead can migrate from freshwater streams to the ocean. They can migrate to and from a lagoon at a river's mouth, or they may stay in the freshwater where they were born. They can even use sections of streams that seasonally go dry but retain isolated pools. They can migrate to the sea at various ages and times within a season and spend varying amounts of time there, then return to a home stream. Steelhead are able to spawn more than once. Females are more likely than males to live after spawning, so they outnumber them on the spawning grounds.

Furthermore, adults that practice one of these life strategies might have progeny that exhibit a different one. For example, an oceangoing parent might produce young that would stay in the freshwater stream and reproduce without attempting an ocean journey.

Steelhead spawn in cool, clear, oxygenated streams that have a certain velocity and gravel size. These conditions are found in the upper tributary creeks of the larger rivers. Here, the female clears out a depression (a **redd**) in which to lay her eggs. The male guards the redd against other males and fertilizes the eggs of the female, which are then covered with a shallow layer of gravel to protect them.

Before juvenile steelhead begin their seaward journey, they undergo **smoltification**, the process that prepares them for survival in salt water. Their tail fins become dark and their scales turn silvery. At this stage, the **smolts**, as they are called, are about six inches long. From mid-March to early May, the outmigration of smolts begins. As they find their way to the ocean, their route may be blocked by a sandbar and they may be forced to spend considerable time in the estuary lagoon formed at the river mouth; this allows the smolts to adapt to saltwater conditions.

Why the ocean odyssey? Because

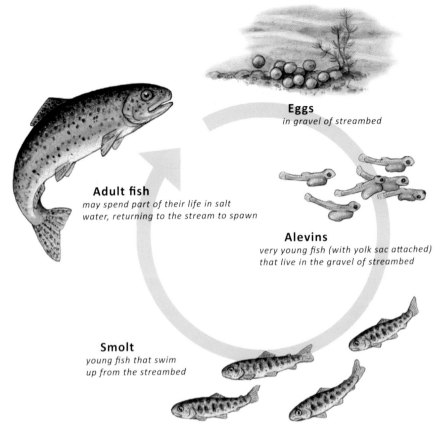

Eggs
in gravel of streambed

Adult fish
may spend part of their life in salt water, returning to the stream to spawn

Alevins
very young fish (with yolk sac attached) that live in the gravel of streambed

Smolt
young fish that swim up from the streambed

Southern Steelhead life cycle

the abundant food in the ocean allows the juvenile steelhead to grow big. One large steelhead documented in the return spawning run on the Santa Clara River measured thirty-three inches long and weighed thirteen pounds. On the Santa Ynez River adult steelhead from two to three feet in length were commonly recorded by anglers. Steelhead returning to freshwater for the second time or more measure the largest.

When the adult steelhead reaches sexual maturity at sea, its extraordinary homing abilities kick in. From thousands of miles away, the steelhead finds its stream of origin. Whether by celestial navigation, the ability to detect the magnetic pull of the earth, an extraordinary sense of smell, or some combination of these, the adult steelhead returns to its natal stream. If, due to drought or human activities, that stream is no longer navigable, the steelhead adapts. It either delays its upstream spawning or enters another available stream.

In our region, steelhead must wait until rains come in late fall, winter, or even early spring. They follow the path of least resistance, swimming up the mainstem channels of major rivers to get to those cool tributary creeks for spawning. Hiding under tree roots and rocks, dodging predators as well as the barriers we have placed in their way, the steelhead undertake their perilous journey back home. Once in freshwater, the male steelhead takes on the appearance of a large coastal rainbow trout, with a rusty lateral stripe and a protruding lower jaw.

In 1997 and again in 2005, scientists concluded that Southern Steelhead were distinct from those to the north, and that they were facing extinction. From the Santa Maria River south to the US–Mexican border, the populations in coastal watersheds such as the Santa Maria, Santa Ynez, Ventura, and Santa Clara rivers were listed as federally endangered; populations from San Luis Obispo to Monterey County are listed as threatened. The listing applies only to those steelhead who exhibit an anadromous life history and whose freshwater habitat occurs below impassable barriers.

When a species is listed as endangered, a plan must be developed to guide recovery. Locally, the National Marine Fisheries Service heads up the effort to restore our rivers so that Southern Steelhead can resume their historic journeys to and from the sea. The threats aren't insurmountable, but they are huge: dams, changes in natural flows, increased water temperatures, reduced flushing of sediments, and introduction of non-native fish (e.g., bass, carp, and catfish) that eat the young steelhead. If you take the long view—that the restoration process will go on for decades—success doesn't seem impossible.

At Arroyo Hondo Creek, where the culvert under the freeway has been modified to link the lagoon at the creek mouth with the upper portion of the creek, an annual steelhead/rainbow trout survey by hydrologist Tim Robinson and colleagues since 2006 suggests there are steelhead occupying the creek. At present, the fish are gaining weight and thriving by migrating downstream to the lagoon and upstream to the spawning grounds. Perhaps some are Southern Steelhead (referred to as "half-pounders"—ten to fourteen inches long), but without genetic testing the biologists cannot say for sure.

At Carpinteria Creek, since 2002 a total of six barriers to steelhead migration have been removed, including modification of stream crossings and debris dams. Now, for the first time in decades, adult steelhead are able to migrate from the ocean upstream to spawning grounds high in Gobernador Canyon.

In downtown Santa Barbara at Mission Creek, steelhead have been observed attempting to swim upstream to Mission Canyon and Rattlesnake Canyon, which contain habitats ideal for spawning and rearing. Historically, Mission Creek was full of steelhead, but with concrete channelization to control floodwaters, the fish have a difficult time completing their journey inland and back out to the ocean.

If you don't believe that steelhead can live in a suburban habitat, stand on the bridge at the Santa Barbara Museum of Natural History in Mission Canyon and look into the deep pools that shelter these beauties. You can see steelhead all right,

Southern Steelhead in Mission Creek, February 2008. Photo by Mark Capelli

but whether they are trapped there forever or will resume their ancestral journey between the mountains and the sea will depend upon our commitment to our rivers and streams—and this special salmon that reflects their ancient rhythms.

Nature Journal
May 10, 2011

Steelhead Musings on the Santa Clara River

The wide, fertile Santa Clara River Valley of Ventura County has been a center for agriculture since the turn of the century. The dark green citrus orchards and plentiful row crops share the valley with the source of its fruitfulness—the Santa Clara River.

This morning the long ridge of South Mountain lies in shade, while the foothills over on the Santa Paula and Fillmore side are bathed in sunlight. Santa Paula Peak stands tall in the Topatopa Mountains on that side of the valley.

I want to get a feel for the Santa Clara River. I want to walk in the floodplain, gaze at the water rushing by. At the western end of the valley near the end of Briggs Road, I park across the street from the car repair shops and metal recycling stores in this neighborhood.

I know the river is somewhere to the south over there, so I start walking, seeking the main channel.

A series of pebbly terraces leads through the forest of willows. Then comes a huge patch of Giant Reed, that unwanted invader. Efforts here at removal of this green-caned imposter are just getting off the ground.

At last I emerge at a major dry side channel. I'm walking in sandy loam. Looking down, I see a rock of solid granite and pick it up. The closest granitic rocks are in the San Gabriel Mountains, fifty miles away, and this rock has made that journey!

Mule Fat—the shrub that pretends it's a willow and certainly looks like one—has an evocative, vinegar-like odor which reminds me of watery places. In wispy, solitary bushes it dots the sandy floodplain.

Descending to the last terrace, I hear the sound of rushing water. The main channel is close.

A river this big is worth admiring. The watery channels merge and separate, divide, and reunite. It is a braided river threading the lifeblood of the land from one side of the wide floodplain to another. After winter storms and heavy rainfall, the river has a mind of its own, its turbulence eroding previous terraces to make new ones, depositing gravel on one sandbar and stealing it from another.

Native plants go with the flow. After a big surge of water, cottonwoods, willows, and Mule Fat may be uprooted, then rebound quickly with new shoots.

Mouth of the Santa Clara River after a winter storm: the sandbar has broken through, creating access to the sea for steelhead in the lagoon at the river's mouth, or upstream for those waiting to go in that direction.

When you watch a big river, the rhythm of the moving water casts a spell. This is no burbling, tumbling coastal creek, but a serious body of water moving swiftly over cobbles and tree roots, sandbars and willow shoots. Murmuring one minute, growling the next, the eddies form and subside, depending upon the obstacles met. Big clumps of debris create deep pools.

I looked at that sunny stretch of the Santa Clara River for a long time and you know what I thought? How perfect for Southern Steelhead this river could be.

It could be a gateway for a restored population of steelhead!

I could picture the juvenile steelhead swimming downstream after a big December spell of rain (like the one we had in 2010), making their way towards the estuary at the river mouth. These would be the immatures, heading for the sea for the first time. Born in the high reaches of Sespe and Santa Paula creeks, they would use the Santa Clara River as a highway to carry them to the sea. Finally, after they reached the lagoon at

the estuary—then, and only with the river's help—they would break free, carried over the breached sandbar by the swirling waters and dumped out into the sea.

The young steelhead can forage now in the ocean and grow bigger than their cousins, the coastal Rainbow Trout. The steelhead just have to bust out and then they're gone for a year or two, and finally, when they need to come back upstream to spawn, they have to wait outside the sandbar at the Santa Clara River estuary for another winter storm to arrive. It can be a long wait. When will it rain hard enough for the sandbar to open up again and allow the river's force to create a channel upstream?

At last, after a two-day downpour, the steelhead seize their chance. They slip back into the brackish water at the river mouth, which has opened up, and they start to battle their way upstream. It's hard, but they can do it—until they encounter an insurmountable barrier: the Vern Freeman Diversion Dam in the lower reaches of the river.

Try as they might, they cannot figure

out a way to get around that structure. And so they languish and may perish, because if they can't surmount that diversion dam, they can't get to the source streams they need—like the cool pools and boulders of Santa Paula Creek, or the rushing riffles of Sespe Creek, where spawning is good.

The best solution would be complete removal of the dam, so that this majestic river could flow freely. But even a properly designed fishway or ramp would be better than nothing. If only the steelhead could swim upstream and get around the diversion dam…

Wouldn't that be one of the best restoration stories in the West?

* * *

Note: Planning sessions have commenced between the United Water Conservation District, which maintains the Vern Freeman Diversion Dam, and other stakeholders in the future of the river. Alternatives to help steelhead recovery on the Santa Clara are being discussed. Biologists are analyzing the best way to provide effective passage over the dam. It will be a slow process, but the Santa Clara River, considered one of the most endangered rivers in the US, may be restored in our lifetime.

Insects of the Riparian Habitat

Insects are essential to animals that live in a freshwater environment. Mayflies, dragonflies, stoneflies, caddisflies, water bugs, mosquitoes, midges, and flies—to name a few—are consumed by steelhead, Coastal Rainbow Trout, and other fishes. In addition, frogs, toads, salamanders, snakes, birds, and bats prey on the millions of insects found in the riparian eco-

system. Spend a summer day birding, hiking, fishing, or swimming near a creek or river, and these hoverers and biters will leave no doubt that they—the insects—are by far the most numerous fauna in the riparian zone.

Insects make a living in myriad ways, each playing a vital role in the ecosystem. Largely due to the decaying leaves and litter in the water and on the stream bank, a rich supply of nutrients is available to them in the riparian zone. Some insects (herbivores) feed on living plants; some insects (carnivores) are predators, pursuing live prey (usually other insects); some insects process dead or decaying organic matter; some insects are parasites.

Aquatic insects—the view from underneath the stream's surface: Imagine for a moment that you are a young steelhead that's been born upstream in a watershed on the South Coast somewhere—it could be in Sespe Creek or Rattlesnake Creek—and if you are going to undertake your life cycle of an ocean journey and return, you need a nourishing diet of insects in order to grow.

Being a juvenile Coastal Rainbow Trout requires a constant search for insects. As the young fish swims along underwater, it notices and consumes the larger prey first. Researchers have evidence that tadpoles, water bugs, and water beetles are favored prey.

Most fish food, however, consists of the odd-looking larval forms of aquatic insects. There's a fantasy world under the surface of the stream, where strange organisms that are unrecognizable to you and me move about. When they become adults they

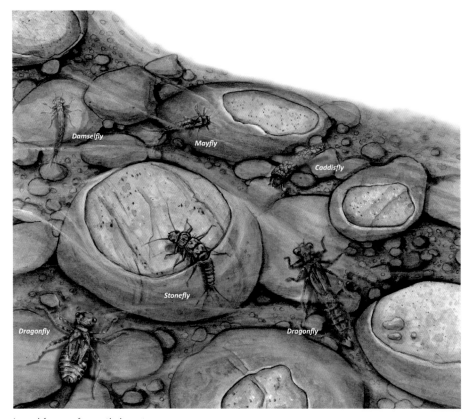

Larval forms of aquatic insects

are familiar, as dragonflies or midges, mayflies or gnats.

For instance, the drab, elongated creature with the big eyes and sharp mandibles that creeps across the muddy streambed will someday become a stunning, airborne dragonfly. The tubular carcass encrusted with pebbles that clambers slowly over the rocks with its head protruding will later, as an adult, become a caddisfly. The weird animal with a feathery tail that hides under that stone is a mayfly—its adult life will be short—ephemeral, to say the least. And the dobsonfly nymph, nicknamed a "hellgrammite," is a cylindrical insect with hair tufts protruding from the sides, completely different from the delicate, lacy-winged, flying adult it will become.

Several orders of insects that provide food for fish have at least one developmental stage in which they are aquatic: **mayflies** (Order Ephemeroptera), **dragonflies** and **damselflies** (Odonata), **stoneflies** (Plecoptera), **dobsonflies** (Neuroptera), and **caddisflies** (Trichoptera). The adults are often seen near water because that's where they lay their eggs. The nymph, or larva, which hatches from the egg, is the aquatic stage in the life cycle. The rather homely nymphs will

Stonefly nymph

metamorphose into beautiful flying insects once they reach adulthood.

Larval stoneflies, mayflies, caddisflies, and dobsonflies are preferred trout food. The emergence of the adult insects is known as "the hatch" by fishermen, who seek to imitate the appearance of the adults with their dry flies.

Mayflies have been called the cattle of aquatic environments because the larvae graze on plant tissues. As nymphs, they may live for several months and are a major source of food for fish and dragonflies. Once the mayfly becomes an adult, it does not feed. It must reproduce, and it only has a few hours, maybe a couple of days, after which it will die. Many anglers use handmade flies that mimic the adult mayfly, filling their fly boxes with "duns" and "spinners," as the winged forms are called.

An interesting experiment by UC Santa Barbara aquatic researcher Scott Cooper showed that a species of mayfly nymph (*Baetis coelestis*) avoided drifting downstream during daytime hours when rainbow trout were present in a stream or pool. Evidently, the nymph gets chemical cues that the trout are present and avoids predation by making its way downstream at night.

Dragonflies and damselflies have powerful chewing mouthparts. (The order name, Odonata, derives from the Greek word for "tooth.") Dragonflies hatch from eggs laid in the water. The larval forms, or nymphs (also called naiads), crawl around on the muddy bottom. They are fearsome predators, eating other insects, tadpoles, fish, and even young salamanders. Lying in wait for prey, the dragonfly nymph snatches a passing victim in its double-hinged lower jaw, which is armed with hooks, teeth, and spiny hairs. Then it retracts its jaw back to the chewing mouthparts for

Dragonfly nymph

Dragonflies and mayflies are examples of aquatic insects that undergo "incomplete metamorphosis": they do not have a pupal stage. After the larva goes through a series of several molts, it climbs out of the water and attaches itself to a nearby plant. It then sheds its final "skin" and emerges as a winged adult. The cast exoskeleton, or **exuvia**, can sometimes be found still hanging on the plant.

Dragonflies and damselflies are related. Dragonflies are robust and hold their wings straight out when perched. Damselfly wings are pressed together in line with the abdomen, so they don't stick out to the side when the insect perches. Dragonflies have enormous compound eyes with excellent vision. While hunting, they employ hawking—aerial pursuit—and sallying tactics. In sallying mode, the dragonfly sits and waits on top of a reed or branch, where it has a good view of the surrounding area. When an approaching insect flies by, the dragonfly sallies out to nab it.

munching. A dragonfly nymph can also rapidly expel water from the tip of its abdomen to jet forward when it needs to escape an enemy.

Common dragonflies in our region are the Common Green Darner, the **Blue-eyed Darner** (*Rhionaeshna*

An adult Vivid Dancer (*Argia vivida*), a common damselfly

An adult Flame Skimmer has just emerged from its exuvia, which remains behind on the vegetation to which the nymph had attached itself.

multicolor), and the **Flame Skimmer** (*Libellula saturata*).

Caddisflies have a unique method of self-protection during their larval stage. Well known to fishing aficionados as "caseworms," the bottom-dwelling larvae construct cases, or tubes, made of silk with sticks and plant fragments attached to camouflage them from hungry fish. Some caddisfly larvae lie stationary within their "houses," with only the head and mouthparts sticking out to grab prey. Some move around with their cases, usually grazing on decaying matter. Powell and Hogue, in *California Insects*, explain the origin of the word "caddis." It dates from sixteenth-century England, where "cadise" referred to cotton or silk. Vendors

wore bits of their wares on their coats as a form of advertisement and were called "cadise men."

Other aquatic insects are somewhat easier to see because their adult forms spend more time on the surface of the water. For example, it is hard to miss the Common Water Strider, indeed one of the most common insects around water in California. These long-legged water bugs that appear to be skating on the surface of the water have long interested scientists. At first it was thought that a waxy coating on the legs, combined with surface tension of the water, was enough to keep the bugs afloat. But in 2004 the strider's secret was discovered. Careful examination of the legs of the bug under a powerful microscope reveals minuscule hairs, all oriented in one direction and scored with tiny grooves, which can trap air and form a cushion that prevents the legs from getting wet. This allows the Common Water Strider to glide about using its middle legs as oars—the front and back legs are for steering—without breaking the surface tension of the water. Striders are predaceous and devour aquatic organisms of all kinds.

Other common water bugs are the **Backswimmer** (*Notonecta shooteri*), which swims upside down and eats mosquitoes and small fish, and the larger **Giant Water Bug** (*Abedus indentatus*). Giant Water Bugs can be over an inch long and are completely aquatic, concealing themselves on the stream bottom until likely prey passes by. Another name for them, "toe biters," refers to the firm grip their front legs exhibit when stepped upon by a human swimmer. To subdue prey, toe biters inflict

The Backswimmer swims belly up while it feeds on mosquito larvae.

The male Giant Water Bug carries eggs that have been deposited by the female on his back, where they will remain until they hatch.

many of which are aquatic in the early stages. The adults, however, are aerial or terrestrial. In mosquitoes, both the larvae (the little "wrigglers," as they're called, that hang from the surface of the water) and the pupae are aquatic. Female mosquitoes have two stomachs—the second one being for blood that they get from a vertebrate animal. They need that blood to stimulate reproduction. Only the females feed on blood; male mosquitoes are nectar feeders.

Midges (Family Chironomidae) in all their stages are a prime source of food for fish and birds. Adult midges, although similar to mosquitoes in body structure, lack biting mouthparts. In spring and summer, male midges fly about in enormous dense swarms, forming clouds over lakes, reservoirs, and streams. In this way they attract females and breeding occurs.

Certain aquatic insects are particularly sensitive to the amount of oxygen available in the water around them, for they need to breathe air while submerged. The larvae of mayflies, stoneflies, and caddisflies require well-oxygenated water, which is found in clear, fast-flowing streams. Because they breathe through delicate, tracheal gills, the presence or absence of these species has been used as a bioindicator of the quality of streams.

Other aquatic insects can get by on less oxygen. For example, the Diptera—the flies, midges, gnats, and mosquitoes—can tolerate the slow-moving or still waters of rivers, lakes, or marshes. They are more widely distributed throughout freshwater wetlands because of their tolerance for less oxygenated waters.

a poisonous bite and then suck up the organs, leaving little behind. The male is responsible for caring for the eggs, which he carries around on his back. He cleans the eggs with his hind legs, then gently rocks them back and forth so that oxygen-rich water will pass over them intermittently.

Most numerous of all the insects in or near freshwater are the members of the order Diptera ("two-winged")—**flies, gnats, midges,** and **mosquitoes**—

Large aggregations of Convergent Lady Beetles overwinter in damp soil near streams, especially in the interior.

Terrestrial Insects: Riparian woodlands contain plants that are hosts to many terrestrial insects—that is, insects which spend most of their lives on land.

Butterflies and moths lay their eggs on host plants which then serve as food for the vegetarian larvae. Mature moths and butterflies are nectar feeders. For example, the **Western Tiger Swallowtail** (*Papilio rutulus*), the **Lorquin's Admiral** (*Limenitis lorquini*), and the **Mourning Cloak** (*Nymphalis antiopa*) use willows as their host plants.

More species of beetles (Order Coleoptera) are found in terrestrial riparian habitats than any other insect. Coleoptera is the largest order in the animal kingdom, so this isn't surprising. One of the more common and easily recognized beetles is the ladybird beetle (Family Coccinellidae), with its deep red coloration and crisp black spots.

In our region, the **Convergent Lady Beetle** (*Hippodamia convergens*) makes a desirable garden visitor because of its appetite for aphids, but where does it spend the winter?

If you've hiked along foothill or mountain streams in fall, winter, or early spring, you will have noticed masses of these "ladybugs" as they overwinter in damp soil and rotting logs. Thousands of the little creatures carpet streamside trails and rocks in a fascinating display of aggregate hibernation. There they will stay, some even buried by snow, until they launch themselves on the spring winds that blow them towards the coastal valleys.

Watch for these masses of ladybird beetles in hibernation along Rattlesnake Creek, along the Fir Canyon Trail, which hugs Davy Brown Creek on Figueroa Mountain, and on Pine Mountain Ridge in Ventura County.

Common Butterflies of Riparian Woodland

1. Western Tiger Swallowtail, *Papilio rutulus*
2. California Tortoiseshell, *Nymphalis californica*
3. Lorquin's Admiral, *Limenitis lorquini*
4. Mourning Cloak, *Nymphalis antiopa*
5. California Sister, *Adelpha californica*

Freshwater Marshes and Vernal Pools

Up to now, we have been discussing one type of freshwater wetland—the riparian habitat. However, two other significant wetlands are found in our region: freshwater marshes and vernal pools. Both are scarce here, compared to the creeks and rivers of riparian systems. Freshwater marshes and vernal pools are located in areas that retain water; the marsh usually has a constant water source, but a vernal pool dries up after winter rains.

Let's discuss freshwater marsh first.

Freshwater Marsh

In our region, freshwater marshes have slowly disappeared. Barka Slough on San Antonio Creek near Vandenberg Air Force Base was formerly one of the largest freshwater marshes in the region.

Many freshwater marshes form naturally at the inland portion of an estuary (see Chapter 5), where low-lying creeks or rivers flow into the sea. Freshwater marshes also occur in a limited way at the margins of lakes, reservoirs, and farm ponds.

Freshwater Oso Flaco Lake is surrounded by the Guadalupe-Nipomo Dunes Complex.

Most lakes in our region were created when dams were built, such as at Lopez Lake, Lake Cachuma, or Lake Casitas, where small patches of marsh grow in sheltered bays around the shores.

Although natural lakes are few and far between, they too have freshwater marsh areas around their perimeters. Examples of natural lakes are: Oso Flaco Lake, one of several small freshwater dune lakes within the Guadalupe-Nipomo Dunes Complex; Zaca Lake in the Santa Ynez Valley, formed by a pair of landslides that slid northward from Zaca Ridge; and Laguna Lake near San Luis Obispo, a remnant of a larger freshwater marsh complex that formed thousands of years ago.

Freshwater Marsh Vegetation

Marsh vegetation grows in bands. Riparian trees and willow thickets occupy the upland areas. Next, a wall of cattails and tules marks the water's edge. Out in the open water, **pondweed** (*Stuckenia* spp.), **duckweed** (*Lemna* spp.) or **Mosquito Fern** (*Azolla filliculoides*) float near the surface, while pale **green algae** (*Spirogyra* spp.) commonly forms large mats in sheltered waters.

The tall, thin stalks of tules are the best indicators of a freshwater marsh. As you approach, a wall of green may block the view of the open water entirely. It is comprised of several kinds of plants: **rushes** (*Juncus* spp.), **bulrushes**, or **tules** (*Schoenoplectus* spp.), **flatsedges** (*Cyperus* spp.), and **cattails** (*Typha* spp.) All may appear indistinguishable to the casual observer, but each is slightly different in the shape and feel of its stem. Tules are the most abundant.

The stalks of tules and cattails push up right out of the shallow, muddy water, often reaching heights of ten to twelve feet. Cattails can be distinguished from tules by their dense, brown flower spikes that look like long hot dogs on sticks.

Tules are the most important plant of our region's freshwater marshes. Both **California Tule** (*Schoenoplectus californicus*) and **Roundstem Tule** (*Schoenoplectus acutus*) bear tiny flowers in large reddish-brown clusters at the tips of their stalks (**culms**). The seeds from the flowers are eagerly sought by many species of birds.

Roundstem Tule's stalk is round, but that of the California Tule is somewhat triangular, especially near the tip. Tule stalks die back each winter and are replaced by new stalks that sprout from underground stems. Tules were formerly more common in California, especially in the Central Valley, and the term "out in the tules" referred to a remote location where few people lived.

Like those of salt marshes, plants growing in freshwater marshes are challenged by a lack of oxygen. The large amount of decomposed organic

Lake Los Carneros, near urban habitat, is a good place to observe a freshwater marsh.

material promotes the growth of bacteria. As bacteria work to break down the organic material, they reduce the oxygen supply even more. But the stems of marsh plants are either hollow or they're filled with **aerenchyma**, a porous tissue that allows air—and oxygen—to travel from the upper, exposed parts of the plants down to their submerged roots.

Birds of the Freshwater Marsh

Gadwalls (*Anas strepera*), **Mallards** (*Anas platyrhynchos*), and **Ruddy Ducks** (*Oxyura jamaicensis*) paddle about in the shallows or slurp the surface-floating duckweed. **American Coots** (*Fulica americana*), those black, lumpish-looking birds with white shields on their foreheads, make nesting platforms hidden in the tules. **Marsh Wrens** (*Cistothorus palustris*) dance up and down the tule stems, scolding at intruders. Male **Red-winged Blackbirds** (*Agelaius phoeniceus*) announce their territories in song, then show off their red shoulder patches to attract mates. Both Red-winged Blackbirds and Marsh Wrens weave their nests

A pair of Mallards swims near tules bordering Lake Los Carneros.

you can study the tules and cattails at eye level.

Other examples of freshwater marsh habitat are at the Ventura Water Treatment Plant/Wildlife Ponds (permission required) and Andree Clark Bird Refuge near the Santa Barbara waterfront.

Vernal Pools

Vernal pools are not as well known or as easy to see as freshwater marshes, but the two habitats are related. A marsh has a steady source of water, usually year-round. A vernal pool is ephemeral; filled by winter rains, it dries up before the long summer.

Vernal pools are perhaps the rarest type of wetland in our region. Our Mediterranean climate makes every drop of water precious; ephemeral pools are transient refuges for endemic plants and animals found nowhere else.

Although a variety of seasonal wetlands exist throughout North America and worldwide, those in California are distinguished by their special flora. An estimated two hundred kinds of plants are associated with vernal pools; nearly a third of those are considered threatened due to habitat destruction.

Vernal pools appear as seasonally wet, shallow depressions, often located in the midst of open grassland. Winter rain fills these basins, turning them into miniature lakes. By late spring or early summer, they succumb to summer drought. They will remain dry for many months.

A vernal pool requires a "perched water table" to keep the collected water from draining out the bottom.

This displaying male Red-winged Blackbird has set up a territory and will attract one or more females to build their nests in the tules.

from the stems of tules. **Virginia Rails** (*Rallus limicola*) and **Soras** (*Porzana carolina*) make loud, harsh calls from the thick stands of reeds.

In winter, the freshwater marsh attracts a variety of ducks, grebes, and herons. They like the calm water, shelter, and abundant food from seeds and floating plants. In spring and summer, swallows swoop low over the marsh, feeding on gnats and midges.

From the boardwalk at Oso Flaco Lake or on the footbridge at the north end of Lake Los Carneros, you can observe the birds that use a freshwater marsh. And you are up high, so

The restored Del Sol Vernal Pool, near the University of California, Santa Barbara

Vernal pool on the Carrizo Plain: concentric rings of flowers bloom as the soil dries up around the pool and growing conditions change.

Inconspicuous vernal pool at More Mesa

The pools are underlain with a fine, sandy loam, and beneath that lies an impermeable layer of clay substrate which keeps the water from seeping through. The impervious layer can be composed of caliche, hardpan, claypan, or bedrock. Vernal pools are often less than three feet deep, sometimes only a few inches.

A vernal pool is a transitional ecosystem. It starts out as an aquatic habitat. Eventually, when the pool dries up, it is a part of the terrestrial landscape. Even if you can't see the mud-caked bottom of the pool after it's dried up, you can tell where a vernal pool has been by the kinds of plants that set it apart from the surrounding annual grassland.

Rare or endangered plants associated with vernal pools in our area are: **coyote thistle** (*Eryngium armatum* and *E. vaseyi*), **Water Starwort** (*Callitriche marginata*), **Wavy-stemmed Popcorn Flower** (*Plagiobothrys undulatus*), **Salt-marsh Aster** (*Symphyotrichum subulatum*), **Southern Tarplant** (*Centromadia pungens* subsp. *australis*), and

331

Hoover's Downingia, an exquisite plant found on the margins of vernal pools in grasslands along Cerro Noroeste Road

several species of rushes and **spike-rushes** (*Eleocharis* spp.), among others. The very colorful, bright blue flower known as **Hoover's Downingia** (*Downingia bella*) surrounds vernal pools on the west slopes of Cerro Noroeste Road near Apache Potrero.

Crustaceans of Freshwater Marshes and Vernal Pools

Freshwater marshes and vernal pools share some of the same creatures. Like their equivalents in the ocean, the filter-feeding zooplankton of freshwater marshes and vernal pools are critical to their ecosystems. Most of them are herbivores, devouring algae and fine detritus. Bacteria on the bottom of the pool transform dead plants into nourishing food for the zooplankton. In turn, the zooplankton are consumed by toads, frogs, salamanders, and birds.

Creatures living in vernal pools must be able to tolerate a wide range of conditions, from flooding to desiccation. Many have an ephemeral existence: they cannot live for long, because they must mature and reproduce before the pool dries up.

One of the advantages of living in a vernal pool is the absence of fish as predators. Fish cannot survive in a pool that is destined to dry up. A healthy vernal pool, therefore, has a rich population of insects and crustaceans that would otherwise be eaten by fish.

Many of the crustaceans in freshwater marshes and vernal pools are so tiny you'll need a hand lens to see them. If you fill a single glass with water from a pond and hold it up to the light, you will see a bewildering diversity of microscopic organisms.

Water fleas (*Cladocera* spp.), **copepods** (*Copepoda* spp.), and **rotifers** (*Rotifera* spp.) swim around, looking the size of pin-pricks. Copepods resemble tiny red dots because they take in pigments, such as carotenids, to protect themselves from ultraviolet radiation. Some zooplankton use their segmented bodies to swim in fits and starts. Others, such as the **seed shrimp** (*Ostracoda* spp.), resemble grains of sand. All are ancient forms of life that were around way before the dinosaurs.

Insects are here, too. Larval forms

A copepod, one of the many microscopic invertebrates found in vernal pools

A triptych of California Clam Shrimp. Two of the individuals are carrying eggs.

of beetles, bugs, mosquitoes, and dragonflies squirm and wiggle their way through the rich soup of pond water. Under a microscope, these creatures are fascinating to watch.

One little crustacean, unique to vernal pools and found in several on the South Coast, is the **California Clam Shrimp** (*Cyzicus californicus*). Clam shrimp are larger than the minuscule water fleas and copepods mentioned above. Adult clam shrimp approach the size of a dime. Their bodies look like shrimp, but they're enclosed by a bivalve shell similar to a clamshell. This gives them protection, and the shrimplike body gives them mobility. Bouncing up and down in the water, clam shrimps churn up the water, trapping detritus, algae, copepods, and rotifers on their feathery appendages.

Before the vernal pool dries up,

clam shrimp will have mated. Similar to several other vernal pool organisms, the female produces **cysts**, or **resting eggs**. Resting eggs survive the parched conditions of a long dry season and only hatch when the pool fills once more with rainwater.

Clam shrimp are favorite foods for shorebirds, herons, and egrets, as well as many kinds of amphibians. When a migrating bird feeds on the animals and plants in vernal pools, it acts as a dispersal agent.

Fairy shrimp (*Branchinecta* spp.), which are related to clam shrimp, are a graceful and delicate species, but they have been extirpated from most South Coast vernal pools. You can still find one species, the **Vernal Pool Fairy Shrimp** (*Branchinecta lynchi*), in ponds around Santa Maria and along Figueroa Mountain Road. After a rainy winter on the Carrizo Plain,

Vernal Pool Fairy Shrimp on the Carrizo Plain

the puddles and ditches around Soda Lake contain several different species of fairy shrimp. They move slowly and gracefully on their backs, beating their legs rhythmically as they swim.

Seasonal changes happen in a vernal pool. After the first rains, the resting eggs of seed shrimp, copepods, clam shrimp, and fairy shrimp hatch out. These first occupants are the herbivorous zooplankton. Later in the season, more insects, such as dragonflies, backswimmers, and diving beetles, will fly in and lay their eggs. Their larvae are carnivores, crawling on the bottom of the pool and eating other invertebrates. Eventually, when frogs, toads, and salamanders hatch, they too will be predaceous carnivores.

In our region, the most accessible vernal pools are located on the coastal terraces of Santa Barbara and San Luis Obispo counties. Unfortunately, they have suffered the same fate as many other freshwater wetlands in the region—destruction by development, overgrazing, road building, and drainage.

Vernal pools are extremely difficult to restore, enhance, or recreate: the delicate balance in a pristine vernal pool is not easily reproduced. However, on the South Coast there have been some impressive successes. At Del Sol Open Space and Vernal Pool Reserve and at Camino Corto Open Space across the street, in Isla Vista off Camino Corto, you can see examples. The Isla Vista Parks and Recreation District has set aside over eleven acres in an urban setting to preserve several of the remaining vernal pools in our region. With the advice of UC Santa Barbara biologists, a diverse vernal pool system was recreated over several years, from 1988 to 1998.

Other vernal pools on the South Coast are located at More Mesa and Ellwood Mesa. In Ojai, the Ojai Meadows Preserve is a good example of a restored pool.

Amphibians of Freshwater Wetlands

Amphibians can be classified into several different families: **Mole Salamanders** (for example, the California Tiger Salamander), **Newts** (California Newt), **Lungless Salamanders** (Arboreal Salamander and Black-bellied Slender Salamander), **Frogs** (Baja California Treefrog), and **Toads** (Western Toad).

Amphibians (the term means "two-lived") have fascinating life histories. As a link between two environments—aquatic and terrestrial—their two lives reflect complex adaptations.

Amphibians play a significant role in the ecosystems of all types of freshwater wetlands, but chiefly in freshwater marshes, ponds, and vernal pools. In these habitats they are the major group of animals that transfer the energy from the invertebrates they eat, i.e., aquatic insects and crustaceans, to those that prey on them, such as

The Baja California Treefrog, commonly heard calling on spring nights

reptiles, birds, and mammals. They can pass that energy on up the food chain. For example, a treefrog that devours a gnat or midge will itself be eaten by a Great Blue Heron. An immature salamander that snags a dragonfly nymph may in turn be gobbled by a raccoon that's patrolling the edge of a pond.

The varied lifestyles of amphibians make generalizations difficult, and space precludes detailed descriptions. Hopefully, the highlights touched on below will pique your interest for further study.

The skin of amphibians is permeable by water, often colorful, and supplied with glands. It can serve as a breathing membrane and protects against dehydration during drought. Mucous glands keep it moist, producing a film that shields the animal from bacteria and facilitates swimming.

Western Spadefoot equipped with a "spade" on each hind foot used to dig beneath the surface of the soil during its terrestrial phase

Poison in the skin glands can help defend against predators. In some toads, the warty protuberances and certain glands at the back of the head exude a poisonous milky substance that can be toxic to humans. Newts have poisonous glands that aren't activated unless the animal is attacked, but their tarichatoxin (TTX) is evidently a powerful neurotoxin. However, TTX is only poisonous in humans if it enters the body through the bloodstream or the digestive tract.

Amphibians have a spectrum of breathing structures. They need to. Many, although not all, are hatched from eggs in water to become larvae.

Tadpoles are the larval form of frogs and toads. As tadpoles, they breathe through gills, and as adults they are terrestrial, breathing through lungs and skin. On the other hand, lung-

Western Toads are frequently seen at night near farm ponds.

less salamanders do not have a larval stage in water, but instead survive in damp places on land. Their skin has a dense network of blood vessels for quick access to oxygen. They also rapidly flutter their throats, which contain moist tissue, fanning the air at

high speed to get more oxygen (see also Chapter 7).

Amphibians have four legs; the hind legs are longer in frogs and toads, for jumping. **Baja California Treefrogs** (*Pseudacris hypochondriaca*, formerly Pacific Treefrog)—the little frogs you are apt to hear in the garden on spring evenings—have toes with adhesive pads or disks to help with climbing. These frogs scramble up and down vegetation with ease. And the Western Spadefoot has a black, sharp protrusion, the "spade," on each hind foot that enables it to dig backwards into the soil. As adults, spadefoot toads spend a part of their lives underground, deep in holes they have excavated.

Adult amphibians are carnivores, feeding on a variety of live animals. They detect their prey by sight and smell. The majority of prey are insects. To aid in catching insects, amphibian tongues can be extended far beyond the mouth opening with lightning speed. Not only does the tongue project well beyond the mouth, it has a sticky uppermost surface that helps in catching and keeping insect prey. Salamanders and some frogs have one or two rows of hinged teeth, recurved towards the back of the mouth. The teeth are used in holding and crushing prey, once the tongue has procured it. Salamanders often wait for prey to appear, but toads actively seek their prey.

Voices of male frogs and toads calling on a spring evening can drown out all other sounds. Especially in places near a potential breeding site—a freshwater marsh, farm pond, or vernal pool—a cacophony of chirp-

Coast Range Newts form a "newt ball" composed of males and one female during the mating season. This photo was taken when the newts were at least a foot underwater.

ing and bleating echoes through the night silence. Frogs and toads croak by forcing air from their lungs over vocal cords in the larynx, filling their vocal sacs like small balloons. When inflated, the vibrating sac carries sound long distances, sometimes even underground and underwater.

These loud springtime calls are the advertising calls of the males. Females can recognize individual males and their calls. This is how frog courtship begins. Not only is the call used to lure females, it is also a way for a male of one species to let another male of that species know that he is present, and this is his space.

Both frogs and toads tend to call in groups. One male, the chorus master, starts the calling sequence. Other males or smaller groups of males join in, one by one. Often there's a pecking order,

with the dominant male being the chorus leader; he's usually the largest, oldest, and most vigorous of the males calling.

Interestingly, the loud choruses of frogs and toads that are reproductively active serve to stimulate the endocrine activity of other males that are somewhat slower in development, bringing them into readiness for mating. Calling may also stimulate ovulation in females.

Frogs, toads, newts, and salamanders are able to migrate to and from breeding sites in an extraordinary show of overland navigation. During the dry summer and fall, when the natal vernal pool or pond has dried up, these animals retreat into abandoned ground squirrel or gopher burrows, culverts, or crevices in rocks and logs to withstand the summer heat and lack of moisture.

Tadpole of a Baja California Treefrog

As soon as the first rains of winter begin to fall, in December and January, perhaps amphibians sense the vibrations on the soil despite the fact that they are sheltering well underground. With each wet, rainy night, they creep closer to the surface. If precipitation is normal and the ponds continue to fill with water, the animals' urge to return to reproduce in the pond where they matured takes over. Migration begins.

Distances vary among species, but some individuals have been known to move a half-mile or more. They move in a line over rough country on a dark, usually rainy night in order to get to a breeding pond. How do they manage to find their way? Biologists have evidence that amphibians use celestial cues, special photoreceptors in the head, and chemical cues. For example, California Newts exude drops of fluid that act as markers. They even use landmarks, such as bushes, trees, and rocks, to navigate.

Reproduction in amphibians can be grouped into two patterns: explosive breeders and prolonged breeders. Western Spadefoot Toads are examples of explosive breeders, using temporary pools to breed whenever conditions are suitable. Their deafening communal chorus attracts females, which arrive more or less together. Mating takes place quickly, and the males scramble to mate with as many females as possible, occasionally having to fight off other males.

In contrast, prolonged breeders tend to go to a more reliable site, such as a freshwater marsh or permanent pond, and breeding extends over a longer period of time. Female Baja California Treefrogs, for example, are attracted to males that call from spaced sites which they defend as territories. Males with the best territories attract the most females. The calls of male prolonged breeders are usually alternated with one another (antiphonal), not given all together like those of explosive breeders.

A Close-up: the Baja California Treefrog

The common Baja California Treefrog, which you can see at Del Sol Vernal Pool, Lake Los Carneros, or in a pond in your backyard, makes a good subject for study.

Let's track its progress from egg to adulthood in a spring season.

Our frog begins its life sometime between November and July as part of a grapelike cluster of eggs laid on submerged vegetation and surrounded by a gelatinous mass. It is one of 400 to 750 eggs, laid in irregular clusters of 9 to 80. From the egg a larval animal emerges, a tadpole.

Tadpoles (polliwogs) breathe through a single gill opening on the left side of the body. The eyes have no lids. The mouth contains upper and lower jaws known as beaks, with minuscule, comblike teeth. Biologists can identify tadpole species by the number and position of the rows of teeth. The head and body appear as one, with a flattened tail with upper (dorsal) and lower (ventral) fin. On either side of the base of the tail, limb buds appear where the hind legs will begin to grow.

Treefrog tadpoles feed by ingesting bacteria, algae, pollen grains, and other small particles. Biologists have observed that tadpoles can specialize in their feeding methods to optimize nutrition. For example, they will go out of their way to swim to the surface to gulp pollen grains, a good source of protein.

Treefrog tadpoles exhibit antipredator behavior by clustering together—just as birds and fish gather for protection against attackers. Benefits of schooling include increased early detection of predators through alarm behavior that passes through the group. When all the tadpoles flee, they can confuse the predator, thereby foiling an attack on a single individual. Tadpole schools are like fish schools or shorebird flocks, in that the nearest neighbors stay a certain distance from each other and swim in the same direction.

Experiments with tadpoles of some frog species show they have an affinity for their own siblings. A genetically based system of kin recognition based on chemical cues has evolved because cooperation in food finding and warning against predators brings tadpole siblings together in an evolutionary advantage.

Even more intriguing are a series of studies done in Napa that illustrate predator-induced changes in prey **morphology** (shape). In other words, tadpoles have the ability to change their morphology if they are reared with certain predators. For example, when **Bluegill** (*Lepomis macrochirus*) were introduced into a pond, the tadpoles' tails and bodies gradually became more elongate, enabling them to swim away faster from the fish. Alternatively, tadpoles reared with predaceous diving beetle larvae (*Dytiscus* spp.) in a pool were seen to grow deeper tails, so that the diving beetle would strike the thick tail rather than the body of the tadpole. Tadpoles from a control group raised in a pond with no predators, when introduced into either of these ponds with predators, did not survive as well.

But back to our little treefrog tadpole: it grows daily, and as it grows, it slowly begins to metamorphose into an adult frog. The longer the pond stays full of water, the more time the tadpole has for gradual transformation. Many studies show that the largest, healthiest tadpoles transform into the largest healthiest adults. If the pond begins to dry up, the tadpole will be forced to accelerate its transformation. Most treefrogs accomplish metamorphosis over a two-month period.

Metamorphosis is all about the radical transformation from one stage in the life of the amphibian to another. Up to now, we have talked only about metamorphosis in the insect world. The metamorphosis of the common, everyday treefrog has elements of wonderful complexity.

Huge changes must occur to our tadpole before it can become a frog. Restructuring involves putting the muscle and cartilage cells together in completely new ways as this intricate organism takes shape.

A tadpole must grow all four limbs. The mouthparts must change into true jaws, teeth, and a tongue; moveable eyelids must form; the lungs need to fully develop. The tail must be reabsorbed into the body. Skin structure must be changed to include keratin layers, and to develop poison and mucous glands. The gut must transform into a true stomach. The long intestine of the vegetarian tadpole must be shortened to that of the carnivorous adult frog.

Upon emerging from the water for a terrestrial life, our treefrog is vulnerable to predators. Although initially well camouflaged in low, moist vegetation around the pond, it will head for higher ground several hundred yards away. Treefrogs can change their coloration to match their surroundings, becoming lighter or darker or losing their spots. However, whether they are of the green or brown color phase is genetically determined and cannot change.

Like others of its kind, this adult treefrog will return to repeat its chorus the following spring at the same pond. *"Re-dip, re-dip, re-dip..."*

Nature Journal
December 18, 2010

Night Driving for Salamanders in the Eastern Santa Maria Valley

"It was a dark and stormy night..." and perfect conditions for California Tiger Salamanders to migrate towards their ponds for mating.

The story goes like this:

Suddenly, an incredible once-in-a-decade storm hits our region. For three days, rain has fallen steadily.

Knowing that it might be a good time to go see salamanders, I call Professor Sam Sweet at UC Santa Barbara to see if he would like some company looking for salamanders on this nasty night. "The nastier, the better," he says.

Sure enough, several hours later I find myself riding shotgun in the back of Sam's diesel truck, with Stuart in the front seat, camera equipment in hand. It's pouring cats and dogs outside, and the wind pushes the truck around as we drive north on US 101 towards the Santa Maria Valley.

I can imagine the salamanders hidden in their ground squirrel burrows, just listening to the raindrops overhead. At first they would ignore the rain, knowing it was too early in the season and that the ponds hadn't filled yet. But as the rain keeps on coming down, hour after hour, day after day, and the moisture seeps deeper and deeper into the soil, perhaps the salamanders hear the rushing of the creeks or the runoff sliding across the roads. Perhaps they sense the moisture plumping up their porous skin. Who knows what their instinct might be telling them? One thing is certain: they will soon journey to the closest pond. It's time for breeding.

Salamanders look to the skyline for guidance. Heading towards the lowest point in the landscape, the animals move downhill because the lowest spot is where the ponds lie.

Meanwhile, the roar and swish of the tires competes with the splash and swish of the windshield wipers and I am straining to hear what Sam has to say about California Tiger Salamanders, an amphibian that so few folks get to see.

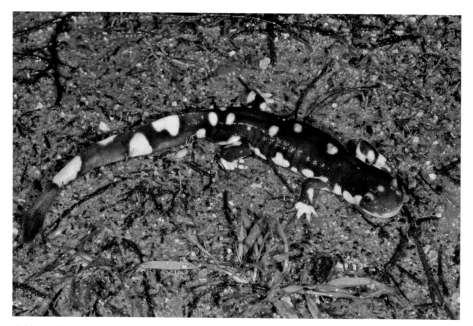

California Tiger Salamander emerges from its burrow on a night of heavy winter rain.

This is my third try at salamander hunting. I've been looking for them since 2001, when I first experienced the disappointment of a late night and no luck.

At last, we turn off the freeway onto country roads. Sam knows all the ponds and their locations around here, but they are hidden away on private property, so our slim chance of seeing a tiger salamander is based on the hope that one will cross the road en route to a pond.

The slick pavement shines in our headlights as we slowly, slowly drive along the side of the road.

Sam hits the brakes, then eases the truck onto the shoulder and gets out. His practiced eye has spotted a California Tiger Salamander! Over six inches long, the animal is a gorgeous, deep, chocolate brown with scattered, bright yellow blotches. Its eyes are bulging, but not frightening. The tail is a keel, and the legs move with elbows sticking out—miniature dinosaurs? Dragons? Just about the most exciting thing that could happen on a rainy night outside Santa Maria!

We get out, struggling with the umbrella, the gusty wind, Stuart's new camera lens, and finally, finally, finally get a good photo of this very cooperative animal.

Later, we see an even larger gravid female—very fat and full of eggs. The females only visit the pond once, mate, then lay their eggs and leave the pond. The males stick around the pond for several months. As Sam says: "They go to the bar every night..."

Sam says that farm ponds built for cattle have actually helped the salamanders stay alive, and their population is more stable than if there were no cattle ponds.

After seeing several more of the marvelous California Tiger Salamanders, we head for home, but not before we have checked the rainy roads again and found a couple of Western Spadefoots and even

Western Toads—all headed for the ponds on a rainy night.

Under cover of darkness and pouring rain, California Tiger Salamanders engage in one of the most spectacular amphibian migrations in California. Crossing paved roads, defying speeding traffic, climbing up and down hillsides, sidling through tall grasses, the animals aim for the nearest pond, usually the one where they spent their larval stage.

Tonight, in this rain, many salamanders will arrive safely.

These were once-in-a-decade conditions for night driving for salamanders! I still can't believe I was there.

The larva of a California Tiger Salamander, showing the prominent, fringed gills that allow it to breathe underwater. The gills will be lost when it metamorphoses into an adult. Photo by Peter Gaede

UC Santa Barbara amphibian expert Sam Sweet filled me in on the details of California Tiger Salamander life history.

When the salamander eggs hatch in the pond, they become carnivorous larvae, eating invertebrates at first, then switching to tadpoles. The tadpoles have to be just the right age, not too big, so that the salamander larvae can catch them. As the pond dries up, the salamander transforms, loses its gills, and becomes terrestrial.

When the salamander leaves the pond, it comes out on the downwind side of the pond, because that's where the humid air is found. As the salamander explores the surrounding area, it sticks its head into a burrow and can determine if it's humid enough for long-term refuge during summer heat. A longer burrow, like that of the California Ground Squirrel, is best. Since ground squirrels and gophers store food and defecate in the burrows, insects are attracted to them. One of the chief foods of salamanders is the **Camel Cricket** (*Ceuthophilus*

The Common Garter Snake is one of several predators of California Tiger Salamander larvae.

californianus), a native cricket with a uniformly arched back. The salamander chooses to glean these insects over others, perhaps because it can easily spot them clinging to the ceilings of the ground squirrel burrows.

The primary predator of California Tiger Salamanders is the **Common Garter Snake** (*Thamnophis sirtalis*), an aquatic garter snake found in the same ponds with salamander larvae. Dr. Sweet describes being in the field, grabbing one of these garter snakes, turning it upside down, and watching as out dropped twenty young

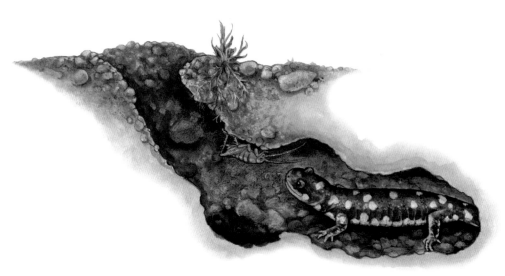

A California Tiger Salamander in its burrow, eyeing a Camel Cricket overhead

salamanders which the snake had just devoured.

Due to the fieldwork of local biologists, the California Tiger Salamander population of Santa Barbara County has been recognized and given the protection it is due by the US Fish and Wildlife Service.

The population in the northern part of the county is a special geographical group of animals, a group which has been isolated for at least a million years. Someday it may be deemed a separate species. (For more on tiger salamanders, see Chapter 2.)

The statewide status of this amphibian can be represented like this:

Population	Federal	State
Sonoma County	Endangered	Threatened
Central Valley	Threatened	Threatened
Santa Barbara County	Endangered	Threatened

* * *

Our journey through the region's wetlands must come to a close.

Like so much in our beautiful land, freshwater wetlands are special, maybe more so than any other habitat we've discussed. Without water, most plants and animals will perish. Humans will suffer drastically.

Our creeks and rivers have been taken for granted. Our marshes and vernal pools were drained and developed. And so it appears that the news is particularly difficult when it comes to freshwater wetlands. Many wetlands have been degraded, destroyed, and defiled simply by their proximity to millions of people.

At the same time, it is the threat of loss that has given rise to new awareness, new action on the part of citizens and government agencies to reverse the damage. If you doubt that we can fix that which we've almost destroyed, then you don't know about the success stories in this chapter.

The mighty Santa Clara River may have turned the corner. Riparian woodlands are being restored and the Least Bell's Vireo is nesting again in certain places along the river. The Southern Steelhead has more of a chance now than it did ten years ago of returning to our region as a viable anadromous fish.

Vernal pools are being restored and enhanced. Tiny crustaceans and rare plants once again flourish in these temporary basins, even if they're surrounded by apartment buildings.

Amphibian populations, previously unmonitored, are in the news now. As a phenomenon, widespread amphibian decline is extremely complicated. There is no smoking gun, and no single process is responsible. But isn't the first step to learn about their complex life cycles and the importance of the quality of the habitat they live in?

Go out and look at tadpoles. Show them to young children. Every kid loves a tadpole and they can see the metamorphosis if you explain it at a local creek. See if you can find a California Newt in one of our streams. Explore Rattlesnake Creek and Mission Creek for any sign of steelhead migrating.

In our region, not every year is a good one for flora and fauna that depend upon wetlands. But the years when the rain comes down all winter long and the land responds with burgeoning creeks and swollen ponds—those are the years we've been waiting for. But they are fleeting.

Get out and enjoy our wetlands as soon as you can.

CHAPTER 10: THE NORTHERN CHANNEL ISLANDS—ISOLATED ECOSYSTEMS AND THEIR SECRETS

The Channel Islands are world-renowned for their wild beauty and the specialized forms of plants and animals that live there.

The four Northern Channel Islands are Anacapa, Santa Cruz, Santa Rosa, and San Miguel. They can be separated geographically and floristically from the Southern Channel Islands, which include Santa Barbara, San Nicolas, Santa Catalina, and San Clemente. These eight islands are often collectively referred to as the California Channel Islands.

From the South Coast of our region, you see the Northern Channel Islands across the Santa Barbara Channel—a glorious view from the crest of the Santa Ynez Mountains at La Cumbre Peak. In summer, their outlines are hazy, their shores bathed in fog; on a clear winter day, their dark blue forms seem pasted against a pewter sky. When storms come over the Pacific, the islands disappear, enveloped in dark clouds. But on a fall day when the offshore winds blow, you can easily make out the pale cliffs of the islands, seemingly close enough to touch.

So close and yet so far.

What is so different about these islands lying only twenty-eight miles away, across the water? Why aren't they simply an extension of the habitats on the mainland that we've talked about thus far in this book?

The Channel Islands are unique, from each other and from the mainland. Their isolation for thousands of years has created a kingdom of plants and animals that are reminiscent of mainland flora and fauna but have diverged into myriad new shapes and sizes.

Islands magnify evolution. Their limited areas make the patterns of evolution stand out.

Aerial view of the Northern Channel Islands. Photo by Bill Dewey

Insular ecosystems, rich in wonder, hold a fascination for all of us. Islands worldwide are havens for the unique and the anomalous. They are incubators for strange, almost mystical creatures; think of the Komodo Dragon, the Tasmanian Devil, the Dodo, the Marine Iguana, and the Moa.

Charles Darwin's theories of evolution were enhanced by what he observed on islands. When Darwin, a careful field biologist and brilliant thinker, accompanied the HMS *Beagle* from 1831 to 1836 on its voyage around the world, he spent time in the Galapagos Islands, in the Pacific Ocean off Ecuador. His observations of animals there helped him arrive at his ideas on the evolution of species. In his first book, *The Voyage of the*

Beagle (1837), he described his experiences for the scientific community. From there, he went on to publish *The Origin of Species* in 1859.

Let's take a trip to the Northern Channel Islands and immerse ourselves in a world apart. Over time, each island has become its own biological microcosm. Assorted species, subspecies, and varieties have evolved; these are forms of plants and animals found nowhere else on earth. They are often smaller or larger, brighter or duller than their mainland relatives. The Island Scrub-Jay and the **Island Fox** (*Urocyon littoralis*) are familiar examples, but there are many more.

Island Biology

We have talked about ecosystems on our planet and how they operate, but on islands the rules are different. By observing the natural history of islands, scientists since Darwin's time have arrived at certain truths about how plants and animals develop. How do plants and animals arrive at an island? How do they adapt to the conditions they find there? Can we predict if they will survive on an island or gradually become extinct?

Dispersal Ability

The first question is how plants and animals get there—how do they disperse? Imagine that Santarosae, the Pleistocene precursor of the Northern Channel Islands, has just emerged from the sea—similar to a volcanic islet that might form somewhere today in the middle of the Pacific. This mound of rock surrounded by ocean is completely devoid of life. What happens next?

The term "**sweepstakes dispersal**" has been used to describe island colonizations, because much of an organism's ability to disperse is pure chance. Some will make it across the ocean, and many won't. Some will thrive on an island, others will succumb to the elements or fail to reproduce once they get there.

Flying is one of the commonest ways to get from the mainland to an island. Migratory birds, bats, and insects are all good colonizers. Birds, especially, are known for their long flights over water. Consequently, bird species from our mainland have colonized the Northern Channel Islands. Those not found on the islands are typically more sedentary species, such as the California Thrasher, California Towhee, Wrentit, Oak Titmouse, and Greater Roadrunner, to name a few.

Swimming is the most challenging method of dispersal. Most large carnivores aren't good swimmers. Perhaps this is why no Coyotes or Mountain Lions are found on the Northern Channel Islands. Herbivores, however, such as deer, hippopotamuses, and especially elephants, have been known to swim distances. (See "The Pygmy Mammoths of the Northern Channel Islands" in this chapter.)

Rafting occurs when animals or plants become stranded on floating debris, particularly storm-borne logs and plant debris that have washed out to sea from the mainland. Some snakes survive by rafting. Although no rattlesnakes are currently found on the Northern Channel Islands, we have fossil evidence that they occurred on San Miguel and Santa Rosa in prehistoric times. Land snails are especially good at rafting, being resistant to desiccation. The flightless endemic silk-spinning crickets (*Cnemotettix* spp.) are thought to have arrived this way.

Air flotation is another manner in which plants, insects, and spiders might have arrived at the islands, especially during strong winds. Many plant seeds have plumes adapted to air dispersal. Spiders, too, are good dispersers, throwing out their strands of silk and hopping on the airwaves.

Plants can colonize islands by **passive transport**, too. For example, migratory birds disperse the small, barbed seeds that attach to their feathers, while fruit may be carried in the gut. Seeds also stick to birds' muddy feet.

What Makes Island Life Different?

Having arrived at the Northern Channel Islands, how do plants and animals adapt to island life?

Size Change: New habitats and climatic conditions give rise to different shapes and sizes. As a former professor of mine used to say, anything smaller than a bread box on the mainland tends to get bigger on islands, whereas anything bigger tends to get smaller.

The term "islandize" is an informal way of describing these changes.

Examples abound in plants. On a pristine island—before livestock are introduced by humans—there are few herbivores to munch on the shrubs, so they may grow bigger and have woodier, stronger stems than the mainland versions of these plants.

On Santa Cruz and Anacapa islands, look for **Santa Cruz Island Buckwheat** (*Eriogonum arborescens*). It's not the low shrub we see on the mainland, but an impressive four-foot-tall plant. **Island Ceanothus** (*Ceanothus arboreus*) grows to twenty feet and has oversized leaves; **Catalina Cherry** (*Prunus ilicifolia* subsp. *lyonii*) is the tree-sized version of our common chaparral shrub **Holly-leaved Cherry** (*Prunus ilicifolia* subsp. *ilicifolia*); and **Island Deerweed** (*Acmispon dendroideus*) is woody and twice as big as any of its mainland congeners.

Among vertebrates, Deer Mice on the islands are all larger than those on the mainland. Another mouse, the **Giant Deer Mouse** (*Peromyscus nesodytes*), found on three of the Northern Channel Islands up until two thousand years ago and now extinct, was several times the size of mainland species. Typically, small mammals like mice evolve to become larger due to an absence of competitors on islands.

Although some small animals tend to grow bigger, some large animals get smaller. The two famous examples of dwarfism from our islands are the **Pygmy Mammoth** (*Mammuthus exilis*) and the Island Fox. Smaller individuals achieve better reproductive success, have smaller ranges, and need less food to survive, so they do well on islands.

Endemism: Endemism is the hallmark of island life. An endemic is a species restricted to a certain location and found nowhere else in the world.

The derivation of multiple species of plants or animals from one ancestor is termed **adaptive radiation** (see also Chapter 4). It's particularly obvious on islands and most noticeable in the plant kingdom. As new species evolve from the original colonizing

Channel Islands Tree Poppy. Like many other endemic island plants, this species is taller and has larger leaves than its mainland counterpart.

population, they take unique forms in order to adapt to life on the island. Each one of those new species is a precious endemic to be admired for qualities all its own.

Of the thirty-eight plants endemic to the Northern Channel Islands, fifteen are found only on a single island. Certain plant families have done especially well in colonizing the islands: live-forevers (*Dudleya* spp.), manzanitas, deerweeds, buckwheats (*Eriogonum* spp.), and dandelions (*Malacothrix* spp.) proliferate in unusual shapes and sizes.

Endemism is evident in all manner of life on the Northern Channel Islands, including not only plants, but snails, insects, reptiles, birds, and mammals.

The Island Scrub-Jay is an original—

endemic to Santa Barbara County alone. No wonder birdwatchers board boats year after year to journey to Santa Cruz Island to see this large, dark blue jay.

Other animals and insects that have assumed novel forms include four endemic subspecies of silk-spinning crickets, related to Jerusalem crickets.

Because it is found abundantly on the adjacent mainland, you would expect the **Striped Skunk** (*Mephitis mephitis*) to occur on the islands, but it is absent. Instead, the **Channel Island Spotted Skunk** (*Spilogale gracilis* subsp. *amphiala*) is the endemic subspecies on Santa Cruz and Santa Rosa islands. It's related to the much less common mainland **Western Spotted Skunk** (*Spilogale gracilis*).

Why isn't the Striped Skunk on the islands? We don't know.

Niche Shifts: Newly arrived organisms fit into ecological niches, or roles, on an island that may be different from those they filled on the mainland.

With less species diversity and less competition, an animal or plant may be able to occur in greater abundance or in a different habitat than it would on the mainland, a phenomenon called **competitive release.**

Among bird species, several examples can be seen on Santa Cruz Island. Although the chaparral habitat on the island is similar to that on the mainland, certain characteristic chaparral birds are absent: there are no Wrentits, Oak Titmice, California Thrashers, or California Towhees. As a result, Bewick's Wrens, **Hutton's Vireos** (*Vireo huttoni*), and Orange-crowned Warblers have become common in chaparral on the island, increasing their numbers in this habitat as compared to mainland chaparral.

In another example of a niche shift, the Island Scrub-Jay has become more of a ground feeder; it also eats pine seeds, since no Steller's Jays or Gray Squirrels are around to preempt that niche. (See "Altered Ecosystems on Islands," later in this chapter, for more on niche shifts.)

Characteristics of Island Communities

Communities of plants and animals on islands are different from those on comparable areas on the mainland. For one thing, species or groups of species may not be represented in the same proportions. For example, because large vertebrates, amphibians, and wingless insects are poor dispersers, they are often scarce or absent on islands.

Furthermore, island fauna and flora may be less diverse than in similar areas on the mainland. Why? Some species have arrived and failed to colonize. Chance plays a big part. Colonizers begin with small populations, often vulnerable to a gentle push over the edge into extinction.

In the essential *A Flora of Santa Cruz Island* (Junak et al.) you can read that several key riparian species on the mainland are absent on Santa Cruz: White Alder, Western Sycamore (although it has been introduced by humans), Fuchsia-flowered Gooseberry, Hummingbird Sage, and California Bay.

Research on the stream fauna found that 94 out of a possible total of 161 insects on the nearby mainland occur on Santa Cruz Island. Entomologists found that aquatic flies (Order Diptera) and beetles (Order Coleoptera) are overrepresented on the island, whereas caddisflies (Order Trichoptera) and stoneflies (Order Plecoptera) are underrepresented. These differences from the mainland fauna may be caused by poor dispersal and colonization techniques inherent in certain insect species, but they could also be due to the impoverished nature of riparian vegetation on the island. Santa Cruz Island has several small streams, but without the riparian plant species mentioned above, certain aquatic insect groups which rely on the presence of twigs and leaves of those taxa in freshwater habitat will not survive.

Another example of how island communities differ from those of the mainland involves the dispersal of tiny insects compared to large ones. In surveys of butterflies and moths (Order Lepidoptera) on Santa Cruz Island, researchers discovered that small, leaf-mining moths (Family Gracillariidae) were better represented than other kinds of moths and butterflies. Collectively, 71 percent of the Central Coast leaf-mining moths have made it to Santa Cruz Island, whereas in the other five groups of lepidopterans surveyed, only 30 to 62 percent of the mainland taxa had reached the island.

The leaf-mining moths are minuscule insects. If they were to fly to the island and lay eggs, all the larvae from one individual could survive by feeding on a single leaf! No wonder they're more successful at adaptation than the larger moths and butterflies, each of whose larvae requires a variety of plants in a larger area on which to feed.

The Northern Channel Islands are revered for the exceptional endemic life-forms that live there. But evolution on these islands isn't static. Island species are prone to extinctions. We know that fluctuations in weather and food supplies, diseases, and human-caused alterations can threaten small populations of any species.

New organisms are continually arriving on the islands. If human influences can be kept to a minimum, island ecological systems will be able to operate without interference. Remember sweepstakes dispersal? Some make it to the islands and some don't. Why is there a Gopher Snake and not a rattlesnake? Why spotted and not striped skunks? Why foxes and not Coyotes? Why frogs and not toads?

The Islands

In order to gather the latest scholarly findings about the California Channel Islands, scientific meetings have been held approximately every five years since 1965. The papers from these proceedings have been compiled into published symposiums. Much of the information in this chapter has been gleaned from the volumes that have been issued thus far—an indispensable resource for those wishing to delve into research on the islands.

Climate

The climate of the Northern Channel Islands is influenced by oceanic currents (see Chapter 3). The cool, nutrient-rich California Current flows southward past Point Conception. However, a portion of the current splits off at the western end of the Santa Barbara Channel, sending a plume of cold water past the northern sides of San Miguel and Santa Rosa and the west end of Santa Cruz.

Santa Cruz Island has nearly the same climate as that of the coastal mainland near Santa Barbara, but the western islands of San Miguel and Santa Rosa have a cooler and moister climate, similar to that of the coast north of Point Conception.

As was discussed in Chapter 3, the prevailing winds in spring and summer blow out of the north or northwest parallel to the coast. San Miguel and Santa Rosa Island sit directly in their path and are constantly windswept. Santa Cruz and Anacapa are more sheltered from these spring winds.

One of the key elements of the climate on the islands is the marine layer. During the dry summers, the cooling fogs and high overcast supplement island rainfall totals. The overhead stratus provides shade that reduces evaporative stress, and at ground level, fog drip provides a source of summer water. Bishop Pines on Santa Cruz Island have been shown to use water from fog drip during the summer, and Torrey Pines on Santa Rosa Island exhibit wider growth rings during periods of increased fog and high overcast.

Oceanic Conditions

The oceanic conditions that control the climate of the Northern Channel Islands influence the species diversity and affinities of each island. The biogeographical break between cold temperature faunas and warm temperature faunas shown by conditions north and south of Point Conception is reflected on the islands, depending upon their position in the archipelago.

The following quote from a paper presented by George L. Hunt and colleagues at the 1980 Channel Islands symposium summarizes the situation:

The Channel Islands provide a meeting ground for northern and southern species of various diverse faunal groups. Forms that typically occur north of the Southern California Bight occur most commonly at the west end of the northern chain [San Miguel, Santa Rosa] and the southern islands show a predominance of species with southern affinities [San Clemente, Santa Catalina].

In other words, the sea surface temperature greatly affects the spe-

cies distribution of marine algae, marine invertebrates, seabirds, and pinnipeds.

One of the ways to illustrate the influence of the gradient of ocean temperatures is to take a species and compare its size from north to south. Comparisons of individual crustaceans and other marine invertebrates have revealed larger sizes at higher latitudes. The upwelled water from Point Conception that circulates near San Miguel and Santa Rosa islands brings the benefit of a richer food supply, such as increased plankton blooms, and this allows the marine organisms found there to grow bigger.

Take the humble Western Sand Crab, which is common on all the islands as well as along mainland beaches. In one scientific study, biologists compared the size of sand crabs found on Santa Cruz, Santa Rosa, and San Miguel islands with those of San Clemente Island, to the south. They correlated their findings with the size of sand crabs on mainland sites from north to south as well.

Presumably, the larger the sand crab, the more access it has to cooler, nutrient-rich waters. Populations of sand crabs sampled on San Miguel and Santa Rosa islands, for example, were more similar in size (i.e., larger) to populations living north of Point Conception than they were to those living on nearby Santa Cruz Island, only six miles away across a narrow channel.

Sand crabs at San Miguel Island and on the mainland's Avila Beach, north of Point Conception, measured 1.18 inches. In contrast, those to the south on Santa Catalina Island and on the mainland at San Clemente State Beach were .86 and .43 inches respectively.

Geology

The Northern Channel Islands are considered **continental islands** because they are not separated by a great distance from our region's shores and they sit on the mainland's continental shelf.

The islands are the emergent portions of a large ridge that runs eighty miles east-west. About eighteen thousand years ago, near the end of the Pleistocene, much of the earth's water was tied up in glaciers, and this lowered sea level about three hundred feet, revealing that the four Northern Channel Islands were connected. Called **Santarosae**, this land mass was four times the land area of the current four islands. After the Ice Age, rising ocean waters separated the islands.

The distance between the eastern tip of Santarosae and the mainland in the vicinity of Ventura was about five miles, a much narrower channel than today. There's no evidence that a land bridge ever connected Santarosae to the mainland.

The geology of the islands is complex. About a dozen types of geologic formations there are absent from the adjacent mainland, but several of these may be correlated with areas hundreds of miles to the south, off San Diego (see Chapter 2).

Anacapa is overwhelmingly volcanic, formed about 16 million years ago, with only a dusting of surface deposits along the trails. Marine terraces formed by the rise and fall of sea levels during the Pleistocene Epoch are more obvious here than on the other islands. The precipitous cliffs show the erosive power of the ocean.

Santa Cruz presents interesting questions for the geologist. A major fault trends east-west, forming a central valley with mountains on either side. The marine sedimentary and volcanic rocks that dominate the landscape north of the fault are about 17 million years old, and they aren't found south of the fault. On the south side of the fault, a complex assortment of rocks, including metamorphic rocks which may be over 170 million years old, abut the much younger rocks of the northern side.

The topography of Santa Rosa is more subdued than that of Santa Cruz, but this island also has a major east-west-trending fault. Although the fault shares the same trend as Santa Cruz, it is offset and may not be related. The rocks on Santa Rosa are less than 55 million years old.

San Miguel is the flattest of all the Northern Channel Islands. Northwest winds buffet the island in summer and are intensified by winter storms. As a result, most of the island is covered by Aeolian (windblown) sand deposits, but rocks older than 65 million years are exposed on coastal cliffs.

Anacapa Island

Anacapa Island, the smallest of the Northern Channel Islands, is the closest to the mainland. It lies fourteen miles off Ventura and is part of Ventura County. The other Northern Channel Islands are in Santa Barbara County.

Anacapa Island appears as three rocky islets: West Anacapa (the

Anacapa Island lighthouse

Giant Tickseed covers rocky terraces of Anacapa Island in spring.

Arch Rock, Anacapa Island

largest), Middle Anacapa, and East Anacapa. Occasionally, when the tide is lowest, you can see that they are attached. Most of the time they're separated by narrow channels of water.

If you fly over West Anacapa Island on an early spring day, the view of **Giant Tickseed** (*Leptosyne gigantea,* formerly Giant Coreopsis) covering the barren, rocky slopes with a forest of yellow daisy blooms is a sight you'll never forget. Giant Tickseed is found on all of the California Channel Islands, and it is also distributed in scattered colonies along the mainland coast from southern San Luis Obispo County to Ventura, near rocky headlands. Still, to see this six-foot-high daisy, with its thick, fleshy stems and lacy green foliage, is a thrill. Giant Tickseed is an example of size change—those woody stems, which die back to brownish stalks in summer, belong on a miniature tree, not a bush daisy.

Seabirds on Anacapa Island

The Northern Channel Islands are well known for the abundance and variety of their seabird colonies. The mixture of cold and warm waters offshore engenders a rich avifauna. Bird species that prefer warmer waters are at the northerly portion of their range, and species inhabiting colder waters are at the southern limits of their range. California Brown Pelicans breed only as far north as the Northern Channel Islands. In contrast, Pelagic Cormorants and Pigeon Guillemots breed only this far south.

Thousands of seabirds choose the islands for nesting because of the rock stacks and inaccessible cliff faces here. Most species of seabirds are especially adapted to nesting in a predator-free environment. They cannot survive where rats, cats, skunks, or foxes prey on the eggs and hatchlings—and sometimes even the adults—of these birds. Thus, the steep, ragged ledges

Western Gull chick

Brandt's Cormorants and Western Gulls on Anacapa Island

Western Gulls have a large nesting colony on Anacapa Island.

provide protection from predators, and an abundant supply of food is nearby in the bountiful sea.

On West Anacapa Island, California Brown Pelicans crowd together in the largest pelican colony anywhere on the Channel Islands. On East Anacapa Island, where a big colony of **Western**

Gulls (*Larus occidentalis*) nests, biologists have been able to measure an increase of over 150 percent in numbers between 1991 and 2007.

The **Scripps's Murrelet** (*Synthliboramphus scrippsi,* formerly Xantus's Murrelet) is a chunky, black-and-white seabird with short wings. This species is an important breeder on Anacapa Island. But murrelets don't nest out in the open; they sequester themselves in rock crevices and sea caves.

Murrelets belong to the family Alcidae, along with the murres, guillemots, auklets, and puffins. Pelagic birds, they only come to land for breeding. Alcids are not strong flyers, but they are deft swimmers beneath the ocean's surface, using their wings as propellers and their feet as rudders. They feed on small fish, squid, and marine invertebrates.

At Anacapa Island, when a pair of adult murrelets finds a nesting site, the female lays one or two eggs. The adults incubate in shifts, the male and female relieving one another as infrequently as once every three days

Scripps's Murrelet nests in sea caves on Anacapa Island.

and sometimes every six! The nest exchange occurs just after dark or just before dawn.

Murrelet eggs are huge in proportion to their bodies; they weigh approximately 22 percent of the adult bird's weight. Young murrelets are precocial: very mobile and well developed immediately after hatching. The young are not fed at the nest. After the second egg has hatched, usually a period of two days, the juveniles must make their way towards the water.

This first nocturnal journey of the hatchling chicks over rocky terrain is unique to murrelets. The chicks, undaunted, follow both adults as they lure the little balls of fluff down towards the water. The adults then fly to the water, continuously calling and encouraging the young. Finally, by scrambling over rocks and tumbling down steep slopes, the chicks reach the shore. There, they are reunited with the parents, who are waiting on the water. For the first time, the young are fed, and the family group moves quickly away from the nesting island to offshore waters. Once the young are at sea, the adults care for them on a regular basis.

Your best chance of glimpsing a Scripps's Murrelet is from the bow of a boat as the bird flushes low and whirrs rapidly off over the water. (See "Altered Ecosystems on Islands," later in this chapter, for more on murrelets.)

But after a trip to Anacapa Island, it is the California Brown Pelicans that everyone remembers. Watching the pelicans' antics as they dive for fish to bring back to their nestlings is like being in the middle of a bombing sortie. After each splashing entry into the sea, the birds come and go, high in the air. Their spectacular dives are the result of excellent eyesight: from heights of sixty to seventy feet, pelicans can spot a school of fish, then

Heermann's Gulls harass a young pelican, attempting to steal the pelican's catch before it's swallowed.

A California Brown Pelican in a plunge dive off Anacapa Island

plunge-dive to grab the prey. Beneath the skin of the pelican's forehead and chest, air sacs cushion the impact of entering the water.

The ocean around Anacapa Island is a well-stocked pantry for the parent birds. Pelican breeding success is dependent upon the availability of Northern Anchovies and sardines. If these fish species have moved into deeper, cooler waters, as during an El Niño event, the nestling pelicans will not get enough to eat and may perish.

Brown Pelicans construct nests on the ground, lining them with sticks and kelp. While incubating, they cover the two to three white eggs with their large, webbed feet; since they don't have brood patches (patches of featherless skin that develop during the breeding season on most birds), pelicans warm their eggs by standing on them. The blood vessels in their feet act as heating pads, and the adults gently roll the eggs to assure that they get evenly warmed.

Pelicans live for a long time, up to thirty years, and they do not breed until they are three to five years old. Colonies like those on Anacapa contain lots of nonbreeders looking for a chance to gain an unoccupied foothold in the colony. (See "Altered Ecosystems on Islands" in this chapter for more on pelicans.)

Santa Cruz Island

Fraser Point, at the extreme west end of Santa Cruz Island, is a carpet of blooms in spring.

In many ways, Santa Cruz Island is the jewel of the Northern Channel Islands. At ninety-six square miles and twenty-four miles long, it is certainly the largest.

In studying islands, biologists theorize that the larger islands close to the mainland are more frequently colonized by mainland species than smaller islands. An example of this phenomenon, Santa Cruz Island possesses the richest fauna and flora of any of the Northern Channel Islands. It has also been the most studied by researchers and students.

An east-west central valley bisects Santa Cruz Island.

Santa Cruz is distinguished by a long central valley which lies between the two ridges that run the length of the island. The north ridge is higher; Picacho Diablo (2,450 ft.) is the highest point on any of the California Channel Islands.

Santa Cruz Island is famous for a beautiful tree, **Santa Cruz Island Ironwood** (*Lyonothamnus floribundus* subsp. *aspleniifolius*). Island Ironwood is known as a **relictual** species, one that's survived in a given place while disappearing everywhere else. Often, islands serve as refuges for species that are unable to survive changing

Island Scrub-Jay and Santa Cruz Island Ironwood

conditions on the mainland. Fossils show that the ironwood genus had a widespread distribution in western North America during the Miocene and Pliocene epochs, six to eighteen million years ago, but now it is only native to Santa Cruz, Santa Rosa, and San Clemente islands.

A tall tree with pinnately compounded, serrated leaves of a lovely pattern, the Island Ironwood is the official Santa Barbara County tree, as well as the logo of the Santa Barbara Botanic Garden, where a fine specimen has been planted at the entrance to the grounds.

Santa Cruz Island Endemic Plants

The flora of Santa Cruz Island is truly remarkable, having seven single-island endemics, more than any of the other islands:

- Santa Cruz Island Manzanita (*Arctostaphylos insularis*)
- White-haired Manzanita (*Arctostaphylos viridissima*)
- Santa Cruz Island Dudleya (*Dudleya nesiotica*)
- Santa Cruz Island Silver Lotus (*Acmispon argophyllus* var. *nesioticus*)
- Santa Cruz Island Bush-Mallow (*Malacothamnus fasciculatus* var. *nesiotica*)
- Santa Cruz Island Gooseberry (*Ribes thacherianum*)
- Santa Cruz Island Lace Pod (*Thysanocarpus conchuliferus*)

Indeed, several of these endemic plants are subspecies or varieties, not yet having acquired full species status. As their appearance and habits diverge from the founder population,

they may gradually assume enough genetic differences to be considered separate species. Or, they may remain subspecies or varieties only, never completely diverging. This is the fascinating way we can track evolution among plants on an island.

On Santa Cruz Island, the animals have evolved, too. Here again, a subspecies may be in the process of developing towards a full species. Their isolation on Santa Cruz has fostered slight differences between the taxa discussed below and those found on the mainland. It's like following evolution step by step.

The Island Scrub-Jay

The Island Scrub-Jay, found on Santa Cruz Island, and the Yellow-billed Magpie, occurring on the mainland, are the only endemic birds of California. You can see both of them in a day in Santa Barbara County! The jay is the only endemic bird on any of the Channel Islands to achieve full species status.

Naturalist Henry Henshaw recognized the Island Scrub-Jay as early as 1875. He collected four scrub-jays on Santa Cruz Island that were larger and darker blue than the mainland jays and concluded the birds were a new species—the Santa Cruz Island Scrub-Jay. But it was not until 1990, with the use of mitochondrial DNA, that this island endemic was confirmed as a genetically separate species from the two other closely related jays, the Western Scrub-Jay and the **Florida Scrub-Jay** (*Aphelocoma coerulescens*).

Island Scrub-Jay ancestry appears to go way back. The species has been shown to have diverged evolution-

Endemic Terrestrial Vertebrates of the Northern Channel Islands

	Anacapa	Santa Cruz	Santa Rosa	San Miguel
AMPHIBIANS				
Channel Islands Slender Salamander	x	x	x	x
REPTILES				
Island Fence Lizard		x	x	x
Santa Cruz Island Gopher Snake		x	x	
BIRDS				
Allen's Hummingbird	x	x	x	x
Island Flycatcher		x	x	x
Island Scrub-Jay		x		
Island Loggerhead Shrike		x	x	
Island Horned Lark		x	x	x
Santa Cruz Island Bewick's Wren	x	x	x	
Dusky Orange-crowned Warbler	x	x	x	x
San Clemente Spotted Towhee			x	
Santa Cruz Island Rufous-crowned Sparrow	x	x		
Island Song Sparrow	x	x	x	x
LAND MAMMALS				
Anacapa Island Deer Mouse	x			
Santa Cruz Island Deer Mouse		x		
Santa Rosa Island Deer Mouse			x	
San Miguel Island Deer Mouse				x
Santa Cruz Island Harvest Mouse		x		
Santa Cruz Island Fox		x		
Santa Rosa Island Fox			x	
San Miguel Island Fox				x
Channel Island Spotted Skunk		x	x	

Endemic to Santa Cruz Island, the Island Scrub-Jay is larger and a deeper blue than the Western Scrub-Jay.

Scrub-Jay. Like several island animals, it's relatively tame around humans.

Comparing Island Scrub-Jay breeding behavior with that of the Western Scrub-Jay reveals interesting differences.

Island Scrub-Jays delay breeding until they are three to four years old, whereas on the mainland, jays breed in their second year. Home territories on Santa Cruz Island are smaller than those of the mainland. The number of Island Scrub-Jay eggs per nest, known as clutch size, is smaller.

These characteristics are the result of an island jay population that has an adult survival rate of 90 percent per year. With a flourishing population and limited space and habitats, Island Scrub-Jay social interactions are tightly structured.

Ornithologists researching breeding habits of this species have noted the birds are monogamous. And once they obtain a territory, they hold onto it for life: they must defend it against "floaters," or nonbreeding birds. These floaters of both sexes roam the island in scattered bands. In winter, 50 percent of the adult jay population consists of non-territorial, nonbreeding floaters; the birds are often found in grasslands or other habitats where breeders are absent. This is different from Western Scrub-Jay nonbreeders, which stay close to breeder territories year-round.

When the breeding season commences, the floaters vie for a chance to succeed to a territory, which only occurs when a member of an established pair dies. For example, if the female of an established pair dies, then an unattached female will attempt to take her place.

arily from the mainland jays over two hundred thousand years ago. Therefore, the Island Scrub-Jay probably colonized the Santarosae landmass well before it broke up into islands ten thousand years ago.

Although the Island Scrub-Jay is unique to Santa Cruz Island today, new fossil discoveries have shown this species was present as recently as a thousand years ago on San Miguel Island. All scrub-jays are generally nonmigratory and incapable of long flights, due to their weakly developed upper wing bones.

The Island Scrub-Jay, a vibrant, deep blue, is larger and heavier and has a longer bill than the Western

Sometimes a floater male and female can usurp a territory from an established pair when one of the established mates has died and the remaining mate is unable to defend it. Or, in another scenario, a floater male and female may be able to carve out a completely new territory in between established territories of paired jays, but this rarely happens.

Island Scrub-Jays are more densely distributed on the island than Western Scrub-Jays on the mainland. For this reason, Island Scrub-Jays have had to disperse into a variety of habitats—oak woodland, chaparral, pine forest, eucalyptus—to accommodate all the birds looking for breeding territories. On the mainland, Western Scrub-Jays occupy mostly chaparral and oak woodland.

Nature Journal
April 5–7, 1991

Visit to Santa Cruz Island

I'm flying high above the Santa Barbara Channel in a plane bound for Santa Cruz Island. Behind us are the snowy peaks of Ventura County and ahead lies the backbone of Santa Cruz Island. As we fly over the island, we see the Bishop Pine forest and the many little canyons, the steep cliffs plunging to the ocean below, everything green and luscious from a rainy spring.

A grassy landing strip near an old barn marks our entry into another world, an island world.

We are transported to Christy Ranch, along with six other visitors, in the back of

a big pickup truck which has been modified with bench seats facing each other. The roads are tortuous; jostling from side to side, we gaze at our new surroundings.

Christy Ranch, a cluster of rustic, whitewashed buildings set among Monterey Cypresses, lies in a sheltered cove. It's been here since the 1850s.

A creek, lined with willows, flows to a deserted beach. I feel as though I'm on the Mendocino Coast a hundred years ago—certainly not offshore of Southern California!

Almost as soon as we set out to explore, we find Santa Cruz Island Bush-Mallow, a lovely, tall endemic with pink flowers. It's begun: the hunt for the island endemics and the thrill of discovering them!

The next day, a trip to Fraser Point—the far westernmost end of the island—ushers us into a windswept, wildflower-strewn landscape. On the way there we notice how the Toyon and Lemonade Berry, familiar shrubs back home, stand on the hillsides as small, solitary trees with wind-pruned tops.

We hike all the way out to the extreme end of the point, the wind tearing at our jackets and hats, the wild beauty of the place enchanting. Views down the precipitous cliffs reveal glossy, black Pelagic Cormorants on nests lined with kelp in rocky enclaves. Far below them the sea howls and the waves spew up spray.

Looking west over the white-capped ocean—across the "potato patch," as they call that especially rough sea channel between Santa Cruz and Santa Rosa Island—we glimpse the shores of Santa Rosa.

All around, goldfields spread in a carpet of bright, bright yellow, interspersed with the lavender of owl's clover stretching forever on this flat terrace.

Candelabra Dudleya, one of several species of *Dudleya* endemic to the Northern Channel Islands

And the live-forevers (Dudleyas), those fantastic green succulents that grow only on the Northern Channel Islands: Santa Cruz Island Live-forever, Greene's Dudleya, and Candelabra Dudleya. Our guide explains that the Dudleyas have spread into several habitats on the island, which is an example of adaptive radiation. That is, they have adapted and changed to fit places not available to them on the mainland.

After a picnic lunch on a sheltered beach, our group climbs to the ridgetop overlooking the north side of Fraser Point. As we cling to the pointy rocks and scramble our way upward, the northwest wind finds us. Whipped and unsteady, I feel as though I might easily slip and fall to my death in the swirling waves far below.

In the back of my mind, I recall that Ralph Hoffmann, one of my idols, met his untimely death in 1932 on San Miguel Island while collecting plant samples for

the Santa Barbara Museum of Natural History. I can understand how it happened— an insatiable curiosity drives the search for these rare plant species, whatever the risk.

Having arrived at the ridgetop, we look down through binoculars at the Dudleya greenei hanging from the cliffs beneath us on the shaded north side of the island, their green rosettes sprouting foot-long stems and little white blooms. At the base of the cliffs far below, a mother Harbor Seal and pup lounge on the rocks. The foamy sea churns around them.

From the windy ridge, the prospect of land and sea, island and mainland, is overwhelming. I will never forget that view.

The next day, we explore part of the inland section. A Santa Cruz Island Scrub-Jay gives us great views: larger, darker blue, thicker bill, and a hoarse, throaty call more like a Steller's Jay's than that of the mainland scrub-jays back home.

Afterwards, while packing up at Christy

Ranch, we watch transfixed as a Santa Cruz Island Fox approaches. It's so unafraid of humans it comes to the back door, interested in the prospect of leftovers.

We are not the first people to come under the spell of Santa Cruz Island. For thousands of years, Native Americans made a good living here from the sea in harmony with the seasons and the quiet.

Is that why Santa Cruz Island seems lost in time? So near and yet so far from the hectic pace of life on the mainland.

Note: Christy Ranch, now owned by The Nature Conservancy, is no longer available to the public. There are day-use picnic grounds and camping facilities on other parts of Santa Cruz Island.

Altered Ecosystems on Islands: From Disaster to Recovery

Before we go on to the other islands, let's make a detour to discussed altered ecosystems. Recall that on an island, the effects of change are magnified. Alterations in insular ecosystems can have disastrous consequences. Disturbances to populations on an island have greater repercussions than on the mainland. Most alterations have originated with human influence on island ecosystems. The challenges are great, but the good news is that recovery and restoration of several key populations are under way.

California Brown Pelican

In the late 1960s, Brown Pelicans were hit hard by the pesticide DDT and its principal metabolite, DDE. These substances concentrated in the top of the food chain, so that by the time a pelican gulped a Northern Anchovy, the bird was ingesting a toxic amount of DDT. This in turn produced DDE, which interfered with calcium deposition during egg laying, resulting in thin-shelled eggs. The eggs broke as the pelicans tried to incubate them.

Our islands are the northernmost nesting location for the California Brown Pelican, a special subspecies which only nests from here south into Baja California. Between 1960 and 1970, California Brown Pelicans were nearly wiped out at island breeding colonies, with zero reproductive success reported. Fortunately, many adult pelicans survived. A colony can sometimes sustain itself for a certain period of time even when reproduction rates plummet.

The California Brown Pelican was listed as endangered in 1970. With the banning of DDT, recovery slowly began. Now, forty years later, there are several thousand breeding pairs on the Northern Channel Islands and the trend is gradually upwards.

The pelican was de-listed (removed from endangered status) as of 2009.

Scripps's Murrelet

Another example of human-caused alteration of an ecosystem occurred with the Scripps's Murrelet, which, like the pelican, breeds on Anacapa Island. Non-native **Black Rats** (*Rattus rattus*) were probably first introduced to the island in 1853 when the ship *Winfield Scott* ran aground on Middle Anacapa. The voracious rats rapidly multiplied, thriving by preying on murrelet eggs, which were an easy target.

From 2001 to 2002, the National Park Service embarked on an ambitious project: they decided to use a rodenticide to eradicate the rats from Anacapa Island in order to stop the decline of Scripps's Murrelets. It worked. There are no longer Black Rats on any part of Anacapa Island.

Studies since that time indicate that the Anacapa population of Scripps's Murrelets has increased. Post-eradication (2003–2010) hatching success in sea caves was 85 percent, compared to just 30 percent pre-eradication (2001–2002). Since all of the California Channel Islands taken together shelter nearly half of the world's total population (ten to fifteen thousand) of Scripps's Murrelets, rat eradication has been a significant step forward for this threatened seabird.

Biologists are hoping that with the success of the rat eradication program, the population of breeding Scripps's Murrelets at Anacapa Island may someday approach that of nearby Santa Barbara Island, where the largest colony in the United States numbers in the low thousands.

Introduced Mammals

Goats, pigs, and sheep were introduced to the islands by early European visitors in the 1800s. When these barnyard animals escaped captivity and reverted to their wild state, their populations exploded. They had no predators, and the islands provided plenty of plants for grazing. Feral pigs, in particular, became a huge problem, for they rooted and dug up many endemic plant species. This was catastrophic for the fragile island ecosystem. And with the native plants gone, invasive weeds thrived.

Enter the National Park Service and The Nature Conservancy. By 2006, administrators and scientists with foresight and funding were able to execute a plan to eradicate the feral pigs on Santa Cruz Island, quite literally saving the numerous endemic plants of our Northern Channel Islands from destruction.

The Eagle Problem

To understand the chain reaction of human influences and niche shifts in an island ecosystem, you might look at the example of the Golden Eagle.

Historically, Bald Eagles were common on the California Channel Islands. They disappeared by the 1960s, helped along by DDT contamination and the resultant eggshell thinning. With the vacancy left by the Bald Eagles, there was no apex avian predator on the islands.

Golden Eagles (*Aquila chrysaetos*) began to move in to take advantage of the availability of abundant prey. They were attracted by the number of feral piglets and sheep. By the late 1980s and early 1990s, sightings of Golden Eagles on Santa Cruz and Santa Rosa had increased dramatically.

Paul Collins of the Santa Barbara Museum of Natural History and his colleague Brian Latta studied the food habits of the nesting Golden Eagles from 2000 to 2007, analyzing prey remains recovered from the eagles' huge nests.

They found that before eradication of feral pigs, Island Foxes comprised 5.9 percent of the prey biomass found in eagle nests on Santa Cruz Island, and feral piglets made up 63.2 percent. After pig removal, however, the biologists made a prey analysis of the one remaining active Golden Eagle nest. It was from this analysis that they were able to document the prey switch from feral piglets to Island Foxes. The foxes made up 45.7 to 57 percent of the nest remains, a huge increase.

Collins and Latta showed that because of the overall paucity of prey on Santa Cruz and Santa Rosa islands, after the pigs were eradicated Golden Eagles shifted to preying upon species they do not eat on the mainland, such as Island Foxes, skunks, Mule Deer fawns, ravens, and various species of gulls; Golden Eagles had changed their diet to take advantage of available prey on the islands.

Between 1999 and 2003, Golden Eagles were captured and translocated in order to save the Island Fox.

The eagles were just doing what they needed to do in order to survive with the pigs gone: eat foxes. This is a perfect example of the unintended consequences of human influences on islands, and their far-reaching implications for whole ecosystems. The absence of the Bald Eagle opened up a chance for the Golden Eagle to move in. The absence of feral piglets caused the Golden Eagle to shift to eating the endangered Island Fox.

Now that goldens—and DDT— were gone, Bald Eagles had a chance. Reintroduction culminated in the hatching of a Bald Eagle chick on Santa Cruz Island in 2006, the first in a half-century.

Since the Golden Eagles' translocation to distant areas, Bald Eagles have once again begun to soar over the islands. In 2012, six known active nests were on Santa Cruz Island, two were on Santa Rosa Island, and one was on West Anacapa Island. It appears that Bald Eagles are back where they belong, thanks to a strategic reintroduction effort on the part of biologists and park personnel. In addition, their presence discourages Golden Eagles from trying to become established again. (You can view the eagles live on the Channel Islands Live Bald Eagle Webcams, http://www.nps.gov/chis/photosmultimedia/bald-eagle-webcam.htm.)

Dissecting an Historic Bald Eagle Nest

Before Golden Eagle translocation, and during the decline of the Island Fox, one question was paramount: how do we know that the Bald Eagles won't prey on Island Foxes the way the Golden Eagles did?

The presence of a historic Bald Eagle nest structure on San Miguel Island held a possible answer.

The Bald Eagle, a huge bird, builds a nest to match its size. The nest structures are tall, bulky piles of sticks, and they're used by generations of eagles. In 2000, when Paul Collins visited this particular long-abandoned nest, he and his colleagues were determined to excavate it.

In the end, they collected almost ten thousand bones, teeth, shells, and other items from the remains of many an eagle meal. With painstaking care, the scientists sorted and identified the contents of this eagle midden. Most of the bones were from seabirds, nearshore fish, and carcasses of dead terrestrial and marine mammals.

Mammals represented only a small percentage of the eagle diet. Of course, this is not to say that Bald Eagles will not ever prey on Island Foxes, but from a historic perspective, it appears that the eagles will choose other prey items first.

The Island Fox

For thousands of years, Island Foxes thrived, until they were brought to the brink of extinction by Golden Eagles after wild pigs were eradicated from the islands. As a result of the dramatic decline in the Santa Cruz Island Fox, the **San Miguel Island Fox** (*Urocyon littoralis* subsp. *littoralis*), and the **Santa Rosa Island Fox** (*U. l.* subsp. *santarosae*), all three of these Island Fox subspecies were listed by the US Fish and Wildlife Service as endangered.

In 2000, some of the Santa Cruz Island Foxes and all from San Miguel and Santa Rosa were captured and placed in on-island captive breeding facilities—a risky undertaking but a necessary one. There were only fifteen individuals each of the San Miguel and Santa Rosa Island Foxes remaining, and perhaps close to sixty still survived on Santa Cruz. Nobody knew whether captive-bred foxes would breed or whether they could be successfully reintroduced, which had to happen on Santa Rosa and San Miguel.

It worked—better than any of the biologists and National Park Service personnel could have predicted. By 2008, captive breeding programs for all three fox subspecies of the Northern Channel Islands had ended and all animals had been released back to the islands. As a result of the reintroduction efforts, the populations of the three endangered subspecies were either stable or increasing. Population monitoring in 2011 estimated there were 393 adult foxes on San Miguel; 280 on Santa Rosa; and 883 on Santa Cruz.

The intriguing little Island Fox is California's only endemic mammal

Santa Cruz, Santa Rosa, and San Miguel Island all have their own endemic subspecies of the Island Fox, the top predator in the Northern Channel Islands ecosystem.

species. About the size of a house cat but much sturdier, how did it get to the islands? How did it adapt so well to island life? What happens in an island ecosystem when the foxes are completely absent, as they were from San Miguel and Santa Rosa for several years during captive breeding?

The Island Fox is an evolved form of its mainland ancestor, the Common Gray Fox. Until recently, it was assumed that fox colonization of the islands was by chance overwater dispersal, such as rafting. However, the paucity of fossil records on the islands prior to human habitation has led some authorities to believe that foxes could have been intentionally introduced to the islands by Native American ancestors of the Chumash peoples. Whether humans brought the foxes to the islands, or whether they were already there, remains from archaeological sites suggest there was a close relationship between the Chumash and the Island Fox. Foxes may have been pets, and they were used in rituals and religious ceremonies.

The lifestyle of the Island Fox shows it's well adapted to insular influences. Because they live in a finite area—an island—paired foxes establish relatively small territories that they maintain year-round. Density is high and there's little change in home range from year to year.

Island Foxes have high survival rates. For example, on San Miguel from 1993 to 1994, adult survival from one year to the next was 100 percent. (This was before the feral pigs were eradicated and hence before Golden Eagles began to prey on the foxes in large numbers.)

Unusual for small foxes like this, the high survival rate is due to the excellent quality of the habitat and the normal absence of predation.

Island Foxes have optimized their requirements to fit perfectly into an island environment. Being omnivores, they feed on a variety of plants and animals in all of the island habitats. Because the foxes have no predators, they can take advantage of daytime hunting. Deer Mice are the most common prey item. Ground-nesting birds and reptiles and amphibians are also eaten. In addition, Island Foxes eat more plant material than do mainland Gray Foxes. Fruits of **prickly-pear** (*Opuntia* spp.) and Toyon provide nourishment.

Rarely do biologists have the opportunity to examine an ecosystem where the top mammalian carnivore has been removed. The extirpation of Island Foxes on Santa Rosa and San Miguel during the captive breeding program (a period of eight years on San Miguel and seven years on Santa Rosa) provided just such an opportunity. Most of the monitoring was on San Miguel Island, where data sets had been established prior to fox removal.

On San Miguel Island, when Island Foxes were removed, Deer Mouse populations soared. On Santa Rosa and Santa Cruz islands, **Northern Harriers** (*Circus cyaneus*) took advantage of the Deer Mouse explosion there and began to nest, showing how the absence of a ground-based carnivore such as the fox can open up a niche for a raptor.

Back on San Miguel, Deer Mouse foraging behavior changed; they sought seeds of plants in open areas, unafraid that a fox might pounce on them. Two island endemic bird subspecies, the **Island Song Sparrow** (*Melospiza melodia* subsp. *graminea*) and the **Dusky Orange-crowned Warbler** (*Oreothlypis celata* subsp. *sordida*)—both of which nest in shrubs near the ground— showed substantial increases during the foxes' absence. Black Rats, which had increased their range and abundance on San Miguel Island while the foxes were gone, became scarce once foxes were returned to the island.

Santa Rosa Island, looking west to Beecher's Bay

Populations of the endemic Channel Island Spotted Skunk that occurs on Santa Rosa and Santa Cruz islands increased dramatically when foxes were in captivity. Furthermore, it was discovered that the skunks on Santa Cruz were now able to access sea caves where seabirds nested. Before this, nobody knew that spotted skunks had this ability. At normal densities, foxes had prevented the skunks from getting to the caves, probably by occupying nearby territories—unwittingly protecting the seabirds.

Santa Rosa Island

Santa Rosa Island is about eighty-four square miles in area, the second largest of the Northern Channel Islands. It lies six miles from Santa Cruz Island and three miles from San Miguel.

Beginning in the early 1900s, Santa Rosa Island was home to a huge cattle-ranching operation owned by Vail and Vickers Cattle Company. Headquarters was at Beecher's Bay, on the northeastern side of the island. All cattle were taken off the island in 1998, and the small herds of introduced Roos-

evelt Elk and Kaibab Mule Deer were removed in 2011.

Santa Rosa is characterized by rolling hills and grassland. After the removal of cattle, native vegetation recovered quickly. Although the plant diversity of Santa Rosa approaches that of Santa Cruz, it is not as ecologically rich.

Santa Rosa Island has five single-island endemic plants:

- **Santa Rosa Island Manzanita** (*Arctostaphylos confertiflora*)
- **Santa Rosa Island Dudleya** (*Dudleya blochmaniae* subsp. *insularis*)
- **Munchkin Dudleya** (*Dudleya gnoma*)
- **Hoffmann's Slender-flowered Gilia** (*Gilia tenuiflora* subsp. *hoffmannii*)
- **Torrey Pine** (*Pinus torreyana* subsp. *insularis*)

Torrey Pine and Munchkin Dudleya on Santa Rosa Island

On the northeast coast of Santa Rosa Island, a wonderful grove of gray-green pines grows. This is the Torrey Pine, the rarest pine in North America. It has one of the smallest ranges of any tree, being

Torrey Pine, one of the rarest pines in the world, on Santa Rosa Island

found only on Santa Rosa Island and in a little patch farther south, on the coast of San Diego County.

Specialists on conifers and island biology have yet to find a satisfactory explanation of how the Torrey Pine got to Santa Rosa Island. Although there's no fossil record of the pine on the mainland, it may have been more widespread at one time, with only these two populations remaining.

Torrey Pines are related to Gray and Coulter pines, which grow on the mainland. The cones of the Torrey Pine are round and fat, and the needles are five to a bundle.

Munchkin Dudleya, another scarce island endemic of Santa Rosa, has only been recognized as a distinct species since 1997. This succulent is tiny, hence its Latin epithet *gnoma*, or "diminutive, fabled being." Munchkin Dudleya thrives on gravelly, vol-

canic soil in a small area along the coast of Santa Rosa Island.

Arlington Springs Man on Santa Rosa Island

Santa Rosa Island is renowned among paleontologists for its Pygmy Mammoth remains. But equally intriguing are the human bones discovered buried thirty feet deep in Arlington Canyon by Santa Barbara Museum of Natural History Curator Phil Orr back in 1959. At the time, the bones were some of the oldest found in North America.

They still are.

Arlington Springs Man was reexamined by modern-day scientists, including Orr's successor John Johnson. At first it was thought the femurs were those of a woman. But later, after careful study of the skeletal remains, it was decided they did, indeed, belong to a man.

The Pygmy Mammoths of the Northern Channel Islands

The Pygmy Mammoths that evolved on San Miguel, Santa Rosa, and Santa Cruz islands in late Pleistocene times have attracted worldwide attention.

In 1994 the first complete Pygmy Mammoth skeleton was discovered and excavated on Santa Rosa Island. It sparked new interest on the part of researchers and the public as to how and why these extinct relatives of modern elephants inhabited the islands.

Mammoths flourished during the Pleistocene. Along with elephants and mastodons, they are members of the mammalian order Proboscidea (animals with flexible noses). For nearly two million years, various forms of mammoths ranged across the Northern Hemisphere.

In North America, when you say "mammoth" most people think of the **Woolly Mammoth** (*Mammuthus primigenius*), a big hairy beast of more northern habitats. But in our region the **Columbian Mammoth** (*Mammuthus columbi*) frequented the mainland of coastal California. Columbian Mammoths stood tall, as high as fourteen feet at the shoulder, and had two long tusks that often crossed in front. Columbian Mammoths were larger than the present-day Asian and African elephants.

Pygmy Mammoth on display at the Santa Barbara Museum of Natural History

Proboscideans evolved into smaller species once they lived on islands. Pygmy Mammoths were pint-sized, standing only six and a half feet high at the shoulder.

Small proboscideans have been found on other islands around the world: in the Mediterranean Sea, off Indonesia and the Philippines, and on Wrangel Island in the Siberian Arctic Ocean. In fact, a dwarfed form of the Woolly Mammoth lived there as recently as thirty-five hundred to four thousand years ago.

On the Northern Channel Islands, paleontologists have discovered both Columbian and Pygmy mammoth remains, although the Pygmies far outnumber the Columbians.

As mentioned earlier, the Northern Channel Islands were one "super island," Santarosae, during periods of lower sea level in the Pleistocene, but there was no land bridge between the islands and the mainland. How did the mammoths get out there?

They swam.

Researchers know that modern Asian Elephants will swim to islands they cannot even see, sometimes as far as twenty-three miles. Picture Santarosae then, four times as big as the present surface of the islands. You can imagine one or two adventurous Columbian Mammoths sniffing the island vegetation and swimming off to explore new territory. Whatever urged them on, mammoths were as good at swimming as modern elephants. As they swam, most of their bodies were underwater, but their heads, eyes, and trunks protruded above the sea.

Once landed on Santarosae, the Columbian Mammoths grew smaller and smaller. They didn't need all that bulk. They didn't need to be tall to graze on the hilly terrain of the islands. The smaller and more agile they were, the more they could climb into nooks and crannies to look for food. And, if resources were scarce, such as during a drought or after a lightning fire, the smaller individuals would be the ones to survive because they required less food and water.

And so, the Columbian Mammoth that emigrated to Santarosae became dwarfed over time; a new species unique to the Channel Islands, the Pygmy Mammoth, evolved.

There is a disadvantage to dwarfing: the little elephants matured, reproduced, and died sooner. Columbian Mammoths routinely lived over seventy years; Pygmy Mammoths were old at fifty. Given the rapidity with which one generation succeeded another, the species of mammoths that swam to Santarosae between forty thousand and twenty thousand years ago, or even earlier, could have become dwarfed in a relatively short period of time, geologically speaking.

Researchers have uncovered fossil bones of small-sized mammoths on the islands since the 1870s. Phil Orr, a curator at the Santa Barbara Museum of Natural History, did much of the exploratory work, from 1945 to 1968 living many months of the year in a primitive camp on Santa Rosa Island. It was not until 1994, however, when geologists discovered the 95 percent complete Pygmy Mammoth skeleton, that excitement began to build.

This skeleton, that of an elderly male animal, was found on a steep cliff in a remote area of Santa Rosa Island, where it had been covered by sand for centuries.

Larry Agenbroad, a paleontologist who specializes in mammoths, was called in to verify the identification of the skeleton and to mastermind its removal, preservation, and age-dating.

With the cooperation of Channel Islands National Park, Agenbroad and a team of scientists airlifted the skeleton by helicopter to Ventura, on the mainland. The original bones, plus fiberglass replicas, were deposited at the Santa Barbara Museum of Natural History. A fiberglass replica is also on display at Channel Islands National Park Headquarters in Ventura.

When did this Pygmy Mammoth—whose fossil remains were exposed on that steep, windswept cliff—meet its death? By using the latest technology, scientists were able to date the bone collagen of this animal to about thirteen thousand years ago.

How and why Pygmy Mammoths met extinction continues to puzzle researchers; the mystery is still unraveling. Intriguingly, human remains found on the islands have recently been dated to overlap the presence there of these diminutive mammoths.

The important question: how old are these bones? Using current radio-carbon dating methods, it has been established that the bones are thirteen thousand years old—much older than the ten-thousand-year age arrived at by Orr. Only one other find in North America has ever been dated to this early age.

The significance here is that humans and Pygmy Mammoths may have coexisted for a brief time on Santa-rosae, at the end of the Pleistocene Epoch. The four Northern Channel Islands would've been joined as one mega-island, Santarosae, and the last of the Pygmy Mammoths would have roamed it. It now appears that the Pygmy Mammoth was resident on the islands from about two hundred thousand years ago until thirteen thousand years ago.

We may never know what was responsible for Pygmy Mammoth extinction. But Arlington Springs Man takes his place alongside the Pygmy Mammoth as one of the two world-famous inhabitants of Santa Rosa Island.

Nature Journal
August 14–16, 1999

Field Trip to Santa Rosa Island

Tonight we're camped at Johnson's Lee on Santa Rosa Island. We're on a Santa Barbara Museum of Natural History field trip and it's my first night on Santa Rosa. What an adventure!

After a delicious dinner in the shelter of the abandoned military base's metal hangar, all of us have retired to our tents to

get a good night's sleep before our excursion tomorrow.

Ha!

Our tent is too tall and, like neophytes, we've placed it in exactly the wrong spot! I swear the wind is going to walk this tent right down the hill and it will land on somebody else's. Flap, slap, shake, jiggle, creak. Repeat. So, that's the part about the wind.

The other really intriguing aspect is the constant scurrying of the Santa Rosa Island Deer Mouse over the top of the tent. (There's an endemic Deer Mouse for

The wild northeast shore of Santa Rosa Island

each of the Northern Channel Islands!) All night long—the patter of little feet. Up one side, across the top, and down the other. Some squeaks and thumps. Then it resumes, up the other side, across the roof, and down. I don't want to think about how many Deer Mice have traveled across our tent tonight, but none have been able to get inside.

I'm thankful...but exhausted.

And then the brilliant clear morning dawns and I forget about my travails of the night before. The wind has calmed, the water of the bay is a vibrant blue, and the golden-brown grasses smell of fresh morning dew. Not a soul around except for our excited group, anticipating the day's events.

We are here with two top experts. Dr. Larry Agenbroad, paleontologist and world authority on the Pygmy Mammoth, and Dr. John Johnson from the Santa Barbara Museum of Natural History, a well-known anthropologist whose knowledge of California Native Americans is legendary.

We load up the vehicles and head for the northwest corner of the island, where Agenbroad has a mammoth site he wants to investigate and Johnson will take us to Arlington Canyon.

Arriving at a bluff-top vantage point, we get out and admire the clear day and the view across to San Miguel Island; from here, the cliff drops off, several hundred feet straight down, to a white beach below. Agenbroad goes off with volunteers in order to prepare a protective plaster jacket for one of the Pygmy Mammoth skeletons he's located on an earlier trip.

The rest of us follow John Johnson down into the ravine known as Arlington Canyon. After hiking down to the excavation site, we learn all there is to know about the island's oldest human remains, "Arlington Man." John's research into Arlington Man's age, and whether he and the Pygmy Mammoths might have lived on the island at the same time, may answer some important questions. This is Anthropology 101, and it's onsite and fabulous!

Then, we hike down to the beach below and watch as the Pygmy Mammoth crew brings up the mammoth bones in a huge bundle and puts them into the back of one of the jeeps.

Later, we drive to a new spot along the western coast. This is where the famous

anthropologist Phil Orr excavated from the 1940s to the 1960s. You can still see the collapsed buildings of Orr's camp.

We learn that because there are no gophers or ground squirrels on these islands, they're ideal for archaeological studies. Things are not disturbed as on the mainland.

As we drive back to camp slowly, bumping along on the rough road, we stop repeatedly. Either Larry Agenbroad or one of his sharp-eyed volunteers spots a fragment of a Pygmy Mammoth vertebra or tusk and we all pile out. How can they discern these mammoth remains from the similar bits and pieces of surrounding rocks?

But then....this is Santa Rosa Island. Everything about it is original. I wouldn't be surprised if a Pygmy Mammoth came strolling towards us from around the next bend in the road.

Anything can happen here.

San Miguel Island

Situated at the northwest tip of the Channel Islands archipelago, San Miguel Island stands desolate, wind-whipped, and wave-pounded. Due to its remote location and relative isolation from humans, this island has an aura all its own. Around it swirls the full force of the cold California Current, sweeping down from Point Conception, twenty-six miles to the north. The current brings the cool fogs and rich upwelled seawater that foster an array of marine life.

In 1542 Juan Rodriguez Cabrillo, the first European visitor, attempted to navigate around Point Conception but was driven back by fierce winds and took shelter in what is now known as Cuyler Harbor at San

Miguel. The story goes that Cabrillo was injured on the island and later died and was buried there. A granite cross has been erected in his memory and overlooks Cuyler Harbor. (Subsequent research uncovered the fact that Cabrillo may have actually been injured on Santa Catalina Island and that he is buried there, not on San Miguel.)

Sand in all its forms dominates the landscape in drifts and dunes that run right through the coastal sage scrub and grasslands.

Strange, pale **caliche** forests have been created where windblown sand encrusts the straight trunks of fossil trees. These calcium casts have preserved the trunks of the ancient vegetation that grew here thousands of years ago.

Of the terrestrial animals, the **San Miguel Island Deer Mouse** (*Peromyscus maniculatus* subsp. *streatori*) and the San Miguel Island Fox are endemic to the island.

But populations of endemics aren't the sole reason for an island's significance. Here at San Miguel, several wide-ranging species have chosen to breed. The impressive pinniped (seal and sea lion) rookeries and the immense colonies of nesting seabirds make San Miguel completely unique.

Point Bennett, at the far western end of the island, has the largest concentration of marine mammal rookeries anywhere along the West Coast. Whether you take a long hike to Point Bennett from Cuyler Harbor (a park ranger must be in attendance) or pass by the point on a boat, you'll be astonished at the sheer numbers of pinnipeds.

Studies comparing six pinniped populations on San Miguel from 1968 to 1998 showed that four species had increased threefold over those thirty years. Another species, the **Steller's Sea Lion** (*Eumetopias jubatus*) had stopped breeding and retreated to its more northerly haunts. Another, more southerly species, the **Guadalupe Fur Seal** (*Arctocephalus townsendi*), had begun to reestablish, starting a new breeding colony. In 1997 the first pup was born in the California Channel Islands in at least 150 years.

The four species that had increased were the California Sea Lion, Northern Elephant Seal, **Northern Fur Seal** (*Callorhinus ursinus*), and Harbor Seal. Researchers recorded eighty thousand California Sea Lions; fifty thousand Northern Elephant Seals; twelve thousand Northern Fur Seals; and twelve hundred Harbor Seals. This is an aggregation of marine mammals unlike any in the world!

Northern Fur Seals, hailing from as far north as the Pribilof Islands, are at the southern tip of their breeding range here. They are joined by California Sea Lions, whose rookery at Point Bennett is the largest in the sea lions' entire range.

Interestingly, all these species appear to be able to coexist on San Miguel. Northern Fur Seals and California Sea Lions compete for breeding space in the spring, but they forage in different areas of the ocean. In contrast, Northern Elephant Seals (also see Chapter 3) and Harbor Seals breed in winter; often they must vie with each other for beaches for pupping, sometimes to the detriment of the Harbor Seals.

Why such diversity here? The answers are obvious enough: distance from human disturbance; intermingling of cold and warm ocean currents; underwater shelf areas close to abundant fish prey; deep, offshore waters for foraging within a day's journey. These are the factors that engender an unbelievably rich marine mammal presence. But the fact that it's all happening at San Miguel Island, just across the Santa Barbara Channel from a bustling center of human population, is what's extraordinary.

The California Sea Lion

In spring at Point Bennett, the deafening barks of California Sea Lions carry for miles. "Sex on the beach" describes the goings-on here. Crowded together, thousands of sea lions fight for dominance, give birth, mate, and nurse. It is a fecund congregation of lumpy brown bodies, some poised on rocks with noses skyward, others lying heaped upon one another, still others galumphing to and from the shore.

Most sea lions hunt at night, locating prey underwater with their large eyes; they pick up the sounds of prey with their whiskers (**vibrissae**), which have been demonstrated to be ten thousand times more sensitive than their ears.

Sea lions feed on anchovies, squid, and shrimp. A peculiar feature of their eating habits is the presence of rocks in their stomachs. Nobody has the answer as to what function the stones might serve; perhaps they aid in digestion, are used as ballast, or help to grind up parasitic worms.

At the rookery, the mature males, bulky at around six hundred pounds, corral harems of ten to twenty females

California Sea Lions are the most common pinniped on San Miguel Island, with a large colony at Point Bennett.

California Sea Lions congregate at deserted beaches on the islands. Photo by Peter Gaede

heightened competition for prey in nearby waters. (See Chapter 3 regarding El Niño impacts on California Sea Lion reproductive success.) In the same study, it was found that female sea lions usually perform shallow dives of short duration.

All this is very interesting, but what the average observer wants to know is how to recognize a sea lion basking in the water. Sea lions often float on their backs with their flippers out of the water. Their high metabolic rate makes them hot after a period of underwater swimming, and airing the wet flippers aids in evaporative cooling. From a distance, the flippers looks like a set of pointy fins sticking up out of the water in a circle.

When swimming, sea lions porpoise forward in swift, undulating motions. In the nonbreeding season they haul out near the mainland on buoys, where they can be seen from shore or from a passing boat.

Seabirds at San Miguel Island

In addition to the tremendous pinniped presence, San Miguel Island hosts throngs of nesting seabirds. The largest rookeries are located just offshore on Prince Island and Castle Rock. Up to twelve species of seabirds breed on or near San Miguel Island, and of those, eight are more common here than on any of the other California Channel Islands. The **Brandt's Cormorant** (*Phalacrocorax penicillatus*), **Cassin's Auklet** (*Ptychoramphus aleuticus*), Western Gull, Pigeon Guillemot, and **Ashy Storm-Petrel** (*Oceanodroma homochroa*) are the most numerous.

Brandt's Cormorants are shiny black birds that stand tall and skinny

and juveniles. Mating takes place in June and July, and pups are born in May and June. Once the breeding season ends, adult males and immatures leave the rookery. But the females, which must nurse the newly born pups for six to eleven months, stay behind.

Researchers have been able to study the foraging behavior of nursing female sea lions at San Miguel. Foraging trips last an average of three to four days and nursing visits back at the rookery last for one or two days, as mother sea lions alternate their feeding and nursing activities.

Female sea lions that are nursing feed most regularly in waters to the northwest of San Miguel Island. A 1996 survey found that during the breeding season females need to travel farther towards the continental shelf and into pelagic waters northwest of the island in order to find enough prey, whereas later on, in the nonbreeding season, prey is available closer to the island. Biologists speculate that this behavior may be due to the density of animals in the breeding colony in recent years, and the

Aerial view of steep Prince Island, just offshore of San Miguel Island. Photo by Peter Gaede

Pigeon Guillemots are one of the most numerous nesting seabird species on San Miguel Island.

A Brandt's Cormorant carrying nesting material. Photo by Peter Gaede

at their nests. From far away they resemble black bowling pins, covering the tops of the flat rocks and level ledges. Masses of Brandt's Cormorants nest in close quarters, then take to the water to dive for fish in large, cooperative groups. Other cormorants, such as the Double-crested and the Pelagic, breed here too, but they're not as numerous as the Brandt's.

In censusing seabirds, biologists have found that certain species are easier to monitor than others. For example, the cormorants, which nest on rock surfaces and open ledges, can be surveyed quite accurately from a distance using binoculars or cameras or even from a small airplane.

But birds like the Cassin's Auklet and Ashy Storm-Petrel, which either

A typical Brandt's Cormorant colony on steep isolated cliffs. Each little dot is a cormorant nest, which is why aerial monitoring is often successful with this species. Photo by Peter Gaede

Ashy Storm-Petrels nest in rock crevices at Prince Island and come and go by night. Photo by Laurie Harvey

dig burrows into the ground or secrete their young in natural cavities and sea caves, are much more difficult to census. Being truly pelagic, auklets and storm-petrels come to land only once a year to nest, and from that nest they come and go only at night. This is why censusing seabird colonies on San Miguel and the other Channel Islands has proved extremely difficult.

A note here about the work of seabird biologists: it's a challenging, time-consuming, and costly process that brings little recognition. A few of the well-known seabird biologists who've worked on the islands—George Hunt, Harry Carter, Frank Gress, and Darrell Whitworth, all of whom have been studying seabirds there since the 1990s—and their predecessors are the ones we should thank. Scaling the steepest sea cliffs, peering into dark sea caves, rappelling down sheer rock faces, these dedicated scientists brave the seas to get population estimates on the most secretive of our seabirds. For Channel

Cassin's Auklets hide themselves in burrows for nesting and only visit the site at night to feed young. Photo by Peter Gaede

Islands National Park, seabird biologist Laurie Harvey conducts most of the baseline surveys of the nesting species annually.

And why monitor seabirds anyway? Because they are another barometer of how we're doing in protecting the environment and these special islands.

A recent analysis by Bird Conservation International found that seabirds

are more endangered than other types of birds. And, because the seabirds nesting in California sample all kinds of ecosystems on land and at sea from Mexico to Alaska, monitoring their presence and productivity tells us a lot about the health of these marine ecosystems.

The Big Picture: A Conversation with Kate Faulkner

For an assessment of recent developments on the islands, I visited Kate Faulkner, Chief of Natural Resources Management, at her office in the Channel Islands National Park headquarters. Channel Islands National Park is comprised of the four Northern Channel Islands plus Santa Barbara Island. (In this chapter, we omit Santa Barbara Island since many authorities do not consider its flora and fauna to have the more northern affinities associated with the Northern Channel Islands.) On Santa Cruz Island, the National Park Service owns 10 percent at the eastern portion, while The Nature Conservancy owns the remaining 90 percent of the island.

Kate Faulkner oversees all the biologists, and the restoration and monitoring groups, in the park. Faulkner has been at Channel Islands National Park since 1990, so she's been involved in most of the projects to restore the health of island ecosystems.

When I asked her about the victories that the National Park Service has had in working with other groups to remove livestock, eradicate rats, and restore native vegetation on the islands, Faulkner outlined the intensive planning and careful logistics that had to be followed in each effort.

Professionals from around the world were called in to help and advise.

She emphasized the amazing significance of the Channel Islands on a bigger scale—viewing them as part of a crucial ecosystem that exists in the eastern North Pacific Ocean.

Connectivity. That word kept coming up. Connectivity in the sense of how the fauna and flora of the islands are influenced by climate, predator-prey relationships, and human interference. Connectivity in the sense of the worldwide significance of the Channel Islands.

"For example, without the islands, there would be few nesting seabirds in Southern California," Faulkner says. "Over 90 percent of the seabirds breeding in Southern California are found on the park islands. Furthermore, seabirds and pinnipeds know no boundaries. They cross geopolitical lines, with birds traveling to islands off Baja to the south and pinnipeds going to the north as far as the Pribilofs in the Bering Sea. And all of them rely on this little pile of rocks for certain parts of their life history. Without them [the islands], the seabirds and pinnipeds are sunk."

Then, Faulkner showed me a fascinating study in which biologists used electronic tagging techniques to track marine vertebrates on their long migrations. Many of these top predators undergo annual migrations from far away to feed in the cool, nutrient-rich waters off the California coast. The tracking data underlines the importance of our offshore waters for seabirds (Sooty Shearwaters), tunas (**Pacific Bluefin**, *Thunnus orientalis*), sharks (**Shortfin Mako**, *Isurus* *oxyrinchus*), cetaceans (Blue Whale), and sea turtles (**Leatherback**, *Dermochelys coriacea*), to name only a few. Although they may breed elsewhere, they travel to the California Current marine ecosystem to forage. The Sooty Shearwater—the most numerous seabird off our shores in spring and summer—makes an annual journey from its breeding islands off New Zealand to feed here!

Looking back over the successes the National Park Service has achieved in restoration on the islands, Faulkner's message was one of hope for the future. There will always be fluctuations in populations, she said, and the challenges will always be there. In the future those challenges may be more out of our control than in the past. Climate change is a big one, or a disastrous oil spill. But if the island ecosystems are healthy, they're in a better position to withstand whatever lies ahead.

Channel Islands National Marine Sanctuary

You can't discuss pinniped rookeries and seabird colonies without focusing on the marine environment that surrounds the Northern Channel Islands. Every bit as splendid and dynamic as anything happening on the islands themselves, habitats offshore of the islands teem with life.

If Channel Islands National Park serves to protect the land-based organisms, Channel Islands National Marine Sanctuary (CINMS) deals with the significant habitats just offshore of the Northern Channel Islands. Designated a sanctuary in 1980, the CINMS extends seaward from the island coasts, surrounding them for a distance of six nautical miles off their shores. In addition to the rich kelp forests, the panorama of underwater sea life includes everything from invertebrates such as spiny lobsters and sea stars to enormous cetaceans like the Blue Whale, which passes through sanctuary waters in migration. CINMS scientists have started aerial surveys to study the passage of the Blue Whales in relation to commercial vessels such as tankers and container ships that move through the Santa Barbara Channel. The potential for collision with these enormous ships creates an ever more perilous situation for the whales as the shipping lanes become more and more crowded. (See Chapter 3 for more on Blue Whales.)

In addition, the CINMS is crucial to the protection of island offshore waters because it includes a network of Marine Protected Areas (MPAs) that have been set aside as a refuge for all sea life. Fishing, both recreational and commercial, is very limited at these special reserves. (The term "Marine Protected Area" covers Marine Reserves as well as Marine Conservation Areas. Limited harvest is permitted in the latter.)

In 2008, five years after the MPAs were established, the various agencies involved in setting them up—including the CINMS—were able to assess the effectiveness of the program. Scientists had monitored the protected areas and noticed changes in marine animals and habitats. They observed higher densities and bigger fish in marine reserves than in the surrounding waters. Larger, healthier fish ("big fat females") will produce more young, which should then spill over into the unrestricted areas of off-shore ecosystems, increasing fish populations everywhere over time.

The MPAs have worked well on the Northern Channel Islands; they have been expanded to include certain areas along the South Coast of our region. Point Conception, Naples Reef, Coal Oil Point, Campus Point, and Goleta Slough are slated for protection off mainland shores.

* * *

We have discussed the many differences between island ecosystems and those of the mainland. The four Northern Channel Islands produce astonishing forms of life unique to each of them.

At the same time, taken together, the Northern Channel Islands are a distillation of several themes that apply to the Santa Barbara region as a whole. The islands illustrate the melding of northerly and southerly oceanic influences. Correspondingly, terrestrial and marine species found there are a reflection of the intermingling of north and south. These concepts are echoed on the mainland and have been emphasized throughout our discussions.

But we cannot forget the gap.

The gap is the distance from the mainland to the islands. It's much farther in terms of species composition than it is in miles across the water. As a result of that gap and its isolating influence, endemism is the hallmark of the islands. Sweepstakes dispersal—what reaches the islands and what doesn't—is the exciting part of the equation.

Go out and see how the islands are different from the mainland and how they're the same. Let a Channel Islands National Park volunteer guide you through the experience. They can bring you up to date on the latest developments at this national treasure.

CHAPTER 11: URBAN PARKS AND BACKYARDS—OUTDOOR ADVENTURES CLOSE TO HOME

We have covered the wildlands of our region from the heights of Mount Pinos to the shores of the Channel Islands, and a good deal of what lies in between on this whirlwind tour of the various habitats of our region.

Dizzy, perhaps overwhelmed, you decide to put the book down and look out the window.

What's out there? You get up from the chair, open the front door and go outside. This is the exciting first step!

Explore your backyard, the vacant lot across the street, a drainage ditch at the end of the cul-de-sac. If there's nothing nearby, walk to the nearest green space or park.

You don't have to visit all the faraway places. You don't have to get into the car. As soon as you step outside, you're in the natural world.

And so this last chapter will bring us home by focusing on the urban and suburban landscapes in which most of us live.

If you are trying to interest a youngster in the outdoor world, the backyard is the beginning. Particularly for young children, and especially if you're a parent, grandparent, or teacher, the importance of exploring the immediate neighborhood cannot be emphasized enough.

Start by observing what's at ground level. An ant hurries across the concrete patio, carrying something white in its mouth. A snail lurks underneath your favorite potted plant. Then a pillbug crawls out from beneath the pot, curling into a tight ball at your touch. In the moist soil of the pot, a squirming earthworm surfaces. Looking up, you notice a Cabbage White butterfly fluttering and eventually landing on the lawn. From the top of a utility pole, a crow caws loudly, its head jerking up and down.

Pond at Alice Keck Park in Santa Barbara

All these species before you've even left the patio!

Urban landscapes are full of animals and plants. You need not go dashing around to find interesting things to study or photograph. Although habitats altered by man vary according to their location, if you're curious you can always discover plants and animals. We owe it to ourselves to learn about the fauna and flora of what's immediately around us.

Look closely and explore locally.

Plants of Urban Parks and Backyards

Native and Non-native: Why Should We Care?

In Chapter 10 we talked at length about colonization on the Northern Channel Islands and which species were able to gain a foothold on the islands and why.

Plant and animal species have long been colonizing new locations around the world, particularly in the past few centuries, as human travel between continents increased. In Southern California we have been inundated with plants and animals from all over. Commercial shipping fosters hitchhikers from other countries. Aquatic interlopers thrive in ships' ballast water; pests are inadvertently introduced on fruits and vegetables; humans transport pets in luggage; misguided individuals think they're doing us a favor by bringing the garden snail from France to eat, or the starling to replicate the birdlife of an English garden.

Not only do we find that we are inextricably linked with other countries culturally and economically, but increasingly our native ecosystems have become melting pots of native

Red Hot Poker plants, native to South Africa, attract a variety of native birds and insects.

and non-native plants and animals. Non-native plants and animals are defined as those that have been transported outside their native range.

At this point, it's impossible to keep out the invaders; widespread attempts to do so have met with mixed results. We could become obsessed with stamping out these foreign colonizers, but at some point we admire their tenacity. After all, those that survive are just doing what they do best—making a living wherever they land on earth.

Unfortunately, though, non-natives do not bring with them natural controls, such as the specialized parasites and diseases that kept them in check in their native habitats back home.

Biologists and naturalists are concerned about the non-native plants and animals that become naturalized, or established, here. If they have the potential to become invasive, spreading rapidly, they harm native ecosystems. Although many, many introduced plants and animals are not invasive, a small percentage are considered pests and are targeted for eradication. The California Department of Fish and Wildlife, the California Invasive Plant Council, and the California Native Plant Society produce official lists of invasive species classified as pests.

Of the plants found in our region, approximately 450 are deemed non-native; they must compete with the 1,500 native plants here for soil, space, and water. For further information about invasive plants to avoid in our region, visit the website of the Santa Barbara Botanic Garden, www. sbbg.org.

The Urban Mix: What Grows in Urban Parks and Gardens?

The term "urban mix" has been borrowed from an excellent book by V. L. Holland and David J. Keil, *California Vegetation,* where some of the ideas discussed below about urban and suburban habitats are developed further.

"Urban mix" refers to the potpourri of non-native and native plants that thrive in our cities, towns, parks, and backyards. Plants from other areas—particularly those from the Mediterranean region, Australia, and South Africa—have been introduced here with great success. Due to its mild climate, this region—especially the city of Santa Barbara—has one of the richest non-native floras for its size anywhere in the United States.

The majority of non-native plant species in California are an accepted part of the landscape, where they have become naturalized over many years. For example, *Schinus molle,* often called the "California Pepper Tree," is not a pepper and is not from California. It was introduced from Peru into the early Mission gardens here and is widely cultivated as an ornamental. **Black Mustard** (*Brassica nigra*), with its bright yellow flowers that decorate our spring hillsides, is another example of a non-native plant from Europe that has been here since the 1700s.

"California Pepper Tree" at San Marcos Foothills Preserve in Santa Barbara

Black Mustard, a non-native plant, splashes yellow highlights everywhere in early spring.

Monterey Pine and **Monterey Cypress** (*Hesperocyparis macrocarpa*) are another example: they are native only to small areas of California around Monterey, but not to our region (with the exception of the Monterey Pines found at Cambria in San Luis Obispo County). It's difficult to believe, but Monterey Pine is the most widely planted commercial pine, and it is found in gardens and parks throughout the world. In all those places, it's a non-native species.

In *Trees of Santa Barbara* by Robert Muller and J. Robert Haller, you can read about the early horticulturalists, such as Joseph Sexton, Francesco Franceschi, and E. O. Orpet, who introduced the lovely assortment of trees which now grace our streets and parks. **Palm** (Family Arecaceae) and **acacia** (*Acacia* spp.), both brought from a variety of far-

away locations, are familiar sights in urban areas.

Native trees, such as Coast Live Oak and California Bay, grow shoulder to shoulder here with non-native **Century Plant** (*Agave americana*) and **Italian Stone Pine** (*Pinus pinea*). Native ceanothus and Western Sycamore share the

Over a dozen species of acacia are cultivated around Santa Barbara.

Bottlebrushes are magnets for hummingbirds year-round, but especially during spring and fall migration.

Blue blossoms of *Echium*, or Pride of Madeira, attract hummingbirds and numerous insects.

same neighborhood park as non-native **Cape Honeysuckle** (*Tecomaria capensis*) and **bottlebrush** (*Callistemon* spp.).

At its best, the urban mix of native and non-native plantings becomes a fertile ecosystem. A variety of insects, birds, and mammals have adapted to life in human surroundings, and they are easy to see. Before moving on to discuss this urban ecosystem and its inhabitants, let's look more closely at one of the most common and most controversial non-native plants: the eucalyptus.

Eucalyptus grows everywhere in our region, not just in urban areas. In windbreaks to shelter farmland, in plantations grown for firewood, in ornamental plantings in backyards and gardens, the eucalyptus tree is often the tallest and most striking aspect of the landscape. At least ten species have become established in the wild in California and hundreds of species grow in parks and gardens.

When we think of eucalyptus trees, most of us picture the **Blue Gum Eucalyptus** (*Eucalyptus globu-*

lus), its tall, graceful branches swaying in the breeze atop a trunk that can reach heights of 150 feet. Other species of eucalyptus come in all shapes and sizes, with flowers of white, pink, orange, or red.

The story of eucalyptus in California is a fascinating one, and the Santa Barbara region plays an important role.

Eucalypti are native to Australia and account for nearly 70 percent of Australian forests. The species was first described by Abel Janszoon Tasman during his voyage of exploration in 1642. On the island of Tasmania, which is named after him, he observed two trees and wrote about them in his journal.

Jump forward a couple of centuries to the gold rush in California, which lured many Australians, who brought with them the idea that eucalyptus should be introduced into the state. W. C. Walker of San Francisco, a nurseryman, was the first person to actually plant eucalyptus from seed in California, in 1853. He was in touch with Baron Ferdinand von Mueller, a renowned German botanist who had moved to Australia. Walker, Mueller, and others began to promote eucalyptus as the perfect tree for firewood, for construction of fences and agricultural implements, and for shade and beauty around houses.

In 1876 Ellwood Cooper of Santa Barbara wrote *Forest Culture and Eucalyptus Trees,* announcing on the title page that it was "the only complete and reliable work on the eucalypti published in the United States." Cooper extolled the virtues of the eucalyptus and proclaimed the need for plant-

Sugar Gum is one of thirty-four eucalyptus species cultivated in Santa Barbara.

ing artificial forests in this barren land devoid of timber. It was also Cooper who planted the first large acreage of eucalyptus in Southern California, on his ranch near Santa Barbara, where he established 150,000 Blue Gum and **River Red Gum** (*Eucalyptus camaldulensis*) trees on one hundred acres.

From there, the boom took off. By the early 1900s, thousands of acres of eucalyptus had been planted, encouraged by state and local governments. The Central Pacific Railroad and later the Southern Pacific Railroad planted millions of trees for ties, poles, posts,

These eucalyptus leaves are heavily infested with a lerp psyllid that was introduced from Australia.

lyptus, the immigrant from Australia, was fully established as a non-native species in California.

Today, several kinds of eucalyptus trees fit beautifully into urban habitats, but dense groves of Blue Gums have become controversial. Many botanists consider this particular species an invasive pest. Blue Gum forests produce lots of litter—downed branches, leaves, bark, and seedpods. Not only is the litter a fire hazard, it has been blamed for the lack of understory in dense stands of eucalyptus. Horticulturalists long thought that the volatile oils these trees exude make it difficult to grow anything under them, but recent research has disproved this theory; it is the root systems of the trees that outcompete other plants.

The fact remains, however, that those volatile oils are an enormous fire hazard. Groves are most flammable after a freeze, when dead branches and foliage have fallen to the forest floor. In a fire, the aromatic oils in the leaves hasten the updraft and entire trees become burning torches. Eucalyptus should be cleared away from buildings for this reason.

But the eucalyptus story doesn't end there.

Recall that non-native plants often do not bring their diseases with them when they immigrate.

This situation changed when one of the most destructive eucalyptus pests, the **Red Gum Lerp Psyllid** (*Glycaspis brimblecombei*), arrived in Los Angeles from Australia in 1998. Soon, the psyllid reached the Santa Barbara region, and it continues to be a presence here in certain stands of eucalyptus.

and firewood. Throughout the early part of the twentieth century, eucalyptus plantations were regarded as get-rich-quick schemes, and thousands more trees were planted.

The bust followed. Once cured, eucalyptus wood warped, cracked, twisted, and became too tough. Unlike the ancient trees used successfully in Australia for building projects, the young California trees did not live up to expectations. The projected yields took too long to be realized. But by the time this was known, euca-

Close-up of a psyllid laying eggs. The sugary, whitish, conelike capsules—lerps—conceal the larvae of the winged adult.

Psyllids are sucking insects that lay their eggs on the succulent leaves and young shoots of many varieties of eucalyptus. The immature psyllids form **lerps**, sugary capsules, which look like tiny white cones clinging to the leaves. Infested trees drop their leaves, and if the trees have been weakened by several years of infestation, they will die.

So now we have an introduced tree, attacked by an introduced insect. The solution: procure an introduced psyllid-specific parasitic wasp to control the psyllid damage. A parasitic wasp (*Psyllaephagus bliteus*) has been introduced from Australia. The female parasitizes the psyllid nymph by killing it, pupating, and emerging, leaving a round emergence hole in the parasitized lerp cover. Voilà! The biological control appears to be working and we observe how a whole *imported* ecosystem operates.

When botanists decry thoughtless introductions of non-native species, they are referring to just such situations. Everything in nature is linked to everything else. And all too often, chemical herbicides rather than natural biological controls must be resorted to in order to curb invasive species.

But don't give up on the Blue Gum. Blue Gum Eucalyptus groves have become extremely important to a variety of wildlife, especially birds and insects. The most famous insect to frequent eucalyptus groves in our region is the beautiful orange-and-black Monarch butterfly. At the **Coronado Butterfly Preserve** at Ellwood Mesa in Goleta, thousands of Monarchs overwinter in clusters, clinging to the leaves and branches of Blue Gum Eucalyptus. The Monarchs have made an adaptive switch

Monarchs overwinter in large colonies in eucalyptus groves at the Coronado Butterfly Preserve at Goleta.

to roosting in eucalyptus trees since the 1870s; before that, they roosted in evergreens and oaks. Blue Gums produce blossoms with nectar, thus feeding the butterflies as well as sheltering them.

Children and adults alike are fascinated by the Monarch, which has been called the best-known butterfly in the world. In fall, Monarchs from the western states migrate to California. From November through February, they shelter in groves of trees near the coast, anywhere from Mendocino to Baja. The largest roost in our region is found at the Coronado Butterfly Preserve; other aggregations in protected areas are located at Camino Real Park in Ventura, and Pismo State Beach and Morro Bay State Park in San Luis Obispo County.

Adrian Wenner, UC Santa Barbara professor emeritus and butterfly expert, says that when butterflies migrate, it's more a question of mass dispersal than purposeful navigation. In spring and summer, West Coast Monarchs fly inland from the coast, following the bloom of food sources towards Utah, Nevada, and other destinations west of the Rockies. In fall, when the days grow shorter, these butterflies use prevailing winds to travel westward. According to Wenner, Monarchs normally fly into the onshore breezes as they migrate back to the West Coast. At times, they rise on thermals and ride Santa Ana winds during offshore flows. By flying in favorable wind conditions, the Monarchs eventually arrive at their traditional wintering sites along the California coast.

It is not known whether Monarchs navigate in the true sense. Some

The distinctive caterpillar of the Monarch

researchers theorize that the butterflies can orient themselves by the sun. Like bees, they can see polarized light, and they may be able to discern differences in polarization across the sky.

When you visit a Monarch roost, go in the morning, before these beauties become active. The butterflies will be dozing, clinging together like orange and black leaves on hundreds and hundreds of eucalyptus branches. From November through February, the roost serves as a refuge from the wind and cold for the fragile butterflies.

Common Butterflies of Urban Habitats

1. Monarch, *Danaus plexippus*

2. Alfalfa Butterfly, *Colias eurytheme*

3. Gulf Fritillary, *Agraulis vanillae*

4. Anise Swallowtail, *Papilio zelicaon*

5. Cloudless Sulfur, *Phoebis sennae*

6. Rural Skipper, *Ochlodes agricola*

7. Fiery Skipper, *Hylephila phyleus*

8. Cabbage White, *Pieris rapae*

Towards the end of their winter lay-over at the roost, the Monarchs mate. Then the females fly inland to search for any of several species of milkweed, including **Narrow-leaved Milkweed** (*Asclepias fascicularis*). This is not a weed but a native plant on which the Monarchs lay their eggs. When the eggs hatch, the caterpillars feed on the milkweed, ingesting a character-istic milky sap. A chemical in the sap, **cardenolide**, is highly toxic, but not to the Monarch. A Monarch caterpil-lar that ingests this chemical will pass it on to the adult; both are then some-what protected from predators.

Most birds will gag the minute they mistake a Monarch for a meal. Some bird species, however, are immune to milkweed toxin; still others have learned to eat only the thoracic mus-cles and abdominal contents, avoid-ing the toxic parts of the butterfly.

A few butterfly species have evolved to mimic the pattern of Mon-archs. The mimic species are edible, but because predators avoid anything that looks like a Monarch, the mimic species are protected, too—another example of Batesian mimicry (see Chapter 7, Burrowing Owls). Further-more, some Monarchs lay their eggs on milkweed species that are less toxic than others. But because the toxic butterflies are more numerous, pred-ators still avoid the nontoxic ones, an example of **automimicry**.

During the spring migration, the first generation of Monarch butter-flies will be followed by at least three or four others. They leapfrog in a northward direction as the season progresses, searching for species of milkweed on which to feed and lay their eggs. Each generation lives but four to six weeks; only the last gener-ation, which lives four to six months, performs the return migration to the winter roost.

When you walk through the thou-sands of butterflies that cluster on the trees, you are looking at the great-great-grandchildren of the indi-viduals that were there last year. They hatched somewhere in the West, and, after a long journey, they have come home to roost.

Creatures of Urban Parks and Backyards

When you're exploring an urban hab-itat, especially with a young child, insects are often the first wild things to catch your eye. A sense of curiosity about butterflies, earthworms, ants, and pillbugs will get you started. It's important for children to know that you are there to observe wildlife and not to harm creatures in any way.

Introducing Children to Nature

In 2006 Richard Louv published a book called *Last Child in the Woods: Saving Our Children from Nature-Deficit Disorder*. The book struck a chord throughout the country. His ideas sparked educators everywhere to rethink their teaching of science and natural history.

Fundamentally, Louv's book says that loss of natural habitat and discon-nection from nature have enormous implications for human health and child development. Earlier, E. O. Wil-son, the famous Harvard biologist who coined the term "biophilia," had argued that "the urge to affiliate with other forms of life" was in our genes.

We just needed to give children (and adults, too, of course) a chance to get outside.

I talked with Elaine Gibson, Nature Education Specialist at the Santa Barbara Museum of Natural History, in August 2011. She spearheaded a campaign called Leave No Child Inside Santa Barbara—a group of institutions and individuals who want to reconnect children with nature. She said that at first she did not believe the situation could be as dire as depicted in Louv's book. However, in her years at the museum, she has observed the first reactions of schoolchildren as they walk outside the classroom and actually get wet in the creek and get dirty. Louv's book is on target.

Initially, children are fearful. When docents lead youngsters across the wooden bridge to the other side of the property, the riparian woodland becomes "the jungle"—whispered in fearful tones.

The most frequently asked questions are "Will it bite?" and "Is it poisonous?" Children are afraid to climb on the big boulders, tentative about putting their fingers in Mission Creek, worried about strange sounds and being outside. When a crow cawed, an eight-year-old asked, "Is that a monkey?"

Don't tell the children to be careful, tell them to be aware. This teaches self-sufficiency, not fear of the unknown.

Too much television and too much indoor time result in fearful responses to being outside. When children watch dramatic nature programs that show footage of sharks and piranhas, they assume these deadly creatures may live in twelve-inch-deep pools in Mission Creek. And who can blame them? This is all unfamiliar; how frightening, to be sitting under a sycamore tree in the leaf litter! Why would we want to dig in the dirt? Icky. Yucky. *Eeeuuuuwww.*

Their parents have been brainwashed about "stranger danger." Children don't play outside alone. They aren't even allowed to ride their bikes a block or two to see a friend. Abductions are in the news. Fear is everywhere, and the children sense it.

At the Museum of Natural History, Gibson and her team in the Education Department have taken a new direction.

First, they are fortunate to have the natural setting that surrounds the buildings at the museum. So, they have taken nature education outside into the best laboratory they could find—the riparian habitat beside Mission Creek. The signs call out this area as "The Museum Backyard." In it, children are encouraged to play imaginary games using natural materials: bamboo timbers to build a fort, logs to walk on instead of balance bars; trees to climb. In order to prevent erosion and damage to the creek bank, children are allowed to access Mission Creek in only one spot.

The Museum Backyard is a place of wonder and delight. Moving water has magic and amuses children for hours. Birds live in the surrounding oak woodland, and a compost pile contains a variety of bugs, beetles, and worms.

The chief point that Louv and educators are making is this: find a ravine, woods, windbreak, swamp, open field, or backyard, and get children outside. Louv calls it the "unofficial countryside."

We extoll the beauty of the habitats in the Santa Barbara region and the creatures that live here, but children don't know what you're talking about until they've been exposed to nature, however close to home it may be.

Once a youngster becomes comfortable outdoors, you hear comments like "Metamorphosis! Awesome!" and "I didn't think I could climb that rock, but I did!"

As Louv says, "The land shapes us more than we shape the land, until there's no more land to shape."

Nature Journal
April 4, 2007

Manning Park, Santa Barbara County

Today I'm with a four-year-old in a suburban park. It rained last night and the sun glistens on the wet pine needles. The grass feels spongy and wet against our shoes. Gophers have dug fresh crescents of dark earth all over the lawn.

My backpack is full of homemade scientific equipment—two small glass jars with air holes poked in the lids, a butterfly net, and a magnifying glass—and some graham crackers and a container of apple juice. The last two items are to nourish the youngster who's holding my hand, my grandson, Alex.

This precious child makes his home in urban Los Angeles. He has to learn that it's okay to get dirty, to get your shoes wet and your hands covered with mud. But he needs encouragement. He's tentative.

Interjecting an element of the "quest for adventure" seems to work best. The kid loves animals, so let's find one!

Sharper eyes than mine find the first critter—a "roly poly," as he calls it. The pillbug plays its part well by immediately curling up into a tight ball. Score one for the pillbug.

"Let's find something else!" Alex is beginning to catch my enthusiasm.

"Eeeuuuuwwww." He sees the earthworms wriggling helplessly, stranded by the night's downpour on the concrete path. I pick them up one by one. We examine many earthworms, speculate upon their movements, put them in the jar, then let them go. Those lying on the pathway are carefully placed back where they belong, in a patch of damp soil.

A line of ants travels up and over a stone wall and down the other side. We decide to follow it. The ant trail ends at the leftovers of yesterday's picnic; food wrappers and bits of bread litter the ground under one of the park's picnic tables. I explain that each individual ant has seized a morsel and is carrying it carefully back to the communal nest for all to share.

Next, Alex spots a garden snail hiding underneath the leaves of an agapanthus. He wants to collect it and name it Willie. Fine. He puts Willie in one of the jars and we watch how the snail slides up the side of the jar on its big, slimy foot.

"Shouldn't we put some leaves in there for it to eat?" he asks. So we pick some oak leaves off the ground, open the jar, and stick them in. Willie appears uninterested, but Alex is proud to be providing for his new friend.

"Oh, look—starlings!" I say, pointing at the trio of black birds with yellow bills that have just landed on the lawn and are walking jauntily around. The starlings

have figured out about the picnic remains and they head over to partake.

I take out the bird identification guide and my grandson immediately pounces on the picture of the European Starling.

"That's the one!" he cries.

I don't tell him it's an introduced species which is often regarded as a pest. It's a bird, and he's excited. I suggest that we make a mark under the picture of each bird we see today. So we get out the marker pen and make a big black dot under the starling.

Argentine Ants transporting their eggs

Alex wants to try out the butterfly net, but we both realize that catching even a Cabbage White butterfly is tricky. They move so fast. We spot one Monarch and Alex is curious. It is on the ground, obviously dead, but still in perfect shape. He says he wants to take the dead butterfly back to the house to study it some more with the magnifying glass, and I say sure. Why not?

And so it goes—our first nature adventure. The city kid has got his shoes wet and his hands dirty, and he knows the names of several species that live in this urban habitat. What a great start! It's definitely time for a snack and self-congratulation all around.

The child who was so afraid to get off the path, to dig in the dirt, to handle a wild creature, has shared many a nature adventure with me since that day.

I don't know who's the luckier one— Alex or me—but I tell this story to encourage you to take a youngster outdoors. Start simply and close to home. Make it fun!

Insects and Related Species in the Backyard

Whether you're exploring an open field, a neighborhood park, or your own backyard, you'll want to know a bit more about a few of the common species. Like the plantings in parks and gardens, many of the creatures have been introduced from other regions of the world and become naturalized here: the **Argentine Ant** (*Linepithema humile*), the **Pillbug** (*Armadillidium vulgare*), and the **Common Earthworm** (*Lumbricus terrestris*), for example.

Non-native species are common in gardens and other disturbed areas. If you bulldoze a vacant lot, the first plants to appear will be the non-native annual grasses, not the natives that grew there before. The same applies to non-native insects and other animals. Humans have excluded native creatures by planting pretty gardens with non-native plants, leaving new niches available for non-native creatures, which often dominate the natives.

Non-native insects, birds, and mammals have adapted well to human habitats. You're going to see some of them in your backyard. To start, envision a journey inside an ant colony.

The Argentine Ant: Introduced from Argentina by boats with sugar and coffee cargo in the late nineteenth and early twentieth centuries, this insect is now established on six continents, including large areas along the Mediterranean and California coastlines.

In our region, trails of tiny, blackish Argentine Ants crawl along the edges of pathways, often near buildings. They nest in moist soil. However, when it rains heavily, these ants may invade kitchen counters and cupboards, seeking a warm, dry place to spend the winter, especially if scraps of food are provided.

If you were an Argentine Ant, you'd be one of an astonishingly successful species…and, you'd be a member of a huge colony. How do you know what to do? What kind of signals do you get from the head of the colony? How do you know where to forage for food? How do you know when an enemy enters the nest?

Guess what? There's no boss in an ant colony. There are queens who lay eggs, but the rest, including you, are workers. Tasks are numerous: patrollers scout the area outside the nest in the morning for food; foragers bring food to the nest; nest maintenance workers construct new tunnels and carry out waste.

Nobody has to tell you what to do. You are equipped with your special genetic signature, broadcast as a pheromone, or odor, so that other ants know that you belong to their colony and not that of strangers. Like all Hymenoptera (ants, bees, and wasps), you're covered with a greasy layer of hydrocarbons. That greasy layer identifies you, and, more importantly,

your task in the colony. You take on the odor of the task you perform. It's your hydrocarbon profile.

As a member of the colony, you use your antennae to communicate, touching hundreds of other ants throughout a typical day. You are part of an interaction network. You react to whatever's going on in the colony. You and the other ants, operating by smell, get the tasks done, whether that means rebuilding the nest after being crushed by a human footstep, or locating the remains of a picnic.

Each moment-to-moment interaction between each ant and others around it makes the colony run. There's no grand oversight or overall plan. Some of the cues are in the environment and others are in the antennae exchanges. Humans call it "control without hierarchy," and it is difficult for us to comprehend.

When you, as an ant, venture outside the nest, your search for food will be based on the number of ants nearby. The presence of lots of ants in the vicinity will cue you to search intensively in that spot—say, under a picnic table. If there aren't many ants nearby, you will travel farther and longer to search for food. As you wander, your pheromone trail will tell other ants where you've been. By following it, they can track you to the new food source.

Because you are an Argentine Ant, your colony is a series of interconnected nests, with trails in between to facilitate transport and communication. However, should you encounter a member of another Argentine Ant colony, one with a different genetic signature, you will not fight. This is not because you're all part of a super-colony (as researchers used to think), but because you do not waste time fighting members of your own kind. Perhaps this is a reason your species is so successful.

Much of the information here about ants was gleaned from Stanford University Professor Deborah Gordon. She has discovered, through her studies of Argentine Ants at the Jasper Ridge Biological Preserve in Northern California, that their impact on native ant communities may be most severe early in the invasion process. Perhaps, in time, native ants will be able to compete with Argentine Ants?

The Common Earthworm: Moving now from our search for Argentine Ant trails, let's stay at ground level and dig around a bit for the Common Earthworm. We have talked about polychaete worms that live in the mud of estuaries (see Chapter 5), but the Common Earthworm is much more familiar. Both belong to the phylum Annelida. The root of the word "Annelida" means ringed, and the name refers to the ringlike body segments of these worms. Each segment of the annelid body looks like the segments before and behind it. It's a very efficient body plan; thousands of worm species inhabit the planet.

The Common Earthworm usually gets our attention after a heavy rain, when many of these reddish-brown wrigglers come to the surface, seemingly stranded on pavements and sidewalks. There's no single explanation for this, but biologists believe that earthworms leave their inundated burrows because the amount of oxygen dissolved in water is less than in air, and therefore they come to the surface to breathe. Or, they may come out of their burrows to search for mates.

Earthworm bodies have a nifty design: a tube within a tube. The long, slimy cylinder that tapers at both ends is the outer tube, and inside that cylinder is another tube that contains the internal organs and the digestive system. They have light-sensitive cells on their outer skin, but no eyes. Simple brains direct the body movement toward light. Earthworms have five hearts, which pump a closed circulatory system of blood vessels. Special organs between the hearts manage the excess calcium in the worms' diet, which they get from eating a lot of dirt. They have no lungs, but breathe oxygen from the air through their skin.

Earthworms move from one place to another by using strong muscles that contract and expand, shortening and lengthening the body after each movement. They maintain permanent underground burrows. When the soil becomes too dry, they curl up in a ball, cover themselves with a mucous cocoon, and estivate until the next rain.

As an earthworm tunnels through the soil, its strong mouthparts eat decayed plant matter, such as leaves and roots, and this passes through the digestive system and comes out as **castings** deposited on the surface. The castings are waste material, full of nutrients and minerals from the soil below that the worm has decomposed. In this way, earthworms are critical to soil health. An earthworm can eat up to one-third its body weight in a day. It's fun to think of these toilers aerat-

Earthworm and sowbug. Unlike the pillbug, the sowbug does not roll up into a ball.

ing the soil by burrowing through it, and improving it simply by eating it.

The downside of the Common Earthworm story is that the species is a non-native introduced from Europe and, as such, has been known to prey on many smaller, less known, native earthworms.

Kids love earthworms. Encourage them to gently handle the worms by saying they tickle when they crawl over your hand. When you explain how important the worms are to plowing up the soil, it's a way of getting rid of the *eeeuuuuwww* reaction which some children—and adults— initially express.

Pillbugs and sowbugs: The roly poly, or pillbug, is another favorite of children. How many critters in a fistful of earth will react immediately to human touch—by rolling up in a ball for protection? The **sowbug** (*Porcellio* spp.) is flatter, larger, and paler

gray and has two taillike structures at the rear of its body. It doesn't roll up into a ball.

Both pillbugs and sowbugs are from the order Isopoda, so they aren't true bugs at all. They belong to the big Arthropod phyllum, which also contains the crustaceans with jointed exoskeletons, like lobsters and

Pillbug

shrimps. Pillbugs and sowbugs are related to the beach hoppers we studied on the sandy beach (Chapter 4).

The majority of the isopods live in the ocean. When they moved onto land, the pillbugs and sowbugs had to adapt to breathing air. They breathe through the underside of their abdomen by exchanging oxygen through special organs. They retain water in their bodies by recycling their digestive fluids and urine. In order to keep their bodies moist, they seek damp environments—under logs, flowerpots, rotting boards—and usually move about at night or on rainy days.

Pillbugs and sowbugs feed on decayed organic litter. They are omnivorous; some gardeners consider them pests because they eat shoots of young plants, but they don't do much damage. And sowbugs do have one trait that endears them to soil analysts: they have the ability to store very high concentrations of metals in their bodies, which can be monitored to study metal contamination of various environments.

Sowbugs and pillbugs have little pouches in which they hold their eggs and protect their young. After the young leave the pouch, they go through a series of molts and become full-grown in a year. Their lifespan is two to three years.

The Brown Garden Snail: There are days when you take a child outside looking for interesting critters and all you can come up with is a **Brown Garden Snail** (*Helix aspersa*). So be it! The snail is worth collecting in a jar for studying purposes.

The Brown Garden Snail was introduced from France into California in the 1850s for fine dining purposes. This escargot may be considered a garden pest because it feeds on vegetables and ornamentals, but it's an excellent example of the class Gastropoda, the snails. Most gastropods are aquatic, but those on land have had to adapt to dry conditions. Every land snail has a large, muscular foot that constantly secretes slimy mucus. The mucus prevents body moisture from being absorbed by the dry ground, and it protects the snail's large foot from sharp objects. It is said that a snail can crawl across a razor without being cut.

The globular shell sculpted into brown spiral bands provides an excellent home for the snail, into which it withdraws when disturbed.

Snails are active at night and on rainy days. During the dry season or in cold weather, they seal themselves up with a thin membrane and attach to tree trunks or fences. Like estivating earthworms, snails can slow down their body processes, then start up again when weather conditions improve.

In our region, large populations of Brown Garden Snails sometimes become established in citrus groves, where they may cause serious damage. Another non-native snail, the **Decollate Snail** (*Rumina decollata*), has been introduced as a biological control on Brown Garden Snails in citrus crops. Although Decollate Snails are voracious predators, feeding on the young and eggs of Brown Garden Snails, they also consume harmless land snails and earthworms, which are beneficial. For this reason, Decollate Snails cannot be released in

The Jerusalem cricket may be parasitized by horsehair worms.

certain California counties. In Santa Barbara and Ventura they are legal, but not in San Luis Obispo County.

The Jerusalem cricket: Another ground dweller—this one a native—that can be seen after a spring rain or by digging in moist soil is the two-inch-long **Jerusalem cricket** (*Stenopelmatus* spp.). These amber-colored crickets are known by several names—"children of the earth" (niñas de la tierra), "sand crickets," and "potato bugs." Due to their large size and rather human-looking heads, Jerusalem crickets have intrigued many an amateur insect observer.

Jerusalem crickets are not poisonous, but they have strong jaws and a nasty bite, so be careful when capturing them to study. For food, they scavenge dead plants and animal matter in the soil, as well as cannibalizing live insects.

In spring, Jerusalem crickets begin drumming with their abdomens against their burrows to lure a mate to the surface. Often, intense wrestling matches ensue between the sexes; after mating, the females frequently kill and devour the males. The female lays her eggs in a little nest in the soil and the immatures may molt as many as ten times before becoming adults.

From here, the story of the Jerusalem cricket takes a strange twist. The cricket is sometimes host to a parasite that looks like a long piece of string, the **horsehair worm** (*Gordia* spp.). When you see your first horsehair worm, it will likely be in a puddle of rainwater or a swimming pool.

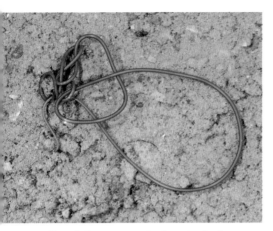

Horsehair worms can be found wriggling around watery habitats once they have emerged from their hosts.

While much of its life cycle is still not completely understood, we do know that the horsehair worm, which can be as long as two feet but is usually shorter, is destined to live and grow inside its host, in this case a Jerusalem cricket.

The story goes like this: male and female worms mate in the water, after which eggs are deposited. When the larvae hatch, somehow they make their way toward land, either by fastening onto vegetation or by burrowing into an aquatic insect as an intermediate host. When the aquatic insect matures and flies to land, it gets eaten by a Jersualem cricket, the final host.

Once the intermediate host has been eaten, the parasitic horsehair worm larva lives and grows inside the digestive system of the Jerusalem cricket. As it feeds on the organs of the cricket, the larval worm eventually drives the cricket to seek out water. When the Jerusalem cricket has arrived at a creek, a rain puddle, or a watering trough, the horsehair worm breaks out, and the cricket dies. The

worm then goes on to live a brief life in the water, mate, and produce eggs, and the cycle begins again.

Although horsehair worms parasitize grasshoppers, beetles, and other crickets, the Jerusalem cricket is the most common host.

In One Cubic Foot of Soil...

So far, we've been talking about the macrofauna in the soil, the big creatures you can see without a microscope.

But to get an idea of the biodiversity in a chunk of soil, give a child a spoon or shovel. Go out in the backyard or to a park and dig in the dirt. Bring home a chunk of the soil and scatter it on a white piece of paper. Have a magnifying glass handy.

Accept the fact that you're only going to see a fraction of the centipedes, millipedes, mites, springtails (see Chapter 7), and nematodes that call the soil home. If you could observe all of them, you'd be counting thousands of organisms—including those invisible to the human eye, the bacteria. Microbiologists are fairly certain that a single spoonful of soil can contain ten thousand different species of bacteria, many of them new to science.

To quote E. O. Wilson in a recent *National Geographic* magazine article (February 2010) entitled "In a Cubic Foot of Soil":

It may seem the whole icky lot of them, and the miniature realms they inhabit, are unrelated to human concerns. But scientists have found the exact opposite to be true....The entire ground habitat is alive....Through their bodies pass the cycles of chemical reactions upon which all of life depends.

Soil creatures are some of the most abundant animals in the world. Living between and among grains of soil, these organisms may be scavengers, predators, or parasites. Essential to the processing of soil, this collection of organisms is at the heart of life on earth because it enables plants to photosynthesize.

Even if you don't have a microscope, you and a youngster can use a magnifying glass to sort through the pin-prick mites, the miniature roundworms (nematodes)—related to horsehair worms—and the many-legged centipedes and millipedes. The pile of soil is alive with creepy crawlies. If you don't know their names, so what? Sharp-eyed children will spot their dif-ferences; the diversity is mind-boggling.

A spade and a magnifying glass can introduce children to a realm of underground dwellers. They just need to get dirty and get outside!

Aquatic Creatures of Backyards and Parks

Visitors to urban habitats with freshwater features such as ponds or creeks always notice the turtles, especially if they're basking on the shoreline. Kids love turtles and if they can find tadpoles too, so much the better.

We learned in Chapter 9 that the presence of water is vital to wildlife. And, since wetlands are rare in our region, those that are located near humans are under great stress from pollution and human interferences.

Freshwater ponds, creeks, and streams in an urban setting are fragile.

Red-eared Sliders—non-native turtles—are common in urban parks.

The Pacific Pond Turtle is our only native freshwater turtle.

They are prone to problems that arise with the introduction of non-native plants and animals. Similar to the reaction to colonization on the Channel Islands, the response to change on these "islands" of fragile wetland is immediate.

The Red-eared Slider: When owners get tired of keeping pet fish, turtles, or frogs in an aquarium at home, they go to the nearest wetland and dump them in the water. For example, at the Andree Clark Bird Refuge in Santa Barbara, a non-native turtle, the **Red-eared Slider** (*Trachemys scripta*), was released years ago and has now spread rapidly throughout the region.

Well-meaning owners think they are doing the right thing by releasing an unwanted pet, but they are doing the exact opposite. Releasing non-native animals into native ecosystems can kill them, promote the spread of disease, or result in the establishment of an introduced species with unknown consequences. If you're no longer able to care for a captive pet,

call a rescue organization for help. In our area, please contact the Santa Barbara Wildlife Care Network or Turtle Dreams for assistance. Do not release pet fish, turtles, frogs, or any other animal on your own.

The Red-eared Slider, a handsome creature with a broad, reddish stripe behind each eye, is the turtle commonly found in our reservoirs, ponds, and urban creeks. From Michigan south to Texas and Louisiana there are three native slider subspecies. However, in Oregon, California, and Arizona, as well as some states in the northeast and in Florida, this non-native subspecies and others have been introduced. And sliders are still being raised on turtle farms and exported to countries around the world. (Another introduced turtle, the **Painted Turtle** (*Chrysemys picta*), can be found at Lake Los Carneros in Santa Barbara County.)

Pacific Pond Turtle: Meanwhile, California's only native freshwater turtle, the Pacific Pond Turtle, is declining in our region and has been listed as a species of special concern by the California Department of Fish and Wildlife. Pond turtles are found basking on the edges of ponds, lakes, rivers, streams, and irrigation ditches. They're generally smaller than Red-eared Sliders and their spotted heads do not have red patches.

During heavy winter storms, pond turtles can be washed down creeks and end up on open roads or on the beach far from their established homes. If you want to help rescue a turtle in distress, remember that it's illegal to possess this species. Be sure to call one of the wildlife organizations mentioned above.

Bullfrogs are native to North America east of the Rockies and have been introduced throughout the West.

Studies have shown that Pacific Pond Turtles in our region mature earlier than those found in the colder climates of Oregon and Washington. Here, a female turtle reaches reproductive age at about four years. Nesting begins in April, when she travels away from the water, sometimes hundreds of feet, to search for a suitable site at which to lay her eggs. In the late afternoon she leaves the creek, seeking a grassy open area with a southern exposure. She spends the night ashore, digging a shallow hole in the ground and laying the eggs. After covering the nest with dirt, the pond turtle returns to the water. Turtle eggs incubate in the warm earth on their own; most require 80 to 120 days to hatch. Incubation temperature dictates the sex of the hatch-lings: males are produced at incubation temperatures below about 86°F, females at higher temperatures. Pond turtle hatchlings, barely an inch long, emerge in late summer. Their greatest predator is the bullfrog.

The Bullfrog: A species that is familiar to all of us, the **Bullfrog** (*Lithobates catesbeiana*) produces the gastronomic delight known as "frog's legs." Native to North America east of the Rockies, the bullfrog has been introduced throughout the West, where it has done well. Paradoxically, the bullfrog appears to be declining in some of its native range while expanding in the West. Bullfrogs live in artificial aquatic habitats, such as agricultural ponds and reservoirs, as well as in a number of rivers and streams in our region. Because they thrive in calm,

Mosquitofish have been introduced to control mosquitoes but, unfortunately, they may escape into native streams.

stagnant water, the creation of ponds on farms and golf courses has provided even better habitat for them than occurs naturally.

The bullfrog—our biggest frog—can reach eight inches in length. They lie submerged in the water, with only their eyes peeking above the surface. To quote from a species account by Gary S. Casper and Russ Hendricks in Michael Lannoo's *Amphibian Declines*, "Adult bullfrogs are voracious, opportunistic predators that employ a sit-and-wait approach and will readily attack any live animal smaller than themselves." In the book, the list of prey items reported for adult bullfrogs fills almost a whole page, beginning with insects and continuing through salamanders, tadpoles, other frogs, fish, turtles, lizards, snakes, rats, voles, bats, and birds.

Bullfrog eggs, tadpoles, and juveniles are in turn preyed upon by birds and a variety of mammals, from raccoons to humans (bullfrogs are a game species in many states). However, the bullfrog, even as a tadpole, is unpalatable to most species of fish, which

is a great protection for the frog. Nevertheless, the adults, when at rest, are very alert. They react immediately when disturbed, making long leaps into deeper water to escape. They utter a loud squawk when fleeing, which warns all the other bullfrogs of danger and initiates an immediate exodus from the shoreline.

Although there's a tendency to blame the bullfrog for declines in populations of native frogs (such as the endangered California Red-legged Frog), it has not been conclusively proven that bullfrogs are solely responsible. Other factors such as habitat alteration and the introduction of predatory fish are equally destructive. One interesting experiment by UC Santa Barbara scientists explored the hypothesis that frequent floods help the Red-legged Frogs and increase the mortality of bullfrogs. During years of heavy rains, the two species may be able to coexist in the same watershed. In addition, the study showed that draining livestock grazing ponds every two years can be effective in controlling bullfrog population density.

When it comes to fish, there are all sorts of examples of the introduction of a non-native species resulting in long-term, unforeseen consequences. For example, the **Mosquitofish** (*Gambusia affinis*), native to the southern and eastern portions of the US, was brought to California as early as 1922. Introduced to control mosquito larvae in ornamental ponds, Mosquitofish should never have been placed in natural aquatic ecosystems here. But, of course, they have escaped into our creeks and rivers, where they prey on more than just mosquito larvae, eating the eggs and larvae of important native amphibians. Recent studies implicate Mosquitofish in declines of the California Newt, Baja California Tree Frog, and **California Tree Frog** (*Pseudacris cadaverina*).

Birds of Backyards and Parks

Perhaps more than any other wild animal, birds have embraced human habitats. Many species have adapted well to life in our backyards and parks.

Luring birds to your garden with feeders and birdbaths is one of the delights of the backyard. Young children, with their keen eyes, are good birdwatchers. They don't even need binoculars, just some encouragement and curiosity. Start early and make a game out of finding new birds that visit the garden. When common birds come to feed on a lawn at a neighborhood park, if you have a child along be sure to name the birds. Looking for new birds is like a treasure hunt, and this entices a youngster!

Spotted Towhee, another of the native birds that are attracted to non-native plantings in parks and gardens

In the coastal communities of our region, where winter temperatures are mild, an enormous variety of birds can be found. Birds do well in the urban mix, often dining on the nectar and fruit from non-native ornamental plantings and using nearby dense shrubbery for cover.

Moreover, several kinds of non-native plants introduced from South Africa or Australia bloom in fall and winter, serving as important sustenance for migrating and wintering birds at a time of year when many native plants are not in bloom.

Increasingly, several species of migratory birds remain in our region

White-crowned Sparrow, a common winter visitor to urban parks and gardens

Great Egret by San Luis Obispo Creek where the creek meanders through downtown San Luis Obispo

Bullock's Orioles feed on nectar and insects found at eucalyptus trees.

rather than completing their journeys to Central America. Some hummingbirds, warblers, tanagers, and orioles—lured by plentiful food in parks and gardens—stop to spend the winter here instead. They are joined by the typical winter visitors, such as **White-crowned Sparrows** (*Zonotrichia leucophrys*) and Yellow-rumped Warblers, which are at home in urban landscapes. Hedges of orange-flowering Cape Honeysuckle and the trees of **Red Bottlebrush** (*Callistemon citrinus*) attract birds to sip nectar from their colorful blossoms.

Christmas Bird Counts in Morro Bay, Santa Barbara, and Ventura have tallied impressive numbers of bird species in twenty-four-hour periods, often in the top five in the nation. This annual census, begun as an alternative to shooting birds—a customary celebration at the turn of the century—has become a tool for mon-

Hooded Orioles use the fibers of palm fronds to construct pendant nests. Photo by Robert Goodell

itoring bird populations in winter throughout the country.

In spring and summer, non-native plantings can provide nesting and roosting spots in backyards and parks. Tall Blue Gum Eucalyptus trees offer good nesting sites for birds

413

This female Allen's Hummingbird nested a foot away from a bedroom window in a Carpinteria garden.

of prey, including **Cooper's Hawks** (*Accipiter cooperii*), **Red-tailed Hawks** (*Buteo jamaicensis*), and **Red-shouldered Hawks** (*Buteo lineatus*). At Goleta Beach and at Morro Bay, Great Blue Herons and Great Egrets have nested in groves of Blue Gum Eucalyptus for decades. Black-crowned Night-Herons and **Snowy Egrets** (*Egretta thula*) use **Weeping Fig** (*Ficus benjamina*), a native of Southeast Asia, for nesting colonies. **Great Horned Owls** (*Bubo virginiensis*) and **Barn Owls** (*Tyto alba*) regularly nest in the fronds in the center of **California Fan Palms** (*Washingtonia filifera*).

Gorgeous yellow-and-black **Hooded Orioles** (*Icterus cucullatus*) gather fibers from the fan palms, from which they weave their hanging nests. The Hooded Oriole pierces the slender frond, then attaches the fibrous pouch by actually stitching the nest to the frond with its sharp bill. You can find oriole nests by looking on the undersides of the dead, shaggy skirts of untrimmed palm trees. The nest is a pale, pendulant orb of fibers.

Migrant and resident hummingbirds feed on a wide variety of native and non-native species of **sage** (*Salvia* spp.), as well as other garden flowers.

The first birds a novice will notice are likely to be the most common. A few are non-native species that have successfully filled the niches around human settlements. For example, the **European Starling** (*Sturnus vulgaris*), the most successful non-native bird in the United States, is a medium-sized, glossy, black bird with a yellow bill. Starlings have adapted so well to human surroundings that they can be found almost anywhere.

414

The Canyon Wren often nests in human-made structures. This nest was in the barn at Arroyo Hondo Preserve.

The story of the introduction of the European Starling is a perfect illustration of how good intentions can go awry.

"And a starling shall be taught to speak." These words from Shakespeare's *Henry IV, Part I* are responsible for every one of the estimated two hundred million starlings that now inhabit the US.

Eugene Schieffelin, a wealthy New Yorker and admirer of Shakespeare, wanted each of the birds mentioned in Shakespeare's plays to live in New York City. Throughout the late nineteenth century, Schieffelin attempted to introduce bird after bird. He was unsuccessful, however, until 1890, when he imported eighty starlings from England. The next year he imported forty more. Every starling you see is a descendant of these birds.

Today starlings are considered a nuisance because they aggressively rob native birds, such as bluebirds and woodpeckers, of potential nesting cavities.

Another bird that has adapted extremely well to human habitation is the **American Crow** (*Corvus brachyrhynchos*), which is a native species. A crow is twice the size of a starling. It's black and it's loud—the *"caw, caw, caw"* call as they fly overhead in a noisy group is familiar to everyone. Members of the family Corvidae, crows are wary, observant, and smart. Having been shot and persecuted in the nineteenth and early twentieth centuries, crows moved from the countryside to urban landscapes, where people do not shoot at them. Like jays and magpies, crows can figure out unfamiliar situations and learn to exploit them for food.

The **House Sparrow** (*Passer domesticus*) and **Rock Pigeon** (*Columba livia*), both introduced from Europe, are hard to miss in downtown areas. But once you get out of the city centers and into suburban habitats, you will find an astonishing number of native birds

Birds that eat seeds, such as grosbeaks, sparrows, and finches, will come to seed feeders; those that don't eat seeds will come readily to water. A dripping faucet, a birdbath, or a recirculating water feature in your backyard will bring tanagers and warblers up close so you can watch them drink and bathe.

Mammals of Backyards and Parks

A few mammals are often seen in backyards: the **Brush Rabbit** (*Sylvilagus bachmani*) and the **Eastern Fox Squirrel** (*Sciurus niger*) are the most common. Rabbit populations are unnaturally high in parks and backyards, where they are protected from their natural enemies, such as hawks, Bobcats, foxes, and Coyotes.

Eastern Fox Squirrels are now aggressively competing with Western Gray Squirrels for urban territories in our region. Fox squirrels were introduced in Los Angeles in 1904, and by 1947 they had spread throughout the Los Angeles Basin. Fox squirrels generally prefer more open habitats than gray squirrels and can often be found foraging on the ground, although they are good climbers, too, and could be a threat to nesting birds.

Except for rabbits and squirrels, most mammals that live near humans hide during daylight hours. They are difficult to observe in backyards or neighborhood parks because they venture out to forage only at night. Orchard fruits, insect-rich garden soil, lush green lawns, and ponds stocked with goldfish or koi provide an easy meal for the Striped Skunk, Northern Raccoon, and Virginia Opossum.

You will see traces of their activities, but it may take a while before you meet them face to face. The paw print in a muddy path, a lingering unpleasant odor under the deck, half-eaten oranges lying on the ground in the orchard, a flower bed dug up...the night visitors have been at work.

Let's set up an imaginary observation post on the patio. Pull up a chair and pretend you have night-vision goggles on. The scenario might go something like this.

Night in the Backyard

When dusk falls and night settles slowly over suburban yards and gardens, nocturnal animals become active.

The first to visit the backyard is a female skunk. She's ambled up the creek bank, headed for the nearest patch of lawn in this backyard that borders a greenbelt. The skunk has left behind three young kits in her den under a thick bundle of brush. At the base of the brush pile, the young kits will lie blind and helpless until they're weaned, in another two months.

Momma skunk moves deliberately, with the gait of a creature who has few enemies. Her black-and-white coat is a sharp warning to other animals, but they already sense she's approaching, by the slight odor coming from her anal scent glands.

The Brush Rabbit seeks shelter in backyards and parks.

Then, a dark shadow flies silently through the trees above the skunk—the Great Horned Owl, the skunk's only serious predator, shows no interest in taking on Momma tonight. Besides, the Great Horned Owl's sense of smell is so poor it certainly has not been alerted by any odor.

Reaching the backyard, the skunk begins the serious business of searching for food. She's hungry. The lawn sprinklers have just been through their cycle and the grass is wet, the soil underneath moist. She digs little pits in the lawn, nosing out the grubs and earthworms that have come to the surface.

As the night progresses and the skunk makes her way towards a nearby hedge and searches for the nests of ground-laying birds, which might be filled with eggs this time of year, another animal appears in the backyard. A raccoon crawls out from behind the old outbuilding where the firewood is stored.

The raccoon, an immature male living on his own, has experience with the goldfish in the garden pond here. They're easy to catch if he waits long enough.

The masked face pattern of the raccoon fools humans into thinking it could be a cuddly pet. Nothing could be further from the truth.

Like all raccoons, this animal bites.

The Great Horned Owl often preys on skunks in urban areas. Photo by Peter Gaede

Although it will search near the back of the house for an open garbage can or two and may enter through a cat door if it smells pet food, you would not want a raccoon—so beautiful in the wild—as a pet.

The raccoon's feet feel the prickly gravel on the path, and it sidles over to the paving stones that surround the artificial pond. From here, it jumps up to the lip of the pond. For appetizers, the raccoon snatches two or three garden snails, shucks them, and pops them into his mouth.

With his extraordinarily tactile front paws, the young raccoon dips into the pond. Tiny hairs located above the claws help the animal feel the slightest movement in the water. His sense of touch, like that of all raccoons, is highly developed.

Flip, splash...got it. The raccoon holds tightly to the slithering gold-fish. When the fish stops struggling, the masked bandit raises its paws to its mouth, and in one gulp, the fish is gone. (Myth: Raccoons have no saliva. Fact: Raccoons frequently feed near water but they have plenty of saliva.)

Next, the raccoon heads for the fruit orchard. The plums have grown ripe and sweet and the raccoon will visit that food source.

Quickly scaling the four-foot-high fence around the orchard, the animal heads towards the largest tree, the one with the most ripe fruit. But the fruit is at the top of the tree, so up goes the bandit. He's almost there when a loud hiss and a faceful of bared teeth greet him.

A possum has got there first.

The possum, a female with young, is in no state to be disturbed, and the raccoon turns around and scuttles back down the trunk in retreat. Raccoons have the unique ability to climb down a tree headfirst; they can rotate their hind feet so they point backward, which brakes their downward momentum.

Meanwhile, the possum, who carries her twelve young snuggled in the furry pouch underneath her abdomen, quickly resumes munching on the ripe plum. When she's finished, she will climb along the branch and down the tree, using her prehensile (grasping) tail and the opposable "thumbs" on her back paws for balance.

The possum, which looks so much like a giant rat, is no relative of rodents. It's a marsupial, the only one native to North America (but not native to the West, however). In some parts of the country it is considered a game animal and hunted for food.

This particular possum has all the wily skills of an animal accustomed to living near humans. Before dawn, she will retreat to a hollow in an oak tree in the vacant lot next door. But first, she has to check out the compost pile for leftover scraps of food.

In the meantime, Momma skunk has been quietly meandering through the flower beds, garnering whatever snails, insects, and grubs she can find, her fluffy tail waving from side to side amid the flowers.

Suddenly, the patio door opens and out comes the homeowner, bouncing golden retriever at his side, patio lights glaring. At once, Momma skunk becomes confused. She can't see well, but she senses the approach of the curious dog. The dog's a puppy, and naturally it will investigate this strange black-and-white visitor to the garden.

With shrill cries of dismay, the owner tries in vain to head off the pet dog. Momma skunk, unable to see her victim but certain she is in danger, turns her back, stamps her feet, hisses, and holds her tail high. No question, she's about to spray.

Just in time, the dog turns on a dime and runs as fast as it can back up onto the patio to the frantic human, who sees where this encounter is going.

And, just in time, the dog has averted a very nasty situation! Skunks can spray from as far away as ten feet and their accuracy is good. As any who've had this experience know, the smell of the chemicals in the spray is like burnt rubber and rotten eggs mixed together.

Skunks are reluctant to spray immediately. But when they do, they can spray more than once, either in a fine mist or a targeted stream of musk.

With all the commotion, the raccoon has scuttled off over the orchard fence and hidden in the closest hedge. He'll be back when the situation calms down. After all, his ability to deal with sealed garbage cans has not yet been tested tonight.

And it is considerable. A couple of scientific studies have shown raccoons to be adept at taking the lids off a variety of container types.

Meanwhile, as the night wears on, lingering into dawn, the female possum nibbles away at the cantaloupe rinds and rotten vegetables she's located in the compost pile.

When daylight comes, the possum, the raccoon, and the skunk fade slowly away from the backyard, retreating to dens and hiding places.

They are not pests, they're just smart. They are looking for food, and humans have made it easy for them. Please do not approach or handle these wild animals.

Night Sounds in the Backyard

At night in the backyard, the smallest creatures make the loudest noises. Aside from the frog chorus (see Chapter 9), there's another night chorus—that of the **tree crickets** (*Oecanthus* spp.). When it's warm, the tree crickets chirp steadily, *"treet-treet-treet,"* on and on and on. Their constant rhythmic pulses reflect the temperature of the surrounding air. The warmer the temperature, the faster they chirp.

The rhythmic symphony of tree crickets on a summer night is a beautiful sound.

Scientific studies have been conducted on certain species of tree cricket that suggest actual formulas for calculating the air temperature from the number of chirps per minute. It works, but it's difficult to do with the faster-chirping species. One formula calls for counting the number of chirps in 14 seconds and then adding 40 to that. So if you heard 25 chirps in 14 seconds, the temperature would be about 65°F.

Only the males call; holding their forewings overhead, they rub a file-like vein at the base of one forewing over the hard surface of the other, and the sound is amplified as the papery parts of their wings vibrate, creating a pulsing trill. The females, equipped with special membranous tissues, are able to detect the males' calls and locate them. The insistent chirping of the tree cricket does not make it any easier

for human ears to locate it, because the sound is ventriloquial and the cricket is small. But female crickets have no problem locating the males.

Related to the tree cricket and the grasshopper in the order Orthoptera, the **House Cricket** (*Acheta domesticus*) sometimes gets into houses and buildings. They hide in cracks and corners, giving away their location by a softer chirping noise. This cricket is usually not part of the night chorus in the backyard.

More Nighttime Visitors: Bats

Other night visitors to the backyard arrive on wings...and they aren't birds. These are the bats—those dark silhouettes that swoop down over the grass or flitter above the trees. When they hunt, their flight pattern is erratic, and they make no sounds that human ears can hear.

The building where these Townsend's Big-eared Bats were photographed was later torn down. Where did the bats go?

Their marvelous lifestyle is completely unique and worth learning about.

First, forget all the stereotypes you've ever heard about bats.

They carry rabies? Yes—only one-half of one percent of bats contract rabies. Recent survey work in California indicates that one in a thousand bats may be incubating rabies; the infected animal will soon become paralyzed and die. Skunk populations have a higher ratio of carrying rabies than do bats. The rule is to never pick up a wild animal that appears to be sick or dying, whether it's a bat, a skunk, a raccoon, or anything else. Be sure your pet dogs and cats are vaccinated against rabies. They are the ones most likely to come in contact with wildlife.

Bats "attack" people at night by fly-ing too close? Not at all. Just because a bat is pursuing an insect—that you can't see—over your head doesn't mean the animal is attacking you. It has located an insect and is chasing the food, not the human.

Don't we have vampire bats that suck human blood? No and no. There are no vampire bats in North America. Three species are found in Mexico, Central America, and South America. They feed on the blood of animals, mostly birds, by inflicting a wound. In the US, there's been only one record of a vampire bat, a wanderer which was captured in Texas, 430 miles north of its usual range in Mexico. So...forget about vampire bats in your backyard; this is part of the misconception that has engendered an irrational fear of bats on the

421

part of the average person. It's time to drop the panicky reaction when you see a bat. Bats are fantastic—not scary.

In our region these beneficial insectivores feed on the multitudinous night-flying insects that swarm in the summer air. An individual bat can catch up to six hundred mosquitoes in an hour; large colonies of bats consume countless billions of insects such as beetles, moths, and many kinds of crop pests. Although there are marked differences in diet depending upon the bat species, all are opportunistic, taking advantage of the hatching period for a particular insect, such as winged termites or caddisflies.

Interestingly, bats sort themselves out in the air column, so that some fly closer to the ground, some fly at a medium height amid the tree canopy, and others go as high as fifteen hundred feet in their nightly searches for food. For example, **Townsend's Big-eared Bats** (*Corynorhinus townsendii*) forage almost exclusively along creek beds by gleaning moths from the foliage of riparian vegetation. **Big Brown Bats** (*Eptesicus fuscus*) forage several yards above the ground, pursuing beetles, stinkbugs, and leafhoppers. **California Myotis** (*Myotis californicus*) come out before dark to feed on small insects they detect near the foliage of oak trees or along riparian corridors.

Bats are like humans: they're mammals that give birth to live young which they nurse. But they are unique and have been placed in a mammalian group of their own, the Chiroptera, meaning "hand-wing." The bones of the bat's wing are equivalent to those of the human arm and

hand, but bat finger bones are elongated and connected by a membrane of skin that forms the wing. Another membrane connects the feet and tail. Although most bats capture insects in their mouths, some use their wing and tail membranes to scoop up insects, which they then reach down and take into their mouths while in flight.

Biologists are just beginning to understand the complexities of **echolocation**, which is how bats navigate at high speeds in total darkness. Echolocation is a thousand times more sophisticated than our fastest computers. The bat emits a series of sounds such as beeps or clicks—their frequencies too high for us to hear—and then judges the location of the echoes that bounce back to its ears. In this way, bats negotiate tricky obstacles or find where the nearest prey is located.

Recently, scientists have discovered a key structural feature of bats that may shed some light on how echolocation works. By taking 3-D images (CT scans) of the bats, they found that a bat's larynx (voice box) is connected to the tympanic bone of the bat's ear. This might help the bat perceive the outgoing signal and perhaps dampen the vibrations to prevent the bat from deafening itself with the sound it produces, which can be one hundred times louder than the reflected echoes.

In another study, scientists showed that bats are able to differentiate the ultrasonic echolocation calls that other bats make as they navigate. Each bat emits calls within a limited range of frequencies, probably as a result of differences in vocal chords. It's like being able to recognize a per-

Tiger moths emit signals that confuse bats' echolocation systems, allowing the moths to escape predation.

son by his or her voice. This would explain why bats don't collide with each other while they're hunting in the dark.

However, in the evolutionary arms race between bats and insects, some insects have developed a defensive repertoire. Moths, crickets, and praying mantids have anti-bat mechanisms to avoid predation: they can hear the ultrasonic sounds emitted by hunting bats. For example, **tiger moths** (Family Arctiidae) and **owlet moths** (Family Noctuidae) possess special tympanums, or "ears," located below the hind wings on their thoraxes. The moths use these structures to measure the distance and intensity of bat echolocation calls, and then they take evasive action when the bat approaches. Furthermore, a study with a tiger moth species found

that the moths emitted signals that could "jam" the bats' sonar. By using ultrasonic clicks, this tiger moth discouraged Big Brown Bats, which ultimately stopped attacking it.

But the bats are fighting back. One of the bats in our area, Townsend's Big-eared Bat, feeds exclusively on moths. Its echolocation calls are softer than those of other bats in order to help it sneak up on moths without being heard.

Over twenty species of bats have been known to occur in the Santa Barbara region. A few only migrate through, others are represented in small numbers. The three most common are the Brazilian Free-tailed Bat, the Big Brown Bat, and the California Myotis.

Let's concentrate on the Brazilian Free-tailed Bat (the southwestern subspecies is often called the Mexican Free-tailed Bat). With a wingspan of twelve to fourteen inches, this species is bigger than the California Myotis and smaller than the Big Brown Bat. Free-tailed bats are so named because at least a third of their tail protrudes beyond the tail membrane.

Brazilian Free-tailed Bats are colonial. In Texas, they gather in huge roosts of up to twenty million in certain caves. In our region aggregations are much smaller. The Brazilian Free-tailed is the bat most likely to be found in buildings, bridges, abandoned mines, and other such structures. They are quite tolerant of urban settings.

This species mates in February and March, giving birth in June. While the mother is hanging head downward, the birth occurs. The young are hairless but have all their milk teeth. Huddled together in tightly packed colonies, the mothers and babies elevate the temperature of the roost, which helps the young bats grow. Despite incredible population densities, mothers returning to the colony after hunting can pinpoint the location of their young within a few inches: each youngster recognizes its mother's voice and calls out to her. Free-tail pups drink almost 30 percent of their body weight in milk daily. Their first flight takes place in about five weeks.

Brazilian Free-tails are aerial foragers and feed on a wide variety of flying insects. They eat flies, moths, plant hoppers, and beetles—many of which are agricultural pests. They also take midges and mosquitoes from the surface of water.

Most bats go into hibernation or migrate south in the winter. Brazilian Free-tails in our region, however, are present year-round, although they may go into torpor as the weather gets colder. Those that roost in the crevices of concrete bridges simply move upwards in the cracks so that they can absorb the warmth generated by the pavement above them. It is difficult to tell if they remain in their maternal roosts, or if they move to other roosting sites during the winter.

An exhaustive study of our regional bat fauna was conducted at Vandenberg Air Force Base by Paul Collins of the Santa Barbara Museum of Natural History and others. The study found ninety-eight bat roost sites and ten bat species on the base, with one or more of the seven most common species found on each roost.

In his 2002 report, Collins discussed other bat sites in our region as well. In San Luis Obispo County bat roosts have been reported at San Simeon State Park (Hearst Castle and San Simeon Creek). At structures scheduled for demolition at Camp Roberts near Paso Robles, eight species of bats were found roosting in fifty-five buildings.

One of the biggest roosts in Santa Barbara County is at the old Garey Bridge over the Santa Maria River, where over five thousand Brazilian Free-tailed Bats have a large colony.

In Ventura County, at the Main Street Bridge over the lower Ventura River, Big Brown Bats and **Yuma Myotis** (*Myotis yumanensis*) roost in a large aggregation of more than one thousand individuals.

Nature Journal
August 25, 2011

Tucker's Grove Bat Roost

Brazilian Free-tailed Bats leave their summer roost underneath a bridge near Tucker's Grove, flying out at dusk.

On a clear summer evening with twilight approaching, I arrive at Tucker's Grove County Park in Goleta. The park is packed with unsuspecting families having dinner and playing portable radios. If only they knew what I know: a famous bat roost lies yards away.

For years, bats have roosted here, underneath a bridge over Cathedral Oaks Road. The bats crawl up inside the concrete crevices of the structure. It's similar to a cave, but it's man-made.

This is a maternity roost, where females gather to give birth to their young. Males roost elsewhere.

Every night, over five hundred bats fly out at dusk to zigzag high in the sky above Goleta Valley backyards, searching for insects.

Stuart and I climb down into the dry creek bed and set up our camp chairs. The smell of bat urine and guano is strong. It's characteristic of Brazilian Free-tailed Bats, which make up the majority of the bats at this roost. They're joined by a few California Myotis and Big Brown Bats.

The loud squeaks and twitters of the bats' social calls issue from the grooves in the cement in the bridge over our heads. The bats are anticipating their night flight; hungry and agitated, they call to one another. Unlike the echolocation calls they'll use later on tonight to find insects when hunting, these social calls are easy for the human ear to pick up.

The bats' twittering gets louder and louder as the sky grows darker. It's past sunset, and I keep looking at my watch, wondering when they will begin to fly out of their concrete crevices.

The camera is all set up: it's focused on a wedge of sky backlit by the waning light. Surely we'll see something?

And then, not all in a mass, but one by one, the bats begin their outflight. They fly so fast that they're out and gone almost before we can click the camera. Bing, bang, bang, bing, out they go. Then a cluster of bats departs. Then a trio. Gradually, the numbers in the roost dwindle. The twitters and squeaks over our heads quiet down.

Group by group, darting and dodging, the bats fly quickly out into the dusk. They have a hard night's work ahead of them.

We notice that some even fly back into the roost again after going out. We aren't sure why. Perhaps they're the young of the year and they're unsure on their "first night out"?

We stay until dark has come. Slowly, we collect our equipment and leave.

If we could only count the number of insects each bat consumes in a night, we could convince people that bats are crucial to the natural world. In other parts of *the Southwest, bats eat fruit and nectar, but here, feeding in the dark, navigating by echoes, these flying mammals are able to sustain themselves on insects alone.*

It's so simple and so important: this historic bat roost, so close to humans. And yet who knew? Who knew that just steps from a public park, a thriving bat colony goes about its business of sweeping the night skies clear of all those annoying mosquitoes?

* * *

The urban habitat is a place where the pressures of a human population constantly push against the boundaries of wildness. At the same time, wild things cross over the interface into the urban mix.

The author and her grandchildren at a back-yard pond

We see this back-and-forth aspect of the natural world in our backyards and neighborhood parks.

Our mild winter climate and proximity to the coast throughout much of the region foster an exceptionally rich urban flora. Everything grows here. It's easy for native and non-native plants to gain a foothold in our backyards and vacant lots. Trees and shrubs from all over the world, but particularly those from a similar Mediterranean climate, have become established. This fertile mix of urban plantings and bits and pieces of wilderness creates the extraordinary beauty of the region, for which it is famous.

Moreover, we can go outside almost every day of the year and discover what nature has to offer.

We are surrounded by opportunities that don't exist in larger cities or harsher climates. In our region you can visit the oak woodland section of a neighborhood park, or study chaparral plants bordering your patio; you can walk along the riparian woodland of a greenbelt surrounded by a suburban housing development. Planted pines create an urban coniferous forest in some parks. Planted palms create a subtropical garden around public buildings.

Think of the plethora of insects, birds, and mammals that live outside your back door! If you care about the natural world, share the discovery of urban nature with others, both young and old.

The mantra: Leave no child *or adult* inside.

APPENDIX A: SEEING FOR YOURSELF—WHERE TO FIND THE HABITATS DESCRIBED IN EACH CHAPTER

Chapter 3: The Ocean

Whale Watching

Virg's Landing at Morro Bay and San Luis Pier in Avila Beach; The *Condor Express* at Sea Landing, Santa Barbara Harbor; Island Packers at Ventura Harbor

Nearshore Waters

Seal Rookeries: Northern Elephant Seal Rookery near San Simeon at Vista Point off Highway 1 (November–May); Harbor Seal Rookery at Carpinteria Bluffs Nature Preserve (December–March)

Watch Gray Whale migration and seabird migration (March–April) from the following observation points:

- Pier at W. R. Hearst Memorial State Beach near San Simeon
- Pier at Cayucos
- Coal Oil Point at Coal Oil Point Reserve
- Goleta Point
- Pier at Goleta Beach County Park
- Mugu Rock

Chapter 4: The Shore

Rocky Shore

- Leffingwell Landing at San Simeon State Park north of Cambria
- Estero Bluffs State Park
- Margo Dodd City Park at Shell Beach
- Hazard Canyon at Montaña de Oro State Park
- Coal Oil Point Reserve
- Mussel Shoals

Sandy Beach

- W. R. Hearst Memorial State Beach
- Cayucos Beach

- Morro Strand State Beach
- Avila Beach
- Pismo State Beach
- Sands Beach at Coal Oil Point Reserve (Snowy Plover/Least Tern Colony March–September)
- Isla Vista Beach
- Goleta Beach County Park
- Arroyo Burro Beach County Park
- East and West Beach along the Santa Barbara waterfront
- Emma Wood State Beach
- Surfer's Knoll off Spinnaker Drive at Ventura Harbor
- McGrath State Beach
- Ormond Beach southeast of Port Hueneme

Dunes

- Morro Dunes Natural Preserve north of Montaña de Oro (on sandspit west of Morro Bay)
- Pismo Dunes Natural Preserve
- Oso Flaco Lake at Guadalupe-Nipomo Dunes National Wildlife Refuge
- Rancho Guadalupe Dunes County Park at the Santa Maria River Estuary (Snowy Plover/Least Tern colony, March–September)
- Dunes between Surfer's Knoll (off Spinnaker Dr. at Ventura Harbor) and the Santa Clara River Estuary (Snowy Plover/Least Tern colony, March–September)
- East end of Ormond Beach (Snowy Plover/Least Tern colony, March–September)

Chapter 5: Coastal Wetlands

Estuary, Salt Marsh, and Lagoon

- Morro Bay State Park marina area
- Baywood Park Beach along Pasadena Dr., Baywood Park

- Sweet Springs Nature Preserve, Baywood Park
- Avila Beach: lagoon at the mouth of San Luis Obispo Creek
- Santa Maria River Estuary
- Santa Ynez River Estuary
- Devereux Slough at Coal Oil Point Reserve
- Carpinteria Salt Marsh Nature Park
- Santa Clara River Estuary Natural Preserve at McGrath State Beach
- Mugu Lagoon from pull-out off Highway 1
- Ormond Beach wetlands at end of Perkins Rd. in Port Hueneme

- Highway 41 between Atascadero and Morro Bay (Cerro Alto Campground)
- Burton Mesa Ecological Reserve adjacent to La Purísima State Historic Park (best viewed from trails within the park)
- East Camino Cielo along the ridge of the Santa Ynez Mountains
- Highway 33 from Wheeler Gorge to Rose Valley Campground
- South-facing slopes of Pine Mountain Ridge along Highway 33 in the Upper Sespe Creek watershed; stop at pull-outs (Derrydale Creek, Potrero John Creek, etc.)

Chapter 6: Coastal Plain and Foothills

Hiking

The best way to get acquainted with these habitats is to hike coastal trails that begin at lower elevations, where coastal sage scrub predominates. Once you leave the coastal plain, the trail will climb into chaparral. For backcountry hiking, consult maps of Los Padres National Forest. Within the national forest, certain designated areas, such as the San Rafael Wilderness and the Dick Smith Wilderness, provide more remote hiking opportunities.

These websites are good for planning day hikes: San Luis Obispo Parks Open Space & Trails Foundation, www.slopost.org/trails.html; SantaBarbara Hikes, www.santabarbarahikes.com; and Ventura County Trails, www.venturacountytrails.org.

Walking or Driving

Coastal Sage Scrub:
- Morro Bay State Park, Cerro Cabrillo Trailhead
- Highway 1 between US 101 and Highway 246
- Paradise Road in the Upper Santa Ynez River watershed (Aliso Loop Trail at Sagehill Group Recreation Area)
- Carpinteria Bluffs Nature Preserve

Chaparral:
- West Cuesta Ridge at summit Cuesta Grade near San Luis Obispo

Chapter 7: Valleys

Coastal Valleys

Relict Association of Northern Plant Species:
- Jualachichi Summit on the Jalama Rd. off Highway 1
- Kinevan Road off San Marcos Pass in the Santa Ynez Mountains
- Refugio Pass at the top of Refugio Road in the Santa Ynez Mountains

Coast Live Oak Woodland:
- Santa Rosa Rd. between Cambria and Black Mountain summit
- Los Osos Oaks State Reserve
- Santa Ynez Mountains: north slopes at Nojoqui Falls County Park; Stagecoach Road west off Highway 154 near San Marcos Pass
- Toro Canyon County Park, Montecito

Valley Oak Savanna:
- US 101 between Atascadero and Paso Robles
- Los Alamos Valley: Los Alamos County Park
- Santa Ynez Valley: Foxen Canyon Rd.
- Los Robles Open Space near Thousand Oaks

Blue Oak–Gray Pine Woodland:
- Santa Margarita Lake
- Shell Creek Rd. off Highway 58
- Pozo and vicinity
- Figueroa Mountain Road
- Sedgwick Reserve (open to the

public on certain weekends or by prior arrangement)
- End of Cottonwood Canyon Rd. off Highway 166 (Bates Canyon Campground)

Interior Valleys

Pinyon-Juniper Woodland:
- Santa Barbara Canyon Rd., eastern Cuyama Valley
- Lockwood Valley Rd. east of Ozena
- Highway 33 between Ventucopa and Pine Mountain summit
- Mil Potrero Highway between Mount Pinos and Cerro Noroeste

Grasslands:
- Cerro Noroeste Rd. between Highway 166 and Apache Potrero Campground
- Wind Wolves Preserve off Highway 166
- Portions of the western end of the Cuyama Valley along Highway 166
- Portions of Carrizo Plain

Saltbush Scrub:
- Carrizo Plain
- Portions of eastern Cuyama Valley: near intersection of Highway 33 and Highway 166

Chapter 8: Mountains

Mixed Conifer Forest

- Figueroa Mountain: summit (Pino Alto Day Use Area, nature trail)
- Pine Mountain Ridge: the dirt road off Highway 33 ends at trailhead for Reyes Peak
- Cerro Noroeste (summit at Campo Alto Campground)
- Mount Pinos: the road up Mount Pinos ends at Chula Vista Day Use area (Iris Meadows)

Subalpine Forest

- Summit of Mount Pinos: walk from Chula Vista Campground on dirt road to summit (1.5 mi.)

Condor Viewing

- "The Forest Service Sign," along Cerro Noroeste Rd. on the Ventura/

Kern County line (see text for details)

Chapter 9: Freshwater Wetlands

Creeks and Rivers with Riparian Woodland

- Salinas River Parkway Project: a series of public parks along Upper Salinas River Watershed in Paso Robles
- Bob Jones Bike Trail (walkers welcome) along the lower portion of San Luis Obispo Creek (proposed to link San Luis Obispo with Avila Beach, but so far only the Avila Beach segment is open)
- Cuesta Park along San Luis Creek in the town of San Luis Obispo
- Santa Ynez River: River Park near Lompoc; Upper Santa Ynez River watershed accessed by several campgrounds along Paradise Rd.
- South Coast of Santa Barbara County: many hiking trails in the coastal canyons follow the creeks (see text for details)
- Arroyo Hondo Preserve (open to the public on certain weekends or by prior arrangement)
- Mission Creek in Santa Barbara runs adjacent to Oak Park, Rocky Nook Park, the Santa Barbara Museum of Natural History, and the Santa Barbara Botanic Garden
- Ventura River: trail/bike path along the river beginning in downtown Ventura and ending at Foster Park (continues as the Ojai Valley Trail to the town of Ojai)
- Santa Paula Creek: the trailhead for East Fork trail is near Thomas Aquinas College off Highway 150; Steckel County Park (may be closed in winter)
- Santa Clara River: Hedrick Ranch Nature Area (open to the public by prior arrangement); other portions of the Santa Clara River Parkway Project to be opened as they are acquired
- Sespe Creek: access via Highway 33

Freshwater Marsh

- At margins of Atascadero Lake, Lopez Lake, Laguna Lake, Oso Flaco Lake, Lake Cachuma, Lake Los Carneros, Andree Clark Bird Refuge, Lake Casitas, Ojai Meadows Preserve in Ojai

Vernal Pools (wet winters only)

- Carrizo Plain, vicinity of Soda Lake
- Figueroa Mountain slopes
- Ellwood Mesa, Goleta
- Isla Vista area: Del Sol Open Space, Camino Corto Open Space
- More Mesa
- Ojai Meadows Preserve

Chapter 10: Northern Channel Islands

Public landings on the Northern Channel Islands are through licensed concessionaires. Island Packers, Inc. (Ventura) and Truth Aquatics, Inc. (Santa Barbara) operate boat excursions depending upon the season. Channel Islands Aviation lands at Santa Rosa Island. All information is available at the Channel Islands National Park Visitor Center in Ventura or online at www.nps.gov/chis.

Chapter 11: Urban Parks and Backyards

A few of the many urban areas where a mixture of native and non-native plantings attracts wildlife:

- San Luis Obispo Creek in downtown San Luis Obispo traverses a planted area with walkways next to shops and restaurants
- Arroyo Grande Creek runs through the oldtown area of Arroyo Grande and is accessible by walkways
- Waller Park and Preisker Park in Santa Maria
- Stow House/Lake Los Carneros in Goleta
- UCSB campus near Isla Vista
- Alice Keck Park in Santa Barbara and Chase Palm Park on the waterfront (Cabrillo Blvd.) in Santa Barbara
- Manning Park in Montecito
- Libbey Park and Soule Park in Ojai
- Arroyo Verde Park and Camino Real Park in Ventura

Natural History Attractions Open to the Public

- San Luis Obispo Botanic Garden
- Avila Beach Marine Institute
- Morro Bay Museum of Natural History at Morro Bay State Park
- Guy C. Goodwin Education Center, Carrizo Plain (December–May)
- Santa Barbara Botanic Garden
- Santa Barbara Museum of Natural History
- Ty Warner Sea Center at Stearns Wharf
- Dunes Center in Guadalupe
- Neal Taylor Nature Center at Lake Cachuma
- Nature Cruises at Lake Cachuma (www.countyofsb.org/parks)
- Coronado Butterfly Preserve, Ellwood Mesa (November–February)
- Channel Islands National Park Visitor Center at Ventura Harbor
- Fillmore Fish Hatchery

Field Trip 1

San Simeon Coast Area

Habitats: Nearshore waters, rocky shore, coastal terrace grassland
Best time to visit: Late fall and winter

- Nearshore waters for migrating Gray Whales and seabirds from the end of W. R. Hearst Memorial State Beach pier and Cayucos Pier (December–April).
- The Northern Elephant Seal colony near Piedras Blancas Lighthouse at Vista Point off Highway 1 (November–May).
- Boardwalk at Leffingwell Landing near Cambria for birding and rocky shore viewing.
- Estero Bluffs State Park north of Cayucos for tidepooling, walking on trails at coastal grassland.

Field Trip 2

Morro Bay Area

Habitats: Sandy beach, rocky shore, dunes, coastal wetlands with salt marsh and lagoon, coastal sage scrub, Coast Live Oak woodland
Best time to visit: Fall through spring

- Morro Strand State Beach: sandy beach.
- Morro Bay State Park: Morro Bay Museum of Natural History, marina area for viewing salt marsh, Cerro Cabrillo Trailhead for hiking in coastal sage scrub.
- Town of Baywood Park: salt marsh viewing from Pasadena Dr. and Sweet Springs Reserve.
- Morro Dunes Natural Preserve (north of Montaña de Oro at the sandspit west of Morro Bay).
- Los Osos Oaks State Reserve: Coast Live Oak woodland.
- Montaña de Oro State Park: Hazard Canyon for tidepooling at minus tides.

Field Trip 3

Carrizo Plain Area

Habitats: Coast Live Oak woodland, Blue Oak–Gray Pine woodland, grassland, saltbush scrub
Best time to visit: Winter and early spring

- Highway 58 from Santa Margarita to Shell Creek Road: spring wildflowers.

Carrizo Plain National Monument:

- Soda Lake Road for birdwatching, spring wildflowers. (Note: Roads in the Carrizo Plain National Monument are impassable after heavy rain, although rainfall is typically less than on the coast.)
- Vernal pools near Soda Lake, depending on rainfall.
- Guy C. Goodwin Education Center for educational materials and orientation (open December–May).
- Wallace Creek: effects of San Andreas Fault and earthquake offset of creek bed.
- Scarp of San Andreas Fault visible at base of Elkhorn Hills in Temblor Range.

Field Trip 4

Cuyama Valley Area

Habitats: Coast Live Oak woodland, Blue Oak–Gray Pine woodland, grassland, saltbush scrub, Pinyon Pine–Juniper woodland
Best time to visit: Winter and early spring

- Highway 166 through Cuyama Valley.
- Side trip to Cottonwood Canyon Road ending at Bates Canyon Campground: spring wildflowers.
- Santa Barbara Canyon Road: Rock formations, views of Pinyon Pine–Juniper woodland habitat. (Note: If you decide to take the dirt road to reach Cuyama Peak, you will need a four-wheel-drive vehicle.)

Field Trip 5

Southern San Joaquin Valley Area

Habitats: Grassland
Best time to visit: Spring and fall
• Cerro Noroeste Road: possible California Condor sightings at the Forest Service sign (fall is best)—see text. In spring, vernal pools, wildflowers.
• Wind Wolves Preserve, off Highway 166: Tule Elk herd, grasslands (native bunchgrasses), possible California Condor sightings.

Field Trip 6

Santa Maria Area

Habitats: Freshwater lake, coastal wetlands, dunes, sandy beach
Best time to visit: Year-round
• Oso Flaco Lake: spring wildflowers on the dunes, waterfowl on the lake in winter.
• Guadalupe: the Dunes Center.
• Santa Maria River mouth: Guadalupe Dunes County Park. (Note beach closure in certain areas, March through September, to protect Western Snowy Plover and California Least Tern nesting).

Field Trip 7

Santa Ynez Valley Area

Habitats: Valley Oak savanna, Blue Oak–Gray Pine woodland, chaparral, maritime chaparral, montane coniferous forest, freshwater lake
Best time to visit: Fall through spring
• Sedgwick Reserve (open to the public on certain weekends or by prior arrangement): Hiking, spring wildflowers, woodland wildlife.
• Figueroa Mountain loop: Figueroa Mountain Road to summits of Figueroa Mountain and Ranger Peak for spring wildflowers, montane coniferous forest birds, mammals; return via Happy Canyon Road through coastal sage scrub and chaparral to Highway 154.
• Lake Cachuma: Eagle cruises, December–March.

• Burton Mesa Ecological Reserve: maritime chaparral habitat visible at La Purísima State Historic Park.
• Santa Ynez River mouth: Ocean Beach Park for birdwatching.

Field Trip 8

Santa Ynez Mountains Area

Habitats: Coastal sage scrub, chaparral, Coast Live Oak woodland, relict association of cool climate hardwoods
Best time to visit: Winter through spring
• East Camino Cielo to La Cumbre Peak: ocean and mountain views, chaparral habitat.
• Kinevan Road and West Camino Cielo adjacent to San Marcos Pass for relict cool association of plants.
• Lower Santa Ynez River Recreation Area, Paradise Rd. to Sagehill Group Campground: Hike Aliso Loop Trail in coastal sage scrub, spring wildflowers.

Field Trip 9

Santa Barbara Coastal Plain Area

Habitats: Ocean, sandy beach, rocky shore, coastal wetlands, coastal sage scrub, vernal pool, freshwater marsh
Best time to visit: Year-round
• Coal Oil Point Reserve for whale watching (spring), birdwatching (fall through spring), tidepooling at minus tides.
• Walk from Coal Oil Point along sandy beach to stairway at west end of Isla Vista (intersection Camino Majorca and Del Playa Dr.).
• In early spring, depending on rainfall, vernal pools along Camino Corto at Del Sol Open Space in Isla Vista.
• Lake Los Carneros County Park at Stow House for a walk around a freshwater marsh/lake (best fall through spring).
Mission Canyon area:
• Rocky Nook Park for riparian streamside vegetation; visit adjacent Santa Barbara Museum of Natural History.
• Trailhead of Tunnel Trail at the end

of Tunnel Road off Mission Canyon Rd. for hiking through chaparral habitat.

Downtown waterfront area:
- Santa Barbara Harbor breakwater for rocky shore birds.
- Sandy beaches: East Beach along Cabrillo Blvd.
- Andree Clark Bird Refuge at east end of Cabrillo Blvd. for birdwatching at a freshwater lake (best late fall through early spring).

Field Trip 10

Carpinteria Area

Habitats: Rocky shore, coastal wetland, coastal sage scrub
Best time to visit: Fall through spring
- Carpinteria Salt Marsh Nature Park, Ash Ave. in downtown Carpinteria: Birdwatching, views of salt marsh vegetation and wildlife.
- Carpinteria Bluffs Nature Preserve (exit US 101 at Bailard Ave.): Carpinteria Harbor Seal Colony visible from overlook on bluffs; coastal trail to Tar Pits Park.

Field Trip 11

Ojai Area

Habitats: Coastal sage scrub, chaparral, montane coniferous forest, freshwater lake, vernal pools
Best time to visit: Winter through early spring at lower elevations, summer at higher elevations
- Lake Casitas Recreation Area: wintering waterbirds, raptors.
- Ojai Meadows Preserve: restored vernal pools and wetlands.
- Highway 33 north of Ojai to observe a variety of habitats: begin by passing through coastal sage scrub, then through chaparral; stop along the way at the various pull-outs along Sespe Creek.
- Pine Mountain Recreation Area: turn east off Highway 33 onto a dirt road that passes through montane coniferous forest. Several campgrounds here provide good habitat for forest birds, mammals. Drive to the end of the road to reach the trailhead for Reyes Peak.

SPECIES LIST

Below is a list of common and scientific names of selected species mentioned in the text, photographs, and art. All species mentioned in the book can be found in the index, but for this list I chose to include only organisms that could be narrowed down to species.

Species not native to the region are marked with an asterisk (*).

References for the Species List

Abbott, Isabella A., and G. J. Hollenberg, *Marine Algae of California.*

Baldwin, Bruce G. et al., eds. *The Jepson Manual: Vascular Plants of California, Second Edition.*

Carlton, James T., ed. *The Light and Smith Manual: Intertidal Invertebrates from Central California to Oregon.*

Chesser, R. Terry et al. "Fifty-third Supplement to the American Ornithologists' Union Checklist of North American Birds."

Collins, P. W., "Checklist to the Amphibians and Reptiles of California's Central Coast," and "Checklist to the Mammals of California's Central Coast."

Dunn, Jon L., and J. Alderfer. *Field Guide to the Birds of North America,* 6th edition.

Hogue, Charles L., *Insects of the Los Angeles Basin.*

ITIS.gov (Integrated Taxonomic Information System).

Love, Milton S. *Certainly More Than You Want to Know about the Fishes of the Pacific Coast.*

Note: More information about these references can be found in the Bibliography.

Marine Algae

Bull Kelp
Nereocystis luetkeana

Feather Boa Kelp
Egregia menziesii

Giant Kelp
Macrocystis pyrifera

Nori
Porphyra perforata

Sea Comb
Plocamium cartilagineum

Tar Spot
Ralfsia pacifica

Vascular Plants

American Dune Grass
Elymus mollis

Alkali Heath
Frankenia salina

Arroyo Willow
Salix lasiolepis

Australian Saltbush *
Atriplex semibaccata

Baby Blue-eyes
Nemophila menziesii

Beach Bur-Sage
Ambrosia chamissonis

Beach Evening-Primrose
Camissoniopsis cheiranthifolia

Beach Sand-Verbena
Abronia maritima

Big-leaf Maple
Acer macrophyllum

Big-pod Ceanothus
Ceanothus megacarpus

Bigberry Manzanita
Arctostaphylos glauca

Bigcone Spruce
Pseudotsuga macrocarpa

Bishop Pine
Pinus muricata

Black Cottonwood
Populus trichocarpa

Black Mustard *
Brassica nigra

Black Sage
Salvia mellifera

Blue Elderberry
Sambucus nigra

Blue Gum Eucalyptus *
Eucalyptus globulus

Blue Oak
Quercus douglasii

Brewer's Lupine
Lupinus breweri

Buckbrush
Ceanothus cuneatus

Bush Lupine
Lupinus arboreus

Bush Monkeyflower
Mimulus aurantiacus

California Bay
Umbellularia californica

California Blackberry
Rubus ursinus

California Buckwheat
Eriogonum fasciculatum

California Coffeeberry
Frangula californica

California Cord Grass
Spartina foliosa

California Fan Palm *
Washingtonia filifera

California Fuchsia
Epilobium canum

California Hedge-Nettle
Stachys bullata

California Juniper
Juniperus californica

California Poppy
Eschscholzia californica

California Sagebrush
Artemisia californica

California Tule
Schoenoplectus californicus

Canyon Live Oak
Quercus chrysolepis

Cape Honeysuckle *
Tecomaria capensis

Cape Ivy *
Delairea odorata

Catalina Cherry
Prunus ilicifolia subsp. *lyonii*

Caterpillar Phacelia
Phacelia cicutaria

Century Plant *
Agave americana

Chamise
Adenostoma fasciculatum

Channel Island Tree Poppy
Dendromecon harfordii

Chaparral Clematis
Clematis lasiantha

Chaparral Yucca
Hesperoyucca whipplei

Coast Live Oak
Quercus agrifolia

Coast Morning Glory
Calystegia macrostegia

Coast Sunflower
Encelia californica

Coastal Lotus
Acmispon maritimus

Coastal Prickly-Pear
Opuntia littoralis

Collinsia
Collinsia childii

Common Eucrypta
Eucrypta chrysanthemifolia

Corn Lily
Veratrum californicum

Coulter Pine
Pinus coulteri

Coulter's Goldfields
Lasthenia glabrata susbp. *coulteri*

Coyote Brush
Baccharis pilularis

Coyote Thistle
Eryngium vaseyi

Cream Cups
Platystemon californicus

Deer Brush
Ceanothus integerrimus

Deerweed
Acmispon glaber

Desert Candle
Caulanthus inflatus

Douglas-Fir
Pseudotsuga menziesii

Dune Lupine
Lupinus chamissonis

Eel-Grass
Zostera marina

Elegant Clarkia
Clarkia unguiculata

European Beachgrass *
Ammophila arenaria

Fiesta Flower
Pholistoma auritum

Fremont Cottonwood
Populus fremontii

Fuchsia-flowered Goose-berry
Ribes speciosum

Giant Reed *
Arundo donax

Giant Tickseed
Leptosyne gigantea

Giant Wild-Rye
Elymus condensatus

Gowen Cypress
Callitropsis goveniana

Gray Pine
Pinus sabiniana

Great Basin Sagebrush
Artemisia tridentata

Great Valley Phacelia
Phacelia ciliata

Hairy Ceanothus
Ceanothus oliganthus

Hillside Daisy
Monolopia lanceolata

Hoaryleaf Ceanothus
Ceanothus crassifolius

Hoffmann's Slender-
flowered Gilia
Gilia tenuiflora subsp.
hoffmannii

Holly-leaved Cherry
Prunus ilicifolia subsp.
ilicifolia

Hoover's Downingia
Downingia bella

Huckleberry
Vaccinium ovatum

Hummingbird Sage
Salvia spathacea

Incense Cedar
Calocedrus decurrens

Iodine Bush
Allenrolfea occidentalis

Island Ceanothus
Ceanothus arboreus

Island Deerweed
Acmispon dendroideus

Italian Stone Pine *
Pinus pinea

Jaumea
Jaumea carnosa

Jeffrey Pine
Pinus jeffreyi

Jimson Weed
Datura wrightii

Kennedy's Buckwheat
Eriogonum kennedyi

La Purisima Manzanita
Arctostaphylos purissima

Large-flowered Phacelia
Phacelia grandiflora

Leather Oak
Quercus durata var.
durata

Lemonade Berry
Rhus integrifolia

Limber Pine
Pinus flexilis

Lompoc Ceanothus
Ceanothus cuneatus var.
fascicularis

Madrone
Arbutus menziesii

Miner's Lettuce
Claytonia perfoliata

Mock Heather
Ericameria ericoides

Monterey Cypress *
Hesperocyparis
macrocarpa

Monterey Pine *
Pinus radiata

Mosquito Fern
Azolla filiculoides

Mountain Whitethorn
Ceanothus cordulatus

Mule Fat
Baccharis salicifolia

Munchkin Dudleya
Dudleya gnoma

Narrow-leaved Milkweed
Asclepias fascicularis

Narrow-leaved Willow
Salix exigua

Owl's Clover
Castilleja exserta

Paintbrush
Castilleja affinis

Parish's Glasswort
Arthrocnemum
subterminale

Parish's Snowberry
Symphoricarpos
rotundifolius

Parry Manzanita
Arctostaphylos parryana

Pepper Tree *
Schinus molle

Pickleweed
Salicornia pacifica

Plain Mariposa Lily
Calochortus invenustus

Poison Oak
Toxicodendron
diversilobum

Ponderosa Pine
Pinus ponderosa

Purple Needlegrass
Stipa pulchra

Purple Sage
Salvia leucophylla

Purple Sand-Verbena
Abronia umbellata

Pursh's Locoweed
Astragalus purshii

Ranger's Buttons
Sphenosciadium
capitellatum

Red Bottlebrush *
Callistemon citrinus

Red Columbine
Aquilegia formosa

Red Willow
Salix laevigata

Redwood *
Sequoia sempervirens

River Red Gum *
Eucalyptus camaldulensis

Roundstem Tule
Schoenoplectus acutus

Salal
Gaultheria shallon

Salt Dodder
Cuscuta salina

Salt Grass
Distichlis spicata

Salt Marsh Bird's-beak
Chloropyron maritimum
subsp. *maritimum*

Saltmarsh Aster
Symphyotrichum
subulatum

Saltmarsh Bulrush
Bolboschoenus maritimus

Sand Almond
Prunus fasciculata var.
punctata

Santa Barbara Ceanothus
Ceanothus impressus var.
impressus

Santa Cruz Island Buck-
wheat
Eriogonum arborescens

Santa Cruz Island
Bush-Mallow
*Malacothamnus fascicula-
tus* var. *nesiotica*

Santa Cruz Island Dudleya
Dudleya nesiotica

Santa Cruz Island Goose-
berry
Ribes thacherianum

Santa Cruz Island Iron-
wood
*Lyonothamnus floribun-
dus* subsp. *aspleniifolius*

Santa Cruz Island Lacepod
*Thysanocarpus
conchuliferus*

Santa Cruz Island
Manzanita
Arctostaphylos insularis

Santa Cruz Island Silver
Lotus
Acmispon argophyllus var.
nesioticus

Santa Rosa Island Dudleya
Dudleya blochmaniae
subsp. *insularis*

Santa Rosa Island
Manzanita
*Arctostaphylos
confertiflora*

Scarlet Bugler
*Penstemon
centranthifolius*

Scarlet Penstemon
Penstemon rostriflorus

Sea Rocket *
Cakile maritima

Sea-Lavender
Limonium californicum

Seacliff Buckwheat
Eriogonum parvifolium

Seaside Arrow-Grass
Triglochin concinna

Singleleaf Pinyon Pine
Pinus monophylla

Sky Lupine
Lupinus nanus

Snow Plant
Sarcodes sanguinea

Southern Tarplant
Centromadia pungens
subsp. *australis*

Southwestern Spiny Rush
Juncus acutus subsp.
leopoldii

Spear Orach
Atriplex patula

Sticky Phacelia
Phacelia viscida

Succulent Lupine
Lupinus succulentus

Sugar Gum *
Eucalyptus cladocalyx

Sugar Pine
Pinus lambertiana

Sword Fern
Polystichum munitum

Tanbark Oak
*Notholithocarpus
densiflorus*

Tidy Tips
Layia platyglossa

Torrey Pine
Pinus torreyana subsp.
insularis

Toyon
Heteromeles arbutifolia

Valley Oak
Quercus lobata

Vandenberg Monkey-
flower
Mimulus fremontii var.
vandenbergensis

Water Starwort
Callitriche marginata

Wavy-stemmed Popcorn
Flower
Plagiobothrys undulatus

Weeping Fig *
Ficus benjamina

Western Blue Flag
Iris missouriensis

Western Mountain Phlox
Phlox austromontana

Western Sycamore
Platanus racemosa

Western Virgin's Bower
Clematis ligusticifolia

Western Wallflower
Erysimum capitatum

Whispering Bells
Emmenanthe penduliflora

White Alder
Alnus rhombifolia

White Fir
Abies concolor

White Sage
Salvia apiana

White-haired Manzanita
Arctostaphylos viridissima

Woolly Paintbrush
Castilleja foliolosa

Yellow Rabbitbrush
*Chrysothamnus
viscidiflorus*

Yellow Sand-Verbena
Abronia latifolia

Yellow Willow
Salix lasiandra

Marine Invertebrates

Bay Ghost Shrimp
Neotrypaea californiensis

Beach Pillbug
Tylos punctatus

Bent-nosed Clam
Macoma nasuta

Black Tegula
Tegula funebralis

Black Turban Snail
Chlorostoma funebralis

Bloodworm
Euzonus mucronata

Blue Mud Shrimp
Upogebia pugettensis

Brittle Star
Amphipholis squamata

California Aglaja
Navanax inermis

California Fat Tellin
Psammotreta obesa

California Horn Snail
Cerithidea californica

California Mussel
Mytilus californianus

California Seahare
Aplysia californica

California Two-spot
Octopus
Octopus bimaculoides

Chink Snail
Lacuna marmorata

Clonal Anemone
Anthopleura elegantissima

Comet Sea Star
Linckia columbiae

Eroded Periwinkle
Littorina planaxis

Fat Innkeeper
Urechis caupo

Fiddler Crab
Uca crenulata

File Limpet
Lottia limatula

Fingernail Limpet
Lottia digitalis

Frilled Venus
Chione undulata

Geoduck
Panopea generosa

Giant Green Anemone
Anthopleura xanthogrammica

Giant Pacific Octopus
Enteroctopus dofleini

Gumboot Chiton
Cryptochiton stelleri

Hermissenda
Hermissenda crassicornis

Krill
Euphausia pacifica

Leaf Barnacle
Pollicipes polymerus

Lewis's Moon Snail
Euspira lewisii

Lined Chiton
Tonicella lineata

Northern Kelp Crab
Pugettia producta

Nuttall's Chiton
Nuttallina californica

Ochre Sea Star
Pisaster ochraceus

Olive Ear Snail
Melampus olivaceus

Owl Limpet
Lottia gigantea

Pacific Egg Cockle
Laevicardium substriatum

Pacific Gaper
Tresus nuttallii

Pacific Littleneck
Leukoma staminea

Pacific Razor Clam
Tagelus californianus

Pacific Rock Crab
Cancer antennarius

Pea Crab
Scleroplax granulata

Pismo Clam
Tivela stultorum

Purple Sea Urchin
Strongylocentrotus purpuratus

Red Sea Urchin
Strongylocentrotus franciscanus

Rough Limpet
Lottia scabra

Salt Marsh Snail
Assimenia translucens

Seaweed Limpet
Notoacmea insessa

Spanish Shawl
Flabellina iodinea

Spiny Lobster
Panulirus interruptus

Starburst Anemone
Anthopleura sola

Striped Shore Crab
Pachygrapsus crassipes

Sunflower Star
Pycnopodia helianthoides

Surf-grass Limpet
Notoacmea paleacea

Volcano Limpet
Fissurella volcano

Western Sand Crab
Emerita analoga

Yellow Shore Crab
Hemigrapsus oregonensis

Terrestrial and Freshwater Invertebrates

Alfalfa Butterfly
Colias eurytheme

Anise Swallowtail
Papilio zelicaon

Argentine Ant *
Linepithema humile

Backswimmer
Notonecta shooteri

Blue-eyed Darner
Rhionaeschna multicolor

Brown Garden Snail *
Helix aspersa

Buckeye
Junonia coenia

Cabbage White *
Pieris rapae

California Carpenter Bee
Xylocopa californica

California Clam Shrimp
Cyzicus californicus

California Dogface
Colias eurydice

California Oak Moth
Phryganidia californica

California Ringlet
Coenonympha tullia

California Salt Marsh Mosquito
Aedes taeniorhynchus

California Tortoiseshell
Nymphalis californica

California Sister
Adelpha californica

Callippe Fritillary
Speyeria callippe

Camel Cricket
Ceuthophilus californianus

Ceanothus Silk Moth
Hyalophora euryalus

Checkered Skipper
Pyrgus communis

Cloudless Sulfur
Phoebis sennae

Common Earthworm *
Lumbricus terrestris

Common Green Darner
Anax junius

Common Water Strider
Aquarius remigis

Common White
Pieris protodice

Convergent Lady Beetle
Hippodamia convergens

Cristina's Timema
Timema cristinae

Decollate Snail *
Rumina decollata

Echo Blue
Celastrina ladon

Fiery Skipper
Hylephila phyleus

Fire Beetle
Melanophila occidentalis

Flame Skimmer
Libellula saturata

Gabb's Checkerspot
Chlosyne gabbii

Giant Water Bug
Abedus indentatus

Globose Dune Beetle
Coelus globosus

Gray Hairstreak
Strymon melinus

Gulf Fritillary
Agraulis vanillae

Honey Bee *
Apis mellifera

House Cricket *
Acheta domesticus

Live Oak Gall Fly
Callirhytis quercuspomiformis

Lompoc Small Blue
Philotiella speciosa subsp. *purisima*

Lorquin's Admiral
Limenitis lorquini

Monarch butterfly
Danaus plexippus

Mormon Metalmark
Apodemia mormo

Morro Shoulderband
Helminthoglypta walkeriana

Mourning Cloak
Nymphalis antiopa

Mylitta Crescent
Phyciodes mylitta

Northern White Skipper
Heliopetes ericetorum

Pacific Coast Tick
Dermacentor occidentalis

Painted Lady
Vanessa cardui

Pajaroello Tick
Ornithodorus coriaceus

Pale Swallowtail
Papilio eurymedon

Pillbug *
Armadillidium vulgare

Red Gum Lerp Psyllid *
Glycaspis brimblecombei

Rural Skipper
Ochlodes agricola

Sara Orangetip
Anthocharis sara

Snowy Tree Cricket
Oecanthus fultoni

Summer Salt Marsh Mosquito
Aedes squamiger

Urchin Gall Wasp
Cynips quercusechinus

Variable Checkerspot
Euphydryas chalcedona

Vernal Pool Fairy Shrimp
Branchinecta lynchi

Vivid Dancer
Argia vivida

Wandering Skipper
Panoquina errans

Western Black-legged Tick
Ixodes pacificus

Western Pygmy-Blue
Brephidium exilis

Western Tiger Swallowtail
Papilio rutulus

Yucca Moth
Tegeticula maculata

Yucca Weevil
Scyphophorus yuccae

Fish

Arrow Goby
Clevelandia ios

Bat Ray
Myliobatis californica

Blind Goby
Typhlogobius californiensis

Blue Rockfish
Sebastes mystinus

Bluegill
Lepomis macrochirus

C-O Sole
Pleuronichthys coenosus

Cabezon
Scorpaenicthys marmoratus

California Halibut
Paralichthys californicus

California Killifish
Fundulus parvipinnis

California Sheephead
Semicossyphus pulcher

Diamond Turbot
Hypsopsetta guttulata

Dolphinfish
Coryphaena hippurus

Garibaldi
Hypsypops rubicunda

Giant Kelpfish
Heterostichus rostratus

Horn Shark
Heterodontus francisci

Jack Mackerel
Trachurus symmetricus

Kelp Bass
Paralabrax clathratus

Leopard Shark
Triakis semifasciata

Longjaw Mudsucker
Gillichthys mirabilis

Mosquitofish *
Gambusia affinis

Northern Anchovy
Engraulis mordax

Ocean Sunfish
Mola mola

Opaleye
Girella nigricans

Pacific Bluefin Tuna
Thunnus orientalis

Pacific Bonito
Sarda chiliensis

Pacific Chub Mackerel
Scomber japonicus

Pacific Sardine
Sardinops sagax

Pacific Staghorn Sculpin
Leptocottus armatus

Senorita
Oxyjulis californica

Shadow Goby
Quietula y-cauda

Shortfin Mako
Isurus oxyrinchus

Southern Steelhead
Oncorhynchus mykiss

Starry Flounder
Platichthys stellatus

Tidepool Sculpin
Oligocottus maculosus

Tidewater Goby
Eucyclogobius newberryi

Topsmelt
Atherinops affinis

White Shark
Carcharodon carcharias

Amphibians

Arboreal Salamander
Aneides lugubris

Baja California Treefrog
Pseudacris hypochondriaca

Black-bellied Slender Salamander
Batrachoseps nigriventris

Bullfrog *
Lithobates catesbeiana

California Newt
Taricha torosa

California Red-legged Frog
Rana draytonii

California Tiger Salamander
Ambystoma californiense

California Tree Frog
Pseudacris cadaverina

Channel Islands Slender Salamander
Batrachoseps pacificus

Monterey Ensatina
Ensatina eschscholtzii

Western Spadefoot
Spea hammondii

Reptiles

Blainville's Horned Lizard
Phrynosoma blainvillii

Blunt-nosed Leopard Lizard
Gambelia sila

California Legless Lizard
Anniella pulchra

California Mountain Kingsnake
Lampropeltis zonata

Common Garter Snake
Thamnophis sirtalis

Gopher Snake
Pituophis catenifer

Island Fence Lizard
Sceloporus occidentalis subsp. *becki*

Leatherback
Dermochelys coriacea

Northern Alligator Lizard
Elgaria coerulea

Pacific Pond Turtle
Actinemys marmorata

Painted Turtle *
Chrysemys picta

Red-eared Slider *
Trachemys scripta

Santa Cruz Island Gopher Snake
Pituophis catenifer subsp. *pumilis*

Southern Alligator Lizard
Elgaria multicarinata

Western Fence Lizard
Sceloporus occidentalis

Western Rattlesnake
Crotalus oreganos

Western Skink
Eumeces skiltonianus

Birds

Acorn Woodpecker
Melanerpes formicivorus

Allen's Hummingbird
Selasphorus sasin

American Coot
Fulica americana

American Crow
Corvus brachyrhynchos

American White Pelican
Pelicanus erythrorhynchos

Anna's Hummingbird
Calypte anna

Ash-throated Flycatcher
Myiarchus cinerascens

Ashy Storm-Petrel
Oceanodroma homochroa

Bald Eagle
Haliaeetus leucocephalus

Barn Owl
Tyto alba

Belding's Savannah Sparrow
Passerculus sandwichensis
subsp. *beldingi*

Bell's Vireo
Vireo bellii

Bewick's Wren
Thryomanes bewickii

Black Oystercatcher
Haematopus bachmani

Black Phoebe
Sayornis nigricans

Black Turnstone
Arenaria melanocephala

Black-bellied Plover
Pluvialis squatarola

Black-chinned Sparrow
Spizella atrogularis

Black-crowned Night-Heron
Nycticorax nycticorax

Blue Grosbeak
Passerina caerulea

Brandt's Cormorant
Phalacrocorax penicillatus

Brant
Branta bernicla

Brown-headed Cowbird
Molothrus ater

Bullock's Oriole
Icterus bullockii

Burrowing Owl
Athene cunicularia

Bushtit
Psaltriparus minimus

California Brown Pelican
Pelicanus occidentalis
subsp. *californicus*

California Condor
Gymnogyps californianus

California Gull
Larus californicus

California Least Tern
Sternula antillarum
subsp. *browni*

California Quail
Callipepla californica

California Thrasher
Toxostoma redivivum

California Towhee
Melozone crissalis

Cassin's Auklet
Ptychoramphus aleuticus

Clark's Grebe
Aechmophorus clarkii

Clark's Nutcracker
Nucifraga columbiana

Common Raven
Corvus corax

Cooper's Hawk
Accipiter cooperii

Costa's Hummingbird
Calypte costae

Dark-eyed Junco
Junco hyemalis

Double-crested Cormorant
Phalacrocorax auritus

Dunlin
Calidris alpina

Dusky Orange-crowned Warbler
Oreothlypis celata subsp. *sordida*

European Starling *
Sturnus vulgaris

Flammulated Owl
Otus flammeolus

Gadwall
Anas strepera

Golden Eagle
Aquila chrysaetos

Golden-crowned Kinglet
Regulus satrapa

Great Blue Heron
Ardea herodias

Great Egret
Ardea alba

Great Horned Owl
Bubo virginianus

Hooded Oriole
Icterus cucullatus

House Sparrow *
Passer domesticus

House Wren
Troglodytes aedon

Hutton's Vireo
Vireo huttoni

Island Flycatcher
Empidonax difficilis
subsp. *insulicola*

Island Horned Lark
Eremophila alpestris
subsp. *insularis*

Island Loggerhead Shrike
Lanius ludovicianus
subsp. *anthonyi*

Island Scrub-Jay
Aphelocoma insularis

Island Song Sparrow
Melospiza melodia subsp. *graminea*

Lawrence's Goldfinch
Spinus lawrencei

Lazuli Bunting
Passerina amoena

Least Bell's Vireo
Vireo bellii subsp. *pusillus*

Least Sandpiper
Calidris minutilla

Light-footed Clapper Rail
Rallus longirostris subsp. *levipes*

Long-billed Curlew
Numenius americanus

Long-billed Dowitcher
Limnodromus scolopaceus

Mallard
Anas platyrhynchos

Marbled Godwit
Limosa fedoa

Marsh Wren
Cistothorus palustris

Mount Pinos Sooty Grouse
Dendragapus fuliginosus subsp. *howardi*

Mountain Bluebird
Sialia currucoides

Mountain Chickadee
Poecile gambeli

Northern Harrier
Circus cyaneus

Northern Mockingbird
Mimus polyglottus

Northern Pygmy-Owl
Glaucidium gnoma

Nuttall's Woodpecker
Picoides nuttallii

Oak Titmouse
Baeolophus inornatus

Orange-crowned Warbler
Oreothlypis celata

Osprey
Pandion haliaetus

Pacific Loon
Gavia pacifica

Pelagic Cormorant
Phalacrocorax pelagicus

Peregrine Falcon
Falco peregrinus

Phainopepla
Phainopepla nitens

Pigeon Guillemot
Cepphus columba

Pink-footed Shearwater
Puffinus creatopus

Pinyon Jay
Gymnorhinus cyanocephalus

Purple Martin
Progne subis

Red-breasted Merganser
Mergus serrator

Red-breasted Nuthatch
Sitta canadensis

Red-breasted Sapsucker
Sphyrapicus ruber

Red-necked Phalarope
Phalaropus lobatus

Red-shouldered Hawk
Buteo lineatus

Red-tailed Hawk
Buteo jamaicensis

Red-winged Blackbird
Agelaius phoeniceus

Rock Pigeon *
Columba livia

Ruddy Duck
Oxyura jamaicensis

Ruddy Turnstone
Arenaria interpres

San Clemente Spotted Towhee
Pipilo maculatus subsp. *clementae*

Sanderling
Calidris alba

Santa Cruz Island Bewick's Wren
Thryomanes bewickii subsp. *nesophilus*

Santa Cruz Island Rufous-crowned Sparrow
Aimophila ruficeps subsp. *obscura*

Scripps's Murrelet
Synthliboramphus scrippsi

Semipalmated Plover
Charadrius semipalmatus

Short-billed Dowitcher
Limnodromus griseus

Snowy Egret
Egretta thula

Song Sparrow
Melospiza melodia

Sooty Shearwater
Puffinus griseus

Sora
Porzana carolina

Spotted Towhee
Pipilo maculatus

Steller's Jay
Cyanocitta stelleri

Surf Scoter
Melanitta perspicillata

Surfbird
Aphriza virgata

Townsend's Solitaire
Myadestes townsendi

Turkey Vulture
Cathartes aura

Violet-green Swallow
Tachycineta thalassina

Virginia Rail
Rallus limicola

Wandering Tattler
Tringa incana

Western Bluebird
Sialia mexicana

Western Grebe
Aechmophorus occidentalis

Western Gull
Larus occidentalis

Western Sandpiper
Calidris mauri

Western Scrub-Jay
Aphelocoma californica

Western Snowy Plover
Charadrius alexandrinus subsp. *nivosus*

Whimbrel
Numenius phaeopus

White-breasted Nuthatch
Sitta carolinensis

White-crowned Sparrow
Zonotrichia leucophrys

White-headed Wood-
pecker
Picoides albolarvatus

Willet
Tringa semipalmata

Wrentit
Chamaea fasciata

Yellow Warbler
Setophaga petechia

Yellow-billed Magpie
Pica nuttalli

Yellow-breasted Chat
Icteria virens

Yellow-rumped Warbler
Setophaga coronata

Mammals

Agile Kangaroo Rat
Dipodomys agilis

American Black Bear
Ursus americanus

Anacapa Island Deer
Mouse
Peromyscus maniculatus
subsp. *anacapae*

Badger
Taxidea taxus

Big Brown Bat
Eptesicus fuscus

Big-eared Woodrat
Neotoma macrotis

Black Rat *
Rattus rattus

Blue Whale
Balaenoptera musculus

Bobcat
Lynx rufus

Botta's Pocket Gopher
Thomomys bottae

Bottlenose Dolphin
Tursiops truncatus

Brazilian Free-tailed Bat
Tadarida brasiliensis

Brush Rabbit
Sylvilagus bachmani

Bryant's Woodrat
Neotoma bryanti

California Gray Whale
Eschrichtius robustus

California Ground Squirrel
Otospermophilus beecheyi

California Myotis
Myotis californicus

California Sea Lion
Zalophus californianus

California Vole
Microtus californicus

Channel Island Spotted
Skunk
Spilogale gracilis subsp.
amphiala

Common Gray Fox
Urocyon cinereoargenteus

Coyote
Canis latrans

Dall's Porpoise
Phocoenoides dalli

Deer Mouse
Peromyscus maniculatus

Eastern Fox Squirrel *
Sciurus niger

Giant Kangaroo Rat
Dipodomys ingens

Gray Wolf
Canis lupus

Grizzly Bear
Ursus arctos

Guadalupe Fur Seal
Arctocephalus townsendi

Heermann's Kangaroo Rat
Dipodomys heermanni

Harbor Seal
Phoca vitulina

Humpback Whale
Megaptera novaeanglia

Island Fox
Urocyon littoralis

Lompoc Kangaroo Rat
Dipodomys heermanni
subsp. *arenae*

Long-beaked Common
Dolphin
Delphinus capensis

Merriam's Chipmunk
Tamias merriami

Morro Bay Kangaroo Rat
Dipodomys heermanni
subsp. *morroensis*

Mount Pinos Chipmunk
Tamias speciosus subsp.
callipeplus

Mountain Lion
Puma concolor

Mule Deer
Odocoileus hemionus

Northern Elephant Seal
Mirounga angustirostris

Northern Fur Seal
Callorhinus ursinus

Northern Raccoon
Procyon lotor

Northern Right-whale
Dolphin
Lissodelphis borealis

Pacific White-sided Dol-
phin
*Lagenorhynchus
obliquidens*

Pinyon Mouse
Peromyscus truei

Pronghorn
Antilocapra americana

Red Fox *
Vulpes vulpes

Risso's Dolphin
Grampus griseus

San Joaquin Antelope
Squirrel
*Ammospermophilus
nelsoni*

San Joaquin Kit Fox
Vulpes macrotis subsp. *mutica*

San Miguel Island Deer Mouse
Peromyscus maniculatus subsp. *streatori*

San Miguel Island Fox
Urocyon littoralis subsp. *littoralis*

Santa Cruz Island Deer Mouse
Peromyscus maniculatus subsp. *santacruzae*

Santa Cruz Island Fox
Urocyon littoralis subsp. *santacruzae*

Santa Cruz Island Harvest Mouse
Reithrodontomys megalotis subsp. *santacruzae*

Santa Rosa Island Deer Mouse
Peromyscus maniculatus subsp. *santarosae*

Santa Rosa Island Fox
Urocyon littoralis subsp. *santarosae*

Short-beaked Common Dolphin
Delphinus delphis

Southern Sea Otter
Enhydra lutris subsp. *nereis*

Steller's Sea Lion
Eumetopias jubatus

Striped Skunk
Mephitis mephitis

Townsend's Big-eared Bat
Corynorhinus townsendii

Tule Elk
Cervus elaphus subsp. *nannodes*

Virginia Opossum *
Didelphis virginiana

Western Gray Squirrel
Sciurus griseus

Western Spotted Skunk
Spilogale gracilis

Yuma Myotis
Myotis yumanensis

Abbott, Isabella A., and G. J. Hollenberg. *Marine Algae of California*. Stanford: Stanford Univ. Press, 1992.

Ackerman, J. T., J. W. Mason, and J. Y. Takekawa. "Seabirds off Southern California." *Sound Waves* 67 (Nov. 2004), pp. 6–7.

Adkins, Jessica Y., and D. D. Roby. "A Status Assessment of the Double-Crested Cormorant (*Phalacrocorax auritus*) in Western North America." USGS-Oregon Cooperative Fish and Wildlife Research Unit report to US Army Corps of Engineers, March 31, 2010.

Agenbroad, L. D. et al. "Mammoths and Humans as Late Pleistocene Contemporaries on Santa Rosa Island." In *Proceedings of the Sixth California Islands Symposium*, ed. D. K. Garcelon and C. A. Schwemm. National Park Service Technical Publication CHIS-05-01. Arcata, CA: Institute for Wildlife Studies, 2005, pp. 3–7.

Agenbroad, Larry D. "*Mammuthus exilis* from the California Channel Islands: Height, Mass, and Geologic Age." In *Proceedings of the Seventh California Islands Symposium,* ed. C. C. Damiani and D. K. Garcelon. Arcata, CA: Institute for Wildlife Studies, 2009, pp. 15–19.

———. "California's Channel Islands: A One Way Trip in the Tunnel of Doom." In *Proceedings of the Fifth California Islands Symposium*, ed. D. R. Brown, K. L. Mitchell, and H. W. Chaney. Santa Barbara: Santa Barbara Museum of Natural History, 2002, pp. 1–6.

———. "New Pygmy Mammoth (*Mammuthus exilis*) Localities and Radiocarbon Dates from San Miguel, Santa Rosa, and Santa Cruz Islands, California." In *Contributions to the Geology*

of the Northern Channel Islands, Southern California, Annual Meeting Pacific Section AAPG, Ventura, California, April 29–May 1, 1998, ed. Peter W. Weigand. Bakersfield, CA: Pacific Section, American Association of Petroleum Geologists, 1998.

Alagona, Peter S. et al. "A History of Steelhead and Rainbow Trout *(Oncorhynchus mykiss)* in the Santa Ynez River Watershed, Santa Barbara County, California." *Bulletin of the Southern California Academy of Sciences* 111, No. 3 (2012), pp. 163–222.

Allen, Sarah G., J. Mortonson, and S. Webb. *Field Guide to Marine Mammals of the Pacific Coast*. Berkeley: Univ. of California Press, 2011.

Ambrose, Richard F., ed. "Coastal Wetland Resources: Santa Barbara County Mainland." Unpublished ms., Environmental Science and Engineering Program, Univ. of California, Los Angeles, 1995.

American Geological Institute. *Dictionary of Geological Terms*. New York: Dolphin Books, 1984.

Anderson, Clarissa et al. "An Empirical Approach to Estimating the Probability of Toxigenic *Pseudo-nitzschia* Blooms in the Santa Barbara Channel." AGU Ocean Sciences Meeting, March 2–7, 2008, Orlando, FL, supplement.

———. "Circulation and Environmental Conditions during a Toxigenic *Pseudo-nitzschia australis* Bloom in the Santa Barbara Channel, California." *Marine Ecology Progress Series* 327 (2006), pp. 119–133.

Arno, Stephen F. *Discovering Sierra Trees*. Yosemite: Yosemite Association and Sequoia Natural History Association, 1973.

Atwater, Tanya, and H. Ehrenspeck.

"Plain English Geology Field Guide for the Western Santa Monica Mountains." In *The Incredible Cenozoic Geologic History of Southern California*, ed. Peter W. Weigand, K. L. Savage, and E. A. Fritsche. Northridge, CA: Dept. of Geological Sciences, CSU Northridge, 2000.

Bakker, Elna. *An Island Called California*. Berkeley: Univ. of California Press, 1984.

Baldwin, Bruce G. et al., eds. *The Jepson Manual: Vascular Plants of California*. Berkeley: Univ. of California Press, 2012.

Barbour, Michael G., Todd Keeler-Wolf, and Allan A. Schoenherr, eds. *Terrestrial Vegetation of California*. 3d ed. Berkeley: Univ. of California Press, 2007.

Barbour, Michael, and J. Major, eds. *Terrestrial Vegetation of California*. New York: John Wiley & Sons, 1977.

Behrens, Michael D., and K. D. Lafferty. "Effects of Marine Reserves and Urchin Disease on Southern Californian Rocky Reef Communities." *Marine Ecology Progress Series* 279 (2004), pp. 129–139.

Benard, Michael F. "Survival Trade-Offs between Two Predator-Induced Phenotypes in Pacific Treefrogs (*Pseudacris regilla*)." *Ecology* 87, No. 2 (2006), pp. 340–346.

Birkhead, Tim. *Bird Sense*. New York: Walker & Co, 2012.

Blakley, Jim. *A Traveler's Guide to California's Scenic Highway 33: From Ojai to Cuyama*. Santa Barbara: Shoreline Press, 2004.

Blanchette, Carol A., B. R. Broitman, and S. D. Gaines. "Intertidal Community Structure and Oceanographic Patterns around Santa Cruz Island, CA, USA." *Marine Biology* 149 (2006), pp. 689–701.

Blanchette, Carol A., and S. D. Gaines. "Distribution, Abundance, Size, and Recruitment of the Mussel, *Mytilus californianus*, across a Major Oceanographic and Biogeographic Boundary at Point Conception, California, USA." *Journal of Experimental Marine Biology and Ecology* 340, No. 2 (2007), pp. 268–279.

Blanchette, Carol A., B. G. Miner, and S. D. Gaines. "Geographic Variability in Form, Size and Survival of *Egregia menziesii* around Point Conception, California." *Marine Ecology Progress Series* 239 (2002), pp. 69–82.

Blanchette, Carol A., Peter T. Raimondi, and Bernardo R. Broitman. "Spatial Patterns of Intertidal Community Structure across the California Channel Islands and Links to Ocean Temperature." In *Proceedings of the Seventh California Islands Symposium*, ed. C. C. Damiani and D. K. Garcelon. Arcata, CA: Institute for Wildlife Studies, 2009, pp. 161–173.

Blanchette, Carol A. et al. "Biogeographical Patterns of Rocky Intertidal Communities along the Pacific Coast of North America." *Journal of Biogeography* 35 (2008), pp. 1593–1607.

———. "Regime Shifts, Community Change and Population Booms of Keystone Predators at the Channel Islands." In *Proceedings of the Sixth California Islands Symposium*, ed. D. K. Garcelon and C. A. Schwemm. National Park Service Technical Publication CHIS-05-01. Arcata, CA: Institute for Wildlife Studies, 2005, pp. 435–440.

Blier, Warren. "The Sundowner Winds of Santa Barbara, California." *Weather and Forecasting* 13, No. 3 (Sept. 1998), pp. 702–716.

Block, B. A. et al. "Tracking Apex Marine Predator Movements in a Dynamic Ocean." *Nature* 475 (July 7, 2011), pp. 86–90.

Boughton, David A. "A Forward-Looking Scientific Frame of Reference for Steelhead Recovery on the South-Central and Southern California Coast." NOAA Technical Memorandum, NMFS, Oct 2010.

Britt, Robert Roy. "Walking on Water: Insect's Secret Revealed." *Live Science*, http://www.livescience.com/62-walking-water-insect-secret-revealed.html. Nov. 2, 2004.

Brontoff, W. N. et al. "Fairy, Tadpole, and Clam Shrimps (Branchiopoda) in Seasonally Inundated Clay Pans in the Western Mojave Desert and

Effect on Primary Producers." *Saline Systems*, http://www.aquaticbiosystems.org/content/6/1/11. Dec. 8, 2010.

Brower, Kenneth. "Still Blue." *National Geographic* 215, No. 3 (March 2009), pp. 139–152.

Brown, Alan K., ed. *A Description of Distant Roads: Original Journals of the First Expedition into California, 1769–1770*. San Diego: San Diego State Univ. Press, 2001.

Brown, Lon R., and L. H. Carpelan. "Egg Hatching and Life History of a Fairy Shrimp *Branchinecta mackini* Dexter (Crustacea: Anostraca) in a Mohave Desert Playa (Rabbit Dry Lake)." *Ecology* 52, No. 1 (1971).

Burroughs, John. *The Birds of John Burroughs: Keeping a Sharp Lookout*, ed. Jack Kligerman. 1908. Reprint, New York: Hawthorn Books, 1976.

CALFED Bay-Delta Program. "Weather Makers—A Look at El Niño and More." *Science News*, http://science.calwater.ca.gov/publications/sci_news_0809_elnino.html. August 2009.

California Academy of Sciences. "Central Valley Vernal Pools," http://www.calacademy.org/exhibits/california_hotspot/habitat_vernal_pools.htm. Accessed Feb. 4, 2013.

———. "Lizards that Fight Lyme Disease," http://www.calacademy.org/science_now/archive. Accessed May 29, 2010.

California Center for Wildlife. *Living with Wildlife: How to Enjoy, Cope with, and Protect North America's Wild Creatures around Your Home and Theirs*. San Francisco: Sierra Club Books, 1994.

California Coastal Commission. *Experience the California Coast: Beaches and Parks from Monterey to Ventura*. Berkeley: Univ. of California Press, 2007.

———. *California Coastal Access Guide*. 6th ed. Berkeley: Univ. of California Press, 2003.

California Invasive Species Advisory Committee. "California Invasive Species List," http://ice.ucdavis.edu/invasives/home/species. Accessed Feb. 4, 2013.

Callaway, R. M., and C. S. Sabraw. "Effects of Variable Precipitation on the Structure and Diversity of a California Salt Marsh Community." *Journal of Vegetation Science* 5, No. 3 (June 2005).

Calsbeek, Ryan, J. N. Thompson, and J. E. Richardson. "Patterns of Molecular Evolution and Diverstification in a Biodiversity Hotspot: The California Floristic Province." *Molecular Ecology* 12 (2003), pp. 1020–1029.

Capelli, Mark H. "Removing Matilija Dam: Opportunities and Challenges for Ventura River Restoration." *Proceedings, U.S. Society on Dams 24th Annual Meeting*. Denver, CO: U.S. Society on Dams, 2004.

Capitolo, P. J. et al. "Aerial Photographic Surveys of Breeding Colonies of Brandt's, Double-Crested and Pelagic Cormorants in Southern California, 2005–07." Unpublished report, Univ. of California, Santa Cruz, Institute of Marine Sciences, 2008.

———. "Comparison of 2007 and 1991 Breeding Population Estimates for Sample Colonies of Western Gulls in Southern California." Unpublished report, Univ. of California, Santa Cruz, Institute of Marine Sciences, 2008.

Carlton, James T., ed. *The Light and Smith Manual: Intertidal Invertebrates from Central California to Oregon*. Berkeley: Univ. of California Press, 2007.

Carter, Harry R. et al. *Breeding Populations of Seabirds in California, 1989–1991*. Vol. 1. Dixon, CA: US Fish and Wildlife Service Northern Prairie Wildlife Research Center, 1992.

Chaney, Ralph W., and H. L. Mason. "A Pleistocene Flora from the Asphalt Deposits at Carpinteria, California." *Contributions to Paleontology*, Carnegie Institution of Washington, March 1933, pp. 47–79.

Chapman, Joseph A., and G. A. Feldhamer, eds. *Wild Mammals of North America*. Baltimore and London: Johns Hopkins Univ. Press, 1982.

Charles, Cheryl et al. "Children and Nature 2008: A Report on the Movement to Reconnect Children to the

Natural World." Children & Nature Network, http://www.childrenand-nature.org/downloads/CNMovement.pdf. Accessed September 7, 2011.

Chatzimanolis, Stylianos, and M. S. Caterino. "Phylogeography of the Darkling Beetle *Coelus ciliatus* in California." *Annals of the Entomological Society of America* 101, No. 5 (2008), pp. 939–949.

———. "Toward a Better Understanding of the Transverse Range Break: Lineage Diversification in Southern California." *Evolution* 61, No. 9 (2007), pp. 2127–2141.

Chelonian Science Foundation. "Western Pond Turtle," http://western-pondturtle.org. Accessed Sept. 5, 2011.

Cheng, Sheauchi, ed. *Forest Service Research Natural Areas in California.* USDA Forest Service Gen. Tech. Rep. PSW-GTR-188, 2004.

Chesser, R. Terry et al. "Fifty-third Supplement to the American Ornithologists' Union Check-List of North American Birds." In *The Auk* 129, No. 3 (July 2012), pp. 573–588.

Chipping, David. *The Geology of San Luis Obispo County.* San Luis Obispo: California Polytechnic State Univ., 1987.

Coan, Eugene V. "Designation of a Neotype for the Pismo Clam, *Tivela stultorum* (Mawe, 1823), and Lectotypes for Synonymous Nominal Taxa (Bivalvia: Veneridae)." *The Veliger* 39, No. 3 (1996): 267–272.

Collins, Charles T., and K. A. Corey. "Territory Acquisition by Island Scrub-Jays: How to Become a Breeder." In *Proceedings of the Sixth California Islands Symposium*, ed. D. K. Garcelon and C. A. Schwemm. National Park Service Technical Publication CHIS-05-01. Arcata, CA: Institute for Wildlife Studies, 2005, pp. 257–262.

Collins, P. W. "Historic and Prehistoric Record for the Occurrence of Island Scrub-Jays (*Aphelocoma insularis*) on the Northern Channel Islands, Santa Barbara County, California." Santa Barbara Museum of Natural History Technical Reports 5, 2009.

———. "Checklist to the Amphibians and Reptiles of California's Central Coast." Unpublished ms. for Santa Barbara Museum of Natural History.

———. "Checklist to the Mammals of California's Central Coast." Unpublished ms. for Santa Barbara Museum of Natural History.

Collins, P. W. et al. "Analysis of Prey Remains Excavated from an Historic Bald Eagle Nest Site on San Miguel Island, California." In *Proceedings of the Sixth California Islands Symposium*, ed. D. K. Garcelon and C. A. Schwemm. National Park Service Technical Publication CHIS-05-01. Arcata, CA: Institute for Wildlife Studies, 2005, pp. 103–120.

Collins, Paul W., C. Drost, and G. M. Fellers. "Migratory Status of Flammulated Owls in California, with Recent Records from the California Channel Islands." *Western Birds* 17 (1986), pp. 21–31.

Collins, Paul W., and H. Lee Jones. "Birds of California's Channel Islands: Their Distribution and Abundance." Unpublished ms.

Collins, Paul W., and Brian C. Latta. "Food Habits of Nesting Golden Eagles (*Aquila chrysaetos*) on Santa Cruz and Santa Rosa Islands, California." In *Proceedings of the Seventh California Islands Symposium,* ed. C. C. Damiani and D. K. Garcelon. Arcata, CA: Institute for Wildlife Studies, 2009, pp. 255–268.

Conil, Sebastien, and A. Hall. "Local Regimes of Atmospheric Variability: A Case Study of Southern California." *Journal of Climate* 19 (2005), pp. 4308–4325.

Conroy, Chris J., and J. L. Newald. "Phylogeographic Study of the California Vole, *Microtus californicus.*" *Journal of Mammology* 89, No. 3 (2008), pp. 755–767.

Coonan, Timothy J., and C. A. Schwemm. "Factors Contributing to Success of Island Fox Reintroductions on San Miguel and Santa Rosa Islands, California." In *Proceedings of the Seventh California Islands Symposium,* ed. C. C. Damiani and D. K. Garcelon. Arcata, CA: Institute for

Wildlife Studies, 2009, pp. 363–376.

Coonan, Timothy J., C. A. Schwemm, and D. K. Garcelon. *Decline and Recovery of the Island Fox: A Case Study for Population Recovery.* Cambridge, UK: Cambridge Univ. Press, 2010.

Cooper, Scott D., and N. Hemphill. "The Effects of Trout on Faunal Assemblages in Stream Pools." Unpublished ms.

Cranshaw, Whitney. *Garden Insects of North America.* Princeton: Princeton Univ. Press, 2004.

Cunningham, Laura. *State of Change: Forgotten Landscapes of California.* Berkeley: Heyday, 2010.

Daane, Kent. "Biological Control of the Red Gum Lerp Psyllid, a Pest of Eucalyptus Species in California." Univ. of California, Berkeley, College of Natural Resources, http://nature.berkeley.edu/biocon/dahlsten/rglp. Sept. 13, 2004.

Dailey, Murray D., D. J. Reish, and J. W. Anderson, eds. *Ecology of the Southern California Bight: A Synthesis and Interpretation.* Berkeley: Univ. of California Press, 1993.

Dallman, Peter R. *Plant Life in the World's Mediterranean Climates.* Berkeley: Univ. of California Press, 1998.

Dana, Richard Henry Jr. *Two Years Before the Mast.* 1840. Reprint, New York: Modern Library, 2001.

Darlington, David. *In Condor Country: A Portrait of a Landscape, Its Denizens, and Its Defenders.* Boston: Houghton Mifflin, 1987.

Davis, John, and A. Baldridge. *The Bird Year: A Book for Birders.* Pacific Grove: Boxwood Press, 1980.

Dawson, E. Yale, and M. S. Foster. *Seashore Plants of California.* Berkeley: Univ. of California Press, 1982.

De Santis, Marie. *California Currents: An Exploration of the Ocean's Pleasures, Mysteries, and Dilemmas.* Novato, CA: Presidio Press, 1985.

DeBlieu, Jan. *Wind: How the Flow of Air Has Shaped Life, Myth, and the Land.* New York: Houghton Mifflin, 1998.

Defenders of Wildlife. "Southern Sea Otter Summary," http://www. defenders.org/sites/default/files/publications/southern_sea_otter_fact_sheet.pdf. Accessed Feb. 6, 2013.

DeLong, Robert L., and Sharon R. Melin. "Thirty Years of Pinniped Research at San Miguel Island." In *Proceedings of the Fifth California Islands Symposium,* ed. D. R. Brown, K. L. Mitchell, and H. W. Chaney. Santa Barbara: Santa Barbara Museum of Natural History, 2002, pp. 401–406.

DeMay, Ida S. "Pleistocene Bird Life of the Carpinteria Asphalt, California." *Contributions to Paleontology* 530 (July 1, 1941), Carnegie Institute of Washington.

Demere, Thomas A. "Early Arikareean (Late Oligocene) Vertebrate Fossils and Biostratigraphic Correlations of the Otay Formation at Eastlake, San Diego County, California." In *Paleogene Stratigraphy, West Coast of North America, Pacific Section,* ed. Mark V. Filewicz and R. L. Squires. Los Angeles: Society of Economic Paleontologists and Mineralogists, 1988.

Denny, Mark W. *Biology and the Mechanics of the Wave-Swept Environment.* Princeton: Princeton Univ. Press, 1988.

Dettinger, Michael. "Fifty-two Years of Pineapple Express Storms across the West Coast of North America." California Energy Commission Public Interest Energy Research Program, CEC-500-2005-004, December 2004.

Dibblee, Thomas W. Jr., "Geology of the Alamo Mountain, Frazier Mountain, Lockwood Valley, Mount Pinos, and Cuyama Badlands Areas, Southern California"; "Geology of the Channel Islands, Southern California"; "Geology of the Santa Ynez–Topatopa Mountains, Southern California"; and "Regional Geology of the Transverse Ranges Provinces of Southern California." In *Geology and Mineral Wealth of the California Transverse Ranges,* ed. D. L. Fife and J. A. Minch. Santa Ana, CA: South Coast Geological Society, 1982.

———. "Geology of the Central Santa Ynez Mountains, Santa Barbara County, CA." *California Division of*

Mines and Geology Bulletin 186, 1966.

Doak, Daniel F. et al. "Understanding and Predicting Ecological Dynamics: Are Major Surprises Inevitable?" *Ecology* 89, No. 4 (April 2008).

Dobson, Andy et al. "Homage to Linnaeus: How Many Parasites? How Many Hosts?" *Proceedings of the National Academy of Sciences* 105, Supp. 1 (Aug. 12, 1008).

Dobson, Heidi E. M. "Bee Fauna Associated with Shrubs in Two California Chaparral Communities." *Pan-Pacific Entomologist* 69, No. 1 (1993), pp. 77–94.

Dooley, J. A., P. B. Sharpe, and D. K. Garcelon. "Movements, Foraging, and Survival of Bald Eagles Reintroduced on the Northern Channel Islands, California." In *Proceedings of the Sixth California Islands Symposium*, ed. D. K. Garcelon and C. A. Schwemm. National Park Service Technical Publication CHIS-05-01. Arcata, CA: Institute for Wildlife Studies, 2005, pp. 313–321.

Doubledee, Rebecca A., E. B. Muller, and R. M. Nisbet. "Bullfrogs, Disturbance Regimes, and the Persistence of California Red-legged Frogs." *Journal of Wildlife Management* 67, No. 2 (2003), pp. 424–438.

Douglas, Paul L., G. E. Forrester, and S. D. Cooper. "Effects of Trout on the Diel Periodicity of Drifting in Baetid Mayflies." *Oecologia* 98 (1994), pp. 48–56.

Doyen, John T. "Biology and Systematics of the Genus *Coelus* (Coleoptera: Tentyriidae)." *Journal of the Kansas Entomological Society* 49, No. 4 (1976).

Dudley, T. L. et al. "Herbivores Associated with *Arundo donax* in California." In *Proceedings of the XII International Symposium on Biological Control of Weeds*, ed. M. H. Julien et al. Wallingford, UK: CAB International, 2008, pp. 146–152.

Dudley, Tom L., and A. M. Lambert. "Completion Report: Biological Control of Invasive Giant Reed (*Arundo donax*)." US Fish and Wildlife Service/Santa Clara River Trustee Council report, December 31, 2007.

Dugan, Jenifer. "Ecological Impacts of Beach Grooming on Exposed Sandy Beaches." *Coastal Ocean Research*, http://www-csgc.ucsd.edu/BOOK-STORE/Resources/PP2003/RCZ174.pdf. October 2003.

Dugan, Jenifer E., and D. M. Hubbard. "Loss of Coastal Strand Habitat in Southern California: The Role of Beach Grooming." *Estuaries and Coasts*, 2009.

Dugan, Jenifer E. et al. "Ecological Effects of Coastal Armoring on Sandy Beaches." *Marine Ecology* 29, Supp. 1 (2008), pp. 160–170.

———. "The Response of Macrofauna Communities and Shorebirds to Macrophyte Wrack Subsidies on Exposed Sandy Beaches of Southern California." *Estuarine, Coastal and Shelf Science* 58S (2003), pp. 133–148.

———. "Macrofauna Communities of Exposed Sandy Beaches on the Southern California Mainland and Channel Islands." In *Proceedings of the Fifth California Islands Symposium*, ed. D. R. Brown, K. L. Mitchell, and H. W. Chaney. Santa Barbara: Santa Barbara Museum of Natural History, 2002, p. 339.

Dunn, Jon L., and J. Alderfer. *Field Guide to the Birds of North America.* 6th ed. Washington, DC: National Geographic Society, 2011.

Easton, Robert. "The Santa Barbara Earthquake: Three Episodes and an Epilogue." *Noticias* (Santa Barbara Historical Society) 36, No. 1 (Spring 1990).

Ehrlich, Paul R., D. D. Murphy, and B. A. Wilcox. "Islands in the Desert." *Natural History* 97 (Oct. 1988), pp. 59–64.

Engblom, Scott B., S. Voland, and T. H. Robinson. "Arroyo Hondo Creek Steelhead/Rainbow Trout Survey." Cachuma Project Biology Staff, unpublished ms.

Eriksen, Clyde H., and D. Belk. *Fairy Shrimps of California's Puddles, Pools, and Playas.* Eureka: Mad River Press, 1999.

Esser, Lora L. "*Eucalyptus globulus.*" *Fire Effects Information System*, http://www.fs.fed.us/database/feis/plants/

tree/eucglo/introductory.html. Accessed Feb. 4, 2013.

Essig Museum of Entomology. "Globose Dune Beetle," http://essig.berkeley.edu/endins/coelglob1.htm. Accessed Feb. 4, 2010.

Faber, Phyllis M. et al. *The Ecology of Riparian Habitats of the Southern California Coastal Region: A Community Profile.* US Fish and Wildlife Service Biological Report 85 (7.27). Washington, DC: Dept. of Interior, 1989.

Fahy, K. A. "The Effect of Habitat Choice, Density and Distribution on Breeding Western Snowy Plovers." Dissertation, Univ. of California, Santa Barbara, 2008.

Failing, Robert M., C. B. Lyon, and J. E. McKittrick. "The Pajaroello Tick Bite." *California Medicine* 116, No. 5 (May 1972).

Feldman, Chris R., and G. S. Spicer. "Comparative Phylogeography of Woodland Reptiles in California." *Molecular Ecology* 15 (2006), pp. 2201–22.

Ferren, Wayne R. Jr. "Carpinteria Salt Marsh: Environment, History, and Botanical Resources of a Southern California Estuary." Dept. of Biological Sciences, Univ. of California, Santa Barbara Herbarium Publication 4, 1985.

Ferren, Wayne R. Jr., and D. A. Pritchett. "Enhancement, Restoration, and Creation of Vernal Pools at Del Sol Open Space and Vernal Pool Reserve, Santa Barbara County, California." Dept. of Biological Sciences, Univ. of California, Santa Barbara Herbarium Environmental Report 13, 1988.

Ferren, Wayne R. Jr. et al. "Review of Ten Years of Vernal Pool Restoration and Creation in Santa Barbara, California." In *Ecology, Conservation, and Management of Vernal Pool Ecosystems,* ed. C. W. Witham et al. Sacramento: California Native Plant Society, 1998, pp. 206–216.

———. "Wetlands of California, Part II: Classification and Description of Wetlands of the Central and Southern California Coast and Coastal Watersheds." *Madroño* 43, No. 1 (1996), pp. 125–182.

———. "Botanical Resources of Emma Wood State Beach and the Ventura River Estuary." Dept. of Biological Sciences, Univ. of California, Santa Barbara Herbarium Environmental Report 15, 1990.

Fiedler, Paul C. et al. "Blue Whale Habitat and Prey in the California Channel Islands." *Deep-Sea Research* 2, No. 45 (1998), pp. 1781–1801.

Fiedler, Peggy L., S. G. Rumsey, and K. M. Wong, eds. *The Environmental Legacy of the UC Natural Reserve System.* Berkeley: Univ. of California Press, 2013.

Fischer, Douglas T. "Ecological and Biogeographic Impact of Fog and Stratus Clouds on Coastal Vegetation, Santa Cruz Island, California." Dissertation, Univ. of California, Santa Barbara, 2007.

Fisher, Robert N., A. V. Suarez, and T. J. Case. "Spatial Patterns in the Abundance of the Coastal Horned Lizard." *Conservation Biology* 16, No. 1 (2002), pp. 205–215.

Force, Don C. "Ecology of Insects in California Chaparral." USDA Forest Service, Pacific Southwest Forest and Range Experiment Station No. PSW-201, 1990.

Ford, Barbara. *Black Bear: The Spirit of the Wilderness.* Boston: Houghton Mifflin, 1981.

Ford, Ray. "Saving the Condor: Robert E. Easton's Fight to Create the Sisquoc Condor Sanctuary." *Noticias* (Santa Barbara Historical Society) 32, No. 4 (1986).

Ford, Raymond Jr. *Santa Barbara Wildfires.* Santa Barbara: McNally & Loftin, 1991.

Foster, Michael S., and D. R. Schiel. *The Ecology of Giant Kelp Forests in California: A Community Profile.* US Fish and Wildlife Service Biological Report 85 (7.2). Washington, DC: Dept. of Interior, 1985.

Fowler, Melinda A. et al. "Hormonal Regulation of Glucose Clearance in Lactating Northern Elephant Seals (*Mirounga angustirostris*)." *Journal of Experimental Biology* 211 (Sept. 2008), 2943–49.

Fraser, Caroline. "Could Re-wilding

Avert the 6th Great Extinction?" *Scientific American,* http://www.sci-entificamerican.com/slideshow.cfm?id=could-re-wilding-avert-6th-great-extinction. Jan. 5, 2010.

Fritsche, A. Eugene, ed., *Sedimentology and Paleontology of Eocene Rocks in the Sespe Creek Area, Ventura County, California.* Pacific Section, Society for Sedimentary Geology Book 74, 1994.

———. *Depositional Environments of Tertiary Rocks along Sespe Creek, Ventura County, California.* Pacific Coast Paleogeography Field Guide 9. Los Angeles: Society of Economic Paleontologists and Mineralogists, 1978.

Fultz, Francis M. *The Elfin Forest.* Los Angeles: Times-Mirror Press, 1927.

Furlong, Laura J., and Adrian M. Wenner. "Stream Fauna of Santa Cruz Island." In *Proceedings of the Fifth California Islands Symposium,* ed. D. R. Brown, K. L. Mitchell, and H. W. Chaney. Santa Barbara: Santa Barbara Museum of Natural History, 2002, pp. 247–255.

Gabil, Margaret P., and L. Rose. *Seashore Syllabus.* Santa Barbara: Santa Barbara Underseas Foundation, 1975.

Gaede, Peter. "Survey for the Belding's Savannah Sparrow at the Carpinteria Salt Marsh Reserve, Santa Barbara County, California." Unpublished ms.

———. "Diet and Feeding Activity at a Flammulated Owl Nest in Idaho." *Western Birds* 34 (2003), pp. 182–183.

Gamradt, Seth C., and L. B. Kats. "Effect of Introduced Crayfish and Mosquitofish on California Newts." *Conservation Biology* 10, No. 4 (Aug. 1996), pp. 1155–62.

Germano, D. J. et al. "The San Joaquin Desert of California: Ecologically Misunderstood and Overlooked." *Natural Areas Journal* 31 (2011), pp. 138–147.

Germano, David J., and G. B. Rathbun. "Growth, Population Structure, and Reproduction of Western Pond Turtles (*Actinemys marmorata*) on the Central Coast of California." *Chelonian Conservation and Biology* 7, No. 2 (2008), pp. 188–194.

Gibson, A. C., P. W. Rundel, and M. R. Sharfi. "Ecology and Ecophysiology of a Subalpine Fellfield Community on Mt. Pinos, Southern California." *Madroño* 55, No. 1 (2008), pp. 41–51.

Gilliam, Harold. *Weather of the San Francisco Bay Region.* 2d ed. Berkeley: Univ. of California Press, 2002.

Going, Barbara M., and T. L. Dudley. "Invasive Riparian Plant Litter Alters Aquatic Insect Growth." *Biological Invasions* 10, No. 7 (2007), pp. 1041–51.

Gordon, Deborah M. "Twitter in the Ant Nest." *Natural History* 119, No. 6 (June 2011).

———. "Colonial Studies." *Boston Review,* Sept./Oct. 2010.

———. "Control without Hierarchy." *Nature* 446 (March 8, 2007).

Gould, S. J. "A Special Fondness for Beetles." *Natural History* 102, No. 1 (1993), pp. 4–9.

Graham, Michael H., J. A. Vásquez, and A. H. Buschmann. "Global Ecology of the Giant Kelp *Macrocystis:* From Ecotypes to Ecosystems." In *Oceanography and Marine Biology: An Annual Review* 45 (2007), pp. 39–88.

Gray, Robert S. "When Mastodons Roamed the Goleta Valley." Santa Barbara Museum of Natural History *Museum Talk,* Winter 1971-72.

Greaves, Jim. "2002 Bird Survey of the Hedrick Ranch Natural Area Property." Oakland, CA: URS Corporation, 2002.

Greaves, Jim, and Z. Labinger. "Site Tenacity and Dispersal of Least Bell's Vireos." *Transactions of the Western Section of the Wildlife Society* 33 (1997), pp. 18–33.

Greene, Michael J., and D. M. Gordon. "Structural Complexity of Chemical Recognition Cues Affects the Perception of Group Membership in the Ants *Linephithema humile* and *Aphaenogaster cockerelli.*" *Journal of Experimental Biology* 210 (Jan. 4, 2007), 897–905.

Grinnell, Joseph. "Up-Hill Planters." *The Condor* 38 (1936), pp. 80–82.

———. "The Burrowing Rodents of California as Agents in Soil Formation." *Journal of Mammalogy* 4, No. 3

(1923), pp. 137–149.

———. "Cuyama Valley." Field Notes, April 22, 1912.

Grinnell, Joseph, J. Dixon, and J. M. Linsdale. *Fur-Bearing Mammals of California*. 2 vols. Berkeley: Univ. of California Press, 1937.

Grinnell, Joseph, and A. H. Miller. *The Distribution of the Birds of California*. 1944. Reprint, Lee Vining, CA: Artemisia Press, 1986.

Hall, Clarence A. Jr. *Nearshore Marine Paleoclimatic Regions, Increasing Zoogeographic Provinciality, Molluscan Extinctions, and Paleoshorelines, California*. Special Paper 357. Boulder, CO.: Geological Society of America, 2002.

Hall, E. Raymond, ed. *The Mammals of North America*, Vol. 1. 2d ed. Caldwell, NJ: Blackburn Press, 1981.

Halsey, Richard W. *Fire, Chaparral, and Survival in Southern California*. San Diego: Sunbelt Publications, 2005.

Hamber, Janet, and Bronwyn Davey. "AC8, AC9 and the Last Days of Wild California Condors," *USFWS Hopper Mountain National Wildlife Refuge Complex*, http://www.fws.gov/hoppermountain/index.html. Accessed Feb. 6, 2013.

Hamilton, Jason G. "Changing Perceptions of Pre-European Grasslands in California." *Madroño* 44, No. 4 (1997), pp. 311–333.

Harden, Deborah R. *California Geology*. Upper Saddle River, NJ: Prentice Hall, 1998.

Harvey, Michael J., J. S. Altenbach, and T. L. Best. *Bats of the United States*. Arkansas Game and Fish Commission, 1999.

Havlik, Neil. "The Temblors: Ugly Duckling of the Coast Ranges." *Fremontia* 33, No. 4 (2005), pp. 15–19.

Hayes, Miles G., and J. Michel. *A Coast to Explore: Coastal Geology and Ecology of Central California*. Columbia, SC: Pandion Books, 2010.

Heller, N. E., K. K. Ingram, and D. M. Gordon. "Nest Connectivity and Colony Structure in Unicolonial Argentine Ants." *Insectes Sociaux* 55 (2008), pp. 397–403.

Heller, N. E. et al. "Rainfall Facilitates the Spread, and Time Alters the Impact, of the Invasive Argentine Ant." *Oecologia* 155, No. 2, pp. 385–395.

Heller, Nicole E., N. J. Sanders, and D. M. Gordon. "Linking Temporal and Spatial Scales in the Study of an Argentine Ant Invasion." *Biological Invasions* 8 (2006), pp. 501–507.

Hildner, K. K. *Guide to Native and Invasive Plants of the Storke Ranch Vernal Pool Open Space*. Santa Barbara: The Coastal Fund of UC Santa Barbara, 2009.

Hinton, Sam. *Seashore Life of Southern California*. Rev. ed. Berkeley: Univ. of California Press, 1987.

Hoffmann, Ralph. *Birds of the Pacific States*. Boston: Houghton Mifflin, 1927.

Hogue, Charles L. *Insects of the Los Angeles Basin*. Los Angeles: Natural History Museum of Los Angeles County, 1993.

Holland, V. L., and D. J. Keil. *California Vegetation*. Dubuque, IA: Kendall/Hunt, 1995.

Holstein, Glen. "Pre-agricultural Grassland in Central California." *Madroño* 48, No. 4 (2001), pp. 253–264.

Hoover, Robert F. *Vascular Plants of San Luis Obispo County*. Berkeley: Univ. of California Press, 1970.

Horn, M. H., and L. G. Allen. "Numbers of Species and Faunal Resemblance of Marine Fishes in California Bays and Estuaries." *Bulletin of Southern California Academy of Science* 75 (1976), pp. 159–170.

Hovore, Frank T. et al. *Santa Clara River Watershed Amphibian and Macroinvertebrate Bioassessment Project Final Report*. Ventura, CA: Santa Clara River Trustee Council, 2008.

Howald, Gregg R. et al. "Eradication of Black Rats from Anacapa Island: Biological and Social Considerations." In *Proceedings of the Sixth California Islands Symposium*, ed. D. K. Garcelon and C. A. Schwemm. National Park Service Technical Publication CHIS-05-01. Arcata, CA: Institute for Wildlife Studies, 2005, pp. 299–312.

Howard, Hildegarde. "A Gigantic Toothed Marine Bird from the

Miocene of California." Santa Barbara Museum of Natural History, Dept. of Geology Bulletin 1 (Feb. 1957).

———. "A New Species of Cormorant from Pliocene Deposits near Santa Barbara, California." *The Condor* 34 (May–June, 1932), pp. 118–120.

Howard, Jeffrey L. "Provenance of Quartzite Clasts in the Eocene-Oligocene Sespe Formation." *Geological Society of America Bulletin* 112, No. 11 (Nov. 2000), pp. 1635–49.

Hubbard, David M., and J. E. Dugan. "Shorebird Use of an Exposed Sandy Beach in Southern California." *Estuarine, Coastal and Shelf Science* 58, Supp. 1 (2003), pp. 41–54.

Human, Vernon. *A Naturalist at Play— In Coastal California and Beyond.* Lompoc, CA: Lompoc Valley Botanic and Horticultural Society, 2004.

Hunt, George L. Jr., R. L. Pitman, and H. L. Jones. "Distribution and Abundance of Seabirds Breeding on the California Channel Islands." In *The California Islands: Proceedings of a Multidisciplinary Symposium,* ed. Dennis M. Power. Santa Barbara: Santa Barbara Museum of Natural History, 1980, pp. 443–459.

Hunt, Lawrence E. "Origin, Maintenance and Land Use of Aeolian Sand Dunes of the Santa Maria Basin, California." Vandenberg AFB: The Nature Conservancy and US Air Force, 1993.

Israelowitz, Meir, S. H. W. Rizvi, and H. P. von Schroeder. "Fluorescence of the Fire-Chaser Beetle *Melanophila acuminate.*" *Journal of Luminescence* 126, No. 1 (2007), pp. 149–154.

Jacob, Udo, H. Walther, and R. Klenke. "Aquatic Insect Larvae as Indicators of Limiting Minimal Contents of Dissolved Oxygen," part II. *Aquatic Insects* 6, No. 3 (1984), pp. 185–190.

James, Sarah E., and R. T. McCloskey. "Lizard Microhabitat and Fire Fuel Management." *Biological Conservation* 114 (2003), pp. 293–297.

Jameson, E. W. Jr., and H. J. Peeters. *Mammals of California.* Berkeley: Univ. of California Press, 2004.

Janowski-Bell, M. E., and N. V. Horner. "Movement of the Male Brown Tarantula, *Aphonopelma hentzi* (Araneae, Theraphosidae), Using Radio Telemetry." *Journal of Arachnology* 24 (1999), pp. 503–512.

Jockusch, Elizabeth L., and D. B. Wake. "Falling Apart and Merging: Diversification of Slender Salamanders (Plethodontidae: *Batrachoseps*) in the American West." *Biological Journal of the Linnaean Society* 76, No. 3 (2002), pp. 361–391.

Johnson, David H. "Systematic Review of the Chipmunks (Genus *Eutamias*) of California." *University of California Publications in Zoology* 48, No. 2 (1943), pp. 63–148.

Johnson, Maile, T. Dudley, and C. Burns. "Seed Production in *Arundo donax?*" *Cal-IPC News* 14, No. 3 (2006).

Johnson, Norman F., and C. A. Triplehorn. *Borror and DeLong's Introduction to the Study of Insects.* 7th ed. St. Paul: Brooks Cole, 2004.

Johnson, Paul S., S. R. Shifley, and R. Rogers. *The Ecology and Silviculture of Oaks.* Oxfordshire, UK: CABI, 2009.

Johnston, Verna R. *California Forests and Woodlands.* Berkeley: Univ. of California Press, 1994.

Jones, B. H. "Upwelling at Point Conception and Its Interaction with the Santa Barbara Channel." Allan Hancock Foundation, Univ. of Southern California, n.d.

Jones, Lee, Paul Collins, and Rose Stefani. "A Checklist of the Birds of Channel Islands National Park." Tucson: Southwest Parks and Monuments Association, 1989.

Jones, Steve. "Ten Thousand Wedges: Biodiversity, Natural Selection and Random Change." In *Seeing Further: The Story of Science, Discovery and the Genius of the Royal Society,* ed. Bill Bryson. New York: William Morrow, 2010, pp. 274–293.

———. *Darwin's Ghost: The Origin of Species Updated.* New York: Ballantine, 2000.

Junak, Steve T. et al. "A Checklist of Vascular Plants of Channel Islands National Park." Tucson: Southwest Parks and Monuments Association, 1997.

———. *A Flora of Santa Cruz Island.* Santa Barbara: Santa Barbara Botanic Garden, 1995.

Junger, Arne, and D. L. Johnson. "Was There a Quaternary Land Bridge to the Northern Channel Islands?" In *The California Islands: Proceedings of a Multidisciplinary Symposium,* ed. Dennis M. Power. Santa Barbara: Santa Barbara Museum of Natural History, 1980, pp. 33–39.

Keator, Glenn. *The Life of an Oak: An Intimate Portrait.* Berkeley: Heyday, 1998.

Keeler-Wolf, Todd. "Ecological Survey of the Proposed Big Pine Mountain Research Natural Area, Los Padres National Forest, Santa Barbara County, California." Unpublished ms.

Keller, Edward A. *Santa Barbara, a Land of Dynamic Beauty: A Natural History.* Santa Barbara: Santa Barbara Museum of Natural History, 2011.

King, Julie, and A. Muchlinski. *Southern California Fox Squirrel Research Project,* http://instructional1.calstatela.edu/amuchli/squirrelform.htm. Nov. 21, 2004.

Klauber, Lawrence M. *Rattlesnakes: Their Habits, Life Histories, and Influence on Mankind.* Abridged ed. Berkeley: Univ. of California Press, 1982.

Koehl, Mimi. *Wave-Swept Shore: The Rigors of Life on a Rocky Coast.* Berkeley: Univ. of California Press, 2006.

Koenig, Walter D., J. M. H. Knops, and W. J. Carmen. "Arboreal Seed Removal and Insect Damage in Three California Oaks." In *Proceedings of the Fifth Symposium on Oak Woodlands,* ed. Richard B. Standiford et al. Albany, CA: USDA Forest Service Pacific Southwest Research Station, 2002.

Koenig, Walter D., J. P. McEntee, and E. L. Walters. "Acorn Harvesting by Acorn Woodpeckers: Annual Variation and Comparison with Genetic Estimates." *Evolutionary Ecology Research* 10 (2008), pp. 811–822.

Koenig, Walter D., and R. L. Mumme. "The Great Egg-Demolition Derby." *Natural History* 106, No. 5 (1999), 32–37.

Kreissman, Bern. *California: An Environmental Atlas and Guide.* Davis, CA: Bear Klaw Press, 1991.

Kruckberg, Arthur R. *Introduction to California Soils and Plants.* Berkeley: Univ. of California Press, 2006.

———. *California Serpentines: Flora, Vegetation, Geology, Soils, and Management Problems.* Berkeley: Univ. of California Press, 1984.

Kuchler, A. W. "Map of the Natural Vegetation of California." In *Terrestrial Vegetation of California,* ed. M. G. Barbour and J. Major. 1977. Reprint, Sacramento: Calif. Native Plant Society, 1988.

Kuchta, Shawn R., and An-Ming Tan. "Lineage Diversification on an Evolving Landscape: Phylogeography of the California Newt, *Taricha torosa* (Caudata: Salamandridae)." *Biological Journal of the Linnaean Society* 89 (2006), pp. 213–239.

Kurten, Bjorn, and E. Andersen. *Pleistocene Mammals of North America.* New York: Columbia Univ. Press, 1980.

Lafferty, Kevin D. "Fishing for Lobsters Indirectly Increases Epidemics in Sea Urchins." *Ecological Applications* 14, No. 5 (2004), pp. 1566–73.

Lafferty, Kevin D. et al. "Food Webs and Parasites in a Salt Marsh Ecosystem." In *Ecology: Community Structure and Pathogen Dynamics,* ed. S. Collinge and C. Ray. New York: Oxford Univ. Press, 2005.

Lanner, Ronald M. *Conifers of California.* Los Olivos, CA: Cachuma Press, 1999.

Lannoo, Michael. *Amphibian Declines: The Conservation Status of United States Species.* Berkeley: Univ. of California Press, 2005.

Lapointe, Francois-Joseph, and L. J. Rissler. "Notes and Comments: Congruence, Consensus, and the Comparative Phylogeography of Codistributed Species in California." *American Naturalist* 166, No. 2 (Aug. 2005), pp. 290–299.

Latta, B. C. et al. "Capture and Translocation of Golden Eagles from the California Channel Islands to Mitigate Depredation of Endemic Island Foxes." In *Proceedings of the Sixth*

California Islands Symposium, ed. D. K. Garcelon and C. A. Schwemm. National Park Service Technical Publication CHIS-05-01. Arcata, CA: Institute for Wildlife Studies, 2005, pp. 341–350.

Lehman, Paul E. *The Birds of Santa Barbara County, California*. Santa Barbara: Univ. of California Vertebrate Museum, 1994.

Lentz, Joan Easton. *Introduction to the Birds of the Southern California Coast*. Berkeley: Univ. of California Press, 2006.

———. "Breeding Birds of Four Isolated Mountains in Southern California." *Western Birds* 24 (1993), pp. 201–234.

———. *Great Birding Trips of the West*. Santa Barbara: Capra Press, 1989.

Lettis, William R. et al. "Quaternary Tectonic Setting of South-Central Coastal California." USGS Bulletin 1995-AA.

Lillywhite, Harvey B. "Effects of Chaparral Conversion on Small Vertebrates in Southern California." *Biological Conservation* 11, No. 3 (1977), pp. 171–184.

Linkhart, Brian D., R. T. Reynolds, and R. A. Ryder. "Home Range and Habitat of Breeding Flammulated Owls in Colorado." *Wilson Bulletin* 110, No. 3 (1998), pp. 342–351.

Linsley, E. G., and P. D. Hurd Jr. "Melanophila Beetles at Cement Plants in Southern California (Coleoptera, Buprestidae)." *Coleopterists Bulletin* 11, No. 1/2 (1957), pp. 9–11.

Little, Crispin T. S. et al. "Early Jurassic Hydrothermal Vent Community from the Franciscan Complex, San Rafael Mountains, California." *Geology* 27, No. 2 (1999), pp. 167–170.

Louv, Richard. *Last Child in the Woods: Saving Our Children from Nature-Deficit Disorder*. Chapel Hill, NC: Algonquin Books of Chapel Hill, 2006.

Love, Milton S. *Certainly More Than You Want to Know about the Fishes of the Pacific Coast*. Santa Barbara: Really Big Press, 2011.

———. *Probably More Than You Want to Know about the Fishes of the Pacific Coast*. Santa Barbara: Really Big Press, 1996.

Lowe, D. W., J. R. Matthews, and C. J. Moseley. *The Official World Wildlife Fund Guide to Endangered Species of North America*. Washington, DC: Walton Beacham, 1990.

Luttbeg, Barney, and T. A. Langen. "Comparing Alternative Models to Empirical Data: Cognitive Models of Western Scrub-Jay Foraging Behavior." *American Naturalist* 163, No. 2 (2004), pp. 263–274.

Mahrdt, Clark R. *Natural Resources of Coastal Wetlands in Santa Barbara County*. Sacramento: Calif. Dept. of Fish and Game, US Fish and Wildlife Service, 1976.

Manolis, Tim. *Dragonflies and Damselflies of California*. Berkeley: Univ. of California Press, 2003.

Martin, Melissa. "Urban Ecosystems," http://depts.washington.edu/open2100/Resources/5_New%20Research/UrbanEcosystems.pdf. Accessed Sept. 8, 2011.

Matocq, Marjorie D., and Francis X. Villablanca. "Low Genetic Diversity in an Endangered Species: Recent or Historic Pattern?" *Biological Conservation* 98 (2001), pp. 61–68.

Matthiessen, Peter. *The Wind Birds*. New York: Viking Press, 1973.

McChesney, G. J., H. R. Carter, and D. L. Whitworth. "Reoccupation and Extension of Southern Breeding Limits of Tufted Puffins and Rhinoceros Auklets in California." *Colonial Waterbirds* 18, No. 1 (1995), pp. 79–90.

McCrary, Michael D., and M. O. Pierson. "Influence of Human Activity on Shorebird Beach Use in Ventura County, California." In *Proceedings of the Fifth California Islands Symposium*, ed. D. R. Brown, K. L. Mitchell, and H. W. Chaney. Santa Barbara: Santa Barbara Museum of Natural History, 2002, pp. 424–433.

McCullough, Dale R., J. K. Fischer, and J. D. Ballou. "From Bottleneck to Metapopulation: Recovery of the Tule Elk in California." In *Metapopulations and Wildlife Conservation*, ed. Dale R. McCullough. Washington, DC: Island Press, 1996.

McMillan, Ian. *Man and the California Condor.* New York: E. P. Dutton & Co., 1968.

McPhee, John. *Assembling California.* New York: Farrar, Straus and Giroux, 1993.

Melin, Sharon R., and Robert L. DeLong. "At-Sea Distribution and Diving Behavior of California Sea Lion Females from San Miguel Island, California." In *Proceedings of the Fifth California Islands Symposium,* ed. D. R. Brown, K. L. Mitchell, and H. W. Chaney. Santa Barbara: Santa Barbara Museum of Natural History, 2002, pp. 407–412.

Messinger, Olivia, and T. Griswold. "A Pinnacle of Bees." *Fremontia* 30 (2003), pp. 32–40.

Miles, Scott R., and Charles B. Goudey, comp. "Ecological Subregions of California: Section and Subsection Descriptions." San Francisco: USDA Forest Service, Pacific Southwest Region, 1997.

Milius, Susan. "Worries Grow over Monarch Butterflies." *Science News,* April 23, 2011.

Miller, A. H. *An Analysis of the Distribution of the Birds of California.* Berkeley: Univ. of California Press, 1951.

Miller, Loye. "Avian Remains from the Miocene of Lompoc, California." In *Studies on the Fossil Flora and Fauna of the Western United States.* Washington, DC: Carnegie Institute of Washington, 1925, pp. 107–117.

Miller, Loye, and Ida DeMay. "The Fossil Birds of California." *University of California Publications in Zoology* 47, No. 4. (1942), pp. 47–142.

Mills, K. L., W. J. Sydeman, and P. J. Hodum, eds. *The California Current Marine Bird Conservation Plan,* Version 1.0. Stinson Beach, CA: PRBO Conservation Science, Stinson Beach, April 2005.

Miner, Melissa C. et al. *Monitoring of Rocky Intertidal Resources along the Central and Southern California Mainland: Comprehensive Report (1992–2003) for San Luis Obispo, Santa Barbara, Ventura, Los Angeles, and Orange Counties.* Camarillo, CA: Dept. of Interior Minerals Management Service, 2005.

Moe, L. Maynard. *A Key to Vascular Plant Species of Kern County, California.* Sacramento: California Native Plant Society, 1995.

Moline, Mark A. "Coastal Upwelling and the Spring Bloom." *Avila Community News,* May 2009.

Mondragon, Jennifer, and Jeff Mondragon. *Seaweeds of the Pacific Coast: Common Marine Algae from Alaska to Baja California.* Monterey, CA: Sea Challengers, 2003.

Monroe, Jeremy B., and J. D. Olden. "Aqua-Rock Climbers." *Natural History* 117, No. 4 (May 2008), p. 64.

Morris, Robert H., Donald P. Abbott, and Eugene C. Haderlie, eds. *Intertidal Invertebrates of California.* Stanford: Stanford Univ. Press, 1980.

Morro Group. "Morro Blue Butterfly Survey and Relocation Report." County of San Luis Obispo, Los Osos Wastewater Facilities Project, Sept. 28, 2004.

Muller, R. N., and J. R. Haller. *Trees of Santa Barbara.* Santa Barbara: Santa Barbara Botanic Garden, 2005.

Muller, Robert. "The Chaparral Is Not Our Enemy." *Santa Barbara Independent,* Dec 24, 2008.

Murray, Steven N., Mark M. Littler, and Isabella A. Abbott. "Biogeography of the California Marine Algae with Emphasis on the Southern California Islands." In *The California Islands: Proceedings of a Multidisciplinary Symposium,* ed. Dennis M. Power. Santa Barbara: Santa Barbara Museum of Natural History, 1980, pp. 325–337.

Norris, Robert M. *The Geology and Landscape of Santa Barbara County and Its Offshore Islands.* Santa Barbara: Santa Barbara Museum of Natural History, 2003.

Norris, Robert M., and R. W. Webb. *Geology of California.* 2d ed. New York: John Wiley & Sons, 1990.

Nosil, Patrik, B. J. Crespi, and C. P. Sandoval. "Host-Plant Adaptation Drives the Parallel Evolution of Reproductive Isolation." *Nature* 47 (2002), pp. 440–443.

Nybakken, James W., and M. D. Bertness. *Marine Biology: An Ecological Approach.* 6th ed. San Francisco: Pearson/Benjamin Cummings, 2005.

Oleson, Erin M. et al. "Behavioral Context of Call Production by Eastern North Pacific Blue Whales." *Marine Ecology Progress Series* 330 (2007), pp. 269–284.

Onuf, Christopher P. *The Ecology of Mugu Lagoon, California: An Estuarine Profile.* US Fish and Wildlife Service Biological Report 85 (7.15), June 1987.

Osgood, Kenric E., and David M. Checkley Jr. "Seasonal Variations in a Deep Aggregation of *Calanus pacificus* in the Santa Barbara Basin." *Marine Ecology Progress Series* 148 (1997), pp. 59–69.

Owings, Donald H., and Daniel W. Leger. "Chatter Vocalizations of California Ground Squirrels: Predator- and Social-Role Specificity." *Zeitschrift für Tierpsychologie* 54, No. 2 (1980), pp. 163–184.

Page, Henry M. "Checklist of Invertebrates (for Carpinteria Salt Marsh)." Unpublished ms.

Page, Henry M., and K. D. Lafferty. "Estuarine and Marine Invertebrates of Carpinteria Salt Marsh." Univ. of California, Santa Barbara, Marine Science Institute. Unpublished ms.

Palmer, Christine. "The 1925 Santa Barbara Earthquake, A 75th Anniversary Commemoration." *Noticias* (Santa Barbara Historical Society) 46, No. 2 (Summer 2000).

Parham, James F., and T. F. Papenfuss. "High Genetic Diversity among Fossorial Lizard Populations (*Anniella pulchra*) in a Rapidly Developing Landscape (Central California)." *Conservation Genetics* 10, No. 1 (2009), pp. 169–176.

Parsons, J. J. "'Fog Drip' from Coastal Stratus, with Special Reference to California." *Weather* 15, No. 2 (Feb. 1960), pp. 58–62.

Pavlik, Bruce et al. *Oaks of California.* Los Olivos, CA: Cachuma Press, 1991.

Phillips, David, and Hugh Nash. *The Condor Question: Captive or Forever Free?* San Francisco: Friends of the Earth, 1981.

Pierson, E. D. et al. *Distribution, Status and Habitat Associations of Bat Species on Vandenberg Air Force Base, Santa Barbara County, California.* Santa Barbara: Santa Barbara Museum of Natural History, 2002.

Pluess, Andrea R. et al. "Short Distance Pollen Movement in a Wind-Pollinated Tree, *Quercus lobata* (Fagaceae)." *Forest Ecology and Management* 258, No. 5 (2009), 735–744.

Powell, Abby N. "Are Southern California's Fragmented Salt Marshes Capable of Sustaining Endemic Bird Populations?" *Studies in Avian Biology* 32 (2006), pp. 198–204.

Powell, Jerry A. "Biogeography of Lepidoptera on the California Channel Islands." In *Proceedings of the Fourth California Islands Symposium: Update on the Status of Resources,* ed. W. L. Halvorson and G. J. Maender. Santa Barbara: Santa Barbara Museum of Natural History, 1994, pp. 449–464.

Powell, Jerry A., and C. L. Hogue. *California Insects.* Berkeley: Univ. of California Press, 1979.

Powell, Jerry A., and David L. Wagner. "The Microlepidoptera Fauna of Santa Cruz Island Is Less Depauperate Than That of Butterflies and Larger Moths." In *Proceedings of the Third California Islands Symposium: Recent Advances in California Islands Research,* ed. F. G. Hochberg. Santa Barbara: Santa Barbara Museum of Natural History, 1993, pp. 189–198.

Priestaf, Iris. "Natural Tar Seeps and Asphalt Deposits of Santa Barbara County." *California Geology* 32 (Aug. 1979), pp. 163–169.

Priestaf, Richard C., and John F. Emmel. "An Extraordinary New Subspecies of *Philotiella speciosa* (Lepidoptera: Lycaenidae) from Coastal Santa Barbara County, California." In *Systematics of Western North American Butterflies,* ed. Thomas C. Emmel. Santa Fe, NM: Mariposa Press, 1988, pp. 283–286.

Quammen, David. *The Song of the Dodo: Island Biogeography in an Age of Extinctions.* New York: Simon and Schuster, 1996.

Quinn, Ronald D., and S. C. Keeley. *Introduction to California Chaparral.* Berkeley: Univ. of California Press, 2006.

Ralls, Katherine, and L. L. Eberhardt. "Assessment of Abundance of San Joaquin Kit Foxes by Spotlight Surveys." *Journal of Mammalogy* 78, No. 1 (1997), pp. 65–73.

Ralls, Katherine, and P. J. White. "Predation on San Joaquin Kit Foxes by Larger Canids." *Journal of Mammalogy* 76, No. 3 (1995), pp. 723–729.

Ralph, F. M., and M. D. Dettinger. "Storms, Floods, and the Science of Atmospheric Rivers." *EOS* 92, No. 32 (Aug. 2011), pp. 265–272.

Ratcliffe, John M. et al. "Adaptive Auditory Risk Assessment in the Dogbane Tiger Moth When Pursued by Bats." *Proceedings of the Royal Society B: Biological Sciences* 278, No. 1704 (2011), pp. 364–370.

Richmond, Jonathan Q. et al. "Population Genetics of the California Red-legged Frog *(Rana draytonii):* Effects of Wildfires on Genetic Diversity…" USGS Western Ecological Research Center, San Diego Field Station, Sept. 2011.

Ricketts, Edward F., Jack Calvin, and Joel W. Hedgpeth. *Between Pacific Tides.* 5th ed. Rev. David W. Phillips. Stanford: Stanford Univ. Press, 1985.

Rissler, Leslie J. et al. "Phylogeographic Lineages and Species Comparisons in Conservation Analyses: A Case Study of California Herpetofauna." *American Naturalist* 167, No. 5 (2006), pp. 655–666.

Roth, V. Louise. "Inferences from Allometry and Fossils: Dwarfing of Elephants on Islands." In *Oxford Surveys in Evolutionary Biology*, Vol. 8, ed. D. Futuyma and J. Antonovics. New York: Oxford Univ. Press, 1992.

Rowe, M. P., R. G. Coss, and D. H. Owings. "Rattlesnake Rattles and Burrowing Owl Hisses: A Case of Acoustic Batesian Mimicry." *Ethnology* 72, No. 1 (1986), pp. 53–71.

Ruano, Saraiya. "The Secret Life of the Flammulated Owl: Territoriality, Unfaithfulness, Forest Fires, Geolocators, and Isotope Ratios." *Birding* (Jan. 2010), pp. 32–36.

Rundel, Philip W., and R. Gustafson. *An Introduction to the Plant Life of Southern California.* Berkeley: Univ. of California Press, 2005.

Russo, Ron. "Confessions of a Gall Hunter." *Natural History* 118, No. 10, pp. 19–25.

———. *Field Guide to Plant Galls of California and Other Western States.* Berkeley: Univ. of California Press, 2006.

Ryden, Hope. *God's Dog: A Celebration of the North American Coyote.* New York: Viking Press, 1979.

Sadava, David et al. *Life: The Science of Biology.* 8th ed. Gordonsville, VA: Sinauer W.H. Freeman, 2006.

Salkeld, Daniel J., and R. S. Lane. "Community Ecology and Disease Risk: Lizards, Squirrels, and the Lyme Disease Spirochete in California, USA." *Ecology* 91 (2010), pp. 293–298.

Santa Barbara Botanic Garden. "The Never-Ending Battle between Native and Invasive Plants." *Ironwood* 19, No. 4 (Fall 2011), p. 1.

———. "Checklist of Birds of the Santa Barbara Botanic Garden." Santa Barbara: Santa Barbara Botanic Garden, 2011.

Santos, Robert L. *The Eucalyptus of California: Seeds of Good or Seeds of Evil?,* http://wwwlibrary.csustan.edu/bsantos/euctoc.htm. Accessed Dec. 3, 2011.

Saunders, Charles Francis. *The Wild Gardens of Old California.* Santa Barbara: Wallace Hebberd, 1927.

Sauvajot, Raymond M. et al. "Patterns of Human Disturbance and Response by Small Mammals and Birds in Chaparral near Urban Development." *Urban Ecosystems* 2, No. 4 (1998), pp. 279–297.

Savage, Donald E., and T. Downs. "Cenozoic Land Life of Southern California." In *Geology of Southern California*, ed. Richard H. Jahns. California Division of Mines Bulletin 170 (Sept. 1954).

Sawyer, John O., T. Keeler-Wolf, and J.

Evans. *A Manual of California Vegetation*. Sacramento: California Native Plant Society, 2008.

Schaffer, Jeffrey P. "California's Geological History and Changing Landscapes." In *The Jepson Manual, Higher Plants of California*, ed. James C. Hickman. Berkeley: Univ. of California Press, 1993, pp. 49–54.

Scheffer, Marten et al. "Why Plankton Communities Have No Equilibrium: Solutions to the Paradox." *Hydrobiologia* 491 (2003), pp. 9–18.

Schick, Katherine N. "Cynipid-Induced Galls and California Oaks." *Fremontia* 30, No. 3, 4 (2002): 15–18.

Schlacher, Thomas A. et al. "Sandy Beaches at the Brink." *Diversity and Distributions* 13 (2007), pp. 556–560.

Schoenherr, Allan A. *A Natural History of California*. Berkeley: Univ. of California Press, 1995.

Schoenherr, Allan A., C. R. Feldmeth, and M. J. Emerson. *Natural History of the Islands of California*. Berkeley: Univ. of California Press, 1999.

Schram, Brad. *A Birder's Guide to Southern California*. Colorado Springs, CO: American Birding Assn., 1998.

Scofield, Douglas G., V. L. Sork, and P. E. Smouse. "Influence of Acorn Woodpecker Social Behavior on Transport of Coast Live Oak (*Quercus Agrifolia*) Acorns…" *Journal of Ecology* 98 (2010), pp. 561–572.

Seabloom, Eric W. et al. "Invasion, Competitive Dominance, and Resource Use by Exotic and Native California Grassland Species." *Proceedings of the National Academy of Sciences* 100, No. 23 (2003), pp. 13384–89.

Seapy, Roger R., and M. M. Littler. "Biogeography of Rocky Intertidal Macroinvertebrates of the Southern California Islands." In *The California Islands: Proceedings of a Multidisciplinary Symposium*, ed. Dennis M. Power. Santa Barbara: Santa Barbara Museum of Natural History, 1980, pp. 307–323.

Shaffer, H. Bradley et al. "The Molecular Phylogenetics of Endangerment: Cryptic Variation and Historical Phylogeography of the California Tiger Salamander, *Ambystoma californiense*." *Molecular Ecology* 13, No. 10 (2004), pp. 3033–49.

Sharp, Robert P. *A Field Guide to Southern California*. 3d ed. Dubuque, IA: Kendall-Hunt, 1994.

Sharp, Robert P., and Allen F. Glazner. *Geology Underfoot in Southern California*. Missoula, MT: Mountain Press Publishing, 1993.

Shaw, William N., and T. J. Hassler. "Species Profiles: Life Histories and Environmental Requirements of Coastal Fishes and Invertebrates (Pacific Southwest): Pismo Clam." US Fish and Wildlife Service Biological Report 82 (11.95), 1989.

Shuford, W. David, and T. Gardali, eds. *California Bird Species of Special Concern*. Camarillo, CA: Western Field Ornithologists, 2008.

Sibley, David Allen. *The Sibley Field Guide to Birds of Western North America*. New York: Alfred A. Knopf, 2003.

Siebert, Charles. "Watching Whales Watching Us." *New York Times*, July 12, 2009.

Simberloff, Daniel. "Impacts of Introduced Species in the United States." *Consequences* 2, No. 2 (1996).

Smith, Clifton F. *A Flora of the Santa Barbara Region, California*. Santa Barbara: Santa Barbara Botanic Garden and Capra Press, 1998.

Smith, Dick. *Condor Journal: The History, Mythology, and Reality of the California Condor*. Santa Barbara: Capra Press and Santa Barbara Museum of Natural History, 1978.

Snyder, Noel, and Helen Snyder. *The California Condor: A Saga of Natural History and Conservation*. London and San Diego: Academic Press, 2000.

Sork, Victoria L. et al. "Mating Patterns in a Savanna Population of Valley Oak (*Quercus lobata* Neé)." USDA Forest Service Gen. Tech. Rep. PSW-GTR-184, 2002.

Sorrells, Trevor R. et al. "Chemical Defense by the Native Winter Ant (*Prenolepis imparis*) against the Invasive Argentine Ant (*Linepithema humile*)." *PloS one* 6, No. 4 (April 2011).

Spangler, Hayward G. "Moth Hearing, Defense, and Communication." *Annual Review of Entomology* 33 (Jan. 1988), pp. 59–81.

Spaulding, Edward Selden. *Camping in Our Mountains*. Santa Barbara: The Schauer Printing Studio, n.d.

Spinks, Phillip Q., and H. B. Shaffer. "Range-wide Molecular Analysis of the Western Pond Turtle (*Emys Marmorata*)." *Molecular Ecology* 14, No. 7 (June 2005), pp. 2047–64.

Sproul, Malcolm J., and M. A. Flett. "Status of the San Joaquin Kit Fox in the Northwest Margin of Its Range." *Transactions of the Western Section of the Wildlife Society* 26 (1993), pp. 61–69.

Stacey, Peter B., and W. D. Koenig. "Cooperative Breeding in the Acorn Woodpecker." *Scientific American* 251 (1984), pp. 114–121.

Stallcup, Rich. *Ocean Birds of the Nearshore Pacific: A Guide for the Sea-Going Naturalist*. Stinson Beach, CA: Point Reyes Bird Observatory, 1990.

Stebbins, Robert C., and N. W. Cohen. *A Natural History of Amphibians*. Princeton: Princeton Univ. Press, 1995.

Stebbins, Robert C., and S. M. McGinnis. *A Field Guide to Amphibians and Reptiles of California*. Rev. ed. Berkeley: Univ. of California Press, 2012.

Steinbeck, John. *Cannery Row*. New York: Viking Press, 1945.

Steinbeck, John, and E. F. Ricketts. *Sea of Cortez: A Leisurely Journal of Travel and Research*. New York: Viking Press, 1941.

Stevens, William K. *The Change in the Weather: People, Weather, and the Science of Climate*. New York: Random House, 1999.

Stewart, Bob. *Common Butterflies of California*. Point Reyes Station, CA: West Coast Lady Press, 1997.

Stoecker Ecological. "Santa Ynez River Steelhead Assessment And Recovery Project," http://www.stoeckerecological.com/santa_ynez_river_stlhd_assessment_recovery_project.html. Accessed Feb. 4, 2011.

———. "Southern Santa Barbara County Steelhead Assessment and Recovery Project," http://www.stoeckerecological.com/southern_santa_barbara_county_stlhd_assessment_recovery_project.html. Accessed Feb. 14, 2011.

Stoecker, Matt W. *Steelhead Migration Barrier Inventory and Recovery Opportunities for the Santa Ynez River, Ca*. Santa Barbara: Community Environmental Council, 2004.

Stoecker, Matt, and E. Kelley. *Santa Clara River Steelhead Trout: Assessment and Recovery Opportunities*. Santa Clara River Trustee Council, 2005.

Storer, Tracy I., and L. P. Tevis Jr. *California Grizzly*. Berkeley: Univ. of California Press, 1955.

Strahler, Arthur N., and Alan H. Strahler. *Elements of Physical Geography*. 4th ed. New York: John Wiley & Sons, 1989.

Stromberg, Mark R., J. D. Corbin, and C. M. D'Antonio, eds. *California Grasslands*. Berkeley: Univ. of California Press, 2007.

Suplee, Curt. "El Niño, La Niña." *National Geographic* 195, No. 3 (March 1999), pp. 73–95.

Swift, Camm C. et al. "Biology and Distribution of the Tidewater Goby, *Eucyclogobius newberryi* (Pisces: Gobiidae) of California." *Contributions in Science* 404. Los Angeles: Natural History Museum of Los Angeles County, 1989.

Sylvester, Arthur G., and G. C. Brown. "Neotectonics and Associated Sedimentation, Ventura Basin, California: A Field Guide." Ventura, CA: Coast Geological Society, Oct. 26, 1997.

Tennesen, Michael. "Testing the Depths of Life." *National Wildlife* 37, No. 2. (Feb./Mar. 1999).

Tesky, Julie L. "*Canis latrans*." *Fire Effects Information System*, http://www.fs.fed.us/database/feis/animals/mammal/cala/introductory.html. Accessed June 7, 2010.

Thorp, Robbin W., P. C. Schroeder, and C. S. Ferguson. "Bumble Bees: Boisterous Pollinators of Native California Flowers." *Fremontia* 30, No. 3, 4 (2002), pp. 26–31.

Timm, Robert M. et al. "Coyote Attacks: An Increasing Suburban Problem." In *Proceedings of the Twenty-First Vertebrate Pest Conference.* Lincoln: Univ. of Nebraska, 2004.

Twisselmann, Ernest G. *A Flora of Kern County, California.* Sacramento: California Native Plant Society, 1995.

Tyler, Claudia M., B. Kuhn, and F. W. Davis. "Demography and Recruitment Limitations of Three Oak Species in California." *Quarterly Review of Biology* 81, No. 2 (2006), pp. 127–132.

Tyler, Claudia M., B. E. Mahall, and F. W. Davis. "Influence of Winter-Spring Livestock Grazing on Survival and Growth of *Quercus lobata* and *Q. agrifolia* Seedlings." *Forest Ecology and Management* 255 (2008), pp. 3063–74.

Tyler, Claudia M. et al. "Factors Limiting Recruitment in Valley and Coast Live Oaks." In *Proceedings of the Fifth Symposium on Oak Woodlands,* ed. Richard B. Standiford. Gen. Tech. Rep. PSW-GTR-184. Albany, CA: Pacific Southwest Research Station, USDA Forest Service, 2002, pp. 565–572.

United States Bureau of Ocean Energy Management, Regulation and Enforcement. "Pinnipeds of the Southern California Planning Area," www.boem. gov. Accessed Feb. 5, 2013.

United States Fish and Wildlife Service. "Stock Assessment Report, Southern Sea Otter," http://www.fws.gov/ventura/species_information/so_sea_otter. Jan. 11, 2013.

———. "California Least Tern (*Sternula antillarum browni):* 5-Year Review, Summary and Evaluation." Carlsbad, CA: US Fish and Wildlife Service, September 2006.

University of California Integrated Pest Management. "Eucalyptus Redgum Lerp Psyllid," http://www.ipm.ucdavis.edu/PMG/PESTNOTES/pn7460. html. Accessed Dec. 3, 2011.

University of Michigan Museum of Zoology. "*Tamias merriami:* Merriam's Chipmunk." *Animal Diversity Web,* http://animaldiversity.ummz. umich.edu. Accessed Oct. 29, 2010.

Usinger, Robert L., ed. *Aquatic Insects of California.* Berkeley: Univ. of California Press, 1956.

Vandergast, Amy G. et al. "Are Hotspots of Evolutionary Potential Adequately Protected in Southern California?" *Biological Conservation* 141 (2008), pp. 1648–64.

Vedder, J. G, and D. G. Howell. "Topographic Evolution of the Southern California Borderland during Late Cenozoic Time." In *The California Islands: Proceedings of a Multidisciplinary Symposium,* ed. Dennis M. Power. Santa Barbara: Santa Barbara Museum of Natural History, 1980.

Wake, David B. "Problems with Species: Patterns and Processes of Species Formation in Salamanders." *Annals of the Missouri Botanical Garden* 93, No. 1 (2006), pp. 8–23.

Walker, Thomas J., and N. Collins. "New World Thermometer Crickets: The *Oecanthus rileyi* Species Group and a New Species from North America." *Journal of Orthoptera Research* 19, No. 2 (2010), pp. 371–376.

Warner, Richard E., and K. M. Hendrix, eds. *California Riparian Systems: Ecology, Conservation, and Productive Management.* Berkeley: Univ. of California Press, 1984.

Weigand, Peter W., ed. *Contributions to the Geology of the Northern Channel Islands, Southern California.* MP-45. Bakersfield, CA: Pacific Section, American Association of Petroleum Geologists, 1998.

Wells, Martin. *Civilization and the Limpet.* New York: Perseus Books, 1998.

Welsh, Hartwell H. Jr. "Bioregions: An Ecological and Evolutionary Perspective and a Proposal for California." *California Fish and Game* 80, No. 3 (1994), pp. 97–124.

Wenner, A. M., J. E. Dugan, and D. M. Hubbard. "Sand Crab Population Biology on the California Islands and Mainland." In *Proceedings of the Third California Islands Symposium: Recent Advances in California Islands Research,* ed. F. G. Hochberg. Santa Barbara: Santa Barbara Museum of Natural History, 1993, pp. 335–348.

Wenner, Adrian M. "Monarch Butterfly Migration in North America: A Critique and Comprehensive Theory." Unpublished ms.

Westerling, Anthony et al. "Climate, Santa Ana Winds and Autumn Wildfires in Southern California." *EOS* 85, No. 31 (Aug. 2004), pp. 289–300.

White, P. J., K. Ralls, and R. A. Garrott. "Coyote–Kit Fox Interactions as Revealed by Telemetry." *Canadian Journal of Zoology* 72, No. 10 (1994), pp. 1831–36.

White, Patrick J., and K. Ralls. "Reproduction and Spacing Patterns of Kit Foxes Relative to Changing Prey Availability." *Journal of Wildlife Management* 57, No. 4 (1993), pp. 861–867.

Whitworth, D. L., H. R. Carter, and F. Gress. "Responses by Breeding Xantus's Murrelets Eight Years after Eradication of Black Rats from Anacapa Island, California." Unpublished report. Calif. Institute of Environmental Studies, Davis, CA, 2012.

Whitworth, D. L., A. L. Harvey, and H. R. Carter. "Cassin's Auklets, Xantus's Murrelets and Other Crevice-Nesting Seabirds at Santa Barbara Island, California: 2009-10 Surveys." Unpublished report. Calif. Institute of Environmental Studies, Davis, CA; Carter Biological Consulting, Victoria, BC; Channel Islands National Park, Ventura, CA; 2011.

Whitworth, Darrell L. et al. "Initial Recovery of Xantus's Murrelets Following Rat Eradication on Anacapa Island, California." *Marine Ornithology* 33 (2005), pp. 131–137.

Wilson, Don E., and R. A. Mittermeier, eds. *Handbook of the Mammals of the World.* Vol. 1. Barcelona, Spain: Lynx, 2009.

Wilson, Don E., and S. Ruff. *The Smithsonian Book of North American Mammals.* Washington DC: Smithsonian Institution, 1999.

Wilson, Edward O. "Within One Cubic Foot." *National Geographic,* Feb. 2010.

Wilson, Robert W. "Pleistocene Mammalian Fauna from the Carpinteria Asphalt." *Contributions to Paleontology* 440 (March 1934), Carnegie Institute of Washington.

Wright, S. A., R. S. Lane, and J. R. Clover. "Infestation of the Southern Alligator Lizard (Squamata: Anguidae) by *Ixodes pacificus* (Acari: Ixodidae)…" *Journal of Medical Entomology* 35, No. 6 (1998), pp. 1044–49.

Yager, David D., and M. L. May. "Ultrasound-Triggered, Flight-Gated Evasive Maneuvers in the Praying Mantis *Parasphendale agrionina.*" *Journal of Experimental Biology* 152, No. 1 (1990), pp. 41–58.

Yanev, Kay. "Biogeography and Distribution of Three Parapatric Salamander Species in Coastal and Borderland California." In *The California Islands: Proceedings of a Multidisciplinary Symposium,* ed. Dennis M. Power. Santa Barbara: Santa Barbara Museum of Natural History, 1980, pp. 531–550.

Zedler, Joy B. *The Ecology of Southern California Coastal Salt Marshes: A Community Profile.* US Fish and Wildlife Service FWS/OBS-81/54. Washington, DC: Dept. of Interior, 1982.

Zedler, Paul H. *The Ecology of Southern California Vernal Pools: A Community Profile.* US Fish and Wildlife Service Biological Report 85 (7.11). Washington, DC: Dept. of Interior, 1987.

Zembal, R., and S. Hoffman. "Status and Distribution of the Light-footed Clapper Rail in California." Environmental Division, Natural Resources Mgmt. Office, Naval Base Ventura County, Point Mugu; US Fish and Wildlife Service; Calif. Dept. of Fish and Game, 2004.

Zimmer, Carl. "The Most Popular Lifestyle on Earth." *Conservation Magazine* 9, No. 4 (Oct.–Dec. 2008).

Useful Websites

Audubon California, www.ca.audubon. org.

Bat Conservation International E-newsletter Archive, http://www.batcon. org/index.php/media-and-info/ e-newsletter.html.

Birds of North America Online (subscription), http://bna.birds.cornell. edu/bna.

California Beetle Project, http://www. sbnature.org/collections/invert/ entom/cbphomepage.php.

California Chaparral Institute, www. californiachaparral.com.

California Department of Fish and Wildlife (formerly Fish and Game), http://www.dfg.ca.gov.

California Herps, www.californiaherps. com.

California Invasive Plant Council, www.cal-IPC.org.

California Native Plant Society, www. cnps.org.

California State Parks, www.parks. ca.gov.

California Wetlands Information System, ceres.ca.gov/wetlands.

California Wildlife Habitat Relationships, http://www.dfg.ca.gov/ biogeodata/cwhr.

Carpinteria Salt Marsh Reserve, UC Santa Barbara, http://carpinteria. ucnrs.org.

Cascadia Research Collective (marine mammals), www.cascadiaresearch. org.

The Cephalopod Page, www.thecepha lopodpage.org.

Channel Islands National Marine Sanctuary, www.channelislands.noaa.gov.

Channel Islands National Park, www. nps.gov/chis.

Coal Oil Point Reserve, UC Santa Barbara, http://coaloilpoint.ucnrs.org.

Conception Coast Project maps, http:// conceptioncoast.org/projects_maps. html.

Educational Multimedia Visualization Center of the Department of Earth Sciences, UCSB (animated geology events), emvc.geol.ucsb.edu.

Friends of the Santa Clara River, www. fscr.org.

Global Invasive Species Database, http://www.issg.org/database/ welcome.

Gray Whales Count, Santa Barbara Channel, www.graywhalescount.org.

Hopper Mountain National Wildlife Refuge Complex (condor recovery program), www.fws.gov/ hoppermountain.

Integrated Taxonomic Information System (ITIS), www.itis.gov.

Marine Science (Genny Anderson), http://marinebio.net/marinescience/ index.htm.

Mountain Lion Foundation, www. mountainlion.org.

National Marine Fisheries Service, www.nmfs.noaa.gov.

NOAA (National Oceanic and Atmospheric Administration weather research), www.noaa.gov.

Salmon/Steelhead Recovery, http://swr. nmfs.noaa.gov/recovery.

San Diego Natural History Museum, http://www.sdnhm.org.

Santa Barbara Museum of Natural History, www.sbnature.org.

Santa Clara River Parkway, http://www. santaclarariverparkway.org.

US Fish and Wildlife Service, www.fws. gov.

US Geological Survey, www.usgs.gov.

Ventana Wildlife Society, www.ventanaws.org species_condors_fieldnotes.

University of California, Berkeley, Museum of Paleontology, www. ucmp.berkeley.edu.

INDEX

Photo by Jennifer Lentz

About the Author

A lifelong resident of Santa Barbara, Joan Easton Lentz has been a serious student of the region's natural history for more than thirty-five years. A naturalist and teacher, she is a research associate at the Santa Barbara Museum of Natural History. This is her fourth book.

Photo by Bruce Reitherman

Peter Gaede has been pursuing his passion for art and nature since childhood. After finishing a degree in biology, he studied scientific illustration at the University of California, Santa Cruz, where he earned a graduate degree. He has completed internships at the California Academy of Sciences, National Geographic Society, and National Museums of Kenya.

Stuart Wilson attended Brooks Institute of Photography and has traveled extensively to photograph rain forest flora and fauna as well as that of the American West. He has taught photography classes at the Santa Barbara Botanic Garden and the Santa Barbara Museum of Natural History and has been widely published in books, calendars, magazines, and DVDs.

Photo by Ron Williams

HEYDAY

into California

About Heyday

Heyday is an independent, nonprofit publisher and unique cultural institution. We promote widespread awareness and celebration of California's many cultures, landscapes, and boundary-breaking ideas. Through our well-crafted books, public events, and innovative outreach programs we are building a vibrant community of readers, writers, and thinkers.

Thank You

It takes the collective effort of many to create a thriving literary culture. We are thankful to all the thoughtful people we have the privilege to engage with. Cheers to our writers, artists, editors, storytellers, designers, printers, bookstores, critics, cultural organizations, readers, and book lovers everywhere!

We are especially grateful for the generous funding we've received for our publications and programs during the past year from foundations and hundreds of individual donors. Major supporters include:

Anonymous (3); Alliance for California Traditional Arts; Arkay Foundation; Judy Avery; James J. Baechle; Paul Bancroft III; BayTree Fund; S. D. Bechtel, Jr. Foundation; Barbara Jean and Fred Berensmeier; Berkeley Civic Arts Program and Civic Arts Commission; Joan Berman; John Briscoe; Lewis and Sheana Butler; California Civil Liberties Public Education Program; Cal Humanities; California Indian Heritage Center Foundation; California State Library; California State Parks Foundation; Keith Campbell Foundation; Candelaria Fund; John and Nancy Cassidy Family Foundation, through Silicon Valley Community Foundation; The Center for California Studies; Charles Edwin Chase; Graham Chisholm; The Christensen Fund; Jon Christensen; Community Futures Collective; Compton Foundation; Creative Work Fund; Lawrence Crooks; Nik Dehejia; Frances Dinkelspiel and Gary Wayne; The Durfee Foundation; Earth Island Institute; The Fred Gellert Family Foundation; Fulfillco; The Wallace Alexander Gerbode Foundation; Nicola W. Gordon; Wanda Lee Graves and Stephen Duscha; David Guy; The Walter and Elise Haas Fund; Coke and James Hallowell; Stephen Hearst; Historic Resources Group; Sandra and Charles Hobson;

G. Scott Hong Charitable Trust; Donna Ewald Huggins; Humboldt Area Foundation; James Irvine Foundation; Claudia Jurmain; Kendeda Fund; Marty and Pamela Krasney; Guy Lampard and Suzanne Badenhoop; Christine Leefeldt, in celebration of Ernest Callenbach and Malcolm Margolin's friendship; Thomas Lockard; Thomas J. Long Foundation; Judith and Brad Lowry-Croul; Michael McCone; Nion McEvoy and Leslie Berriman; Michael Mitrani; Moore Family Foundation; Richard Nagler; National Endowment for the Arts; National Wildlife Federation; Native Cultures Fund; The Nature Conservancy; Nightingale Family Foundation; Northern California Water Association; The David and Lucile Packard Foundation; Alan Rosenus; The San Francisco Foundation; Greg Sarris; Savory Thymes; Roselyne Chroman Swig; Swinerton Family Fund; Sedge Thomson and Sylvia Brownrigg; TomKat Charitable Trust; The Roger J. and Madeleine Traynor Foundation; Lisa Van Cleef and Mark Gunson; Patricia Wakida; John Wiley & Sons, Inc.; Peter Booth Wiley and Valerie Barth; Dean Witter Foundation; The Work-in-Progress Fund of Tides Foundation; and Yocha Dehe Community Fund.

Board of Directors

Guy Lampard (Chairman), Richard D. Baum, Barbara Boucke, Steve Costa, Nik Dehejia, Peter Dunckel, Theresa Harlan, Marty Krasney, Katharine Livingston, Michael McCone (Chairman Emeritus), Sonia Torres, Michael Traynor, Lisa Van Cleef, and Patricia Wakida.

Getting Involved

To learn more about our publications, events, membership club, and other ways you can participate, please visit www.heydaybooks.com.